* write anti-trust paper
  ↳ become a pharma + ATT
     - expert?

→ info- privacy after all?

Privacy

* internet anti-trust

Patent Wars

Patent Wars

How Patents Impact Our Daily Lives

THOMAS F. COTTER

OXFORD
UNIVERSITY PRESS

OXFORD

UNIVERSITY PRESS

Oxford University Press is a department of the University of Oxford. It furthers
the University's objective of excellence in research, scholarship, and education
by publishing worldwide. Oxford is a registered trade mark of Oxford University
Press in the UK and certain other countries.

Published in the United States of America by Oxford University Press
198 Madison Avenue, New York, NY 10016, United States of America.

Library of Congress Cataloging-in-Publication Data
Names: Cotter, Thomas F., 1961– author.
Title: Patent wars: how patents impact our daily lives / Thomas F. Cotter.
Description: Oxford [UK]; New York: Oxford University Press, [2018] |
Includes bibliographical references and index.
Identifiers: LCCN 2017052310 | ISBN 9780190244439 (bb: alk. paper) |
ISBN 9780190244446 (updf) | ISBN 9780190244453 (epub)
Subjects: LCSH: Patent laws and legislation—United States. | Patent suits—United States.
Classification: LCC KF3114 .C68 2018 | DDC 346.7304/86—dc23
LC record available at https://lccn.loc.gov/2017052310

1 3 5 7 9 8 6 4 2

Printed by Sheridan Books, Inc., United States of America

To my children

Mark the spirit of invention everywhere, thy rapid patents,
Thy continual workshops, foundries, risen or rising,
See, from their chimneys how the tall flame-fires stream.
—Walt Whitman, from *Song of the Exposition*

CONTENTS

ACKNOWLEDGMENTS

First off, I'd like to express my thanks to the University of Minnesota Law School and our former dean, David Wippman, for granting me leave during the fall semester of 2016 to devote time to this project; and to Dean Wippman and our current dean Garry Jenkins for providing me with summer research grants. Thank you also to my former faculty assistant, Victoria Jackson, who has gone on to bigger and better things, and to my research assistants, especially Sung Woo (Matt) Hu, Michael Sikora, Travis Waller, and Tianziang (Max) Zhou.

Some portions of this book are based in part on previously published work, including (1) *A Burkean Perspective on Patent Eligibility*, 22 Berkeley Technology Law Journal 855 (2007); (2) *A Burkean Perspective on Patent Eligibility, Part II: Reflections on the (Counter)Revolution in Patent Law*, 11 Minnesota Journal of Law, Science & Technology 365 (2010); (3) *Introduction* to Symposium on Intellectual Property, Development, and Human Rights, 14 Florida Journal of International Law 147 (2002); (4) *Market Fundamentalism and the TRIPs Agreement*, 22 Cardozo Arts & Entertainment Law Journal 307 (2004); (5) *Patents, Antitrust, and the High Cost of Health Care*, 13 Antitrust Source No. 4 (Apr. 2014), https://www.americanbar.org/content/dam/aba/publishing/antitrust_source/apr14_cotter_4-8f.authcheckdam.pdf; and (6) *Pragmatism, Economics, and the* Droit Moral, 76 North Carolina Law Review 1 (1997). In addition, portions of certain chapters may appear in adapted form in a forthcoming book of which I am a coauthor, titled *Redesigning Patent Law*, which I also hope will be published in the near future by Oxford University Press.

For his insightful comments and criticism of the entire manuscript, I am deeply indebted to Norman Siebrasse, whose unwillingness to settle for facile analysis I have come to appreciate more and more over the past several years. For their comments, criticism, or willingness to provide advice on individual chapters or groups of chapters, I thank in particular Dr. Amy Calhoun,

Jessica Clarke, Kevin Collins, Ralph Hall, Jill Hasday, Claire Hill, Christopher Holman, JaneAnne Murray, Brett McDonnell, Barbara Noah, Bill Page, Daniel Schwarcz, Michael Tonry, Andrew Torrance, and Peter Yu. Whether I followed your recommendations or not, I greatly appreciate the effort you devoted to providing me with feedback. Any errors or lapses in judgment, of course, are mine alone.

Finally, I thank David McBride and Claire Sibley at Oxford University Press for shepherding this project through to completion. And I thank my students and professional colleagues over the years for challenging me to hone and defend the views presented in this book.

PROLOGUE

A Typical Day

Your digital alarm clock wakes you up, as usual, at 6:00 A.M. You yawn, get out of bed, perhaps make a stop at the bathroom, then slap on some clothes and go for a quick run. When you get home, you shower, remember to take your daily medication, and get dressed for the day. You then wander over to the kitchen. Fortunately, you remembered to program your coffee maker before you went to bed last night, so you pour yourself a cup. You turn on your smartphone or tablet to read the daily news while you munch on your cornflakes. At 8:00 sharp, you start your morning commute. By 8:30, you have arrived at work, sat down at your desk, and turned on your office computer. Another day awaits.

How many patented inventions do you think you've used by 9 A.M.?

Let's start at the beginning. Beds and bed linens have been around for a while, and, as we'll see, patents are available only for *new* inventions, something that (roughly speaking) hasn't been done before. Assuming that you sleep in a conventional bed, then, you might expect that the frame, mattress, pillows, covers, and any other such conventional items don't embody any patented components; but actually, they might. Crate & Barrel, for example, advertises its Simmons Beautyrest mattress as having "a layer of patented Transflexlon Comfort Technology foam," while Select Comfort, the maker of Sleep Number beds, holds 27 US and 37 foreign patents relating to the design and function of its products; and surely you've seen or heard the ubiquitous commercials touting Mike Liddell's patented My Pillow.[1] A quick search of various publicly searchable databases discloses that there are plenty of other issued patents and pending patent applications covering mattresses, beds and bed frames, and even bed covers (though some of these patents appear to relate to specialized beds, such as those used in hospitals). Perhaps even more likely, if your linens or sleepware

are made of cotton, is that the seed from which the cotton was grown was genetically modified to be resistant to pests and is subject to patents owned by Monsanto Company.

To be sure, the mere fact that someone has obtained a patent on a new invention doesn't necessarily mean that the invention or design is or will be commercially successful. You've surely heard the old saw that if you build a better mousetrap, the world will beat a path to your door; but the fact is that many, perhaps most, patents are never used at all, much less incorporated into commercially successful products. (And yes, people are still getting patents on mousetraps—though I'm not aware of any lately that have transformed their inventors into millionaires. Let's hope you don't have to deal with any mousetraps during your morning routine.) Moreover, not every issued patent is actually valid; as we'll see, about 40–50 percent of all US patents that are the subject of patent infringement lawsuits and are litigated to judgment ultimately are declared invalid in whole or in part. Be that as it may, there's a pretty good chance that, one way or another, your bedroom set incorporates or is derived from one or more patented inventions—though it's also possible that you escaped any direct contact with the patent system while you dozed beneath your covers. (Even then, it's conceivable that you had some *indirect* contact with the patent system, if for example some component of your HVAC system or another structural feature of your house or apartment is patented.) But it's still only 6 A.M.

The next thing you did was shut off your alarm clock. Alarm clocks are not very new either, and even digital clocks with LED displays have been around for a few decades now. Patents typically remain in force for less than twenty years, so any patents that covered the original 1970s-era technology almost certainly have long since expired. But again, a search will show that there are still plenty of people out there patenting, or attempting to patent, alarm clocks that include features such as "random offset alarm" (designed to make it more difficult for you to ignore the alarm and go back to sleep), or that insert an alarm into objects such as pillows. Perhaps only a small number of these innovations are ever likely to find their way into your home, but some may; Brookstone's website, for example, lists several utility and design patents relating to clocks and other products. Or perhaps you're one of those people who use their smartphone as an alarm clock—and as we'll see below, smartphones embody thousands of potentially patentable features. So while it's hard to generalize, depending on how old your device is and how many "bells and whistles," literally or metaphorically, it contains, it's possible there could be one or more patented features embodied in your digital timepiece.

The next step in your morning ritual may have been to use the bathroom—but I'll grant you some privacy and return to the bathroom later, when you're likely to spend more time there anyway. For now, let's assume that after taking care of the essentials you decided to go for your morning run or other exercise. (If it's more likely you would sleep in, meditate, or have a cigarette, you can skip this part—though by way of information, there are several patents in existence on electronic cigarette technology, as well as on smoking cessation devices.) How likely is this part of your daily routine to involve any patented inventions? Again, it's hard to generalize, but patented inventions or designs could intrude upon your morning exercise in a number of different ways. Consider first your shoes. Although some athletic shoes may embody no patentable features, other models incorporate patented inventions intended for purposes such as reducing stress or increasing stride, or patented *designs* relating to the shoe's appearance.* (Nike, for example, has a large portfolio of US and foreign patents. Since 2012, Nike and adidas have locked horns over the validity of Nike's patent on its popular Flyknit model, first in Germany and later in the United States.[2]) Another possibility is that one or more patents may read on some device you use during your morning workout—a high-end pedometer or heart monitor, for example, or an exercise bike or treadmill. (Most of these products will also bear various trademarks, such as a brand name or other source-identifying features, but for now our focus is just on patents for new inventions and designs. I'll explain a little more about trademarks and how they differ from copyrights in Chapter 1.)

After completing your exercise routine, you decide it's time to shower and dress. In your bathroom, you're sure to encounter several patented compounds and devices. A quick look at all the bottles, containers, and devices in a typical American bathroom is likely to confirm that at least a few of them (somewhere on their packaging or housing) list some US patent numbers or references to "patents pending." Among the more likely suspects would be products such as contact lens solution, razors (manual and electric), electric toothbrushes, tooth whitening strips, and (improbable as it may seem) dental floss. Another is cosmetics; Estée Lauder, for example, tout the company's "25+ patents and patents pending worldwide." As with most of the other patents you've encountered already, most of these probably do not cover an entire class of products, but rather some functional component, such as the chemical formulation of a specific ingredient or an electronic or mechanical feature of a device. One possible exception, however, relates to drug patents, which often cover (or "read on," in patent lingo) a specific medication. If you take some sort of daily medication, there's a good chance that the product is still subject to patent protection—if not in the original formulation of the chemical compound, then

---

* Most countries award some form of protection for qualifying industrial designs. In the United States, qualifying designs are accorded a form of patent protection, which I will briefly discuss in Chapter 1. Except for one important recent case involving smartphone designs, however—see Chapter 9—the book's principal concern will be with patents for new inventions, not designs.

perhaps in some "new and improved" version relating to its dosage or form—though it's also true that many once-patented drugs are now off-patent and thus (in theory, at least) subject to generic competition.

Your next stop, the kitchen, is likely home to many more patented inventions—ranging, potentially, from, well, the range and other appliances like that nifty coffee maker, to the very food and drink you consume. Most corn that US consumers ingest is genetically modified to be resistant to glyphosate-based herbicide, for example, so (as with the sleepware example above) there's a reasonable chance that the seed from which the product (in this case, corn flakes) is derived is subject to one or more of Monsanto's patents. Yet while these patents are important (and controversial), it is your smartphone or tablet that houses a veritable treasure trove of patents on a dizzying array of functional (and possibly even some nonfunctional) features. The specific numbers will vary depending on what sort of device you use, but a conservative estimate is that a typical smartphone embodies several hundred patented features, relating not only to the device's internal hardware, but also to some of the things the device enables you to do (e.g., a "method, system, and graphical user interface for providing word recommendations means for communicating over wireless networks")[3] and possibly even including the way it looks (design patents, again). The 4G network that enables the smartphone to communicate involves several *thousand* patents, and by one estimate there are over 250,000 active patents—representing one in six active patents today—that impact smartphones. Of course, you probably don't use all of these patented features over breakfast—and you might never use some of them, depending on your likes and interests. But just in the course of turning on the device and skimming the daily news on the web or with some app, you are likely to have made use of several potentially patented inventions. Similarly, when you switch on your computer at the office later in the morning, you will start using some of these same and other patents. (As with the other examples above, your kitchen ritual also is likely to involve encounters with many trademarks and, particularly in the course of skimming the daily news, *copyrighted* content such as newspaper articles and photographs. I'll say a little more about copyright—which subsists in works of authorship such as these, as well as in motion pictures, music, and software—in Chapters 1 and 5. But again, our interest for now is simply with the patented inventions and designs.)

Unless you walk to work (and don't wear those patented shoes), your morning commute is also likely to involve the use of patented technology—if you drive to work, potentially quite a lot of it. The average gasoline-powered automobile may incorporate patented inventions relating to a host of features including engines, transmissions, fuel injector systems, and so-called "soft parts" such as seats and luggage racks. (Indeed, one of the more important US Supreme Court patent cases this century, which we'll come across in Chapter 1, involved the question of whether a new type of automobile pedal was sufficiently nonobvious to merit a patent.) Cars that incorporate more cutting-edge "green" technologies, or that are powered by alternative energy sources, may contain many more, numbering perhaps in the hundreds.[4] (Chances are you're not using a self-driving car just yet, but—not surprisingly—there's an ever-increasing number of patents on various aspects of these vehicles as well.) Alternative methods of transportation, including bicycles, motorcycles, and mass transit, also frequently incorporate patented components. Recent litigation between Trek Bicycle and a company called Split Pivot, for example, involved competing patents relating to bicycle suspension systems, as did a concurrent suit between dw-link and Giant Bicycle. If you take the subway to work, on the other hand, you may be riding over patented railway couplings and using a smart card embodying patented technology to buy your pass and access the tracks. Indeed, several recent lawsuits have involved claims of patent infringement relating to smart cards, though the validity of many of these patents is hotly contested.[5]

But wait—is it possible that we're missing the most obvious way in which your morning ritual involves the use of patents? What about your own body? Perhaps you've heard something over the past few years about whether it's possible to patent human genes. Could it be that your own body houses genes that are patented—and therefore owned—by somebody else? Are you possibly trespassing on someone else's property simply by virtue of being alive? Or is someone else trespassing on *your* property interest in your own body by asserting ownership over your genes?

Actually, the correct answer to all of the above questions is a simple no. Patents on genes—DNA sequences and other related compositions and methods—have indeed been in the news lately, but in 2013 the US Supreme Court decided that naturally occurring DNA is nonpatentable (although synthetic, that is, human-made DNA, can still be patented).[6] Rest assured, however, that even before this Supreme Court ruling no one was claiming ownership of the genes that reside within your own body. All that gene patents ever covered—or continue to cover, in the many countries in which genes remain patentable subject matter—are DNA sequences that have been *isolated* from their naturally occurring state, that is, genes that have been removed from the body or synthesized in a lab. To be sure, even with this qualification gene patents have been highly controversial, as we shall see, perhaps for good reason. But, thankfully, it's not very likely you'd be making use of any once or future *patented* genes during your morning rush to the office.

So, to answer the question posed above, how many patents have you encountered during the first three hours of your waking life on a typical day? Results may vary, of course, depending on your habits, interests, and lifestyle, but if you are a typical consumer in North America, Europe, Japan, China, or

South Korea, the number probably ranges from somewhere in the low hundreds to several thousand. We are, quite literally, awash in patents to an extent that might have seemed startling just a generation ago.[7] Patented technologies and designs pervade our lives like the air we breathe. Except for those of us who belong to communities, such as the Amish, that have chosen to follow a radically different way of life, it is virtually impossible to escape these many encounters with patented products. Barring some catastrophe, there seems to be little, if any, prospect of materially reversing the trend—though the number of patents issued *can* vary a bit from year to year, and as we will see the legal standards regarding what sorts of things can be patented are also subject to change.

How Did It Get to Be this Way? Does It Matter?

It hasn't always been so. Scholars have traced the origins of the modern-day patent system to Renaissance Italy and Elizabethan England, but patent law didn't really take off until the nineteenth century; and its ubiquity is certainly a modern-day phenomenon. The number of "utility patents" (patents for new inventions) granted annually in the United States first reached the four-figure mark in 1854, the five-figure mark in 1867, and the six-figure mark in 1994. In 2015—the most recent year for which such statistics are available at the time this book went to press—the US Patent and Trademark Office (USPTO) granted 298,407 patents.[8] For the first time ever, the United States awarded fewer patents than China, which issued 359,316; Japan, South Korea, and the European Patent Office (EPO) rounded out the top five. Patent infringement litigation now makes up a substantial portion of the federal judiciary's docket, with over 4,000 patent infringement lawsuits filed in 2016;[9] and most US law schools now have one or more patent scholars among their faculty—a big change from, say, thirty years ago, when the number of patent scholars at top US law schools probably could have fit comfortably into a (now-obsolete) phone booth.

Nevertheless, outside of Silicon Valley and a small number of other research hubs, the average person probably knows very little about the subject of patent law—apart from what they might read in the paper from time to time about controversies over gene patents, patent "trolls," or a handful of prominent disputes involving smartphone or pharmaceutical companies. In addition, what people do know, or think they know, about the patent system often comes with a great deal of ambivalence. For many people, the intuition that inventors deserve some sort of reward for their contribution to society—that they have a moral entitlement to profit from their inventions—is strong. Nevertheless, most of the lawyers, economists, and other people who make a living from studying the patent system—including me—find this sort of argument, rooted in a "natural law" perspective, unpersuasive, for reasons I will explore in Chapter 2. Instead, most of us believe that the patent system (in theory, at least) derives its justification from some form of utilitarianism—roughly speaking, that patents serve the greater good by making the world a better place than it otherwise would be. More specifically, the conventional argument is that granting exclusive rights in inventions for a period of time provides a necessary incentive for inventors (and those who fund them) to devote time, money, and other resources to developing (and disclosing how to make and use) new products and services, as opposed to merely copying existing ones. Indeed, this justification seems to be at the root of the Patent and Copyright Clause (article I, section 8, clause 8) of the US Constitution, which authorizes Congress to "promote the progress of science and useful arts, by securing for limited times to authors and inventors the exclusive right to their respective writings and discoveries." (According to the US Supreme Court, in the idiom of the eighteenth century "science" referred to knowledge generally, and so promoting the "progress of science" is viewed as the rationale for investing authors with exclusive rights in their writings, i.e., copyright rights.[10] Promoting the "useful arts" is the job of patent law.)

One obvious problem, however, is that while (just about) everyone agrees in principle that innovation is a good thing, the extent to which a patent system is *necessary* to generate the "optimal" level of innovation, and what the features of such a system ought to be, remains elusive. In addition, as economists are eager to tell us, for every benefit there is some corresponding cost; and the patent system is no different. Most of us have experienced these costs in one form or another. We know, for example, that when drugs come off patent, competition often (though not always!) enables us to pay lower prices because generic drugs are now available; by contrast, while the patent is in force, the patent owner's right to exclude others from making or selling the invention enables the owner to set a price that is higher than it otherwise would be. Less obvious, but arguably more important, is the fact that every new invention necessarily builds on that which came before it. Sir Isaac Newton's observation, "If I have seen further it is by standing on the shoulders of giants," still rings true. Practically speaking, however, this means that every time a company wants to make a product embodying a new invention, it may have to obtain permission, in the form of a license, from some other company that owns the rights to some earlier, now-improved-upon, innovation that is embodied in the new invention. In the aggregate, these costs sometimes can be quite high. In addition, for some people, the mere idea that genes or living organisms or other types of nontraditional subject matter can be patented at all seems positively revolting. Though not easily quantifiable, from the standpoint of economics this "yuck factor" can be viewed as a cost as well, at least in terms of the psychic toll it takes among people who disapprove.

(Whether such psychic tolls *should* factor into any sort of policy analysis, however, is another issue.)

Although the specific examples would have been different, this ambivalence is as old as the patent system itself. Throughout history, judges and others have often characterized patents as "monopolies," and while modern-day economists believe that this label is not always, or even usually, correct, there is a kernel of truth in it: the whole point of having a patent system is to encourage invention by offering temporary protection from competition. Most patents don't actually achieve this goal because, as I noted above, most patented inventions are not commercially successful: a "monopoly" over something that nobody wants is pretty much meaningless from an economic point of view. But as with the drug example above, some patents *do* enable their owners to charge higher prices than would be possible in a more competitive market—the very definition of "market power," which in extreme cases can amount to full-blown monopoly. Nevertheless, the patent system rests upon the premise that the underlying tradeoff between *access* and *incentives* is worthwhile—that is, that patents may result in our paying more and having limited access to certain things in the short run, while in return providing an incentive for people to invest in inventing those things, so that over the long run society derives far more benefits than costs. (For that matter, there could be net benefits even in the short run, if the patent system induces the invention of, say, a cancer vaccine that otherwise would not exist at all. Paying a monopoly price to obtain a cancer vaccine may seem bad, but it's better than developing cancer.)

The problem is that no one really can say for sure, at any given point in time, how close a given patent system comes to achieving the goal of generating a surplus of social benefits over costs—let alone the *maximum attainable* surplus of benefits over costs, which would be the point of optimal innovation. Anyone who's ever studied patent law has encountered, probably multiple times, the economist Fritz Machlup's famous dictum (written in 1958) that "No economist, on the basis of present knowledge, could possibly state with certainty that the patent system, as it now operates, confers a net benefit or a net loss upon society . . . . If we did not have a patent system, it would be irresponsible, on the basis of our present knowledge of its economic consequences, to recommend instituting one. But since we have had a patent system for a long time, it would be irresponsible, on the basis of our present knowledge, to recommend abolishing it."[11] Sixty years later, it's not clear that we're any closer to resolving the dilemma posed by Machlup; and this uncertainty over whether the patent system achieves its goals is especially troubling because the stakes often seem so high. According to most economists, invention—and its offspring, innovation, a term that economists use in a more technical sense to refer to the *commercialization* of a new invention—is what drives the modern economy.[12] Not only are vast sums of money at stake, but more importantly people's livelihoods—their very lives, in some instances—may depend on whether the benefits of the patent system outweigh the costs. Indeed, not only are the benefits and costs inherently unquantifiable, but reasonable minds may not even agree on what counts as a benefit or a cost. From an ethical standpoint, is it appropriate to confer exclusive patent rights in, say, a new drug, so as to induce firms to invest in developing newer and even better medicines, if the consequence of conferring such rights is a price increase that may put the medicine out of reach of some consumers? Moral philosophy may not offer any clear answer to this question— and, happily, the question need not always *be* resolved, if for example there are alternative means available either for inducing invention or for ensuring access. Nevertheless, the so-called "incentive–access" tradeoff remains a persistent, and troubling, aspect of the patent system (and of other intellectual property rights, including copyright and trade secrets).

The Plan of this Book

The preceding discussion provided some examples of how patents pervade many aspects of our daily lives, and briefly outlined some of the public policy questions that every patent system must resolve—whether up front and explicitly, or implicitly in the way the system operates. Not surprisingly, patent lawyers and others whose livelihood depends upon the existence of a patent system generally view patents in a favorable light, though they differ among themselves in their support for various proposals to improve or reform certain aspects of the system. Many economists and others who have less of an obvious stake in the game tend to agree that, in general, patents generate more benefits than costs, though there is a distinct minority that views matters in a much less favorable light. By contrast, among some other segments of society the view is decidedly mixed, with professional associations such as the American Medical Association, various consumer and public interest organizations such as the American Civil Liberties Union (ACLU), and nongovernmental organizations (NGOs) such as Doctors Without Borders, focusing more on the "access" part of the incentive– access tradeoff and thus taking a more skeptical view of the steady expansion of patent law over the past decades.

For the nonspecialist who might read about these disputes from time to time in the *Wall Street Journal*, the *New York Times*, or other outlets, blogs, or websites, sorting through these conflicting views and arriving at an educated opinion may seem daunting. And yet it is, I believe, important that the average citizen develop some understanding of, and ability to contribute to, these ongoing debates. For the outcomes of these debates do have an impact on our lives and the lives of others; and while it may be impossible to know with absolute certainty what an optimal patent system would look like (or whether it would exist at all), I am enough of a believer in reason and rationality to think that we often can make evidence-based educated guesses as to whether one side or another has the better argument with respect to altering, strengthening, or weakening any given aspect of the patent system. (That said, I'm also convinced by arguments such as those put forward by Jonathan Haidt in his book *The Righteous Mind* that our underlying temperaments and personalities strongly influence our moral and political beliefs.[13] I'll have more to say about this topic later in the book, but for now I'll simply state my belief that reason can and should play an important role in debates over public policy, while admitting that it would be foolish to believe that our perspectives can ever be entirely dispassionate and impartial.)

And so this book is written with you, that educated nonspecialist reader, in mind, in the hope that it will make it easier for you to understand and—if you so choose—as a citizen, consumer, voter, or investor, to try to influence the ongoing evolution of a body of law that affects so much of our daily life and work. The book is divided into nine chapters, each of which will assist you in understanding the relevant issues and, I hope, drawing your own conclusions regarding this brave new patent-populated (or is it patent-infested?) world.

The first two chapters are devoted to a basic overview of patent law, its justifications and critiques, and its gradual expansion over the past thirty years. In particular, Chapter 1 provides something of a crash course in the basics of patent law in the United States (and, to some degree, other major economies), discussing matters such as what a patent is, the conditions under which inventors are entitled to obtain patents, and what a patent entitles an inventor to do (and what it doesn't). Some simple examples will help to make the discussion comprehensible, and I will make some brief points about how various aspects of patent law relate to the overall purpose, discussed above, of encouraging the invention and disclosure of new technology. Chapter 2 will then subject some of these explanations to closer analysis: what exactly does contemporary economic theory and empirical evidence tell us about patents as a tool for encouraging invention and disclosure, and what implications can we draw from the evidence?

Chapters 3, 4, and 5 will then focus on one specific set of modern-day controversies, namely the question of whether certain *types* of inventions or discoveries—including DNA sequences, methods of diagnosing disease, business methods, and computer software—should be patentable at all. As noted above, in 2013 the US Supreme Court decided that, contrary to US practice as it had existed for the past thirty years or so, human genes are patent-ineligible. (Many other countries still permit gene patents, however, subject to some qualifications.) For some observers, this decision was obviously right, for one of two reasons: either because they believed (incorrectly) that such patents allowed private companies to assert ownership of genes in individual human bodies, when in fact gene patents covered only DNA sequences that had been isolated from, and existed outside of, the human body; or because they believed (more plausibly) that gene patents threatened to raise the cost of medical diagnoses and experimentation to an unacceptable level. Others contended, however, that higher costs and limited access are the necessary price we pay, in the short term, for the long-run benefits generated by the patent incentive; and that, in any event, it's simply too difficult to define an unpatentable "product of nature" in any principled way because every physical thing is simply a combination or modification of material found in nature. Many of these same arguments and policy considerations can be brought to bear, with some modifications, in regard to patents on diagnostic methods as discussed in Chapter 4.

I will review the evidence for and against these views and suggest that one problem in many of the analyses to date has been the focus on the patentability of genes and other subject matter in isolation from other aspects of the patent and health care systems. In some countries, the costs associated with gene patents may be mitigated through the availability of an experimental use exception in patent law and of universal health care programs that constrain the ability of patent owners to charge monopoly prices.[14] Given the inability of courts to order such holistic reforms, however, the US patent system was left with two unattractive options: either to admit the patentability of both isolated DNA sequences and of diagnostic methods, on the ground that the resulting higher prices and access limitations are no different in kind from the higher prices and access limitations that result from patents on, say, life-saving drugs; or to deny patentability, and thus potentially to undermine the incentive to engage in some forms of cutting-edge research on the ground that the short-term costs are too high. It may be that the latter option is to be preferred, particularly if other incentive systems (such as government and private funding of basic research, coupled with first-mover advantages) remain untouched and can take up much of the slack; but the recognition that whichever rule a court or legislative body adopts may wind up allocating life-saving benefits to one group or another should lead us to question simplistic views of gene patents as either an obvious good or evil.

As for the subject of Chapter 5, business methods and software, the question of patentability may seem less tragic, but (if anything) all the more salient given the explosion in the number of business and software-related patents that occurred from, roughly, the early 1990s through the early 2010s. To many observers, the majority of these patents did little, on balance, to stimulate innovation. Rather, critics charged, these types of patents tended to be of low quality, while also being uniquely susceptible to abuse on the part of patent trolls (the subject of Chapter 8). Moreover, some companies acquired patents in these fields mostly for defensive purposes—to fend off, or to be able

to retaliate in the event of, patent infringement lawsuits filed against them—
with the result that acquisitions of patents and patent portfolios sometimes
has been likened to an arms race. As is the case with real arms races, however,
there may be good reasons to suspect that, in a better world, many of the resources spent on the acquisition of new weapons (here, patents) could be put
to more productive uses. (The premise is that companies would still develop
innovations in these fields, but without the need to obtain, license, or enforce
patents relating to them.) Proposals to "ban the bomb" by eliminating software and business methods patents altogether nevertheless raise concerns that
at least *some* of these patents might induce invention that otherwise would
not occur—and, perhaps more importantly, that it isn't as easy as you might
think to define exactly what "software" or "business methods" *are*. In a world
in which many products use software, after all, a ban on software patents
might require rather fine (and perhaps easily evaded) distinctions between
unpatentable software and patentable software-related art. Others argued that
software and business methods actually weren't uniquely bad in comparison
with other patents, and that reforms short of abolition were a more sensible
solution to perceived problems. In any event, as we shall see, since 2010 the
Supreme Court has made it increasingly difficult (though not impossible) to
obtain valid patent rights in software and business methods, with many of the
battles now fought out in new types of administrative-law proceedings that
Congress created only in 2011.

The next two chapters will focus on, among other things, some current
debates relating to the patenting of drugs. Here the focus is somewhat different
from the preceding chapters, since most observers agree that drug patents play a
crucial role in encouraging the development of new medicines. At the same time,
however, concerns are widespread that drug companies sometimes wield their
patents in a manner that is potentially harmful to public health, for example by
impeding the marketing of lower priced generic drugs. In this regard, Chapter 6
takes up the question of whether, or to what extent, drug patents contribute to
the high cost of health care in the United States. To get a better handle on the
topic, this chapter also will introduce you to a couple of other bodies of law that
interact with patents in this sphere, namely food and drug law (which permits
companies to market new drugs and medical devices only when they are proven
safe and effective), and antitrust or competition law. For many people, antitrust
appears to conflict with patent law, inasmuch as patents are (sometimes correctly) viewed as statutory monopolies, while the whole purpose of antitrust law
is to *reduce* the market distortions caused by monopolies. In reality, the tension
between these two bodies of law is often not quite as stark as people make it out
to be, though there are some areas of real conflict; and while patents do indeed
play a role in keeping the price of drugs high, I shall argue, it has sometimes been

the failings of regulatory and antitrust law that have enabled firms to manipulate the health care system to their advantage.

Chapter 7 then takes a more global perspective by introducing you to, among other things, the Trade-Related Aspects of Intellectual Property Rights (TRIPS) Agreement, one of many treaties administered by the World Trade Organization (WTO). Since 1995, TRIPS has obligated WTO members to extend patent protection to drugs, though this obligation was deferred for a period of time with respect to developing countries, and has been further postponed with respect to the least-developed. Nevertheless, by the early twenty-first century, many of these developing countries had begun to think twice about the wisdom of enforcing patents on drugs, and they sought assurances from the WTO that they could compel drug patent owners to license at least some of their patents at below-market prices. The WTO's TRIPS Declaration of 2001 largely affirmed the developing countries' position, though, as it turned out, expectations that this would lead to the widespread compulsory licensing of patents were soon deflated. These disappointments notwithstanding, I will argue that the developing countries' efforts to loosen some of the obligations set forth in TRIPS probably made sense. At the same time, compulsory licensing is hardly a panacea; and for the poorest of the poor, the vagaries of patent law often have little impact for good or ill. Rather, other tools for improving both the development of and access to health care must be both cultivated and extended.

The final chapters address two aspects of contemporary patent law that have garnered considerable attention over the past five to ten years in both the United States and abroad. The first, discussed in Chapter 8, is the rise of patent assertion entities (PAEs), more popularly known as patent trolls, which buy up patents and then seek to license—or litigate—their use by others. Actually, PAEs sometimes are able to generate revenue simply by threatening to file suit, given the confluence of a number of factors including: (1) the huge volume of patents in existence, which often is too high for any company to have carefully searched before launching a new product; (2) the vague language with which these patents often have been drafted, resulting in uncertainty as to precisely what they cover; (3) the high likelihood that allegedly unauthorized uses of these inventions are inadvertent, that is, the result of independent invention by the user—a factor that nevertheless does not excuse infringement, which is a strict liability tort requiring no showing of intentional copying; and (4) the potential for ruinous liability if a court were to order an infringer suddenly to cease infringing (and possibly to pay monetary damages for past infringement as well). (Recall from above just how many patents are potentially embodied in a smartphone, and imagine the consequences if the unintentional infringement of any one of them could lead to shutdown.) In recent years, Congress has considered several different ways of addressing the trolling phenomenon, and many of the states already have enacted their own anti-troll measures. I'll discuss several of these possible solutions, as well as the broader question of whether trolling really is a serious problem—whether it constitutes a tax on innovation, more than a means of inducing new innovation—or whether these concerns are overblown. (To cut to the chase, I'll explain why I think the concerns are indeed serious, though less so as of mid-2017 than they appeared only a year or two ago.)

Chapter 9 will then discuss some aspects of the "smartphone wars" that, over the past few years, have embroiled firms such as Apple, Samsung, and Google/Motorola in litigation spanning the globe. Here, many (though not all) of the relevant patents are so-called *standard-essential patents* (SEPs). As the name implies, a firm that wants to market a product in a particular industry must be sure that the product conforms to agreed-upon technical standards (for example, relating to the exchange of information over wireless networks). Standard-setting organizations (SSOs) often require their members (which, in the case of standards relating to wireless communications, comprise just about all of the major players, including device manufacturers) to agree to license their patents on "fair, reasonable, and nondiscriminatory" (FRAND) terms. Unfortunately, the meaning of FRAND is often unclear, and (as in the patent trolling example above) the risk that a firm could be ordered to stop selling its products if it is unable to reach agreement with the patent owner over the terms of a FRAND license sometimes can be quantified in the billions of dollars. Efforts in the United States, Europe, and elsewhere, to reach an appropriate framework for dealing with SEP owners' obligations to license their patents on FRAND terms are ongoing as of this writing. In this regard, I will suggest some ways in which courts and regulatory agencies could deploy patent law (or, less promisingly I think, antitrust law) to reduce the risk of SEPs resulting in industry holdups.

A Final Word

As you may have gathered from the preceding discussion, this book not only describes what the law currently is (in the United States and, to a lesser extent, other major patent jurisdictions) but also competing visions—including my own—for what it should be. Thus, by the time you get to the end of book, you'll know something about patents generally, as well as some specifics about matters such as gene patents, TRIPS, and FRAND. But you'll also know where I and others stand on these and other leading issues of the day, and why—for example, why I believe one argument, theory, or body of evidence is more credible than another when it comes to questions such as whether genes or software should be patented—and you can judge for yourself whether the reasons supporting these views hold water or not. In all honesty, though, I'm less interested in convincing you that I am right than in prompting you to think through (and rethink) your own views, based on a deeper understanding of the subject. Enabling you to reach your own conclusions is, from my perspective, the most important purpose of this book.

For it's not a stretch to say that the content and practice of modern patent law reflects its makers, users, and enforcers—that is to say, *us*—with all of the good and bad aspects of our collective character: our striving toward knowledge and creativity; our greed and ego; even, to allude once again to Jonathan Haidt's analysis, our diverse views on matters of equality, desert, and sanctity. So throughout this book my message will be to listen carefully to what I have to say and weigh it accordingly; then trust your own judgment about how, if at all, the patent system needs to be reformed. Just don't trust your own judgment *too* much: it's always possible that further information will call your settled beliefs into question. Especially when the subject is patents—the body of law most closely related to science and technology—it's important for you and me both to keep an open mind, and to follow the evidence, wherever it may lead.

Patent Wars

What Exactly *Is* a Patent?

As I discussed in the Prologue, we encounter patented inventions pretty much everywhere we go: in combination, the big five (the United States, China, Japan, South Korea, and the European Patent Office [EPO]) alone grant almost a million new ones every year, and there are over 2.5 million US patents in force today.[1] Not surprisingly, many people's professional lives today require them to read patents, to negotiate patent licensing agreements, or at least to understand some of the relevant business and legal issues to which patent law pertains. If you're one of those people—an engineer or research scientist, perhaps, or an employee of a pharmaceutical or smartphone company, to name just a few possibilities—you may already be familiar with all or most of what I will be covering in this chapter, and you may want to move on to the succeeding chapters right away. If you're not one of these people, however, this chapter will provide you with a basic understanding of what a patent is, and how the patent system works (or sometimes fails to work, as the case may be), and it will enable you to better comprehend the rest of this book. I'll begin by trying to dispel some common *mis*understandings before proceeding with an overview of what patents are and what they enable their owners to do. Most of what follows will relate to *utility patents*—patents for new inventions—but I'll say a little about design and plant patents at the very end.

Some Common Misunderstandings

Throughout the centuries, people have made use of myths and other stories to explain, console, or offer inspiration to deal with the challenges posed by everyday life. You might think that the hard-nosed, science-infused world of technology and invention would be largely immune from this tendency, but it's not. For many people (including some who should know better) the patent system derives its justification from what is sometimes referred to as the "myth of the solitary genius." What follows is my version of the story, with a few embellishments.

Once upon a time, there was a solitary genius (call him Steve—for some reason or another, in this mythical world, the protagonist is almost always a guy)[2] who spent all of his spare time, day and night, toiling away in his garage to invent what no one had ever invented before. (Since we're dealing in clichés here, let's call Steve's project the "better mousetrap.") Steve devotes all his mental and physical energy, to say nothing of his life's savings, to turn his vision into reality, even when it means neglecting such creature comforts as proper nutrition, sleep, or personal hygiene. (Perhaps he has more than a little in common with that other hackneyed character, the starving artist.)[3] Eventually, though, it all pays off. Steve's unique combination of brilliance and persistence leads him to his breakthrough, and he proves the naysayers wrong by perfecting his better mousetrap. Steve then fills out some paperwork and sends it off, along with a working model of his invention, to the Patent Office in Washington, DC (Actually, the full name of this agency is the United States Patent and Trademark Office, or USPTO, and today it's headquartered just outside the DC city limits in Alexandria, Virginia). The office reviews Steve's application, makes sure the invention lives up to its claims, and then issues Steve a patent, conferring upon him a statutory monopoly over his new device. From then on, all Steve needs to do is sit back and wait for the world to beat that long-anticipated path to his door. Fame and fortune no doubt await.

As myths go, this one's not bad. Perhaps it inspires some young people (boys and girls both, one would hope) to study hard, work diligently, and dream big: after all, they could be the next Thomas Edison (or Steve Jobs, or Bill Gates, or whoever). And like most good myths, it bears just enough of a relation to reality—or to what many of us would like reality to be—that it can almost seem plausible. People like Thomas Edison and Steve Jobs really did work long, hard, sometimes solitary hours, to perfect their ideas; and they certainly met with enormous commercial success. As a result, people sometimes express concern that certain enacted or proposed changes to patent law will weaken patent rights in such a way as to have a detrimental effect on small, independent inventors, whom they claim are the "backbone" of innovation.[4]

Like many myths, however, the story of the solitary genius glosses over more than a few inconvenient facts—among them, that most inventors aren't solitary and they aren't geniuses. As for solitariness, most patented inventions today are the work of teams of inventors who are employed by corporations or universities, and who earn a salary (perhaps supplemented by a contractual right to share in royalties or other perks).[5] More fundamentally, as I noted in the Prologue, at least since Isaac Newton, if not earlier, scientists and engineers have understood that few if any great technological ideas spring full-formed like Athena from the head of Zeus; rather, new ideas necessarily build on that which came before. Invention therefore is typically a form of collaboration among creators in real time (e.g., Steve Jobs and Steve Wozniak) and across the decades (e.g., Steve Jobs benefiting from the insights of earlier pioneers in the fields of computer science, electrical engineering, and—according to Jobs himself—calligraphy).[6] As for genius, perhaps its presence or absence depends on how one defines the term. Assuming, however, that the term refers, roughly, to someone who comes up with an idea that is far, far ahead of its time, genius also turns out to be pretty uncommon in the inventive sphere. As Stanford University Law School Professor Mark Lemley has written, "new ideas are often either 'in the air' or result from changes in market demand or the availability of new or cheaper starting materials."[7] As a result, near-simultaneous invention by two or more teams of inventors working independently of one another is so prevalent as to be virtually the norm. Nor is this a new phenomenon; near-simultaneous invention appears to have been as common in the days of Thomas Edison and Alexander Graham Bell (both of whom raced neck-and-neck with others in the development of, respectively, electric lighting and telephony) as it is today.[8] This is not to suggest that there are no geniuses in the inventive sphere, of course; but it does appear that genius is the exception, not the rule. Fortunately, even the law manages to get this point right, with the Supreme Court long ago explicitly disavowing any implication that a patentable invention must reflect the "flash of creative genius."[9]

A second way in which the myth departs from reality is with regard to the premise that, in order to obtain a patent, inventors have to actually *make* something. They don't. Formally, as a matter of legal doctrine the act of "invention" requires two conditions. The first is "conception," which is sometimes defined as "the formation, in the mind of the inventor, of a definite and permanent idea of the complete and operative invention."[10] So, if you steal an invention from someone else, you're not the person who conceived it and you cannot, lawfully, obtain a patent. The second condition for an act of invention to occur is referred to as "reduction to practice"; the term seems to suggest that the invention must be, well, *practiced*, in the sense of actually performed or accomplished. And that certainly is one way to show that you have invented something: to engage in what patent lawyers refer to as an "actual" reduction to practice, meaning that the inventor builds a working model of the invention and ascertains that it works to achieve its intended purpose. So if Steve wants to build a model of his better mousetrap, he should go for it. He can even send the model along with his patent application if he really wants to, though inventors usually don't do that anymore.[11] Law being law, however, an alternative way of proving that you are an inventor is to engage in a "constructive"—or as a cynic might put it, imaginary— reduction to practice, which consists of merely filing a valid patent application. In other words, the inventor doesn't have to actually *build* anything, but only describe *how* to build it in terms that would enable someone familiar with the relevant field of technology to make and use it. (More on this "enablement" requirement of patent law below.) Of course, the description must be such that the Patent Office can be reasonably confident that the invention will, in fact, work if built—though curiously, the burden of coming forward with reason to *doubt* that the invention will work rests with the Patent Office, rather than the burden resting on the applicant to prove that it *does* work.

A third, related, way in which the myth is at odds with reality concerns its implicit premise that inventors necessarily invent complete and tangible end products—things like lightbulbs, telephones, airplanes, and so on. Sometimes they do, of course. Perhaps the most commonplace modern-day example is in the pharmaceutical field, where patents often read on the compounds that comprise the active ingredients in patented drugs.[12] But utility patents can read on any of four types of subject matter, namely machines (sometimes referred to as apparatuses); compositions of matter (drugs are an example); articles of manufacture (any other sort of physical thing); and processes, also known as methods.[13] (A combination of machines or of methods is called a "system" and would be considered a type of a machine or method, as the case may be.) Subject matter falling into any of the first three of these categories is necessarily tangible, but there is no requirement that it comprise an entire, saleable product. Indeed, in some industries—information technology is a notable example— patents often read on relatively small parts of a larger device. As Stuart Graham and Saurabh Vishnubhakat point out, for example, smartphones incorporate not only software patents, but also a range of other technologies relating to displays, microprocessors, signal processing and transmission, and compression.[14] Moreover, the fourth category, processes, need not be tangible at all, though (as we shall see in Chapter 5) the law is at present a bit unclear regarding the extent to which patentable processes must *pertain* to something physical. (A process that, say, turns straw into gold obviously effects a physical transformation of one thing into another; but what about a process that converts digital input into digital output?)

A fourth problem is that the myth, at least as I described it above, glosses over all of the work that goes into the process of applying for a patent. Briefly stated, the application must describe the invention in some detail and stake out a "claim" to the invention's boundaries, within which others may not trespass. Although individual inventors are permitted to write and defend their own patent applications (in legal jargon, to act *pro se*), it's usually advisable to leave to professionals the work of patent drafting and "prosecution," the latter term referring to the process of shepherding the application through the Patent Office. Both lawyers and nonlawyers may qualify as such professionals, by passing the USPTO's special patent bar exam. (Even to sit for the exam, however, an aspiring patent lawyer or "patent agent," the latter being the term used to refer to nonlawyer patent drafters/prosecutors, normally must have taken a specified combination of qualifying graduate or undergraduate science, math, or engineering courses. No special training is required for lawyers to engage in other types of patent-related work, though, such as patent litigation in federal court or negotiating patent licenses.) Nevertheless, despite their small numbers in comparison with, say, criminal or divorce lawyers, patent lawyers and agents are not especially hard to find; and compared with some lawyers, their fees are not terribly steep. In the United States, the average fee for drafting and prosecuting a patent application is (roughly) in the $10,000-or-so range,[15] though complex or contested applications can wind up costing much more. Suffice for now to note that the job of drafting and prosecuting a patent application that successfully makes its way through the Patent Office, that is difficult for others to design around (I'll explain what this means shortly), and that (if necessary) will hold up in court, is not a simple task.[16] After the application is submitted it is, eventually, subjected to an examination by a qualified patent examiner, and there often will be ongoing discussions between the patent lawyer or agent and the examiner concerning such issues as whether the invention as claimed is patentable, whether the application should be amended, or whether it should be divided up into two or more separate applications. Most applications are published eighteen months after filing, and overall the process of obtaining a patent for a new invention usually takes two or three years, though it can take less or more time depending on the circumstances.

A fifth problem with the myth is one that I already alluded to in the Prologue: the cliché about the world beating a path to the inventor's door. The truth is that often the world couldn't care less: many, probably most, patents are never commercially successful.[17] Furthermore, of those that are, very few live up to the hype of being statutory "monopolies" in any meaningful sense. To an economist, a monopoly exists when only one entity supplies the vast majority of a product or service for which there are no adequate substitutes; the monopolist's privileged position enables it to charge a higher price, and to produce less output, than would a group of competitive firms. So understood, the use of the term "patent monopoly," which one sometimes still encounters (even in judicial opinions), seems a bit odd. Often there is *no* demand for the patented article, and describing the ownership of something that no one wants as a monopoly is just plain silly.

Other times, there is some consumer interest in the patented invention, but not so much as to confer upon the inventor anything resembling a full-blown monopoly. As we shall see, just because an invention qualifies for a patent does not necessarily mean that it performs *better* than the existing alternatives; and for most patented goods, there exist a range of better-or-worse substitutes with which the patented good competes. (The US Supreme Court came around to recognizing this point only in 2006.)[18] It's also worth noting that, technically, a patent does not confer upon the inventor any *affirmative* right to make, use, or sell the invention him- or herself. Legally, a valid patent confers only a *negative* right to enjoin (stop) others from making, using, or selling the invention without permission or to obtain monetary damages for their unauthorized use. The relevance of this distinction between affirmative and negative rights is that some patented products cannot be lawfully made, used, or sold, even by the patent owner, until other conditions are in place. A common example is a patented drug, which in the United States cannot be marketed until the Food and Drug Administration (FDA) concludes that the drug is safe and effective, a matter that is usually not resolved until several years after the patent has issued.[19] Given that patent rights generally expire twenty years after the date on which the patent application is filed, this means that the *effective* patent term for pharmaceuticals—the period of time within which the patent owner can actually market the invention free of competition—often consists of only ten years or less, though in the United States it is possible to obtain some extension of the patent term to compensate for regulatory delay.

Finally, even if an inventor happens to own a patent on an invention that promises substantial technical or other benefits over other alternatives, the patent is only worth what others are willing to pay for permission to make, use, or sell products embodying the patented technology. That amount could be substantial, but only if the patent owner is willing to commercialize or license the invention, and to enforce it against parties who infringe (that is, who make, use, or sell the invention without authorization or a valid legal defense). All of these activities are expensive—litigation especially so, though its costs affect both the party filing suit and the defendant[20]—which explains why many inventors are better off assigning or licensing their rights to someone (an employer, perhaps, or a patent troll) who is in a better position to bear these costs. (I'll return to this topic in Chapter 8.) Even then, however, as I noted in the Prologue, over 40 percent of all patents subject to federal court validity challenges are invalidated in whole or in part (though, again, it's hard to know whether these patents are representative of all issued patents).[21] In addition, a majority of the patents litigated to judgment in new proceedings that the 2011 American Invents Act (AIA) authorized the USPTO's Patent Trial and Appeal Board (PTAB) to conduct also wind up being invalidated in whole or in part. (More on the AIA later in this chapter, and on the new PTAB proceedings in Chapter 5.) Though one might conclude from such figures that the Patent Office is derelict in its duty by issuing so many invalid patents, the reality is that each examiner is expected to spend no more than about twenty hours of time processing any given application over the two- or three-year prosecution period. A more rigorous examination procedure, while perhaps desirable in theory, might slow things down enormously or require huge expenditures to hire more patent examiners[22]—though recently the Government Accounting Office has recommended some ways to improve patent quality at the margins, such as through improving examiners' ability to search the prior art (more on what that means shortly).[23]

In any event, the likelihood that a patent eventually might be invalidated in a judicial or administrative proceeding affects how much someone will be willing to pay to use the patent *ex ante*. Given all of these obstacles and what might appear to be a rather slim probability of hitting the jackpot, you might wonder why anyone would go to the trouble of getting a patent in the first place. It's a fair question, but there are some rational answers. One is that patent protection really is a key element to the financial health of companies in some industries— most notably pharmaceuticals, where the upfront costs of research and development are very high and the need to exclude competition for a period of time so as to recoup these costs is substantial. (More about this topic in Chapters 2 and 6.) Another is that many companies feel they can't afford not to get patents if all of their competitors are doing so—the "arms race" I referred to in the Prologue. In addition, some patent scholars have noted that venture capitalists often consider the number of patents a start-up firm has accumulated when deciding whether to offer the start-up financing.[24] The theory is that although patents may be an imperfect signal of firm value, they offer *some* evidence of value that otherwise might be difficult to uncover, given that a start-up is, by definition, not yet widely or publicly traded. Finally, Kennedy School Professor Mike Scherer suggested a few years back that some inventors may seek patents for much the same reason that some people play lotteries: not because it is a prudent investment, but rather because the possibility of a huge, though improbable, payoff appeals to some would-be entrepreneurs who, unlike many of us risk-averse types, like a good gamble.[25]

So ... What Exactly Is a Patent?

At the most literal level, a utility patent is a document issued by a government agency—or by some other authority to which multiple governments are members, such as the EPO—entitling its owner to exclusive rights in a new invention for a period of time. In most countries, including the United States, that period of time begins running on the date the patent is granted and expires twenty years after the date on which the application was filed—although it sometimes can be extended for various reasons or, more commonly, may terminate early due to the owner's decision not to pay the periodic maintenance fees that are necessary to keep the patent in force. The rights conferred by a patent are usually viewed as a form of personal property that can be bought, sold, or licensed. (A license is, technically, a permission to make, use, or sell, and the patent owner who chooses to license may do so on an exclusive basis—e.g., promising Company A that it will license Company A and no others—or on a nonexclusive basis, e.g., promising to license Company A but reserving the right to license as many others as the patent owner wishes.) If the owner discovers someone making, using, or selling a product or process that falls within the scope of the patent's claims, without the patent owner's authorization, the owner may go to court and demand an injunction and/or monetary damages. Some patent owners' business models depend upon the ability to obtain an injunction, which ensures that the owner faces no competition from other firms that would like to make, use, or sell the patented invention; whether this exclusivity amounts to a full-blown monopoly over some well-defined product market, however, depends upon whether there are adequate substitutes for the patented product, as discussed above. Other patents owners, who may lack the capacity to make, use, or sell the patented product themselves, may prefer to license their rights in exchange for royalties.

(There are, by the way, a few exceptions that sometimes enable someone who has engaged in the unauthorized use or sale of a patented invention to avoid liability for infringement. The most common is the first-sale or "exhaustion" doctrine, under which a person who lawfully purchases a patented article is free to use or resell the article without consent of the patent owner. I'll discuss some of the nuances of this doctrine in Chapter 7. Another is "experimental use," which in many countries exempts certain experimental uses of patented inventions from liability. In the United States, however, the common-law version of this exception applies only when the experiment is done entirely "for amusement, to satisfy idle curiosity, or for strictly philosophical purposes"[26]—which is to say, just about never, although there is a somewhat broader experimental use defense that applies when, for example, a generic drug company experiments on a patented invention for the purpose of submitting information to the FDA.[27] Note also that, although independent invention is common—which in turn means that people often infringe others' patents inadvertently, that is, without even being aware of the patent's existence—independent invention is not a defense to patent infringement, which is a strict liability tort.[28])

One of the first things I do when I teach my introductory intellectual property or patent law courses is to show my students some real patents, so that they have some concrete examples to anchor their understanding of the terms and concepts we will be covering throughout the semester. A good one to use for teaching purposes, because the nature of the invention is relatively simple for newcomers to the field to comprehend, comes from my former colleagues at the University of Florida, David Saliwanchik and Jeff Lloyd, who for several years taught patent drafting and prosecution while maintaining their own busy practice in Gainesville and Orlando. The first page of the fourteen-page Fregley et al. patent is reproduced in Figure 1.1. (You can easily find the full text online from the USPTO's Patent Full-Text and Image Database.) Recall from above that the process of obtaining a patent like this one begins with the patent attorney or agent drafting an application, most of the content of which consists of information that ultimately will be found in the issued patent, subject to whatever amendments are made during the prosecution.

The first things to notice are, at the top left of the patent document, the words "United States Patent [19]," underneath which it reads "Fregley et al." The "[19]" and other bracketed numbers found on the cover page are called "INID" codes, for "Internationally Agreed Numbers for the Identification of (bibliographic) Data." These are used by most of the world's patent systems to make it easy for people reading foreign patents to identify the relevant portions of the document.[29] "19", for example, identifies the office or organization that issued the patent. "Fregley et al." are the inventors (in patent law, sometimes referred to as the "inventive entity.") They are more fully identified a few lines down as Melvin J. Fregley, R. Malcolm Privette, and Robert Cade, of Gainesville, Florida. (Dr. Cade was the inventor of Gatorade—the name refers to the University of Florida Gators—and the invention claimed here is also a type of sports beverage.) The top right lists the patent number (4,981,687) and the date of issue (January 1, 1991). (As we will see throughout this book, a common shorthand for referring to issued patents is by their last three digits, e.g., '687.) The modern numbering system in the United States began in July 1836, so from that date through the beginning of 1991 the United States issued about 5 million patents. Since 1991, the USPTO has issued more than 4 million more.

Moving back to the left-hand column, you'll find the invention's title[30] ("Compositions and Methods for Achieving Improved Physiological Response to Exercise") and, as noted, the names of the inventors. US patent law requires that all of the inventors be named in the patent application and that each one file an oath or declaration to the effect that he or she believes himself or herself to be an inventor of the claimed subject matter.[31] Historically, US patents have issued in the name of the actual inventor or inventors as well, even if those individuals (as here) have already assigned their rights to an employer. A recent change now permits the patent to be issued in the name of the assignee, who is legally the owner of the patent; this conforms to the long-standing practice of other major patent systems.[32] Even before this change took effect, however, assignees (like the University of Florida in the example) were permitted to prosecute applications if they filed the required proof of the assignment with the USPTO. Assignments made after the patent is granted (say, from the University of Florida to Startup Inc.) may, but are not required to, be recorded with the USPTO. Absent a recording, however, a person accused of infringement may

United States Patent [19]

Fregly et al.

[11] Patent Number: 4,981,687

[45] Date of Patent: Jan. 1, 1991

[54] **COMPOSITIONS AND METHODS FOR ACHIEVING IMPROVED PHYSIOLOGICAL RESPONSE TO EXERCISE**

[75] Inventors: Melvin J. Fregly; R. Malcolm Privette; Robert Cade, all of Gainesville, Fla.

[73] Assignee: University of Florida, Gainesville, Fla.

[21] Appl. No.: 378,582

[22] Filed: Jul. 17, 1989

Related U.S. Application Data

[63] Continuation-in-part of Ser. No. 226,027, Jul. 29, 1988, abandoned.

[51] Int. Cl.^{5} A61K 47/00; A61K 33/14; A61K 31/70; A61K 31/52

[52] U.S. Cl. 424/439; 424/679; 424/680; 514/23; 514/264; 514/557; 514/738

[58] Field of Search 424/439, 606, 679, 680; 514/53, 264, 557, 738, 23

[56] **References Cited**

U.S. PATENT DOCUMENTS

4,042,684	8/1977	Kahm .
4,322,407	3/1982	Ko .
4,839,347	6/1989	Franz 514/53
4,874,790	9/1989	Stanko 514/557

OTHER PUBLICATIONS

Maughan, R. J. and M. Gleeson (1988), "Influence of a 36h Fast Followed by Refeeding with Glucose, Glycerol or Placebo on Metabolism and Performance During Prolonged Exercise in Man," The Eur. J. Appl. Physiol. 57:570–576.

Gleeson, M., R. J. Maughan, and P. L. Greenhaff (1986), "Comparison of the Effects of Pre-Exercise Feeding of Glucose, Glycerol and Placebo on Endurance and Fuel Homeostasis in Man," The Eur. J. Appl. Physiol. 55:645–653.

Miller, J. M., E. F. Coyle, W. M. Sherman, J. M. Hagberg, D. L. Costill, W. J. Fink, S. E. Terblanche, and J. O. Hollszy (1983), "Effect of Glycerol Feeding on Endurance and Metabolism During Prolonged Exercise in Man", Medicine and Science in Sports and Exercise 15(3): 237–242.

Terblanche, S. E., R. D. Fell, A. C. Juhlin–Dannfelt, B.

W. Craig, and J. O. Holloszy (1981), "Effects of Glycerol Feeding Before and After Exhausting Exercise in Rats," J. Appl. Physiol. 50(1):94–101.

Allen, D. Y., and L. M. Reidesel (1985), "Overhydration Following Ingestion of Glycerol Solution," (Environ. Physiol. (3713–3720), p. 1046 (abstract).

Reidesel, M. L. (1987), "Oral Glycerol Solutions as a Deterent to Dehydration During Heat Exposure", Department of the Air Force Report, AD–A118746.

Meuli, L. E., T. Lyons, M. L. Reidesel (1988), "Plasmid ADH and Aldosterone Levels Following Glycerol Induced Hyperhydration," Exercise II (1309–1314), p. a521.

Felig, P., A. Cherif, A. Minagawa, and J. Wahren (1982), "Hypoclycemia During Prolonged Exercise in Normal Men," N. Engl. J. Med. 306(15):895–900.

Riedesel, M. L., D. Y. Allen, G. T. Peake, and K. Al–Quattan (1987), "Hyperhydration with Glycerol Solutions," J. Appl. Physiol. 63(6):2262–2268.

Lyons, T. P., M. L. Riedesel, and L. E. Meuli (1988), "Physiological Costs of Exercise Following Hyperhydration with Glycerol," Temperature Regulation I (35–40), p. 323 (abstract).

Ferguson, M., and M. M. O'Brien (1960), "Heat Stroke in New York City: Experience with Twenty–Five Cases," NY State J. Med. 60:2531–2538.

Costill, D. L. and K. E. Sparks, (1973), "Rapid Fluid Replacement Following Thermal Dehydration," J. Appl. Physiol. 34(3):229–303.

Greenleaf, J. E. (1979), "Hyperthermial and Exercise," Int. Rev. Physiol. 20:157–208.

Primary Examiner—Mukund J. Shah
Assistant Examiner—E. C. Ward
Attorney, Agent, or Firm—Saliwanchik & Saliwanchik

[57] **ABSTRACT**

Disclosed here are novel compositions and methods which can be used to reduce or prevent adverse physiological effects of physical exercise or environmental exposure. The novel compositions comprise fluids containing water, sugar, electrolytes, and a substance which is non-toxic to man or animals, can be rapidly absorbed through the gastrointestinal tract, prevents decreases in blood volume, and acts as an energy source.

8 Claims, 7 Drawing Sheets

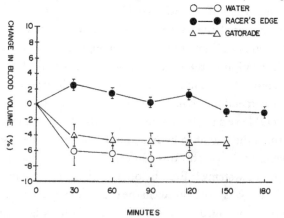

Figure 1.1 US Patent No. 4,981,687, Front Page

have a difficult time figuring out who actually owns the patent at issue; this lack of transparency with respect to ownership has become a point of contention in the recent debates over patent "trolls," as we shall see in Chapter 8.

Still looking at the left-hand column, you'll see that the patent discloses a filing number, the application date, and information about a related application. (Sometimes an inventor files an initial application upon which subsequent applications are based.) Next comes a listing of more codes that classify the field of invention and indicate what classes of "prior art" the examiner considered in determining whether the invention was patentable. The remainder of the first column and most of the second column on the right-hand side of the cover page lists various US patents and other "references" cited in the patent. I will discuss later in the chapter why this sort of information is relevant. The cover page then concludes with the names of the examiners and the patent lawyers or agents; an "abstract," or brief summary of the invention; and, in this example, a drawing. Drawings are required "where necessary for the understanding of the subject matter sought to be patented."[33] The actual patent contains seven pages of drawings.

The heart of the patent comes next and takes up all of the remaining six pages (the ones with numbered columns 1–12, if you consult the full text of the patent). This is called the specification, and it contains two parts: a "description" and "claims." The description portion is required to disclose technical information relating to the invention. More precisely, it must satisfy two requirements. First, under US law, the so-called "written description" requirement obligates the inventor to disclose information demonstrating that she is "in possession" of the claimed subject matter. If this sounds confusing, it's because it is; as noted above, the inventor is not required to actually reduce the invention to practice before filing a patent application, so "possession" in this context hardly connotes the everyday meaning of that term. Put simply, the written description requirement is probably best understood as a tool for keeping the inventor honest, by limiting the reach of her rights to that which was within her grasp at the time she filed her application. The other requirement, which is somewhat more intuitive, is referred to as "enablement," and it requires the inventor (as stated in the Patent Act) to disclose "the manner and process of making and using" the invention "in such full, clear, concise, and exact terms as to enable any person skilled in the art to which it pertains, or with which it is most nearly connected, to make and use the same."[34] The basic concept is reasonably straightforward. As I will discuss in more detail in Chapter 2, one of the purposes of patent law is to encourage inventors to disclose their inventions, rather than keeping them secret (as trade secret law permits), so that others may learn from these discoveries, consider ways of improving upon them, and upon expiration of the patent practice the invention freely. The enablement requirement satisfies this purpose, by obligating the inventor to disclose her discovery in sufficient detail to allow a person skilled in the "art"—the relevant field of technology—to make and use the invention "without undue experimentation" (this last part being a judicial gloss on the statute). Of course, as with other aspects of patent law, determining what the concept requires as a practical matter is not always easy. The Patent Office and the courts sometimes have to exercise judgment in determining how much detail must be disclosed, how much skill to attribute to the person skilled in the art, and how much additional experimentation on the latter's part would be "undue."[35]

Finally, the patent concludes with one or more "claims." As I mentioned earlier in this chapter, the claims establish the boundaries—the periphery—of the patent owners' rights.[36] An analogy is often made to a real estate deed, which sets forth the "metes and bounds" of a homeowner's property. Some patents conclude with just one claim, others with tens or even hundreds. Figure 1.2 reproduces page 14 of the Fregley et al. patent, which concludes with eight claims, starting toward the bottom of column 11 with the words "We claim."

The first thing you may have noted about the eight claims is that each one is exactly one sentence long. That's no accident; each claim *must* be exactly one sentence long, even if that means that some sentences wind up being very lengthy.

4,981,687

11

dehydration accompanying prolonged exposure to cold temperature, the quantity of fluid ingested may be less than that which is necessary to achieve the desired effects in hot climates.

The ratio of ingredients in the composition may also be adjusted for changing environmental or physiological conditions. For example, in cold weather, the composition may contain a greater concentration of glycerol and a reduced concentration of electrolytes. Also, for individuals who desire a lower calorie drink, the sugar may be replaced with an artifical sweetener such as aspartame. For individuals who are concerned about high blood pressure, the drink can contain reduced concentrations of sodium.

EXAMPLE 10

The composition of the subject invention may also be prepared in a dehydrated, powder, or concentrate form for convenience of sale or shipment. When formulated in this way, the product could be reconstituted by the addition of water. The preparation of such a product in the dehydrated, powder, or concentrate form is well known to those skilled in the art. See for example, U.S. Pat. Nos. 4,042,684 and 4,322,407.

We claim:

1. In a beverage comprising water, sugar, and electrolytes, an improvement wherein said beverage further comprises glycerol in a concentration of from about 0.5% to about 5.0%.

2. The beverage, according to claim 1, wherein the concentration of said glycerol is about 1.0%.

12

3. In a beverage comprising water, sugar, and electrolytes, an improvement wherein said beverage further comprises pyruvate.

4. The beverage, according to claim 3, wherein the concentration of said pyruvate is about 1.0%.

5. In a beverage comprising water, sugar, and electrolytes, an improvement wherein said beverage further comprises caffeine in a concentration of about 50 mg/l to about 5000 mg/l.

6. In a beverage comprising water, sugar, and electrolytes, an improvement wherein said beverage further comprises one or more of the following ingredients: glycerol in a concentration of from about 0.5% to about 5.0%; pyruvate; and caffeine in a concentration of from about 50 mg/l to about 5000 mg/l.

7. The beverage, according to claim 6, comprising the following ingredients:

Ingredient	Approximate Concentration
potassium	2 meq/l
sodium	26 meq/l
glucose	4%
pyruvate	1%
caffeine	150 mg/l
water	balance.

8. A method for ameliorating the effects of physical exertion, said method comprising the administration to a person in need of such amelioration a composition of claim 7.

* * * * *

Figure 1.2 US Patent No. 4,981,687, Claims

You also may have thought some of the language sounded a bit stilted: all those "wherein"s and "said"s, for example. Again, that's no accident. Stilted or not, that's the type of language that patents often are drafted in, and if a patent drafter tried to be more creative and use something other than the standard terminology, it might be less clear what was intended.

Now take a close look at claim 1: "We claim, in a beverage comprising water, sugar, and electrolytes, an improvement wherein said beverage further comprises glycerol in a concentration of from about 0.5 percent to about 5.0 percent."[37] If you break it down, the claimed beverage has four parts—known in patent law as "elements" or "limitations"—water, sugar, electrolytes, and glycerol in a con-centration of from about 0.5 percent to about 5.0 percent. Assuming the claim is valid, it covers ("reads on") any beverage having those four elements. A beverage that consists exclusively of 4 percent sugar, 2 percent glycerol, 5 milliequivalents per liter (meq/l) potassium (an electrolyte), and water would clearly fall within the scope of the claim 1. So would a beverage that is 4.5 percent sugar, 2.5 percent glycerol, 8 meq/l phosphate (another electrolyte), and water. But what about a beverage identical to this last one, except that it also contains 100 milligrams per liter of caffeine? This would fall within the scope of claim 6, but would it also fall within the scope of claim 1? In other words, does claim 1 cover a beverage made up *only* of the four claim elements, or does it read on any beverage having those four elements regardless of whether other elements are present too? Here again, patent law shows its formal side: the use of the word "comprising" means that the claim is an "open" claim, so that it reads on any beverage having the four elements, whether additional elements are present or not. Had the drafter used the word "consisting," the claim would be "closed," meaning that it would read on a beverage having *only* the four listed elements. Most of the time, there's no reason to use the closed claiming format, unless the drafter is concerned that adding another element would render the invention inoperative (and thus make the claim invalid).

Claim 1 is also broader than all the other claims, though this is a less obvious point. Students completing their first patent drafting assignment often assume that longer claims are broader, but in fact the opposite is usually true (assuming the claims are all "open"): the shorter the claim, the more embodiments it covers. Compare claim 1 with claim 6, for example. Claim 6 includes everything in claim 1, plus two more elements, pyruvate and caffeine. This means that the universe of beverages falling within the scope of claim 1 is larger than the uni-verse of beverages falling within the scope of claim 6. The same is true for claim 2, which incorporates claim 1 by reference but limits the glycerol element to a concentration of about 1.0 percent. A claim like claim 2 that references another claim by reference is called a "dependent" claim; claim 1, the referenced claim, is an "independent claim." (Notice that claim 7 is also dependent—it references claim 6—and claim 8, the only method claim in the patent, is dependent from claim 7.) You might wonder what the point is of following a broad claim (claim 1) with a narrower claim, but there is a good reason: if the patent examiner were to reject, or a court were to invalidate, claim 1, perhaps claim 2 would survive and would cover some potentially infringing compositions, though not as many as claim 1.

But why might an examiner or a court conclude that claim 1 is invalid? We'll be talking about a variety of possible reasons shortly, but I've already alluded to a couple: written description and enablement. These two requirements are closely related to the claims: a claim that is very broad will need a correspondingly broad enabling description, and the written description will have to demonstrate that the inventor is in "possession" of the broadly claimed invention. The broader the claim, the greater the risk of failing one or both of these requirements. At the same time, narrow claims tend to be less valuable because they don't cover many embodiments, or are easy for others to avoid infringing by substituting or changing an element or two—a process known as "designing around" the patent. (To infringe, a product or process must contain all of the elements of at least one claim. Omit or change one element and, generally speaking, there's no infringement.)[38] There are other potential claim drafting pitfalls as well, some of them highly technical, which we need not go into here. Suffice to say that trying to capture in words a new invention—something that hasn't been done before, at least not in the precise way the inventor has done it—in a manner that is as broad as the law will allow, but not so broad as to risk invalidation, is not easy. Patent professionals earn their money.

All of these potential claim drafting problems also relate to yet another aspect of patent law—claim *construction*, or how the USPTO and the courts interpret claims. You might think that because lawyers draft and courts interpret so many other types of complex documents—contracts, wills, and so on—that patent claim construction would be pretty much standardized by now. But while there are various standards, or "canons of construction," that courts employ to interpret patents, patent claim construction often remains very much a wild card. Empirical evidence shows, for example, that in some years the United States Court of Appeals for the Federal Circuit—the court that hears all appeals in patent matters in the United States—has reversed trial court rulings on claim construction at rates that exceeded 40 percent (though the percentage has gone down in recent years).[39] Claim construction is also one of the many aspects of patent litigation that tends to drive up costs. For approximately the past twenty years, most U.S. courts have held pretrial hearings (known as *Markman* hearings, after a U.S. Supreme Court decision[40]) at which each party presents its evidence, often including expert testimony, as to the meaning of disputed claim terms. The trial judge then makes a ruling and, unless the matter settles, the case proceeds to trial. Only after the trial court has entered judgment at the conclusion of trial does the losing party get to appeal (subject to some exceptions not relevant here). If the trial judge's decision on the meaning of disputed terms is reversed on appeal, the appeals court normally will send the entire matter back to the trial court for a new trial on infringement. On the other hand, a claim that "fail[s] to inform, with reasonable certainty, those skilled in the art about the scope of the invention" is considered "indefinite" and thus invalid.[41]

While we're on the topic of trials and appeals, I may as well say a few words here about patent enforcement. In the United States, a patent owner who believes his or her rights are being violated may file a complaint for patent infringement in federal district court in just about any locale ("venue") in which the defendant does business. This has led, over time, to a significant amount of what lawyers refer to as "forum shopping"—that is, filing the complaint in a district court that is believed to be more advantageous to patent plaintiffs than to defendants (see Chapter 8). Sometimes this is simply a matter of choosing a court where the judges are likely to have substantial experience with the intricacies of patent law, or to keep cases moving quickly (though the time to trial is almost never less than a year and often much more). One district that became very popular for other reasons over the past fifteen to twenty years was the Eastern District of Texas, which mostly hears cases in the towns of Marshall and Tyler, Texas. In the United States (alone among the nations of the world) patent litigants have a constitutional right to trial by jury, and the district's popularity among patent owners was due to the perception that Eastern District juries (and judges) tended to favor patent owners.* (As we'll see in Chapter 8, however, a 2017 Supreme Court decision has made it more difficult for patent owners to initiate litigation in places like the Eastern District with which the typical defendant has few connections.) Sometimes potential infringement defendants can turn the tables by filing first, in a forum more favorable to their interests, what is known as a "declaratory judgment action," which (in this context) would ask the court to declare that the party filing the action is not infringing a specific patent and/or that the patent is invalid. Would-be defendants sometimes do this when they

---

* To be clear, none of this suggests conscious bias, much less corruption; patent owners didn't always win, and there were other venues that could be more favorable to a particular owner's claims. Rather, the perception was that local juries tended to be relatively sympathetic to patent owners, both in terms of win rates and damages awards, and that local rules and practices as adopted and administered by the judges also tended to work in favor of patent owners. For further discussion and citations to the relevant studies, see Chapter 8. As you can imagine, patent litigants keep track of such things.

have reason to believe they are in danger of being sued. In the United States, however, you can't simply go into federal court and request what is known as an "advisory opinion" on some legal issue that interests you; as a matter of constitutional law, there has to be an actual "case or controversy." Parties who have received cease-and-desist letters threatening infringement litigation would almost always be able to request declaratory relief, but aside from this relatively bright-line rule the law is still in flux regarding just how concrete a nascent dispute must be in order for there to be a "case or controversy" sufficient to permit a court to entertain an action for a declaratory judgment.[42] (In addition, though, as noted previously there are now procedures within the USPTO for challenging patent validity outside of federal district court, which I'll return to in Chapter 5.)

Once the matter is in court, each party is entitled to pretrial discovery, which means that each can request the other to turn over documents and other tangible things (unless the documents are subject to, say, the attorney–client privilege) and to require potential witnesses to submit to pretrial depositions—question-and-answer sessions, under oath and transcribed, at which both sides to the dispute (but not the judge) are present. This too is a major factor in the cost of litigation in the United States, where discovery is much more extensive than just about anywhere else. Costs can be particularly high in patent cases, where each side is likely to hire expert witnesses (typically outside specialists in fields such as engineering or economics) to offer opinions on matters requiring specialized knowledge. In any event, if the matter neither settles nor is disposed of on the basis of a pretrial motion, it eventually proceeds to trial.[43] Over 70 percent of US patent infringement cases are now tried before juries, which is a major change that has taken place over the last thirty years; in the 1980s, the average was below 15 percent.[44] Concerns over runaway juries and the potential for ruinous liability, justified or not, are one reason that foreign entities in particular dread being hauled into court in the United States (though they might not mind so much being plaintiffs).[45] My own research confirms the assumption that damages awards tend to be much larger in the United States than anywhere else, though there probably are many nonjury factors (including the size of the market) that affect this result, and substantial damages awards are not unheard of elsewhere.[46]

As noted above, at the conclusion of trial, the losing party may appeal to the Federal Circuit, a specialized court that Congress created in 1981 to hear, among other matters, appeals in patent infringement matters (as well as appeals filed by inventors who dispute the USPTO's decision that their inventions are not patentable). This was a notable development at the time, because the United States historically has not made much use of specialized courts. In addition to recognizing the potential advantages from having a specialized court that could develop expertise in the factual and legal complexities of patent matters—a factor that nevertheless did not lead to the creation of specialized patent *trial* courts,[†] which are now found in many countries—Congress was also concerned that some of the regional circuit courts of appeal (the federal courts that hear appeals in most other instances, based on where the case was tried) were deciding issues of fact and law in a manner that was disproportionately unfavorable to patent owners, and that this was harming American innovation. So Congress created a specialized court, the Federal Circuit, in the expectation that it would interpret patent rights in a manner that would be more friendly toward patent owners. In the opinion of most commentators, this expectation has largely been vindicated, though subject to exceptions in some specific areas of patent law.[47] From the Federal Circuit, it's possible for the disappointed litigant to petition the US Supreme Court to hear its case. On average, though, the Supreme Court agrees to hear no more than a handful of patent cases in any given term.

One final matter relevant to enforcement that people often ask is this: if an inventor has a patent in one country (say, the United States), is the patent enforceable only in the United States or anywhere in the world? The answer is, only in the United States. Patent rights are *territorial*, meaning that they are enforceable only in the country (or region, as with the EPO) in which they are granted. Therefore, an inventor who wants to obtain patent protection in multiple countries must file multiple patent applications. This can be quite burdensome—and expensive, since each patent office demands its own fees—although various multilateral treaties allow for some streamlining of the process. Under the Paris Convention, for example, an agreement to which most of the world's nations are parties, the date on which the inventor files in one Paris Convention member state is deemed to be the date on which she files in another, as long as the second filing occurs within twelve months of the first.[48] (We'll see why this can be important in a minute.) The Patent Cooperation Treaty further eases the process, by enabling the inventor to file a single international application designating those states in which the inventor wishes to obtain patent protection.[49] (The European

---

[†] In 2011, however, the Administrative Office of the US courts selected fourteen federal district courts to participate in a ten-year pilot program intended to "encourage enhancement of expertise in patent cases." Within these districts, certain judges are designated to hear patent cases. If another judge in such a district is randomly assigned to a patent matter, that judge has the option of declining the case and having it assigned to one of the designated judges. For analysis of the program at the five-year mark, see Margaret F. Williams et al., Patent Pilot Program: Five-Year Report Prepared for the Court Administration and Case Management Committee of the Judicial Conference of the United States (Fed. Jud. Ctr. Apr. 2016), https://www.fjc.gov/sites/default/files/2016/Patent%20 Pilot%20Program%20Five-Year%20Report%20(2016).pdf.

Patent Convention does something similar, though only for the nations which are members of that treaty.) Eventually, though, patent prosecution and enforcement are left up to each individual member state or regional authority.[50] Finally, as we shall see in Chapter 7, many aspects of substantive patent law—what types of inventions must be patentable, what rights patent owners must be granted, and so on—have been harmonized over the past two decades (for better or worse) as a result of the TRIPs Agreement.

Technical Requirements for Obtaining a Patent: Inventorship

US patent law has undergone some significant changes just in the past few years. In September 2011, President Obama signed into law a patent reform bill known as the Leahy-Smith America Invents Act, or AIA.[51] The act was the culmination of several years of political wrangling to address various perceived deficiencies in the US system. The first in a series of patent reform bills had been introduced as early as 2005; some of these draft bills included measures that would have modified, among other things, the way damages are calculated and something known as the "inequitable conduct" doctrine, discussed below.[52] Many of these provisions were controversial; as we will see in coming chapters, for example, firms in the software and IT industries have been much more concerned about damages issues than have the pharmaceutical companies, for whom those issues have tended to be less important. Eventually the opposition to some of these proposed reforms, coupled with the fact that courts had begun addressing some of these issues themselves, led the bills' sponsors to delete or dilute some of the more contested provisions. What ultimately passed in 2011 was, nevertheless, a complex piece of legislation that makes some far-ranging changes to US practice. And, even without some of the provisions that had caused tension between the software/IT sector and the drug companies, the AIA still managed to contain enough changes to outrage some of the more tradition-minded segments of the US patent community. The bill's various provisions went into effect in stages, with the most important changes only taking effect in March 2013.

The AIA's two most important changes were, first, the adoption of a modified version of a "first to file" standard for determining which inventors are entitled to patents; and second, the adoption of the new proceedings I alluded to above for challenging patent validity before the PTAB rather than initially in federal district court. I'll hold off discussing this latter change until Chapter 5 and limit myself here to explaining first-to-file. As I mentioned earlier, frequently two or more inventive entities, working independently and without knowledge of one another, may both be working on the same or a very similar invention at approximately the same time. Both may wind up filing patent applications at roughly the same time (say, within a year or so of one another). Assuming that the invention at issue is patentable—that it meets all the criteria I'll be talking about in a few minutes—and that only someone who "invents," in the sense of conceives and reduces to practice, is eligible to obtain a patent—the obvious question is, which inventor gets the patent?[53] The two most obvious options would be to award the patent either to the first to invent or to the first to file. (In theory, you could have a system that awarded *both* parties a patent, but that would create difficulties down the road—would someone wanting to use the patented technology have to obtain permission from both patentees or just one?—and to my knowledge no patent system has ever gone this route.)

Of course, the issue only comes up if the first-to-invent is not also the first-to-file. Experience in the United States indicated that this was actually not a *very* common occurrence; most of the time, the first-to-invent was also the first-to-file, and the Patent Office could politely show the second comer to the door. Inevitably, though, there will be a nontrivial number of cases in which the first-to-invent is the second-to-file, and so patent systems must develop a rule to favor one party or the other. For some people, the choice is obvious: the first inventor seems like the one who "deserves" the patent more. In addition, perhaps a rule awarding the patent to the first-to-file would put smaller, less sophisticated, or less wealthy inventors at a disadvantage in comparison with their well-heeled rivals. For others, the choice of first-to-file might seem equally obvious: it should be a piece of cake to determine who was the first to file, in comparison with determining who was the first to invent. Think back, again, to what it means to invent: the inventor must both conceive and reduce the invention to practice. Determining when someone conceived (mentally) the invention almost always requires some sort of evidentiary hearing, with witnesses and documents to evaluate; determining if and when someone actually reduced to practice, if that is what allegedly happened, also can present evidentiary difficulties and opportunities for fraud. (Things could get even more complicated if Inventor A conceived first but reduced second, and a country took the position—as the United States did—that the first to conceive was the one who deserved the patent, but only if she was "reasonably diligent" in attempting to reduce the invention to practice.) One might question whether the difficulties involved in resolving these matters would be worth the effort—particularly if one believes that the purpose of patent law is *not* to reward inventors as such, but rather to reward inventors only as a means for providing benefits to the public. We'll talk about this issue more in the next chapter, but for now note simply that, on one view, the party who is providing the greater benefit to the public is, arguably, the first-to-file, because a patent issuing from the first-filed application is likely to disclose the invention, and to fall into the public domain, sooner than the second-to-file.[54]

In any event, debates like this have been going on for decades, and by the end of the twentieth century the consensus among the nations was pretty clear: first-to-file is the way to go. Canada and the Philippines were the last countries to switch from first-to-invent to first-to-file, in 1989 and 1998, respectively. Last, that is, except for the United States, where a combination of inertia and nostalgia for the small inventor kept the first-to-invent rule in place until, by the second decade of the twenty-first century, support for a changeover was finally broad enough to result in legislative action. Thus, for applications filed on or after March 16, 2013— the AIA provided that the change would go into effect eighteen months after the president signed the bill, in order to provide time to transition over to the new system—the patent goes to the first-to-file, not the first-to-invent.

Well, sort of; the AIA is actually more complicated than that, for the following reason. Prior to the AIA, the United States had a rule that provided the inventor with a "grace period," which meant that an inventor could obtain a patent even if she published a written description of the invention or publicly used or sold the invention, for a year or less before filing her patent application. No patent would issue, however—in patent language, the inventor would be "statutorily barred"—if the inventor (or someone else, including another, independent, inventor) effected a publication, use, or sale *more* than one year before the filing date. The rule could sometimes be complex in its application—for example, courts had to come up with standards for determining what, exactly, counted as a "public use"—but its underlying purpose was reasonably clear: the rule allowed the inventor to test the market a bit before deciding whether to proceed with a patent application. The rule also was intended to accommodate small or unsophisticated inventors, who otherwise might have inadvertently lost their right to patent by making a premature disclosure. Of course, the one-year duration of the grace period was somewhat arbitrary—it actually was two years for much of the nineteenth century—but the point of limiting the grace period to a defined term was to prevent the inventor from abusing her rights by disclosing her invention and then postponing her decision whether to seek patent protection indefinitely. Anyway, the AIA still provides for a one-year grace period, although the way the new law is written leaves the resolution of some issues, the answers to which were reasonably clear under the old law, uncertain. For example, under the old law, an inventor who used a trade secret process to make products that she sold to the public could not wait more than a year to file a patent application; the process was deemed to be in "public use," even if the public could not readily discover it and it remained a trade secret. At present, opinions differ on whether the new law retains or changes this rule. Perhaps Coca-Cola could someday patent its secret formula, if the AIA changed the long-standing rule.

To return to the first-to-file issue, the new law accommodates the traditional grace period with the first-to-file system in the following way. Suppose that Alice the Inventor invents a new machine in January, publicly discloses her invention in March, and files for a patent application in September. Alice can still get a US patent, even if Ivan the Innovator independently invented the same machine in February, kept it a secret, and then filed his patent application in June (before Alice). Ivan is the first to file, but Alice still gets the patent, which leads some people to refer to the new system as a "first-to-file-or-disclose," rather than as a pure first-to-file, system. But that's a bit of a misnomer as well, because if Ivan had disclosed his invention in, say, February (before Alice's disclosure), but not filed his application until October (after Alice's filing), the new law (unlike the old) would preclude *either* party from getting the patent. So, yes—it's complicated, and perhaps unnecessarily so. Most other countries have managed to get along well enough without offering the inventor *any* grace period.[55] Moreover, as a practical matter, a patent lawyer would advise an inventor who wants to obtain patent protection in *other* countries as well as in the United States not to disclose the invention at all prior to filing her first patent application, because doing so most likely would preclude patentability anywhere but in the United States. (This issue recently came up in one of the smartphone patent cases Apple filed in Germany; a German court invalidated an Apple patent based on evidence that Steve Jobs had disclosed the invention before filing his first application covering it.[56]) In an increasingly global marketplace, the grace period therefore might seem a bit anachronistic, unless other countries were to adopt a comparable grace period (which is a possibility, though for now a remote one).

To summarize where we are so far, to obtain a valid patent you must, first of all, be an inventor (either singly or jointly with someone else with whom you've collaborated). If you stole the idea from somebody else, you're not the inventor and cannot, lawfully, obtain the patent. (Proof that you "derived"—stole—the idea from someone else would result in the application being rejected or, after the fact, in the patent being invalidated.) Second, even if you are *an* inventor, if someone else independently invented first, it is that party, not you, who is entitled to a patent under a first-to-invent system. No country uses the first-to-invent standard anymore for newly filed applications, but there are, and will be for nearly twenty years to come, hundreds of thousands of US patents that were examined and issued under that system. (Early in 2017, for example, the USPTO issued a decision in a pre-AIA inventorship dispute arising out of work done by rival teams relating to the Crispr-Cas 9 gene-editing technology.[57]) Third, even if you are the first inventor, if you're the second to file you won't be entitled to a patent under a pure first-to-file system. (You still might, under some limited circumstances, in the United States, as we have seen.) Fourth, if you publicly disclose your invention prior to filing your application, this would be a ground for rejecting your application in most countries, and even in the United States if the disclosure occurred more than one year before filing. Assuming that you successfully negotiate all of these mine fields, however, there are still plenty of reasons why the Patent Office might deny your application or, if not, why a court someday might invalidate your patent. There are, in other words, a host of additional conditions that must be in place for the invention to be patentable—most importantly, patentable subject matter, disclosure, utility, novelty, and nonobviousness. Let's turn to these other conditions next.

Technical Requirements for Obtaining a Patent: Patentable Subject Matter

The first of these—patentable subject matter or patent eligibility—is one that I've alluded to already. Section 101 of the US Patent Act states that "[w]hoever invents or discovers any new and useful process, machine, manufacture, or composition of matter, or any new and useful improvement thereof, may obtain a patent therefor, subject to the conditions and requirements of this title." Thus, a patentable invention can fall into any of four categories: machines, processes (methods), articles of manufacture, or compositions of matter. Excluded from this list, according to the case law, are laws of nature, naturally occurring products of nature, and abstract ideas. (Also excluded is any sort of nonfunctional subject matter, such as works of literature or art, which are covered by copyright law. Design patent law, which I will discuss briefly at the end of this chapter, covers nonfunctional industrial design.)[58] There is a certain logic to these exclusions, as we shall see—principally the concern that, because natural laws, products of nature, and ideas are the fundamental building blocks from which all new inventions are derived, conferring exclusive rights upon such subject matter would generate far more social costs than benefits. And in the vast majority of cases, the distinction is easy to draw: a new diabetes drug is patentable subject matter, whereas the Higgs Boson is not. (Just to make sure we're clear on this, stating that a new drug is patentable subject matter is not, by itself, to state that the drug is patentable. Patentable subject matter is just one requirement for patentability, in addition to those I've discussed already and those I will discuss below.) Problems arise, however, in applying the distinction between patentable and unpatentable subject matter to certain things that have become very important in the modern world but which either did not exist, or which few people bothered to attempt to patent, until recent decades: things such as human-created life forms (clearly patentable nowadays in the United States and many countries, though still controversial in some quarters); DNA sequences; medical, diagnostic, and therapeutic methods; business methods; and computer software. Debate often centers on arcane legal issues, such as whether a DNA sequence isolated from the human or other animal body is or is not a product of nature, or whether patent law implicitly requires that an invention pertain to the "technological arts"; so stated, however, these issues often do no more than raise other questions, such as how to define such terms as "products of nature" or "technology." Underlying all the legal posturing, however, are important policy questions, among them whether recognizing patent rights in such nontraditional subject matter helps or hinders the progress of technology and, if so, at what cost. I'll be discussing these issues in depth in subsequent chapters; as we will see, the law in the United States in particular as it relates to these topics has become quite complicated.

Technical Requirements for Obtaining a Patent: Disclosure

The second requirement—disclosure—is one that I have discussed already as well: the patent application must provide a written description of the invention, and must enable a person of skill in the art to make and use it. The other principal disclosure requirement in the United States is that the inventor, and anyone else associated with prosecuting the application, must disclose any "material" information—roughly, any information of which the inventor or other person is aware that would affect the patentability of the invention. Let's say, for example, that I am aware that someone else has already invented a device very similar to the device for which I am seeking patent protection. (As we'll see in a few minutes, the other device might anticipate or render obvious my invention.) I might hope that the patent examiner will never discover the other device's existence and will grant me a patent. Nevertheless, I am under an ethical obligation to disclose any such information of which I am aware, though not to go out and find information of which I am *not* aware. The consequence of not disclosing such information is that, if a court later determines that I intentionally failed to disclose material information, I may be found guilty of "inequitable conduct" and my patent rendered unenforceable.[59] To my knowledge, few countries other than the United States have adopted this sort of rule—though in extreme circumstances the failure to disclose material information might lead to other consequences (such as violations of competition law) in both the United States and abroad.[60] Until fairly recently, the ability to plead inequitable conduct as a defense to patent infringement provided patent defendants with a formidable tool, because even though the defense was only rarely successful, the harsh penalty imposed when a court *did* find inequitable conduct had a certain *in terrorem* effect. In any event, in 2011, the Federal Circuit tightened the requirements for proving inequitable conduct, to the point where it now is pleaded much less frequently and is more difficult to prove.[61] Many observers, including me, believed that many of the disputes arising from the pre-2011 inequitable conduct standard had little if anything to do with sound patent policy and that the changes were long overdue, but the debate is not over.

Technical Requirements for Obtaining a Patent: Utility

A third requirement—utility, as it is known in the United States, or "capable of industrial application," as it is referred to elsewhere—is often the easiest to satisfy.[62] Most fundamentally, utility requires only that an invention work—not that it work better, or more efficiently, than a prior invention, but simply that it work to achieve some minimal human purpose. So understood, this requirement excludes very little, other than perpetual motion machines and other such "inventions" that can't work because they would violate the laws of physics. Occasionally people question why we need such a requirement at all; a patent on a fantasy invention (say, a method for breeding unicorns) is hardly a ticket to riches. But such patents would serve no positive social good, either, and there is (apart from the risk that people would waste the Patent Office's time trying to patent such things) a potential for fraud, if some consumers were to conclude, incorrectly, that a patent amounts to some sort of governmental seal of approval.[63]

This potential for fraud leads to another question, however, namely whether the utility doctrine should be used to prevent people from obtaining patents on fraudulent or otherwise harmful inventions. In the United States, this idea was first floated in an old case, *Lowell v. Lewis*,[64] in which US Supreme Court Justice Joseph Story, by way of rejecting the argument that a patented invention must work better than other existing devices, asserted that "All that the law requires is, that the invention should not be frivolous or injurious to the well-being, good policy, or sound morals of society. The word 'useful,' therefore, is incorporated into the act in contradistinction to mischievous or immoral. For instance, a new invention to poison people, or to promote debauchery, or to facilitate private assassination, is not a patentable invention."[65] These statements are what lawyers refer to as *dictum* (or by the plural form, *dicta*), meaning that they were unnecessary to the resolution of the case and not necessarily controlling in future cases. Nevertheless, Justice Story's dictum provided a basis for the Patent Office and the courts from time to time to reject or invalidate applications for such "immoral" inventions as gambling games, seamless stockings (disguised to look like they had seams, which were the fashion in the 1920s), and a process for making unspotted tobacco leaves look spotted (fashion again).[66]

Many of the applications of the "moral utility" doctrine seem silly today, and the Federal Circuit in 1999 put the doctrine to rest, at least as it relates to allegedly fraudulent inventions.[67] Moreover, many commonly patented inventions (e.g., contraceptives, erectile dysfunction drugs) are likely to offend *somebody's* moral scruples, while others (e.g., weapons, e-cigarettes) certainly *can* be harmful. (Nuclear weapons are an exception to this libertarian approach; there's a federal statute specifically forbidding patents on "inventions useful solely in connection with special nuclear material or atomic weapons.")[68] Nevertheless, it may be possible that moral utility could provide a basis for denying patent protection to some inventions, the practice of which would shock the conscience. When activists Stuart Newman and Jeremy Rifkin filed a patent application for a part-human, part-animal "chimera" in 1995, for example—they hadn't actually reduced one to practice, but were trying to attract publicity to the potential misuse of genetic engineering—the USPTO initially denied the application for lack of moral utility. (Subsequently, the Office asserted instead that human organisms did not constitute patentable subject matter.)[69] Perhaps the USPTO would take a similar position in other such cases. Many other countries recognize an analogous limitation on patentability known as *ordre public*, under which patents may be denied to inventions the practice of which would violate fundamental public policy.[70]

A final aspect of utility that has arisen from time to time relates back to the idea that an invention is useful if it satisfies some minimal human need. How minimal is that? The case law in the United States provides that an invention that merely satisfies intellectual curiosity, or that only *might* prove beneficial for some reason someday, is not sufficiently "useful."[71] Not many inventions are excluded by this rule, however; it's clear, for example, that a drug can be (and most are) patented before the clinical studies that the FDA requires as proof of safety and effectiveness have been completed.[72] One (fairly) recent case in which the Federal Circuit applied the utility doctrine to deny a patent, however, is *In re Fisher.*[73] *Fisher* involved an application to patent express sequence tags (ESTs)—DNA fragments that can be used for purposes such as providing the source material that can be used in a process called the polymerase chain reaction to duplicate specific genes. The Federal Circuit held that merely reciting the general purposes for which researchers may use ESTs was insufficient to demonstrate the utility of the *particular* ESTs that Fisher claimed to have invented. Had the inventor been able to describe the utility of the specific genes that the fragments would have helped to duplicate, the case might have come out the other way.[74] Many observers agree with the result in *Fisher*, out of concern that patenting such small fragments would have impeded others' research to a greater extent than it would have stimulated new research on ESTs in particular. Again, though, *Fisher* is an unusual case; *almost* all claimed inventions meet the modest requirements of the utility doctrine.

Technical Requirements for Obtaining a Patent: Novelty

The next requirement is that the invention be novel, or new. In a *very* rough sense, this means that the application must claim something that hasn't been invented before—though a moment's reflection will suggest why, standing alone, this could never be a very precise definition of novelty. An initial problem with defining a novel invention simply as "one that hasn't been invented before" relates to timing: *before what*? A patent system needs to define the date from which novelty is to be measured. The term often used for this date is the "critical date," and its identity depends on whether the system is first-to-file, first-to-invent, or some other variation. So perhaps we could modify the proposed definition to state that an invention is novel if no one else had invented it before the critical date—the date of invention in a first-to-invent system, the date of filing in a first-to-file system, some other date in some other hypothetical system. This helps to clarify the inquiry a bit, but it still leaves many other issues unresolved.

Suppose, for example, that the claimed invention is a chemical compound. Prior to the critical date, however, a chemist (call her Marie) accidentally synthesized the very same compound in her laboratory in Paris, without "conceiving" what it was or reducing it to practice; she then discarded it. Marie, in other words, *made* the invention, but she clearly didn't "invent" it. (Recall from above that an actual reduction to practice requires not only making the invention, but also appreciating that it works to achieve its intended purpose, something that logically can't happen if Marie didn't realize she'd made the compound in the first place. A constructive reduction to practice requires filing a patent application, which Marie also didn't accomplish.) Should Marie's previous making of the claimed compound disqualify the applicant, who understands what the compound is and what it does, from obtaining a patent? (The applicant *must* know these things, or else he won't be able to make an "enabling" disclosure.) Should the answer be different if Marie understood what the compound *was*—she knew its composition—but lacked any idea what it did?

You might respond that, in the two preceding cases, no one (perhaps not even Marie, in the first case) would have sufficient knowledge of Marie's earlier creation of the claimed compound, so perhaps the patent system can simply ignore such remote possibilities. But let's change the facts again: suppose this time that Marie understood what she had made (though maybe not what it can be used for) and that she disclosed the identity of the compound and how she made it in a European scientific publication (which the applicant, however, had not read). Should Marie's disclosure preclude the applicant, who independently discovered the same compound and identified a use for it, from obtaining a patent? What if instead Marie had published her results only in her long-forgotten doctoral dissertation, the only extant copy of which resides somewhere in the archives of the Sorbonne? Should it matter whether those archives are accessible to researchers—and if so, how accessible must they be? Finally, what if the compound Marie made or disclosed is not *exactly* the same one the applicant made, but rather only a very similar compound—one that, say, is identical except that it lacks one additional methyl (CH_3) group? Alternatively, what if the claimed compound combines two *separate* compounds that Marie had previously synthesized?

What I've tried to do in the preceding two paragraphs is to lay out, by way of examples, some of the many issues that a patent system must resolve in trying to determine whether a claimed invention is "novel." I'll now try to explain those issues in a somewhat more systematic fashion.

The first issue to be resolved is the timing—the "before what"—issue, which I've already discussed. Its resolution is the most straightforward, depending on whether the system is first-to-file, first-to-invent, or some other variation. Thus in the United States prior to the AIA, the critical date for novelty purposes was the date of invention; post-AIA, the relevant date is, as in other countries, the date of filing. (Complicating matters in the United States, however, is that the critical date for *statutory bar* purposes—the grace period—remains one year before the date on which the application was filed. But let's move on.)

The second issue involves determining what subset of all inventions (or makings, or disclosures, or whatever) that existed prior to the critical date *count* for purposes of evaluating an invention's novelty. Patent lawyers refer to the universe of things that count as the "prior art" or "prior art references." (So now you understand why the Fregley et al. patent that I excerpted earlier in this chapter mentioned various prior art references. Those were the things the patent examiner considered in evaluating the invention's patentability, or that the inventors themselves called to the office's attention and successfully distinguished from their invention.) In terms of the preceding hypotheticals, then, the relevant questions included whether an invention that was merely made and then discarded is within the prior art; whether disclosures made in scientific journals or doctoral dissertations can fall within the prior art; whether, to qualify as prior art, such disclosures must, like a patent application, inform a person of skill in the art both how to make and use the invention; and whether it matters where the disclosure was published, or how easy it would be for someone to come across it. Each patent system must resolve these matters for itself. In the United States prior to the AIA, for example, prior art included, among other things, inventions that, prior to the applicant's date of invention, were "known or used" in the United States; were "made" in the United States and not abandoned, suppressed, or concealed; or that were described in a printed publication anywhere in the world.

Moreover, to qualify as prior art, the reference only has to inform a person skilled in the art how to make *or* use, not both; and the reference must have been "reasonably accessible" to the public, but need not have been widely known. Applying these rules, an invention that Marie made only in Paris and then discarded wouldn't have been prior art for two reasons: because it wasn't made in the United States and because it was abandoned. Her disclosure in the scientific journal probably would have been, however, while the status of her doctoral dissertation would require more facts concerning its accessibility. Under the new law, by contrast, the United States, like most other countries, considers prior art to include anything that was "available to the public," anywhere in the world, prior to the date of filing.[75] The switch from a so-called "relative novelty" standard (novelty determined, in some instances, only in light of an invention's accessibility within the United States) to an "absolute novelty" standard (consider prior art existing anywhere in the world) will make it marginally more difficult for inventors to obtain US patents.

The third issue concerns how to use the prior art: is an invention novel unless it is found in one single prior art reference, or does it lack novelty if it consists of two or more prior art references in combination? And does the prior art reference (or references) have to be identical to the claimed invention, or only close? The answers here, fortunately, are simple. An invention lacks novelty—to use a synonymous term, is "anticipated" by the prior art—if prior to the critical date there is a single qualifying prior art reference that contains all of the elements of the claimed invention, arranged in the same functional relationship. Thus if Marie disclosed in one single qualifying prior art reference, such as the journal article, a compound identical to the one the applicant is attempting to patent, the claimed invention lacks novelty and is unpatentable. If the invention's elements exist in the prior art only if one combines two or more references, however, or if the elements are not identical, the claimed invention is novel; it is not anticipated by the prior art. It could still falter on one on the remaining hurdles, however—most likely the next (and last) one, nonobviousness.

Technical Requirements for Obtaining a Patent: Nonobviousness

That issue is as fugitive, impalpable, wayward, and vague a
phantom as exists in the whole paraphernalia of legal concepts.
     —Judge Learned Hand, in *Harries v. Air King Products Co.,*
                    183 F.2d 158,162 (2d Cir. 1950)

The last of the requirements for patentability is one of the more difficult to describe: the requirement of nonobviousness (or "inventive step," as many systems refer to it). The basic idea is that, even if novel, some inventions are simply not a sufficient advance over the prior art to merit a patent. But what does it mean to say that an invention is (or is not) a sufficient advance? What is "sufficient"?

One possibility—dare I say the most obvious?—is to focus on technology: is the invention a significant technological advance over the state of the art? But this doesn't really advance the ball very far. How significant should an invention be for a patent to issue? If we require it be *highly* significant, revolutionary, a work of genius, we'll grant very few patents. Maybe that would be just as well; twentieth century Supreme Court Justice Hugo Black is reported to have said that in all his years as a judge he "had seen only one real invention—the airplane—and he wasn't even certain about that one."[76] Except for those who would abolish patents altogether, however, most observers over the decades have concluded that, if you're going to have a patent system, the nonobviousness standard shouldn't be quite *that* high: most inventions, though perhaps clever, are not the work of genius. So how high should the standard be? Should we grant patents on inventions that took people in the field by surprise? What if it was predictable that someone eventually would solve a particular technical problem, but no one knew precisely how or when? Should the patent system reward the industrious grind who tried every conceivable solution to a given problem before hitting upon the one that worked, or does a "nonobvious" solution have to reflect some additional technological *je ne sais quoi*?

Another possibility to consider would be to base the nonobviousness doctrine on some sort of economic footing. A view common among economists is that, ideally, the patent office would grant patents only for inventions that would not have been invented, but for the existence of the patent incentive. Perhaps, then, we could define a nonobvious invention as a novel invention whose existence is attributable to—was induced by—the existence of the patent incentive. Nevertheless, many scholars have hesitated from embracing this "inducement" theory[77] out of concern that we simply can't *know* which inventions would have been created absent the patent system. Even if we happened to know that the prospect of obtaining a patent motivated a specific inventor (or more likely, her employer) to invest in developing the invention, there might be no way of telling whether someone else would have been equally motivated without the prospect of the patent reward. Perhaps most inventions would have been created *eventually*. In response, we could revise the proposed criterion to state that an invention is nonobvious if it wouldn't have been created quite so soon in the absence of the patent incentive, but this merely begs the question of what "quite so soon" means.

These problems have bothered courts and patent scholars for years, and yet it often seems that patent law has made little headway in providing adequate answers. For now, all I'll try to do is to explain briefly what the current state of the law is, and where some of the uncertainties still lie.

Something like a nonobviousness doctrine has been part of US law virtually from the beginning. In a famous letter responding to a litigant's request for advice on a patent dispute, Thomas Jefferson once asserted that a "mere change of form" or material "should not give title to a patent";[78] and, in 1851, the US Supreme Court appeared to vindicate Jefferson's view when it held that a porcelain door-knob was not sufficiently inventive to merit protection.[79] A nonobviousness re-quirement nevertheless wasn't explicitly mentioned in the Patent Act until 1952, when Congress enacted what remains—subject to various amendments, in-cluding those introduced by the AIA—the current version of the US Patent Act. The applicable provision is section 103, which in relevant part states that "a patent for a claimed invention may not be obtained . . . if the differences between the claimed invention and the prior art are such that the claimed invention as a whole would have been obvious . . . to a person having ordinary skill in the art to which the claimed invention pertains. Patentability shall not be negated by the manner in which the invention was made." According to the Supreme Court's 1966 decision in *Graham v. John Deere Co.*, the second sentence was intended to dispel the notion (which the Supreme Court itself had created in an earlier case) that an invention must reflect the "flash of creative genius."[80] All that is required is that the invention is "beyond the skill of the calling," that it "evidence more ingenuity and skill than that possessed by an ordinary mechanic acquainted with the business."[81]

More precisely, in making a nonobviousness determination, the examiner or the court should, first, ascertain the scope and content of the prior art—essentially, all the references it would consider in determining novelty, though for nonobviousness purposes only if the references are from the "same field of endeavor" or are "reasonably pertinent" to the problem the inventor was attempting to solve.[82] Second, the decisionmaker attempts to determine the "level of ordinary skill in the pertinent art."[83] Third, it evaluates the differences between the prior art and claimed invention, with an eye to whether the differences are such that the claimed invention would have been obvious as of the critical date to a "person having ordinary skill in the art"—a fictional con-struct sometimes referred to by patent lawyers by the acronym PHOSITA.[84] (You may recall that we've encountered a very similar concept before—the en-ablement doctrine's hypothetical "person skilled in the art.") For reasons we've already discussed, however, the application of this third step—determining whether the differences are such that the claimed invention would have been obvious to the PHOSITA—is itself hardly obvious. In *Graham*, the Supreme Court did little to clarify it, other than to note the potential relevance of certain factors (usually referred to as "secondary considerations"), such as the commer-cial success of the invention; whether it addressed a long-felt but previously un-solved need; and whether others had tried and failed to solve the problem the invention addresses.[85]

In the years following *Graham*, courts continued to struggle with the meaning of the third step. Consider, for example, a claimed invention comprising four elements, which we can refer to as A, B, C, and D. Suppose there are two relevant prior art references, one containing A and B, and the other containing C and D. Should a court simply substitute its own inexpert judgment for whether the combination of AB and CD was more than the work of a skilled mechanic? Or suppose that the prior art consisted of ABCX, and the inventor thought to substitute element D for X. Work of a skilled mechanic, or invention? Is there any principled way of determining whether the substitution likely would have occurred to someone, even absent the patent incentive? As Justice Potter Stewart put it in another (equally vexing) legal context—how to recognize obscenity— is it all just a matter of "I know it when I see it"?[86]

The Federal Circuit thought not. Not long after it was created in 1982, the court developed a test that was to govern for over twenty years, until the Supreme Court decided to enter the fray once again. Known as the "teaching, suggestion, or motivation," or TSM, test for determining nonobviousness, it asked whether the prior art itself would have taught, or suggested, or motivated a person of ordinary skill to make the substitution, combination, or other solution embodied in the invention.[87] To its defenders, the TSM test provided an objective basis for determining nonobviousness: the examiner, or the court, would simply look to the teachings of the prior art, rather than to their own intuition about what is "inventive." As such, the TSM test may counter the human tendency toward "hindsight bias." Once the magician reveals how he did his trick, it often seems obvious in retrospect. Hindsight is twenty-twenty.[88]

The shortcomings of this approach, however, should be equally evident. Sometimes the prior art may not *expressly* teach, or suggest, or motivate anything: it simply *is*. Consider, for example, a patent obtained by Tropicana in 2000, on orange juice prepared by "harvesting a very early season orange cultivar" selected from among four varieties of (unpatented) oranges developed at the University of Florida; extracting and collecting the juice; and blending it with another orange juice source to make a "product having a Color Number in excess of 33 CN units, while also exhibiting sensory qualities substantially equivalent to the sensory qualities of Hamlin orange juice."[89] (Hamlin oranges are commonly blended with other varieties to make juice.) The Patent Office granted the application, presumably because it was unable to locate any express teaching, suggestion, or motivation in the prior art it reviewed that would have led a person of ordinary skill in the art of preparing orange juice to follow precisely these steps. Another invention that was scrutinized under a very narrow understanding of TSM was the jack-o-lantern trash bag at issue in *In re Dembiczak*.[90] The Federal Circuit engaged in a detailed analysis of the relevant prior art— which included such things as conventional garbage bags, a book describing how to make crepe-paper jack-o-lanterns, and an article describing how to make paper-bag pumpkins stuffed with newspaper—before soberly concluding that none of this material clearly taught toward the claimed invention.

To be sure, courts sometimes were less demanding than one might have expected from cases such as *Dembiczak*, and were willing to find an *implicit* teaching, suggestion, or motivation in the PHOSITA's level of skill or the nature of the problem to be solved. (Even the court in *Dembiczak* recognized this possibility, though it found no such implicit teaching there.[91]) And some questionable patents wound up being weeded out, eventually. In 2001, a group of rival citrus growers challenged Tropicana's orange juice patent by requesting the USPTO to conduct a proceeding known as a "reexamination." As a result, Tropicana in 2008 agreed to "disclaim" the forty-seven claims of the patent and to let the patent lapse for failure to pay maintenance fees. And despite the Federal Circuit's reversal of the Patent Office's nonobviousness ruling in *Dembiczak*, it appears from a search of the USPTO's database that the inventors never did wind up getting a utility patent on their Halloween trash bag. But a challenger could hardly count on the examiner or a court applying the "implicit" version of TSM (which, in any event, threatened to undermine the test's perceived predictability); and the common wisdom at the time was that a challenger had to "connect the dots" in order to stand a chance of proving obviousness.[92] The end result was to be expected: over the years, the USPTO issued a very large number of patents that, in the opinions of many observers, were of low quality (in the sense of being, at best, only marginally nonobvious).

Coincidentally, at the same time that the law on nonobviousness was becoming ever more friendly to patent applicants, the Federal Circuit also was issuing rulings to the effect that most software-related inventions and business methods were patent-eligible. Because these two fields in particular were fairly new to patent law, many people were concerned that there was a dearth of recorded prior art from which examiners could pinpoint a relevant teaching, suggestion, or motivation; and that, as a result, the USPTO was approving far too many software and business method patents that were factually, but not legally, obvious. (I'll return to this perceived problem in Chapter 5.) Relatedly, by some measures, the USPTO was granting 70 percent or more of all utility patent applications—a much higher percentage than in the EPO, which generally has had a better reputation for quality control.[93]

By the first decade of the twenty-first century, enough critical voices were making themselves heard that both Congress and the Supreme Court decided to take on some of the perceived dysfunctionalities of the US patent system. The AIA was the ultimate result of Congress's intervention (and may not be the last word yet). As for the Supreme Court, it "heard, decided, or granted certiorari in six patent cases in 2006, more than in any year since 1965"[94]—including one that addressed the test for nonobviousness, *KSR International Co. v. Teleflex Inc.*[95] (I'll be discussing some of the other cases the Court took on during that and subsequent terms later in the book.) In *KSR*, the invention was a combination of a modular electronic sensor attached to a fixed pivot point of an adjustable automobile pedal assembly; the principal purpose of the combination was "to provide a simpler, smaller, cheaper adjustable electronic pedal."[96] Each element of the combination was in the prior art, but the Federal Circuit had concluded that the art did not teach, suggest, or motivate the combination because none of it was intended to solve the precise problem the inventor had attempted to solve ("a simpler, smaller, cheaper adjustable electronic pedal"). The Supreme Court reversed, holding that TSM was not the only standard for judging nonobviousness; rather, the Patent Office and the courts should apply "common sense," a term Justice Anthony Kennedy used five times during the course of the opinion.[97] The Court also stressed that a PHOSITA is not an "automaton," but rather a person of "ordinary creativity" who might be expected to try to solve problems by combining prior art references, even if those references did not directly address the problem the inventor was trying to address.[98]

So does this mean we're back to "I know it when I see it"? Not necessarily. The Court did provide some more specific guidance, upon which the USPTO and the Federal Circuit have since elaborated. Among the relevant considerations now are such matters as whether the claimed invention combines prior art elements in a manner that yields a predictable or an unexpected outcome, and whether "exogenous" technological developments (such as the development of the Internet) readily lend themselves to new applications (such as conducting auctions over the Internet).[99] In any event, a recent study by Professor Jason Rantanen indicates that *KSR* has had an impact. Rantanen finds that the Federal Circuit has gone from finding nonobviousness in 54 percent of patent infringement cases in which the issue was addressed prior to *KSR*, to only 43 percent afterward.[100] Perhaps patent quality is slowly but surely improving.

Other Types of Patents, Other Types of Intellectual Property

Before ending this chapter, I should say just a few words about other types of patents, as well as other forms of intellectual property. As noted earlier, most countries, including the United States, confer a type of patent or patent-like protection on industrial designs. One recent high-profile case involving design patent rights (discussed in greater detail in Chapter 9) pitted Apple against Samsung, which was accused of copying Apple designs directed to the appearance of the iPhone.[101] Historically, though, design patents have been much less prominent than utility patents; in 2015, the USPTO granted nearly 300,000 utility patents, but only about 26,000 design patents.[102] Design patents are examined for novelty, nonobviousness, and ornamentality (instead of utility), and they last for a period of fifteen years after grant.[103] Industrial designs are registered in much larger numbers in the European Union (more than 90,000 in 2015) and in astonishingly larger numbers in China (close to half a million).[104] Some observers believe we will soon see an upsurge in the number of design patents granted and litigated in the United States as well, perhaps as companies come to view design as an increasingly more important contributor to the success of products such as athletic shoes and electronics. Until now, though, with the exception of a few unusual cases, design patents have played a much less visible role in US law.

So too for plant patents. In 1930, Congress enacted the Plant Patent Act, which authorizes the USPTO to grant patents on new and distinct varieties of asexually reproducing plants. Given the difficult of describing a plant in words, Congress specified that the written description only has to be "as complete as is reasonably possible," but otherwise the provisions that apply to utility patents apply equally to plant patents.[105] In 1970, Congress enacted the Plant Variety Protection Act (PVPA), which is separate from the Plant Patent Act and administered by the Department of Agriculture, and which confers a twenty-year term of protection on sexually reproducing plant varieties that are new, distinct, uniform, and stable.[106] Other countries have broadly similar laws, most of which conform to one of two versions of an international treaty known by its French acronym, UPOV (for *Union internationale pour la Protection d'Obtentions Végétales*, or Union for the Protection of Plant Varieties).[107] An exception under the earlier versions of UPOV, known as the "farmer's privilege," allows farmers to save and reuse patented seed. The more recent version of UPOV, however, allows member states to abolish the farmer's privilege, and a movement to encourage developing countries to adopt the second version of the treaty has been met with some resentment.[108] Within the United States, plant patents have come to play even less of a role than design patents, with the USPTO granting only a little over 1,000 plant patents, and the Department of Agriculture 521 PVPA registrations, in 2015.[109] One reason may be that inventors of new plant varieties are not required to go the plant patent route, but rather may seek and obtain utility patents if their inventions satisfy the relevant criteria.[110] (The concern about not being able to describe a plant has been alleviated by allowing inventors to satisfy the requirement by depositing a sample.) Another is that utility patent law does not recognize a farmer's privilege, which exists under the PVPA. The patents that Monsanto and other major agricultural companies assert these days tend to be utility patents, not plant patents.

The other major forms of intellectual property rights are copyrights, trademarks, and trade secrets.[111] I've already mentioned a little bit about them and will not belabor the point, except to make sure that the distinction between these types of rights and patents is clear. A copyright subsists in an original work of authorship, such as a literary work, a musical composition, or a motion picture; under current law, protection does not expire until seventy years after the author's death. Although copyright and patent law originally developed in somewhat parallel fashion, today the nature of the rights conferred is quite distinct, and there is not much overlap between the two bodies of law. One exception is with respect to industrial design, which can be protected both by copyright (though often is not, for reasons we need not go into here) and by design patent law. Another is computer software, because copyright may subsist in the code itself, while a patent covers the functional aspects of a program (a point I will come back to in Chapter 5). As for trademarks, these are words or other symbols that identify a unique product or service, such as the name "Coca-Cola," or the Quaker Oats man (known to oatmeal mavens as "Larry"). Again, there's not much overlap with patent law, except to the extent that people occasionally assert a form of trademark protection (known as "trade dress") in the distinctive design of a product—something that could, conceivably, also be covered (or have been covered in the past) by a utility or design patent. Of course, a product could incorporate all three of these types of intellectual property in different ways: an ingredient in a cosmetic might be patented, for example, while the brand name of the cosmetic is a trademark, and the labeling might be protected by copyright.

Finally, a trade secret is any form of secret information that confers a competitive advantage upon its owner: the primo example is the formula for Coca-Cola, but there are plenty of more humble trade secrets in things like customer lists as well. Many trade secrets involve subject matter that would not be patentable for one or more reasons (obviousness, for example), but this is not always the case. An inventor who has kept secret a potentially patentable invention therefore must choose between retaining his trade secret or seeking a patent—but he can't do both, because once the Patent Office publishes a patent application, the invention is no longer secret. In many cases, inventors are better off opting for a patent, because patent rights are stronger than trade secret rights inasmuch as the latter are violated only if someone literally steals the trade secret or discloses it in violation of some duty of confidentiality; independent invention and subsequent use by another person is perfectly lawful as far as trade secret rights, but not patent rights, are concerned. But there are exceptional cases, where reverse-engineering someone's trade secret has proven so difficult that no one has succeeded in doing it for decades, or perhaps even centuries (again, think Coca-Cola); in such cases, had the owner gone the patent route, his rights would have lapsed long ago. Thus, while many trade secrets (such as customer lists) have only a relatively short-term commercial value, or eventually cease to be secret because someone else reverse-engineers, independently discovers, or publishes the once-secret information, a small number of trade secrets are, at least potentially, immortal.

Summary

If you've made it to the end of this chapter, you now know more about patents than do most nonspecialists: what patents look like, how they are obtained and litigated, and how they differ from other forms of intellectual property. At this point, we're almost ready to start talking about some of the most news-worthy, and controversial, aspects of patent law—gene patents, generic drugs, business methods, trolls—but there's still one more bit of background to make this discussion meaningful. What is the point of having a patent system in the first place? I've alluded to some possibilities already, of course; the traditional rationales are to encourage both invention and the *disclosure* of that which has been invented. But it's important to understand these rationales a little more deeply: why do governments consider patents necessary to stimulate invention, as opposed to some other means to this end? *Are* patents necessary, as a matter of empirical fact? What other reasons might there be for granting exclusive rights in inventions, and how persuasive are these alternate rationales? These are the questions the next chapter addresses; for answers, we may need to look not just to the history of science and technology, but also to the "dismal science" of economics and (perhaps) even a bit to moral philosophy. Liberal arts majors take note: patent law is for you, too.

2

Why Patents?

Chapter 1 provided an introduction to what a patent is, the conditions that must be satisfied for a valid patent to issue, and the rights that accrue to the owner of a valid patent. I've also mentioned that the most common argument in favor of having a patent system is that patents provide an incentive for the creation and disclosure of new inventions. In this chapter, I'll discuss this and other economic arguments for and against patent rights in greater detail. As we'll see, although most patent lawyers and scholars—including me—buy into one or more of the economic rationales for patents to some degree, a few defend patents and other forms of intellectual property on the basis of nonutilitarian moral theories derived from the writings of John Locke (1632–1704) and Immanuel Kant (1724–1804). These latter theories do not reflect my own views, but they pose some interesting challenges to the more conventional perspective.

The Standard Model: Patents Induce Invention and Disclosure

When I ask my students at the beginning of a new semester why we have a patent system, there are usually two—or sometimes three—different answers I may get. The most common one is that patents encourage invention. I imagine that most of the students giving this answer might have come up with it on their own, even if they hadn't done the assigned reading. (In law school, students typically are assigned some readings before the first day of class.) After all, these are second- or third-year law students who've had some experience by now in thinking about *why* different bodies of law and legal doctrines exist; and they've probably given some thought to these matters before, since they aren't required to take patents or intellectual property law to graduate and are taking the class because they're already interested in the subject. Many of them also come to class with some prior understanding of patents or other forms of intellectual property, either from other classes they've already taken or from real-world work experience. So it's not surprising that they get the answer "right," in the sense that the predominant explanation for the patent system is that it encourages invention, and most of us think that invention is a good thing.

There is another possible explanation that I suspect is more likely to occur to nonlawyers, and which some students (and inventors) also find compelling: namely, that the inventor *deserves* a patent for having created something new. Many people feel, intuitively, that their ideas belong to *them*; and that patents (and copyrights and trademarks and other forms of IP) are property for the very same reason that land is property, and tangible goods are property, and shares of stock and other intangible things are sometimes property. And those reasons are . . . well, for many of us, they just *are*. But let's see if we can pin things down a little more firmly.

For some, respect for property rights may be rooted in religious tradition: "Thou shalt not steal." But even if we set aside the whole question of separation of church and state, appeals to religious tradition have always seemed (to me) to come up short in the context of intellectual property. As far as we know, none of the great religious figures of the past (Moses, Buddha, Jesus, Mohammed . . . the list goes on) had anything to say about the desirability (or not) of granting patents for new inventions. Unlike laws concerning murder, theft, real estate, and so on, patent law is a latecomer in human history, emerging on a widespread scale only in the past few centuries. (So too for copyright. Trademark protection, which protects against commercial deceit, arose in rudimentary form a bit earlier, but it's not central to our discussion.) To the extent religion has anything to say about respecting IP rights, it's more of a modern-day phenomenon, based perhaps on the idea that citizens generally should obey the law; so if the law says that inventions are property, there's a religious duty to respect that property. But that still doesn't tell us why the law imposes that duty— and, in the modern world, religious organizations if anything are more likely to oppose than to advocate certain expansions of patents and other IP rights (for example, to essential medicines or human-created life forms).

Another possibility is to ground patents and other IP rights in one or another system of moral philosophy. One of the leading contenders for this role is the idea, associated with the writings of the English philosopher John Locke, that people have a natural right to the fruit of their labor. Another, often associated with Immanuel Kant, is that property is essential to human freedom, because it enables us to pursue the ends we choose for ourselves as autonomous individuals. Whether either of these rationales, which might justify the institution of private property generally, makes a compelling case for conferring exclusive rights in inventions or other intangible subject matter is a matter we'll come back to later in the chapter. Yet another possible moral justification derives from utilitarianism—roughly, the idea that laws should promote the greatest good (utility) for the greatest number.[1] In the present context, this would mean that governments should confer patents not to protect the inventor's investment of labor in a new invention, or to respect her autonomy as an individual, but rather because conferring patents serves the broader public interest: patents, somehow, make the world a better place. This justification, of course, leads us back to the initial proposal that patents are nothing more than a means to the end of promoting invention. Under this view, the patent system should reward inventors *only* to the extent that doing so is consistent with the overarching purpose of benefiting the public by stimulating new invention.

A third possible response to the question of "Why patents?" is one that I don't hear as much from students—though perhaps this reflects nothing more than the fact that at the places I've taught the students mostly have tended to occupy the political mainstream. But another way of viewing the matter is to put aside all the highfalutin rhetoric about morality and autonomy and the public good, and to recognize that the patent system—like many other laws and legal institutions—mostly works for the benefit of powerful interest groups. You can spin this story in either a leftward or a rightward direction. From a left perspective, the primary effect of patent laws is to reward the lobbying efforts of well-connected industries—pharmaceutical and agricultural chemical companies are a convenient, and perhaps sometimes an appropriate, bogeyman here—while impoverishing the rest of society. At the other end of the political spectrum, some libertarians—people who generally advocate a minimalist state—decry patents and other forms of IP as an imposition on individual liberty; after all, patents are sometimes thought of (whether accurately or not) as governmentally granted *monopolies*. (Other libertarians take a more favorable view of patents as a form of *property*, the protection of which is one of the few things that even a minimalist state *ought* to engage in.) More generally, many economists (not just those on the left and right ends of the spectrum) are wary of "regulatory capture," a term used when an industry effectively gains control of those arms of the state that are supposed to be regulating it. To be fair, there is arguably less regulatory capture in the patent context than in the realm of copyright law, where the entertainment industry has actually written much of the legislation that Congress has enacted over the past generation. Nevertheless, many observers believe, with some justice, that for much of the last three decades both the USPTO and the Federal Circuit have understood their role as being, largely, one of supporting the interests of patent owners—for example, in adopting a broad definition of patentable subject matter and a narrow definition of nonobviousness, prior to subsequent corrections from the Supreme Court.

Be that as it may, the idea that patents encourage invention, and that patent laws should be crafted to carry out this purpose, remains the dominant justification among patent lawyers and scholars. At this point, it seems appropriate to elaborate a bit on what it means to encourage invention, and how patent laws might be an effective means to this end. Perhaps the best place to begin is by posing the question, what would happen if patents were to vanish tomorrow? Would inventors stop inventing? Didn't anybody do any inventing before there were patent laws? The answer to the last question, of course, is yes. Someone (or, almost certainly, some *ones*) invented the wheel, clothing, agriculture, various types of tools, plows, weapons, and all manner of other things, long before it occurred to anyone to invent a patent system. So doesn't this show that patents are not absolutely necessary to stimulate invention?

Well, yes; so maybe the answer is that patents stimulate *more* invention than would otherwise exist. This is a better answer but still incomplete: what is it about invention that (perhaps) demands some form of government intervention in the form of handing out patents to inventors? To answer this question, it's necessary to think a bit about the cost of copying. Skip forward a few millennia to the fifteenth century, when Johannes Gutenberg invented the moveable type printing press in Germany. Up until the invention of the printing press, copying manuscripts was extremely labor-intensive: think of all those monks copying Bibles and other works by hand. Not surprisingly, before the fifteenth century, we also don't encounter any copyright laws either; copying was expensive and most people were illiterate, so what would be the point of having a law that targeted such a marginal social activity as copying books? Eventually, though, by fits and starts the reduction in the cost of copying made it more worthwhile for people to invest in writing (and in learning to read); simultaneously, it also made copying other people's work a much more attractive option than it had been previously. Over time, governments came around to the view that it might be a good idea to grant authors and publishers some freedom from competition for a period of time, in order to recoup their costs of production.[2]

A roughly similar phenomenon happened in the realm of invention. By 1474, the city-state of Venice had standardized a system whereby anyone who built a new invention could receive a right to exclude others from making the invention for a period of ten years.[3] (Many of these early patents were for inventions imported into Venice from elsewhere; there was, as of yet, no requirement that the patentee himself be the inventor.) In England, the process was, to some extent, standardized in 1623, with the enactment of the Statute of Monopolies. The statute was an attempt on the part of Parliament to rein in the sovereign's practice of granting monopolies—exclusive rights even in such commonplace goods as iron or salt—to political favorites: the capture theory before it had a name, if you will. These grants were memorialized in "letters patent"—letters bearing the king's seal but "patent" in the sense of "lying open" to public examination. From an early date, patents were public records, of a sort. (We still use the word "patent," derived from the Latin word for "to lie open," in this sense: for example, an ambiguity that is apparent on the face of a document is a "patent" ambiguity. Patently obvious, isn't it?) Anyway, the Statute of Monopolies forbade the sovereign from granting any more of these monopolies, *except* for new inventions. Over the years, the system slowly evolved in England and elsewhere into something more closely resembling the modern-day patent system.[4]

The broader point is that as the cost of copying someone else's invention decreased over the years, due to the spread of scientific knowledge and to improvements in the technology that enables copying, the more persuasive the case might have appeared for immunizing inventors from competition for a period of time, in order to allow them to cover their costs of invention. More formally, as long as the cost of copying is less than the cost of inventing, from a purely mercenary point of view, it's a better strategy to copy than to invent, particularly since inventing itself is a risky activity: what seems like a great idea initially might not ever pan out. But if everyone adopts the strategy of copying rather than inventing, invention grinds to a halt, and the public loses out on the benefits of new invention. Of course, invention *won't* grind to a halt entirely: some inventions will be difficult to copy, and for these inventions in particular it will be advantageous to be the first in the market (the so-called "first-mover advantage," which we'll talk about more below). But there will be fewer inventions, in a quantitative sense; and many of those that are invented will remain closely guarded trade secrets, which undermines the goal of widespread disclosure. The patent system solves both problems, by conferring enough protection against copying to stimulate more new inventions, and by requiring, in exchange for this conferral of exclusive rights, that inventors publicly disclose how to make and use their inventions—the "patent bargain." The result is a sort of virtuous circle, with patents inducing both invention and the disclosure of scientific knowledge, which in turn stimulates yet more invention and more disclosure, and on and on.

This, in a nutshell, is the basic economic theory of patents, and most patent lawyers and commentators believe that it captures enough of reality to continue to offer a convincing explanation both for the existence of a patent system and for many of the specific features of that system. Broadly speaking, the theory promotes patents as a means for inducing the technological progress that most of us view as offering deliverance from the life of disease, drudgery, isolation, and boredom that we imagine, with some justice, characterized much of the premodern world. To be sure, not literally *everyone* thinks or has thought that technology is such a great thing; Mahatma Gandhi, the Amish, and machine-smashing Luddites of nineteenth-century England all number among the doubters—as does the occasional nutcase like Unabomber Ted Kaczynski. And even the majority of us who happily embrace our modern conveniences surely have our doubts from time to time, whether they be directed toward the "dark

Satanic mills" of Victorian England (or contemporary China) or the role of fossil fuels in causing climate change in the twenty-first century. But most of us also probably view technology as the only realistic hope of solving the many problems our planet faces from hunger, contagion, environmental degradation, and other possibly looming catastrophes. Which is not to say that patents are the only, or even the most important, tool we have for achieving technological progress—or that achieving progress by means of patents is cost-free. As economists never tire of reminding us, it's necessary to consider both the benefits and the costs, including the opportunity costs of forgoing alternatives. So let's spend some time thinking about those costs and the alternatives.[5]

Probably the most obvious cost of a patent system is the cost of monopoly. As I've mentioned, most patents don't result in monopolies, if by monopoly we mean a situation in which only one seller offers a product for which there are no reasonable substitutes. Occasionally, though, patents do enable their owners to exercise monopoly power, as in the case of a new drug for which there really are no adequate substitutes; other patents enable their owners to price above the competitive level for a period of time, even if they fall short of conferring full-blown monopoly power. From an economic standpoint, this is surely a cost, though not necessarily for the reasons that would occur to non-economists. A non-economist might think it a cost that prices go up, but to the extent a price increase only transfers income from consumers to monopolists, aggregate wealth (that is, the sum of monopolist and consumer wealth) remains the same, so to an economist there is no net *social* loss. Of course, this assumes that a transfer of $1 from consumer to monopolist lowers the consumer's happiness (utility) by the same amount that it raises the monopolist's; and this assumption may be false, if (as economists also sometimes assume, and as common sense would suggest to most people) an additional dollar earned has less of an impact on a wealthy person than on a poor person. (The term for this phenomenon is "diminishing marginal utility.") Moreover, many people care about the distribution of wealth and not only its aggregate amount; and perhaps an increasingly inegalitarian distribution of wealth has other negative social consequences, as many social scientists believe.[6]

But what bugs economists the most about monopoly is not the distributional consequence but rather the fact that, in the short run at least, aggregate wealth under monopoly is less than what it would be under competition. A monopolist maximizes profit by producing less output, and charging a higher price for it, than would a company that faced competition. (Technically, as you may remember if you ever took a college economics course, a monopolist maximizes profit by equating marginal revenue with marginal cost, rather than by pricing at marginal cost as a perfectly competitive firm would.)[7] The monopolist is better off, and consumers as a whole are worse off, than either would be under competition.

The important point, however, is that the monopolist's gain is, in a purely quantitative sense, less than the amount of consumers' loss; consumers lose more than the monopolist gains. This surplus loss, referred to by economists as the "deadweight" loss, is what makes monopoly inefficient in the short run. There is less aggregate wealth than there would be under a competitive system.[8]

Notice, however, my use in the preceding paragraph of the term "short run." (To an economist, the short run is the opposite of the "long run," the time within which a company could replace its fixed assets.) It's possible that, *over time*, a monopoly could make society as a whole better off than it would have been had the monopoly never existed. Joseph Schumpeter, a mid–twentieth-century Austrian-born US economist, posited that economies grow through a process of "creative destruction," whereby companies compete to become monopolists through the introduction of new products and services that displace the old. No one monopolist can hold on to its position forever, though, and so the process constantly repeats as new technologies consign their predecessors to the dustbin of history. On this view, monopoly is a stimulus that drives innovation, and with it the growth brought about by creative destruction.[9] To be sure, not everyone buys into Schumpeter's analysis in all its details, but many modern-day economists agree that innovation is the principal engine of economic growth. Formal economic models try to describe the process mathematically.[10] What this means is that it might make sense to tolerate some degree of short-term monopoly if the effect of doing so is to induce innovation and, hence, long-run growth. And when you think about it, this pretty much is what the patent system is intended to do: to encourage companies to invent by offering them the prospect of becoming short-term monopolists. Seen in this light, the short-term monopoly costs that may arise from having a system of patent rights are simply the price society pays to obtain the benefits of long-run growth; it's a trade that works out well for society in the long run. (As I suggested in the Prologue, for example, it may be a pain to pay a monopoly price for a new drug, but it's better than succumbing to the disease the new drug cures.)

Of course, all of this assumes that the patent system is, indeed, necessary to induce the inventions that lead to long-run growth. Whether that assumption is true is an empirical matter, and if it turns out to be false (for all or even just for some industries) society may be paying monopoly costs that it would be better off avoiding. Plus, there's the question of how *much* monopoly is necessary to induce an inventive effort in the first place. If patent rights lasted forever, for example, instead of terminating after twenty years, the reward accruing to patent owners would be higher and might induce even more innovation. But the monopoly costs (and other costs, to be discussed below) would also be correspondingly higher, and at some point society would wind up paying more than it would be likely ever to get back. Patent systems, not surprisingly, try to constrain these monopoly costs in various ways, even while recognizing that dangling the lure of monopoly profits to attract invention is a necessary part of any patent system.

Getting back to the issue of costs, patent systems certainly generate other costs in addition to the cost of monopoly. One is the administrative cost of having a patent system, which requires establishing a patent office, hiring examiners, training lawyers and judges to deal with patent matters, and so on. For wealthy countries, this may not be such a big deal, though for the developing countries I discuss in Chapter 7 it sometimes might be. Another set of costs—which actually may be the most important of all—is what economists refer to as "transaction costs." These are the costs a person would incur to enter into a transaction; in some instances, these costs can derail what would otherwise be advantageous deals. Suppose, for example, that you have an heirloom you'd be willing to sell for $100. If it would cost you more than $100 (in terms of money, time, and other resources) to find potential buyers, negotiate with them, and reach an agreement, it's not worth it, even though in a transaction-cost–free world some potential buyer might have gladly entered into the exchange. Alternatively, if you expect your transaction costs to top out at, say, $50, it's worth going ahead with your plan to sell the item, but if there were some way to reduce transaction costs the exchange would be all the more attractive to both parties; the gains from trade would be higher. The example is a homey one, but the basic concept is significant, because transaction costs pervade the economy. Over the past fifty years, economists have come to appreciate how various types of legal rules, organizational structures, and contractual provisions can be understood as tools for reducing transaction costs—and other potential bargaining obstacles, including the risk of opportunistic behavior (the risk that one transacting party will take advantage of a situation after the other is locked in, a subject I'll come back to in Chapters 8 and 9).[11] Generally speaking, the reduction of transaction costs and other bargaining obstacles is a good thing.

In some respects, patents themselves reduce transaction costs by making it easier to market and access new technologies. To see why, imagine that you develop (what you think is) a great new improvement in the design of solar panels. You may lack the capital to start your own firm to make the panels, however, or to conduct an extensive marketing campaign. What do you do? One possibility would be to contact other firms that have the ability to market the product, and try to interest them in your idea. Another would be to look for investors who might be willing to fund your own expansion efforts. You face a risk, however, that once you disclose your idea to others, they might decide to use it without your consent and without compensating you; you'd like to disclose your idea to potential investors or licensees without incurring that risk. So you might try to interest people in your idea by disclosing it at a sufficient level of generality that you don't give out the key ideas until your prospective business partners sign a confidentiality agreement. But those partners also face a risk that after you disclose your idea they might realize it's something they've already considered. (Maybe they're working on a similar project already.) Consequently, they'd prefer not to sign the confidentiality agreement until they know what they're getting into; they'd rather not risk being dragged into a lawsuit someday over whether they used *your* idea or some idea they already had. But then we get back to the initial problem, that you don't want to disclose your idea until you have an assurance of confidentiality. So there's a bit of a chicken-or-the-egg problem: you don't want to disclose until you're certain the other side won't betray your trust, but the other side doesn't want to commit to confidentiality (or compensation) until they know what your idea is.

These problems are not necessarily insurmountable—people license trade secrets every day—but they do exist, and in some instances they can derail, or render more costly than is desirable, transactions that might be in both parties' interest. The name for this problem is "Arrow's Information Paradox," after Kenneth Arrow, a Nobel Prize-winning economist who (among his many other contributions to his field) devoted a portion of his career to the economics of information and innovation. The point here is that patents solve the paradox. Once the patent issues, investors and licensees can understand the nature of the invention and make something of an informed decision about whether it's worth their time; but they can't use it without the inventor's permission, because that would be infringement. For this reason, the disclosure function of patents serves not only to spread scientific knowledge, but also to reduce transaction costs so that the parties who can most efficiently make, use, or sell a new technology will be able to do so.

Patents nevertheless are a double-edged sword, because they also can *generate* their own peculiar transaction costs. Each time a manufacturer wants to use someone else's patented technology, it has to negotiate a license and/or pay a royalty, so there's a transaction cost. Moreover, because technology is cumulative, over time any given device is likely to incorporate many individual parts or methods that were, at some point, patented. If patents lasted forever, it wouldn't take long before it would cease to be cost-effective to market new devices, because the accumulated transaction costs would eat up all or most of the profits to be earned from sales. (To be sure, patent owners might realize that too, and not demand royalties that would be too burdensome. But maybe not; economic models predict that, where ownership of the underlying patents is disperse, the cumulative royalties demanded by patent owners will be higher than if ownership were concentrated in one single patentee.)[12] Fortunately patents don't last forever, but the basic insight remains: the more relevant patents there are, the greater the transaction costs. The problem of "royalty stacking," which we will encounter in Chapter 9 with regard to the Smartphone Wars, presents an extreme example (if and when it exists) of transaction costs run amok. Or, to cite an example from Chapter 1, suppose that the Federal Circuit had decided that ESTs were patentable after all (and that the Supreme Court decision on gene patenting had gone the other way as well). A scientist whose research required her to make and use a specific DNA sequence might have to pay royalties not only to the person who owned the patent on the entire sequence but also to the holders of patents on the EST fragments that compose the sequence. The risk is that at some point the potential benefits to be earned from making or using the sequence would be swamped by the aggregate transaction costs. Professors Michael Heller and Rebecca Eisenberg refer to this problem as the "anticommons," to distinguish it from what economists refer to as the "tragedy of the commons," which occurs when resources such as fisheries are overused because no one has enforceable property rights to exclude anyone else or to manage the resource efficiently. By contrast, the anticommons problem can arise when there are *too many* fragmented property rights, such that transaction costs threaten to exceed the potential gains from trade.[13]

The broader point of the preceding discussion is that patent rights that are too strong—that last too long, or read on too many embodiments, or subsist in minor innovations or fragmentary subject matter—can be just as bad as patents that are not strong enough (and therefore provide an insufficient incentive to invent and disclose). From an instrumental perspective, patent laws should be designed with these potential benefits and costs in mind; or to put it another way, if you were a social planner, you'd want to manage the incentive–access tradeoff that I referred to in the Prologue in such a way as to maximize the benefits and minimize the costs. More specifically, you might imagine a diagram that looks something like Figure 2.1, where the x-axis represents patent strength, and the y-axis the surplus of social benefits over costs.

I hasten to note that the diagram merely presents a way of *thinking* about the patent system, and not to measure patent strength or costs or benefits in any quantitative sense. (If it were possible to construct a curve that actually mirrored empirical reality, for all we know that curve might look very different. Indeed, if the patent abolitionists whom we'll meet shortly are correct in asserting that patents generate more costs than benefits, the entire curve would lie below the x-axis.) Nevertheless, the diagram conveys a key insight shared by most patent scholars: rights that are too weak won't provide enough of an incentive to invent and thus will generate a smaller surplus of benefits over costs than is desirable; but at the same time, rights that are too strong will generate so many monopoly and transaction costs that the net benefit of having a patent system is lower than it otherwise could be. The ideal patent system would confer rights that are "just right," in the sense of inducing the maximum surplus of benefits over costs (where the curve is at a maximum point on the y-axis). The problem

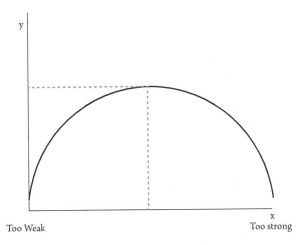

Figure 2.1 Maximizing the Surplus of Social Benefits over Social Costs

is that nobody knows how to do this; since there is no agreed-upon metric for measuring patent strength or for quantifying all the possible benefits and costs that might be attributed to a patent system, pinpointing the sweet spot where the surplus is highest is impossible. Perhaps the best we can do is to develop a sense of whether any given change to the existing system—moving from first-to-invent to first-to-file, tightening up the nonobviousness doctrine, what have you—would be more likely to move us toward or away from the ideal. A combination of economic theory and empirical evidence may enable us to make reasoned judgments in this regard. Even then, however, we shouldn't expect the sort of consensus that surrounds scientific models, like the theory of evolution by natural selection or the standard model of particle physics, that have survived decades of attempts at falsification. Patent law's "standard model," in other words, is not just incomplete, like physics'; rather, it falls within the domain of the *social* sciences, where our data are less subject to quantification and our conclusions are necessarily more tentative and context-dependent. We do our best with what we have.

Alternatives to Patents

So far I've presented what I've referred to as the standard model, namely that patents provide an incentive to invent and to disclose that otherwise would be undermined by the presence of free-riding copiers. But patents are not the only available tools for encouraging invention and disclosure. Before we take a serious stab at comparing the costs and benefits of patents, we need to know what these other options are and to evaluate their strengths and weaknesses as well. Perhaps they work better than patents for encouraging certain types of inventions, and for others, worse.

First off, as I described it above, the standard model posits that patents make the most sense when the cost of copying is less than the cost of inventing, because when these conditions are present copying promises a bigger payoff than inventing. But sometimes the cost of copying isn't less than the cost of inventing, in which case patents may not be necessary to stimulate invention after all. There are two factors at play here. First, it may not be very costly to invent certain things; not every invention costs millions of dollars to create. (Pharmaceuticals do, but in terms of R&D expenditures they're in a class by themselves.) Second, it may be very expensive to copy certain things. As it happens, the small-molecule compounds that make up the active ingredients in pharmaceuticals turn out to be relatively easy to copy (witness the generic drug industry). This combination of high creation costs and low copying costs makes pharmaceuticals the poster child for patent protection; if the pharmaceutical industry doesn't need patents, nobody does. In other industries, the cost of creation may be lower but the cost of copying also may be low, or at least low enough that copying still makes more sense as a business plan—unless, that is, the inventor has some other way to prevent the copying of subject matter that is inherently copy*able*. The inventor might rely on trade secrecy or contract, for example, to keep others from copying his product. But these often are not very good alternatives, either for the inventor or for society. From the inventor's standpoint, trade secret protection is (usually) weaker than patent protection because others lawfully may independently invent or reverse-engineer the secret—or even make use of someone else's deliberate misappropriation of it. Trade secrets are also harder to license, as we saw above; and society suffers to the extent that useful information remains secret. Similarly, contractual restraints on copying have their limits, not only due to transaction costs but also because a contract between the inventor and any given user does not bind a third party to whom the user transfers or discloses the product. (In legal jargon, there is no privity of contract between the inventor and the third party.) Patent rights, by contrast, as a species of property are good against the world, and thus offer a stronger incentive to create, if one is necessary.[14]

On the other hand, where the cost of copying is inherently high—or at least high enough to shield the inventor from competition for a substantial period of time—the standard model doesn't provide a very persuasive rationale for allowing patent protection (though perhaps other rationales do, as we will see). In other words, maybe first-mover advantages are sufficient to induce invention in some industries, because by the time the invention is copied the first-mover will have earned enough revenue to cover the costs of inventing, or will have established a reputation that will enable him to continue earning an above-average profit even in the face of competition. (As we'll see, for example, some consumers prefer brand-name drugs even when generic copies are available.) If first-mover advantages are sufficient to induce invention, the economic rationale for patent protection falls away; from the public's standpoint, patents are all cost and no benefit. But are there any real-world industries that fit this pattern?

According to two of today's leading patent abolitionists, economists Michele Boldrin and David Levine, *most* industries fit this description.[15] Boldrin and Levine argue that a combination of factors—among them, high copying costs in some sectors, capacity constraints that limit the profitability of new entry in others, and inventors' ingenuity in deriving profit from related products or services, such as the provision of advice on how best to exploit the invention—suffice to confer substantial benefits on being the first in the market with a popular product.[16] In another paper, Boldrin, Correa, Levine, and Ornaghi report that they find "no statistically significant relationship between measures of productivity . . . and patenting activity";[17] and they point to numerous other empirical studies finding that strengthening (or in some countries, introducing) patent laws has had little or no impact on rates of innovation.[18] Another frequently cited study, however, by Cohen, Nelson, and Walsh, concludes, on the basis of a survey administered to 1,478 R&D laboratories in the United States in 1994, that while patents "are still not one of the major mechanisms in most industries when the views of all firms are considered . . . they can be counted among the major mechanisms of appropriation in a more sizeable minority of industries," including pharmaceuticals and agricultural chemicals.[19] (Moreover, as we'll see shortly, there are several *other* economic rationales for patents that, to some observers, provide an adequate justification even if the incentive rationale is weak.) Consistent with the results reported by Cohen et al., most economists reject Boldrin and Levine's call for patent abolition; in the words of economist Josh Lerner, the majority "agree[s] that some intellectual property protection is better than no intellectual property protection at all," while recognizing that "this does not mean that very strong protection is better than a more moderate level of protection."[20]

Perhaps it's also fair to conclude that economists, like most of us, are reluctant to take bold leaps into the unknown, and thus greatly prefer reform of the most clearly dysfunctional aspects of the system to outright abolition. As Graham and Vishnubhakat put it, "[w]ithout strong evidence of the superiority of such a large change in the institutional environment in which innovation and economic activity occurs, a 'do away with patents' alternative cannot be fairly categorized as a hypothetical ideal."[21] I tend to agree, though I understand that the view expressed by Graham and Vishnubhakat may be more of a philosophical or attitudinal position than a strictly scientific one.

Yet another possible alternative to a patent system would be to fund invention through a system of private or public grants, rewards, or prizes. Historically, prizes were one of the principal tools for motivating invention; a famous example is the British government's decision in 1714 to award prizes to inventors who made improvements in the calculation of longitude at sea.[22] Today the X Prize Foundation, Netflix, and other organizations from time to time announce that they will award prizes for new inventions; among the recipients have been the inventors of a private space vehicle and of an algorithm for better guessing which movies consumers want to see, based on their past viewing habits.[23] Another form of funding is a grant awarded by a public or private funder to enable someone to carry out a research project. (Tax benefits, in the form of deductions or credits awarded for expenditures on R&D, are in economic substance very similar.) Many grants, however, target basic research, which may have no immediate commercial payoff in sight and thus is often financially too risky for for-profit organizations to fund; retrospective awards for lifetime achievement such as the Nobel Prize or the Field Medal in mathematics also generally reward basic research. By contrast, the patent system (as we will see) is reserved for *applied* research, that is, research that is intended to result in some marketable product or service in the relatively near term. Of course, the dividing line between basic and applied research is not always clear; and in theory one could imagine a patent system that rewarded basic as well as applied research or a more extensive use of grants, rewards, or prizes for applied research/inventions.

One drawback in using grants, rewards, or prizes to stimulate invention, however, is that the funder must somehow figure out what reward is needed to stimulate the desired activity; and for all but retrospective awards, the funder must also decide, in advance, what projects are worth funding.[24] The patent system, in contrast, is more decentralized in nature: millions of inventors decide what to invent, and the market, rather than a central planner, ultimately judges what the resulting inventions are worth. This is an advantage, if one believes (as many economists do) that over a wide range of activities, and over the long term, the market— comprised of millions upon millions of individual actors—is more "intelligent" than any one person or institution can ever be. Put another way, although patents are intended to induce inventors to invest in creating and disclosing new inventions, by offering them the hope of recouping their investment through the exclusion or licensing of others for a period of time, the ultimate goal of the patent system isn't to compensate inventors (some of whom, after all, may be wasting their time inventing products that nobody wants). Rather, the goal is to enable inventors to reap whatever reward the market bestows upon them in exchange for the use of their inventions. In theory, this reward, based on what people are willing to pay for the invention in view of its advantages over alternatives, should be at least roughly commensurate with the inventor's contribution to the art.[25]

On the other hand, the market may be less than ideal for allocating resources toward research that commands only a small market value but which may be eminently worth doing for some other reason. Examples would include not only the basic research that may be too risky for for-profit organizations to carry out on an efficient scale, but also research into rare or otherwise neglected diseases. Private and public philanthropy therefore may be better suited to encourage this type of research. One such public philanthropic effort is the Orphan Drug Act, under which the US government provides additional funding, tax benefits, and exclusive marketing rights to drug companies that conduct research into diseases affecting small populations.[26] Similarly, private organizations such as the Gates Foundation have led global efforts to reduce malaria, river blindness, and other diseases that devastate the developing world. One way to harness the technical expertise of the private sector for such projects might be through the use of "advance market commitments" (AMCs), whereby a funder would offer in advance to purchase at a premium over the market price a specified quantity of, say, a newly developed vaccine meeting specified performance criteria, with the patent owner contractually obligated thereafter to sell any additional quantities at a specified low price.[27] A consortium of five countries and the Gates Foundation announced the first such AMC, to encourage the development of a pneumococcal conjugate vaccine, in 2007.[28]

Other Economic Rationales for Patents

Scholars have proposed several other possible economic rationales for having a patent system. The best-known of these, Professor Edmund Kitch's "prospect theory," draws on a historical analogy to make its point. As Kitch explains, in the late nineteenth century a system developed under which the first person to discover mineralization on a tract of federal land was entitled to file a claim, which entitled him to the exclusive right to develop the claimed mineral "prospect." This right of first possession, according to Kitch, was efficient because the claimant could then decide how to manage and coordinate the development of the prospect, and thus could prevent wastefully duplicative efforts on the part of rival claimants. Kitch argued that patents are a lot like these mining prospects. Early on, the inventor, like the mining claimant, doesn't know whether the prospect will have any commercial value; an invention might turn out to have immense value or it might be a dud. And, like '49ers heading out to the Gold Rush, there often will be many people—here, rival inventors—all hoping to claim the same territory. Awarding the patent to a single claimant enables that claimant to decide how best to develop the prospect. Someone who comes up with a great idea for applying or improving the claimed invention can seek out the patent owner, pitch her idea, and if successful license the use of the patent to develop the improvement. The point is that the patent owner can efficiently coordinate these follow-up improvements, in a manner that avoids wasteful duplication.[29]

A number of patent scholars find the prospect theory insightful, not only as a fresh explanation for patents generally but also as an explanation for various features of patent doctrine: for example, why independent invention or improvement is not a defense to patent infringement (because allowing such a defense would destroy the prospecting function); why courts often have seemed to grant "pioneering" inventions broad scope (because these are the sorts of inventions that are likely to generate numerous improvements); and perhaps even why laws of nature are not patentable (supposedly, because they can't be improved).[30] Others cite the prospect theory as showing how patent law promotes not just invention, but also innovation, in the sense of the commercialization of invention: patents enable inventors to coordinate follow-up investment not only in improvements over the patented invention, but also in efforts to commercialize it.[31] The Achilles Heel of the theory, however, has always been the lack of empirical evidence that, outside the realm of pharmaceuticals and perhaps a few other outliers, the world of invention works in the way the theory describes. Roger Beck was the first to take notice of how many years typically pass before an invention *is* commercialized, while Robert Merges and Richard Nelson catalogued case studies in which the initial inventor, rather than efficiently coordinating investment in follow-up improvements, seemed more content to rest upon its laurels.[32] The theory nevertheless has its adherents within the legal academy; and it has more than a little affinity with a Schumpeterian-influenced economic theory known as "competition for the market," which posits that innovation is better served by encouraging firms to compete for temporary dominance than by keeping markets competitive.[33] Some recent economic research nevertheless suggests that, both as an empirical and a theoretical matter, moderately competitive markets actually do a better job of stimulating innovation.[34]

Another possible justification for patents turns the prospect theory on its head, in a sense. To understand how, it's helpful to address first the concept of patent "races." A patent race occurs when two or more inventive entities race to invent, and patent, the same thing. As I noted in Chapter 1, near-simultaneous invention is commonplace; as a result, patent races are common too. One possible consequence of races, however, is that there's a lot of wasted effort going on, since only one firm can succeed in getting a patent—and once it does, it can exclude the others from using the invention even if they independently invented.[35] Some people therefore view all the duplicative effort that goes into patent races are yet another cost of the patent system.

More technically, patent races threaten to dissipate the expected "rents" from the exploitation of patented technologies. In this context the word "rent," as used by economists and not in its everyday sense, refers to the profit you earn by engaging in a specific course of conduct, above the profit you would have earned from engaging in your next-best available alternative course of conduct.

Superstar athletes enjoy very large economic rents, because the difference between their salaries and what they would earn from their next-best alternative (say, teaching high school PE) is astronomical. Similarly, a few superstar
patents— for example, a patent on a blockbuster drug—may generate extraordinary economic rents. In the patent context, however, a potential problem is
that all or much of that rent may be dissipated when many firms engage in a race.
If the expected rent from a new invention is, say, $1 billion, and five firms each
compete by spending $250 million to develop the invention, the firms' aggregate
payoff is actually negative. To some observers, the possibility of such outcomes
not only is wasteful; it also potentially reduces the incentive for participants to
enter the race at all, and thus diminishes the incentive to invent. (Apparently
the incentive is not often reduced to zero, though, or we wouldn't observe any
racing, or patenting, in the real world; many firms still see a need to compete,
even if they know that only one of them will emerge victorious.)[36]

In any event, the prospect theory is partly a response to this perceived problem,
since it views patents as a way of minimizing races, and thus rent dissipation, in
the market for follow-up improvements (though not in the market for the initial
invention). But other scholars view patent races more favorably. As Mark Lemley
notes, even if only one firm succeeds in obtaining the raced-for patent, others may
wind up inventing other, unforeseen products along the way; or they may benefit from the know-how they develop through competing in the race. Moreover,
patent races, like real races, motivate their participants to move fast—faster than
they might in the absence of a patent system, since the winner gets to exclude
the losers—and faster invention, presumably, benefits the public. On this view,
the fact that patent law may stimulate races is a feature, not a bug; even if most
inventions would be invented in the absence of a patent incentive, patent law
serves the public interest by encouraging races and thus speedier invention.[37] As
always, however, the problem (as Lemley recognizes) is that there isn't much in
the way of actual data to verify (or refute) the theory. And there probably is some
reason to worry about one particular manifestation of patent races—the "arms
race" phenomenon that I mentioned in the Prologue, whereby firms compete in
acquiring patents mostly for the *defensive* purpose of warding off or responding
to accusations that they themselves are engaged in patent infringement. Even if
patent races are, on balance, a good thing, this particular offshoot of some patent
races really *does* seem like a cost that could be avoided if patents didn't exist.

Finally, as I noted in the preceding chapter, some scholars view patents as
serving a signaling function, in the sense of providing potential investors with a
means for estimating the value of start-ups and other non–publicly traded firms.
(An analytically similar argument is that having a strong patent system attracts
foreign investment and thus is particularly useful for developing countries. We'll
return to the merits of this argument in Chapter 7.) This signaling may well be

a benefit, to the extent start-ups contribute value to the economy. As with the other theories noted above, however, it's impossible to predict what the effect would be if patents ceased to exist. Would venture capitalists find other tools for predicting value, and how would those tools compare to patents? Even if the alternative signal were a little "noisier," would the social cost be lower than the cost attributable to the patent system? We simply don't know.

Ultimately the problem, as Professor John Golden puts it, can be analogized to "frustration"—a term used by physicists to describe a state in which interactions among correlated particles can prevent a researcher from getting two particles to spin in the same desired direction.[38] A more down-to-earth example (which isn't "frustration" in the quantum physics sense, but can be frustrating in the everyday sense) would be of an automobile designer who wants to increase a vehicle's safety, style, and comfort while simultaneously reducing the cost of production. Achieving all of those goals to the extent desired may be impossible, and tradeoffs may be necessary. But the problem in patent law goes deeper. As we've seen, most (though not all) economists believe that patents have a comparative advantage over other possible tools for stimulating the production of at least some inventions (and their disclosure). Even so, this modest insight isn't very informative when it comes to crafting legal standards to attain the optimal tradeoff between incentives and access. Beyond these problems, though, there's also no consensus on which, if any, other goals patent law *should* serve—prospecting? signaling? encouraging or discouraging patent races?—let alone when it might be appropriate to trade off one such goal for another. A pure incentive-to-invent theory, for example, *might* suggest a relatively minimal, though not nonexistent, patent system, while the prospect theory favors one that is more robust. Developing a patent law that predictably maximizes the surplus of social benefits over costs would require resolving these conflicts by first deciding which of the possible goals are really desirable and which are not. Even then, the impossibility of quantifying all of the potentially relevant costs and benefits suggests that anyone who tells you, with confidence, that any given change to patent law would surely lead to more (or less) innovation is selling you a bill of goods. There is, and probably will always be, a large degree of uncertainty in predicting which changes, if any, would better serve the public good.

The Moral Philosophy Alternative

It is the uncertainty mentioned above that motivates some patent scholars to look for alternative justifications for IP rights within the field of moral philosophy. At first blush, this quest might seem quixotic. To many observers, moral philosophy hardly seems like a bastion of certainty, having failed over the course of several millennia to provide universally convincing answers on topics ranging from justice, war, and sex, to abortion, the death penalty, and animal rights. Economics at least has pretensions of being a science, and perhaps occasionally can fill the bill; supply and demand are not make-believe, after all. But moral philosophy? *Please.*

This view is unnecessarily harsh, even philistine, though frankly it may contain a kernel of truth. For what it's worth, I for one find it difficult to take seriously the views of those who dismiss economics as a pseudoscience while proposing alternatives that often rest on much more contentious, and tenuous, foundations. (There are plenty of such alternatives on display in academia, on both left and right.) And at the end of the day, after years of reflection on the matter, I honestly *don't* find the leading nonutilitarian justifications for IP rights all that persuasive. Nevertheless, it would be premature to dismiss these alternatives without giving them their due; I'm hardly infallible and, like many others, you may find these alternatives more persuasive than I do. As noted previously, in the present context the two principal contenders are theories derived from the writings of Locke and Kant.

The Lockean theory is principally based on Locke's analysis of the just acquisition of property rights, as explained in a portion of his 1690 *Second Treatise on Government: An Essay Concerning the True Original Extent and End of Civil Government.*[39] In chapter V, Locke presents the following puzzle: if, as Locke believed, at the beginning of time God created the world and gave it to human beings to enjoy in common, where does the institution of private property come from? More to the point, is private property morally justifiable? Locke concludes that the answer to the latter question is yes, based on another fundamental premise: that "every man has a property in his own person" that no one "has any right to but himself."[40] From this premise, Locke then proceeds to the heart of his argument, in paragraph 26:

> The labour of his body and the work of his hands, we may say, are properly his. Whatsoever, then, he removes out of the state that Nature hath provided and left it in, he hath mixed his labour with it, and joined to it something that is his own, and thereby makes it his property. It being by him removed from the common state Nature placed it in, it hath by this labour something annexed to it that excludes the common right of other men. For this labour being the unquestionable property of the labourer, no man but he can have a right to what that is once joined to, at least where there is enough, and as good left in common for others.

Locke elaborates on his theme by imagining a person in the primordial state of nature, going about picking acorns or apples for his own nourishment. In

Locke's view, the gatherer acquires a property interest in these items by using his labor to appropriate them from the commons; someone who were to take an apple or acorn from the gatherer would be harming him by, in effect, taking his labor without his consent.[41]

As the apple and acorn examples suggest, all of the illustrations Locke uses throughout the essay involve tangible things; none of them involve what we would refer to today as intellectual property. This is hardly surprising, given the relative unimportance of patents and copyrights in Locke's day.[42] Nevertheless, many subsequent theorists (who need not share Locke's theological premises about a beneficent creator) have argued that Locke's analysis is largely sound and that it applies equally well to intangibles, including inventions and works of authorship. (My reference to inventions and works of authorship as "intangibles" might strike some readers as odd; inventions and works of authorship such as books are tangible things, right? Actually, no. A patent covers an invention in the sense of an inventive *principle*—something that can be embodied in tangible things such as machines or compounds, but which is defined exclusively by the scope of the patent grant. Similarly, copyright subsists in intangible *works*, such as strings of words or images, which *can* be embodied in tangible things such as books, film, computer files, and so on.) To see how, you first have to imagine there being a "commons" of ideas analogous to the commons of natural resources that Locke imagined existed at the dawn of time. An inventor or author then comes along and mixes her labor with the commons to produce something new. Someone who copies the author's or inventor's work therefore appropriates the author's or inventor's labor; and, as in the examples involving tangible things, this appropriation of another's labor without consent constitutes a moral wrong. This in a nutshell is the Lockean theory, although modern writers also note that Locke's famous "proviso"—that a person may appropriate property from the common only as long as "there is enough, and as good left in common for others"—provides some built-in limitations on IP rights as well. One might argue, for example, that the Lockean theory is consistent with the rule in the United States that you can't patent an abstract idea or law of nature because exclusive rights in such subject matter wouldn't leave "enough and as good" for others to produce their own works.

I suspect that many of the people who find Locke's theory attractive do so because they share an intuition that being a free-rider—or opportunist, or parasite, or whatever other term of opprobrium strikes your fancy—is a bad thing. For sound evolutionary reasons, nobody wants to be a sucker. But on closer inspection a Lockean-based theory of IP rights seems weak, for a variety of reasons.[43] To my mind, the biggest challenge is that, unlike the things Locke himself wrote about to illustrate his theory—apples, acorns, and so on—intangibles can be used by many people (in theory, an infinite number) without depleting the source. If I compose a song or write a poem, for example, as many people as the spirit moves can sing the song or recite the poem without using it up. Similarly, if I invent a new small-molecule compound, as many people as have the equipment to do so may make the drug without destroying the inventive principle: the formula for making the drug is not consumed by others' use. To use an economic term, tangible resources like apples, acorns, and land are *rivalrous* in consumption: my consumption of a specific apple deprives you of the ability to consume that same apple, and only a limited number of people can physically occupy the same tract of land at any one time. One person's use rivals another's. By contrast, intangibles like songs and inventions are nonrivalrous, in the sense that anyone can sing my song, or make my molecule, without depriving me of the ability to do so as well.*

To be sure, a Lockean might respond that someone who uses my intellectual creation without my permission is still taking a free-ride on my labor, just as in the examples involving tangible goods. Nevertheless, the point remains that free-riding doesn't have the same consequence for intangibles as for tangibles and thus arguably makes the moral offense, assuming there is one at all, much less severe. Moreover, as applied to intangibles, the Lockean theory runs up against the observation that free-riding on others' creations is pervasive—so much so that most of the time we don't even realize that we're doing it. To refer back, once again, to Sir Isaac Newton, we all stand on the shoulders of giants—or perhaps more accurately, we all stand on the shoulders of everyday men and women (and the occasional genius) who have enriched human knowledge through their contributions to the arts and sciences. If every use of any such contribution, down through the ages, had to be authorized or compensated, the world as we know it would come to a stop. Even more obviously, we all use skills and information that others have taught us over the years. I may well owe my grade-school teachers a debt of gratitude for teaching me to read; and presumably they were paid in money (though probably not very much) at the time. But no one

---

* In this sense, inventions and works of authorship are what economists refer to as "public goods," things like national defense and highways and parks, my consumption of which does not, at least over a wide range of activity, deprive you of the ability to consume as much as you want as well. You also can't easily exclude someone from using these types of things once they become available, just like, in the absence of legal protection, you can't easily exclude someone from copying your invention or work of authorship once it becomes widely known. Because the market is likely to undersupply such nonrivalrous, nonexcludable goods due to the presence of potential free-riders, governments often provide these goods instead by financing their production through taxation and then making them freely available to everyone. As applied to invention, however, that sort of solution—having the government invent everything and then tax us to pay for the underlying R&D, rather than relying on a patent system—probably wouldn't work very well, for the reasons discussed above in connection with grants, prizes, and awards.

seriously thinks that every time you read a sentence the law should compel you to contribute to your teachers' retirement funds; at some point the ride necessarily becomes free.[44] Maybe the rule should be different for inventions and works of authorship, but if so it's not clear exactly why.

In response, some Lockeans argue that the labor theory doesn't suggest that every use of another's intellectual contribution must be authorized or compensated from now until the end of time. As we've seen, according exclusive rights in some contributions (newly discovered laws of nature, for example) may substantially interfere with others' abilities to make their own contributions and thus violate the "enough and as good" proviso. Moreover, at some point, free-riding may simply become too attenuated or difficult to trace to its distant sources, and perhaps there has to be some sense of proportion between the labor expended to create something and the reward granted.[45] Or maybe exclusive rights should last only as long as it would take someone else to create the very same thing—or at least should be subject to an independent invention defense, as in trade secret law—though such a constraint would hardly be consistent with patent law as it currently exists, and it's not clear who would have the expertise to decide what the appropriate term of protection for any given creation should be. Or perhaps we're not focusing clearly enough on the harm that free-riding causes: if someone records my song (or synthesizes my molecule) without my permission, that person is potentially depriving me not of the use of the creation, but of the ability to make a living as a creator. That *is*, potentially, a serious harm. The problem is that this argument seems to presuppose an existing right to make a living by selling the rights to my creative works—that is, it presupposes that patent and copyright laws already exist—which purportedly is what the Lockean theory is trying to prove in the first instance. Either that, or Lockeans are implicitly adopting a utilitarian theory that patent and copyright laws are needed to stimulate creative effort (or viewing Locke himself as a proto-utilitarian, as some Locke scholars do); but if so, it's hard to see the point of going through the whole labor-as-the-basis-of-property exercise to begin with.

Alternatively, some scholars have tried to ground IP rights in a theory of personal autonomy derived from the writings of Immanuel Kant. Kant actually wrote a little about IP—specifically, authors' rights—in an essay titled *On the Injustice of Copying Books*.[46] In that work, Kant distinguished between the book as an *external thing*—which its publisher (and, thereafter, a purchaser) may possess and alienate just as he may possess and alienate other external things—and the book as the author's *discourse or speech*. In Kant's view, the mere ownership or possession of a book does not entitle the owner to copy it, because copying would interfere with the author's prerogative of deciding when and how he will communicate, through his authorized publisher, with the public. For Kant, the author's interest in deciding how and when to speak is an inalienable part of his personality; the author therefore may license, but can never alienate, the right to copy his work. Moreover, as a mere agent, the publisher is obligated to present the work according to the author's wishes. The author's freedom to express his inner being to the public, without alteration, remains paramount.

Kant's views on authors' rights, as later supplemented by Hegel and by a line of legal philosophers, has had a substantial impact on the development of European copyright law—in particular, the concept of authors' "moral rights" to have their works presented to the public in a manner that is consistent with their artistic vision.[47] This all may seem rather far removed from the world of patents, however, since most people don't think of inventions as embodying the inventor's inalienable personality or artistic vision. But in his book *Justifying Intellectual Property*, Rob Merges outlines a broader Kantian-based theory of IP law that centers on Kant's views of the importance of private property *generally* in enabling us to realize our potential as autonomous, self-defined actors. As Professor Merges explains, Kant's Principle of Universal Right obligates the state to recognize private property as a necessary precondition for individuals "to expand their range of freedom—their autonomy."[48] (Of course, the state also is obligated to restrain those uses of property that would impinge on others' freedom and autonomy.) In this light, Merges views *intellectual* property as merely one type of property that enables individuals to "pursue the ends they set for themselves"; patent rights in particular can "enhance the independence of highly skilled people who make a specialized technology input . . . to have more say over their work, more control over their professional fate—more autonomy."[49] On this view, patents are not simply a means to the end of inducing invention, but also in significant measure a means for enabling individuals to realize their potential.

Merges's Kantian perspective makes a powerful case for the role of private property ("stable, durable claims over objects") in enabling individuals to pursue their own ends as they see fit.[50] I nevertheless remain skeptical of his use of Kantian theory to defend *intellectual* property rights in particular, especially patents. To the extent the argument boils down to the role of professional autonomy in enabling us to pursue our chosen ends, I'm willing to concede that such autonomy can be an immense source of satisfaction. (University professors like me, and like Merges, have about as much professional autonomy as anyone on the planet.) Citing autonomy as a rationale for patents nevertheless seems odd. Most workers, after all, don't get to rely on patenting their creations to achieve autonomy, assuming they ever get to achieve it at all. Indeed, if we were to take seriously the idea that expanding professional autonomy is a moral imperative, it seems to me we would be talking about things like workers' councils, guilds, unions, or other means for enhancing workers' rights—though these would surely have their costs as well as benefits—rather than something as narrowly focused as a patent system. What's so special about inventors, as compared with everyone else?

To be fair, as I've already noted I tend to agree that patents probably play some role in motivating invention and disclosure, and thus that they contribute to technological progress; and technological progress, like private property in Merges's account, plays a role in enabling us to better pursue the ends we set for ourselves, to the extent it enhances our ability to live longer, healthier, more socially and intellectually rich lives. Once again, though, this brings us back to some sort of utilitarian argument—that patents make the world a better place—which in my view remains the only defensible reason for having a patent system in the first place. Put another way, if there were convincing evidence that patents *didn't* promote the progress of the useful arts—or that progress could be attained just as well through less socially costly means—I for one have a difficult time seeing what the point would be of keeping the patent system in place, even though abolishing it might deprive inventors of one potential source of self-actualization. Perhaps they could find other sources, like gardening.

In any event, even if Kant (or Locke, for that matter) provides a defense of sorts for having a patent system, at the end of the day that defense may not have all that many implications beyond a few obvious ones: for example, that patents should have a limited duration, and should not be so broad or absolute in nature as to unduly interfere with others' ability to engage in their own self-actualization. Merges largely concedes as much, concluding that "[a]n understanding of IP that embraces creator autonomy directs us to resolve close cases, those where the costs and benefits of IP protections are in doubt, in favor of creators."[51] So perhaps all he's really advocating is a rule that "ties go to the creator," which seems reasonable enough. Reasonable, that is, until we stop to realize that just about *every* case is one in which, potentially, "the costs and benefits of IP protections are in doubt." Should creators therefore always win?

Summary

The most widespread justification for patent rights is that patents stimulate invention and disclosure—at least up to the point at which patent rights become so broad or so numerous that they begin to generate more social costs than benefits. Unfortunately, no one knows precisely where that point lies. Given the difficulty of quantifying all the potentially relevant costs and benefits—or perhaps even reaching consensus on precisely what *counts* as a cost or benefit— the goals of maximizing the surplus of benefits over costs is, strictly speaking, impossible.

Coupled with the lack of robust empirical evidence that patents do play a dominant role in stimulating invention and disclosure in a wide range of industries, these problems have led some observers to advocate abolishing patents altogether, or else to seek refuge in some other, nonutilitarian theory; but I think either response would be an overreaction. I find the nonutilitarian theories weak, for reasons discussed above; and while we may never be able to devise a patent system that achieves the utilitarian ideal of maximizing benefits over costs, we *can* attempt a reasoned analysis of whether various proposed modifications of the present system would be more or less likely to move us in the direction of that ideal. As we will see in forthcoming chapters, in recent years empirical studies have provided us with a good deal of evidence about how some aspects of the patent system actually work. Some of this evidence challenges certain assumptions on which the standard model is based, while other evidence provides support. The point is that we can learn, and are learning, more about the empirical reality of how the patent system affects innovation and access, and in principle we should be able to use this knowledge to improve that system. Progress may be incremental, at times excruciatingly slow; but that is not, in my view at least, a reason to abandon the effort and junk the system altogether.

3

Genes

Early in her career, University of California geneticist Dr. Mary-Claire King became interested in studying whether certain types of breast cancer could be traced to hereditary genetic mutations. At the time, prevailing wisdom did not favor this line of inquiry; although science could link certain relatively rare diseases to genetic abnormalities, the epidemiology of more common diseases such as breast cancer was thought to be too complex to trace to individual genetic mutations. King and her team eventually proved the conventional wisdom wrong when, in 1990, they announced their discovery of a genetic "marker"—a DNA fragment located on the long arm of chromosome 17—the presence of which substantially increased the probability that a subject would develop breast cancer over the course of her lifetime.[1] The discovery of the marker lent credence to the hypothesis that a hereditary mutation or mutations of a specific gene played an important role in the etiology of some breast cancers.

Subsequent research by King and others led to the identification of other relevant markers, and thus helped researchers gradually to home in on the precise location and composition of the posited gene, which King labeled "*BRCA1*."[2] Several different research teams, including King's, competed to "sequence" the gene—that is, to determine the sequence of organic molecules, known as nucleotides, of which the gene is composed—but the winner was a team led by Dr. Mark Skolnick at the University of Utah. In 1994, Skolnick's team announced that it had succeeded in identifying *BRCA1*, as well as several mutations to the gene.[3] Meanwhile, a team in the UK headed by Michael Stratton discovered on chromosome 13 a different gene, labeled *BRCA2*, that also appeared linked to hereditary breast cancer.[4] Stratton and his colleagues partially sequenced the gene in 1995,[5] but Skolnick's team claimed to be the first to isolate and sequence the entire gene.[6] Research further demonstrated that, absent a mutation, *BRCA1* and *BRCA2* code for complex proteins, referred to as the BRCA1 and BRCA2 polypeptides, that suppress tumors. Certain mutations inhibit the production of these proteins, and when these mutations are passed down to offspring they greatly increase the risk that the offspring will develop cancer. According to the

National Cancer Institute, altogether the mutations at issue probably account for somewhere between 5 and 10 percent of all cases of female breast cancer and 15 percent of all cases of ovarian cancer; and they increase the lifetime risk of developing breast or ovarian cancer from a baseline of, respectively, 12 percent and 1.4 percent, to a range from 45–65 percent for breast cancer and 11–39 percent for ovarian cancer.[7] (Of course, the presence of the mutations does not guarantee that a subject will develop cancer, and most women who do develop breast cancer don't carry these mutations.) It still remains uncertain why these mutations are associated with higher risks of breast and ovarian cancers in particular.

The controversial part of the story came when Skolnick's team, through its assignee Myriad Genetics (a start-up cofounded by Skolnick), filed patent applications on, and obtained patents for, the isolated *BRCA1* and *BRCA2* genes and other related discoveries. Ultimately, this set the stage for an epic Supreme Court battle that concluded in 2013, when the Court held that isolated human genes are not patentable subject matter, but that so-called "complementary DNA" or "cDNA" sequences are.

This chapter takes up the issue of gene patents: what they are, the arguments for and against them, and where the law has for now settled in the wake of the Supreme Court's ruling. In order to better understand the legal and policy issues, though, it first may be helpful to present a little background on the underlying science. (If you're already familiar with how DNA works, you may want to skip this part.) From there, after a brief overview of Myriad's patents we'll proceed to the legal developments in the field of biotechnological patents, from the Supreme Court's 1982 decision that human-created life forms are patentable to the 2013 *Myriad* decision and beyond. I'll also explain how some other countries have dealt with these issues and why, in my view at least, a more "holistic" approach to public health would be a sensible way to balance the costs and benefits of patents on biotechnological inventions.

Genes

The nucleus of every human cell contains 23 pairs of chromosomes made of deoxyribonucleic acid (DNA).[8] DNA is a macromolecule arranged in a "double helix" structure, first modeled in 1953 by James Watson and Francis Crick based on data obtained by Rosalind Franklin. Each of the two strands that make up the double helix is made of nucleotides, which in turn consist of a sugar (deoxyribose), a phosphate, and one of four nitrogenous bases: adenine (A), cytosine (C), guanine (G), or thymine (T). Each of the four bases in turn naturally bonds with one of the other bases located on its companion strand: A bonds with T by means of two hydrogen bonds, while three hydrogen bonds bind G with C. The result is a long chain of "base pairs," as depicted in Figure 3.1. For reasons we will see momentarily, one of the two strands of a DNA molecule is referred to as the coding or "sense" strand, while the other is the template or "antisense" strand.

You can also imagine a strand of DNA as a sequence of nucleotides, like this:

ATTGTCAACGAATGCAACTGGAAGGTTATGGCATAACCTTCT
ATGCCCTGATAACTG

When a cell divides within the human body, the chromosomal DNA replicates by means of an enzyme known as DNA polymerase. The enzyme cleaves the double helix in two and synthesizes a corresponding sense or antisense strand that bonds with each cleaved strand. The result is the formation of two perfect copies of the previous DNA molecule. (Well, mostly perfect; the error rate is approximately one in a hundred million.) Subsequently, there may be some transposition or "gene-jumping" on individual chromosomes, as well as (within the

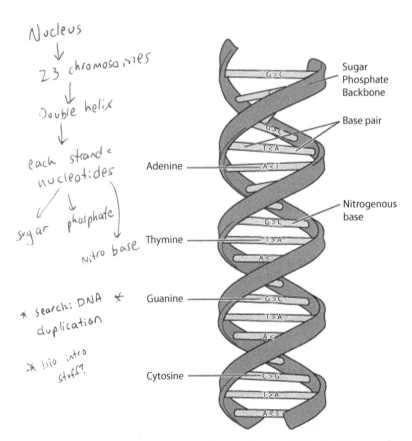

Figure 3.1 DNA Structure and Bases (Source: Wikipedia Commons)

sex cells) the crossover of genetic material between chromosome pairs, though none of this is particularly relevant to our story.

The term "gene" refers to a region of a chromosome that codes for either the production of a protein, within the cell's ribosomes, or various types of ribonucleic acid (RNA), such as the ribosomic RNA (rRNA) that makes up the ribosomes themselves. Estimates vary a bit, but there are at least 20,000 protein-coding genes in the human body,[9] and most of them are "polymorphic," meaning that they naturally occur in more than one variation. These variations tend to be fairly small. Sometimes two or more alleles of the same gene express the exact same protein, while in other instances (for example, the genes that determine eye color) these differences may result in the expression of different proteins. The alleles that commonly occur in nature are referred to as "wild types." Occasionally, though, an allele may contain a mutation— a nucleotide that normally would be present may be missing, for example, or other unexpected ones inserted into the sequence—in which case the protein or RNA produced by the gene also may be different from the more commonly expressed versions. These mutations can be either hereditary or "somatic" (acquired); some are harmless or, in rare cases, advantageous (hence allowing for evolution by means of natural selection to occur). Others, however, are potentially harmful; as we will see, certain mutations to BRCA1 and BRCA2 fall into this category.

I mentioned RNA above, and it is this acid that forms the intermediate step in the progression from DNA to protein. RNA is chemically similar to DNA in that it consists of nucleotides comprising a sugar (ribose, as opposed to deoxyribose), a phosphate, and a base, but RNA's four bases are A, C, G, and uracil (U) in place of T. Sequences of three RNA nucleotides, called triplets or codons, code for each of the twenty amino acids that form complex molecules known as polypeptides, which in turn fold themselves into proteins. To progress from DNA to protein, an enzyme called RNA polymerase initiates a process, known as transcription, at a portion of a gene called a promoter. RNA polymerase binds to a portion of the antisense DNA strand and causes that portion temporarily to separate from its corresponding sense strand. RNA polymerase produces RNA nucleotides that bind to the DNA strand—C binds with G and G with C, A binds with T, and U with A—until, assuming the process is successfully completed, the RNA polymerase reaches a termination signal at the end of the gene. A protein known as Rho factor then causes the DNA–RNA complex to unwind, so that the RNA strand (now called "pre-messenger RNA" or pre-mRNA) detaches and the antisense strand rebinds with the sense strand. Due to their binding properties, the triplets (codons) located on the pre-mRNA will be a mirror image of the triplets (referred to as "anticodons") residing on the antisense strand—that is, UUU corresponds to a DNA sequence of AAA, CCC corresponds to GGG, and so on—and will be identical to the codons located on the relevant portion of the antisense strand, except for the substitution of U for T.

The pre-mRNA undergoes one further transformation before exiting the nucleus. This is needed because DNA and pre-mRNA typically contain long stretches that don't code for anything. These noncoding regions are referred to as "introns" (the coding regions are "exons"), and the effort to uncover the precise function of these noncoding regions (once referred to dismissively as "junk DNA") is at present a matter of intense interest.[10] In fact, the average gene contains 8.8 exons and 7.8 introns,[11] with the noncoding DNA including the introns making up about 97 percent of a full-length gene.

In order to go from pre-mRNA to protein coding, the next thing to happen is that the introns detach from the pre-mRNA, while the exons are spliced together to form (mature) "messenger RNA" (mRNA). The mRNA then exits the nucleus for the ribosome, where the genetic instructions will be "translated" into a polypeptide chain—a protein—with the help of another molecule, "transfer RNA" (tRNA). tRNA consists of an amino acid at one end and a triplet (anticodon) at the other. Except for the untranslated regions (UTRs), the mRNA codons will bind with their corresponding anticodons (again, AAA binds with UUU, and on and on) on the tRNA. There are sixty-four possible codons—that is, sixty-four possible triplets of the bases A, C, G, and U—but there are only twenty amino acids. This means that some amino acids are coded for by more than one codon. (The amino acid leucine, for example, is coded for by UUA, UUG, CUU, CUC, CUA, and CUG.) Combinations of the twenty amino acids form polypeptides, which then fold themselves into proteins. The end result is the specific protein, made from the polypeptide chain, which, we can now say, was encoded by the initial DNA sequence. Consistent with this process, the naturally occurring *BRCA1* and *BRCA2* genes normally encode for proteins that work to suppress tumors.

One other thing to note before moving on is that it is often difficult to use a DNA sequence (for genetic engineering, for example, or as a "probe" to test whether a corresponding sequence is present in a sample) if you have to use the *entire* sequence containing introns and exons. Fortunately, through a process known as "reverse transcription," a researcher can take mRNA (which, remember, lacks introns) and reverse-transcribe it to a corresponding single-stranded DNA sequence; for example, the reverse transcription of mRNA codon ACU would be TGA. The end result is an exact copy of the sense strand of the original DNA sequence from which the mRNA derived, minus the introns. This intron-less DNA is referred to as "complementary DNA" or cDNA. For some applications, the single-stranded cDNA is all that is needed; for others, the enzyme DNA polymerase is used to create a double-stranded cDNA containing both sense and antisense strands.

Myriad's Patents

As you may recall from Chapter 1, even before the Supreme Court's 2013 decision in *Myriad* it was clear that "products of nature" were not patentable subject matter. So what exactly did Myriad think it could patent within the letter of the law? As we will see, until 2013 the rule the USPTO applied was that genes that had been isolated from their natural state were *not* products of nature, and thus were potentially patentable inventions. On this view, the DNA sequences for *BRCA1* and *BRCA2* were not patentable as long as they remained in their natural state, the human body; but once someone isolated a sequence from its natural state—for example, by extracting it from a human subject and cloning it in a laboratory, which is what Myriad did—that isolated sequence would no longer be a product of nature, because in nature you don't find DNA sequences in isolation from their surrounding genetic material.

To illustrate, Claim 1 of Myriad's US Patent No. 5,747,282, dated May 5, 1998, reads as follows:

> What is claimed is:
> 1. An isolated DNA coding for a BRCA1 polypeptide, said polypeptide having the amino acid sequence set forth in SEQ ID NO:2.[12]

Most of the terms used in this claim are defined somewhere in the patent's written description. An "isolated" DNA sequence, for example, "is one which is substantially separated from other cellular components which naturally accompany a native human sequence or protein . . . . The term embraces a nucleic acid sequence . . . which has been removed from its naturally occurring environment, and includes recombinant or cloned DNA isolates . . . ."[13] The patent further defines "recombinant nucleic acid" as one that "is not naturally occurring, or which is made by the artificial combination of two otherwise separated segments of sequence," while the term "BRCA1 polypeptide" refers to a "polypeptide encoded by the BRCA1 locus, variations or fragments thereof." The terms "polypeptide," "encode," and "BRCA1 locus" are all defined as well, with the "BRCA1 locus" including "all allelic variations of the DNA sequence" that code for "a BRCA1 polypeptide, fragment, homolog, or variant, including, e.g., protein fusions or deletions," and that "possess a sequence which is either derived from, or substantially similar to a natural BRCA1-encoding gene or one having substantial homology with a natural BRCA1-encoding gene or a portion thereof." Finally, "SEQ ID NO:2" is defined as a specified sequence of 1,863 amino acids beginning, as always, with methionine and ending with tyrosine. (The USPTO requires the use of sequence identification numbers, abbreviated "SEQ ID NO," to identify DNA sequences.)[14] Altogether, the definitions span

why?

columns 17–28 and take up six pages, not including the sequence listings, which run from columns 67–154 and thus take up another forty-four pages.

The upshot is that Claim 1 does *not* read on DNA sequences in their nonisolated, naturally occurring state within the human body, but rather only on an isolated sequence that codes for the normally-functioning, wild type *BRCA1* polypeptide; this would appear to include both the entire double-stranded gene and its cDNA counterpart. (Take away the introns and you still have a sequence that codes for the protein.) Nevertheless, some ambiguities remain. Suppose, for example, that a researcher were to extract (and reassemble in the lab, using a technique I will describe below) chromosome 17 in its entirety. That chromosome includes the *BRCA1* gene, among many others. Would the researcher be infringing Claim 1, because the *BRCA1* gene has been isolated "from other cellular components which naturally accompany a native human sequence"—for example, the proteins known as histones around which cellular DNA winds like thread on a spool? Or does "isolated" in this context mean something like "separated from the other genes on chromosome 17?" Or what if the isolated "product" consists of thousands of DNA or cDNA fragments which the researcher *could* reassemble, like pieces of a jigsaw puzzle, into a facsimile of the entire gene? As we will see, researchers usually have no reason actually to do this; but is such a reassembly necessary to infringe the claim? Because of the unusual procedural posture of the *Myriad* litigation, as explained shortly, no court ever held a *Markman* hearing (see Chapter 1) to determine Claim 1's precise boundaries. Even after the Supreme Court decision, then, it remains somewhat unclear whether any of the parties to *Myriad* actually *were* infringing Claim 1; I'll come back to this point at the end of the chapter.

Moving along, Claim 2 of the '282 Patent recites "the isolated DNA of Claim 1, wherein said DNA has the nucleotide sequence set forth in SEQ ID NO:1," and "SEQ ID NO:1" is defined as a cDNA having 5,914 base pairs, beginning with a 120-nucleotide UTR before commencing with ATG (the DNA version of the start codon, for methionine) and concluding with TAC (for tyrosine) followed by a stop codon (TGA) and a 203-nucleotide UTR. As discussed in Chapter 1, dependent claims like Claim 2 function as a sort of insurance policy, intended here to preserve a claim to an isolated cDNA sequence even if the broader Claim 1 were invalidated (as, indeed, it eventually was).

Some of the other claims of the '282 Patent are even broader than Claim 1, however. Claim 5, for example, recites "an isolated DNA having at least 15 nucleotides of the DNA of Claim 1," and thus covers *BRCA1* fragments, as well as the entire sequence. (Presumably the claim drafter meant 15 nucleotides in the same sequence as claimed in Claim 1, not just 15 nucleotides in common, since all DNA is made up of only four different nucleotides.) According to the

fragments vs sequence?

probe?

p?

specification, "this number of nucleotides is usually about the minimal length required for a successful probe that would hybridize specifically with a BRCA1-encoding sequence." If you remember the discussion of ESTs in Chapter 1, this will sound familiar, because ESTs are often used as probes. A researcher uses small bits of single-strand DNA to test for the presence of corresponding DNA in a sample by "hybridizing" with it. Columns 21–22 of the written description explain that one could use such fragments to probe for mutations that are associated with a predisposition to cancer, as well as to determine whether mRNA that encodes *BRCA1* is present in a sample. Claim 7 recites the cDNA sequences for four mutations to the wildtype *BRCA1* gene that had been discovered in study participants, while Claims 8 through 17 recite compositions and methods for replicating *BRCA1* or *BRCA1* polypeptide (or portions of them) in the lab. Claims 18 and 19 read on kits for detecting *BRCA1* mutations, and Claim 20 a method for screening potential cancer therapeutics by comparing samples of altered *BRCA1* genes in the presence and absence of compounds suspected of being cancer therapeutics.

Like the '282 Patent, Myriad's patent on the *BRCA2* gene (US Patent No. 5,837,492, dated November 17, 1998) begins with claims to an isolated DNA (in this case, an isolated DNA coding for a *BRCA2* polypeptide comprising a specified amino acid sequence) and to the corresponding cDNA. In a few respects, however, '492 is broader than '282. For example, it claims all mutated versions of *BRCA2*, as well as a long list of specific mutations. Myriad also obtained several other patents relating to *BRCA1* and *BRCA2*, including patents on altered forms of *BRCA1* and methods for detecting mutations.

For all of these patents, the USPTO concluded that the issued claims—including the claims to isolated DNA sequences—recited patentable subject matter and satisfied all of the other requirements of patentability (novelty, nonobviousness, and so on) as well. If valid, the claims reciting isolated DNA sequences would enable Myriad to prevent others from engaging in the unauthorized manufacture, use, or sale of identical isolated sequences. Note, however, that none of the claims would render it illegal to make or use a *nonisolated* DNA sequence within one's own body—nor could they, consistent with constitutional protections against involuntary servitude. Nonetheless, many people recoil at the notion that DNA, whether isolated or not, should be viewed as a patentable "invention." For many people—and, as we'll see, the Supreme Court—DNA is an unpatentable product of nature. Before we proceed any further in examining the Court's opinion, however, and its resolution of the other claims in suit, it's worth spending some time considering the conventional rationales for not allowing products of nature to be patented, and how these rationales have evolved over the years. What exactly *is* a product of nature, and why can't you patent one?

Products of Nature

As noted in Chapter 1, section 101 of the US Patent Act states that "[w]hoever invents or discovers any new and useful process, machine, manufacture, or composition of matter . . . may obtain a patent . . . ." The inclusion of the words "invents *or discovers*" might lead you to think that section 101 authorizes the USPTO to award patents not only to inventors but also to people who discover naturally-occurring, but previously unknown, processes (for example, the process by which the HIV virus insinuates its way into cells), or who discover new species, organisms, minerals . . . *genes* . . . anything that could be thought of as a "composition of matter." (The Act doesn't define the word "discovers," though it does define "invention" as "meaning invention or discovery." Big help there.) Nevertheless, courts and commentators have long agreed that naturally-occurring products of nature are not patentable: that, in fact, you do have to invent something, not just discover it, to obtain a patent. Sometimes the application of this rule is easy: the case law simply wouldn't permit the USPTO to award a patent to someone who discovers a new species lurking in the Brazilian rain forest, for example. But other cases are not so obvious. Genes are one such example, but there are plenty more: cases in which someone has patented, or tried to patent, an otherwise naturally-occurring thing (for example, a gene, protein, or hormone) that has been isolated from its natural state. For many people, isolated genes are still just genes, that is, products of nature, but clearly there is (or was at one time) a degree of ingenuity that went into figuring out how to isolate them from their natural state and replicate them in the lab. As always, the question is ultimately one of policy. *Should* isolated products of nature be regarded as (potentially) patentable inventions? At what point should a product that has been altered in some manner be deemed sufficiently distinct from its naturally-occurring form that it becomes (again, potentially) patentable? Perhaps more fundamentally, why not allow someone to patent a product of nature?

It's probably easiest to address the last of these questions first. The conventional wisdom is that, like laws of nature and abstract ideas (which we'll discuss in the next two chapters) products of nature should be in the public domain, because they form the fundamental "building blocks" (or "basic tools") of future invention—and thus the social costs of patenting them would exceed the benefits. More specifically, the argument is that, although authorizing the patenting of newly discovered species or other preexisting subject matter conceivably could produce some social benefits—maybe more people would be motivated to go out and discover them—grants or other such incentives also are available tools for motivating these types of discoveries, and may be better suited for this role. (Recall from Chapter 2 the distinction between basic and applied research. While the line between the two is sometimes easier to assert than to discern, by most accounts patents are better suited for motivating applied than basic research, which often has no short-term commercial payout.) At the same time, the social costs of permitting patents on products of nature could be high, if such patents would impede other researchers from conducting their own investigations. Thus, even if the availability of patent protection would encourage *some* additional investment in discovering products of nature beyond what is available by ways of grants or other incentives, at the margin these benefits would be less than the potentially enormous monopoly and access costs.

As we'll see, the Supreme Court largely adopted this "building block" argument in the *Myriad* case. As we'll also see, however, while many people find this rationale compelling for excluding products of nature from patent eligibility, the rationale is not without its problems. For one thing, while it may be that (in principle) the decision whether to classify something as a product of nature turns on some sort of implicit cost–benefit analysis, it's not exactly obvious how courts or other policymakers are supposed to *know* when the costs begin to outweigh the benefits. Maybe the benefits of extending patent protection to, say, newly discovered species would be higher than posited above, even if we consider the availability of alternatives such as grants; or maybe the costs wouldn't be as high as is sometimes imagined. Myriad wasn't really going to lay claim to the genes residing in your own body, after all—though as discussed below, Myriad's patents did enable it to charge a high price for screening services, and could have deterred some research uses as well (albeit the evidence supporting this latter point is debatable). Moreover, even if one grants these negative impacts substantial weight, you could make a similar argument about the effect of many other inventions, including drugs, which clearly *are* patentable. The question then becomes whether the social costs associated with patenting the things courts classify as "products of nature" are systematically higher than the social costs of patenting other, more conventional, subject matter. Maybe they are, but assertions standing alone are not evidence.

Perhaps a better rationale for excluding products of nature is that they often don't seem to fit very well with the underlying logic of a system of patent rights. Again, let's assume I discover a new species and were (in theory) able to patent it. I'd still be vulnerable on several other grounds. Is the species really *novel* if it was out there, albeit undetected, all the time? Is it "useful" in the narrow, patent-specific sense of that term? How can anyone be certain that I really *was* the first to discover what's been out there all this time? Is there something incongruous, even offensive, about parceling out exclusive rights to prevent others from making, using, or selling a species that has been in existence for millennia?

Some of these objections might seem to apply with even more force to genes and other subject matter found within human (or other animal) bodies. Even if no one could actually detect Gene X until modern technology enabled this to happen, it was there, all the time, performing its natural function. In that sense, one could say that it was "inherent" in the prior (human or nonhuman) art and therefore lacks novelty. It's also the case that some genes are detected before anyone knows exactly what they do, so many of them might (technically) lack utility in the sense of an articulable purpose for which a human researcher could employ them. Of course, these objections would be independent grounds for denying a patent anyway: even if an invention is clearly patentable subject matter, if it lacks novelty or utility, then it isn't, at the end of the day, patentable. For some patent scholars, these sorts of thought experiments prove the point that we really don't need restrictions on patentable subject matter as such: we could reach the "right" result by applying standard patent doctrine relating to novelty and utility (and, in appropriate cases, nonobviousness as well), without engaging in what some perceive as the metaphysical dispute over what distinguishes an invention from a product of nature. For others, though, a little redundancy isn't necessarily a bad thing. If there are multiple reasons to think that something shouldn't be patentable, you should be more confident in reaching that conclusion than if there were only one.

Most fundamentally, just about everyone would find it morally offensive if the first person to discover Gene X could prevent others from making or using Gene X within their own bodies. Surely no one could force your cells to stop making Gene X, even if they had a legal right to do so, but even if they "only" had a right to demand payment this would seem to contravene fundamental concepts of human liberty and autonomy as enshrined in, among other places, the Thirteenth Amendment: "Neither slavery nor involuntary servitude, except as a punishment for crime whereof the party shall have been duly convicted, shall exist within the United States . . . ." (If paying someone so that you may continue to use your genes isn't a form of slavery, it's hard to know what is.) And while it may be quite unlikely that anyone actually *would* insist that you pay them for your body's use of your own genes, why have a legal standard that makes even a remote risk of such a nightmarish outcome possible?

All of this suggests that there are some reasonably good if not airtight arguments for excluding preexisting, naturally occurring subject matter—especially subject matter residing within the human body—from the scope of patent protection. The hard part, as I said above, comes in determining how far the "product of nature" concept should extend beyond these examples. What about products that have been extracted, isolated, refined, or changed in some way from their naturally-occurring state? Is there a sensible place to draw the line between patentable and unpatentable? Rather than considering that question in the abstract, it might be helpful to consider some of the cases that preceded *Myriad*, over the course of more than a century, in trying to flesh out the definition.

On the one hand, some cases from the nineteenth to mid-twentieth centuries appeared to stand for the proposition that you can't get a patent on an extracted or refined version of a naturally-existing product of nature. One of the leading cases was an 1874 Supreme Court decision, *American Wood Paper Co. v. Fibre Disintegrating Co.*,[15] which involved a patent claiming "a pulp suitable for the manufacture of paper, made from wood or other vegetable substances, by boiling the wood or other vegetable substances in an alkali under pressure, substantially as described." In invalidating the patent, Justice Strong stated:

> There are many things well known and valuable in medicine or in the arts which may be extracted from divers substances. But the extract is the same, no matter from what it has been taken. A process to obtain it from a subject from which it has never been taken may be the creature of invention, but the thing itself when obtained cannot be called a new manufacture.

In the very next sentence, however, the Court states that the extract in question "may have been in existence and in common use before the new means of obtaining it was invented, and possibly before it was known that it could be extracted from the subject to which the new process is applied." Ultimately the Court concluded that the pulp lacked *novelty* because it had been reduced to practice by someone else prior to the inventors' date of invention. Justice Strong's assertion that extracts are nonpatentable subject matter is, therefore, *dictum*—a statement of opinion that, while possibly persuasive, is not controlling on future courts.

Arguably more relevant is a series of (non–Supreme Court) decisions stating or holding that a product that has been purified or refined from its natural state is not a patentable article. The earliest of these is an 1889 decision of the Commissioner of Patents, *Ex parte Latimer*, which involved a claim on a pine needle fiber from which the inventor, by means of a process he had developed, removed certain naturally-occurring impurities. In rejecting the claim, Commissioner Hall stated:

> It is not asserted . . . that the product, which is the result of applicant's process, is in any manner affected or produced by the process, or that its natural condition as a fiber has in any wise been affected, changed, or altered . . . . It is also well known that the pure fiber after it has been eliminated from the natural matrix of the leaf or stalk or wood in which nature forms and develops it is essentially the same thing and possesses the same construction. The chemical formula for this cellulose . . . is the same.

It cannot be said that the applicant in this case has made any discovery . . . any more than to find a new gem or jewel in the earth would entitle the discoverer to patent all gems which should be subsequently found, so that generally it may be said that fiber such as is described in this application is old . . . .[16]

Commissioner Hall expressed some discomfort with this result, noting the "alleged invention is unquestionably very valuable, and . . . of immense benefit . . . ." He even suggested some ways that future inventors might be able to avoid the same fate, stating that if the process "had another final step by which the fiber . . . were changed, either by curling it or giving it some new quality or function . . . the invention would probably cover a product."[17] Latimer himself nevertheless was out of luck. Although *Latimer* itself would not be cited in a judicial decision for several decades—and, according to legal historian Christopher Beauchamp, may not have been representative of Patent Office practice at the time, under which some patents did issue for extracted natural products[18]—a later series of cases from the 1920s and 1930s rejected such claims, though it's sometimes difficult to tell whether the basis for the decision was lack of patentable subject matter, novelty, or nonobviousness.[19] As noted in Chapter 1, in earlier times, courts sometimes viewed all three of these concepts as all falling within the broader rubric of "inventiveness."

Finally, a third body of cases dealt not with extracted or refined products but rather with products of nature to which some (arguably) modest change had been made. The leading case here is a 1931 Supreme Court decision, *American Fruit Growers, Inc. v. Brogdex Co.,*[20] in which one of the claims in suit recited "fresh citrus fruit of which the rind or skin carries borax in amount that is very small but sufficient to render the fruit resistant to blue mold decay." The Court held that the fruit was not a patentable "manufacture" because the "[a]ddition of borax to the rind did not produce from the raw material an article for use which possesses a new or distinctive form, quality, or property." The rule therefore seems to be that transforming a product of nature into a potentially patentable article requires giving it some "new or distinctive form, quality, or property." Beyond the immediate facts of the case, however, the opinion doesn't provide much insight into how courts should discern in future instances what counts as "new or distinctive form, quality, or property."

On the other side of the ledger are a handful of (again, non–Supreme Court) cases from the late nineteenth and early twentieth centuries one of which was to become, for a time, the foundational decision on products of nature—in part because it was authored by one of the giants of US jurisprudence, Judge Learned Hand.[21] For lawyers reading this book, Hand needs no introduction. For nonlawyers, it's fair to say that Hand is usually considered one of the greatest legal thinkers of all time. Although never appointed to the Supreme Court, Hand sat for nearly forty years (1924–61) on the United States Court of Appeals for the Second Circuit, at the time probably the most influential court in the nation aside from the Supreme Court; and his opinions on a wide range of topics, including constitutional law, torts, antitrust, and intellectual property remain widely cited to this day. Fifteen years before ascending to the Second Circuit, the thirty-seven-year-old Hand left private practice to begin his judicial career as a federal trial court judge in Manhattan. An early case over which he presided was a patent dispute, *Parke-Davis & Co. v. H.K. Mulford Co.*[22]

The case involved two patents relating to a hormone/neurotransmitter known alternatively as epinephrine or adrenaline. (Epinephrine is the term used more frequently in US scientific and medical circles, but the words refer to precisely the same compound.) As you're probably aware, the body naturally produces the hormone as part of its "fight or flight" response to threats. Medicinally, epinephrine also is used to treat cardiac arrest, asthma, and anaphylaxis, among other conditions, because the hormone constricts the blood vessels, dilates the bronchi, and improves heart muscle function, thus increasing a patient's heart and respiratory rates. (It's also the active ingredient in the EpiPen device, which we'll encounter in Chapter 6.) The compound was discovered in the adrenal glands of mammals in the late nineteenth century, and its use for medicinal purposes seemed apparent. Epinephrine extracted from animal tissue often carried with it some of the surrounding glandular tissue as well, however, and thus raised collateral risks of infection or death.

In the early twentieth century, Jokichi Takamine, a Japanese-born chemist residing in the United States, perfected a method for extracting and purifying the hormone so that it could be used more safely in humans.[23] Takamine obtained two US patents, which he assigned to the US drugmaker Parke-Davis. The principal claim of the first of these (the '176 Patent) was for "[a] substance possessing the herein-described physiological characteristics and reactions of the suprarenal glands in a stable and concentrated form, and practically free from inert and associated gland-tissue," while the second ('177 Patent) recited "a substance consisting of the blood pressure raising principle of the suprarenal glands chemically combined with a non-suprarenal substance whereby the stability of a water solution of said blood pressure raising principle is maintained." Technically, '176 covered a purified form of the hormone in the form of a chemical base, while '177 claimed the base treated with an acid to form a water-soluble salt. Parke-Davis marketed the product under the trademark "Adrenalin," and sued a competitor for infringing the two patents. Judge Hand found both patents valid and infringed; our concern here is with his rulings on validity.

First, as for '176, the question Judge Hand addressed was whether the base was anticipated by the prior art extracts, and he concluded that it was not because all of the prior art was in the form of a salt. The products therefore were not identical. Hand went on to state, however, that:

> Nor is the patent only for a degree of purity, and therefore not for a new "composition of matter." As I have already shown, it does not include a salt, and no one had ever isolated a substance which was not in salt form, and which was anything like Takamine's . . . . But, even if it were merely an extracted product without change, there is no rule that such products are not patentable. Takamine was the first to make it available for any use by removing it from the other gland-tissue in which it was found, and, while it is of course possible logically to call this a purification of the principle, it became for every practical purpose a new thing commercially and therapeutically. That was a good ground for a patent. That the change here resulted in ample practical differences is fully proved. Everyone, not already saturated with scholastic distinctions, would recognize that Takamine's crystals were not merely the old dried glands in a purer state, nor would his opinion change if he learned that the crystals were obtained from the glands by a process of eliminating the inactive organic substances. The line between different substances and degrees of the same substance is to be drawn rather from the common usages of men than from nice considerations of dialectic.

Hand further concluded that the '177 Patent (covering a salt) was valid because none of the prior art salts was free from the inert and associated gland tissue.

If you read the above passage carefully, you may have wondered how Hand could have stated that "even if it were merely an extracted product without change, there is no rule that such products are not patentable," given that *Latimer* appears both to state and apply that supposedly nonexistent rule. Of course, Hand wasn't obligated to follow *Latimer*—a federal district court is free to disagree with a legal interpretation by the Commissioner of Patents—and, as I will argue below, Hand's rule may be better than the one proposed by Commissioner Hall. But shouldn't Hand have been upfront in rejecting *Latimer*, instead of simply ignoring it? Maybe so, but apparently neither party bothered to bring *Latimer* to the attention of the young trial judge who, as of 1911, still had a ways to go before attaining his eventual status as legal legend. (The patent examiner who had been assigned to review Takamine's applications *was* aware of *Latimer*, however, and he initially rejected the claims for the isolated hormone. It was only after several years of prosecution and amendment that the examiner apparently was convinced that Takamine's compositions were, in the words of *Latimer*, sufficiently "changed" by the addition of some "new quality or function" to qualify as patentable subject matter.[24]) In any event, the omission might not have mattered: Hand was aware of, but distinguished, *American Wood Products*, and as support for his ruling he cited two other recent appellate decisions that *had* allowed patents to issue on purified or new forms of chemical compounds, where the new form resulted in a much more useful product.[*]

Hand's judgment in favor of Parke-Davis was affirmed on appeal,[25] but for several decades thereafter the case was cited only sporadically by other courts.[26] The opinion probably was more famous for an entirely separate point, namely Hand's expression of frustration at "the extraordinary condition of the law which makes it possible for a man without any knowledge of even the rudiments of chemistry to pass upon such questions as these." Hand suggested that Congress should consider authorizing the use of technical advisers in such cases. (One hundred years later, federal law now permits judges to appoint their own experts, but with few exceptions they rarely do so.) By 1958, however, Hand was at the peak of his prestige among lawyers and judges, and a federal appellate court in Richmond, Virginia cited his decision in *Parke-Davis* in finding a vitamin B_{12} active composition produced from fungi constituted patentable subject matter.[27] Over the next half-century a broader view of patentable subject matter gradually began to win approval, as evidenced most clearly by the Supreme Court's 1980 decision in *Diamond v. Chakrabarty*.

In the early 1970s, Dr. Anand Chakrabarty, a young microbiologist working for General Electric Company in Schenedectady, New York, was researching naturally-occurring plasmids that were capable of degrading complex hydrocarbons. (Plasmids are circular DNA structures that are separate from the chromosomes. They are found in bacteria and some other organisms.) Specifically, Chakrabarty and colleagues identified plasmids that "specify a degradative pathway"—that is, they code for enzymes that enable a microorganism to convert a "primary substrate" (camphor, octane, salicylate, or naphthalene, all of which are constituents of crude oil) into a "some simple common

---

[*] Harkness argues that these cases, *Union Carbide Co. v. American Carbide Co.*, 181 F. 104 (2d Cir. 1910), and *Kuehmsted v. Farbenfabrik of Elberfeld Co.*, 179 F. 701 (7th Cir. 1910), were "largely irrelevant to the issue of whether a purified product of nature could be patented" because the patents in suit read on, respectively, a "new form of crystalline calcium carbide" and "a greater purification of a man-made chemical." Jon Harkness, *Dicta on Adrenalin(e): Myriad Problems with Learned Hand's Product-of-Nature Pronouncements in* Parke-Davis, 93 J. PAT. & TRADEMARK OFF. SOC'Y 363, 390 n.190 (2011). Beauchamp, by contrast, reads the two cases as standing for the proposition that "a commercially significant advance in purification constituted a meaningfully new product," and that Hand was actually bound by the *Union Carbide* holding. *See* Christopher Beauchamp, *Patenting Nature: A Problem of History*, 16 STAN. L. & TECH. REV. 257, 295 (2013). Either way, Hand's opinion is the one that over time came to be most closely associated with the principle that products isolated or refined from their natural state were patentable subject matter.

metabolite, a normal food substance."[28] Chakrabarty succeeded in developing a process for introducing two or more of these plasmids together into a single host bacterium of the genus *Pseudomonas*; when the bacterium replicated, the plasmid combinations too would be passed along to another generation. Put another way, Chakrabarty had invented a species of bacteria that did not exist in nature, and which (it was believed) would be useful in cleaning old spills.[29] Chakrabarty then filed a patent application, claiming not only the process for engineering the bacteria but also the oil-hungry bacteria themselves. Eight years later, Chakrabarty's case would wind up before the US Supreme Court.

The path to the Supreme Court began when the patent examiner assigned to review the application rejected the claims to the bacteria on two grounds: first, that the bacteria were unpatentable products of nature; and second, on the separate ground that living things are unpatentable. Chakrabarty appealed to the Patent Board of Appeals and Interferences (predecessor to today's PTAB), which affirmed on the second ground. The board reasoned that, in enacting a Plant Patent Act in 1930, Congress signaled its understanding that (outside the context of that act) living things generally were not patentable: why else would Congress have gone to the trouble of enacting a law permitting a certain class of living things to be patented, if living things generally had been patentable all along? Chakrabarty requested reconsideration, then appealed again, this time to the Court of Customs and Patent Appeals (CCPA), the predecessor court to the Federal Circuit. When the CCPA sided with Chakrabarty, the USPTO sought further review in the Supreme Court.[30]

In a 5–4 decision, the Supreme Court agreed that Chakrabarty's bacteria constituted patentable subject matter.[31] Writing for the majority, Chief Justice Burger viewed the matter as a simple matter of statutory construction: section 101 of the Patent Act says "[w]hoever invents . . . *any* new and useful . . . manufacture, or composition of matter . . . may obtain a patent therefor . . .'; "any" means "any," and Chakrabarty's bacteria qualify as both "manufactures" (articles produced "from raw or prepared materials by giving these materials new forms, qualities, properties, or combinations") and "compositions of matter" ("all compositions of two or more substances," including those formed by "chemical union . . . whether they be gases, fluids, powders, or solids").[32] According to Chief Justice Burger, it's clear that Congress intended for section 101 to be given broad scope. The House of Representatives Committee Report that accompanied the 1952 Patent Act, for example, "inform[s] us that Congress intended statutory subject matter to 'include anything under the sun that is made by man . . . .'"[33] (As we'll see in Chapter 5, the Court appears to have taken that statement from the legislative history somewhat out of context, but so it goes.)

Further, the majority insisted, the bacteria were *not* naturally occurring products of nature, because they didn't exist in nature, but rather were a "product of human ingenuity." On this issue, the Court distinguished a 1948 precedent, *Funk Bros. Seed Co. v. Kalo Inoculant Co.*,[34] that involved six naturally-occurring species of bacteria that help certain plants to extract nitrogen from the air. Though it had been thought that each species had a mutually inhibitory effect on the others, so that the six could not be packaged together, the inventor (Bond) discovered strains of each species that did not have this effect and obtained a patent on the combination. *That* patent was held invalid—it was not an "invention"—because the combination did not change the way in which the bacteria naturally functioned. By contrast, Chakrabarty's bacteria had "markedly different characteristics from any found in nature."[35] Of course, the plasmids in those bacteria continued to code for the same enzymes they had before, though perhaps the act of getting them to coexist in a single cell seems more inventive than does Bond's aggregation of the six naturally-occurring strains in *Funk Bros.*

The Court also was not persuaded that Congress was taking a stand, one way or the other, on the patentability of living things when it enacted the Plant Patent Act in 1930. As we saw in Chapter 1, one of the motivations behind enacting the Plant Patent Act was the concern at the time that plants couldn't be described in such a way as to qualify them for utility patent protection. Another was that, on the authority of *Latimer*, the Patent Office otherwise might have considered even human-bred hybrids as unpatentable products of nature. Neither concern, according to the majority, signaled a position on the broader question of whether describable human-created life forms could receive utility patent protection. (In response, the four dissenting justices thought there would have been little point in enacting a Plant Patent Act if life forms were otherwise patentable, but this view failed to carry the day.)

In addition, the majority rejected the argument that it should await express congressional authorization before extending patent protection to subject matter that Congress couldn't have had in mind when it enacted section 101. Lots of inventions are unforeseeable, after all, and encouraging their creation is pretty much the point of having a patent system in the first place. Finally, the Court noted arguments that it should exercise caution in the face of the potential dangers of genetic engineering:

> Scientists, among them Nobel laureates, are quoted suggesting that genetic research may pose a serious threat to the human race, or, at the very least, that the dangers are far too substantial to permit such research to proceed apace at this time. We are told that genetic research and related technological developments may spread pollution and disease, that it may result in a loss of genetic diversity, and that its practice may tend to depreciate the value of human life.

In response, however, the Court suggested both that resistance would be futile—patentability "may determine whether research efforts are accelerated by the hope of reward or slowed by want of incentives, but that is all"—and, more importantly, that it is the role of Congress and the President to make such weighty policy decisions, not the courts.[36]

Thirty years later, it may be tempting to wonder what all the fuss was about. Patents on genetically modified organisms are commonplace both in the United States and abroad, and, in the opinion of many commentators, the availability of such protection played a key role in the growth of the biotechnology industry in the 1980s and beyond.[37] The decision nevertheless upset many people at the time, and it remains controversial among some environmentalists and religious leaders to this day. For one thing, although the facts of *Chakrabarty* involved a microorganism, the Court's reasoning would seem to apply to genetically modified macroorganisms as well; and, indeed, both the USPTO and its counterparts in other countries have allowed patents to issue on higher life forms.[†]

Some were (and are) concerned about the possible unforeseen consequences of genetic engineering, as recognized in the Supreme Court's opinion, or bristle at the thought that humans are playing God. (Recall from Chapter 1 Stuart Newman's attempt to draw attention to the issue by filing a patent application on a chimera.) On the other hand, just because life forms are patentable doesn't mean that genetic engineering itself must be unregulated or even legal. Again, you'll recall from Chapter 1 that owning a patent doesn't authorize you to *do* anything, other than stopping someone else from making, using, or selling your invention; marketing a drug without approval of the FDA, for example, is illegal even if you happen to own a patent on the drug. The same reasoning disposes of the argument that patents on living organisms amount to "owning life": patents don't affirmatively confer any ownership over physical things but only the intangible right to exclude others from making, using, or selling those things. (And of course, people do own many living things, both plants and animals, and this is usually not very controversial, which makes the "owning life" objection a bit hard to understand.) Nevertheless, for some people, the potential risks of genetic engineering outweigh the benefits, while for others the practice remains morally problematic. And if you disapprove of genetic engineering generally, I suppose it makes sense to disapprove of policies such as patent protection that are likely not only to encourage it but that might seem to stamp a governmental seal of approval on it.

[†] Two major exceptions are Canada, where the Supreme Court held that the "Oncomouse"—a mouse that was genetically engineered to be susceptible to developing tumors—was not patentable subject matter, and China. Both countries allow microorganisms to be patented, however.

The first patents on recombinant (non-naturally occurring) DNA sequences followed shortly in the wake of *Chakrabarty*,[38] and by the late 1980s the USPTO had begun issuing patents on isolated, naturally-occurring DNA sequences.[39] In 1991, when a case involving a patented gene (coding for the human protein erythropoietin) first came before the Federal Circuit, the infringement defendant challenged patent validity on several grounds including nonobviousness, but not lack of patentable subject matter.[40] Meanwhile, in 1990, Professor Rebecca Eisenberg restated the holding of *Parke-Davis* as standing for the proposition that an isolated or purified product of nature that possesses practical utility constitutes patentable subject matter,[41] and that interpretation reflected the mainstream view as embodied, for example, in the USPTO's 2001 Revised Utility Guidelines.[42] Altogether, prior to the *Myriad* decision the USPTO had issued thousands of patents relating to DNA sequences, and other countries took a similarly liberal approach. A frequently cited statistic that 20 percent of all human genes have been patented,[43] however, has been debunked. Although many patents *mentioned* DNA sequences somewhere in the written description or claims, a much smaller percentage specifically *claimed* a DNA sequence.[44]

The *Myriad* Controversy

You might wonder why it took so long for the question of whether human genes are patentable subject matter to come before the courts. One answer is that, after *Chakrabarty* (and another case we will encounter in Chapter 5 on software patents), both the USPTO and the Federal Circuit gradually adopted a very broad view of what sorts of inventions are eligible for patent protection. At least in the view of many patent lawyers, therefore, there was nothing particularly surprising about the extension of patents to isolated gene sequences; and, as in cases like the one involving erythropoietin, it remained (and remains) the case that gene patents can still be challenged on a number of other grounds, including utility, enablement, and nonobviousness. Another reason is that, until recently, only someone who had been sued (or reasonably believed he was about to be sued) for infringement would have been allowed to challenge the validity of a US patent on the ground that the claimed invention is not patentable subject matter. Since most of the infringement litigation involving gene patents pitted one drug or biotech company or research university against another, neither side really wanted (or, realistically, could have expected from the Federal Circuit) a ruling that genes were unpatentable. And while many scientists reportedly made and used patented DNA sequences without bothering to obtain a license—while others expressed concern about the potential chilling effects of such patents on research—gene patent owners never brought suit against any of these entities, who (had they been sued) might have been motivated to mount a subject matter challenge.[45]

Aside from individual scientists and researchers, however, there were a few parties who might have been motivated to challenge gene patents under the right circumstances. As documented by Gold and Carbone,[46] Myriad in particular made a number of public relations mistakes, both in the United States and abroad. In the United States, it used its patents to exclude potential competitors in the market for breast cancer screening tests, and it charged high prices to physicians and hospitals who wanted to use those tests—both of which practices, of course, its patents if valid entitled it to do, but neither of which generated much goodwill either. A competitor or a hospital that defied the patents and induced an infringement lawsuit could have raised lack of patentable subject matter as a defense, but again given (what seemed at the time) the unlikelihood that the defense would prevail, apparently all of these potential defendants either agreed to accept a license or avoided having their use of the patented technologies come to Myriad's attention.

By the late 2000s, however, the law relating to who could challenge an existing patent had changed somewhat. In *MedImmune, Inc. v. Genentech, Inc.*,[47] the Supreme Court held that the Federal Circuit's test for determining which potential accused infringers could preemptively sue for a declaratory judgment—a declaration from a court that they were not infringing or that the patent at issue was invalid—was too strict. This finally set the stage for a challenge to the long-simmering controversy over gene patents, by enabling the American Civil Liberties Union (ACLU) to coordinate a civil action, brought by a nonprofit scientific organization (the Association for Molecular Pathology) and several organizations and individuals against the USPTO and Myriad, seeking a declaration that Myriad's gene patents were invalid for lack of patentable subject matter.[48] Before proceeding with a discussion of how the litigation played out, however, it might be useful to take a step back and ask in precisely what ways researchers or physicians might be infringing the Myriad patents I've discussed above.

First off, many people seem to think that merely sequencing the patented genes would necessarily infringe the Myriad patents, assuming those patents were valid; but that isn't necessarily the case. Sequencing a gene is a complex process. To begin, a researcher could extract a cell sample from a subject—for example, by means of a cheek swab. The DNA (which contains multiple genes) can then be extracted through a simple process. It is then cleaved (segmented) at certain points by means of restriction enzymes derived from bacteria, resulting in the production of DNA fragments most of which will consist of portions of a single gene. These fragments can then be cloned, by binding them with plasmids to create a "vector," introducing the vector into a host cell (often a bacteria or yeast cell), and letting the cell reproduce over and over again. The end result is a library of millions of copies of individual DNA fragments; libraries like this now exist at universities and research institutions throughout the world. There are also libraries of cDNA fragments produced by a process that starts with the mRNA instead of with double-stranded DNA.

To sequence the DNA, a researcher would take identical segments of double-stranded DNA and heat them up so as to "denature" (split) them into complementary single strands. She would then introduce millions of "free" (unbound) nucleotides to the mix, some of which would be "dideoxy" nucleotides—meaning that they lack one of the hydroxyl (OH) groups found in most nucleotides—and these special nucleotides are modified so that they fluoresce in different colors in the presence of ultraviolet light. She would also add some short DNA sequences known as "primers," which bind to complementary portions of the single strands, and an enzyme (often a Taq polymerase) which attaches to the primer and begins a chain reaction by pulling in free nucleotides and binding them to the single strand (A with T and vice versa, and C with G and vice versa). When one of the dideoxy nucleotides binds, it terminates the chain reaction due to the lack of additional hydroxyl group. The researcher therefore ends up with thousands or millions of double-stranded DNA segments of varying length. By various means, these can be arranged by length and their terminating points "read" by a computer that detects the fluorescent light corresponding to each of the four bases. The computer then outputs the sequence of the segment. Since no one segment necessarily corresponds to an entire gene, however, further analysis (carried out by computer) is performed to determine which segments fit together.

You might analogize the process described above to putting together a jigsaw puzzle—though perhaps only in a metaphorical sense, since the act of sequencing as such does not require that anyone actually put the segments together to replicate the original gene. If the researcher *does* want to "make" an entire gene, however, in isolation from the rest of the genome, that can be done as well, once the sequence is known. Often, though, there is no particular reason to make the entire gene, introns and all. If the purpose of the endeavor is to produce the protein for which the gene codes, for example, the cDNA will work just as well and will be easier to use because it is shorter. The researcher therefore could splice together cDNA segments already existing in the lab, or produce her own cDNA from a library of DNA by means of reverse transcription.

Another possibility is that a researcher or forensic scientist will want to analyze a person's DNA for the presence of certain markers. Over 99 percent of the DNA in your body is the same as in mine. The parts that differ can be used to tell us apart, or to determine the probability that we are closely related. They also might signal the presence of a mutation, such as the mutations to *BRCA1* and

BRCA2 that are associated with an increased cancer risk. To perform this sort of testing, a researcher would take a DNA sample as above; cleave the DNA with restriction enzymes; reproduce those portions that are of interest (e.g., segments that tend to vary the most from one individual to another, or that may include known mutants), often by means of the polymerase chain reaction or other known techniques; and then use short-sequence DNA probes to determine the composition of these segments. For these purposes, there normally would be no reason to go to the trouble of reproducing an entire gene—though the portion of interest (e.g., the portion with the relevant biomarker that correlates with increased susceptibility to a particular disease), might include both coding and noncoding regions.[49]

Getting back to the case, the *Myriad* plaintiffs filed their complaint in federal district court in New York, and the matter was assigned to a long-serving and highly respected judge, Robert Sweet. Both the challengers and the patent owner moved for summary judgment—a common procedural device that enables a court to dispose of a case without proceeding to trial, if there is no "genuine issue of material fact" and one side or the other is entitled to judgment as a matter of law.

On March 29, 2010, Judge Sweet stunned much of the patent bar when he issued a lengthy opinion holding that isolated DNA and cDNA sequences were invalid for lack of patentable subject matter. In Judge Sweet's view, neither the isolated DNA nor cDNA sequences were "markedly different," to use the Supreme Court's phrase in *Chakrabarty*, from naturally-occurring DNA, since they all conveyed precisely the same genetic information found in the latter. Judge Sweet pointedly rejected Learned Hand's *Parke-Davis* dictum, noting that Hand's statements about patentable subject matter had never been expressly adopted by any higher court (and, in Judge Sweet's view, were directly contrary to controlling Supreme Court case law such as *Funk Brothers*); and he dismissed the argument that cDNA is different from naturally occurring DNA as nothing more than "a lawyer's trick."[50] Judge Sweet also concluded that Myriad's challenged method claims were invalid, a matter we will return to in the next chapter.

Myriad appealed to the Federal Circuit and, to few people's surprise, that court reversed (though by a 2–1 vote), holding that isolated DNA and cDNA are patent-eligible. The challengers then petitioned for Supreme Court review, but that Court—which had just decided a case (*Mayo v. Prometheus*, discussed in the next chapter) on the patentability of diagnostic methods—simply remanded (sent back) the case for reconsideration. Hearing the case on remand would be the same three-judge panel that had heard the first appeal: Judge Alan Lourie, a longtime Federal Circuit judge who also holds a PhD in chemistry; Judge Kimberly Moore, a former law professor who holds a graduate degree in electrical engineering from MIT; and Judge William Bryson, a former government lawyer who once clerked for Supreme Court Justice Thurgood Marshall.

Again, to few people's surprise, on remand the Federal Circuit stuck to its guns and reversed Judge Sweet 2–1. Writing for the majority, Judge Lourie emphasized the structural differences between naturally-occurring and isolated DNA:

> It is undisputed that Myriad's claimed isolated DNAs exist in a distinctive chemical form—as distinctive chemical molecules—from DNAs in the human body, *i.e.*, native DNA. Natural DNA exists in the body as one of forty-six large, contiguous DNA molecules . . . .
>
> Isolated DNA, in contrast, is a free-standing portion of a larger, natural DNA molecule. Isolated DNA has been cleaved (*i.e.*, had covalent bonds in its backbone chemically severed) or synthesized to consist of just a fraction of a naturally occurring DNA molecule . . . . Accordingly, *BRCA1* and *BRCA2* in their isolated states are different molecules from DNA that exists in the body; isolated DNA results from human intervention to cleave or synthesize a discrete portion of a native chromosomal DNA, imparting on that isolated DNA a distinctive chemical identity as compared to native DNA.[51]

A fortiori, cDNA is patentable subject matter because it is even further removed from the state in which it exists in nature. Judge Lourie further dismissed arguments that recognizing isolated DNA sequences as patentable subject matter would be analogous to allowing someone to patent a chemical element by isolating it from the earth, or a leaf by snapping it off a tree, because in neither of these cases does someone create a new molecular entity.

Concurring in the judgment that isolated DNA is patent eligible, but not for the same reasons articulated by Judge Lourie, Judge Moore concluded that cDNA is (to use the magic words) "markedly different" from naturally-occurring DNA because of its lack of introns. She was less convinced that the different structure of isolated DNA by itself was enough to render it "markedly different," however, and instead focused on the question of whether the differences confer a new utility on the claimed invention. For the short segments, Judge Moore concluded, the answer was yes, because unlike naturally-occurring sequences these segments can be used (as probes or primers, for example) to achieve a new purpose. Judge Moore was not convinced that the isolated full-length sequences had a new utility; nevertheless, given the fact that the USPTO had been granting such patents for thirty years, that several thousand of them were still in force, and that Congress had never once intervened to change matters led her to conclude that the court should defer to the industry's "settled expectations" that even the isolated sequences were patent-eligible.

Judge Bryson dissented in part. Like the others, he believed that cDNA was sufficiently different from natural DNA to qualify as patent-eligible. Nevertheless, Judge Bryson concluded that the isolated DNA sequences were not patentable, because their *informational content* was precisely the same as the informational content of naturally-occurring DNA. Judge Bryson also expressed concern that allowing patents on isolated sequences would hinder future research, and (unlike Judge Moore) he was unpersuaded that the USPTO's long-standing practice of granting such patents was entitled to deference.

The Supreme Court Opinion

As was expected, the plaintiff again filed a petition for Supreme Court review, and the Court granted the petition. Over fifty individuals and organizations filed amicus (friend-of-the-court) briefs, urging the Court either to affirm or reverse. Oral argument was held in April 2013, and on one of the last days of the 2013 term the Court delivered its unanimous opinion that, while cDNA is patentable, isolated DNA is not.[52]

Writing for the Court was Justice Clarence Thomas. After explaining the basics of DNA[53] and setting forth the facts of the dispute, Justice Thomas disposed of the legal issues in short order. For Justice Thomas, "Myriad's principal contribution was uncovering the precise location and genetic sequence of the *BRCA1* and *BRCA2* genes," and the principal question was "whether this renders the genes patentable." With the Court having phrased the question this way, it was pretty clear what Justice Thomas's answer would be. Merely finding the location of the gene was an act of discovery, not invention; who could disagree with that? But what about the act of isolating the gene from its natural state: didn't that create something that is not found in nature? Not according to the Court, because unlike Chakrabarty, "Myriad did not create anything. . . . [S]eparating that gene from its surrounding genetic material is not an act of invention," and the claims are not

> saved by the fact that isolating DNA from the human genome severs chemical bonds and thereby creates a nonnaturally occurring molecule . . . . [T]he claims understandably focus on the genetic information encoded in the BRCA1 and BRCA2 genes. If the patents depended upon the creation of a unique molecule, then a would-be infringer could arguably avoid at least Myriad's patent claims on entire genes . . . by isolating a DNA sequence that included both the BRCA1 or BRCA2 gene and one additional nucleotide pair. Such a molecule would not be chemically identical to the molecule "invented" by Myriad. But Myriad

obviously would resist that outcome because its claim concerned primarily with the information contained in the genetic *sequence*, not with
the specific chemical composition of a particular molecule.[54]

The Court was similarly unimpressed with Judge Moore's argument about
deferring to USPTO practice. On the other hand, the Court's logic led it to conclude that the cDNA sequences were patentable, because these molecules generally do not exist in nature. Finally, the Court noted that none of the method
claims were before it (the Court had agreed to hear the case only as it related to
the product claims), and that nothing in the opinion addressed the patentability
of recombinant DNA.

So What Does It All Mean?

The *Myriad* opinion clearly holds that naturally-occurring DNA sequences are
not patentable subject matter, regardless of whether they have been "isolated"
from the human body. The Court's reasoning appears to be based on two premises: first, that the claimed sequences were, in substance, claims to naturally-
occurring *information* which is identical whether it exists within or outside the
body; and second, that this information is a "basic tool" of scientific research.
Although both premises contain a kernel of truth, I will argue below that neither premise necessarily supports the Court's conclusion that isolated DNA is
unpatentable; nor does the result really get to the heart of what I view as the
fundamental policy issue, namely the impact of gene patents on research and on
health care costs.

Consider first the "information equivalency" rationale. I'll admit that this rationale has some intuitive appeal: a sequence of nucleotides is, after all, rightly
viewed as a code that can result in the production of a protein. But it's not clear
to me that the Court really understood or appreciated the implications of this
rationale. In the portion of the opinion quoted above, Justice Thomas seems
to rest his conclusion that the *BRCA1* claim is "really" a claim to information
on the ground that Myriad would resist the idea that adding a single nucleotide (which would create a slightly different compound while incorporating
the same information) would avoid infringement. But as we saw in Chapter 1,
any time an applicant uses the "open" claiming format the claim reads on the
claimed invention *and anything else added on.* (The Myriad claims do not use
the magic word "comprising," but in the view of most patent professionals those
claims would be understood as open claims.) Put another way, Justice Thomas's
observation that the addition of an additional element would not avoid infringement is true of the vast majority of patent claims, not just gene patents. If

DNA sequences are unpatentable information for this reason, then so are most other inventions.

More fundamentally, in a broad sense *all* patent claims really *are* nothing more than claims on information.[55] As you may recall from Chapter 1, a patent claim normally is not limited to the specific embodiment or embodiments the inventor herself has made or envisioned, but rather to any process or tangible thing that embodies or incorporates the inventive principle as expressed in the claim language. For this reason, patents (and, with appropriate adjustments, other forms of intellectual property) are correctly viewed as rights in *intangibles*, rather than as rights to physical objects.

In any event, the informational equivalency rationale for holding DNA unpatentable seems especially weak when you consider that the Court found the cDNA claims to be patentable because the cDNA sequences at issue do not occur in nature: in Justice Thomas's words, "[a] lab technician unquestionably creates something new when cDNA is made."[56] True enough; except for very short cDNA sequences—which the Court noted may be indistinguishable from naturally-occurring DNA sequences, and therefore *un*patentable[57]—the structure of a human cDNA molecule is different from anything you'd find in nature. But the informational content is precisely the same as that of the corresponding DNA molecule, because both molecules code for the very same protein. The fact that the Court found the cDNA sequences to be patentable makes the informational equivalency rationale seem like something of a makeweight.[58]

Legal reasoning aside, though, maybe the opinion is right on policy, and this is where the second rationale ("basic tools") comes in. As Justice Thomas noted earlier in his opinion, the exclusion of products of nature from the scope of patentable subject matter is intended to avoid the "danger that the grant of patents would 'tie up' the use of [the basic tools of scientific and technological work] and thereby 'inhibit future innovation premised upon them.'"[59] Whether this is a compelling rationale for excluding isolated DNA sequences depends upon the factual premise that isolated DNA sequences are, indeed, "basic tools" (and *if* they are, upon the inference that the costs of conferring protection on such tools outweighs the benefits, something that the Court must have implicitly assumed to be the case). And this, I think, is where the case becomes genuinely difficult. On the one hand, as I've tried to explain above, the need for researchers to make or use *isolated* genes *in their entirety* actually may be quite scant. Researchers generally *don't* need to do this to sequence a gene, or to test a patient's DNA for the presence of a mutation, or even for purposes of experimentation. On the other hand, researchers *do* use relatively short stretches of DNA (or cDNA) for all of these purposes, and *Myriad* holds that these DNA segments are not patentable either (though the cDNA may be, as above). If one views these *segments* as "basic tools," excluding *them* from the scope of patent eligibility may make sense

(though again, only if the added benefits from conferring patent protection outweigh the costs). But are the segments basic tools?

In one sense, clearly yes. Prior to *Myriad*, scientists who conducted research
in genetics often had few options but to use patented sequences for which there
were no substitutes—that is, to infringe or license. Studies by John Walsh and
others nevertheless showed that neither Myriad nor other DNA patent owners
attempted to assert their rights against such experimental uses, even though such
uses technically would have appeared infringing.[60] (As I noted in Chapter 1,
the "experimental use" defense in US patent law is extremely narrow—much
narrower than in most other countries.) Thus, even in the absence of a formal
exception, it would appear that DNA patent owners largely tolerated (and/
or failed to detect) unauthorized experimental uses, and that the predicted
"anticommons" or patent thicket did not arise. Moreover, if DNA patent owners
had filed such suits there's no guarantee they would have won. At least some such
claims might have been vulnerable to invalidation on both utility grounds (as in
In re Fisher) or on the ground that someone else had isolated them first (thus
anticipating them). Indeed, that may well have been the case in *Myriad* itself. If
the claims were construed to encompass the *BRCA1* or *BRCA2* gene isolated
from the human body but not reassembled, for example, they probably would
have been anticipated by the prior art; so too for the short segments.[61]

Nevertheless, just because no one has sued so far does not prove that no one
ever will. The next "anticommons" could be just around the corner, and even a remote risk of liability might deter some researchers from going forward—though
if so, one might wonder why the Court's holding does not extend to cDNA too,
since for practical purposes it's probably more of a "basic tool" than is DNA.
And of course DNA patent owners sometimes *did* sue to prevent unauthorized
commercial uses, such as (for example) when Myriad sued competing providers
of diagnostic genetic testing. These lawsuits kept the prices of diagnostics high
and thus, potentially, out of the reach of some potential patients; it also left some
patients who wanted second opinions out of luck. On the other hand, these sorts
of consequences are not limited to the field of *genetic* tests. By design, the patent
system enables the price of any patented diagnostic method (or drug or medical device or whatever) for which there are no good substitutes to be higher
than it would be under competition. Is there anything about DNA sequences
that demands a different result? Moreover, since *Myriad* did not forbid the
USPTO from continuing to issue patents on diagnostic methods or on cDNA,
it was hardly a foregone conclusion that the price of genetic diagnostics would
decrease, at least not until these arguably valid patents expired. Indeed, shortly
after the Supreme Court's decision, Myriad filed suit against other competing
diagnostic testing outfits, based upon Myriad's surviving claims. (Ultimately,
though, things didn't turn out well for Myriad on this front either. In 2014, the

Federal Circuit concluded that the method claims at issue were unpatentable in light of the *Mayo* decision discussed in the following chapter.)

There also are some other troubling implications of *Myriad* that so far have received relatively little attention. Although the question presented was whether human genes are patentable, there is nothing in the Court's reasoning that would suggest a different outcome for DNA sequences found in other species. To the extent DNA patents *do* serve to encourage research, there could be less effort devoted to making and using naturally-occurring nonhuman DNA (though perhaps the patentability of nonhuman cDNA suffices). (Note, however, that in some prokaryotic organisms all naturally-occurring DNA *is* cDNA; there are no introns.) It's also not clear whether the Court meant to exclude from patentability other products that are isolated from their natural state, like Takamine's adrenaline or, in more recent years, claims to isolated compounds such as erythropoietin, which is used for treating anemia and other conditions. These products may not seem as "information-ish" as DNA, and maybe they seem less like "basic tools" as well; but they *are* naturally occurring, and if the isolation of naturally occurring products isn't enough to transform them into patentable subject matter, then claims to these substances also would appear to be problematic after *Myriad*.[62] Further, while some research reported a decrease in the rate of scientific publications about genes that were the subject of patents,[63] thus suggesting that patentability may have been hampering the dissemination of useful information, a recent study by Sampat and Williams concludes that on average gene patents haven't hampered follow-on innovation.[64]

Finally, a lack of patentability could generate the perverse consequence of encouraging greater reliance on trade secrecy (or, again, reducing the incentive to discover useful information in the first place). Indeed, the latest front in the ACLU's challenge to Myriad is a lawsuit claiming that, under federal health care law, at the request of a patient Myriad is obligated to release that person's genomic test notwithstanding any assertion on the part of Myriad that such information constitutes a trade secret.[65]

My own view is that, although some limitations on patentable subject matter serve a useful purpose of keeping ideas and laws of nature in the public domain— and, as discussed in subsequent chapters, of preventing patents from impinging on important liberty or autonomy interests—these restrictions should be fairly minimal. Patentable subject matter doctrine is a very rough tool for balancing social costs and benefits—and often an unnecessary one due to other available doctrinal limitations such as nonobviousness and novelty. And it's hardly clear that gene patents cannot coexist with other fundamental values. Most other developed countries permit them, while addressing the social costs (potential restrictions on research and on access to health care) through an experimental use defense (for researchers) and (for doctors and patients) a universal health care system that limits the prices that patent owners may charge for drugs and diagnostic tools.[66] (From the inventor's standpoint, better a constrained monopoly than none at all.) Of course these options are first and foremost legislative ones, not something the Supreme Court in *Myriad* could have proposed as a possible compromise (even if one could, somehow, imagine the justices wanting to do so). And perhaps such a compromise would still leave unresolved the intuition of many people that gene patents are just wrong. If, as many researchers believe, we often come up with reasons to justify our moral beliefs (rather than the other way around), anything short of a ban on gene patents might have seemed unacceptable to large segments of the population.

As a practical matter, though, the compromise the Court did choose (distinguishing DNA from cDNA) may do very little to address research and access costs. On the other hand, perhaps it won't do much to harm incentives, either, if the existence of the patent incentive turns out to be relatively unimportant to research in this field or if the continued patentability of cDNA suffices for most, though not all, purposes.[67] Over time, it may come to appear that the principal significance of *Myriad* is its insignificance, at least in comparison to the Court's comparatively less-heralded opinion on diagnostic methods in *Mayo v. Prometheus*. It is to this matter that we now shall turn our attention.

4

Diagnostic Methods and
Personalized Medicine

As I've mentioned in previous chapters, under US law patentable subject matter—the types of inventions that are *potentially* patentable, assuming they meet all the other requirements (novelty, nonobviousness, and so on)—includes machines, processes, articles of manufacture, and compositions of matter, but not laws of nature, abstract ideas, or naturally-occurring products of nature. Chapter 3 discussed the last of these exclusions, culminating in the Supreme Court's decision that naturally-occurring human DNA, even when isolated outside the body, is an unpatentable product of nature. This chapter takes up the question of what it means to exclude "laws of nature" from patent protection. As with products of nature, although the basic idea that laws of nature are unpatentable sounds simple, reasonable, and intuitive, its application to a range of real-world discoveries—including some that pertain to the nascent field of personalized medicine—is both controversial and unclear.

To understand the rationales behind the law of nature exclusion, let's start with a simple (albeit fanciful) example of the concept and work our way forward. Specifically, suppose that Sir Isaac Newton had been able to patent the law of universal gravitation (or Charles Darwin the principle of evolution by natural selection). But wait, you say—those aren't inventions, they're discoveries; and in any event, they aren't machines or processes or articles or compositions, and thus don't fit within any of the four categories of patentable subject matter. Common sense, after all, tells us that the law of gravity and evolution existed independently of any human being having conceived of them—for that matter, independently of humans themselves ever having existed. (Some philosophers of science may debate whether there *is* any principled distinction between invention and discovery, but for present purposes I'll assume a realist position—that the law of gravity, for example, is not simply a social construct, and that it expresses an objective truth, even if subsequent developments in physics have revealed it to be only an approximation, albeit an extremely good one for the vast majority of human purposes to date, of some deeper reality.) As we've seen, though, the Patent Act (literally) says that "[w]hoever invents *or discovers* any new and useful process," etc.; and a clever patent lawyer wouldn't have too difficult a time characterizing a law of nature as *some* sort of "process," for example, "a process in which a first particle attracts a second particle, wherein the force of the attraction is directly proportional to the product of the masses of said first particle and second particle and inversely proportional to the square of the distance between said first and second particles." And in any event the deeper question is *why* laws of nature shouldn't be patentable, not whether a given version of the Patent Act permits or forbids this result.

Fortunately, there *are* plenty of reasons why people probably shouldn't be allowed to patent newly discovered laws of nature. For one thing, it's absurd to imagine trying to enforce a patent on something like the law of gravity: no matter what a court might say, Newton really couldn't exclude others from using gravity without his permission. (I guess he could ask for damages, but come on.) Moreover, even if in some imaginary sci-fi universe it were possible for the state to forbid someone from using the law of gravity (or to require payment for its use), doing so would interfere with our deeply held intuitions concerning human liberty and autonomy (though maybe in some sci-fi dystopia those concepts wouldn't exist). After all, people (and everything else, for that matter) were making use of the law of gravity long before Newton figured it out, and there is, literally, no way for anyone to stop doing so even in regions of the universe in which its impact is faint. If demanding a toll for nonvolitional conduct such as complying with the law of gravity isn't an interference with human liberty and personal autonomy, what is?

In addition, as discussed in previous chapters there are other incentive schemes intended to encourage the sort of basic research that sometimes leads to the discovery of new laws of nature, including grants, prizes, and rewards. These may or may not be at their optimal level at any given time and place, but they do exist, and they may be better suited than the patent system would be for promoting research that has no immediate commercial prospect. Relatedly, one might argue that whatever *additional* incentive might flow from allowing patents to issue on laws of nature, that benefit would likely pale in comparison with the potential monopoly and transaction costs resulting from the exercise of exclusive rights, particularly if we're talking about a claim to something of universal application such as the law of gravity or natural selection. Beyond this, there are more elaborate theories of why laws of nature are not patentable, including Grady and Alexander's gloss on Kitch's prospect theory (because laws of nature can't be improved, there's no point in granting someone the exclusive right to develop the "prospect")[1] and Michael Green's argument that IP rights would undermine the norms of science by discouraging unauthorized efforts to replicate the discoverer's claimed results.[2]

Overall, then, it's probably not too surprising that you can't patent a law of nature—and that, as with products of nature, there are multiple legal rules that reinforce this exclusion. Thus, in addition to failing patent law's subject matter hurdle, attempts to patent some laws of nature also would run aground on the novelty requirement because they are "inherent" in the prior art: people have been using the law of gravity, well, ever since there were people, so in that sense there was nothing "new" about the law when Newton discovered it.[3] In addition, in some instances the first person to discover a law of nature might not be able to identify a specific, practical use for it, and thus might encounter problems satisfying the utility requirement. Gravity has plenty of specific practical applications, to be sure, but other laws of nature (like, say, the cosmological constant that reflects the accelerating expansion of the universe[4]) do not. And in yet other cases, the discoverer might claim so broadly as to run afoul of the enablement or written description requirements; we'll come across an example from a famous nineteenth-century case shortly.

Up to now I've been using the law of gravity as an example of a law of nature, because it's easy to show that allowing someone to patent such a law would be a bad idea for many, many reasons. But not all examples are going to be this easy: indeed, as you probably noticed, I haven't even defined the term "law of nature" yet. In my defense, I'll note that philosophers of science don't all agree on what counts as a law of nature either. Would an appropriate definition include only principles of biology, physics, chemistry, and other "hard" sciences, or would it also include such things as mathematical discoveries, principles of economics, or even moral philosophy? (Perhaps these latter examples fit more comfortably under the rubric of unpatentable "abstract ideas" rather than "laws of nature," to the extent it matters. We'll take them on in Chapter 5.) More surprisingly, perhaps, the courts and the USPTO have never clearly defined the term either—though in some of its training materials for examiners the USPTO now refers to unpatentable "natural principles" that are "the handiwork of nature and occur . . . without the hand of man," and which include laws of nature, natural phenomena, and naturally occurring relations or correlations.[5] Thus, for example, under the USPTO's reading of the case law I'll be getting to shortly, an unpatentable natural principle would include "the relationship between blood glucose levels and diabetes," as well as "a correlation that occurs naturally when a man-made product, such as a drug, interacts with a naturally occurring substance, such as blood, because the correlation exists in principle apart from any human action."[6] Claiming such correlations as one's patentable invention therefore would be a no-no—even though it's not likely that the social costs if we *did* confer patent protection would be anywhere near what the costs of the hypothetical patent on gravity would be.

Be that as it may, suppose that I tried to draft around the exclusion by claiming as my invention *a method of diagnosing diabetes*, based on a patient's blood glucose level: would *that* be distinct enough from the natural principle it-self? After all, as Rebecca Eisenberg observes, as a product of human judgment a diagnosis hardly exists independently of the human actor who makes it.[7] On the other hand, if one reason for rendering laws of nature unpatentable is the con-cern over invading human liberty and autonomy interests, maybe the fact that diagnostic methods involve the exercise of human judgment *should* render them unpatentable. Unlike, say, a patent on the law of gravity, such patents wouldn't necessarily prohibit nonvolitional conduct, but should it be possible to violate patent law by engaging in a mental act? Or what if I added an additional claim limitation, instructing the physician after having determined the concentration of glucose in the patient's blood to record it, relay it to the patient, or administer a particular treatment? Should any of those additional instructions be enough to distinguish the method from the underlying natural principle?

The question, in other words, is whether we should exclude from patent eli-gibility only claims to laws of nature *as such*—the hypothetical patent on the law of gravity, let's say—or some broader class of *applications* of laws of nature. The problem, if we go this latter route, is that all inventions necessarily involve the application of laws of nature, so if the exclusion goes beyond the bare minimum we may wind up having to draw some rather fine lines between patentable and nonpatentable applications. If we want to avoid overdoing it, then, should we ex-pand the exclusion only to claims that, if enforced, might be viewed as invading important liberty or autonomy interests, such as (perhaps) the diagnostic method discussed above? Or should the exclusion be limited to claims reading on discoveries that offer no present commercial benefit (and which therefore should be excluded on utility or other grounds anyway)? Or would it be better to exclude a much broader category of claims, such as those whose novelty or inventiveness resides only in the law of nature itself, or which would "preempt" all or most practical applications of that law (whatever that means)? Where do we draw the line?

A Brief Detour: Medical and Surgical Procedures

We'll come back to these questions in a few minutes, but for now I want to di-gress a bit into a distinct but related topic of inquiry, namely the patentability of medical and surgical methods. Depending on how we answer the questions I'm temporarily deferring, of course, some such methods, like the hypothetical method for diagnosing diabetes, may be indistinguishable from laws of nature. But let's consider something that would seem, on any reasonable interpreta-tion, to be readily distinguishable from a law of nature—say, a new method for grafting skin onto burn victims, or a new technique for coronary bypass surgery.

Surely these are "methods" for accomplishing some specific, practical end, and therefore would seem to be patent-eligible. But is there nevertheless something odd about the prospect of a physician or surgeon patenting such a method, and then refusing to license others to perform it? Would such a practice violate medical ethics, and if so should that be of concern to patent law?

The answers to *these* questions actually can differ quite a bit from one country to another. Article 53(c) of the European Patent Convention, for example, states that "European patents shall not be granted in respect of . . . methods for treatment of the human or animal body by surgery or therapy and diagnostic methods practised on the human or animal body." This sounds simple enough, though there sometimes are close questions whether a given method involves surgery, therapy, or diagnosis (a method for drawing blood? acupuncture?), and in practice there are some ways to skirt the prohibition (for example, by claiming the use of a product such as a drug *in* surgery, therapy, or diagnosis).[8] The United States, by contrast, has never had an analogous statutory prohibition on medical method patents, though in one well-known case from 1862 a federal court invalidated a patent granted to Drs. Charles Jackson and William Morton on "a method of rendering patients insensible to pain during surgical operations" through the administration of sulfuric ether. According to the court, the principle that "well-known inhalation of well-known agents (in increased quantities) would produce a state of the animal analogous to complete intoxication accompanied with total insensibility to pain" was a "mere discovery"[9]—in contemporary terminology, an unpatentable law or principle of nature. The USPTO nonetheless began granting a small number of medical and surgical patents as early as the 1920s.[10] Among them was a 1992 patent granted to ophthalmologist Dr. Samuel Pallin for performing sutureless cataract surgery, and in 1993 Pallin sought to enforce his patent against a surgeon affiliated with Dartmouth Medical College.[11]

Pallin's lawsuit turned the question of surgical patents into something of a *cause célebre*. The American Medical Association (AMA) soon declared the enforcement of such patents a breach of medical ethics, due to the risk that such enforcement could result in some patients being denied the optimal level of care (either because the patent holder wouldn't license the patent, or would charge a royalty that placed the use of the method beyond what some patients or, more likely, some insurance companies would be willing or able to pay).[12] Which may be true—though when you think about it, how is this any different from the risk that patents on drugs will raise prices and thus result in some patients being denied the optimal level of care? If one is a breach of ethics, why not the other? In fact, many countries *did* refuse to issue patents on drugs until relatively recently, a topic we will discuss in Chapter 6. But as I've mentioned in earlier chapters, the pharmaceutical industry is also just about everyone's paradigm example of an industry that *needs* patent protection, due to a combination of high R&D costs and low costs of copying. (Not that people don't have beefs with the pharmaceutical industry, as you know and as we'll see in greater depth in Chapter 6. But for the most part even the industry's loudest critics agree that drug patents are necessary to stimulate innovation.) So perhaps, to hearken back to a theme I advanced in Chapter 2, it's ultimately more a matter of economics than morality. Drug patents may be a necessary evil, but surgical method patents probably *aren't*, in general, necessary to induce invention and disclosure: the costs incurred by surgeons to develop new techniques typically—though not inevitably—are low, and the incentive to develop and publicize such techniques is high even absent a boost from the patent system.[13] Moreover, according to Professor Katherine Strandburg's analysis of the *Pallin* case, in general surgeons benefit more from a system whereby each user can improve upon one another's work, than from a system of exclusive rights.[14] Or maybe it's all a matter of, once again, autonomy—in this case, the autonomy of doctors to treat their patients as they see fit, without the risk of liability for patent infringement. Surgical patents, in other words, might interfere with the doctor–patient relationship in a way that drug patents don't, since as a practical matter drug companies aren't very likely to sue doctors for prescribing or using infringing drugs. (They'd sue the makers or distributors of those drugs instead, as we'll see in Chapter 6.)

So did Congress take the AMA's advice and prohibit the patenting of surgical techniques? Well, not exactly. Shortly after the *Pallin* case itself settled,[15] Congress enacted a compromise, codified as section 287(c) of the Patent Act, which does not forbid the issuance of surgical patents but instead renders them unenforceable against medical practitioners and the institutions that employ them.[16] Future Dr. Pallins can hang their patent certificates on the walls of their waiting rooms to impress their patients, in other words, but they can't sue other doctors for infringing their patents. Even so, there are some loopholes. First, a doctor's unauthorized practice of a patented method would still be, technically, an act of infringement. Therefore, if for example the patented technique involves the use of a special piece of equipment—say, a specially designed medical device—the patent owner may be able to sue the device maker (whom the statute *doesn't* exempt from liability) for contributory or induced infringement. Second, the statute only exempts practitioners and their institutions from liability for performing "medical or surgical procedures," which the statute itself doesn't define but which, according to most analysts and in contrast to article 53 of the European Patent Convention, doesn't include diagnostic or therapeutic methods (such as our hypothetical method for diagnosing diabetes, or the methods at issue in two recent Supreme Court decisions we'll be coming across shortly). As is often the case in US patent law, the operative principle appears to be one of avoiding simple rules that nonspecialists can readily comprehend.

Laws of Nature Revisited

Let's return now to laws of nature. As you might imagine, patent attorneys have tried out various strategies over the years to come as close as possible to patenting laws of nature, with mixed results. In what is probably the most well-known example, the Patent Office in 1848 awarded Samuel F. B. Morse a reissue patent covering not only the telegraph (for which Morse is rightly remembered as a pioneering inventor) and Morse Code, but also for something much broader. As Morse stated in his (in)famous claim number eight: "I do not propose to limit myself to the specific machinery or parts of machinery described in the foregoing specifications and claims; the essence of my invention being the use of the motive power of the electric or galvanic current, which I call electro-magnetism, *however developed* for making or printing intelligible characters, letters, or signs, at any distances, being a new application of that power, of which I claim to be the first inventor or discoverer" (emphasis added).[17] As others have observed, this claim, if valid, would have covered virtually *any* use of electromagnetism to make signs (though, of course, it would have expired long before anyone could have developed such applications as, say, television or the Internet).[18] Ultimately, the Supreme Court concluded that the claim was invalid— though in doing so the Court didn't say anything about laws of nature as such. Rather, it appeared to rest its holding on the observation that claim eight was "too broad," in that it would require future inventors who developed new ways of using electricity to make signs to obtain permission from Morse (even if they used entirely different equipment).[19] Thus, in modern terminology, a possible ground for invalidation might have been that Morse didn't enable the "full scope" of claim eight, or that his written description didn't show that he was in "possession" of the claimed subject matter. Nevertheless, the case has come to be viewed as authority for the proposition that you can't patent a law of nature, and as we'll see it continues to be cited for that principle today. In another famous nineteenth-century case, by contrast, this one involving the invention of the telephone, the Supreme Court affirmed Alexander Graham Bell's claim five which recited "[t]he method of, and apparatus for, transmitting vocal or other sounds telegraphically, as herein described, by causing electrical undulations, similar in form to the vibrations of the air accompanying the said vocal or other sounds, substantially as set forth."[20] What saved the claim from the same fate as Morse's eighth was the use of the words "as herein described" and "substantially as set forth," which limited the application of the principle underlying early telephony to the general features that Bell himself claimed to have invented.[21]

As it turned out, a hundred or so years later the principle that laws of nature are unpatentable appeared both firmly established and rarely applicable. In the wake of *Diamond v. Chakrabarty* and another case involving computer software that we'll discuss in the next chapter, by the early 2000s the Federal Circuit and the USPTO had come around to the view that any claimed invention that was "useful, concrete, and tangible"—which is to say, just about anything that achieved some practical, replicable result—was patent-eligible.[22] But then the tide began to turn, and the first chink in the armor happened to be a case involving a diagnostic method, *Laboratory Corp. of America Holdings v. Metabolite Laboratories, Inc.*[23] In the mid-1980s researchers had discovered a correlation between elevated levels of total homocysteine (an amino acid) in human bodily fluid and deficiencies of folate (vitamin B_9) or cobalamin (vitamin B_{12}). In 1990, they obtained a patent, claim 13 of which recited "[a] method for detecting a deficiency of cobalamin or folate in warm-blooded animals comprising the steps of: assaying"—that is, testing—"a body fluid for an elevated level of total homocysteine; and correlating an elevated level of total homocysteine in said body fluid with a deficiency of cobalamin or folate."[24] The patent eventually made its way into the hands of Metabolite Laboratories, which filed suit against LabCorp for inducing physicians to infringe the patent. Metabolite won at trial, and the Federal Circuit affirmed without even addressing the question (which LabCorp itself had not emphasized at trial) whether claim 13 covered a principle of nature, namely the relationship between elevated homocysteine levels and vitamin deficiencies.

This result surprised few observers at the time, given the Federal Circuit's then-prevailing views on patentable subject matter. What *did* surprise many people was when the Supreme Court—contrary to the advice of the US Solicitor General, to whom the Court often defers when deciding whether to accept a case for review—agreed to hear LabCorp's appeal on the question of whether it was "permissible to patent a correlational relationship in a medical test result, such that a doctor necessarily infringes on the patent simply by thinking about the relationship after looking at the test result."[25] A further surprise was then in store just a few months later, when a majority of the justices apparently had second thoughts and dismissed the appeal as having been "improvidently granted."[26] So the Federal Circuit and USPTO's expansive interpretation of the scope of patentable subject matter would remain in place, for now; but the fact that the justices had signaled an interest in the topic was lost on no one, and Justice Breyer (joined by Justices Stevens and Souter) filed a dissenting opinion arguing that the Court should have retained and decided the appeal. And it was pretty clear what the three dissenters thought the result should be: characterizing claim 13 as "instruct[ing] the user to (1) obtain test results and (2) think about them," Justice Breyer concluded that the claim "simply described the natural law at issue in the abstract patent language of a 'process.' "[27] The dissenters further expressed doubt that "useful, concrete, and tangible" were the exclusive criteria for determining what sorts of inventions or discoveries are patentable.[28]

LabCorp was a washout, but it was now only a matter of time until the Court would revisit the law of nature doctrine—which it did in 2012, in *Mayo Collaborative Services v. Prometheus Laboratories*.[29] As described in the opinion, physicians sometimes treat patients suffering from certain autoimmune disorders such as Crohn's disease and colitis with an (unpatented) drug, thiopurine, the effectiveness of which varies depending on how quickly the patient metabolizes the drug. The underlying discovery made by two Canadian researchers was that if, after the patient ingested the drug, certain metabolites in the patient's bloodstream (referred to in short form as 6-TG and 6-MMP) registered above or below certain specified levels, the dosage was either too high or too low to be safe and effective (and thus would need to be adjusted). Prometheus eventually came into possession of two resulting patents claiming the steps of (1) administering thiopurine to a patient suffering from an autoimmune disorder and (2) determining the level of the relevant metabolite (6-TG or 6-MMP) in the patient's blood, (3) wherein certain specified concentrations of the metabolite would indicate a need to adjust the dosage up or down. For a time, Prometheus sold test kits and licensed the patents to the Mayo Clinic; but when Mayo stopped buying the kits and developed its own tests, Prometheus sued, claiming that the Mayo tests infringed the Prometheus patents.

This time Justice Breyer got his wish. Writing for a unanimous Court, Justice Breyer invoked *Morse* and other vintage cases for the proposition that patent law shouldn't "inhibit further discovery by improperly tying up" or "preempt[ing]" future uses of natural laws, which he described as "basic tools of scientific and technological work"; and he rejected the argument that granting exclusive rights in narrow natural principles (like the correlations at issue here) should be treated differently from granting rights in broad ones (like the law of relativity).[30] The difficult question remains how to distinguish an unpatentable law of nature from something that a good patent lawyer will argue is a patentable process involving the *application* of a law of nature. To understand the Court's response to this question, recall from previous chapters that lawyers often think of patent claims as a series of "elements" or "steps" or "limitations" which for convenience can be designated with letters, for example "I claim a therapeutic method comprising steps A, B, and C." Thus, in the present context, one could think of administering the drug as step A, determining the level of 6-TG in the blood as step B, and the "wherein" clause alluding to the correlation as step C. The issue, then, as the Court framed it, was whether any of the instructions in these steps added enough of substance to the law of nature recited in step C to distinguish the claim from a mere restatement of that law—for, in Justice Breyer's words, it isn't enough simply to recite a law a nature and say "apply it."[31] Rather, the claim must "add enough . . . to allow the processes . . . to qualify as patent-eligible processes that apply natural laws," and "[p]urely 'conventional or obvious' '[pre]-solution activity' is normally not sufficient to transform an unpatentable law of nature into a patent-eligible application of such a law."[32] Or, to put it another way, "a process that focuses upon the use of a natural law [must] also contain other elements or a combination of elements, sometimes referred to as an 'inventive concept,' sufficient to ensure that the patent in practice amounts to significantly more than a patent upon the natural law itself."[33]

Unfortunately for Prometheus, the Court didn't think there was enough of an "inventive concept" in steps A, B, and C to "transform" the underlying law of nature into a patentable invention. In particular, as the Court saw it steps A and B were "conventional" and "obvious," and step C in effect nothing more than a recitation of a law of the nature—the fact that certain concentrations of 6-TG and 6-MMP indicate a need to adjust the dosage. Summing up, Justice Breyer wrote:

> The upshot is that the three steps simply tell doctors to gather data from which they may draw an inference in light of the correlations. To put the matter more succinctly, the claims inform a relevant audience about certain laws of nature; any additional steps consist of well-understood, routine, conventional activity already engaged in by the scientific community; and those steps, when viewed as a whole, add nothing significant beyond the sum of their parts taken separately. For these reasons we believe that the steps are not sufficient to transform unpatentable natural correlations into patentable applications of those regularities.[34]

Analysis and Subsequent Developments

Mayo thus breathed new life into the law of nature doctrine—and combined with other cases limiting the scope of patentable subject matter, including *Myriad* and those discussed in Chapter 5, has made life for patent applicants in certain fields more challenging. The remaining issues for us to consider here are whether *Mayo*'s analysis of the law of nature exception makes sense from the standpoint of public policy, and the implications of the case for the patentability of diagnostic and therapeutic methods—and for personalized medicine more generally.

As I mentioned at the outset of this chapter, there are two principal (and nonexclusive) reasons for excluding laws of nature from the scope of patentable subject matter: one rooted in concerns over unduly restricting human liberty and autonomy, the other in a more utilitarian assessment for social costs and benefits. Focusing first on concerns over liberty and autonomy, I argued above that this rationale provides one plausible explanation for why, say, the law of gravity shouldn't be patentable. But does it have any implications for patents involving narrower concepts like the correlations at issue in *LabCorp* and *Mayo*, which, unlike the law of gravity, most of us never encounter in our daily lives—and the significance of which (as Professor Eisenberg reminds us) depends on the exercise of human judgment?

The answer, in my view, is yes—though standing alone, this rationale would support a somewhat narrow exclusion from patentability. To see why, recall from above Justice Breyer's characterization of *LabCorp* claim 13 as instructing the user to "(1) obtain test results" by assaying a patient's bodily fluid to determine its homocysteine level, and "(2) think about them." The first step, in isolation, was in the prior art and therefore was, in the language of *Mayo*, "conventional" and "obvious." In effect, then, if claim 13 were valid it would render infringing the combination of performing an act (step 1) that was in the public domain, and then (step 2) "thinking about" it, that is, mentally applying the correlation to make a diagnosis. Put another way, the only thing that would distinguish this claim from the prior art—and thus the only thing that would allow the state to penalize a doctor for otherwise lawful conduct—would be the performance of a step that could be done entirely within the doctor's head. But can an act of patent infringement be completed merely by *thinking* about something? Can the government confer exclusive rights on one person to demand payment from another for "thinking patentable thoughts"? In fact, some recent Federal Circuit decisions have found certain processes unpatentable on the basis of a "mental steps" doctrine,[35] the precise contours of which remain a bit unclear but which I and others have previously argued should be understood as forbidding claims like claim 13 that are distinguishable from the prior art only by reason of an additional step that can be performed mentally.[36] Excluding such a claim from the scope of patentable subject matter therefore might appear to safeguard the individuality and integrity of the human mind. Even DNA patents, after all, were never thought to read upon DNA within the human body itself.

Beyond the preceding example, perhaps some other steps one could imagine adding to claim 13 would also give rise to undue burdens on liberty, autonomy, or other important interests that in other contexts we would expect the law to protect. Suppose, for example, that claim 13 included a third step that instructed the user to inform the patient of the resulting diagnosis. Absent telepathy, this step can't be performed mentally; but one might nevertheless view it as an intrusion on the doctor–patient relationship, or maybe even on constitutional guarantees of free speech and privacy, to make the act of orally communicating a diagnosis to a patient the key to patent validity (and consequently to liability for infringement). Again, some commentators (including me) have argued that unless we want courts hearing patent cases to weigh in on such weighty constitutional issues—and we probably *don't* want that, given a long-standing legal tradition that courts should avoid deciding constitutional issues when they don't really have to[37]—patentable subject matter doctrine, operating at the subconstitutional level, should lead to the invalidation of claims that threaten to invade such protected interests.[38]

On the other hand, a test based exclusively on liberty and autonomy concerns wouldn't preclude claims that included steps (no matter how conventional or obvious) that *didn't* implicate those concerns. To illustrate, suppose that in *LabCorp* there was a third claim element expressly instructing the administration of a folate/cobalamin tablet in response to having detected an elevated level of total homocysteine in a patient's bloodstream; and that prior to the inventors' discovery of the correlation, no one would have prescribed this treatment based on the presence of an elevated total homocysteine level.[39] The presence of the hypothetical third step would thus ensure that the "point of novelty"—that which distinguishes the claim as a whole from the prior art—does not reside in a purely mental step. (Ignoring mental step 2, steps 1 and 3 individually may be in the prior art but the combination of 1 and 3 is not.) Thus, unless you buy into the libertarian critique that *all* patents are unethical because they impose *some* limitations on human liberty and autonomy (see Chapter 2)—or the argument referenced earlier in this chapter that *all patents relating to medical care,* including drug and medical device patents, are unethical because they inhibit optimal treatment—such a claim would appear to pass muster, because forbidding someone from practicing this combination of claim steps wouldn't impose any unusual burden on liberty or autonomy, at least no more so than lots of other patents do.[40]

Generalizing a bit, perhaps we could say that under this proposed interpretation some or all *diagnostic* methods would be vulnerable on subject matter grounds because the only thing that distinguishes them from the prior art is a mental step, but that *therapeutic* methods would be unaffected. But then again, maybe not. Suppose for example that the claim in *Mayo* was rewritten to require (1) administering thiopurine, (2) determining the level of the relevant metabolite, (3) inferring whether this level corresponded to the need to adjust the dosage up or down based on the newly discovered correlation, and (4) adjusting the dosage accordingly. (If you reread the claim in the actual case, you'll notice that the "wherein" clause doesn't *literally* require the physician to do anything, even if the metabolite level indicates the need for a higher or lower dosage.[41]) So now we would have a claim reciting four steps of, respectively, administering, measuring, inferring, and adjusting. The problem is that everything except the "inferring" step was in the prior art—doctors previously had been adjusting thiopurine dosages if the metabolite levels appeared too high or low, albeit without knowing precisely what level corresponded to "too high" or "too low"[42]—and thus the point of novelty would reside only in the mental (inferring) step. So even if the correct principle is that an inference-type claim is patent-eligible as long as it includes a nonmental step that distinguishes the claim as a whole from the prior art, this still might result in some therapeutic patents being rejected. The simple formula that diagnostics are suspect while method of treatment claims are not doesn't appear to be quite right—even if, as some have posited, the *Mayo* opinion itself might be premised on some such distinction between diagnostics and therapeutics.[43]

Moreover, a broader reading of *Mayo* would appear to preclude the patentability of my hypothetical *LabCorp* claim—the one that included a third step of administering a folate/cobalamin tablet—if, as of the critical date, the act of administering the tablet would have been a conventional, routine response to the presence of a total homocysteine corresponding to a folate or cobalamin deficiency.[44] As a matter of legal doctrine, this broader reading—which would require that the nonlaw of nature steps exhibit some degree of "inventiveness," not just novelty—may be closer to what the Court had in mind. In litigation brought by Myriad Genetics, for example, on claims involving methods for detecting the presence of mutations to the *BRCA* genes, the Federal Circuit wasn't swayed by the fact that the methods involved using gene probes or primers for purposes of comparing a patient's DNA with the nonmutated "wild type."[45] Similarly, at issue in the recent *Ariosa Diagnostics, Inc. v. Sequenom, Inc.* case was a patent issued in 2001 to Oxford University's Isis Innovation Limited for a noninvasive prenatal diagnosis method involving the use of cell-free fetal DNA (cffDNA).[46] As the term suggests, cffDNA is noncellular fetal DNA that is found in the bloodstream of pregnant women. In the late 1990s, a research team led by Dr. Dennis Lo of the Chinese University of Hong Kong and Oxford's Dr. James Wainscoat discovered that cffDNA also could be detected in the mother's serum and plasma—two products that, up until then, hospitals routinely discarded—and in much greater concentrations than were detectable from whole blood.[47] As described in the opinion, Lo and Wainscoat thereafter used "a combination of known laboratory techniques" to develop a method that poses fewer risks to the fetus than do comparable methods that require sampling the placenta or the fetus itself, "for detecting the small fraction of paternally inherited cffDNA in maternal plasma or serum to determine fetal characteristics, such as gender."[48] Thus, for example, claim 1 recites "A method for detecting a paternally inherited nucleic acid of fetal origin performed on a maternal serum or plasma sample from a pregnant female, which method comprises" (1) amplifying (that is, creating multiple copies by means of the polymerase chain reaction) a paternally inherited cffDNA from the sample, and (2) detecting the paternally inherited cffDNA within the sample (by using ethidium bromide to "stain and visualize" the paternally inherited amplified cffDNA).[49]

Isis Innovation in turn licensed the patent to an American company, Sequenom, which markets a test kit that uses the claimed methods. In 2011,

Ariosa and another of Sequenom's competitors filed actions for a declaratory judgment of invalidity. The district court agreed that the methods were unpatentable under *Mayo*, and in 2015 a panel of the Federal Circuit affirmed. Writing for the court, Judge Jimmie Reyna concluded, first, that claim 1 and the other claims in suit were directed to "naturally occurring phenomena," in that the method starts and ends with naturally-occurring cffDNA.[50] Second, the court held that because the amplification and detection steps were conventional and routine as of the date of invention, the claims lacked an "inventive concept sufficient to 'transform'" the phenomena into patentable processes.[51] The court also rejected Sequenom's argument that, because "there are numerous other uses of cffDNA aside from those claimed in the . . . patent," the method does not "preempt" all uses of cffDNA and therefore should be patent-eligible. While noting that "[t]he Supreme Court has made clear that the principle of preemption is the basis for the judicial exceptions to patentability," and that "preemption may signal patent ineligible subject matter," the court concluded that "the absence of *complete* preemption does not demonstrate patent eligibility" (emphasis added).[52] Citing *Mayo*, the court could find no principled distinction between broad and narrow laws of nature or natural phenomena.[53]

This reading of *Mayo* may well be correct as a matter of law, but is it sensible? One argument against the framework as applied in cases like *Ariosa* is that it substitutes what typically would be a careful examination of other possible validity problems (such as obviousness or written description) for an ad hoc inquiry into whether the combination of steps other than the principle of nature is conventional and routine. In this sense, the inquiry seems to replicate what Rob Merges and John Duffy refer to as the "Nature's Library" fiction, under which a newly discovered law or product of nature is treated as if it were in the prior art, even though (as one Federal Circuit judge recently put it) "an inventive concept can sometimes come from discovery of an unknown natural phenomenon, not just from unconventional application of a phenomenon."[54] The inquiry also can seem both formalistic and yet (paradoxically?) unpredictable as well. In a recent update intended to assist patent examiners in evaluating patent eligibility, for example, the USPTO presents several hypotheticals involving a method for detecting a protein known as JUL-1, the presence of which indicates that a person suffers from julitis, an autoimmune disease.[55] The agency's analysis begins reasonably enough by stating that a method comprising "obtaining a plasma sample from a human patient; and . . . detecting whether JUL-1 is present in the plasma sample by contacting the plasma sample with an anti-JUL-1 antibody and detecting binding between JUL-1 and the antibody" would be patent-eligible, because it is directed to a detection process, not a law or product of nature. The addition of a third step, however, instructing the user to diagnose julitis would doom the claim because now it would recite a correlation (between the presence of JUL-1 and julitis) that "is a consequence of natural processes"; and the first two steps (which were okay when they were the *only* two steps, remember?) are recited at such a "high level of generality," and are so "well-understood, routine, and conventional," that they fail to add an "inventive concept" to the natural process. *Adding* a step, in other words—which as we've seen results in a narrower, not a broader, claim—would render the claim patent-ineligible on the basis of a legal doctrine that supposedly is all about avoiding the preemption of further innovation; go figure. If, however, the drafter had added a fourth step instructing the user to "administer[] an effective amount of anti-tumor necrosis factor (TNF) antibodies to the diagnosed patient," the claim would have survived— even though steps 1, 2, and 4 were previously known to the art—because now the combination of claim steps "amount to more than merely diagnosing a patient with julitis and instructing a doctor to generically 'treat it.'" Again, I'm not necessarily critiquing the UPSTO's interpretation of the law, which may well be correct (though one might debate the USPTO's judgment that the first JUL-1 claim is patentable subject matter, in light of *Ariosa*); but how applicants in such instances are supposed to predict which combinations of known steps are sufficiently inventive to overcome a rejection is, in my view, anyone's guess.

These doctrinal issues aside, as indicated above a liberty-and-autonomy rationale alone probably wouldn't sustain this broader reading of *Mayo*; but perhaps a broad reading of the case can be defended on a purely utilitarian comparison of social costs and benefits. In this regard, however, a possible concern is that *Mayo* and other similar cases could retard investment not just in diagnostics and therapeutics generally, but even more problematically in a field that could lead to radical improvements in public health, namely personalized medicine. To understand why, consider that conventional medicine works largely on the basis of statistical averages: well-conducted studies can predict, say, what percentage of patients are likely to benefit from a given treatment regime, and ideally this knowledge allows doctors and patients to make informed judgments as to the costs and benefits of that treatment in the typical case. But often there is considerable variation among individuals' responsiveness to treatment based on genetic and environmental differences. A commonly cited example involves the drug Herceptin, which was developed specifically to treat the 25–30 percent of breast cancer patients whose cancer cells express a protein known as HER-2.[56] Differences among individuals also can result in certain commonly prescribed drugs providing little or no benefit in comparison with alternatives for a majority of patients (though that doesn't necessarily mean that the drugs are ineffective; they're just not any more effective than other treatments).[57] The promise of personalized medicine is that doctors will be able to evaluate an individual's likely response to a course of treatment based on a statistical comparison of how others who share the relevant biological "markers" have fared from that treatment—a goal that, when attained, avoids unnecessary expense and human suffering. But if *Mayo* and other similar cases materially reduce the incentive to discover the relevant biomarkers and how they interact with drugs and other treatments, the forgone benefits could be much higher than any savings attributable to fewer patents. (Indeed, even a narrower reading of *Mayo* could have this effect, albeit to a lesser degree, insofar as it would render unpatentable some diagnostics and even some therapeutics, as discussed above.)[58]

Even so, it's still possible that the social benefits from validating patents like the ones in *LabCorp, Mayo,* and *Ariosa* are negligible, if the costs of developing diagnostic and therapeutic methods are in general sufficiently low that other policy options—including grants for basic research, first-mover advantages, and the availability of patents on drugs, devices, and other products that are *used* in diagnosis and therapy—would continue to provide a sufficient incentive to develop and commercialize new methods. (Of course, even if this is the case, it's hard to see why the patentability of methods like the ones described above in the julitis example should turn on the vagaries of claim drafting, which bear little relation to any relevant economic considerations. A better rule might be simply to remove patent protection for diagnostic and therapeutic methods altogether.) So far, the leading study addressing the cost of developing diagnostic tests is a 2010 report of the Secretary of Health and Human Service's Advisory Committee on Genetics, Health, and Society, which estimated the cost of developing a laboratory-based genetic test at about $8,000 to $10,000.[59] The study noted that the cost of developing diagnostic test *kits,* however, which are regulated by the US Food and Drug Administration (FDA), can be substantially more, because the FDA treats the kits as a form of medical device the safety and efficacy of which, depending on the device's classification, sometimes must be established by means of expensive clinical testing.[60] So-called laboratory-developed tests (LDTs), which are performed in-house by a test developer (such as Myriad) at present are not subject to this requirement, but a 2014 FDA proposal to include LDTs within the scope of FDA regulation probably would have significantly increased the cost of commercializing diagnostic tests across the board.[61] (Some observers expressed concern that this proposal, coupled with reductions in recent years to the amount that Medicare and private insurers will reimburse for such tests and with the limitations on patentability that I've been discussing in this chapter, would have created the perfect storm to drive away investment in the field.[62] The FDA has since announced that it was not going forward with the proposal as originally announced.[63]) Moreover, some worry that relying exclusively on the availability of patents on drugs and other products to encourage investment in "companion" diagnostic methods would bias efforts against the discovery of so-called *prognostic* methods that can reduce the need for certain drugs and treatments, or of methods like the one at issue in *LabCorp*, *Mayo*, and *Ariosa* that don't require the use of patented products at all.[64]

That said, scholars have proposed a variety of fixes that wouldn't require overturning *Mayo* but which might compensate for its potential negative impact on investment. These include greater public investment in developing genetic databases (in other words, more subsidization of the basic research that underlies this field);[65] authorizing the FDA to grant short periods of regulatory exclusivity for new diagnostic methods, which would enable developers to recoup some of their costs without the need for a patent; and modifications to the FDA approval and Medicare reimbursement processes, so that these pose less of a disincentive for developing new diagnostics.[66] On balance, these approaches might be more cost-effective than restoring patent protection for the full range of diagnostics, though they would require both careful tailoring and congressional action to implement. For the government to take no action, however, either along the lines just suggested or by reversing *Mayo*, does appear to pose serious risks to innovation in the field of personalized medicine. Thus, as I suggested at the conclusion of the previous chapter, *Mayo* is likely to have a much greater practical impact than the gene-patenting dispute at issue in *Myriad*. Patents on human genes may fire the imagination, but maybe the less conspicuous cases on diagnostics are the ones that policymakers and the public really should be paying attention to.

5

Software and Business Methods

In the preceding two chapters, I've discussed how the courts and USPTO have come to understand patent law's exclusion of products of nature and laws of nature from the scope of patentable subject matter. The third, and remaining, category of patent-ineligible subject matter is "abstract ideas"—a concept that itself can seem a bit abstract, once you start trying to pin down exactly what it means. Abstraction, after all, is a matter of degree. To borrow an illustration from copyright law—the relevance of which in a book about patents will, I hope, become apparent over the course of the next few pages—suppose that I were to up and quit the law prof business and try my hand at writing plays. The literal text of my hypothetical play—the complete sequence of words and other symbols as arranged on the pages of my manuscript—would be the work's least abstract, most concrete embodiment. A close paraphrase would be a slightly more abstract embodiment, while a detailed summary (think *Cliff's Notes*) would be more abstract still. A less detailed summary would be even more abstract, and on and on, until at some point you might be left with nothing more than a one-sentence description: "It's a play about two star-crossed lovers."[1]

To visualize what I'm talking about, you could think of the play as embodying varying layers of abstraction, from the least abstract, most concrete embodiment at the tip to the most abstract, least concrete embodiment at the top, as depicted by the inverted triangle in Figure 5.1.

Of course, there are lots of plays which, if you had to summarize them in a sentence, would fit within the description at the top layer—"it's a play about two star-crossed lovers"—whereas at the other end of the spectrum (at the tip of the triangle), no matter how conventional or trite the plot may be, it's very unlikely that another author would independently create another play having literally the identical sequence of words as mine. Not surprisingly, copyright law confers protection on the literal text (assuming it's original to the author, and not itself copied from someone else), but it wouldn't have allowed Shakespeare (or whoever first came up with the idea before him) to corner the entire market on star-crossed-lover plays. The tough cases are the ones in between, where

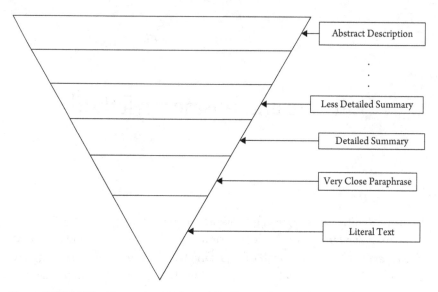

Figure 5.1 The Idea-Expression Dichotomy in Copyright

someone appropriates, say, certain plot elements from the original or patterns some of her characters after the first author's. A task that courts sometimes have to face in copyright law, therefore, is to determine just how far the author's copyright extends beyond the literal text—or to put it another way, whether the copyist has appropriated elements that are too "abstract" to merit copyright protection. Often there is no easy way to resolve the matter, other than by making some rough-and-ready determination of how many other works independently make use of similar elements, how if at all the lack of protection is likely to impact authors' incentives to create and publish, and how much of a disadvantage the copyist would face if she couldn't use those elements in her own, potentially competing work. One way or another, though, courts sometimes have to decide where the dividing line lies between copyrightable expression and uncopyrightable ideas or facts. Thus, at each layer of the inverted triangle, at least certain aspects of the work may be unprotectable because it is not original to the author, or in the public domain, or essential to any treatment of the subject matter at issue. As we move up the triangle from the tip to the base, less and less of what we encounter at each layer is subject to copyright protection, until at some point we cross entirely beyond the realm of copyrightable expression, selection, or arrangement.

Patent law sometimes presents an analogous dilemma of having to determine how abstract is too abstract[2]—particularly, though not exclusively, when it comes to claims involving the use of computer software or methods of doing business. As was the case for claims involving products of nature or laws of nature, at times it might seem equally (or more) plausible to resolve the matter by resort to other legal doctrines: a claim that is abstract in the sense of not being limited to a specific practical application would lack patentable utility, for example, while a claim that enables someone to monopolize an entire abstract concept might run afoul of written description, enablement, or claim definiteness doctrines. Be that as it may, just as it has breathed new life into the exclusions for products of nature and laws of nature, the Supreme Court has revitalized the abstract ideas exclusion as well, to the extent that it is now one of the most frequently invoked reasons for rejecting or invalidating claims involving business methods and software. As a result, although software-related inventions and business methods remain, in principle, potentially patentable, in practice a large percentage of claims in these fields are now either rejected by the USPTO or invalidated if challenged in court. In this chapter, we'll see how this came to pass; and I'll suggest some reasons for thinking that, while software and business patents do indeed pose some unique challenges to the operation of an efficient patent system, the courts may be applying the wrong tools to address the problem.

Software

Although the idea of programming a device to carry out a set of calculations can be traced to such forerunners as the nineteenth-century polymath Ada Lovelace and the great twentieth-century mathematician Alan Turing, it wasn't until the late 1940s that computers had any *stored* programs—software—as such.[3] In the very earliest computers designed prior to and during World War II, programmers would physically alter the computer's *hardware*—its electromechanical circuitry—when they wanted to give the device a new task to carry out. By the mid- to late 1940s, however, researchers in the United Kingdom and the United States had begun to figure out how to store a set of instructions in the "memory" of a computer, which instructions could then be recalled and executed at the user's command—an advance that enabled the further development of general-purpose computers that could perform a wide variety of tasks without having to be manually rewired each time. The earliest efforts instructed the computer in the language that, as Turing foresaw, computers can "understand," namely a sequence of 1's and 0's that direct the opening and closing of electrical circuits in a programmed sequence to make computations. By the mid-1950s, however, engineers had developed more human-friendly languages such as COBOL and FORTRAN, in which a programmer could write her instructions and which, by means of another program known as a compiler, would then be translated into computer-friendly binary code. The programmer-written instructions are often referred to as "source code," and the resulting strings of 1's and 0's "object code."

Both forms of code fall within the category of "software," the term coined to distinguish code from computer hardware.

When computer engineers write code they often begin by breaking down the general purpose or goal of the program into discrete subtasks or "modules." A flow chart is often helpful to depict the relationships among the modules, which constitutes the overall structure or architecture of the program. (Figure 5.2 is a flow chart taken from the patent that was granted in response to the US Supreme

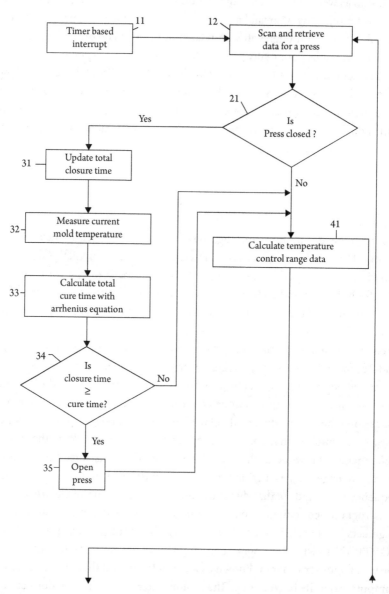

Figure 5.2 Flow Chart from US Patent No. 4,344,142

Court's 1981 decision in *Diamond v. Diehr*, which we'll be talking about shortly.) The modules are, essentially, individual programs within the program, which receive data in accordance with specified parameters or "data structures." (Courts sometimes have referred to modules as subroutines, though it is probably more accurate to use the term "subroutines" to refer to certain sequences occurring within modules.) The modules in turn are made up of algorithms, that is, sequences of steps for processing data. To borrow an example from the first US Supreme Court software patent case, an algorithm might specify the sequence of steps to follow to convert a binary-coded decimal number such as 0101 0011—which corresponds to the number 53 in base 10 because 0101 and 0011 in base 2 equal, respectively, 5 and 3 in base 10—into its pure binary number counterpart of 110101.[4] At the lowest layers of abstraction, source code, converted by the compiler into object code, instructs the computer to carry out the algorithms.

Now, I'm not aware of anyone who ever questioned whether computers, as physical machines, were patentable subject matter. (One of the most prominent early computer-related patent disputes, for example, *Honeywell Inc. v. Sperry Rand Corp.*, involved among other things the question of whether John Mauchly and J. Presper Eckhart had derived the invention of the automatic electric digital computer from an earlier pioneer, John Atanasoff. Judge Earl Larson's 1973 opinion addresses a huge number of issues relating to the validity and enforceability of the various patents in suit, but it doesn't say a word about patentable subject matter.[5]) Nevertheless, the question of whether computer *software*—code—was subject to any form of IP protection took a while to come to the attention of legal policymakers; and when it did, most of the initial focus was on copyright, not patents. After all, as discussed above source code (at least) is just a sequence of words, numbers, or other symbols, and thus in form no different from other types of written works that are subject to copyright protection. Following this reasoning, by the mid-1960s the US Copyright Office had begun to register computer programs as copyrightable works of authorship; and in 1976 when Congress enacted a comprehensive revision to the copyright statute, it published a legislative history stating that the new law's definition of protectable "literary works" (works "expressed in words, numbers, or other verbal or numerical symbols or indicia, regardless of the nature of the material objects, such as books, periodicals, manuscripts, phonorecords, film, tapes, disks, or cards, in which they are embodied") was broad enough to encompass computer programs. In 1980, following recommendations made by the Commission on New Technological Uses of Copyrighted Works (CONTU), Congress amended the copyright statute again by adding a definition of "computer program" as "a set of statements or instructions to be used directly or indirectly in a computer in order to bring about a certain result," and another provision that specifically referred to the infringement of computer programs.[6] From that point on, it was clear that original source and object code would both be subject to copyright protection. This result has remained controversial among some copyright scholars, who argue that computer programs are more functional in nature than many other copyrightable works and that copyright's term of protection (which, as I noted in Chapter 1, often lasts for more than one hundred years) is far too long for a type of work any exemplar of which will surely obsolesce long before the copyright terminates. Nevertheless, the copyrightability of source and object code is now embodied in international treaties that would be difficult to renegotiate even if there was the political will to do so, which there isn't. So copyright is certainly an option for the creator of a new program.

You might think that the decision to recognize computer programs as copyrightable works of authorship would have resolved most of the relevant legal questions about the protectability of software; and that's true if we're talking about the literal code itself. But suppose that a firm hires someone to create a new program for, say, tracking its inventory throughout various storage and distribution centers. If a competitor were to copy the resulting code without the consent of the copyright owner, it would be liable for copyright infringement; if, on the other hand, the competitor independently created its own program for tracking inventory, it wouldn't. By analogy to the playwrighting example with which I opened this chapter, at most the competitor has copied only the *abstract idea* of an inventory-tracking program; and the first firm's copyright in a specific program no more entitles it to monopolize the use of that idea, than would the first playwright's copyright in a specific text entitle him to prevent others from independently creating their own plays on the theme of star-crossed lovers. Between these two polar cases, however, are the intermediate ones in which the second author, without necessarily copying the literal text of the first, borrows something more than just the abstract idea: in the play example, maybe the plot or characters, or in the computer example perhaps the modules into which the structure of the program is divided. As in the play example, the question here is whether the second comer nevertheless has taken an original expression or selection or arrangement in which copyright subsists; or, alternatively, has copied something that (while not as abstract as the bare idea of an inventory-tracking system) is still *too* abstract to qualify for copyright protection. Since this is a book about patent law, not copyrights, I won't go into all the detail of how the courts have come around to resolving such questions, but will merely note that they do so in a manner that is consciously patterned after the playwrighting example. Depending on the specific facts and circumstances at issue in a given case, then, a defendant's "nonliteral" copying of, say, the program's subroutines for carrying out certain functions may or may not amount to copyright infringement.

A second option for the programmer would be to protect the code as a trade secret. This option is not mutually exclusive to copyright; and it might even protect some fairly abstract features of the program, as long as those features are, among other things, secret, that is, neither generally known nor readily ascertainable by proper means (see Chapter 1). But therein lies (from the owner's perspective) one of the potential defects of trade secret protection, since information no longer qualifies as a trade secret once it becomes generally known to the industry. Relatedly, trade secret law prevents only the disclosure or use of secret information in violation of a duty of confidentiality, or its acquisition by "improper means." Trade secret law therefore provides no protection against reverse engineering, which is viewed as a *proper* means of uncovering another person's trade secret; and once the secret is reverse engineered (or independently discovered) its status as a trade secret may be lost. Furthermore, even if someone improperly acquires another's trade secret, or uses or discloses it in violation of a duty of secrecy, if that person reveals the trade secret to the world it's no longer a trade secret and others are free to use it as they please (though the person who engaged in the initial act of wrongdoing can still be punished).

A third possible option would be to apply for some sort of patent, for if this option is viable it might seem to offer a more robust form of protection than either trade secret or copyright law—the former for the reasons I've just discussed, the latter for reasons we'll come to in a minute. In order to satisfy patent law formalities, of course, the programmer would have to dress up the program as some sort of invention, but that shouldn't be too hard. Most programs, after all, are intended to accomplish some functional purpose such as managing inventory, to use the example from above; and as we've seen, software is really just a more efficient substitute for hardware, from which one might conclude that if hardware is patentable than software should be too. Thus, a competent patent lawyer should be able to draft a claim reciting a method for accomplishing some useful purpose (e.g., managing inventory) by means of a computer program that executes a specified sequence of functions; or, more creatively, a machine (i.e., a general purpose computer) that has been programmed to execute such a program, or maybe even an "article of manufacture," namely a computer-readable storage medium (such as a disk) from which a computer may execute such a program.

The point of this exercise would be to protect the program at a higher level of abstraction than is available under copyright alone—something that patent law makes possible if a claim reads on many functional embodiments of the underlying inventive principle. Thus, while a copyright on a program for managing inventory will cover other programs that use substantially the same source or object code, and perhaps *some* of the program's nonliteral features, a valid patent on a novel and nonobvious method for managing inventory by means of a computer program will cover any such method using any software to carry out the specified sequence of claim steps; and those claim steps frequently are drafted at a fairly high level of generality. (Also, as we've seen, in copyright law independent creation is a defense, whereas in patent law independent invention, though commonplace, is not.) At least until recently, for example, it often wasn't necessary even to disclose the underlying algorithms for carrying out the claimed function unless the claim was explicitly drafted in something called a "means plus function" format.[7] A June 2015 Federal Circuit decision now requires a greater number of claims to disclose the relevant algorithms,[8] though precisely at what level of specificity remains an open question;[9] and the inventor still doesn't have to disclose any actual code. (Relatedly, until the Supreme Court's 2014 *Nautilus* decision a claim was not subject to invalidation on the ground of indefiniteness unless it was "insolubly ambiguous."[10] Such a standard encouraged drafters to write ambiguous claims—as long as the ambiguity wasn't "insoluble"—and thus compounded the difficulty of determining the precise scope of patent claims.) Thus, while a patent on a specific computerized process for managing an inventory system probably wouldn't entitle the owner to exclude *every* such process, the patent likely would cover a greater share of potential embodiments than would the copyright in a specific inventory program. In visual terms, patent law draws the line between what is protectable and what is not somewhat higher up the inverted triangle than does copyright, as depicted in Figure 5.3.

Or does it? The preceding discussion assumes that the hypothetical inventory management claim doesn't present a patentable subject matter problem; and until fairly recently, it probably wouldn't have. But as with products of nature and laws of nature, the law of abstract ideas has undergone a sea change since the mid-2000s, so that nowadays a great many software-related claims are vulnerable on the ground that they are, in substance, nothing more than abstract ideas. To see how we got where we are today, let's return again to the 1960s, around the time the Copyright Office started registering copyrights in computer programs. It didn't take long for somebody to figure out that if you could get a *patent* on a software-related invention, the resulting claims potentially would be much more difficult for competitors to design around, and patent attorneys began experimenting with drafting software patent claims. Eventually, the matter reached the US Supreme Court. In fact, it reached the Court three times within the course of a decade (from 1972 to 1982), before the Court revisited the topic in 2010.

The Trilogy

The first time the Supreme Court ever had to deal with the patentability of a software-related invention was in the 1972 case of *Gottschalk v. Benson*,[11] which involved an application filed back in 1963 on behalf of two Bell Labs engineers

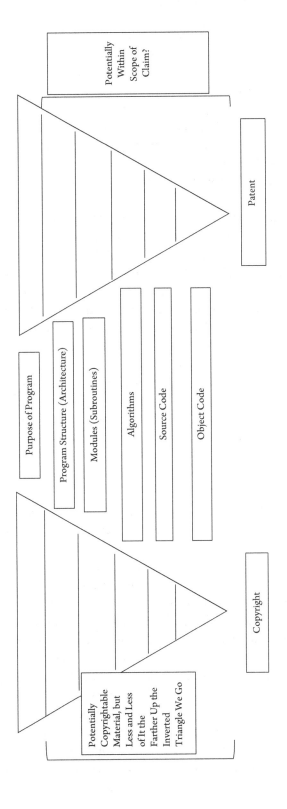

Figure 5.3 The Idea-Expression Dichotomy in Relation to Software

titled "Conversion of Numerical Information." At issue were two claims, both involving use of the algorithm I mentioned above for converting binary-coded decimal numbers into pure binary numbers. (The first claim was drafted so that it would read on any use of the algorithm performed on a general purpose computer; the second arguably would have read on any use of the algorithm, period, including in one's head.) Characterizing the algorithm at the core of the two claims as an unpatentable idea, the Supreme Court held that the claims themselves were unpatentable because they "would wholly pre-empt the mathematical formula and in practical effect would be a patent on the algorithm itself."[12] At the same time, however, the Court attempted to limit its holding by noting that the claims "were not limited to any particular art or technology, to any particular apparatus or machinery, or to any particular end use," and stated that it was not establishing a general rule that computer-related art was per se unpatentable.[13] Six years later in *Parker v. Flook*,[14] the Court again rejected a claim involving the use of a computer, this time in connection with a catalytic hydrocarbon conversion process for reducing toxic emissions from an automotive engine. The claims at issue in *Flook* recited methods for calculating an "alarm limit" in such a process by means of an algorithm that would process a relevant variable (temperature, pressure, or flow rate) and then "update" the limit during the transient operation of the vehicle. If the limit exceeded a certain value, this might signify "the presence of an abnormal condition indicating either inefficiency or perhaps danger."[15] The Court held the claims unpatentable, primarily because the final, nonalgorithmic step of actually adjusting the alarm limit to the updated number was "conventional or obvious." As in *Benson*, however, the Court tried to limit its holding by stating "a process is not unpatentable simply because it contains a law of nature or a mathematical algorithm."[16]

Four years later, the Court reversed course in *Diamond v. Diehr*,[17] a case decided less than a year after the Court held in *Diamond v. Chakrabarty* that human-created bacteria were patentable. At issue in *Diehr* was the patentability of "a method for operating a rubber-molding press for precision molded compounds with aid of a digital computer." In particular, the claimed process recited the steps of programming a computer to repeatedly perform something known as the Arrhenius equation, an algorithm first proposed almost a hundred years earlier for determining the relationship between temperature and at the rate at which a chemical reaction would occur; constantly providing the computer with the temperature inside a rubber-molding press; and automatically opening the press when the computer determined that the rubber had been completely "cured," that is, was ready for use.[18] (The flow chart reproduced in Figure 5.2 is taken from the patent that eventually issued in this case.) The process was an improvement over the state of the art because conventional techniques could not accurately monitor the temperature inside the press and thus determine the optimal cure time.[19] This time, a majority of the justices viewed the invention as a potentially patentable process—"a mode of treatment of certain materials to produce a given result," "an act, or a series of acts, performed upon the subject-matter to be transformed and reduced to a different state or thing"—that was not excluded from patentability merely because it employed a mathematical equation and a computer.[20] In reaching this result, the Court cited the *Flook* Court's statement that "insignificant postsolution activity will not transform an unpatentable principle into a patentable process,"[21] but it viewed the "post-solution" (that is, nonalgorithmic) steps here as more than merely "insignificant." The Court also noted that the claims didn't preempt all uses of the Arrhenius equation, even though the lack of complete preemption hadn't been enough to save the claims at issue in *Flook*; and it was a bit hard for some observers to see why the nonalgorithmic steps in *Diehr* were any more significant than the nonalgorithmic step (updating the alarm limit) at issue in *Flook*. In the minds of many—including the four dissenting justices, all of whom were part of the *Flook* majority—*Diehr* simply overruled *Flook* without explicitly saying so.

In the years immediately following *Diehr*, both the USPTO and the Federal Circuit struggled to apply the now-governing legal standards in a consistent and predictable fashion. By the mid-1990s, the Federal Circuit had settled on a very broad interpretation of patentable subject matter—namely, the "useful, concrete, and tangible" standard that I mentioned in the preceding chapter. Leading the way was Judge Giles Rich who, as a judge on the Court of Customs and Patent Appeals in the 1970s, had embraced a broad view of patentable subject matter in the case that eventually made its way to the Supreme Court as *Diamond v. Chakrabarty*. (Judge Rich had adopted a similarly expansive view with respect to software-related inventions in some of the lower court decisions that preceded *Diehr*.) Writing for the court in the 1994 decision *In re Alappat*, Judge Rich held that a machine programmed to perform an algorithm for improving the electronic waveform displayed on a digital oscilloscope was patent-eligible because it was not just a "disembodied mathematical concept," but rather a specific machine that produced a "useful, concrete, and tangible result."[22] A year later, in *In re Beauregard*, the USPTO withdrew its objection to the patent-eligibility of software on a disk—disks are articles of manufacture, after all!—and from then on, such "Beauregard" claims would be patent-eligible as long as the software performed some useful, concrete, and tangible function.[23] And just before the turn of the century the Federal Circuit in *AT&T Corp. v. Excel Communications, Inc.* rejected the argument that process claims are patentable "only if there is a 'physical transformation' or conversion of subject matter from one state into another."[24] (The AT&T patent in suit had claimed a process for generating a message record for interexchange telephone calls, the end result of which was a "signal useful for billing purposes.") The case therefore made it clear that the

Federal Circuit wasn't requiring inventions to be "concrete" and "tangible" in any *literal* sense, but rather only, as the USPTO later put it, "not abstract" and "substantially repeatable."[25]

Business Methods

Paralleling the preceding developments in the patentability of software-related inventions was a similar development with regard to methods for doing business. (Actually, the two often dovetailed, since many business methods are or can be implemented by software.) At least until the early 1990s, conventional wisdom among patent lawyers had long been that business methods were not patentable. Not that there was a lot of case law on the topic, mind you. Neither the Supreme Court nor the Federal Circuit had ever addressed the topic; and most of the cases that had were fairly old and had talked about the patentability of business methods only in *dicta*, albeit *dicta* that many observers viewed as a pretty accurate reflection of the law. To the extent anyone sought a rationale for this exclusion, it was sometimes that commerce simply wasn't one of the "useful arts" to which the Constitution refers when it authorizes Congress to grant patents "[t]o promote the Progress of . . . useful Arts";[26] or that the long history of a *lack* of attempts by inventors to patent business methods reflected a common understanding, which Congress implicitly approved, that business methods weren't patentable. (The belief that, with rare exceptions, inventors never even tried to patent business methods nevertheless appears to be inaccurate. In a 2012 study of patents granted from 1790 to 1836, Professor Michael Risch reports that about 8 percent could be broadly classified as involving business methods, which he defines as methods that are "not particularly technological," including "ways to manipulate information, including methods of measurement, writing or drawing, or teaching."[27] None of them appear to have had much of a market impact, however, and to my knowledge none of the truly great nineteenth or early twentieth century innovations in ways of doing business—such as, for example, Montgomery Ward's method of selling goods to rural customers by mail order—were ever patented.[28]) Further, from the standpoint of economic theory one might question whether, in general, businesses really *need* an additional incentive to invent and commercialize methods to improve their own operations, since they stand to benefit from those improvements and (arguably) need to continue developing them to remain competitive, even if the improvements are susceptible to copying. Of course, patents also disclose new inventions so that others can learn from them, improve upon them, and freely practice them once the patents expire. But arguably the patent incentive isn't usually necessary to achieve this purpose either, because many business methods are either self-disclosing or, conversely, so difficult to reverse-engineer that their owners would prefer the trade secret option anyway; think of Google's search algorithms. Thus, for a variety of reasons and at least through the end of the 1980s, most patent practitioners and scholars were of the view that business methods were protectable, if at all, through first-mover advantages or by contract or trade secret law—but not by patents, regardless of how novel or useful or nonobvious the innovation might have been.

The exclusion of business methods from the scope of patent protection nevertheless began to unravel in the early 1990s, when the USPTO began to grant an increasing number of patents on what were, for all intents and purposes, methods of doing business. To see how this came about requires a little further background.

First off, let's be clear that there is no standard, agreed-upon definition of what a business method *is*. (For purposes of a type of administrative review I'll discuss toward the end of this chapter, the 2011 America Invents Act [AIA] defines a "covered business method" as "a patent that claims a method or corresponding apparatus for performing data processing or other operations used in the practice, administration, or management of a financial product or service." This helps a bit, though reasonable minds continue to differ on exactly what the term embraces, and it's probably best not to view it as a comprehensive definition of the term "business method" as used in other contexts.) In a study published in 2006, for example, Allison and Hunter argued that "the term is probably indefinable," but then went on to suggest that "[b]roadly speaking, a business method patent covers a business practice or technique"—a definition they recognized as "circular" but which would include methods "relating to advertising, shopping, sales, purchasing, financing, insurance, human resources activities, and specialized forms of communication within business firms," and perhaps other practices as well.[29] They also noted, however, that "[p]atents on software-implemented business practices constitute the vast majority of such patents" and thus for purposes of their study they considered business method patents as a "subset" of software patents. By contrast, Risch's definition from above (methods that are "not particularly technological," including "ways to manipulate information, including methods of measurement, writing or drawing, or teaching") is much broader.

A second bit of background information is that patent applicants are obligated to classify their inventions based on field of technology. Until recently, the United States followed the (surprise!) US Patent Classification (USPC) System, under which each patent would bear an original or primary classification, of which there were 475, and a subclass, of which there were approximately 165,000. Inventions that taught more than one concept would bear additional cross-classifications.[30] (I briefly alluded to patent classes in Chapter 1 when discussing the Fregley et al. patent. If you look back, you'll see that the patent's original class/subclass was 424/439, which represents "Drug, Bio-Affecting and Body Treatment Compositions/Food or Edible as Food for Pharmaceutical Carrier." It also included lots of cross-classifications.) On January 1, 2015, the United States transitioned to a new system, the Cooperative Patent Classification (CPC) System, which is jointly managed by the USPTO and the European Patent Office (EPO). For purposes of this background discussion, however, we'll focus on the USPC.

One of the agency's long-standing classes under the USPC was Class 235 ("Registers"), which covered cash registers and other counting devices. In the late 1960s, the agency split off two new computer classes from Class 235, Classes 364 and 395, for business and cost/price methods and systems, then in 1997 it abolished these and created a new Class 705 for "Data Processing, Financial, Business Practice, Management or Cost/Price Determination."[31] Most of the available descriptive statistics on the number of business method patents therefore are based on Class 705 and its predecessor classes—though there are many other patents that the USPTO assigned to other classes, such as Class 235 or Class 700 ("Generic Control Systems or Specific Applications") that many people would consider to be business method patents.[32] In addition, the USPTO maintains statistics on the numbers of patents issued by USPC class, with the caveat that the "classification need not correspond to any classification that was assigned to the patent at the time of issue since the classification system is continuously undergoing revision and since classifications that are assigned to patents are continuously updated to reflect these revisions."[33] (Thus, the statistics published for Class 705 would include patents that were previously classed under Classes 364 or 395.) Until being superseded by the CPC, Class 705 had come to include "a collection of 20+ financial and data processing areas," including "data processing in specific enterprises such as Insurance, Stock/Bond trading, Health Care Management, Reservation Systems, Postage Meter Systems (Computerized) as well as more general enterprise functions such as Electronic Shopping, Auction Systems, and Business Cryptography."[34] Anyway, notwithstanding the conventional wisdom that business methods were unpatentable, USPTO statistics show that from 1977 through 1995 the agency had already issued over 1,879 patents that would have been assigned an original or cross-classification of Class 705; and, for the specific years 1995–97, the numbers increased from 195 to 254 to 367, respectively.[35] Prior to 1990, according to the agency, these "patents were heavily focused on computerized postage metering and cash register systems," apparently reflecting the class's evolution from "Registers," but "by the end of 1994 heavier emphasis was placed on financial transaction systems which moved postage metering to the second place category."[36]

It didn't surprise a lot of people, then, when in 1998 the Federal Circuit (in yet another opinion by Judge Rich) laid to rest what it described as the "ill-conceived" business methods exception.[37] The case, *State Street Bank & Trust Co. v. Signature Financial Group, Inc.*, involved a Class 705 patent that the USPTO had issued on a data processing system for implementing an investment structure used in administering mutual funds. The district court had held the claims invalid, but the Federal Circuit (citing *Alappat*) reversed, holding that "the transformation of data, representing discrete dollar amounts, by a machine through a series of mathematical calculations into a final share price" constituted a "practical application of a mathematical algorithm, formula, or calculation, because it produces a 'useful, concrete, and tangible result'—a final share price momentarily fixed for recording and reporting purposes."[38]

Finally, in 2005 a panel of USPTO administrative law judges kicked away one of the last remaining obstacles to the patentability of business methods by ruling that patents don't even have to pertain to technology at all. At issue in *Ex parte Lundgren* was a method for compensating a firm manager for reducing the firm's exposure to the risk of liability for violating the antitrust laws; none of the steps of the invention required the use of a computer or other equipment.[39] The examiner had rejected the application on the ground that the claims read on subject matter "outside the technological arts, namely an economic theory expressed as a mathematical algorithm without the disclosure or suggestion of computer, automated means, apparatus of any kind." The appellate panel reversed, citing *AT&T* for the proposition that "a process claim that applies a mathematical algorithm to 'produce a useful, concrete, tangible result without pre-empting other uses of the mathematical principle, on its face comfortably falls within the scope of § 101'" and rejecting the need for any inquiry into whether an invention is "technological" in nature. Thus, with the apparent blessing of the Federal Circuit and the USPTO, business method patents could now come out of the closet, as it were, no longer having to pass themselves off as something they were not.

The Flood of Software and Business Method Patents

The predictable result of the developments noted in the preceding paragraphs was a substantial increase in the number of software and business method patent applications and grants. The number of Class 705 patents issued annually, for example, rose from 711 in 1998 to 1,358 in 2010.[40] To be sure, as a percentage of all patents granted, these are small numbers—ranging from less than one-half of one percent in 1998, to slightly more than one-half of one percent in 2010.[41] As noted above, however, focusing on Class 705 alone underestimates the overall number of business method patents, given the difficulty of defining exactly what counts as a business method, and the fact that many patents reading on what would appear to be business methods under any reasonable definition were classified in classes other than 705.

As for software patents, again we run into a definitional problem since as Stuart Graham and David Mowery observe "no widely accepted definition of 'software patent' exists."[42] James Bessen's proposed definition of software patents as "patents that use a logic algorithm for processing data that is implemented via stored instructions residing on a disk or other storage medium or in read-only memory"[43] nevertheless seems plausible—though depending on how you interpret it, it could encompass a great deal of subject matter. Lots of technologies use software to accomplish their ends, after all. (To borrow an example from Mark Lemley, the Toyota Prius's "hybrid gasoline-electric engine works because the car has a sophisticated controller that decides when to draw power from the gasoline engine and when from the battery. That controller is a piece of software. Is the hybrid car engine a 'software patent'?")[44] In any event, one technique that researchers have used to estimate the number of software patents is to focus on the patent classes in which they would expect to find a disproportionate number of such patents (however one defines them). For example, Graham and Mowery identified twelve USPC classes accounting for 67.9 percent of the patents issued from 1987 to 2003 to the six largest US producers of personal computer software. (The twelve include several with the principal heading "Data Processing.")[45] They reported that "the share of all US patents accounted for by software patents grew from 2.1 percent to 7.4 percent of all issued US patents between 1987 and 1998," although "the share of patents in these twelve US classes has remained between 6.9 and 7.5 percent of overall patenting during 1999–2003."[46] Using similar criteria,[47] Garry Gabison's more recent study estimates that the number of software patents granted annually from 2004 to 2013 climbed from about 15,000 to a little under 40,000—a percentage increase of more than 150 percent, in comparison with an approximate 70 percent increase in the total number of patents granted during that time—accounting for about 13 percent of all issued patents by 2013.[48] These estimates are slightly lower than Bessen's estimate of about 40,000 software patents granted annually by 2009, based on a somewhat broader mix of patent classes.[49] Because all of these studies rely on patent classification, however, which doesn't always track very closely with the underlying technology— indeed, lawyers can manipulate it to some degree to increase their chances of a favorable prosecution—they all risk including some patents that are not software patents at all while missing others. By contrast, studies based on text searches of terms believed to be associated with software patents generated somewhat higher numbers of these patents—almost 25,000 for the year 2002, for example, in a study by Bessen and Hunt[50]—but also risked generating a fair number of false positives.[51]

Whatever the precise numbers actually may have been, it was pretty clear by the late 2000s that the USPTO was granting at least a few tens of thousands of software and business method patents every year, and that these patents accounted for a growing proportion of all issued patents—probably at least 10 percent, and very likely more. To be sure, by itself this wasn't necessarily a bad thing. Software and business methods are important elements of any modern economy, after all; and maybe there was a surfeit of innovation going on in these fields in comparison with others. Further to this point, advocates of software and business method patents argued that there's no good reason categorically to exclude innovations in these fields from the scope of patent protection. As noted above, in principle anything the software accomplishes could be accomplished, albeit less efficiently, with hardware. Moreover, finance and other business-related fields are important areas of scholarly inquiry and innovation: so why not allow for the patenting of novel, useful, and nonobvious improvements in, say, "financial engineering?"[52] Finally, any effort to exclude business methods and software from patent eligibility would require a definition of what these things *are*, which as we've seen is not necessarily easy; and whatever definition policymakers might agree upon, you can be sure that attorneys would try to come up with ways of drafting around it. As some saw it, encouraging such gamesmanship would be socially wasteful as well as futile.

For many other people, however, the increasing volume of software and business method patents provided cause for alarm. Some associated the abandonment of the need for showing a physical transformation or a nexus to technology with a proliferation of patents on trivial inventions, such as methods for exercising a cat,[53] for taping and cutting hair,[54] and for swinging on a swing.[55] Of course, patents like these probably had little if any commercial value and were unlikely to be enforced—and thus, like many patents throughout history, were problematic only to the extent they wasted patent examiners' time and resources. Similarly notorious were the tax shelter patents—that is, patents on methods for exploiting loopholes in the tax code to reduce one's liability to Uncle Sam. From the standpoint of patent policy, it's a little hard to see why the government would need (or want) to encourage the invention of new methods for reducing its own tax receipts—though since most people aren't wealthy enough to use tax shelters anyway, the overall impact of these patents too may not have been all that substantial. (Congress in any event effectively eliminated tax shelter patents when in 2011 it included in the AIA a provision stating that "any strategy for reducing, avoiding, or deferring tax liability . . . shall be deemed" within the prior art.[56] By this act of statutory legerdemain, any methods for sheltering tax henceforth would be considered obvious or lacking novelty. No offense intended, tax lawyers.) Potentially more serious, however, because of their broader applicability, were a large number of patents in the field of electronic commerce. Among the most widely cited examples were Amazon. com's patent on one-click shopping,[57] which for many observers symbolized the USPTO's practice of granting patents on obvious applications of standard Internet technology to standard business practices; and Priceline.com's patent on a method for conducting a reverse auction over the Internet,[58] one of a class which Allison et al. have described as "contain[ing] claims of a sufficiently broad nature that the invention could form the foundation for an entire business, or line of business, on the Internet."[59]

One widely voiced critique of patents like these was that the USPTO simply wasn't well-positioned to find nonpatent prior art references that might have resulted in some of them being rejected or invalidated for lack of novelty or for obviousness. As it turned out, though, research published by John Allison and Emerson Tiller (and others) in the early to mid-2000s cast serious doubt on this particular argument. Applying some standard measures that economists use to es- timate patent quality (including "number of prior art references, type of prior art references, number of claims within the patents, number of inventors, and time spent in the PTO before issuance"), Allison and Tiller instead concluded that software-implemented business methods did not appear to be "uniquely deficient" compared to patents in other fields.[60] Of course, as these authors were quick to point out, the fact that the quality of the typical business method patent may have been comparable to that of patents in other fields doesn't imply anything about that overall level of quality; and there are reasons to think that quality in most fields of invention could stand a bit of improvement. As noted earlier in this book, for ex- ample, about 40 percent of all litigated patents ultimately are invalidated. Moreover, patent examiners bear the burden of proving that a claimed invention in *not* pat- entable (rather than the inventor bearing the burden of showing that it *is*), and are expected to spend no more than about 20 hours total on any given application. As a result, mistakes inevitably will be made. Further, if the various legal requirements for patentability are too easy to satisfy, the agency can wind up granting patents that contribute relatively little to the state of the art; and during the period of time that Allison and Tiller conducted their studies, the nonobviousness bar in partic- ular probably *was* too low. As discussed in Chapter 1, prior to the Supreme Court's 2007 decision in *KSR*, the Federal Circuit often required strict proof that the prior art taught, suggested, or motivated a person of ordinary skill to combine the rel- evant references before those references could be used to reject or invalidate a patent on obviousness grounds. As a consequence, a somewhat larger percentage of applications for inventions of marginal social value probably did succeed in getting through the system prior to 2007 than after—though again that would be true for all fields of invention, not just business and software.

Nevertheless, critics worried that even if business method and software patents were on average no worse than other patents in terms of quality, they threatened to inflict disproportionate harm, for several reasons. First, studies have confirmed the intuition that business method and software patents are more likely to be litigated, and to be invalidated in litigation, than are other patents.[61] In fact, the most frequently litigated business and software patents have fared particularly poorly in litigation,[62] though again questions of whether frequently litigated patents and patents litigated to judgment are representative of all patents within a particular class are hard to answer. Second, as discussed earlier in this chapter, until recently the Federal Circuit permitted inventors to draft broadly functional, often ambiguous, software claims, with the result that patents like Priceline.com's potentially could read on a vast range of Internet-related business activities. But while there may be good reasons to construe the claims for "pioneering" inventions very broadly, most inventions aren't pioneering. To the extent that claim drafting rules permitted software and business method patents to read more broadly on average than most patents, critics argued that the rewards accruing to such patents often exceeded their actual contribution to the art.[63] Worse yet, such broad patents risked ensnaring a huge range of inadvertent infringers, thus giving some credence to the notion that software patents in particular imposed a type of "innovation tax" on independent inventors.[64] Add in the fact that a disproportionate share of software and business patents (broadly construed) wound up in the hands of patent assertion entities (PAEs)—who, for reasons we'll see in Chapter 8, on balance are more likely to demand royalties or to litigate than are the practicing entities that make or sell products—and you have an enormous potential for what economists refer to as "rent seeking," that is, conduct intended to reap private rewards at the public's expense. Finally, even many practicing entities that otherwise might have been happy to do without them wound up developing or acquiring software patents (again, broadly construed) as bargaining chips to use in the event of a lawsuit brought by another practicing entity.[65] As with the literal arms races in which countries sometimes engage, even if the weapons are never used their development and acquisition imposes social costs that could be avoided if détente were a viable option.

Backlash: Bilski and Alice

Such were the defenses and critiques of software and business method patents that were being bandied about when, in the mid-2000s the Supreme Court began signaling its renewed interest in patent law. As I mentioned in Chapter 1, in 2006 the Court heard, decided, or granted cert in six patent cases. These included the

LabCorp matter discussed in the preceding chapter, as well as *KSR* (argued in 2006, decided in 2007), the case that tightened the standard for determining whether an invention is nonobvious. Among the other patent cases the Court decided in 2006–07—all of which, by the way, resulted in reversing or overruling the Federal Circuit—was *eBay Inc. v. MercExchange, L.L.C.*, in which the Court held that even when a patent owner prevails at trial, it isn't *automatically* entitled to an injunction—a court order that the defendant stop infringing—but rather, in some cases, may only recover a judgment for monetary damages.[66] We'll talk more about injunctions and damages in the last few chapters of this book, but I bring the *eBay* case up now simply to point out that, in a concurring opinion joined by three other justices, Justice Anthony Kennedy specifically mentioned "[t]he potential vagueness and suspect validity of some" business method patents as a potentially relevant consideration in deciding whether to grant an injunction.[67]

These developments were not lost on the Federal Circuit and the USPTO, which soon began to backtrack a bit on their understanding of patentable subject matter. In particular, early in 2008, the Federal Circuit decided to hear a subject matter case, *In re Bilski*, "en banc"—meaning that all of the active judges on the court would participate in the decision. (Except for certain emergency petitions which might be temporarily addressed by one single justice, the US Supreme Court always hears cases en banc. Federal appellate courts, by contrast, usually sit in panels of three judges, and only agree to hear cases en banc when a majority of the judges believe that the matter is of unusual importance—for example, when the court needs to resolve a conflict among its own prior decisions.) At issue was a patent application filed by inventors Bilski and Warsaw for, as the Federal Circuit succinctly described it, "a method of hedging risk in the field of commodities trading."[68] Essentially, the patent claimed a method whereby an intermediary would minimize the risk to consumers and providers of a commodity (such as coal) of a fluctuation in the price of the commodity, by agreeing to purchase it from the one and sell it to the other at fixed prices based on historic averages.[69] Parsing the Supreme Court's *Benson-Flook-Diehr* trilogy for clues on how to distinguish a patentable method from an abstract idea, Chief Judge Paul Michel settled on three core principles: first, that "[a] claimed process is surely patent-eligible . . . if: (1) it is tied to a particular machine or apparatus, or (2) it transforms a particular article into a different state or thing" (the so-called "machine or transformation" test); second, that patentable methods must not preempt all practical uses of a fundamental principle; and third, that "the recited machine or transformation must not constitute mere 'insignificant postsolution activity.'"[70] Applying these standards here, the court found that the claims were not "tied" to any machine or apparatus, and didn't transform anything other than information.[71] Along the way, the court rejected the *Alappat/State Street Bank* standard that any "useful, concrete, and tangible" invention was patent-eligible.

At the same time, however, the majority disavowed any reliance on a "techno-logical arts" doctrine, and rejected the argument that business methods were per se unpatentable.[72]

From there, the case made its way to the Supreme Court, which heard oral argument in November 2009. Since the Court usually issues opinions just a few months after argument has taken place, by early 2010 those of us who follow patent issues were expecting the Court any day to issue its expected clarification of what had once again proved to be a thorny area of the law. Would the Court affirm or reverse? Would it decide once and for all whether business methods are patentable? Would it define what an abstract idea is? Would it say anything about technological arts, or mental steps, or the need for "particular machines" or physical transformations? But as the months ticked by and the 2009–10 term began drawing to a close, the Court still hadn't issued its opinion, and tensions began to mount. What was going on behind the justices' closed doors?

Finally, on June 28, 2010—the last day of the Court's 2009–10 term—the Court issued its opinion (or rather, opinions) in the case now titled *Bilski v. Kappos*.[73] The upshot was that Bilski and Warsaw lost, 9–0, with all nine justices agreeing that the claimed invention was nothing more than an abstract idea. (Technically, then, the Supreme Court affirmed the Federal Circuit's judgment.) By itself, this wasn't so surprising, since all but one of the Federal Circuit judges had concluded largely the same thing, and few people expected the Supreme Court to be more favorable to the patent applicants than the lower court had been. What *was* surprising to some was the division among justices on the question of whether business methods were patentable, as well as the min-imal guidance the Court provided to determine *when* a method recites nothing more than an abstract idea.

First, in an opinion joined by four other justices, erstwhile business method skeptic Justice Kennedy began by reaffirming that abstract ideas, along with laws of nature and products of nature, fall outside the scope of patentable sub-ject matter. As for how one should go about spotting an abstract idea, however, Justice Kennedy was less specific, calling the Federal Circuit's machine-or-transformation test only "a useful and important clue," not the "sole test," for determining whether a claimed invention qualifies as a potentially patentable process.[74] Second, while reiterating his concern that "some business method patents raise special problems in terms of vagueness and suspect validity," Justice Kennedy concluded that nothing in the patent statute categorically excluded business methods from the scope of patentable subject matter.[75] Nevertheless, characterizing risk-hedging as "a fundamental economic practice long prevalent in our system of commerce," the majority concluded that Bilski's claims, even if limited to the fields of commodities and energy markets, recited nothing more than an unpatentable idea.[76]

Much longer than Justice Kennedy's opinion was a separate opinion authored by Justice Stevens, joined by three other justices, which argued that, based on history and tradition, business methods simply weren't the type of methods Congress had in mind when it enacted section 101.[77] Justice Stevens's opinion actually reads more like a majority than a concurring opinion, beginning with a detailed recitation of the facts and procedural posture of the case. Many people believe that this explains the delay in deciding Bilski's appeal: that Justice Stevens initially had been tapped to write a majority opinion holding that business methods were per se unpatentable, but that somewhere along the way Justice Kennedy changed his mind and wound up writing what would now be a majority opinion reaching the opposite conclusion. In any event, on the question of whether business methods are patentable, Justice Stevens ultimately lost the day—though he did succeed in showing that the "anything under the sun that is made by man" quote, found in the legislative history of the 1952 Patent Act and cited by Justice Kennedy (and by the majority in *Diamond v. Chakrabarty*, see Chapter 3) in support of a broad view of patentable subject matter, probably was intended to mean something quite different. If anything, the full quote ("A person may have 'invented' a machine or a manufacture, which may include anything under the sun that is made by man, but it is not necessarily patentable under section 101 unless the conditions of [this] title are fulfilled") suggests that Congress understood the Patent Act to impose meaningful limits on patentability—though whether those limits should be rooted in patentable subject matter doctrine or principally in considerations of novelty, utility, and nonobviousness, is debatable.[78]

So the guiding principle remained, then, that abstract ideas are not patentable. But what exactly *is* an abstract idea? Shortly after the *Bilski* opinion was published, the USPTO got to work drafting some guidelines that stated, among other things, that the presence of "general concepts" such as "basic economic practices or theories" or "mental activity" could be "a clue that the claim is drawn to an abstract idea," while also noting that the machine-or-transformation test remained relevant even if not dispositive.[79] For many observers, however, the *Bilski* opinion appeared to clarify very little, and the courts' and agency's application of *Bilski* to specific cases often seemed ad hoc and unpredictable. Meanwhile the law of patentable subject matter in other fields continued to evolve, as evidenced by the Supreme Court's 2012 decision in *Mayo* and its 2013 decision in *Myriad*. Still, the Supreme Court hadn't said anything definitive about software, as such, since its 1970s-era trilogy, and before long conflicting views of how to apply the more recent Supreme Court teachings to software-related inventions began to emerge among the lower courts. Expectations therefore ran high when the Federal Circuit in 2012 agreed to consider en banc the patent-eligibility of certain method, system, and *Beauregard* (software-on-a-disk) claims in *CLS Bank International v. Alice Corp. Pty. Ltd.*[80]

As described by Federal Circuit Chief Judge Randall Rader, the claims in *Alice* all involved "a trusted third party settl[ing] obligations between a first and second party in order to eliminate 'settlement risk,'" that is, "the risk that only one party will meet its payment obligation"—essentially, the performance of an escrow transaction—with the system and *Beauregard* claims explicitly invoking the use of software to carry out the invention.[81] Reading the claims themselves doesn't make for the most scintillating reading, but if you want to get a sense of what the fuss was all about, try parsing the following claim, which was representative of the method claims in suit:

> A method of exchanging obligations as between parties, each party holding a credit record and a debit record with an exchange institution, the credit records and debit records for exchange of predetermined obligations, the method comprising the steps of:
> (a) creating a shadow credit record and a shadow debit record for each stakeholder party to be held independently by a supervisory institution from the exchange institutions;
> (b) obtaining from each exchange institution a start-of-day balance for each shadow credit record and shadow debit record;
> (c) for every transaction resulting in an exchange obligation, the supervisory institution adjusting each respective party's shadow credit record or shadow debit record, allowing only these transactions that do not result in the value of the shadow debit record being less than the value of the shadow credit record at any time, each said adjustment taking place in chronological order; and
> (d) at the end-of-day, the supervisory institution instructing ones of the exchange institutions to exchange credits or debits to the credit record and debit record of the respective parties in accordance with the adjustments of the said permitted transactions, the credits and debits being irrevocable, time invariant obligations placed on the exchange institutions.[82]

Got that? Unfortunately, the resulting opinions in the case—five of them, amounting to nearly seventy pages in the Federal Reporter—were only slightly more comprehensible. All told, six of the ten participating judges voted to affirm the district court's conclusion that the method and *Beauregard* claims were not patent-eligible, and divided 5–5 on the question of whether the system claims were. (When an appellate court is evenly split like this, the lower court's disposition of the question is affirmed without setting any precedent. So in effect the Federal Circuit affirmed the unpatentability of the system claims too.) Few people therefore were surprised when the Supreme Court granted cert to (it was hoped) bring some order to what had become a chaotic body of law.

A few months later, the Supreme Court issued its unanimous opinion in *Alice Corp. v. CLS Bank International*,[83] which as of this writing remains the Court's latest word on the subject of patentable subject matter. Like the *Myriad* opinion from the preceding year, the opinion was authored by Justice Clarence Thomas—though it appears to owe more to the framework Justice Breyer developed in *Mayo* than to *Myriad* (or *Bilski*), as shown by Justice Thomas's description of the test for analyzing patent claims of whatever type:

> First, we determine whether the claims at issue are directed to one of those patent-ineligible concepts. If so, we then ask, "[w]hat else is there in the claims before us?" To answer that question, we consider the elements of each claim both individually and "as an ordered combination" to determine whether the additional elements "transform the nature of the claim" into a patent-eligible application. We have described step two of this analysis as a search for an "'inventive concept'"—*i.e.*, an element or combination of elements that is "sufficient to ensure that the patent in practice amounts to significantly more than a patent upon the [ineligible concept] itself." [84]

Applying this standard, the Court concluded, first, that the "claims are drawn to the abstract idea of intermediated settlement," which like the hedging concept at issue in *Bilski* was a "fundamental economic practice long prevalent in our system of commerce."[85] Second, the Court found that "the method claims, which merely require generic computer implementation, fail to transform that abstract idea into a patent-eligible invention."[86] Further:

> Considered "as an ordered combination," the computer components of petitioner's method "ad[d] nothing that is not already present when the steps are considered separately." Viewed as a whole, petitioner's method claims simply recite the concept of intermediated settlement as performed by a generic computer. The method claims do not, for example, purport to improve the functioning of the computer itself. Nor do they effect an improvement in any other technology or technical field. Instead, the claims at issue amount to "nothing significantly more" than an instruction to apply the abstract idea of intermediated settlement using some unspecified, generic computer.[87]

Finally, the Court concluded that the system and *Beauregard* claims failed "for substantially the same reasons"; the recitation of specific hardware for carrying out those claims was "purely functional and generic."[88]

The Aftermath of *Alice*

One gets the sense from reading the Supreme Court's *Alice* opinion—which clocks in at a mere fifteen pages, or about one-fifth of what it took the Federal Circuit to dispose of the matter—that the Court just doesn't think that these patentable subject matter questions are all that difficult. And maybe that's right: maybe it takes a generalist court like the Supreme Court to see the forest for the trees. Still and all, it's hard to step away from cases like *Alice* and *Bilski* without wondering whether the Court could have provided a little more guidance on how to spot an abstract idea, or how if at all the "inventive concept" that now must be present to overcome a subject matter rejection differs from the inventive concept that must be present to demonstrate nonobviousness. (Indeed, critics might charge that the Court has merely moved what should be the core of a nonobviousness inquiry to the forefront—though without all of the surrounding legal doctrine, such as the "person having ordinary skill in the art" [PHOSITA] or the secondary considerations, that normally would be part of such an inquiry.) Be that as it may, the Court now appears to view its subject matter decisions as an application of the two-part *Mayo/Alice* framework; and it's up to the USPTO and the courts to flesh out what, if anything, remains of the patentability of software and business methods post-*Alice*.

As for what *does* remain, the short answer may be "not much." True, the USPTO still issues some patents on software-related inventions and on business methods. According to some initial analyses, however, the percentage of business and software-related applications the USPTO is now approving has sharply plummeted post-*Alice*, with a large percentage of the rejections explicitly based on lack of patentable subject matter.[89] Many business method and software patents also now wind up being invalidated in trials conducted before a body within the USPTO called the Patent Trial and Appeal Board (PTAB). As I mentioned in Chapter 1, the enactment in 2011 of the AIA effected two far-reaching changes in US patent practice. The first of these—the replacement of a first-to-invent standard with a first-to-file-or-disclose standard for determining which of two or more independent inventors is entitled to a patent—is the one I discussed at some length in Chapter 1. The second big change, however, was the introduction of three new types of proceedings whereby interested persons can challenge the validity of issued patents within the USPTO, rather than in federal district court. These proceedings—known as inter partes reviews (IPRs), postgrant reviews (PGRs), and postgrant reviews of covered business method patents (CBMs)—garnered considerably less public attention in 2011 but actually may be having the deeper impact on the overall working of the patent system. Indeed, former Chief Judge Rader has referred to these proceedings as "death squads killing property rights," though as I see it if a patent isn't valid, it isn't property at all. Passions nevertheless sometimes run high among patent lawyers, believe it or not.

(I should note, by the way, that in June 2017—shortly before this book went to press—the US Supreme Court granted cert in a case called *Oil States Energy Services, LLC v. Greene's Energy Group, LLC*, to decide whether IRPs violate the US Constitution "by extinguishing private property rights through a non-Article III forum"—that is, an administrative agency, rather than a federal district court—"without a jury." I'm not going to go into the details of the legal arguments here, but I'll be surprised if the Court finds IPRs to be unconstitutional. If, however, you're reading this in 2018 or 2019 and, contrary to my prediction, the Court *has* gotten rid of IPRs, you may as well skip the next couple of paragraphs of this chapter while I lick my wounds.)

The basic idea behind all three of these proceedings was to enable validity challenges to proceed in an administrative-law forum that would be cheaper and speedier than litigation in federal district court. (All three types of proceedings are supposed to terminate within at most two years from the challenger's filing of the petition requesting the institution of such a proceeding. Infringement cases that proceed to trial take, on average, a little under two and a half years to judgment—an average that has gone up a bit in recent years, probably due in part to judges staying infringement litigation pending the outcome of an administrative validity challenge.[90]) First, a person can request a PGR (which is similar to a proceeding known in many countries as an "opposition") to challenge the validity of a patent on any applicable ground—subject matter, novelty, whatever— but only within nine months from the date the patent issued. The PTAB will then "institute" the proceeding (that is, permit it to proceed to trial before a panel of administrative law judges) if it finds that the petitioner has made a prima facie case that at least one claim is invalid.[91] More popular so far among challengers, however, are IPRs, which can be requested at any time after the nine-month window for a PGR has passed.[92] Again the challenger must present a prima face case that at least one claim is invalid, though unlike with PGRs the only applicable grounds for challenging validity are novelty and nonobviousness, and only on the basis of previously issued patents or printed publications. The third type of proceeding, a CBM, is only available to challenge the validity of "covered business method patents," which the AIA defines as patents claiming "a method or corresponding apparatus for performing data processing or other operations used in the practice, administration, or management of a financial product or service, except that the term does not include patents for technological inventions."[93] A person can request a CBM only after having been sued for or charged with infringement, but as with PGRs the challenger can raise any validity arguments, including lack of patentable subject matter.[94] The AIA designated CBMs (but not PGRs and IPRs) as a "transitional" program that would end after eight years, though Congress has considered extending their authorization further out.

The legal standards surrounding these new proceedings are evolving, complex, and controversial—and for the most part beyond the scope of a book like this intended for a general audience. Suffice it to say, though, that requests for the institution of IPRs and CBMs have exceeded expectations. And while it may not be fair to call them "death squads," since the USPTO denies a substantial plurality of requests to institute review, and another plurality settles either before or after institution,[95] those that proceed to trial pretty much can expect the worst. According to the USPTO's statistics, over 80 percent of instituted IPR petitions that proceed to trial result in invalidation of some or all of the challenged claims; and over 80 percent of the instituted claims that the USPTO classifies as "electrical/computer" and that proceed to trial are invalidated or disclaimed by the patent owners. For CBM petitions that proceeded to trial, 97 percent so far have been invalidated in whole or in part, with lack of patentable subject matter a ground in close to half of these invalidations.[96]

Similarly, for those cases that are litigated in federal district court, *Alice* appears to be having a significant impact on judges' willingness to invalidate patents on subject matter grounds. According to Silicon Valley litigator Robert Sachs, who has been keeping track of the relevant case law on his firm's "Bilski Blog," as of April 30, 2017, federal district courts had granted more than 60 percent of dispositive motions to invalidate claims on section 101 grounds, with (according to Sachs's earlier updates) software and business method patents the most common targets.[97]

Meanwhile, as of that date the Federal Circuit had rejected section 101 challenges in only eight out eighty-eight appeals.[98] One of them involved diagnostic methods and is mentioned in the notes to Chapter 4. The remaining seven involve either business methods or software, and for present purposes I'll focus on two of them, *DDR Holdings, LLC v. Hotels.Com, L.P.* and *Enfish, LLC v. Microsoft Corp.*, to see what sufficed to salvage these patents from invalidation.[99] *DDR Holdings* involved a patent on a system that, upon "activation of a hyperlink on a host website—such as an advertisement for a third-party merchant—instead of taking the visitor to the merchant's website . . . generates and directs the visitor to a composite web page that displays product information from the third-party merchant, but retains the host website's 'look and feel.'"[100] This invention, the majority held, was patent-eligible because the claims didn't "merely recite the performance of some business practice known from the pre-Internet world along with the requirement to perform it on the Internet," or "broadly and generically claim 'use of the Internet' to perform an abstract business practice."[101] As for *Enfish*, the claims recited a "self-referential" model of arranging data for a computer database, by including all of the relevant "data entities in a single table, with column definitions provided by rows in that same table."[102] Noting that the model's design "disclose[d] an indexing technique that allows for faster searching of data than would be possible with" more conventional models, and "allow[ed] for more effective storage of data" and greater "flexibility in configuring the database," the court viewed the claims as being directed not to abstract ideas "for which computers are invoked merely as a tool," but rather to "an improvement in computer functionality itself"—that is, the sort of thing that even the *Alice* Court conceded would remain patent-eligible.[103] Much more common, however, were cases like *Planet Bingo, LLC v. VKGS, LLC*, in which the court concluded that claims reciting a program "used for the generic functions of storing, retrieving, and verifying a chosen set of bingo numbers against a winning set of bingo numbers" involved nothing more than an abstract idea and "purely conventional" steps to be performed by a computer.[104]

Suffice to say that software and business method patents may not be dead, but it clearly is much more difficult to obtain and maintain them than it was as recently as ten or even five years ago. Cases like *Enfish* also suggest that in some ways US practice is converging with that of the EPO, which has long required software and business method claims to demonstrate a technical solution to a technical problem.[105] At the end of the day, maybe this isn't such a bad standard—though if indeed this is where US law too ultimately comes to rest, it might be helpful if the courts and the USPTO stopped speaking in terms of undefinable abstract ideas, and came up with a workable definition of "technical" or "technology." (For what it's worth, building on others' proposed definitions I've previously suggested that an invention is technological if it harnesses the forces of nature in some stable, predictable, and reproducible manner to achieve a practical end result.[106]) Or perhaps it would it have been more sensible simply for Congress or the Supreme Court to say that business methods and software are per se unpatentable, rather than to chip away at them one at a time—though, as I've suggested earlier, such an approach raises its own difficult definitional questions and risks weeding out some useful innovations for which, conceivably, the existence of the patent incentive might have proved crucial. Consequently, I'm inclined to think that a vigorous nonobviousness doctrine coupled with meaningful restrictions on overly "functional" claiming would have been preferable both to categorically excluding software and business methods and to the current, almost-but-not-quite-categorical, approach that emerges from *Alice*. Whether I'm right or not, though, it's clear that US practice as it relates to these types of inventions has changed enormously within a relatively short time frame, from being one of the most permissive in the world to one of the strictest. For better or worse, for many business and software-related inventions patentability now appears to be nothing more than an abstract idea.

6

Drugs

When I began writing this chapter in the fall of 2016, there were days on which national media coverage would shift from its obsessive focus on the bizarre US presidential campaign to another subject that at times could appear almost equally surreal: the price of prescription drugs, for which Americans were expected to spend $328 billion in 2016 alone.[1] In August 2016, for example, US Senator Amy Klobuchar made national headlines with her call for a public hearing and investigation into Mylan N.V.'s decision to raise the list price of the EpiPen injectable epinephrine device, which retailed for $100 or less in 2007, to $609.[2] In September, the *Wall Street Journal* devoted a front-page story to how Sovaldi and other new drugs—which can eliminate hepatitis C entirely in over 90 percent of patients, but carry a list price of $54,000 to $94,000 per person for a twelve-week regimen—were threatening to bust the budgets of several state prison systems. (Seventeen percent or more of state prison inmates are believed to carry the disease.)[3] Other coverage focused on the list price, amounting to tens of thousands of dollars annually, for certain new cancer drugs[4] and biologics (biologics are a type of complex molecule) used for treating severe inflammatory diseases;[5] and these stories were hardly isolated instances. Even before the EpiPen dustup, both the US Senate and the House of Representatives had held public hearings on drug prices,[6] with much of the testimony focusing on two companies in particular—Valeant Pharmaceuticals, which since 2010 more than quintupled the price of certain drugs it acquired from other firms;[7] and Turing Pharmaceuticals, which in 2014 acquired marketing rights to Daraprim (a drug used for treating toxoplasmosis) and immediately raised the price from $13.50 to $750 a pill.[8] (Few people shed a tear when Turing's former CEO, a thirty-two-year-old hedge fund manager named Martin Shkreli, was arrested and charged with an unrelated count of securities fraud involving a different firm.)[9]

Since then, although Mylan and some other drug companies have tempered their price hikes a bit in the wake of adverse publicity, the overall picture hasn't changed much. According to a report published in February 2017 by Express Scripts, a large pharmacy benefits management organization, from January 2008 to December 2016 "the average price for the most commonly used [prescription] brand-name drugs" rose 208 percent, while the consumer price index during that time rose only 14 percent.[10] One year earlier DRX, a firm that publishes comparative pricing information, reported that, based on "a survey of about 3,000 prescription drugs . . . prices more than doubled for 60 and at least quadrupled for 20 since 2014," and that "about 400 formulations of brand-name drugs went up at least 9.9 percent since early December" 2014;[11] and in 2014 the US Centers for Medicare and Medicaid Services estimated that prescription drug spending would increase at an annual 6.3 percent rate from 2016 through 2025.[12] How, if at all, the Republican Congress's effort, unsuccessful as of July 2017, to replace the Affordable Care Act ("Obamacare") might impact this trend remains to be seen, but few if any analysts anticipate a substantial decrease in the growth rate, let alone a reversal, anytime soon.

Whether you were familiar with any of the above stories before now, if you happen to reside, or at some point in your life have resided in, the United States, you probably already have first-hand knowledge of how complicated and expensive the US health care system can be. And if you've ever lived for an extended period of time in, say, Canada or Western Europe or Japan, you may have first-hand experience of how much *less* complicated and expensive health care typically is in those places, by way of comparison. The EpiPen, for example, still retails for about $100 in Europe, where there are several competing brands of epinephrine autoinjectors, and in Canada.[13] Daraprim costs 66 cents a pill in the UK.[14] And as for health care generally, the United States spends about $10,000 per person as of 2017—approximately twice as much as other developed countries.[15] To be sure, the US system also has much to be proud of. For one thing, the quality of health care available to those who can afford or otherwise have access to it is extremely high: for example, although US life expectancy in 2016 fell slightly, at 78.6 it remains a full three years higher than it was just thirty years ago;[16] many diseases and conditions that would have killed people only a few decades ago are now curable; and while others (such as AIDS) remain for now incurable, many patients are able to live long, productive lives with the assistance of newer and better therapeutics. Moreover, much of the research and development that results in new drugs and methods of treatment is done at American research universities or by drug companies that either are headquartered or that have substantial presences here.[17] And even when it comes to prescription drug prices, the news isn't all bad. According to Express Scripts, generic (that is, nonpatented) drugs comprise over 85 percent of all filled prescriptions, and the average price of generics decreased by almost 75 percent from 2008 through 2016.[18]

And yet the negatives are all too apparent as well. Health care costs not only continue to increase, but often are enormously higher than what patients and insurers in other developed countries pay; at the same time, these higher costs don't translate into a longer life expectancy at birth than is enjoyed by residents of Canada, Japan, and much of Europe.[19] Indeed, except for the absence of any redeeming humor, the manner in which drugs and health care services in the United States are priced can sometimes seem like something dreamed up by a Kafka or an Ionesco–as described by *New York Times* reporter Elisabeth Rosenthal in her 2013 series on US health care, "products can simply disappear and prices for vital medicines can fluctuate far more than they do for a carton of milk."[20] The obvious question is why US consumers pay so much more for health care: is patent law the principal culprit, or are there other reasons?

I'll argue in this chapter that, although patents clearly do play a role in raising health care costs—particularly the cost of prescription drugs—their impact is offset to some degree by substantial countervailing benefits (though I believe that policymakers could do more to rein in some of the price impact without materially impacting incentives). Furthermore, it's clear that patents aren't the only reason for the high cost of prescription drugs, let alone for health care costs generally. Canada, Japan, the UK, and the member states of the European Union (EU) all confer patent protection on drugs, too, after all; and while Americans spend over $300 billion on prescription drugs every year, this (admittedly very large) number accounts for only about 10–15 percent of total health care spending in the United States.[21] Moreover, as noted above 85 percent of pre-scription drugs are generics—and these include some of the drugs at issue in the vignettes that led off this chapter. (Daraprim, for example, went off-patent many years ago, while epinephrine was first synthesized in 1906. Meridian Medical Technologies, which licenses the exclusive marketing and distribution rights to the EpiPen to Mylan, holds four patents on features of its injection device, how-ever.)[22] Much of the blame for high drug and other health care costs therefore is attributable not to patents, but to other aspects of the legal environment, in-cluding (at times) lax antitrust enforcement and a regulatory system that is ripe for gaming. I'll discuss some of these issues at the end of the chapter.

From Research to Marketplace

Initially, though, it may be helpful to understand a bit more about how prescrip-tion drugs get to the market in the first place.[23] The process starts with basic research, such as the identification of a "target" gene or protein associated with a disease. Much, perhaps most, of this basic research takes place in universities and other nonprofit institutions, and is funded in whole or in part by the fed-eral government, often by an agency known as the National Institutes of Health (NIH). Identification in turn may lead to further "validation" studies, which if promising may motivate applied research to discover a new drug to act against the target. (Traditionally this work has centered on studying small molecules, which form the active ingredients of most prescription drugs, though in recent years a growing percentage of it has involved biologics.) This discovery process often involves screening hundreds, thousands, or even millions of compounds; modifying some of them, for example to reduce toxicity; and if all goes well, identifying one or more "candidates" for preclinical (nonhuman) testing, for example on mice. Although NIH funding sometimes covers applied as well as basic research (and the lines between the two are not always entirely clear), private industry undertakes or funds much of the study of drug candidates and provides the majority of funding in the United States for preclinical studies. Overall, for-profit firms fund about 70 percent and nonprofit entities about 30 percent of the entire process, from basic research through the end of clinical trials discussed below.

Next, if a particular drug candidate shows promise at the preclinical stage, it's likely that the sponsoring drug or biotech company will begin the process of seeking approval from the US Food and Drug Administration (FDA) to market the drug to the public. It's also likely that the inventors will apply for a patent, which poses two questions we should stop to consider before moving on. The first is ownership. In the United States, if the inventors are employees of a private firm that self-funded the applied research resulting in the invention, their employment contracts almost certainly require them to assign their rights to their employer (e.g., a drug or biotech company). The same is likely true if the inventors are employees of a university or research institution. To the extent the applied research was funded in whole or in part by the federal government, however, the rule at one time was that ownership of any inventions resulting from that research vested in the federal government, rather than in the university or research institution that employed the inventors. Congress overturned this rule in the 1980s by enacting legislation (the Bayh-Dole Act and the Stevenson-Wydler Technology Innovation Act) that now enables the recipients of federal funding to obtain patent protection. The reason for the change was the perception that the federal government often was not well-positioned to exploit or license such inventions itself, and that (even though taxpayers already had funded the research that led to the inventions' development) patents would serve the public interest by encouraging universities and other research institutions to *commercialize* them, typically by licensing or assigning rights to others. (The "other" may be a start-up founded by the researchers themselves or an unrelated entity such as a drug company.)[24] By most accounts, Bayh-Dole and Stevenson-Wydler have largely succeeded in facilitating the commercialization of drugs and other inventions resulting from taxpayer-funded research. (The Acts' impact with regard to the commercialization of other fields of technology may be positive as well, though some observers have questioned the extent to which this is so.)[25]

The second patent-related issue to consider at this point is one of timing. As you may recall from Chapter 1, you can apply for a patent at a fairly early stage in the process—long before you've had an opportunity to conclude all of the clinical studies on safety and effectiveness as described below—though not *too* early, that is, before you can identify a specific and substantial use for the claimed invention. (When researchers *do* jump the gun, and apply before they have a sufficient basis for believing that the compound will work to achieve its intended purpose, the patent application is subject to rejection on utility, written description, or enablement grounds.)[26] As it turns out, the preclinical stage is usually when the inventors have enough information to file a patent application, and they certainly don't want to wait any longer than is necessary.

As you also know from Chapter 1, however, just having a patent doesn't mean that you yourself can make, use, or sell the patented invention. The present situation illustrates the point, because whether you have a patent or not you can't start selling a drug until the FDA is convinced that it is safe and effective, and the FDA's standard for evaluating effectiveness is (by design) substantially higher than the USPTO's. Thus, if a drug candidate looks promising as a result of the preclinical research described above, the next step toward obtaining FDA approval is to file something called an Investigational New Drug (IND) application. The IND will describe the preclinical studies, the indications (uses) for which the preclinical studies suggest the drug may be effective, and the clinical trials the applicant intends to perform to further investigate the drug's safety and efficacy. Assuming that the FDA gives the go-ahead to proceed with the proposed clinical trials, the first round (Phase I) typically involves administering the drug to a small number of healthy volunteers over the course of a few months, to test such matters as safety and dosage. (Volunteers for clinical trials are usually compensated, and the conditions of their participation first must be approved by the testing institution's Institutional Review Board [IRB]. The number of clinical trials each year is staggering: government website ClinicalTrials.gov lists over 260,000 studies since 2000, including over 90,000 in the United States.[27]) Estimates vary concerning how many drugs that are the subject of an IND transition from Phase I to Phase II, with the FDA reporting 70 percent and other studies reporting lower figures.[28]

Phase II involves administering the drug to a larger group of subjects who have a particular disease or condition for a period of a few months up to two years, to assist in evaluating the drug's effectiveness and any side effects. Between 20 and 33 percent of the drugs that make it to Phase II then proceed on to Phase III,[29] which typically consists of at least two large-scale trials lasting for one to four years and involving hundreds or thousands of volunteers. (Phase III trials normally are randomized controlled trials [RCTs], meaning that there will be a control group that doesn't take the drug or that takes a placebo, to enable a meaningful statistical assessment of the drug's likely effects. Testing also is usually double-blind, meaning that neither the participant nor the administering entity knows whether the participant is receiving the drug or a placebo.) According to the FDA, about 25–30 percent of Phase III trials are successful, though some other estimates are lower (about 10 percent).[30] If the Phase III trials are successful, the sponsor will file a New Drug Application (NDA) or, for biologics, a Biologic License Application (BLA), basically a petition asking the FDA to approve the drug for marketing. The FDA then subjects the NDA or BLA to internal review, and though it can–and sometimes does–deny an application outright, more often if the agency has questions or concerns it will require further testing or clarification as a condition of approval. According to one recent study, the FDA ultimately approves about 86 percent of NDAs/BLAs.[31] Once the drug is approved, it's listed, along with any "related patent and exclusivity information," in the FDA's publicly accessible "Orange Book."[32]

All of this testing takes time and money, of course. As for time, it's been estimated that on average it takes eight years or more from the submission of the IND to approval of the NDA,[33] which means that once a drug is approved for marketing several years of patent protection probably already have elapsed. To provide the drug company with an opportunity to recoup its investment, federal law permits patent term extensions of up to five years to compensate for time spent in clinical studies and for securing FDA approval.[34] In addition, the Food Drug and Cosmetic Act (FDCA) provides sponsoring firms with various terms of exclusivity independent of patent law, though if the drug is patented this FDCA-mandated exclusivity normally expires before the patent does. For example, if the NDA covers a "new chemical entity" (NCE), generic drug manufacturers cannot apply for permission to market a generic equivalent of the drug for five years (four if the generic firm plans to challenge patent validity or infringement) following approval of the NDA.[35] (I'll have more to say about generic drugs shortly, and about other FDCA exclusivities later in the chapter.)

As for money, according to a recent note published in the *Journal of the American Medical Association*, the NIH and other US agencies fund less than 10 percent of clinical studies registered on the ClinicalTrials.gov website. Drug and biotech firms fund about 36 percent, while a category denominated "all others," which includes "non-US governmental agencies, organizations, universities, and other funders, mainly from outside the United States," fund the remainder.[36] However funded, the clinical studies themselves nevertheless are usually undertaken by universities and other research institutions, often after an intermediary organization known as a contract research organization (CRO) hooks up a particular drug company with a particular institution for purposes of conducting the clinical trials. The fact that drug companies fund such a large percentage of trials sometimes has given cause for concern, since the companies presumably want the drug to be approved and the recipients know this. A few years ago, drug companies' alleged manipulation of the clinical studies leading up to the approval of Vioxx and Avandia (both of which wound up being pulled from the market due to serious side effects) led to calls for greater transparency regarding study protocols and test results.[37] In September 2016, the FDA promulgated stricter regulations for the registration of clinical studies on ClinicalTrials.gov.

But how much money are we talking about? Here's where things get a bit sticky. Drug companies that are members of the industry trade association PhRMA claim that they spend more than $51 billion, or about 18 percent of their sales revenue, on research (including both preclinical and clinical studies) annually.[38] And this may well be true: as noted above, the clinical studies alone can involve thousands of participants, and millions of people have participated in them. On the other hand, drug companies have resisted calls for the public disclosure of their specific research and development costs, and this lack of transparency has made the academic study of drug company R&D challenging.[39] By far the best known studies are those published by DiMasi, Grabowski, and Hansen (DGH) under the auspices of the Tufts Center for the Study of Drug Development (CSDD). (The CSDD receives funding from major drug companies.) The authors' methodology, as described in their most recent (2016) study, involves the analysis of data provided by "a confidential survey of . . . new drug and biologics R&D costs" incurred through 2013 by "[t]en multinational pharmaceutical firms of varying sizes."[40] In particular, the authors obtained a sample of 106 investigational compounds drawn from a population of 1,442 investigational drugs and biologics in the CSDD database. All of the sampled compounds were "self-originated" in the sense that "[t]heir development and synthesis up to initial regulatory marketing approval was conducted under the auspices of the surveyed firm," and they consisted of eighty-seven NCEs and nineteen new biologic entities (NBEs) for which the initial clinical testing began during the period 1995–2007.[41]

The goal of this and the authors' previous studies is to estimate the drug companies' average cost per approved, self-originated NCE/NBE, from the synthesis or isolation of the compound through the completion of Phase III trials.* To understand their methodology, consider the following hypothetical.

---

* Just to be clear, the authors estimate the cost the drug companies incur beginning with drug discovery, defined here as "the point of compound synthesis or isolation," with "discovery and preclinical development costs . . . grouped and referred to as pre-human costs." *id.* at 21–22 and n.5. The authors explain how they estimated these pre-human costs at pages A.4 to A.5 of the study's appendix A, available at http://ars.els-cdn.com/content/image/1-s2.0-S0167629616000291-mmc1.docx.

(I'll get to the real numbers shortly, but I think this simple example will make matters a bit easier to understand.) First, for drugs entering Phase I, suppose that the cost incurred from synthesis or isolation through the completion of pre-human testing is $10 million. Second, suppose that there is a fifty-fifty chance of transitioning from Phase I to Phase II and from Phase II to Phase III, and that the overall probability of completing Phase III is exactly 25 percent. Finally, suppose that the average cost incurred in Phase I is $10 million; in Phase II, $50 million; and in Phase III, $100 million. In isolation, the out-of-pocket cost for developing the one drug in four that completes Phase III and is approved is $10 million (pre-human testing) + $10 million (Phase I) + $50 million (Phase II) + $100 million (Phase III) = $170 million. However, if the hypothetical drug company were to earn "only" $170 million from sales of this drug, it would go out of business, because its overall costs, including the costs of developing the three duds, was $280 million. The average out-of-pocket cost per *approved* drug, therefore, would be $280 million. In addition, if you wanted to measure these costs as an economist would, you'd take into account the time value of money. For example, if it takes on average four years to proceed through Phase III, and assuming for the sake of simplicity that you incur the associated $100 million cost on Day 1 of that phase, for the duration of Phase III you've tied up $100 million that you could have invested somewhere else. If you could have earned 10 percent simple interest annually on that $100 million, the real cost of Phase III is $140 million, not $100 million. The $40 million you didn't earn but could have is what economists refer to as "opportunity cost." Add that to the $280 million out-of-pocket cost, and you have a grand total of $320 million per approved drug.

Applying the methodology just described to the *actual* cost, time, and probability data DGH derive from information provided by the drug companies and from public domain information, the authors report in their 2016 paper that (1) the average out-of-pocket, pre-human testing cost per approved drug from synthesis or isolation was $430 million; (2) the average out-of-pocket clinical testing cost per approved drug was $965 million; and (3) a total cost per approved drug, including an opportunity cost premised on the assumption that the drug companies could have earned a 10.5 percent rate of return from other investments during the relevant time period, was $2.558 billion.[42] If these figures are accurate, they indicate that the drug companies need to earn at least $2.558 billion per approved NCE or NBE to make it worth their while to continue investing in the development of these types of drugs.

Actually, the figures don't *quite* mean that. Much of the expense incurred would be tax deductible, and the resulting tax deductions would reduce the real costs incurred by the drug companies for the investment; so unless there are other substantial costs omitted from consideration a pretax expenditure of

$2.558 billion almost surely overstates the actual average cost of developing a drug. Critics have noted this point,[43] though DGH are clear that they are reporting only pretax expenditures. They also argue that trying to estimate the after-tax expenditure would have been enormously complex, given that tax rates differ over time and jurisdiction.[44] Of course, even if we assume, arbitrarily, that tax deductibility reduces the actual cost by, say, one-third or even one-half, we still have an average cost per approved drug of more than a billion dollars, assuming that the rest of the analysis is sound.

But is the rest of the analysis sound? Aside from the tax issue, criticisms have taken two principal forms. First and foremost is the fact that the data on which the analysis is based are confidential, which means that other researchers don't have access to, and therefore can't replicate, the authors' estimates. Two studies published by Federal Trade Commission economists in 2006 and 2010, however, have applied DGH's methodology to publicly available information about drug development costs (culled from "press releases, academic presentations, and other public information about drugs in development"), and came up with estimates that actually were somewhat higher than DGH's.[45] In addition, DGH present details on their own "validation efforts," based on publicly available information, which they claim show that their estimates are "if anything, conservative."[46] Still and all, and without casting any aspersions on the integrity of the DGH research team, without the underlying data their findings must be taken with a grain of salt.

Second, some commentators have leveled more technical criticisms (including the tax issue noted above) against the DGH papers, some more persuasive than others. One critique is that the authors shouldn't have included the time value of money in their calculation, because if a drug company "doesn't invest in research and development, it won't be a drug company anymore."[47] The assertion may be true, but it doesn't negate the need for an accurate cost estimate to include opportunity cost. (Whether the drug companies should be compensated for their opportunity cost—or for any other costs, for that matter—is another issue, as is any debate over the 10.5 percent rate of return on alternative options.) Another criticism is that the study's focus on self-originated NCEs and NBEs may not be representative of the cost of developing drugs *generally*, inasmuch as the cost of basic research often is undertaken by the NIH and other public-sector funders rather than by drug companies. (Moreover, research by Ashley et al. shows that, for a large portion of important drug discoveries over the past several decades, the public sector has played a more meaningful role than the drug companies in funding the applied research as well.[48]) Critics also note that the majority of applications submitted to the FDA are not for NCEs and NBEs, but rather for such things as new uses of, or variations on, existing drugs, for which development costs are likely to be much lower.[49] DGH's studies do make it clear, however, that the authors are estimating the average cost per approved, self-originated NCE/NBE, and not the average cost of approved drugs generally. To be fair to the critics, though, public statements from the drug companies' trade association, PhRMA, to the effect that the "average cost to develop one new approved drug—including the cost of failures" is $2.6 billion,[50] don't exactly highlight those nuances.

The bottom line is that we really don't know how much drug and biotech companies spend to bring new drugs to the market—though it's probably fair to assume that for newly discovered molecules, the cost is (at least) somewhere in the hundreds of millions of dollars, including the offsetting effects of the time cost of money and the value of tax deductions and credits. It's also fair to assume that, while not every new drug or biologic is "self-originated" as defined above, some are, while others are funded at least in substantial part by drug and biotech firms. Finally, it's reasonable to assume that the drug and biotech firms aren't willing to fund this activity out of the goodness of their hearts. Thus, if we think that society benefits from the discovery and commercialization of new drugs, we need some mechanism to encourage firms to keep at it; and patents are one obvious tool for achieving this goal. Indeed, as I've mentioned before, most innovation economists view the pharmaceutical industry as the paradigm example for which patents (or some other method of social assistance) are crucial, given the high costs of invention (whatever they actually turn out to be) and the comparative ease of copying (as discussed in the next section). Seen in this light, when drug companies deploy patents to charge monopoly prices, the patent system is working as intended, because the expectation of monopoly pricing presumably is what lures companies into bearing the R&D costs from which the public ultimately benefits. Put another way, if any industry needs patent protection, it's the drug industry; and while it may be burdensome (or worse) if drug companies charge monopoly prices in exchange for life-saving drugs, it's better than not having the drug developed at all, or having it developed much later in time.

Nevertheless, the fact that patents may encourage the development of new drugs doesn't necessarily mean they're the only, or even the best, policy tool for achieving this result. As discussed in earlier chapters, some economists think that prizes might work better than patents under some circumstances—though probably the strongest case for prizes is for neglected diseases for which market demand is low, a matter to be discussed in more detail in Chapter 7.[51] And even if patents are in general better than other alternatives for encouraging the development of new drugs, the optimal policy may not be to permit patent owners to charge whatever the market will bear under any and all circumstances. Public utilities, for example, often are viewed as a type of "natural" monopoly, because permitting a single firm to provide electricity to a given locale may avoid the need for inefficiently duplicative infrastructure, and are subject to price regulation for this reason.[52] Of course, not all drug patents confer monopoly power, and drug companies are not natural monopolies in the preceding sense. Nevertheless, some form of price regulation—whether direct price regulation of some sort or, as in many countries, the adoption of a single-payer health care system in which government negotiates the price of all prescription drugs[53]—in principle could both preserve the incentive to develop (and patent) new drugs while reducing the ability of drug companies to charge substantially more than is necessary to recoup their investment. In a related vein, Brennan et al. recently proposed that the US government could make greater use of an already-existing federal statute, 28 USC § 1498, which allows the government and government contractors to use patented inventions subject only to an obligation to pay fair market value (essentially, a court-determined reasonable royalty).[54]

To be sure, one potentially serious drawback of any such reform is that it would put future innovation at risk because the relevant government actors— lacking sufficient information about costs and benefits, or sensitive to political pressure, as the case may be—might set prices too low to adequately compensate patent holders for their investments. (This is also one of the most frequently stated concerns about the compulsory licensing of patented inventions, something that we'll come back to in Chapter 7.) Any such system therefore would have to be carefully designed and administered to ensure that the risk of negative consequences is remote. But maybe some experimentation along these lines would be worthwhile; as drug company critics are quick to point out, after all, profits earned by the major drug companies are consistently among the highest of any industry,[55] and drug companies' marketing expenditures routinely exceed the amounts they claim to spend on R&D.[56] And when profits from the sale of a given drug substantially exceed even the $2.6 billion figure PhRMA touts as the cost of bringing a new drug to market, as those profits sometimes do, it's a bit hard to credit concerns that a price cap would materially depress incentives. In their proposal for the expanded use of § 1498, for example, Brennan et al. notes that the sales revenue *already realized* from the sale of the new drugs for treating hepatitis C exceeds $36 billion. They argue that future sales of the drugs would still be profitable at a price of less than $1,000 for a course of treatment, given its low production costs; and that such a drastic price reduction (from a current actual price of up to $90,000) would constitute a tremendous gain for consumer welfare.[57]

Alternatively, there may be ways that policymakers could modify patent law itself to rein in the price of prescription drugs—though to my mind, some of these solutions are potentially more problematic than a carefully designed single-payer system would be. For example, yet another frequently heard criticism of the drug companies is that much of the research they undertake is devoted to copycat or "me-too" drugs that are only marginally better, if at all, than existing alternatives.[58] (By "me-too drugs," by the way, I don't mean "generic," that is, nonpatented, drugs. "Me-too" drugs perform much the same function as an existing drug but may be covered by their own patents. Think Viagra and Cialis, for example.) In a perfect market, of course, a product that's no better than other, unpatented alternatives wouldn't be able to command any price, let alone a monopoly price, above the marginal cost of production. Therefore, if me-too drugs command a premium, it must be either because (1) they actually do offer some benefits over alternatives for some subset of patients, for reasons suggested in Chapter 4's discussion of personalized medicine; or (2) the market is sufficiently imperfect, perhaps due in part to advertising or other peculiar features of the US health care system discussed later in this chapter, that drug companies are able to sell me-too drugs above marginal cost despite their lack of benefits over comparable products.[59] My own guess, though that's all it is, is that the truth lies somewhere in-between—which, if true, would render other proposed solutions, such as a heightened utility or nonobviousness requirement to screen out drugs that offer few new benefits, potentially overbroad.[60] Instead, proposals to limit *insurance* coverage of me-too drugs absent compelling evidence that they work better for some subset of patients—something that, as noted later in this chapter, often isn't done today in the United States—might work better, since they wouldn't require anyone (such as a patent examiner) to indulge in potentially fallible speculation about the effects of a drug far in advance of clinical testing.

Finally, it's worth noting that, despite its many imperfections, patent law already operates to reduce patent owners' ability to extract supracompetitive profits under certain circumstances. As we've already seen, disclosure doctrines prevent firms from patenting an entire class of compounds beyond what they can describe and enable.[61] For better or worse, the Supreme Court has limited the patentability of diagnostic methods and human genes, while Congress has restricted owners of surgical procedure patents from enforcing them against medical practitioners.[62] In addition, something called the doctrine of "double patenting" operates to prevent drug companies from patenting obvious variations over their own previously patented drugs,[63] while the doctrine of inherency precludes drug companies from stringing out protection by patenting metabolites which the body naturally produces upon ingestion of a prior art drug.[64] (As we'll see in the next section, though, another body of law, antitrust, sometimes can play a role in this space as well, since neither inherency nor double patenting entirely eliminates firms' ability to hold on to their customer base by patenting relatively minor variations over existing drugs—practices known as "evergreening" or "product hopping.") Finally, while the practice (largely unknown outside the United States) of permitting patent owners to file continuations—separate applications for variations derived from an initial "parent" application—in the past may have contributed to evergreening, amendments passed early in the

2000s have to a large extent limited drugmakers' ability to use continuations to ward off generic competition.[65] Thus, while in many instances patents may enable firms to charge prices that are substantially higher than necessary to recoup their R&D, at least in other respects patent law plays a positive role in dampening potential negative effects.

To recap where we are so far, then, I've argued that the cost of bringing new drugs to market is very high, even if the drugs that form the basis of DGH's $2.6 billion estimate are not representative of the whole. Unless we figure out some other way to stimulate investment in the development of new drugs, therefore, patent protection remains crucial; and patent law itself keeps in check at least some of the social costs of having a patent system. In addition, it's important to keep in mind that drugs account for only 10–15 percent of US health care spending (which is still a lot of money, to be sure); and, as we'll see shortly, drug *patents* aren't always the reason for high drug *prices*. That said, at the end of the day US consumers pay a lot more for prescription drugs than do consumers in other countries; and our disinclination thus far to regulate drug prices surely plays a role in enabling this state of affairs to persist. Finally, while I don't want to be understood as accusing drug companies of being nothing more than greedy actors who exploit hapless consumers, drug companies sometimes have contributed to the problem in various ways, including by violating the antitrust laws. It is to this subject that we now turn.

Generic Drugs and Antitrust Law

Figuring out how to make a generic (bioequivalent) copy of a patented drug normally isn't too difficult or time-consuming for experienced generic drug manufacturers,[66] so once the patent expires you'd expect them to enter the market with lower priced alternatives to brand-name drugs. If generic firms also had to conduct clinical studies, however, to prove that their drugs were safe and effective, they would be faced with a serious dilemma: how would they recoup the cost of those studies without having patents of their own to protect them from competition? Fortunately, the 1984 Hatch-Waxman Act enables the maker of a bioequivalent drug to bypass this requirement by relying on the brand-name firm's clinical studies to prove safety and effectiveness. (The application filed by the generic firm is called an Abbreviated New Drug Applications [ANDA] because it can rely on the existing clinical studies as described in the brand-name firm's NDA. To give the brand-name firm some time to recoup its costs, however, potential generic competitors have to wait at least four years from the date of NDA approval.)[67] In addition, the maker of the generic drug must certify that the generic won't infringe any Orange Book–listed patent covering the brand-name drug, or that any such patent (if there is one) is invalid. To further encourage generic firms to file ANDAs, Hatch-Waxman also provides that the first generic firm to obtain FDA approval is entitled to 180 days of exclusivity from *other* generic firms.[68]

(Under the Biologics Price Competition and Innovation Act of 2009, there is an analogous pathway for the approval of "biosimilars"—generic versions of biologics, the development of which is technologically much more demanding than the development of generic small-molecule drugs.[69] The legal framework, which courts only recently have begun to interpret, is also even more complicated than the framework under Hatch-Waxman. My discussion here will concentrate on Hatch-Waxman only.)

Two problems nevertheless can impede the speedy entry of generic drugs to the market. The first is that in recent years the number of ANDAs filed annually grew much faster than the number of FDA employees who review these applications, which led to a tremendous backlog of ANDAs. Legislation enacted in 2012, however, authorized the FDA to collect user fees from generic drug applicants to pay for, among other things, additional FDA personnel. As a result, the backlog has decreased substantially. [70] Going forward, the agency's goal is to complete the initial review of all newly submitted ANDAs within fifteen months; the agency also prioritizes applications for potential "first generic" drugs.

A second problem is that there are various ways in which brand-name firms can try to exclude potential generic competitors from the market, the legality of which often depends on how courts interpret and apply federal and state antitrust laws. As I mentioned in the Prologue, antitrust (or "competition" law, as it is often called abroad) is a body of law that, roughly speaking, is intended to keep markets competitive. In the United States, the principal federal statutes are the Sherman, Clayton, and Federal Trade Commission Acts, all of which were enacted more than a hundred years ago. The relevant language of all three statutes can sound rather vague. Section 1 of the Sherman Act, for example—the most important of the three statutes for our purposes—renders illegal "every contract, combination . . . or conspiracy, in restraint of trade," while section 2 condemns any person who "shall monopolize, or attempt to monopolize,"[71] but the statute never spells out what a "restraint of trade" is or what the term "monopolize" means. And when you think about it, every contract literally restrains (some) trade, and at least some patents confer monopoly power; but it would be a strange world in which antitrust law forbade all patents (what would be the point of granting them in the first place?), and an even stranger one in which it forbade all contracts. Fortunately, no one advocates for such a literal approach to the statute. Instead, the conventional view is that in passing the antitrust laws Congress in effect delegated to the courts the responsibility of developing a body of "common law"—that is, judge-made law—based on the gradual accumulation of more and better knowledge of the competitive impact of various types of transactions and combinations.[72]

(For some nonlawyers reading this, the idea that courts sometimes "make" law might seem, at best, surprising, and at worst like some radical plot to undermine democracy through judicial fiat. Actually, though, judges in the Anglo-American tradition for centuries have been, in effect, making law—including much of the common law of contracts, torts, and property—through articulating and adapting legal principles to the facts of individual cases. The debate today between liberal and conservative legal scholars, though sometimes presented for popular consumption as centering on the question of whether judges should or shouldn't "make" law, is often more about whether judges whenever possible should defer to the literal text or traditional understanding of constitutional and statutory provisions, or instead read those texts in view of the judges' understanding of their underlying purpose, society's evolving moral standards, or other such considerations. As far as antitrust law is concerned, though, even conservative textualists like the late Justice Antonin Scalia mostly have agreed that Congress intended for the courts to develop a common law of competition.)[73]

As matters played out, courts over time came to the conclusion that *certain* contracts, combinations, or conspiracies among firms are so likely to impede the workings of a competitive market, and so unlikely to have any redeeming *pro*competitive qualities, that these agreements should be considered "per se" illegal—meaning that the court will condemn them without any detailed inquiry into their actual purposes and effects. The clearest example is when two or more competing firms conspire to fix the prices they'll charge to buyers of their products. If the conspiring firms acting together have the ability to charge a higher price and produce fewer units of output than would be the case in a competitive market, the firms' behavior in the aggregate will approximate that of a profit-maximizing monopolist; and as we saw in Chapter 2, economic theory predicts that consumers' losses under such an arrangement will exceed the monopolist's gain, leaving both consumers and society as a whole worse off. Moreover, it's not likely that firms would agree to such an arrangement unless, collectively, they possessed the ability to set market prices and output, because otherwise their plan would be undercut by others who are not parties to the conspiracy; thus, the legal system conserves on adjudication costs by not bothering to inquire whether *in fact* the conspiring firms in the aggregate possessed market power. In addition, because courts view the policy behind the Sherman Act as one of promoting competition, the firms wouldn't get anywhere in court by arguing that they should be allowed to price-fix, because vigorous competition in their industry is a bad thing (perhaps because it makes the firms' employees work too hard or puts their jobs in jeopardy, or because the market can't efficiently sustain more than one or a small number of competitors due to economies of scale in production). Rather, if the argument to be made is that competition is undesirable in some particular setting, it's up to the advocates of that view to lobby Congress for an antitrust exemption. For good or for ill, depending on one's point of view, Congress on occasion has granted antitrust exemptions in whole or in part to entities including labor unions, the insurance industry, and major league baseball, but not to the drug industry.

Unlike agreements to fix prices, however, most contracts between firms are not per se illegal, but rather potentially would be subject to antitrust scrutiny under something called the Rule of Reason. To illustrate, suppose that two automobile manufacturers agree to form a joint venture—a partnership of sorts to achieve a specific, limited end—to design a new type of energy-efficient engine. For all other purposes, the two firms will remain independent; but for the purpose of developing the new engine the idea is that both will benefit from pooling money and talent. As part of the joint venture agreement, however, the firms agree not to individually develop a competing engine prototype, because (they say) doing so would undercut their motivation for working together. (I wouldn't agree to work with you on a project, after all, if I thought you were likely to keep your best ideas to yourself or to steal my ideas, and then beat me to the marketplace with your own product.) This hypothetical noncompete agreement is clearly a restraint of trade, of sorts, but it has at least a plausible procompetitive rationale, namely to encourage the firms to work together to create a new product that neither could achieve as efficiently on its own. Thus, if the government or a private entity were to challenge the noncompete as a violation of antitrust law, a court wouldn't condemn the agreement as per se illegal, but rather would consider its actual or likely effect on competition. And unless there was something odd about the agreement—say, the firms promised not to compete against each other in the market for automobiles, something that doesn't seem reasonably necessary to achieve the joint venture's purpose of developing a new engine— a court probably would conclude that the procompetitive benefits outweighed the potential for anticompetitive harm, and absolve the parties of liability.

Similarly, with respect to monopolization (the subject covered by section 2 of the Sherman Act), the courts have taken a less-than-literal approach. According to the Supreme Court's 1966 decision in *United States v. Grinnell Corp.*, section 2 doesn't forbid the mere possession of monopoly power, but rather "the willful acquisition or maintenance of that power as distinguished from growth or development as a consequence of a superior product, business acumen, or historic accident."[74] The basic idea is that section 2 forbids only predatory or exclusionary conduct—as, for example, when a monopolist (usually defined for present purposes as a firm with at least a 70 percent share of the relevant market) engages in "predatory pricing" by temporarily pricing below cost to drive would-be competitors from the market, in the expectation that it will be able to make up its losses down the road. Here again some version of the Rule of Reason often comes into play, since the monopolist's conduct might be ambiguous in terms of its purposes and effects. Charging a low price that potential competitors can't meet, for example, actually makes consumers better off in the short run, and only *eventually* makes them worse off if the structure of the market is such that the monopolist can absorb losses until its potential rivals are gone and thereafter raise prices to monopoly levels without attracting more would-be competitors (something that might be possible if there are substantial barriers to entry, such as regulatory obstacles, that would make it very costly for new firms to enter and compete). Moreover, it's possible that the monopolist's ability to charge lower prices is due to, say, greater efficiencies in production or use of superior technology, rather than to a scheme to drive out competitors. In order to determine whether the challenged conduct constitutes a violation of section 2, therefore, courts would need to closely consider the structure of the market, and whether the monopolist's justification for its conduct (if credible) outweighs the risks of long-run anticompetitive harm.

The preceding paragraph suggests three additional points worth noting before returning to the drug industry. The first is that, under contemporary antitrust law, the fact that conduct by a single firm or group of firms may harm other firms is not by itself reason to condemn the conduct, if at the same time it promises to make consumers better off. This was not always the case. At least for a period of time in the early to mid-twentieth century, the conventional wisdom as reflected in Supreme Court opinions and other sources was that antitrust was, to some degree, intended to promote "fair" competition by protecting small businesses from being undercut by larger competitors. Within antitrust law, there remains one outpost of this way of thinking known as the Robinson-Patman Act (actually part of the Clayton Act, as amended) which when applicable forbids some forms of price discrimination. For the most part, however, antitrust law has long since moved away from this protectionist stance toward a focus on consumer welfare. When a big firm like Wal-Mart (or Amazon) lowers its prices, for example, due to its superior distributional network, its ability to bargain with suppliers, or the wages it pays its employees, this may harm local mom-and-pop stores; but it isn't any concern of antitrust, absent proof of collusion with other competitors or conduct like predatory pricing, since consumers presumably benefit from the lower prices. (Consumers who might prefer not to shop at Wal-Mart due to its labor policies or its impact on local business are of course free to do so. The point is that antitrust doesn't make that decision for them, but rather lets the market—that is, consumers themselves—decide the matter; as noted above, it's not a good antitrust argument that say that competition, in this case from Wal-Mart, is bad in and of itself.) This change in antitrust jurisprudence, from a focus on competitors to a near-exclusive focus on consumers, was hastened by the rise to prominence of the so-called "Chicago School" of economics, which emphasized the benefits of free markets and less governmental intervention in the economy. (The term "Chicago School" derives from a group of economists and law professors who were particularly active at the University of Chicago during the 1960s and 1970s.) Chicago School economics began to influence the Supreme Court's antitrust case law in the 1970s, as well as the views of the antitrust enforcement agencies—the Antitrust Division of the Department of Justice (DOJ) and the Federal Trade Commission (FTC)—in the 1980s. For the most part, though, over the past generation economists on both the right and the left have come to agree that antitrust should focus on improving consumer welfare as opposed to the welfare of individual competitors; and while there are differences at the margin, the general consensus has been that antitrust should intervene in the market only when there is a sound basis in theoretical and empirical economics for predicting that a challenged practice will result in some combination of higher prices, lower output or quality, or less innovation. To the extent one believes that consumers are making unwise or uninformed decisions (say, in buying low-priced goods at Wal-Mart at the expense of the local hardware store or bodega), the remedy if there is to be one must lie outside of antitrust.[75]

A second point is that contemporary antitrust law is more concerned about ensuring that markets are reasonably competitive than it is about any particular outcome. As noted above, it's not an offense for a firm merely to possess monopoly power, as long as it acquired it monopoly by means of "a superior product, business acumen, or historic accident."[76] The implicit premise is that, as long as the monopolist is not deterring potential rivals through exclusionary or predatory behavior, it will only be a matter of time before one or more of those rivals succeeds in overthrowing today's monopoly. (Think back to the discussion of Schumpeter in Chapter 2.) Moreover, the goal of becoming a temporary monopolist may be what motivates firms to try harder to come up with newer and better products; on this view, for the law to penalize someone for succeeding would undermine the overarching goal of promoting consumer welfare. Relatedly, it follows that if it's not an antitrust violation merely to *be* a monopolist, it's also not a violation to *act* like a monopolist by charging a higher price and producing fewer units than one would expect to encounter in a market characterized by the presence of multiple firms. Put another way, it's not an antitrust violation for an otherwise lawful monopolist merely to charge a monopoly price. Judges generally like this rule, since it means that they don't have to determine what a "fair" price would be (something that they're not obviously well-positioned to do). So do most economists (including those on the left), principally on the ground that in competitive markets high prices signal opportunities for other firms to enter and compete. At the same time, none of this necessarily means that price regulation is always a bad idea. Governments generally do regulate the prices that may be charged by public utilities and other "natural" monopolies, for example, and as suggested above, I think it's possible that public health would improve if government to some degree regulated the price of prescription drugs. Any such regulation, however, would require careful implementation and would in any event exist outside of antitrust law, not within it.

A third point is that an invention (patented or not) for which there are no close substitutes is one type of "superior product" that may enable its owner lawfully to enjoy monopoly power. Indeed, as I've noted repeatedly, that's the whole *point* of patent law: to lure firms to invest in the creation, disclosure, and commercialization of new inventions in return for exclusive rights that may enable them temporarily to exercise monopoly power. Nevertheless, it's easy to see why people might view antitrust and patent law as diametrically opposite bodies of law—one promotes monopoly, while the other condemns it—and this perspective sometimes has informed the way in which the courts and agencies have approached certain practices and transactions involving patents (and copyrights too, for that matter). For a period of time in the mid-twentieth century, for example, the courts and agencies looked with suspicion on a wide range of patent- and copyright-related practices—including what a DOJ official memorably referred to in a 1970 speech as the "Nine No-No's," e.g., certain types of exclusive licenses and conditions on the use or resale of patented products.[77] This view of patents and antitrust as being in inherent tension nevertheless is a bit simplistic, since as we've seen most patents don't really confer monopoly power. More fundamentally, both bodies of law can be viewed as tools for improving consumer welfare: antitrust law by keeping markets competitive, and patent law by contributing to the innovation that makes consumers better off in the long run. (In this sense, patent law ideally promotes what economists refer to as "dynamic" or long-run consumer welfare, in contrast to the "static" or short-run consumer welfare that is impacted by the deadweight loss resulting from monopoly pricing. See Chapter 2.) This perspective is reflected in the *Antitrust Guidelines for the Licensing of Intellectual Property*, first published by the DOJ and FTC in 1995 and revised in 2017, which take the position that "the same general antitrust principles" apply "to conduct involving intellectual property that . . . apply to conduct involving any other form of property."[78] This is an improvement over the agencies' earlier perspective, but in turn it may be a bit simplistic too: there may be instances in which patent and antitrust law really *do* conflict, and the courts have to choose between emphasizing one at the expense of the other. As we'll see, some of the disputes involving generic and brand-name drugs arguably fall within this zone of ambiguity.

To return then to the Hatch-Waxman Act, suppose that the would-be maker of a generic drug files an ANDA and certifies that the patents allegedly covering the brand-name drug are either invalid or not infringed by the proposed generic. Assuming that the patent owner doesn't concede the point, the statute provides the owner with a 45-day window to file suit against the generic for . . . well, for what? At the time it files the ANDA, the generic firm isn't selling any quantities of the generic drug yet. (It better not be, because merely filing an ANDA doesn't equate to FDA approval.) Presumably it's *made* some quantities of the drug in order to gear up for filing the ANDA, but Hatch-Waxman excuses any such acts that are "solely for uses reasonably related to the development and submission of information" to the FDA.[79] So what can the brand-name drug company sue the generic for at this point in time?

The answer is, for what the case law refers to as "technical" infringement—or, perhaps more accurately, *possible* technical infringement, since the firm filing the ANDA may be correct in asserting that the patents at issue are invalid or not infringed. More specifically, in order to speed up resolution of the inevitable dispute between the applicant and the patent owner, Hatch-Waxman defines the submission of the ANDA as an act of infringement (even though at the time of submission the applicant hasn't yet made, used, or sold any infringing products),[80] and permits the patent owner to file suit upon receiving notice of the submission. If the owner does so within 45 days, the statute automatically "stays" the FDA from approving the ANDA for thirty months. As you may imagine, thirty more months of monopoly protection can be worth a lot of money, so patent owners under these circumstances don't waste too many opportunities to file suit. Once the lawsuit is filed, the normal litigation process can begin, with the parties taking discovery and filing motions in the expectation of a possible trial down the road. (As of 2016, the median time for patent infringement cases to proceed to trial was two and a half years,[81] which happens to coincide with the duration of the automatic stay.) The other possibility is that the case will settle. The vast majority of civil and criminal cases wind up settling, after all, and in this respect patent cases are no exception. But in the present context this is also where the possibility of antitrust liability is highest. Why so?

In brief, the answer is that the patent owner has a lot more to lose than does the ANDA filer. Suppose, for example, that during the period in which the patent owner faces no competition from makers of generic drugs it earns $500 million annually in sales of the patented drug. Once a generic firm enters, the two firms will split the market, with the generic firm catering to consumers who are more price-sensitive and the (former) patent owner to consumers who are willing to pay more for the brand-name drug. (Remember that for at least 180 days, there won't be any *other* generics in the market, unless the former patent owner decides to market its own "authorized" generic during that time, as it sometimes does. More about this shortly.) Given the generic's lower price, however, and the likelihood that a majority of consumers will buy the generic, the two firms'

aggregate profits from sales of the brand-name and generic drug are likely to
be less than $500 million. For the sake of argument, let's assume that the ge-
neric expects to earn $100 million and the brand-name firm $200 million for
the first year following generic entry. Obviously, the brand-name firm would be
better off if it could keep the generic off the market—which is precisely what it's
entitled to do if its patent is valid and the generic infringes. On the other hand,
if the brand-name firm simply paid the generic $100 million to stay out of the
market, the generic would be no worse off and the patent owner would be better
off (in the amount of $200 million*) than if the matter proceeded to trial and the
brand-name firm lost its exclusivity. Of course, the brand-name firm is worse off
in comparison with a state of the world in which the matter proceeded to trial
and it won, in which case it would retain its $500 million in profit and might
even pocket some monetary damages for the profits it lost for the time period,
if any, during which the generic actually was selling infringing products. (Its
attorneys' fees would be higher, though, if the matter proceeded to trial instead
of settling. According to the American Intellectual Property Law Association
(AIPLA), the mean cost of ANDA litigation with more than $25 million at stake
is $1.15 million through the end of discovery, motions, and claim construction,
and $2.6 million through the end of trial and appeal.)[82] But if the brand-name
firm thinks that the odds of losing at trial are sufficiently high, it may decide it's
better served by paying off the generic and keeping the market to itself until the
patent expires. Alternatively, the parties could agree to allow the generic firm
to enter the market a bit earlier than the date on which the patent is set to expire (though not as early as it would enter if it won the litigation), either with
or without a cash payment from the patent owner to the generic firm. Or the
payment could be in the form of something other than money: an alternative
used in some recent settlements has been for the brand-name firm to agree not
to launch its own "authorized" generic to compete against the ANDA filer.

   From an antitrust perspective, however, the problem with this sort of
arrangement is that normally you can't pay a potential competitor to stay out
of the market: that's one of those offenses, like price fixing among competitors,
that's considered per se illegal under the Sherman Act. These settlements also
look fishy to a lot of people because most of the time (you would think) when
parties settle patent litigation it's the *defendant* who pays something to the
plaintiff, not the other way around. Consider a typical case in which the patent
owner sues a defendant who allegedly has been selling infringing products
to consumers: if both parties peg the owner's odds of winning at trial to be

---

* If the generic enters, it earns $100 million and the brand-name firm earns $200 million.
If the brand-name firm pays the generic $100 million to stay out, the generic still winds up with
$100 million and the brand-name firm earns $500 million − $100 million = $400 million.

70 percent, and that in the event of a win the defendant will have to pay the plaintiff $10 million in damages, it would make sense to avoid the expense of going to trial by agreeing for the defendant to pay the plaintiff $7 million, which is the actuarial value of what the owner can expect to recover if the matter is litigated to judgment. (The actual numbers might be adjusted to reflect the time value of money, the expected savings of attorneys' fees, or the parties' differing expectations of the likely outcome at trial or their tolerance for risk.) For many observers, however, the fact that in ANDA cases the plaintiff is paying the defendant only strengthens the intuition that the parties are simply colluding to share a monopoly profit at the expense of consumers. Moreover, since the payment seems to going counter to its "normal" direction, and the defendant is usually agreeing to delay entry, these settlements are often referred to as "reverse payment" or "pay for delay" agreements.

On the other hand, though, if the brand-name firm proceeded to trial and won, it would be legally entitled to exclude the generic competitor until the patent expired—or until someone else, maybe another would-be generic competitor, succeeded in invalidating it. (There's no legal obstacle to another firm filing an ANDA and trying its luck against the patent owner. The fact that the patent owner won the trial against the first ANDA applicant does not create any precedent that must be followed in a lawsuit against a second applicant. Even if successful at trial, though, a second ANDA applicant wouldn't be able to market its generic drug until the first applicant enjoyed its 180 days of exclusivity, a fact that may discourage the second applicant from coming forward.) In addition, the fact that money is going from plaintiff to defendant may not be as odd as it seems, given the strange way in which litigation conducted under the Hatch-Waxman Act arises. Recall from above that as of the date the brand-name firm files suit for "technical" infringement, the defendant hasn't actually made or sold any infringing products—which means that this isn't like the typical patent infringement suit in which, if the plaintiff wins at trial, the defendant is likely to owe the plaintiff some money.[83]

Further, as suggested above, the brand-name firm potentially has a lot to lose—including, but not limited to, the additional attorneys' fees incurred by not settling—if the trial court finds for the defendant, and it may simply be willing to pay to avoid that risk. In fact, some economic models of reverse payment settlements suggest that (at least up to a point) these settlements can be consistent with a reasonably high likelihood that the patent owner would have prevailed on the merits.[84] Nevertheless, as shown in recent papers by Edlin et al., in any case in which the parties settle for a reverse payment exceeding their avoided litigation costs, they *could* have settled instead on terms permitting earlier generic entry without a reverse payment. Forbidding reverse payments therefore would on balance result in earlier generic entry, which would seem to benefit consumers.[85] Moreover, the empirical evidence, as gathered by the FTC, shows that brand-name and generic firms can (and often do) settle their disputes without resorting to reverse payments.[86] Other empirical work by Scott Hemphill and Bhaven Sampat reports that, in the majority of ANDA settlements with reverse payments, the patents in suit were "secondary" patents—that is, patents involving some variation on the initial patent covering the drug's active ingredient. According to Hemphill and Sampat, patent owners are less likely to win nonsettled lawsuits involving secondary patents, which is at least suggestive that reverse payments are more common for ANDA cases involving relatively weak patents.[87]

In any event, suppose that the brand-name and generic firm agree to a settlement under which the generic is allowed to enter the market a year prior to patent expiration (but a year later than if the case had gone to trial and the generic had won), in exchange for the brand-name firm's agreement to pay the generic $100 million (a not atypical sum). Suppose further that the FTC or a private entity (for example, an insurer) then files suit against the settling parties for violating the antitrust laws. Should a court find the agreement to be per se illegal, because the brand-name firm is simply paying a competitor to stay out of the market? Or should the court dismiss the antitrust claim, because the agreement to delay generic entry was consistent with the patent's potential exclusionary scope (the so-called "scope of the patent" test)—that is, because the patent entitled the brand-name firm to exclude the generic, perhaps for even longer than the period of time to which the parties agreed, as long as the patent is valid and infringed? Or should the court try to guess at the likely outcome of the patent litigation, and find for the antitrust plaintiff if it believes the generic firm would have prevailed but for the settlement; or find for the antitrust defendants if it believes the brand-name firm would have won? This last option, involving the court trying to guess at the likely outcome, would involve applying some form of the Rule of Reason, and might seem to be the most intellectually satisfying, but it also seems impractical: in effect, it would require the court hearing the antitrust case to conduct a patent infringement trial within the antitrust trial, with both of the parties to the settlement now motivated to show that the patent case would have resulted in victory for the brand-name firm. (It also would undermine the benefits, in terms of conserving on attorneys' fees and judicial resources, of having settled the patent case.) Alternatively, might there be some way to predict what would have happened if the patent case had gone to trial, based on more limited evidence, such as the amount of the payment? For example, suppose that (as was sometimes the case) the money transferred from brand-name to generic exceeded the profit the generic had projected it would earn from sales of the generic drug. At least in this situation, it's hard to see how the settlement could be anything *other* than an anticompetitive agreement to split monopoly profits, since it leaves the generic firm better off than it would have been if the patent had been found invalid or noninfringed (the best result the generic could have anticipated in litigation). But should courts condemn settlements even when the payment is less than the generic's forgone profit, and if so what level of payment is too much?

Courts began struggling with these issues in the late 1990s, with a few concluding that the settlements were per se illegal, while the majority opted for the more forgiving "scope of the patent" test. In 2012, however, one federal appellate court adopted the FTC's proposed "quick look" approach, under which a court would presume that a reverse payment settlement was illegal, but the settling parties themselves could try to rebut the presumption. With the various federal appellate courts now in open conflict, the Supreme Court finally agreed to take up the matter in *FTC v. Actavis, Inc.* Writing for a 5–3 majority, Justice Breyer concluded that the correct standard for evaluating reverse payment settlements was the Rule of Reason.[88] Recognizing, however, that courts and parties have legitimate reasons for wanting to avoid conducting a patent trial within an antitrust trial, Justice Breyer indicated that it is permissible to infer what would have happened in the infringement suit based on the size of the payment:

> An unexplained large reverse payment itself would normally suggest that the patentee has serious doubts about the patent's survival. And that fact, in turn, suggests that the payment's objective is to maintain supracompetitive prices to be shared among the patentee and the challenger rather than face what might have been a competitive market— the very anticompetitive consequence that underlies the claim of antitrust unlawfulness. The owner of a particularly valuable patent might contend, of course, that even a small risk of invalidity justifies a large payment. But, be that as it may, the payment (if otherwise unexplained) likely seeks to prevent the risk of competition. And, as we have said, that consequence constitutes the relevant anticompetitive harm. In a word, the size of the unexplained reverse payment can provide a workable surrogate for a patent's weakness, all without forcing a court to conduct a detailed exploration of the validity of the patent itself.[89]

As for what constitutes a "large" payment, the Court further elaborated:

> The reverse payment, for example, may amount to no more than a rough approximation of the litigation expenses saved through the settlement. That payment may reflect compensation for other services that the generic has promised to perform—such as distributing the

patented item or helping to develop a market for that item. There may be other justifications. Where a reverse payment reflects traditional settlement considerations, such as avoided litigation costs or fair value for services, there is not the same concern that a patentee is using its monopoly profits to avoid the risk of patent invalidation or a finding of noninfringement. In such cases, the parties may have provided for a reverse payment without having sought or brought about the anticompetitive consequences we mentioned above.[90]

Reasonable minds may differ, but as I read these passages the majority actually came pretty close to adopting the "quick look" approach while denying it was doing so. In particular, the opinion seems to indicate that the antitrust plaintiff doesn't have to directly prove that the patent probably would have been found invalid but-for the settlement. Rather, the court may infer that the probability of invalidity was high, and that the agreement constituted an illegal conspiracy, if the payment exceeded the plaintiff's avoided litigation costs (perhaps estimated on the basis of the AIPLA data cited above); the settling parties would then have the burden of proving that the amount paid actually was consistent with avoided expenditures, or was compensation for other services the generic firm agreed to provide (whatever those might be). Although the lower courts are still working out the details, the most recent appellate decisions construing *Actavis* seem consistent with this reading. The appellate cases also have concluded (correctly, in my view) that a "payment" from brand-name to generic doesn't have to be, literally, money, but rather can consist of any other benefit, such as an agreement not to market an authorized generic.[91]

How much these developments will affect the price and availability of generic drugs nevertheless remains to be seen. The FTC once estimated that reverse payment agreements cost consumers $3.5 billion per year,[92] so if the *Actavis* decision eliminates losses of this magnitude, the result is certainly an improvement to consumer welfare. Even so, and even assuming some adjustment for inflation, the amount saved probably won't amount to more than about 1 percent of the $328 billion, noted at the beginning of this chapter, that Americans were expected to spend on prescription drugs in 2016. Reining in reverse payments therefore is a step in the right direction, but it's hardly a panacea for the rising cost of pharmaceuticals in the United States.

Another practice that drug companies are alleged sometimes to engage in to prolong their exclusivity is referred to as "evergreening" or "product hopping." As I mentioned earlier in this chapter, a doctrine within patent law known as "double patenting" prevents a patent owner from obtaining a second patent on an obvious variation over the first patented invention. Drug firms nevertheless routinely obtain secondary patents like those discussed by Hemphill and Sampat, which for example might cover alternative formulations or new methods of delivery (e.g., liquid versus pill form). As long as these secondary inventions are sufficiently nonobvious to survive a double patenting challenge, they sometimes can provide the drug companies with a means for extending their effective period of exclusivity, since the term of protection for the secondary patent is measured from the date on which the application for the secondary (not the primary) patent was filed. To illustrate, suppose that the owner of a patented, FDA-approved, drug files an NDA or supplemental NDA (sNDA) for a new formulation of the drug; and that, once approval is obtained, the company invests in converting doctors and patients over to the new formulation. Even though the active ingredient in the new formulation is the same, the sponsor is still entitled to a period of exclusivity—albeit now only for three years—before anyone else can file an ANDA for the drug covered by the secondary patent. Of course, the generic firm could file—perhaps already has filed—an ANDA for the drug covered by the primary patent, and it can try to compete with the brand-name firm by selling a generic version of the original formulation. But often such efforts will be impeded due to a patchwork of state laws governing when pharmacists may unilaterally substitute a generic for a brand-name drug. For example, in *Abbott Labs. v. Teva Pharmaceuticals USA, Inc.*, Abbott filed a series of NDAs for different formulations of a drug called TriCor, and after each NDA was approved, Abbott changed the code for the old version in the National Drug Data File to read "Obsolete." The code change allegedly limited the marketability of generic versions of TriCor by preventing pharmacists from substituting the generic for the new brand-name formulation.[93] Similarly, in *New York ex rel. Schneiderman v. Actavis PLC*, the brand-name firm withdrew Namenda IR, a twice-daily Alzheimer's drug for which the patent was about to expire, and introduced a new, once-daily version called Namenda XR. As in *Abbott*, the substitution allegedly disadvantaged would-be generic competitors, because pharmacists couldn't lawfully substitute IR for XR, and doctors might be reluctant to switch Alzheimer's patients back to IR once they had become accustomed to the once-daily regimen.[94]

I mention *Abbott* and *Schneiderman* because these are two of the only cases to date in which courts have shown themselves willing to entertain an antitrust claim based on an economic theory known as "predatory innovation." (In *Abbott*, the court denied Abbott's motion to dismiss the antitrust claim outright, after which I believe the case settled; in *Schneiderman*, it affirmed a preliminary injunction preventing Actavis from pulling Namenda IR from the market.) The basic idea is that sometimes the social benefits of an innovation are so slight in comparison with the social costs that the introduction of the innovation should be deemed an unlawful attempt to maintain a monopoly, in violation of Sherman Act section 2. Traditionally, courts have been reluctant to entertain such theories, on the grounds that they aren't well-positioned to determine when the necessary conditions for liability are present, and fear unduly chilling innovations from which consumers may wind up deriving substantial benefits.[95] (In economic terms, one would say that the risk and cost of judicial error potentially are high.) These concerns are legitimate ones, and the exercise of antitrust oversight in this sphere accordingly should be undertaken with caution. But prudence shouldn't amount to a complete abdication of responsibility either. The social cost of not intervening also is potentially high, when the evidence presents strong reason for concluding that the drug company's course of conduct in introducing a new formulation to the market will put generic competitors (and cost-conscious patients) at an unnecessary disadvantage. Moreover, at least in cases like *Schneiderman*, the risk of inadvertently discouraging innovation seems slight, as long as the remedy is simply to require the brand-name firm to refrain from pulling the original formulation off the market for a period of time.

Nonetheless, although these developments in the law of predatory innovation are welcome, I'd be surprised if they made a big dent in the overall cost of prescription drugs—though perhaps in combination with a more vigorous antitrust enforcement generally the impact would be enhanced. In a recent paper, for example, Michael Carrier and Carl Minniti argue that Mylan's provision of EpiPen devices to schools on condition that the recipients not keep other brands of autoinjectors on hand impeded the development of those other brands and may violate the Clayton Act's prohibition on anticompetitive exclusive dealing arrangements.[96] In a similar vein, a 2009 report from the Government Accountability Office speculated, albeit without providing detailed analysis, that increased concentration within the drug industry—a matter of potential concern to antitrust regulators—had contributed to drug price increases by limiting competition.[97] (More about the law of mergers shortly.) More recently, some legal scholars have argued that drug companies sometimes delay generic entry by filing so-called "citizen petitions" with the FDA, alleging that a generic drug for which FDA approval is pending may suffer from safety problems.[98] This conduct, however, often is immune from antitrust scrutiny due to *Noerr-Pennington* immunity, which in a nutshell means that because you have a First Amendment right to petition the government, the act of petitioning doesn't violate the antitrust laws unless the petition is nothing more than a sham. Proving that a petition is a sham requires evidence that it is objectively baseless and subjectively motivated by a desire to impede competition, and is quite difficult (though not impossible) to sustain.[99]

Nonetheless, there is only so much that antitrust law can do to keep drug prices in check, given that US antitrust law (correctly, in my view) doesn't provide a warrant for courts directly to regulate price. If price regulation is in fact desirable, then we need some other means–whether it be 28 USC section 1498 or a full-blown system of universal health care—to achieve it. Any such system, however, must be carefully designed and operated to avoid undermining the incentive to invest in the development of new drugs. Even if it doesn't *really* cost $2.6 billion to develop the average FDA-approved drug, as PhRMA contends, we're probably talking at least a few hundred millions of dollars, and, for a broad range of drugs, patents probably are necessary to induce that investment. That said, it hardly follows that drug companies should be free to do whatever they want with their state-sanctioned monopolies.

Other Factors that Make Health Care Costly

Because this book is about patents, this chapter mostly focuses on pharmaceutical patents and their impact on the cost of prescription drugs. Before concluding, however, it's important to note that drug patents are only one component driving up the cost of health care in the United States and that there are several other factors that play as great or an even greater role. In the interest of completeness, I sketch them out briefly below.

Since we were just talking about antitrust, I'll start by noting that antitrust law arguably has failed to constrain health care costs in matters having little or nothing to do with drugs or drug firms. The most obvious example is with regard to hospital consolidation, which began to take off in the early 1990s. Economists refer to an industry characterized by only a small number of firms as an "oligopoly," and while there is no single economic theory of how oligopolistic firms will set prices and output, under many plausible scenarios the smaller the number of firms, the greater the risk they will collude either explicitly or tacitly. Thus when a market has only a small number of competitors to begin with, and two of them merge (or one acquires the other), the risk of anticompetitive harm goes up. Section 7 of the Clayton Act, however, prohibits anticompetitive mergers; and another piece of legislation, known as Hart-Scott-Rodino Act and incorporated into the Clayton Act, requires that for any proposed merger involving assets over a given threshold (the current minimum is $80.8 million) the merging partners must submit detailed information to the antitrust enforcement agencies to enable them to decide whether to oppose the combination in court (or require the partners to satisfy certain conditions, such as the divestiture of certain assets, to avoid trial).[100] Merger law is complicated, but the basic idea is that the agencies will evaluate the evidence to predict whether, on balance, the proposed combination will reduce or enhance competition in the relevant market. All other things being equal, the greater the concentration within the market—as measured by something called the Herfindahl Hirschman Index (HHI), which sums the squares of the market shares of each firm in the market so that, for example, in a market consisting of four firms each with a 25 percent share the HHI would be 2,500—the greater the risk of anticompetitive harm. Even so, under the agencies' current approach, concentration levels aren't always key, and there may be offsetting efficiencies suggesting that, on balance, the merger will make consumers better off by reducing the cost of doing business and thus, potentially, prices.

In any event, since the early 1990s there have been 1,000 hospital mergers or acquisitions in the United States, including more than 500 between 2007 and 2012.[101] Concentration within health care markets, not surprisingly, has steadily risen; according to Cory Capps and David Dranove, as of 2009 the average metropolitan statistical area HHI in the market for hospital ownership was "roughly 4700," far above the level (2,500) the agencies consider highly concentrated.[102] The agencies themselves lost six consecutive cases against hospital mergers between 1993 and 1995 and did not block a single one for over a decade.[103] Thomas Greaney has argued that, in permitting these mergers, the courts simply assumed away preexisting market imperfections with respect to such fundamental matters as geographic and product market definitions.[104]

The empirical evidence appears to be consistent with Greaney's critique. In a report published in 2006, William Vogt and Robert Town stated that the "great weight of the literature" to date showed that hospital consolidation "raised prices by at least five percent and likely by significantly more."[105] A 2011 update by Town and Martin Gaynor reported, on the basis of empirical studies published since 2006, that increases in hospital market concentration had led to increases in the price of hospital care; that hospital mergers in concentrated markets had generally led to significant price increases ("most exceeding 20 percent"); and that for certain procedures, concentration reduced quality while competition had the opposite effect.[106] Although the tide had begun to turn somewhat in the early 2000s, with the FTC notching several victories against proposed hospital mergers, the number of hospital mergers has climbed from 66 in 2010 to over 100 in 2015 and 2016.[107] In the somewhat depressing view of health economist Roger Feldman, "health care mergers may be too numerous for antitrust to be a meaningful strategy," though Feldman recommends lowering the thresholds that would trigger federal antitrust review as well as greater involvement on the part of state regulatory agencies.[108]

A second problem is the lack of transparency within which the US system operates, which allows multiple opportunities for gaming. Only within the last few years, for example, has the federal government made available hospital chargemasters (price lists) for common inpatient and outpatient services[109] and published regulations requiring the disclosure of pharmaceutical company payments to physicians.[110] Even so, as Steven Brill points out, "[p]harmaceutical and medical device companies routinely insert clauses in their sales contracts prohibiting hospitals from sharing information about what they pay and the discounts they receive."[111] According to the Government Accountability Office, this lack of transparency "raises questions about whether hospitals are achieving the best prices possible."[112] In addition, health care providers are reimbursed based on how medical procedures are coded and where they are carried out, which not only makes matters less transparent but also serves to increase transaction costs, with armies of workers now having to be trained both to code and to interpret codes.[113] The transparency deficit makes competition on the basis of price more difficult than it otherwise would be.

Third is the fact that the vast majority of health care–related products and services in the United States are funded through either private or public insurance.[114] Now, insurance is a wonderful thing, in that it enables us to reduce the impact of many of the unavoidable risks that we encounter in everyday life. But insurance also has two soft spots that are particularly aggravated in the United States. The first is known as "moral hazard," which in essence means that "[p]eople may change their behavior . . . once they know they will not bear the full consequences."[115] In the market for health care, moral hazard discourages actors at virtually every stage of distribution to externalize many of the relevant costs. Doctors, for example, often have little reason to consider the cost of the drugs or procedures they prescribe and whether those costs are justified in view of the benefits of those treatments in comparison with alternatives. (They also may be influenced, consciously or not, by drug company representatives who parcel out free goodies.)[116] Consumers often don't bear the full cost up front either, though rising copays and deductibles may be making some of them think twice (or more). Of course, insurers and pharmacy benefits managers care about price, and often they can negotiate lower prices, discounts, or rebates for covered medications; but they're also often bound by law to pay for a specified formulary of drugs, whether or not those drugs are actually better or more cost-effective than alternatives.[117] In addition, unlike in other countries, US law forbids our largest public insurer—Medicare—from using its bargaining power to negotiate for lower drug prices.[118] Medicare *does* decide how much to reimburse physicians for various services, and private insurance companies often follow Medicare's lead in this regard. Critics contend, however, that a number of factors—including the formula by which reimbursement rates are set, the specialist-dominant nature of the committee that advises Medicare on these rates, and the fact that (contrary to practice elsewhere) many physician services in the United States are delivered on a fee-for-service basis—create perverse incentives for physicians to structure treatment in ways that inflate prices.[119] Lack of transparency strikes again.

A second problem with insurance is adverse selection: people who don't expect to get sick may prefer to go without insurance, so that as a result the risk pool is disproportionately composed of people who are, or expect to be, sick—which in turn encourages insurers to raise premiums, which then induces more relatively healthy people to drop out, and on and on (the so-called "death spiral"). The Affordable Care Act was supposed to reduce this problem by coupling a prohibition on discriminating on the basis of preexisting conditions with a requirement that most everyone obtain "minimum essential coverage" or pay a penalty.[120] For a variety of reasons, however, including the fact that the penalties aren't high enough to induce everyone to join, several insurance companies either have dropped out of the state health insurance exchanges or substantially raised their premiums.[121] By contrast, single-payer systems not only reduce administrative costs but also avoid the death spiral by requiring everyone to participate in the risk pool.[122]

A fourth factor contributing to the high cost of health care is that firms can sometimes exploit FDA law to the detriment of consumers. As we have seen, certain provisions of federal law provide qualifying drugs with periods of exclusivity from competition, independent of patent protection: a generic drug maker has to wait three to five years, depending on the circumstances, before filing an ANDA, and the first-filing ANDA applicant is entitled to 180 days of exclusivity vis-à-vis other generic firms. Creative use of these provisions can enable anticompetitive pay-for-delay agreements and product hopping, as discussed above. But there are several other exclusivities available for qualifying drugs and devices, including seven years of exclusivity for "orphan" drug indications for conditions affecting fewer than 200,000 people in the United States and six months of additional exclusivity for conducting pediatric clinical studies. (There are yet other exclusivities for biologics, qualifying antibiotics, and other products and methods.)[123] To be sure, Congress's decision to enact these exclusivities may have been well-intentioned; and in principle exclusivities can improve social welfare by providing an additional, more finely tailored set of incentives than can patent law. (Recall that patent protection comes with a standard twenty-year term, which however can be extended a bit to compensate for regulatory delay.) But they also may provide opportunities for gaming. Critics have charged, for example, that sponsors sometimes conduct pediatric investigations of drugs that are only rarely used to treat children, in order to obtain the additional six months of exclusivity (which applies to all indications, not just pediatric ones), and seek orphan drug exclusivities in the expectation that doctors will prescribe these drugs for more lucrative off-label (that is, non-FDA-approved) uses (which doctors are allowed to do).[124] Another prominent example arose after the FDA announced an Unapproved Drugs Initiative, a program intended to motivate sponsors to conduct clinical studies of drugs that have been in use since before the FDA began requiring proof of effectiveness in 1962. In line with this program, in 2009 URL Pharma, Inc. obtained three years of exclusivity to market colchicine—the first documented use of which to treat gout dates back to the sixth century A.D.—for conducting a one-week clinical study that observers have argued added little to what was already known about the drug. URL promptly raised the price from 9 cents to $4.85 per pill.[125]

There are other possible problems with the drug and device approval process besides these. For example, in approving drugs and devices, the FDA doesn't take into account matters such as cost effectiveness, access, and affordability; nor does it require sponsors to investigate a drug's effectiveness compared to other drugs, which arguably leads to the approval of drugs that offer few if any benefits over existing products. [126] Critics also variously argue that in certain respects FDA approval still takes too long and is too strict, while in other regards (particularly as related to medical devices) it may not be strict enough.[127] I don't claim any special expertise relevant to these latter critiques, but I am intrigued by a proposal, often touted by free-market advocates, that would allow the FDA to approve a drug or medical device that already has been approved in another comparable country or set of countries, such as the European Union or Japan.[128] Such a "reciprocity" process might allow, for example, the makers of the epinephrine autoinjectors sold in Europe immediate access to compete within the United States. To be sure, there's some risk that other countries might not employ sufficiently rigorous safety standards; in this regard, critics of reciprocity often note that thalidomide, which was marketed as an anti–morning sickness drug in Canada and Europe in the late 1950s and 1960s but was never approved for marketing in the United States, was eventually proved to cause birth defects. Nevertheless, it's hardly clear that the standards applied in these countries today are riskier than those employed by the FDA; and whatever risk *does* arise from letting approved drugs into the United States must be balanced against the risk that *not* letting them in will cause even greater harm by restricting access based on price. On balance, I'd be inclined to give reciprocal approval a try, though whether it would have a major effect on drug and device prices remains unknown.

Finally, according to the Center for Responsive Politics, the health industry spent more than half a billion dollars on federal government lobbying in 2016.[129] Not surprisingly, reform can be difficult to achieve in such a money-saturated environment; and the Supreme Court's gradual chipping away of meaningful campaign finance reform in the name of free speech probably doesn't help. Relatedly, in the forty years since the Supreme Court first extended First Amendment protection to commercial speech, the Court has held unconstitutional a Vermont law that attempted to constrain health care costs by restricting the sale to pharmaceutical companies of "pharmacy records that reveal the prescribing practices of individual doctors,"[130] as well as a federal law that prohibited certain ads by compounding pharmacies.[131] In addition, FDA regulations[132] and commercial speech doctrine permit drug companies to engage in direct-to-consumer advertising, a practice that is absent from almost every other country and is widely believed to contribute to the high cost of US health care.[133]

At the end of the day, it's hard not to conclude that some form of universal, single-payer health care along the lines of what is found in Canada, Europe, and elsewhere would be an improvement over our current high-cost system. But despite the fact that universal care has been championed over the years by such luminaries as (Republican) President Teddy Roosevelt[134] and the (emphatically nonsocialist) economist Friedrich von Hayek,[135] polls indicate that large numbers of Americans still view even the rather mild version of universal care that is embodied in the Affordable Care Act with disdain. (With rising copays and deductibles, this frustration is understandable, though to its credit the act has succeeded in substantially reducing the numbers of uninsured.) And to be fair, universal health care is hardly perfect: the litany of its unintended consequences, including sometimes long waits for services and spartan facilities, is well-documented too. Perhaps innovation ultimately would suffer as well if Americans weren't so willing to fund it by paying higher prices for drugs, devices, and other health-related products and services (though this hardly suggests a rationale for approving protectionist policies that have nothing to do with innovation). And maybe there is some better alternative to both our current system and the single-payer model, though for now I remain somewhat skeptical.[136] In any event, and for better or worse, over the course of more than a century we have collectively chosen a different model for the provision of health care than has much of the developed world; and if we are unwilling to change, we must accept the bitter with the sweet. As Pogo would say, "we have met the enemy and he is us."

7

Developing Countries

Imagine you're the leader of a country that's either small or poor (or both). "Small" and "poor," of course, are comparative terms, so for the sake of discussion let's assume, arbitrarily, that your country has a population of less than 10 million or a per capita income within the bottom quartile. Your country therefore might be small and rich, like Switzerland or Singapore; or it could populous and poor, like Bangladesh or Tanzania; or it could be small in both population and income, like (say) Laos or Benin. Regardless of where exactly your country fits within this framework, I'd guess that, if you care about improving the lives of the people you serve, you'd probably like for your country to be more innovative. But what does that mean, exactly? Well, for one thing, I'd assume that you'd like your country's industries to be more active in developing and commercializing new inventions and technologies. I'd also guess that you'd want the citizens of your country to enjoy the benefits of innovations that are developed elsewhere, so that your people can live longer, more fulfilling and productive lives. (Your views concerning what sorts of innovations are desirable nevertheless may vary quite a bit depending on your country's cultural makeup, religious traditions, and relations with its neighbors.) To be sure, if you're a poor country, the obstacles to achieving these goals are going to be far greater than if you're rich. Small countries that are rich are likely to start with many advantages, including generally higher levels of education, better infrastructure and public health systems, and stable and responsive governments—though not all well-off countries enjoy these advantages in equal measure, and some poor countries fare pretty well with regard to at least some of them. Whatever your country's starting point may be, however, I'll assume that you perceive innovation to be one of the keys to prosperity, so that (subject to the constraints you have to operate within) you'd like for your country to be more innovative.

Should your country have a patent system?

At first blush, this might seem like a strange question to ask, for a couple of reasons. The first is that it simply may be hard to imagine any country today *not* having a patent system of some kind—just as it's hard to imagine any country today not having roads, bridges, hospitals, schools, courts, a national defense system, and some sort of legislative body that professes to represent the people's interest. Issuing patents just seems like one of the things that modern nations— even including such microstates as Andorra, Monaco, and San Marino—*do*. As I noted in Chapter 1, however, patents are territorial in the sense that a patent in Country A is enforceable only in Country A and not in Country B; and, in principle, it's entirely up to Country B whether to issue any patents or not. Nevertheless, the intuition that it's odd for any modern country not to have a patent system is correct. Indeed, for reasons we'll get to shortly, it would be difficult nowadays for any country that wants to engage in substantial international trade to resist having one—though according to one source, as of February 2015 there were still a small number of holdouts, and a few others that merely register patents issued somewhere else.[1]

A second reason it might seem strange to ask whether a small or poor country should have a patent system relates to my discussion throughout this book of the benefits and costs of patents. To summarize, the principal theoretical justification for patents is that they encourage people to invest in creating, disclosing, and commercializing new inventions, by providing inventors with a period of time to try to recoup their investments without interference on the part of free riders. Further, while patents aren't the only available tools for accomplishing these goals—and they need not be the exclusive tool upon which governments rely for accomplishing them—in theory patents promise certain advantages over alternatives such as reliance on first-mover advantages, which may not be sufficient especially for subject matter like drugs; grants and prizes, which require funders to predict in advance what needs to be invented and to follow through on promises to compensate; or trade secrets, which impede widespread disclosure. In addition, most though not all innovation economists believe that the empirical evidence (such as it is) generally supports the theory that patents promote innovation, while recognizing that reasonable minds may differ over the precise contours that an optimal patent system would take. Seen in this light, then, why *wouldn't* you have a patent system, if the experts (well, most of them) think that patents by and large serve the public interest? Is there something different about small or poor countries that might lead them to tally up the benefits and costs of patents a little differently?

Here the answer is, maybe yes. Consider: if your country is either small or poor, it's probably not going to generate too many patentable inventions on its own. To be sure, you might predict that small, wealthy nations like Singapore (population 5.6 million) or Luxembourg (population 580,000) will be able to generate a lot of new inventions relative to their populations. But in sheer numerical terms that's still a small population of potential inventors (and consumers), and no matter how industrious the Singaporeans and Luxembourgeois may be, it's hard to imagine them developing anything approaching the sheer quantity of inventions produced by much larger industrial powerhouses. A small country's patent system therefore isn't likely to induce a *huge* number of new inventions, all other things being equal. (The same goes for a poor country, given its comparative economic disadvantages.) Moreover, if inventors who reside in a small or poor country have the option of obtaining patents in other, larger markets— which, as we will see, they do under the oldest multilateral patent treaty, the Paris Convention of 1883—they may still have a fairly robust incentive to invest in developing new inventions even in the absence of a domestic patent system.[2] (A multilateral or plurilateral treaty, by way, is an agreement or convention to which several nations are parties. Agreements between just two nations, which we will also encounter in this chapter, are referred to as "bilateral.") In addition, manufacturers within a small or poor country can learn how to make and use the inventions claimed in foreign patents simply by reading those patents, since by definition patents are public documents. (Language could be a problem, though in the modern world most of the patents you'd have any interest in copying probably will be written in one of just a handful of languages: English, Chinese, Japanese, Korean, German, or French. Further, the most valuable inventions are likely to be covered by counterpart patents in several countries in several languages.) Finally, consumers within the small or poor country will pay lower prices if domestic manufacturers can make and sell products that are patented elsewhere, without having to pay patent royalties. From the perspective of such a country, then, it might seem that it would be much more sensible *not* to have a patent system: domestic inventors' incentives aren't likely to be affected all that much, and domestic consumers won't have to pay a premium for domestically-made products that are subject to patent protection elsewhere. Free riding makes sense.

In fact, this pretty much was the strategy employed by the Netherlands and Switzerland in the nineteenth century. The Netherlands abolished its patent system in 1869, while Switzerland "had no patents until the country adopted a rudimentary patent system in 1888 and switched towards a full-fledged system in 1907"[3] (five years after hiring the man who was to become the most famous patent examiner of all time, Albert Einstein). The strategy appears to have had some impact on the types of inventions on which Dutch and Swiss inventors concentrated, which tended toward things (like scientific instruments, food processing, and industrial chemicals) that back in the day were hard to reverse engineer and thus could be adequately protected as trade secrets.[4] You might think that this would be a pretty good strategy for a small country today too, especially a poor one. Why should a developing country have a patent system, if it doesn't have many domestic inventors who will take advantage of it, and if its citizens would have to pay higher prices to (mostly) foreign companies in exchange for patented products?

There may be some flaws in this approach, however. One argument sometimes made in support of the extension of patent protection to small or poor countries is that often you can't really learn everything there is to know about how best to make and use a patented technology merely by reading published patents. Instead, optimal use may depend on the willingness of the patent owner to share unpatented know-how and new ways of practicing the invention that may not be disclosed by the patent itself. (Recall from Chapter 1 that inventors don't have to update their patent applications to reveal any newer or better methods of use that they discover after the date of filing.) Foreign patent owners in particular may be unwilling to share such information with potential licensees in small countries absent the assurance, which a patent provides, that the technology to which such know-how pertains can't be used without their consent. More generally, foreign firms may be less willing to invest in countries that lack a system of enforceable patent rights. (To be sure, foreign investment might rub some inhabitants of a developing country the wrong way because of its potential impact on local autonomy. If, however, a particular country decides that attracting foreign investment would be economically worthwhile, the argument goes, setting up an effective patent system is one way to signal the country's receptivity to foreign business.) Advocates also sometimes argue that patents can stimulate the development of inventions the principal market for which consists mostly of developing countries, such as medications for treating diseases that are endemic to the developing world. If that's true, it would be best if all the countries that are likely to benefit from such inventions extended similar patent protection, because otherwise the incentive for each of them will be to wait for one of the other affected countries to patent the medicine and then to free-ride; but if they all follow this strategy, there may never be an adequate incentive to develop the new drug.[5]

In fact, there actually is some empirical evidence to support the theory that a system of intellectual property rights attracts technology transfer, foreign investment, and the introduction of new products to domestic markets. Branstetter et al., for example, report that between 1982 and 1999 US multinationals "significantly increase[ed] technology transfer to" sixteen countries (ranging from the Philippines and Indonesia at the poorer end of the spectrum to Japan at the richer) that had adopted stronger IP rights regimes.[6] Hu and Png's study of fifty-four industries and seventy-two countries from 1981 to 2000 concludes that the adoption of strong patent rights correlated with faster economic growth, though the correlation was stronger for patent-intensive industries and higher income countries,[7] while a study by Kyle and Qian covering sixty countries for the period 2000–13 reports that drug patents facilitated the introduction of new drugs into poorer countries, with price discrimination offsetting expected price increases.[8] In an earlier paper studying countries that extended patent protection to drugs between 1978 and 2002, however, Qian cautions that patents alone did not appear to stimulate domestic innovation, but rather that "domestic innovation accelerates in countries with higher levels of economic development, educational attainment, and economic freedom"; and that "there appears to be an optimal level of intellectual property rights regulation above which further enhancement reduces innovative activities."[9] Other research is consistent with Qian's conclusion that strengthening IP rights can be beneficial, though only when development is already above some minimum level and when other positive factors are in place.[10]

In addition, to date the evidence is scant that patents have provided much of an incentive for domestic or foreign inventors to develop inventions of interest mostly to developing countries. One problem is that, for many developing countries, market demand (as measured by what governments or individuals are willing and able to pay) often isn't strong enough to motivate Western drug companies to invest much in developing treatments for what are often referred to as "neglected" diseases, such as malaria.[11] Other tools, such as prizes or advance market commitments (AMCs) as discussed in Chapter 2, therefore may be necessary to induce adequate investment in this space. Moreover, as Qian suggests, the evidence that stronger patent policies may induce foreign investment and the provision of new products doesn't necessarily mean that stronger patent rights are desirable without exception. As we'll see below, the arguments in favor of compulsory licensing of essential medicines are in my view strong (though compulsory licensing is hardly a panacea for the problems faced by the developing world). The overall welfare effects of strong IP rights also must take into account not only the potentially positive impact of increased foreign investment and technology transfer, domestic innovation, and in some cases the provision of higher quality goods, but also (as noted above) the potential negative impact of higher prices for patented goods. Additional effects may include the displacement of local firms that previously operated without regard to IP rights.[12] On balance, then, the effect of increased IP protection is likely to vary depending on many specific factors, including the stage of a country's economic development.

Nonetheless, in recent decades just about every country in the world *has* adopted a patent system that, in terms of its general features, is pretty similar to what you'd find in any other country. To be sure, there are many differences in the details; and sometimes there can be substantial gaps between the "law on the books" and the law that one actually encounters in practice. Still, since the 1990s the vast majority of the world's nations have obligated themselves to abide by a host of "minimum standards" with regard to patents, as a condition of their ability to participate in the global system of free trade that is overseen by the World Trade Organization (WTO). This chapter will trace out how this state of affairs came to be, as well as the inevitable backlash that ensued from encouraging developing countries to enact and enforce strong patent laws. I'll also briefly examine some related issues concerning protection for plants, seeds, and traditional knowledge (TK).

From the Paris Convention to TRIPS

Do you have any idea where the next World's Fair will be held? Neither did I, until I looked it up. As it turns out, since 1928 an entity known as the Bureau International des Expositions (BIE) has regulated most but not all of the events billed as "World's Fair" or "Expo," with the major ones taking place in calendar years ending in a 0 or 5 (the next one, in 2020, will be in Dubai) and smaller, specialized expositions in between (the one in 2017 was in Astana, Kazakhstan).[13] I imagine it might be fun to attend one someday, though I doubt they will ever again attract as much attention as, say, the (non-BIE-sanctioned) 1964 New York World's Fair or Chicago's 1893 Columbian Exposition, both of which continue to live on in popular culture. (The New York fair, for example, provided one of the settings for Disney's 2015 film *Tomorrowland,* while the Columbian Exposition—which featured the public premiere of the Ferris Wheel, the moving walkway, and shredded wheat cereal—was one of the subjects of Erik Larson's 2002 bestseller *The Devil in the White City.*) By contrast, I'm guessing that a century from now no one's going to be writing a popular history or producing a mass market film about Astana's Expo 2017. No offense, people of Astana, but World's Fairs just aren't what they used to be.

At one time, though, international expositions were high-profile events at which the nations of the world would showcase new inventions. (Petra Moser's research on expositions provided the data from which it was possible to infer, as noted above, that nineteenth-century inventors tended to focus on different types of innovations depending on whether or not their countries granted patents.) Prior to the opening of the 1873 Vienna Exposition, however, US inventors expressed concern about the requirement, under Austria-Hungary's 1852 Patent Act, that patented inventions be "worked," that is, practiced, within the empire within one year of grant.[14] In response, the American minister to Austria-Hungary, John Jay II, successfully proposed that Austria-Hungary provide for the temporary protection for inventions exhibited at the exposition, as the UK and France had done during their expositions earlier in the century. The

Vienna Exposition also provided an opportunity for delegates from several countries to get together to discuss a possible multilateral patent law treaty. Follow-up meetings in Paris in 1878, 1880, and 1883 eventually led to the conclusion of the first such multilateral treaty, the Paris Convention for the Protection of Industrial Property. Since 1883 the Paris Convention has been revised six times, most recently in 1967 in Stockholm, and today 177 nations are members. The Convention deals with patents, trademarks, and some other forms of "industrial property" and unfair competition, though not copyright. (Copyright got its own treaty, the Berne Convention, in 1886.)

The Paris Convention establishes two major principles of relevance here. First, the Convention provides for "national treatment," meaning that each member state must confer on nationals of any other Paris Convention member state at least the same level of protection with respect to patents and trademarks as it confers upon its own citizens or subjects: in other words, as far as patents and trademarks are concerned, you can't discriminate against nationals of other Paris Convention member states.[15] Second, for patents the Convention provides a twelve-month period of priority, meaning that if an inventor wants to obtain patent protection in multiple Paris Convention member states, any application she files in a member state within twelve months of the filing of her first application will be treated for most purposes as if it had been filed on the date of the first application.[16] Thus, if the inventor files a patent application claiming ABC in the United States on April 2, 2010, and in Canada within twelve months— say, on March 21, 2011—Canada will review her application to determine if the claimed invention was novel and nonobvious as of April 2, 2010, not March 21, 2011; any prior art references that were first publicly disclosed in the interim will have no effect on the patentability of the invention in Canada. This is helpful to inventors, since it may take some time for them to draft and file applications in all of the other countries in which they might want to obtain patent protection. (A follow-up agreement known as the Patent Cooperation Treaty [PCT], which was concluded in 1970, further simplifies the process by enabling inventors to file a national application, usually in the inventor's home country or region, followed by a single international application which then is entitled to the Paris Convention's twelve-month priority period and may serve as a request for protection in as many other PCT countries as the inventor wishes.) Today, both the Paris Convention and the PCT, along with a host of other international IP treaties including the Berne Convention, are administered by a United Nations agency known as the World Intellectual Property Organization (WIPO).

There are other features of the Paris Convention that we don't need to go into here, but I should note two additional points before moving on. The first is that the Paris Convention establishes very little of what lawyers refer to as "substantive" law—meaning, in the present context, that it doesn't say anything at all about, for example, what sorts of inventions member states may or must recognize as patent-eligible, or about the requirements for obtaining a valid patent, the activities that constitute infringement, or the term of patent protection.[17] As a result, the Paris Convention by itself doesn't do much to harmonize different countries' patent laws; rather, it tolerates a broad range of national rules and standards. In fact, the Convention doesn't obligate members to have *any* patent system at all: all it requires, in conformity with the principle of national treatment described above, is that *if* a member offers patent protection it must offer it to nationals of other members on terms that are no less favorable than those it applies to its own citizens or subjects. This explains how, as I noted earlier in this chapter, both Switzerland and the Netherlands managed to become charter members of the Paris Convention in 1884 without actually having a patent system in place; since they didn't offer patents to their own citizens, they weren't violating national treatment by refusing to offer patents to foreigners.

Second, like many international treaties the Paris Convention lacks an effective means for compelling other members to live up to their own obligations under the treaty. Treaties among nations are sometimes analogized to contracts among private parties, and in a manner analogous to what would happen in connection with a contract dispute article 28 of the Paris Convention permits a member that believes another member is in breach of its treaty obligations to bring an action before the International Court of Justice in the Hague (sometimes referred to as the "World Court").[18] In practice, however, no country has ever brought a Paris Convention dispute before the World Court. Moreover, the treaty allows countries that are becoming members of the Convention to declare that they'll opt out of article 28 altogether. The United States is one of many countries that has so declared; so if, say, Canada thinks the United States is reneging on one of its obligations under the Paris Convention, Canadian and US diplomats can try to resolve the matter through negotiation and see where that leads, or failing that Canada might consider imposing trade or other sanctions on the United States, though doing so might risk provoking retaliation. But that's about it. (It's a little hard to imagine anyone taking a violation of the Paris Convention seriously enough to go to war over it, thank goodness.) This lack of an effective system for resolving disputes is a defect of which, as we'll see, the drafters of the Agreement on Trade-Related Aspects of Intellectual Property Rights (TRIPS) were well aware.

IP Rights and Free Trade

Unlike the Paris Convention and most of the other international treaties relating to IP, TRIPS, which entered into force in 1995, is not administered by WIPO but rather by the WTO—an international organization that describes itself as "a forum for governments to negotiate trade agreements" and "a place where member governments try to sort out the trade problems they face with each other."[19] Each of the 164 countries that are members of the WTO is a party to a set of treaties relating to international trade, including TRIPS. (Members aren't allowed to pick and choose among the treaties; once you become a member of the WTO, in other words, you're bound by all of the WTO treaties. The WIPO-administered treaties are different, in that a state could be a member of, say, the Paris Convention and not the Berne Convention, or vice versa.) A legitimate question to ask is why an international treaty relating to IP is included within a set of treaties relating to free trade. What's the connection, if any, between IP and free trade?

A good place to start is by defining what free trade is. A simple definition of free trade would be "a system under which two or more nations trade with one another freely." Under a system of free trade between Nations A and B, for example, Nation A would be free to export goods to Nation B without having Nation B erect trade barriers such as tariffs or import restrictions, and vice versa. In addition, both nations would want to make sure that neither one can give its own domestic producers any unfair advantages, such as subsidies. The theory behind free trade, which can be traced back to the classical economic thought of Adam Smith and David Ricardo, is that if both Nation A and Nation B trade freely with one another aggregate wealth in both countries will be higher than it would have been in the presence of trade barriers. In particular, the economic theory of comparative advantage holds that, if Nations A and B each specialize in producing whatever goods they're best at producing and then trade some of those goods for goods made in the other state, Nations A and B will each create a larger surplus of wealth than if each one tried to produce everything it needed on its own (what economists refer to as "autarky"). For example, if Nation A can produce a pair of running shoes at a cost of $50 and Nation B can produce the same shoes at a cost of $5, consumers in Nation A will be better off if Nation A imports the shoes from Nation B than if they have to buy the shoes from a higher cost domestic producer. (The relative price of the goods Nation A exports, however, will go up.) More importantly, because resources in the aggregate are being used more efficiently, aggregate wealth in A and B will be higher than if each country tried to go it alone or to impede the flow of trade. Further, firms in both countries will have an incentive to produce better goods at lower cost if they face competition, or potential competition, from foreign firms; and consumers stand to benefit from this increase in competition, both in the long and the short run.

Mainstream economists generally support free trade for the reasons outlined above, subject to some qualifications. One qualification, known as the "infant industry" argument and sometimes associated with (among others) Alexander Hamilton, is that developing countries (such as the United States, in Hamilton's day) may need to protect their industries for a period of time to enable them to grow to an efficient scale. Many economists would concede the point, though some would caution that it's easy to overestimate how much protection an infant industry really needs, and to underestimate the difficulty of lifting protective tariffs once they're no longer needed. In addition, since the 1970s economists have developed models of how, in the presence of certain conditions, governments sometimes could improve domestic welfare by engaging in "strategic" or "managed" trade. For example, in a market characterized by economies of scale in production such that only one firm is destined to survive over the long run, or conversely in an industry in which expenditures on research and development are likely to produce knowledge spillovers that would benefit other domestic firms, government policies that benefit domestic firms at the expense of foreign competitors in theory could result in larger domestic social welfare gains that would be possible under free trade. As with the infant industry argument, however, any such policies would have to be undertaken with caution: free trade might still dominate over managed trade if government actors lack adequate information (e.g., about whether the necessary conditions that favor managed trade are present, or what the optimal amount of the subsidy should be), or if foreign firms are likely to retaliate. As a result, as Paul Krugman sums up the mainstream view, "[t]here is still a case for free trade as a good policy, and as a useful target in the practical world of politics," even if the new economic thinking shows that it's more of a "reasonable rule of thumb" than a policy that's always right.[20]

One obvious problem, however, is that while free trade may increase a country's aggregate wealth as measured by conventional metrics such as gross domestic product, among individuals there will be both winners and losers. Firms that export more products will be better off, as will workers in those industries and consumers who buy a lot of imported goods. Workers in industries that can't compete with cheaper foreign goods, on the other hand, risk losing their jobs and thus, even if the prices of many of the goods they consume are lower, are likely to be worse off if they can't find new jobs at similar wages. And while in theory it would be possible to redistribute some of the gains from trade so as to make everyone better off, as a matter of political reality this is often a pipe dream; and some losses, like the loss of dignity that comes from having a regular job, arguably couldn't be compensated by money anyway.[21] (US government programs to help retrain workers who've lost their jobs due to foreign competition also don't appear to have been much help so far.[22]) Morals aside, one might also question whether it's politically sound to outsource most of a country's unskilled or low-skill jobs to other countries: as I've noted already, inequality has been on the increase over the past few decades and among its potentially negative consequences is a loss of social cohesion and solidarity. (I've often wondered whether, at some point, free trade risks undermining the political stability that makes free trade possible in the first place; though of course free trade is hardly the only force that has contributed to inequality in the West, and on a global scale it's probably *reduced* inequality by expanding trade with the developing world.[23]) On the other hand, almost *any* government policy, like any technological change, is going to make some people better off and some worse off in comparison with the status quo; and it's at least worth asking whether it's fair to consumers to impose tariffs to protect, say, textile workers, if the effect is to raise the price of clothes consumers buy. Protectionism also might not seem very fair to workers in developing countries, who are more likely to emerge from poverty as a result of increased global trade. Of course, those workers might be working for low wages and under appalling conditions, and this too seems unfair, both to them and to workers in higher income countries who can't compete on those terms. True, working in a sweatshop may be preferable to the even worse poverty that might be one's lot in life if the sweatshop didn't exist—though the dichotomy may be a false one. According to some analyses, the portion of the price of, say, a garment made in a developing country that goes toward wages often is so minuscule that it could be substantially increased without having much of an effect on demand.[24] Some observers also favor linking trade with improvements in labor and environmental standards, thought economists by and large have been hesitant to embrace such proposals.[25]

In any event, even if you're convinced that on balance the benefits of free trade generally outweigh the costs (as I am), the fact that those benefits are prospective and disperse, while the losses tend to be concentrated and tangible, means that free trade advocates often have faced an uphill battle in convincing politicians to rally to their cause. The United States, for example, dating back to Hamilton's support for infant industries, imposed high tariffs and other trade barriers for much of its history. In the nineteenth and early twentieth centuries, the Republican Party in particular was the champion of high tariffs, even though in more recent decades (prior to its turn to a populist stance as epitomized by Donald Trump) Republicans have been more likely than Democrats to support free trade (the latter tending to be more in alignment with organized labor, environmental groups, and other entities that are often skeptical of free trade). Even so, it was a Democratic president (Bill Clinton) who presided over the establishment of the North American Free Trade Agreement (NAFTA) and the WTO in 1990s—which if anything goes to show that at least for a period of time both major parties in the United States had largely embraced a commitment to freer trade, as did leaders in many other advanced economies at the time. (I say "freer" trade, because in probably every country you'll find interest groups that lobby, sometimes successfully, for the maintenance of subsidies or other trade barriers that favor them, though of course there are also plenty of organized groups pushing for open markets.)

Freer trade gained momentum during the latter part of the twentieth century in part due to historical circumstances and experience.[26] One of the principal examples that economists often cite in support of free trade is the enactment of the Smoot-Hawley Tariff Act of 1930, by which the United States raised its tariffs to their highest levels in history. As many economists at the time feared, this increase only worsened the global depression by provoking retaliation from other countries; in turn, the depression contributed to the coming war by stoking political extremism and weakening confidence in democratic governance. During World War II, the sentiment among many of the Allied leaders was that trade, development, and economic stability would reduce the risk of another war. Thus in July 1944, with events now appearing to favor an Allied victory, delegates from forty-four governments assembled in Bretton Woods, New Hampshire for the United Nations Monetary and Financial Conference, usually referred to as the Bretton Woods Conference. There they drafted a proposal for a postwar international financial system consisting of three principal parts: an International Monetary Fund (IMF), which would assist governments in stabilizing exchange rates and provide short-term economic assistance; an International Bank for Reconstruction and Development, or "World Bank," which would provide longer term assistance to the war-ravaged nations of Europe and to lesser developed countries; and an International Trade Organization (ITO), which would administer matters relating to international trade, labor standards, and other subjects. As it turned out, the IMF and the World Bank got off the ground shortly after the war but the ITO never did, with US concerns over its potential loss of sovereignty often cited as a major reason for the ITO's failure.

Early in 1947, however, at a time when the ITO was still viewed as viable, President Truman invited delegates from twenty-three nations to participate in negotiations on the reduction of tariffs, which Truman believed would help revive Europe's economies. The conference took place in Geneva, Switzerland, and resulted in a tariff reduction agreement known as the General Agreement on Tariffs and Trade (GATT). Feeling at the time was that GATT would be just one component of a more comprehensive agreement or set of agreements to be administered by the ITO, but after the ITO's failure GATT developed what Thomas Dillon has called a "quasi-organizational status" of its own.[27] The next few decades witnessed periodic "rounds" of trade negotiations and new agreements concluded within the GATT framework. In 1986, delegates convened in Punta del Sol, Uruguay, for a new round of negotiations that concluded in 1993 with the "Final Act Embodying the Results of the Uruguay Round of Multilateral Trade Negotiations." The Final Act comprises a number of separate agreements (known collectively as the "Uruguay Round Agreements"), including the Agreement Establishing the World Trade Organization (whose job is to administer the other treaties that make up the Uruguay Round Agreements), as well as new agreements addressing trade in agriculture, textiles, services, and other subjects. One of these new agreements was TRIPS. I'll discuss some of the details of TRIPS shortly, but for now will note only that TRIPS requires all member states of the WTO to adhere to certain common standards of protection with respect to IP rights—standards that were stronger, in some respects, than what some countries previously had been willing to adopt.

The postwar movement toward freer trade blossomed outside of the GATT framework as well. In 1951, six European states (Belgium, France, Italy, Luxembourg, the Netherlands, and West Germany) formed a quasi–free trade zone known as the European Steel and Coal Community, which later morphed into the European Economic Community or Common Market and eventually expanded into the European Union (EU).[28] At present (and until "Brexit" is finalized), the EU comprises a twenty-eight-nation political and economic federation that includes most of the European states and that requires its members to adhere to the principles of free movement of goods, services, labor, and capital. (Four non-EU nations—Iceland, Liechtenstein, Norway, and Switzerland—are members of something called the European Free Trade Agreement. The first three but not Switzerland also are members, along with all of the EU states, of the European Economic Area [EEA], which follows the principle of free trade within the internal European market.) On the other side of the Atlantic, the United States and Canada in 1987 entered into the Canada–United States Free Trade Agreement, and, along with Mexico, the two nations entered into the North American Free Trade Agreement (NAFTA) in 1993. NAFTA includes several provisions relating to IP, though NAFTA's provisions on patents aren't greatly different from what we find in TRIPS.

I've now spent a few pages discussing the arguments for and against free trade, along with the run-up to the establishment of the WTO, but I still haven't explained the connection between free trade and patents: *why* does GATT 1994 include a treaty on IP, of all things? One reason, according to some commentators, was the recognition that products and services embodying IP rights had become an extremely important component of international trade, and that the ways in which nations regulated IP could either facilitate or hinder that trade. Rules like Austria-Hungary's long-ago "working" requirement, for example, arguably made it more difficult for foreigners to compete; analogously, by tolerating the sale of counterfeit trademarked or copyrighted goods a country could give its domestic producers an advantage over foreign trademark and copyright owners. Thus, in the words of one writer, "[w]hile strong intellectual property rights were once believed to create possible trade barriers, today the international exchange of goods is threatened by insufficient or nonexistent intellectual property rights . . . . It has been discovered that the absence of adequate protection of intellectual property or the existence of excessive protection can undermine the benefits derived from the elimination of high tariffs and the reduction of nontariff barriers."[29] Relatedly, there's the argument noted above that a system of strong IP rights stands to benefit everyone, including the developing countries, by encouraging technology transfer, foreign investment, and the development of new products and services.

Whether the extension of strong IP rights as embodied in TRIPS really does work to the benefit of developing countries nevertheless remains a matter of dispute. As we've seen, the empirical evidence to date suggests that while there are some potential benefits from adopting IP laws, those benefits are more likely to be realized in the higher-income developing countries; and there are potentially some substantial costs as well. Indeed, the more skeptical literature on TRIPS argues that the treaty disproportionately benefits the developed countries, with the skeptics themselves divided into two camps. The more positive view sees TRIPS as part of a larger bargain that stood to benefit both the rich and poor, albeit in different ways. Thus, while the wealthier countries stood to gain more from stronger IP rights than did the poorer countries, the successful conclusion of the Uruguay Round required the wealthy to make a number of concessions to the poor, including a reduction on trade barriers in products such as textiles and agricultural products; the promise of greater technical assistance and investment, as discussed below; and (as also discussed below) a method for settling disputes that shielded developing countries from the imposition of unilateral trade sanctions.[30] The more pessimistic view, by contrast, views the developing countries either as having been coerced into signing off on TRIPS or as having failed to appreciate the treaty's significance.[31] (Personally, although I find the empirical evidence that IP laws can benefit developing countries fairly convincing, I recognize that developing countries are not uniform in terms of their relative development, resources, political structure, and other relevant characteristics. Perhaps all of the views described above have some kernel of truth.)

TRIPS itself articulates several key principles. First, consistent with the more positive perspectives noted above, article 7 (titled "Objectives") states that the protection and enforcement of IP rights "should contribute to the promotion of technological innovation and to the transfer and dissemination of technology, to the mutual advantage of producers and users of technological knowledge and in a manner conducive to social and economic welfare, and to a balance of rights and obligations." Relatedly, article 8 (titled "Principles") states that, "in formulating or amending their laws and regulations" members may "adopt measures necessary to protect public health and nutrition, and to promote the public interest in sectors of vital importance to their socio-economic and technological development, provided that such measures are consistent with the provisions of this Agreement"; and that "[a]ppropriate measures, provided that they are consistent with the provisions of this Agreement, may be needed to prevent the abuse of intellectual property rights by right holders or the resort to practices which unreasonably restrain trade or adversely affect the international transfer of technology." As we'll see shortly, however, just a few years after TRIPS entered into force a debate arose over whether the other provisions of the treaty *should be read in light of* articles 7 and 8, thus arguably providing for a measure of flexibility in the interpretation of those other provisions; or whether the other provisions *should be understood as already embodying* the objectives and principles, in which case those provisions might be interpreted more strictly.

Second, TRIPS adopts a principle that we've encountered already in connection with the Paris Convention, national treatment—the idea that you can't treat nationals of other member states worse than you treat your own citizens or residents.[32] Third, subject to some exceptions TRIPS requires that nations also follow the most-favored-nation principle, which means that any additional protection they extend to nationals of any WTO member must be offered to nationals of all WTO members.[33] For example, if the United States and South Korea, both WTO members, were to conclude a separate bilateral agreement requiring South Korea to extend copyright protection to US authors for the life of the author plus seventy years, South Korea would have to offer that benefit to nationals of all other WTO member states.

Fourth, TRIPS requires that all WTO members maintain certain minimum standards with respect to the protection of patents, trademarks, copyrights, and some other forms of IP. It does so first by incorporating by reference most of the key provisions of the Paris and Berne Conventions, including the Paris Convention's rules concerning priority.[34] Thus, whether a WTO member is a party to these other treaties or not, it's bound *as a WTO member* to follow the standards laid out in those treaties. In addition, TRIPS includes a large number of provisions relating to the enforcement of IP rights. Member states must allow IP owners to seek redress in court for the infringement of their rights, for example, and must make available effective remedies such as damages and injunctions.[35] Most important for our purposes, however, is that TRIPS requires members to maintain a variety of substantive IP standards not found in any of the earlier treaties; we'll see what those rules are for patents shortly.

Finally, though, before proceeding to substance, it's important to note that since TRIPS is a WTO-administered treaty, any WTO member that believes another member is in violation of TRIPS (or of any other WTO-administered treaty) can make use of the WTO's dispute resolution procedure to try to resolve the matter. Briefly stated, if negotiations between the affected countries fail to resolve the dispute, the parties can present their case before the WTO Dispute

Settlement Body, which will eventually issue a ruling. (The losing party can appeal the ruling to the WTO's Appellate Body.) If, at the end of this process, the accused country is found to be in violation, the WTO may authorize the complaining party to impose trade sanctions as a means for coercing the violator into compliance. In this respect, TRIPS goes beyond the Paris Convention and other earlier treaties, which as we saw earlier don't provide an effective mechanism for resolving disputes. Since most of the Paris and Berne Convention provisions are incorporated by reference in TRIPS, however, a WTO member that has reason to believe that another member isn't following, say, the Paris Convention's rules concerning priority, now has a more effective means for trying to compel the scofflaw to change its practice.

So what exactly are the substantive provisions of TRIPS relating to patents? Most of them won't seem very surprising in comparison with US law, but some of them did require substantial changes to other countries' laws. For example, article 27 of TRIPS requires that, subject to some exceptions, "patents shall be available for any inventions, whether products or processes, in all fields of technology, provided that they are new, involve an inventive step and are capable of industrial application"; and that "patents shall be available and patent rights enjoyable without discrimination as to the place of invention, the field of technology and whether products are imported or locally produced."[36] (The terms "new," "inventive step," and "capable of industrial organization" correspond to the US requirements of novelty, nonobviousness, and utility.[37]) The exceptions permitted under article 27 are that members may exclude, first, inventions that lack what I referred to in Chapter 1 as "moral utility," meaning roughly that the practice of such inventions would contravene some fundamental public policy. Second, article 27 permits nations to exclude "diagnostic, therapeutic, and surgical methods," which as discussed in previous chapters many nations do. (In the United States, the validity and enforceability of such methods are constrained by Patent Act § 287 and more recently by the *Mayo* decision.) Third, nations may exclude "plants and animals other than micro-organisms."[38] The negative implication is that nations must consider human-created living organisms like Dr. Chakrabarty's bacteria to be patent-eligible but not higher life forms like the Oncomouse or new varieties of plants. (Members that exclude plants from utility patent protection, however, are required to offer some alternative form of exclusive rights, such as the plant patents I briefly discussed in Chapters 1 and 3. I'll return to the subject to plant patents at the end of this chapter.)

Notice, however, that subject to the preceding exceptions article 27 requires members to offer patent protection to all "fields of technology," including, presumably, pharmaceuticals. For countries that *didn't* previously extend patent protection to drugs, this was a substantial, and as you can imagine, controversial change. (Indeed, until fairly recently even some of the developed countries didn't allow drug patents. Italy didn't until 1978, and Spain until 1992.[39]) Nevertheless, since TRIPS doesn't define the term "field of technology," a member state probably could take the position that business methods—and perhaps software, too—are ineligible for patent protection because they're not sufficiently "technological" in nature. On the other hand, article 27's prohibition on discrimination as to field of technology might indicate that whatever standards a country adopts with regard to patents must be the same for all fields of technology, whatever those are. (There is an ongoing debate, however, about whether some *differentiation* among fields might be permissible, at least under some circumstances.[40]) This runs contrary to the recommendation of some scholars who believe that a sensible patent system would provide a greater incentive for fields such as pharmaceuticals that are cost-intensive and a lesser incentive for others—though the counterargument, that different rules for different fields of technology would only encourage industries to curry favor to be counted among the favored few, is in my view more persuasive.

Moving along, article 28 of TRIPS requires that members shall confer upon patent owners the right to prevent the unauthorized manufacture, use, offer for sale, sale, and importation of patented inventions during the term of patent, as well as the right to assign, transfer, or license their rights; and article 33 mandates that the term of protection "shall not end before the expiration of a period of twenty years counted from the filing date." These articles actually required Congress to make a couple of tweaks to US law: first, by conferring upon patent owners the right to prevent "offers to sell," which the patent statute hadn't explicitly mentioned before; and second, by changing the patent term from seventeen years from the date of grant to a term that begins on the date of grant and ends twenty years from the date of filing.

Article 28 also drops a footnote stating that the rights conferred upon patent owners are subject to TRIPS article 6, which in essence says that member states are not obligated to adopt any particular "exhaustion" or "first-sale" doctrine, a topic I haven't discussed until now.[41] The basic concept, which the United States and other countries apply to copyrights and trademarks as well as patents, is that once the IP owner has authorized the sale or other transfer of ownership of a product embodying her IP right, the lawful owner may resell (and, in the patent context, use) the product without having to obtain any further permission from the IP owner; the patent owner's right to control the subsequent use or resale of the article is "exhausted" at the point of first sale. Thus, under US law, once you buy your computer or smartphone the owners of the many patents lawfully embodied in those devices have no right based on patent law to prevent you from using those inventions or from reselling the devices. (Repairs, by the way, are considered permissible uses, but you're not permitted to "remake" the invention altogether because the sale doesn't exhaust the "making" right.

Litigation sometimes ensues over whether the owner of a patented product has engaged in a permissible repair or an impermissible making.) The exhaustion rule generally conforms to people's settled expectations of what they may do with the tangible products they own, though there are other possible theoretical justifications we don't need to go into here.[42]

For our purposes, the main thing I want to highlight is that TRIPS articles 6 and 28 allow nations to decide for themselves whether to apply a regime of "national" exhaustion, meaning that only domestic sales exhaust the patent owner's rights, or "international" exhaustion, meaning that a lawful sale anywhere in the world exhausts those rights. (There are other possible variations including "regional" exhaustion, under which exhaustion within a specific region such as the EEA is triggered by an authorized sale anywhere within that region.) Until recently, the Federal Circuit interpreted US patent law as embodying the principle of national exhaustion, so that sales occurring outside the United States wouldn't exhaust US patent rights, even if the patent owner authorized those sales. Thus, if an invention was patented in both the United States and, say, France, a person who lawfully purchased a product incorporating that invention in France would be infringing the US patent owner's rights if he imported the product into the United States, or used or sold it here. In May 2017, however, in *Impression Products, Inc. v. Lexmark International*, the US Supreme Court held that US law follows a regime of international exhaustion, based in part on the Court's concern about national exhaustion impeding the flow of international commerce.[43] For the time being, however, this ruling is unlikely to result in the mass importation into the United States of patented pharmaceuticals sold at cheaper prices abroad, given that FDA law also forbids the unauthorized importation of pharmaceuticals, whether protected by patents or not. Both the FDA and the drug companies nevertheless have long tolerated US citizens' importation of small quantities of cheaper drugs from Canada and Mexico.[44] (For what it's worth, I'm inclined to think that a regime of international exhaustion is preferable from the standpoint of global welfare. Readers who wish to follow up on this point should consult the preceding endnote.)

TRIPS also contains two provisions regulating the conditions that member states may impose on the exercise of patent rights. First, article 30 states that "[m]embers may provide limited exceptions to the exclusive rights conferred by a patent, provided that such exceptions do not unreasonably conflict with a normal exploitation of the patent and do not unreasonably prejudice the legitimate interests of the patent owner, taking account of the legitimate interests of third parties." An example of an exception that would be permitted under article 30 is the "experimental use" defense, under which third parties are allowed to make and use patented inventions for purposes of experimentation.[45] (The US experimental use exceptions are much narrower than those applied in other countries, as I noted in Chapters 1 and 3.) Article 30 also probably tolerates a variety of other narrow exceptions. One, which many countries have adopted, is to exempt private noncommercial uses of patented inventions from the scope of infringement liability.[46] The United States hasn't adopted this exception, however, so if your smartphone (say) incorporates some patent-infringing component, technically you're liable for using that feature even if you have no idea that the patent exists. (We'll come back to the subject of end-user liability in Chapter 8.) Another, which the United States did not fully embrace until enactment of the AIA in 2011, is to allow someone who invents a process or machine and maintains it as her trade secret to continue using it in her own business, even after someone else independently invents and patents it.[47]

Second, article 31 imposes a number of conditions on the compulsory licensing of patents, something that I've alluded to earlier in this book. The basic idea is that sometimes a nation may wish to compel the patent owner to license the right to make, use, or sell the patented invention, either to the government itself or to third parties, at some government-determined price. The United States generally has avoided ordering the compulsory licensing of patents, subject to a few exceptions. One, which I noted in Chapter 6, is that the United States government has a right to make and use—and to authorize government contractors to make and use—patented inventions pursuant to a federal statute, 28 USC § 1498, in exchange for reasonable compensation. (Many of these uses over the years have been for military purposes, though as I noted in Chapter 6, the government arguably could employ the statute more aggressively in an effort to lower the price it pays for drugs.) Second, the Bayh-Dole and Stevenson-Wydler Acts that I mentioned in Chapter 6, as well as the Plant Variety Protection Act and the federal Clean Water Act, all authorize the government to order compulsory licensing under some circumstances, though to date the government has never exercised its authority to do so under these statutes.[48] Third, courts occasionally have ordered patent owners to license their patents at court-determined royalties (or for free) as a penalty for certain antitrust violations. Fourth, as we'll see in more detail in Chapter 9, since 2007 in about 25 percent of the cases in which US patent owners have prevailed at trial, the court has declined to issue an injunction and instead has ordered the infringer to pay a court-determined royalty covering the defendant's future use of the technology. (Although the Federal Circuit doesn't consider this last example to be a type of compulsory licensing, since the court isn't requiring the patent owner to make the patent available to *anyone* who's able to pay the court-determined royalty,[49] the government clearly *is* compelling the patent owner to license the patent to a specific defendant.)

In other countries, by contrast, governments at one time frequently employed compulsory licensing, particularly in connection with drug patents. Until 1993, for example, Canada routinely compelled the owners of pharmaceutical patents to license their patents to generic drug manufacturers, as a means of controlling the price of drugs.[50] Other countries from time to time also have required compulsory licensing as a penalty for the patent owner's failure to "work" the patent domestically. (The Paris Convention sets some limits on how long a government must wait before it imposes compulsory licensing as a penalty for failure to work but otherwise tolerates the practice. Nevertheless, the United States, unlike Austria-Hungary among others, has never imposed a domestic working requirement. Again, we'll come back to this issue in Chapter 8.) A third common situation in which governments may compel the licensing of a patent occurs when one person has a "dominant" patent and another invents an improvement that includes the dominant patent. (If you think back to Chapter 1, imagine that the dominant patent claims elements A, B, and C, and that the improvement comprises elements A, B, C, and D.) If the improvement itself is sufficiently novel and nonobvious it can be patented too, but the owner won't be able to practice the improvement without permission of the dominant patent owner (who in turn won't be able to practice the improvement without permission of the owner of the improvement patent). This is known as the "blocking patents" scenario, since the patents block each of the owners from practicing the improvement. Many countries reserve the right to respond to blocking patents by imposing compulsory licensing.

Economists have long debated whether compulsory licensing of patents is a good idea. A conventional argument *against* compulsory licensing is that patents are best protected by what economists refer to as a "property rule," which means that the owner has a right to exclude others (if necessary, by getting a court to issue an injunction), rather than by means of a "liability rule," which means that in the event of a dispute the owner has a right only to recover monetary compensation. Some legal rights typically are protected by property rules, others by liability rules. If you trespass on my land, for example, I'm usually entitled to enforce my rights by getting the sheriff to evict you (though I'd be entitled to monetary damages for any quantifiable harm your presence caused me to suffer during the interim), whereas if you breach your contract with me I'm usually entitled only to sue you for monetary damages. One reason that is often cited for protecting patents (and other types of IP) by means of a property rule is that it's difficult to value IP assets. The economic value of a patented technology to a prospective user is the profit or other benefit she expects to derive from the use of the technology, in comparison with the benefit she would expect to derive from using the next-best alternative. Thus, if I could expect to earn $1 million from using an unpatented, public domain technology to make the products I sell to consumers, and $2 million if I used a more efficient patented technology, the value of the patent to me is $1 million. Presumably I'd be willing to pay up to $1 million for a license to use it, and if the patent owner is willing to accept

$1 million or less we'll strike a deal. (If not—if the patent owner thinks he could earn more by using the patent himself and excluding me, or by licensing the patent to someone else on an exclusive basis, he'll refuse me. That's the market working, however, not a market failure.)

Anyway, the conventional wisdom is that it's hard for a third party, such as a court or other government agency, to determine what that value *is*; and, to the extent we think it's important to "get it right" in order to preserve the patent incentive scheme, we might prefer to leave it to the parties to negotiate their own deal rather than having a court try to do it for them. Put another way, if courts are likely to award damages that systematically either over- or underestimate the value of the invention in comparison with alternatives, the result would be that patents would be either stronger or weaker than they should be. As a result, the public would wind up paying either too much for the invention in view of the benefits it provides, or not enough to make it worthwhile for would-be users to negotiate with the patent owner for the right to use the invention. In the latter case, would-be users may just as well infringe and, if necessary, pay a modest court-determined royalty. Knowing that that's the likely outcome in advance, the patent owner would then be motivated to license the technology at a modest rate—which is terrific, if the patent incentive isn't really necessary to stimulate invention, but not so good in the long run if it is. In that case, a property rule might better serve the public interest, because the would-be user then has an incentive up front to negotiate with the patent owner, based on the parties' best estimates of the benefit of the invention in comparison with alternatives. (If the defendant decides to infringe anyway and gets caught, under a property-rule regime the court will order the defendant to stop using the invention, in which case the parties can negotiate a license at that point, based on their estimates of the value of the invention. Knowing that this is the likely outcome in advance, they're motivated to negotiate early and avoid court.)

By contrast, if we think that it's not too difficult for courts to determine an appropriate royalty, we might prefer a liability rule under which, in the event of infringement, the user will be ordered to pay court-determined damages for any past and future infringement. (Of course, both parties are still better off negotiating a license, if they can, in order to avoid the cost of going to trial.) After all, if damages are fully compensatory in the sense that they replicate the bargain the parties themselves would have struck prior to the infringement, the patent owner is no worse off than it would have been under a property rule; and not allowing an injunction avoids the risk that the patent owner will be able to negotiate a royalty that exceeds the value of the invention, in a case in which the defendant accidentally infringes and is thereafter locked-in to the infringing technology (a topic we'll come back to in the next two chapters' discussion of patent trolls and the smartphone wars). Alternatively, maybe the government doesn't or shouldn't care about "getting it right," in the sense of accurately estimating the market value of the technology: rather, it just wants to keep prices low for the immediate benefit of consumers. As above, such a strategy makes sense if the patent incentive is irrelevant, though in that case maybe it would make more sense to abolish patents altogether and be done with it. (On the other hand, if the patent incentive actually does benefit consumers in the long run, the widespread adoption of such a strategy would threaten to impoverish everyone—though you can see why any individual country might have an incentive to free-ride, if it can.) In either case, a liability rule might, in theory, enable a court or agency to set monetary compensation at an appropriate level below the amount the patent owner otherwise could demand.

You can see why the stakes may be particularly high when we're talking about something like pharmaceuticals. On the one hand, allowing the drug companies to reap an appropriate reward is important if, as I suggested in Chapter 6, the ability to recoup high R&D costs is what drives drug companies to invent new drugs. On the other hand, the resulting high prices can also mean that the drug will be priced out of reach for some of the people who need it the most. (By definition, a monopolist's profit-maximizing price will exclude consumers who are willing to pay a price above the marginal cost of production but who won't or can't pay the monopoly price.) In the case of life-saving drugs, such restrictions on access can result in unnecessary suffering and death, which may seem like a good reason to restrict patent owners from charging the monopoly price. One possible response, then, as I suggested in Chapter 6, is some form of price regulation, which in fact is how many countries though not the United States respond to the problem. Another possible response is compulsory licensing, under which the government compels the drug company to license, on terms set by the government, the right to make and sell the patented invention either to the government itself or to third parties. Both price regulation and compulsory licensing, however, risk the possibility that the government will set the price too low to provide adequate compensation, so that in the long run the incentive to invent and market newer and better drugs will diminish. The empirical evidence on the effect of compulsory licensing on the incentive to invent nevertheless is ambiguous. Economist Mike Scherer, for example, "reported a decline in patenting activity among 38 firms subject to compulsory licensing antitrust decrees from 1954–56, but he found no significant decline in R&D based on a similar survey of 44 firms conducted in 1975."[51]

TRIPS doesn't place any explicit restriction on the grounds a government may cite for requiring compulsory licensing, but article 31 does impose a host of conditions that governments must satisfy before they do so. For example, article 31(b) states that a government may not permit compulsory licensing unless "prior to such use, the proposed user has made efforts to obtain authorization from the right holder on reasonable commercial terms and conditions and . . . such efforts have not been successful with a reasonable period of time. This requirement may be waived by a Member in the case of national emergency or other circumstances of extreme urgency or in cases of public non-commercial use." The general rule, therefore, is that someone who wants the government to issue a compulsory license is supposed to first negotiate with the patent owner, on (undefined) "reasonable commercial terms and conditions," and that the government may issue the license only if such efforts are rebuffed—except in cases of (undefined) "national emergency or other circumstances of extreme urgency," or public non-commercial uses (like the US government's use of patents for military purposes). Beyond this, article 31 specifies, among other things, that the scope and duration of the use must be "limited to the purpose for which it was authorized"; licenses must be nonexclusive, generally nonassignable, and "authorized predominantly for the supply of the domestic market"; authorization "shall be liable . . . to be terminated if and when the circumstances which led to it cease to exist and are unlikely to recur"; the patent owner must be paid adequate remuneration; and there must be an opportunity for judicial review of the license and the remuneration. These conditions stand in stark contrast with the Paris Convention, article 5A of which imposes only some modest limits on the practice (for example, by obligating member states that require patent owners to work their patents to wait for at least three years before resorting to compulsory licensing for failure to work).[52]

Finally, TRIPS provided developing countries with a somewhat longer period of time to conform their laws to the TRIPS Agreement generally and to the patent provisions in particular.[53] As a general matter, nations that were members of the WTO as of the date the WTO treaties entered into force (January 1, 1995), had a period of one year (that is, until January 1, 1996) to conform their laws to TRIPS. (The United States made the changes it deemed necessary, such as changing the way the patent term is calculated, in a statute Congress enacted in December 1994, which became effective in June 1995.) TRIPS permitted developing country members, however, to delay implementing the agreement (except for the provisions on national treatment and most-favored-nation status) until January 1, 2000, and they were given until January 1, 2005, to extend product patent protection in any fields of technology for which they did not offer patent protection as of January 1, 1995. (As noted above, for many developing countries pharmaceuticals were one such field.) Further, *least*-developed countries (LDCs) were given until January 1, 2006, to apply any portions of the agreement other than national treatment and most-favored nation status.[54] In addition, TRIPS included provisions promising that developed countries would provide assistance to the developing countries and LDCs. In particular, article 66(2) provides that "Developed country Members shall provide incentives to enterprises and institutions in their territories for the purpose of promoting and encouraging technology transfer to least-developed country Members in order to enable them to create a sound and viable technological base," while article 67 states that "developed country Members shall provide, on request and on mutually agreed terms and conditions, technical and financial cooperation in favour of developing and least-developed country Members," including "assistance in the preparation of laws and regulations on the protection and enforcement of intellectual property rights as well as on the prevention of their abuse" and "support regarding the establishment or reinforcement of domestic offices and agencies relevant to these matters, including the training of personnel."

Developing countries and LDCs taking advantage of these extensions nevertheless had to start accepting receipt of patent applications for drugs and agricultural chemicals as of January 1, 1996, and once those countries got around to reviewing these applications, they'd have to examine them based on the prior art as it existed as of the date of filing. This rule was known as the "mailbox" rule, because countries had to have a metaphorical "mailbox" available for accepting patent applications. Another transitional provision—known as the "pipeline" provision, because it required protection for drugs that were "in the pipeline"—required that developing countries and LDCs would have to extend exclusive rights for a period of time to drugs that had been cleared for marketing in their home country and in the developing country or LDC, even though the patent application covering those drugs in the developing country or LDC was still pending. In the late 1990s, the United States and the EU both commenced proceedings against India for failing to apply these two rules. The WTO ruled for the complainants, after which India amended its domestic law.[55]

Doha and Its Aftermath

It didn't take too long for the battle lines to form. In 1998, a consortium of thirty-nine drug companies commenced an action in South Africa to have a new law permitting the importation of generic AIDS drugs into the country declared unconstitutional.[56] While this case was pending, the United States initiated an action against Brazil before the WTO, arguing that Brazil's domestic working requirement, which threatened certain AIDS drug patents with forfeiture, violated TRIPS. Both lawsuits attracted a lot of bad publicity, however, and by mid-2001, the drug companies had withdrawn their complaint in South Africa, and the United States and Brazil reached a settlement of the WTO dispute.[57]

Meanwhile, preparations were under way for a WTO Ministerial Conference to be held in Doha, Qatar, in November 2001, with development issues the principal item on the agenda.[58] In the months leading up to the conference, some developing countries began staking out a position in favor of a conference declaration to the effect that developing countries have the right to resort to compulsory licensing to combat public health emergencies; that TRIPS article 31 must be interpreted in light of the principles and objectives set out in articles 7 and 8; and that nations are permitted to use compulsory licensing to supply drugs to markets which do not have the manufacturing capability to engage in meaningful compulsory licensing themselves. The United States, Switzerland, and to a lesser extent the EU initially objected to these proposals, arguing among other things that the flexibility the developing nations wanted was already provided for in the TRIPS provisions allowing poor countries a longer time to conform their laws to the treaty.

Then came 9-11, followed by the anthrax scare, the latter of which led the US government to consider invoking 28 USC § 1498 to compel the licensing of ciprofloxacin in the event of a widespread outbreak of anthrax.[59] Under the circumstances, the West's opposition to the developing countries' agenda began to soften a bit. Shortly before the Ministerial Conference opened the United States, Switzerland, and the EU abandoned their hard line positions, and the member states of the WTO unanimously adopted a compromise text titled "Declaration on the TRIPS Agreement and Public Health," which I'll refer to as the TRIPS Declaration.[60]

The TRIPS Declaration consists of seven paragraphs. The first three affirm the members' recognition of "the gravity of the public health problems afflicting many developing and least-developed countries, especially those resulting from HIV/AIDS, tuberculosis, malaria and other epidemics"; the need for TRIPS "to be part of the wider national and international action to address these problems"; and both the importance of IP "for the development of new medicines" and "concerns about its effects on prices." The substantive provisions of the Declaration then begin with paragraphs 4 and 5, which state:

4. We agree that the TRIPS Agreement does not and should not prevent members from taking measures to protect public health. Accordingly, while reiterating our commitment to the TRIPS Agreement, we affirm that the Agreement can and should be interpreted and implemented in a manner supportive of WTO members' right to protect public health and, in particular, to promote access to medicines for all.

    In this connection, we reaffirm the right of WTO members to use, to the full, the provisions in the TRIPS Agreement, which provide flexibility for this purpose.

5. Accordingly and in light of paragraph four above, while maintaining our commitments in the TRIPS Agreement, we recognize that these flexibilities include:

   a. In applying the customary rules of interpretation of public international law, each provision of the TRIPS Agreement shall be read in the light of the object and purpose of the Agreement as expressed, in particular, in its objectives and principles.

   b. Each member has the right to grant compulsory licenses and the freedom to determine the grounds upon which such licenses are granted.

   c. Each member has the right to determine what constitutes a national emergency or other circumstances of extreme urgency, it being understood that public health crises, including those relating to HIV/AIDS, tuberculosis, malaria and other epidemics, can represent a national emergency or other circumstances of extreme urgency.

   d. The effect of the provisions in the TRIPS Agreement that are relevant to the exhaustion of intellectual property rights is to leave each member free to establish its own regime for such exhaustion without challenge, subject to the [most-favored nation] and national treatment provisions of Articles three and four.

Paragraph 6 then recognizes that nations with insufficient pharmaceutical manufacturing capability might not be able to make effective use of compulsory licensing, and directed the Council for TRIPS (the body responsible for administering the agreement) "to find an expeditious solution to this problem and to report to the General Council [of the WTO] before the end of 2002."[61] Paragraph 7 closes by "reaffirm[ing] the commitment of the developed-country members to provide incentives to their enterprises and institutions to promote and encourage technology transfer to least-developed country members pursuant to Article 66.2," and by extending the date by which LDCs had to conform their patent laws with respect to pharmaceuticals from January 1, 2006 to January 1, 2016.

At first blush, the TRIPS Declaration seems like a major victory for the developing countries. As those countries had hoped, the Declaration recognizes that TRIPS should be interpreted "flexibly," in light of its purposes and objectives, and in a manner "supportive" of its members' right to protect public health. Moreover, although TRIPS article 31 remains in effect, members are free to consider public health crises as "a national emergency or other circumstances of extreme urgency" that allow them to dispense with the need to negotiate with patent owners before resorting to compulsory licensing. Moreover, the WTO had now committed itself to coming up with "an expeditious solution" for countries with insufficient manufacturing capabilities to make "effective use" of compulsory licensing, and it extended the time period for LDCs to comply with the bulk of the TRIPS provisions for another ten years. In light of these concessions, you might expect that in the years following Doha there's been a flurry of compulsory licensing of essential medicines for the benefit of developing countries and LDCs.

Think again. Once the initial euphoria had worn off, it became apparent that things weren't going to move all that fast after all. 2002 came and went without the Council for TRIPS having found the promised "expeditious solution" for the benefit of countries with insufficient manufacturing capabilities to make effective use of compulsory licensing. In August 2003, however, the General Council issued a decision titled "Implementation of Paragraph 6 of the Doha Declaration on the TRIPS Agreement and Public Health," which I'll refer to as the "Implementation Decision," setting out a policy under which members with inadequate manufacturing capabilities could pair up with members who were willing to export generic copies of patented drugs.[62] The basic idea was that an exporting nation could issue a compulsory license for the production and exportation of the drug, while the importing nation issued a corresponding compulsory license of importation. (Eligible importing members were defined as including all LDCs, as well as any developing countries that filed an appropriate notification.) As noted above, however, one of the many conditions that TRIPS article 31 imposes is that compulsory licensing "shall be authorized predominantly for the supply of the domestic market of the Member authorizing such use," so in order to effect the Implementation Decision the General Council agreed to waive this requirement as long as, among other conditions, the importation license "specifies the names and expected quantities of the product(s) needed," and the exportation license authorizes the export of only the specified amount. Further, the exporter must ensure that the generic products are "clearly identified as being produced under the system set out in this Decision through specific labelling or marking," such as "special packaging and/or special colouring/shaping of the products themselves, provided that such distinction is feasible and does not have a significant impact on price," and before shipment begins it must post on a website information about the quantities being supplied and their distinguishing features. The exporter also must notify the WTO of the grant, and it's still required to pay the "adequate remuneration" referred to in article 31. The importing member in turn is supposed to take reasonable measures to ensure that the imported products are not diverted for re-exportation to other countries. Finally, the text makes clear that the Implementation Decision was intended simply to be an interim measure, since the Council committed that it would terminate "on the date on which an amendment to the TRIPS Agreement replacing its provisions takes effect for that Member. The TRIPS Council shall initiate by the end of 2003 work on the preparation of such an amendment with a view to its adoption within six months." The WTO promptly congratulated it-self for having "removed the final obstacle to cheap drug imports."[63]

2003 and 2004 nevertheless came and went without the adoption of the proposed amendment, and without any notifications being filed by either el-igible importing or exporting nations.[64] In December 2005, however, the General Council announced that the members of the WTO had agreed to amend TRIPS by adding a new provision, article 31bis, which would (drum roll, please) . . . codify the Implementation Decision by adding its language to the text of TRIPS.[65] (It took two years just to do that?) Technically, however, the new ar-ticle wouldn't take effect until two-thirds of the WTO members formally ratified it. The General Council set a deadline of December 1, 2007, for the members to do so, but the deadline was thereafter extended. It was only in January 2017 that the WTO secured the necessary two-thirds approval for article 31bis finally to enter into force.[66]

And how has the Implementation Decision fared in the interim? In July 2007, a mere four years after the "final obstacle to cheap drug imports" allegedly had been removed, Rwanda filed the first-ever notification under the system, stating its intent to license the importation of a specified quantity of an AIDS drug from Canada; Canada followed up in October 2007 with its notice declaring that it was granting Apotex, Inc. a compulsory license to export that quantity to Rwanda.[67] So far, this remains the only instance of anyone taking advantage of the interim solution. As stated by Beall and Kuhn, "[t]his well-studied episode illustrated many pitfalls in the existing . . . system, including a variety of costly bureaucratic delays and a price that was still higher than for comparable Indian generics."[68] Little wonder, then, that there wasn't much enthusiasm for ratifying an amendment that simply codifies the failed Implementation Decision.

So has Doha actually accomplished anything of value to developing coun-tries? Maybe. There have been a few notable examples of compulsory licensing since 2001, including Brazil's issuance of a compulsory license for the manufac-ture of efavirenz, an AIDS drug, and Thailand's authorization of the compulsory licensing of two AIDS drugs, a heart disease drug, and three anticancer drugs.[69] Beall and Kuhn's 2012 study, however, could identify only "24 unique interna-tional CL [compulsory licensing] episodes from 1 January 1995 through 6 June 2011," collectively involving "40 drug patents for 22 unique pharmaceutical products." (Two countries, though, Ghana and Zimbabwe, authorized the com-pulsory licensing of all antiretroviral drugs [ARVs].) According to the authors, half of these twenty-four episodes "ended specifically in the announcement of a CL . . . but the great majority ended in some kind of price reduction for the potential issuing nation, whether via CL, VL [voluntary license], or discount." Two-thirds of the episodes involved ARVs. Eleven of the twenty-four occurred between 2003 and 2005, however, and the authors conclude that the volume of compulsory licensing has substantially tailed off since then.[70] On the other hand, since drug companies are aware of the possibility of being subject to compulsory licenses, they may be more willing to voluntarily lower their prices; and governments may be emboldened in some instances to construe their patent laws narrowly, thus making it more difficult to keep certain patents in force at all.[71]

Then again, maybe compulsory licensing was never all that it was cracked up to be in the first place. As I noted in an article I published back in 2004, several practical factors can constrain a country's ability to make and distribute drugs pursuant to compulsory license, "among them the need to have an established industrial sector in place that can engage in reverse engineering and production of the invention covered by the patent, and the need for an adequate legal and administrative system to oversee the compulsory licensing procedure."[72] (Of course, if a country is only compelling the licensing of the importation of a drug from somewhere else, concerns about domestic production are allayed somewhat.) Patents also aren't the only obstacles impeding access to essential medicines; in fact, about 95 percent of medicines the World Health Organization (WHO) includes in its Model List of Essential Medicines (MLEM) are off-patent, and the remaining 5 percent (mostly ARVs) are not subject to patent protection in many LDCs.[73] There's also some risk that widespread compulsory licensing could result in retaliation on the part of developed countries in the form of trade sanctions, and that drug companies would be less eager to provide drugs and technical assistance in such environments.[74] (Some of the research cited earlier in this chapter, you may recall, suggests that patents have played a positive role in encouraging drug companies to introduce new drugs in poor counties, and that lack of effective patent protection can have the opposite effect.[75]) Moreover, as stated in the recently issued *Report of the United Nations Secretary-General's High-Level Panel on Access to Medicines,* "[t]here are many reasons why people do not get the healthcare they need, including, inter alia, under-resourced health systems, a lack of sufficiently qualified and skilled healthcare workers, inequalities between and within countries, regulatory barriers, poor health education, unavailability of health insurance, exclusion, stigma, discrimination *and* exclusive rights" (emphasis added).[76]

Nevertheless, as the last part of that final quoted sentence indicates, IP rights do play *some* role in raising the cost of and, presumably, access to health care. Bilateral and plurilateral treaties such as the much-debated Trans-Pacific Partnership (TPP) also often include provisions going beyond what TRIPS itself requires, by including what are referred to as "TRIPS-Plus" provisions. These may include, for example, rules (all of which are found in US law) preventing generic manufacturers from having access to the patent owner's clinical data for a period of time; linking the approval for marketing of a generic drug to the lack of patent protection for the original version; and according drug patents some additional period of exclusivity to make up for regulatory delay in approving the drug for marketing.[77] Some of these new agreements also envision the use of something called the Investor-State Dispute Settlement (ISDS) process, under which private entities sometimes can require the governments to submit to mandatory arbitration.[78] Critics argue that the potential use of the ISDS procedure could chill poorer countries into overcompliance with their treaty obligations with respect to, among other things, IP, which is considered a qualifying "investment."[79]

As I suggested earlier, however, the development of newer and better treatments for diseases that are endemic to the developing world may depend less on conventional patents and more on alternatives such as AMCs. The UN report cited earlier, for example, calls for greater coordination among governments to implement such alternatives in order to "delink" R&D costs from price:

> Building on current discussions at the WHO, the United Nations Secretary-General should initiate a process for governments to negotiate global agreements on the coordination, financing and development of health technologies. This includes negotiations for a binding R&D Convention that delinks the costs of research and development from end prices to promote access to good health for all. The Convention should focus on public health needs, including but not limited to, innovation for neglected tropical diseases and antimicrobial resistance and must complement existing mechanisms.[80]

The report also recommends the adoption of international norms favoring greater transparency with regard to such matters as the extent of patent protection for medicines and vaccines, as well as the cost of R&D. As for the extent of patent protection, while it's true that all issued and many pending patents are public documents, the report notes that "patent information is often confusing, incomplete, and fragmented."[81] As a result, as Reed Beall observes, "[a]ccurate patent information on MLEM products is not readily available in most countries, which may act as a deterrent to potential manufacturers and exporters of essential medicines, who may erroneously believe there is patent protection where there is none."[82] To rectify this problem, the report recommends that WIPO establish and maintain a comprehensive, standardized, and publicly accessible database of patents relating to medicines and vaccines.[83] Second, with regard to R&D expenditures, the report notes a recent study by the nonprofit Drugs for Neglected Diseases Initiative (DNDi) that estimates its own average cost of developing new chemical entities for neglected diseases, including the cost of failures, was between $130 and $190 million.[84] The report cautions that this figure may not be directly comparable to the much higher figure reported by DiMasi et al., which we encountered in Chapter 5, "given the significant disparities in R&D costs depending on the health technologies in question and the costs of operation,"[85] but rightly notes that it would be helpful nonetheless to have more verifiable data on what the costs of drug development really are. The report also recommends greater efforts to make transparent the terms of voluntary licenses and the results of clinical trials.[86]

Finally, though, it's important to reiterate that health care in the developing world depends not only on the availability of old and new medicines at affordable prices, but also on a host of other public policies, including (depending on the country) measures to improve health care infrastructure and to ensure the adequate training of medical personnel, the reduction of corruption and unnecessary bureaucracy, and the availability of public or private health insurance.[87] Efforts to ramp up the use of AMCs, compulsory licenses, and projects like those undertaken by DNDi are in my view crucial, but even so they remain only partial solutions to an extremely complex and multifaceted problem.

Plants, Seeds, and Traditional Knowledge

To close out this chapter without unduly prolonging it, I'll say just a few words about two other matters that are of special importance to some developing countries—namely protection for plants and seeds, and for traditional knowledge (TK). Readers who find these issues particularly interesting will at least understand the basics, and know where to search for further information and discussion.

First, as recounted in Chapter 1, US law enables the inventor of a new variety of plant to obtain exclusive rights under the Plant Patent Act (for nonsexually reproducing plants), the Plant Variety Protection Act or PVPA (for sexually reproducing plants), or a utility patent. US plant patents nevertheless aren't very popular these days, because inventors of new plant varieties can opt for utility patent protection instead, and utility patent protection is potentially stronger than plant patent protection for reasons we'll get to in a moment. In addition, as of 2017, seventy-five nations including the United States are parties to the Union Internationale pour la Protection d'Obtentions Végétales (Union for the Protection of Plant Varieties, or UPOV), an international treaty which obligates members to provide exclusive rights ("breeder's rights") for new varieties of plants. (As we saw earlier in this chapter, TRIPS article 27 permits nations to exclude plants from the scope of utility patent protection, but if they do so they must provide for some other form of exclusive rights. Plant patent rights that conform to UPOV would suffice.) UPOV dates back to 1961 but has been revised several times since then, most recently in 1978 and 1991. Most of the nations that are members of UPOV have ratified the 1991 text, but a few (including many in Latin America) remain parties to the 1978 version only.

Any country that wants to become a member today, however, would have to join UPOV 1991, and the 1991 version requires members to provide breeders with a stronger set of rights than the rights available under UPOV 1978. One difference between the two versions of the treaty, which I alluded to in Chapter 1, is that UPOV 1978 permits the individual farmer who's lawfully acquired and used protected seed to grow crops to harvest and to save some of the seed produced by those crops for use during the next growing season, something known as the "farmer's privilege."[88] Under UPOV 1991, by contrast, member states are free to recognize the farmer's privilege if they want, but they're not obligated to do so.[89] The United States, which adheres to UPOV 1991, recognizes a limited farmer's privilege under the PVPA,[90] but not under the Patent Act or the Plant Patent Act—which explains why developers of new types of seeds, such as Monsanto, prefer to go the utility patent route. (For example, Monsanto owns utility patents on genes and plant cells that are genetically modified to tolerate glyphosate-based herbicide, and it incorporates this technology into its Roundup Ready soybean seed. Farmer Vernon Bowman lawfully purchased some of this some seed and, after using it to plant a crop, saved some of the seed harvested from that crop and used it the following year to plant a second crop. Monsanto sued, and in 2013 the Supreme Court ruled in its favor, holding that although the exhaustion doctrine would permit the farmer to use and resell any seed he bought from Monsanto, it didn't exempt the unauthorized "making" of new seed from that seed, or the use or sale of plants derived from that seed.[91]) Advocates of farmers in the developing world (and elsewhere) sometimes express concern that, even though UPOV 1991 permits member states to retain the farmer's privilege, countries that adopt that treaty would have to affirmatively enact the privilege (in other words, it's not the default principle under the newer treaty).[92] In addition, UPOV 1991 expands, among other things, the scope of protectable subject matter, the rights conferred upon breeders, and the minimum term of protection.[93]

A second set of issues surrounds the use of what is often broadly referred to as "traditional knowledge" or TK. WIPO defines TK as "a living body of knowledge passed on from generation to generation within a community" that "often forms part of a people's cultural and spiritual identity," and states further that "WIPO's program on TK also addresses genetic resources (GRs) and traditional cultural expressions (TCEs)." WIPO itself is working on negotiating international agreements addressing IP and GRs, TK, and TCEs.[94] For present purposes, we'll be focusing mostly on the more utilitarian forms of TK.

To illustrate the concept, suppose that the inhabitants of a developing country disclose some TK to a researcher—say, that a particular plant is useful for certain medicinal purposes. If the researcher later makes some novel, nonobvious improvement over this TK, she may be able to obtain a patent on the improvement in her home country. When this happens (and it sometimes has) it doesn't always sit well with the people or the country that was the source of the TK. In recent years, for example, the Government of India has objected to attempts to assert IP rights in the United States and Europe in derivatives of the neem tree, turmeric, and Basmati rice, among others.[95] Among the questions that may arise in relation to such practices are whether there is any obligation (in law, morality, or public policy) to attribute the source of the TK, to obtain the source's informed consent before disclosing or using it, or to share any profit resulting from its exploitation.

The ethical and policy arguments are in my view genuinely difficult.[96] On the one hand, one could argue that since you can't validly patent (say) a naturally occurring plant, or a method that someone else invented or that's in the public domain, a patent that improves upon TK (or GR) does no one any harm. If anything, the patent enriches the general public by providing something new and useful. Put another way, when patents encourage the invention and disclosure and commercialization of novel and nonobvious subject matter, they're doing what they're supposed to do; and from the public's standpoint, there's no reason to compound the social costs of patents by making it unnecessarily difficult to obtain them or by requiring the compensation of people who freely made some useful but unpatentable contribution to what later became a patented technology.

On the other hand, many people feel that such a view shortchanges some important ethical issues. Building on Locke's theory of labor as the basis of property, for example (see Chapter 2), one might argue that indigenous people have a right to be compensated for the labor that went into developing the TK—though there may be difficulties in determining who, precisely, among a group is entitled to compensation for developing or disclosing the TK, particularly if it was developed long ago. Perhaps more convincing are the moral intuitions that many of us share (from whatever source we may derive them) that human decency and respect for others requires obtaining informed consent before exploiting subject matter that, in WIPO's description, "forms part of a people's cultural and spiritual identity," and that sharing the benefits of this information with the source can help in some small degree to mitigate the grossly unequal distribution of global wealth and power. And maybe there are even good utilitarian arguments for requiring consent and compensation. Perhaps indigenous people will become unwilling to disclose or even preserve their TK or GR, if they believe that the recipient of this information is going to keep all the benefits for itself—or if they're worried that somewhere down the road they'll have to start paying for access to the patented version of the TK or GR (an improved version of a crop, for example), once the patented version becomes the standard and the original becomes unmarketable.

As for the international *legal* issues surrounding the use of TK and GR, the two most important documents to date are the UN Convention on Biological Diversity, sometimes referred to as the "CBD" or "Rio Convention,"[97] and the 2010 Nagoya Protocol to the CBD.[98] The CBD arose out of the Earth Summit held in Rio de Janeiro, Brazil, in 1992, and it includes two articles that are directly relevant to TK and GR. First, article 8(j) (titled "In-Situ Conservation") states that each member nation "shall, as far as possible and as appropriate . . . [s]ubject to its national legislation, respect, preserve and maintain knowledge, innovations and practices of indigenous and local communities embodying traditional lifestyles relevant for the conservation and sustainable use of biological diversity and promote their wider application with the approval and involvement of the holders of such knowledge, innovations and practices and encourage the equitable sharing of the benefits arising from the utilization of such knowledge, innovations and practices."[99] Second, article 15 (titled "Access to Genetic Resources") states that "the authority to determine access to genetic resources rests with the national governments and is subject to national legislation," and that "[a]ccess, where granted, shall be on mutually agreed terms." Article 15 further requires outsiders to obtain prior informed consent prior to accessing GR, and states that each member "shall take legislative, administrative, or policy measures . . . with the aim of sharing in a fair and equitable way the results of research and development and the benefits arising from the commercial and other utilization of genetic resources with the Contracting Party providing such resources. Such sharing shall be upon mutually agreed terms."[100] The Nagoya Protocol builds upon this framework by requiring prior informed consent for access to GR and TK, and states that "benefits arising from the utilization of genetic resources as well as subsequent applications and commercialization shall be shared in a fair and equitable way with the Party providing such resources."[101]

You probably won't be too surprised to learn that the United States has never ratified either treaty. (In fact, it's the only nation other than Vatican City that hasn't ratified the CBD.[102]) As of August 2017, however, 100 states or other entities including the EU have ratified the Nagoya Protocol. Following ratification and the treaty's entry into force, the EU in 2014 enacted a regulation codifying its member states' obligations to obtain (and document) informed consent for the use of TK and GR, and to share the benefits derived from the utilization of TK associated with GR on fair and reasonable terms.[103] As of this writing, there isn't much literature yet on how states and private entities are complying with the regulation, and to my knowledge the regulation's provisions haven't yet been interpreted by any court. Critics worry that the provisions requiring informed consent and sharing based on "utilization" of TK associated with GR, if read broadly, could prove quite onerous, because at some point the use of knowledge (as opposed to physical things) can be very difficult to identify and trace. (As discussed in Chapter 2, information is intangible, nonrivalrous, and to some degree nonexcludable; as a result, we are able to stand on the shoulders of the giants and not-so-giants who came before us.) Then again, maybe these concerns will prove exaggerated; or the burdens of compliance, such as they are, won't seem so burdensome once people become accustomed to them.

I don't know about you, but I'm eager to see how these debates over seeds, TK, and patents and essential medicines continue to play out over the next few years. Moral norms evolve, sometimes in unexpected ways, and almost anything is possible; but perhaps most of us in the developed world eventually will come to view such matters as the compulsory licensing of life-saving drugs or the protection of TK and GR as being as essential to the moral fabric of our society as are, say, the prohibitions on slavery and torture. The majority of the world's people, after all, reside in the developing world. Maybe the time is ripe to accord their lives and traditions a greater measure of respect and concern. If we do, I'm guessing that, in the decades to come, they'll have a lot to teach us.

8

Trolls

Scandinavian folklore often depicts trolls as frightening, bad-tempered, antisocial creatures of questionable hygiene (which perhaps explains their antisocialness just a bit). Think of the troll who's the nemesis of the Three Billy Goats Gruff, for example—or, if you prefer more high-culture references, the trolls who inhabit the Hall of the Mountain King in Ibsen's *Peer Gynt* (cue up the iconic music by Grieg), or Beowulf's foes Grendel and Grendel's mom (possibly trolls), or the child-snatching beast immortalized by Goethe and Schubert, the *Erlkönig* (actually an evil elf, but close enough in my book). Portrayals of scary trolls like these have continued into the modern era, in settings including Tolkien's Middle Earth, games like *Dungeons and Dragons* and *World of Warcraft*, and the imaginatively titled horror films *Troll, Troll 2,* and *Troll 3.* Nevertheless, in modern-day pop culture you may be more likely to encounter the cuddly, so-ugly-they're-cute variety of troll, such as the miniature fuzzy-haired dolls that Danish sculptor Thomas Dam made famous back in the 1960s and that Dreamworks resurrected for its 2016 film titled, brace yourself, *Trolls.* Or, if you're a parent or grandparent of small children, you're surely familiar by now with the kindly trolls who advise Anna and Kristoff in Disney's *Frozen* and who, no doubt, will soon have the opportunity to reprise their song-and-dance routines in the inevitable *Frozen 2.*

Parents still read *The Three Billy Goats Gruff* to their children, however; and the persistence of the more sinister connotations of the word "troll" is evident from the use of the term in connection with two high-profile contemporary phenomena. First, there are the so-called "Internet trolls," those gentle souls who use the Internet to disseminate fake news, fish for personal data, or engage in the online harassment of people with whom they disagree. Second, and more relevant to our purposes, is the *patent troll*—an entity which is often portrayed, like the storybook troll who lurks under the bridge waiting for the goats to pass by, as springing upon its unsuspecting victims to demand an undeserved tribute. The term "patent troll" is said to have arisen in the early 2000s when executives at Intel were trying to come up with a milder synonym for "patent extortionist," a term the company had used against a firm that had sued Intel for patent infringement (and that, having taken umbrage at the "extortionist" rap, subsequently sued the company for libel as well). In a 2001 interview, Intel Assistant General Counsel Peter Detkin described a patent troll as "somebody who tries to make a lot of money from a patent that they are not practicing, have no intention of practicing and in most cases never practiced," and the name has stuck ever since.[1] (In fact, the term has since been applied, fairly or not, against a company called Intellectual Ventures that Detkin himself left Intel to join.) Since then, the term has seeped into public consciousness through a variety of sources, including (sometimes comic) video and radio segments, as well as ad campaigns urging legislative action to stop patent trolls.[2] In response, a number of state legislatures have enacted anti-troll laws, as we shall see, though to date the impact of these laws appears to be fairly minimal. Even President Obama took up the call by reviving the extortionist meme, referring to trolls as "folks [who] don't actually produce anything themselves. They're just trying essentially to leverage and hijack somebody else's idea and see if they can extort some money out of them."[3]

But is the accusation of extortion fair? After all, anyone who sues or threatens to sue for patent infringement must in fact own an actual patent (otherwise they really *are* just extortionists), and, as we have seen, all issued patents are presumed valid. As we've also seen, however, in a substantial percentage of cases that are litigated to judgment the accused is able to rebut that presumption and have the patent invalidated, and/or the court concludes that the defendant isn't actually infringing the patent. So is the concern that the infringement actions initiated by patent trolls are even weaker than the run of the mill—and if so, is that concern valid? For that matter, what *is* a patent troll, exactly? In the quotes above both Detkin and Obama refer to the fact that trolls don't make any products—in the jargon of patent law, they fall within the category of patent owners known as "nonpracticing entities" or "NPEs"—but historically lots of patent owners have sought to make money from licensing their patents to others rather than by making or selling products themselves, and such arrangements aren't necessarily indicative of anything sinister. After all, the United States (unlike, say, Austria-Hungary in the 1870s) has never required patent owners to "work" their patents; and perhaps an efficient division of labor can result when one person specializes in creating new inventions while another does the work of making and selling products that embody those inventions. Self-employed individual inventors, for example, like Chapter 1's hypothetical inventor of the better mousetrap, often aren't well-positioned to produce and market their inventions themselves; neither are the research universities whose professors, as discussed in Chapter 6, often develop patentable inventions that are used for medical or other purposes. For many people, then, what makes a patent owner a troll isn't the fact that it's an NPE, but rather that (unlike the individual inventor or the university) the stereotypical troll buys up patents that the original owner is neither practicing *nor* licensing, and then seeks out firms to license (or, if necessary, sue for infringement). Moreover, often these targeted firms were not previously aware of the patent at issue, but rather independently developed their allegedly infringing products. (As you may recall from Chapter 1, independent invention is common but, because patent infringement is a strict liability tort, it's not a defense to a claim for infringement of a valid patent.) Still, it's worth exploring whether there's anything intrinsically wrong with the practice of buying, licensing, and enforcing previously unlicensed and unenforced patents; as we'll see, there are nontrivial arguments on both sides of the question. Furthermore, since use of the word "troll" seems to prejudge which side is right, most commentators aspiring for some degree of objectivity prefer to use the more neutral term "patent assertion entity" or "PAE" to designate businesses that, in the words of the Federal Trade Commission (FTC), "acquire patents from third parties and seek to generate revenue by asserting them against alleged infringers" which "already use . . . the patented technology."[4] For the remainder of this chapter, then, I'll use the term "PAE" rather than "troll" except when I'm quoting someone else or the context requires that I resort to the more popular, but also more loaded, word "troll."

I'll begin by drawing on the existing empirical literature on PAE characteristics, including the FTC's 2016 study *Patent Assertion Entity Activity*, to sketch in somewhat greater detail exactly what PAEs are and how they differ from non-PAE patent owners: *are* PAE-owned patents weaker on average than other patents that are asserted in litigation, for example, and do they fall disproportionately into one or two fields of technology? Do all PAEs follow the same business model, or are there important differences among them? I'll also highlight what the economic literature has had to say thus far about the likely effects of PAEs on innovation and on the economy more generally. My own view, informed by this literature, is that in several respects the patent system as it currently operates enables PAEs to extract private benefits at public expense—a phenomenon that economists refer to as "rent-seeking." In the second part of this chapter, I'll suggest some possible reforms to the patent litigation system which I believe would help to alleviate these problems, while still respecting the role that patents can play in encouraging innovation.[5]

What PAEs Are, and Why It Matters

As noted above, the FTC defines PAEs as businesses that "acquire patents from third parties and seek to generate revenue by asserting them against alleged infringers" which "already use . . . the patented technology." This definition neatly captures the core idea that PAEs buy patents from some earlier owner who hasn't been licensing or enforcing them; hunt around for entities that they believe are using the invention without authorization; and then "assert" those patents against the alleged infringers, either by sending a letter demanding that the accused agree to license the patented technology for a sum of money, or by commencing litigation. Since the PAE isn't making or selling any products, however, the ultimate purpose of any such litigation would not be to exclude the infringer from the market, but rather to strengthen the PAE's hand in licensing negotiations.[*] A patent owner that doesn't fit this model—say, because it's enforcing patents that it's using or that it's owned all along, or because it's actually transferring technology to someone who isn't already using that technology— is by definition not a PAE. That's not to suggest that all firms that fit the PAE business model are bad (though people who are critical of PAEs believe that the model does lend itself to abuse, as we shall see), or that all firms that don't fit are good; but rather simply to acknowledge that when people talk about PAEs (or "patent trolls") this is the concept they usually have in mind. The questions we then need to address are whether firms that fit within this definition of PAE are meaningfully different from non-PAEs; what *are* the critics' concerns about PAEs; and are those concerns justified?

Several empirical studies have helped to shed light on how PAEs are different from other patent owners. First off, let me say a few words about the FTC study, which in my view is the most authoritative source to date. The study is based in large part on information the agency obtained under its statutory authority to collect confidential business information from private entities for the purpose of conducting studies like this one. Altogether, the study analyzed information from 22 Responding PAEs with over 2,500 "Affiliates and other related entities," of which 327 had engaged in patent assertion by sending demand letters, litigating, or licensing.[6] ("Affiliates" are defined for purposes of the study as including parent companies, subsidiaries, divisions, and any other person or persons over which a responding firm exercised supervision or control.[7] As we'll see shortly, PAEs often comprise numerous affiliated corporations.) According to the agency, the data disclose "two distinct PAE business models for generating revenue through patent assertion: Portfolio PAEs and Litigation

---

[*] As I've mentioned previously, in patent law a license is simply a permission to make, use, or sell the patented technology. Patent owners who choose to license their inventions sometimes do so on an exclusive basis, which typically means that they're agreeing to license just one entity, or "licensee," and not to allow that licensee's competitors to have access to the technology. A patent owner who grants licenses on a nonexclusive basis makes no such commitment. Whether a strategy of exclusive or nonexclusive licensing will maximize the patent owner's expected profits may depend both on the characteristics of the market and on the patent owner's interest, if any, in expending resources to protect its licensee against competitors.

PAEs."[8] Portfolio PAEs are entities that "negotiate[] licenses covering large portfolios, often containing hundreds or thousands of patents ...."[9] These PAEs are "highly capitalized ... often rais[ing] money from investors that included both investment funds and manufacturing firms."[10] (Intellectual Ventures, the firm that Peter Detkin joined after leaving Intel, would fall within the definition of a Portfolio PAE.) During the period of time studied (January 2009 through mid-September 2014) Portfolio PAEs generated approximately 80 percent of the revenue reported by responding PAEs, even though they accounted for only 9 percent of the reported licenses in the study.[11] Litigation PAEs, by contrast, "typically sued potential licensees and settled shortly afterward by entering into license agreements with defendants covering small portfolios, often containing fewer than ten patents." Litigation PAEs filed 96 percent of the cases in the study and accounted for 91 percent of the reported licenses, but only 20 percent of the reported revenue, or approximately $800 million.[12] Litigation PAEs, in other words, appear to engage in many more, but less lucrative, acts of patent assertion.

Several characteristics are common to the PAEs that were the subject of the FTC study. First, over 75 percent of PAEs' patents were software-related.[13] Second, the licenses the Study PAEs negotiated tended to be nonexclusive, and the royalties were usually payable as a lump sum rather than as a "running" royalty equal to a percentage of the revenue earned from sales of infringing products over time.[14] (Although conventional wisdom holds that patent owners *generally* prefer running royalties, the use of lump-sum royalties cuts down on PAEs' cost of monitoring the licensee's use,[15] as does the granting of nonexclusive as opposed to exclusive licenses.) Third, Litigation PAEs tended to be thinly capitalized, and they operated largely through Affiliates that themselves are structured as Limited Liability Companies (LLCs). This form of corporate organization means that the Affiliates don't have to publicly disclose the identities of their shareholders, and also that, unless a court takes the unusual step of "piercing" the corporate veil, their assets can't be used to satisfy a judgment entered against another Affiliate. Most of the studied Affiliates each owned one patent, or a small number of patents acquired from a distinct patent owner, and the LLC form ensures that the licensing revenue from that patent won't be commingled with the assets of other Affiliated firms.[16]

Fourth, while Portfolio PAEs typically sent demand letters to initiate licensing negotiations, and usually concluded negotiations without filing suit, Litigation PAEs were less likely to send demand letters prior to filing suit, and even when they did they generally did not negotiate licenses until after having initiated litigation.[17] Contrary to some observers' expectations, however, most of the studied PAEs sent fewer than twenty demand letters, and most recipients didn't receive more than one demand from any family of Affiliated PAEs.[18] Nevertheless, there were some firms that departed from this practice. One of the most notable was a firm called MPHJ Technology Investments, whose 101 subsidiaries sent demands to thousands of small businesses threatening suit for the infringement of certain "scan to email" patents, in some instances proposing a settlement amounting to $1,000 or $1,200 per employee. In 2015, the FTC threatened to sue MPHJ for unfair or deceptive trade practices, after which MPHJ eventually agreed to a consent order forbidding it from making misleading representations about the patent licenses it had granted to others, and from falsely representing its intent to file suit for infringement.[19]

The FTC study focused on a subset of all PAEs and thus didn't try to estimate the full extent to which PAEs have contributed to the increase in patent litigation, or what percentage of all patent infringement actions are filed by PAEs. Other studies have attempted to do this, however, and while estimates vary to some degree, almost all of them agree that PAEs have been responsible for (at least) a large plurality of the patent infringement actions filed over the past several years. And make no mistake about it—the number of infringement actions filed annually has substantially increased over the past generation, from a little over 1,000 in 1991 to over 5,000 in 2015, before declining to about 4,500 in 2016.[20] To be sure, even today the amount of patent litigation per issued patent is much smaller than it was during some periods in the past. According to Christopher Beauchamp, who refers to the period running roughly from the mid-1840s to the mid-1880s as the nation's "first patent litigation explosion," "[i]n 1850 New York City and Philadelphia alone had ten times more patent litigation, per US patent in force, than the whole United States did in 2013."[21] Many of the complaints one hears today about patent trolls were directed then against patent "speculators," or "sharks," some of whom employed much the same business model that PAEs do today.[22] Eventually the number of lawsuits fell, however, perhaps due to the reform of practices that (for instance) made it easy for patent owners to obtain both patent term extensions and "reissue" patents that expanded the scope of their claims. (Defenders of PAEs sometimes point to the prevalence of patent litigation in the nineteenth century as evidence that PAEs today do not present a serious problem, though it's never been clear to me how that conclusion follows. Lots of things were worse, from our standpoint, in 1880 than they are today, but that hardly means that there's no need for further improvement.)

Anyway, while researchers differ somewhat in their estimates, most studies have concluded that in recent years PAEs have accounted for at least 40 percent of all patent infringement lawsuits filed, with some putting the number over 60 percent.[23] So it's probably fair to say that PAEs are responsible for much of the increase in patent litigation over the past decade, though again this fact by itself doesn't tell us whether PAE behavior is socially desirable or not. It is consistent, however, with the expectation expressed by many observers that PAEs would be less hesitant than operating companies to resort to litigation, since the latter have to take into account the possibility that if they file suit (say, against a competitor for selling infringing products) they might be counter-sued for infringing some patent owned by the accused—something that PAEs generally don't have to worry about, since by definition they're not making or selling any products, infringing or otherwise. (Since PAEs don't have customers, they also don't have to be too worried about courting backlash from the "end users" of their patented technology by suing *them*, as opposed to the companies that make the products those end users use, for patent infringement. By contrast, imagine the marketing disaster that a company like Apple would suffer if it started suing people who own Samsung phones for using those devices in some way that infringes one of Apple's patents.[24]) In addition, PAEs also benefit from what economists refer to as "economies of scale" in litigation, meaning here that filing suit often is marginally less costly for the PAE than for an operating company, since PAEs are more likely to retain counsel on a contingency fee basis; to sue numerous defendants using largely identical legal pleadings; and in some places to take advantage of procedural technicalities, such as mandatory early discovery, that disproportionately disadvantage defendants, as discussed later in this chapter.[25] ("Discovery," by the way, is the term used for the pretrial exchange of potentially relevant evidence, as governed by the Federal Rule of Civil Procedure and local court rules.)

So now for the crucial question: *is* PAE behavior socially desirable or not? Are PAEs good for innovation, because they can license and litigate efficiently, and thus can provide small inventors with a better chance of recouping their investments in R&D? Or does their activity constitute more of a "tax" on other innovators who actually make products and sell them to the public? To try to answer this question, one trio of researchers looked at the effect on stock market valuations of companies that had been sued by NPEs for patent infringement between 2006 and 2010, and estimated that the average annual cost of NPE litigation during that period came to over $80 billion.[26] (Recall from above, however, that PAEs are a subset of all NPEs, with the latter class also including individual inventors and research universities.) Another study by two of the same three authors used data disclosed by the ten largest publicly traded NPEs to come up with a more conservative estimate that NPE litigation cost the economy $29 billion in 2011.[27] Both studies have received a fair amount of media attention, as well as criticism based on what some researchers perceive as methodological problems with both estimates.[28] Unless you want to delve into the weeds of these academic debates, however, you'll probably find it more instructive to consider what the literature reveals about more specific impacts of PAE behavior, for example on accused infringers and on start-ups, so let's turn to that body of work instead.

First, as noted above, for the most part PAEs don't transfer technology to would-be users, but rather target firms that already are present in the market and allegedly using the patented invention. Now, if most of these targets were shameless copiers, you might feel that they had it coming; but in fact most of them probably aren't.[29] As I noted in Chapter 1, near-simultaneous independent invention is a common occurrence, and it's likely that in the majority of patent infringement lawsuits the defendant is an inadvertent (alleged) infringer.[30] Of course, inadvertent infringement is still infringement; and in principle it might have been possible for the accused infringer to have discovered the patent at issue before making and selling its own product. (I say "might," because the defendant may have committed to a particular technological solution while the application for the patent in question was pending and not yet published.) In practice, however, it isn't always so easy to uncover the relevant patents in advance, particularly in fields in which technology is quickly changing, or in fields (such as software and business methods) where the claims themselves can be opaque.[31] PAEs therefore may have an incentive to assert claims for infringement not only when the claims appear relatively strong, but even when they're not—the latter in the hope of extracting a nuisance settlement (a payment to make someone go away) from a defendant who's already committed to a particular technological solution and cannot reverse course without eating the costs it's already incurred, or incurring substantial additional costs to design around. And in fact, the FTC study shows that 77 percent of the assertions by responding Litigation PAEs settled for less than $300,000—an amount that is less than the estimated median cost of litigating even a small-stakes patent infringement suit through the end of discovery—and that over 30 percent settled for less than $50,000.[32] (The cost estimate, by the way, comes from the American Intellectual Property Law Association, which every year publishes estimates of the median cost for various types of IP-related legal services. For 2017, the reported mean cost of defending against an NPE-filed infringement action with less than $1 million at stake was $238,000 through the end of discovery and claim construction, and $547,000 through the end of trial and appeal; costs are higher for cases with more money at stake.[33] Conventional wisdom holds that patent litigation, which tends to make heavy use of expert witnesses in both technology and economics, is on average more costly than any other type of litigation.) This strongly suggests that Litigation PAEs are settling the majority of their claims for their nuisance value, a result that is hard to square with any sort of coherent innovation policy. (Portfolio PAEs, by contrast, settled 65 percent of their cases for $1 million or more.)[34] Other studies also have shown that PAEs tend to lose a disproportionately large percentage of their cases that don't settle, but rather go to trial[35]—a result that is not all that surprising, if, as the FTC study indicates, PAEs mostly own software patents, which as we saw in Chapter 5 are among the least likely to prevail in litigation.

Second, while both Litigation and Portfolio PAEs often assert their patents against manufacturers, they also sometimes target end users who, as the FTC notes, "likely have little information about how the products may infringe and, therefore, may be less well positioned to defend an infringement complaint than the product's manufacturer."[36] (As we saw above, for example, MPHJ targeted hundreds of small businesses that used allegedly infringing scanner technology. Another PAE, Innovatio IP Ventures LLC, sued numerous coffee shops, cafes, grocery stores, and hotels that made wireless Internet access available to their customers. In this latter case, however, the makers of the allegedly infringing equipment eventually intervened and later settled the consolidated cases.)[37] Other empirical studies report that PAEs frequently target start-ups and firms that are flush with cash from initial public offerings[38]—and (surprise!) that these firms are noticeably less likely to innovate after having been sued.[39] This strategy makes a lot of sense if you're a PAE, but again it's hard to reconcile with any sort of sound innovation policy, particularly if the alleged infringement is inadvertent or the infringement claim weak. The only possible counterargument would be that the assertion of patents against end users and start-ups promotes innovation by funneling a substantial portion of PAE licensing revenue back to the inventors who assign their rights to PAEs, to recoup their R&D costs. So far, however, the empirical evidence doesn't appear to provide strong support for the hypothesis that individual inventors derive substantial benefits from PAE activity.[40]

Another feature of US patent litigation that, until recently, appears to have favored PAE litigation was the dominance of the Eastern District of Texas as a "venue" for patent litigation. As noted in Chapter 1, although the Federal Circuit hears all appeals in patent infringement cases, the United States doesn't have a specialized patent or IP trial court, as some countries do. Nevertheless, over the past decade or so a surprisingly large percentage of all US patent litigation—in 2015, *over 40 percent* of it—was filed in one single court, the United States District Court for the Eastern District of Texas.[†] The Eastern District's rise to prominence was due to two factors, the first being a 1990 Federal Circuit decision that reinterpreted the federal statute that governs where patent litigation may be filed, in a way that permitted firms that distributed their products throughout the United States to be sued for patent infringement in just about any of the nation's ninety-four federal trial courts.[41] The other factor was the district's adoption of various rules and procedures that appeared systematically

---

[†] In case you're not up on your Texas geography, the Eastern District's biggest city is Plano (population 274,000), and its next biggest—and where most of the patent cases were filed—are the cities of Marshall (118,000) and Tyler (100,000). It is a largely rural district, and no major corporations are headquartered there.

to work to the benefit of patent owners. As documented by Professors Daniel Klerman, Greg Reilly, Jonas Anderson, and others,[42] these advantages included: (1) a relatively short time to trial (speedier civil trials generally tending to benefit plaintiffs, who control the timing of the lawsuit's filing); (2) a disinclination on the part of Eastern District judges, compared to judges in other districts, to grant summary judgment, which also tends to favor plaintiffs by ensuring that the case will proceed to trial unless it settles; (3) a local rule requiring the parties to exchange relevant documents within just a few months of the filing of the case, even in the absence of a formal discovery request, thus putting disproportionate pressure on defendants to settle; (4) the court's reluctance to transfer cases to other districts that would have been more convenient to parties and witnesses; and (5) until a change brought about by the America Invents Act (AIA) in 2011, liberally permitting patent owners to join multiple defendants together in one single action, thus lowering the cost to patent plaintiffs (who didn't have to file as many separate actions), while potentially disadvantaging defendants (who had to share trial time to defend themselves). Patent owners generally, and NPEs in particular, also enjoyed a higher "win rate" in the Eastern District in comparison with other popular districts, and the median damages awarded for patent infringement in the Eastern District (about $10 million from 1997 to 2016) were higher than the national median of just under $6 million during that period.[43] As one might expect, NPEs have accounted for at least a substantial plurality of the patent infringement actions filed in the Eastern District in recent years,[44] and potential litigants sought to create goodwill among the locals. Samsung even built a skating rink across the street from the federal courthouse in Marshall.[45]

The Eastern District's day in the sun nevertheless may now be at an end. In May 2017, the Supreme Court in *TC Heartland LLC v. Kraft Foods Group Brands LLC* held that the Federal Circuit's interpretation of the patent venue statute had been incorrect, and that plaintiffs may sue only in the district corresponding to the defendant's state of incorporation, or the place in which the defendant allegedly infringed and had a "regular and established place of business."[46] A patent infringement lawsuit against a manufacturer incorporated in, say, California therefore could take place in California, or in any district in which the firm itself allegedly infringes and has a "regular and established place of business"— but probably not (as before) any district into which it merely shipped the product through established distribution channels for sale to consumers.[47] As this book goes to press, it appears that the District of Delaware, where many US corporations are headquartered, will probably become the leading venue for patent litigation; prior to *TC Heartland* Delaware was already the second most popular district for patent litigation, though NPE success rates there have been about average for NPEs generally (and much lower than in East Texas).[48]

How this will play out over the next few years therefore remains, for now, anyone's guess.

If the above discussion is correct in asserting that PAEs generally don't transfer technology, and that a large portion of PAE cases settle for their nuisance value and target end users and startups, I'm inclined to agree with PAE critics that PAEs probably have done more harm than good. That said, I also think it's important not to overreact, for example by curtailing the potentially efficient division of labor that can result from nonpracticing patent owners being able to license and enforce their patents. (As others before me have observed, it's not the identity of the patent owner that ultimately matters, but rather the conduct. Moreover, PAEs are hardly the only entities that exploit the patent system for their own benefit, though as noted above operating companies may be more cautious about initiating litigation due to the risk of countersuit. This caution, however, is in part due to patent law's "arms race," see Chapter 1, which itself is arguably a waste of social resources.) The better strategy to deal with the problematic consequences of PAE behavior therefore is, in my view, to reform those features of the patent system that enable patent owners (whether PAEs or not) to engage in socially costly rent-seeking. Efforts to improve patent quality, for example by winnowing out overly broad software and business method patents as discussed in Chapter 5, may go a long way to achieving this goal independently of any reform specifically targeting PAE behavior. In the next two sections, however, I'll focus on a handful of additional reform measures that would apply to all patent owners and that, I will argue, would enhance the working of the patent system for the greater good.

Possible Reforms: Remedies

I talked a little about patent remedies (damages and injunctions) in the preceding chapter in the context of compulsory licensing, where I laid out the conventional arguments in favor of awarding injunctions to IP owners who prevail in litigation—as well as some situations in which courts would be well-advised to depart from this general rule and award compensatory damages not only for the past harm suffered, but also for the future losses resulting from the defendant's continued use of the invention. In the following pages, I'll discuss some ways in which the law of patent remedies can affect PAE-initiated litigation, and propose a few modifications of existing practice. (We'll return to the issue of remedies one more time in Chapter 9's discussion of litigation involving smartphones, where there are yet more complicating factors to consider.)

As I mentioned in Chapter 7, the principal argument in favor of awarding injunctions is to avoid requiring a court to determine the value of the technology in suit, which is the sort of thing you might expect the parties to have a better grasp on than a judge. Notwithstanding the valuation problem, however, I also proposed that where there is reason to believe that the defendant couldn't easily avoid the infringement in advance, and it would be unduly costly to design around the patent if a court subsequently forbade its use, the better rule may be to deny an injunction and permit the use to continue subject to a court-determined ongoing royalty, because in such a case an injunction may enable the patent owner to extract a "holdup" royalty exceeding the technology's value in comparison with the next-best alternative. (More technically, a royalty negotiated under the threat of an injunction may reflect not only the technology's value over alternatives, but also some portion of the cost the defendant already has incurred to implement that technology—its so-called "sunk" costs, which may go to waste if it has to abandon the technology and start over—as well as the additional costs or forgone benefit, if any, of switching to some alternative.)[49] These conditions are often present in PAE cases, where patent assertion typically occurs after the accused has adopted a technology that allegedly infringes some (software or other) patent. To be sure, as we've seen, PAEs don't actually litigate many cases to trial or win the ones they do, so they're not often in a position to threaten a defendant with immediate shutdown—though it's not as if this has *never* happened. Some readers may remember how in 2006 a PAE by the name of NTP, Inc. obtained an injunction and compelled BlackBerry maker Research In Motion to pay $612.5 million to avoid going dark, a development from which BlackBerry arguably never fully recovered.[50] Providing PAEs with the right to injunctive relief under such circumstances certainly strengthens their bargaining power, but not necessarily in a way that serves the public interest.

Anyway, until about ten years ago, the Federal Circuit applied a rule under which prevailing patent owners like NTP were automatically entitled to injunctions, absent exceptional circumstances; but just a few months after the NTP settlement the US Supreme Court held in *eBay, Inc. v. MercExchange LLC*[51] that injunctive relief is discretionary, not automatic. A court therefore should consider whether the patent owner will suffer "irreparable" harm if it doesn't get an injunction, or whether instead an award of monetary damages will suffice, as well whether either party or the public will suffer undue hardship if an injunction is or is not entered. As a result of the *eBay* decision, practicing entities that prevail against their competitors typically still get injunctions since they often have a legitimate interest in market exclusivity.[52] PAEs, by contrast, generally don't get injunctions, since (among other things) they don't face irreparable harm if they can't exclude nonexistent competitors. A royalty in payment for a nonexclusive license is usually all the PAE ultimately hopes to achieve, and courts can award an ongoing royalty, similar in function to a compulsory license, in place of an injunction if the PAE prevails at trial. At least in this respect, then, the courts appear to have gotten things right.

On the other hand, there are several features of the US law of monetary damages that may encourage rent-seeking litigation. I'll talk about some of the ways that courts calculate reasonable royalties and profits in the next chapter, and suggest some changes, but for now I'll focus on three issues that may continue to cause problems even when injunctive relief is off the table. The first relates to the ongoing royalties that courts now award when they don't enter injunctions. To illustrate the problem, suppose for example that the court awards a royalty for past infringement equal to 5 percent of the defendant's revenue from sales of infringing products prior to judgment; this is the amount, in other words, that the court believes will adequately compensate the patent owner for the licensing revenue it would have earned had the defendant first approached it for a license. What then should the royalty rate be for the future infringing sales the defendant will be permitted to make absent an injunction? According to the Federal Circuit, the trial court may award a rate that is higher than the rate awarded for past infringement, on the theory that the patentee is now in a much stronger bargaining position.[53] In practice, courts tend roughly to double the rate,[54] though in some cases they've increased it even more.[55] From an economic standpoint, however, if the principal economic reason not to enter an injunction is to avoid holdup, it makes little sense to award a royalty that exceeds the value of the invention and thus replicates the risk of holdup that the denial of an injunction was supposed to avoid in the first place.[56] Someday, I hope, the Federal Circuit will revisit this issue and correct its error.

Second, US patent law allows courts to award "enhanced" damages of up to three times the damages the patent owner actually suffered, if the court concludes that the infringement was "willful" or "egregious" (or some other nasty-sounding adjective).[57] In recent years, courts haven't actually awarded enhanced damages all that often,[58] and again, in the present context where most infringement may be inadvertent, the risk of incurring them may often be remote. Nevertheless, it's still a risk; and the Supreme Court's 2016 decision in *Halo Electronics, Inc. v. Pulse Electronics, Inc.*,[59] which removed some of the impediments to awarding enhanced damages that the Federal Circuit had erected, has increased that risk significantly. *Halo* now gives the district courts more discretion than they previously had to award enhanced damages (albeit only for willful infringement), and pending further application by the courts the decision for now leaves open the possibility that the continued use of a patented invention after being sued for infringement could, in some instances, be considered "willful" even if it initially was inadvertent.[60] Most other countries, by contrast, don't award enhanced or punitive damages for patent infringement (or for anything else); and while there's certainly an argument that courts should assess some sort of penalty

in extreme cases—for example, to deter intentional wrongdoing that otherwise might go undetected and unremedied—it's also important to consider
the possibility that the risk of incurring enhanced damages might "overdeter"
companies from engaging in lawful conduct. This might happen, for example,
if the company reasonably, but incorrectly, believed either that the patent in
suit was invalid, or that its effort to design around the patent had resulted in a
noninfringing product.[61] In his concurring opinion in *Halo*, Justice Breyer noted
these risks and recommended the "careful application" of enhanced damages,
"to ensure that they only target cases of egregious misconduct."[62] Let's hope that
the courts follow his advice.

Third, as noted earlier, because the cost of patent litigation is so high,
Litigation PAEs often settle with accused infringers for payments that are less
than the latter's expected cost of defending itself in court. From the perspective of the accused, settling such a case often is a good business decision, because even when defendants prevail at trial they usually have to pay their own
attorneys' fees. The rule that each party bears its own fees is called the "American
Rule," to contrast it with the "English Rule" followed in the United Kingdom
(and, for that matter, much of the rest of the world) under which the loser pays
the winner's fees. True, even in the United States there are some exceptions to
the American Rule; in antitrust and civil rights cases, for example, the prevailing
plaintiff generally is entitled to recover compensation for the fees it reasonably
has incurred. But patent litigation mostly conforms to the American Rule, in
that the statute permits courts to award attorneys' fees to the prevailing party
only in "exceptional" cases;[63] and until recently the Federal Circuit's case law
interpreting the word "exceptional" made it very difficult for the victorious party
to recover its fees. In 2014, however, the Supreme Court in *Octane Fitness, LLC
v. Icon Health & Fitness, Inc.*[64] held that courts should consider the totality of
the circumstances when deciding whether to award fees. As a result, judges now
appear to be somewhat more willing to award prevailing defendants their fees,
for example, when the evidence shows that the infringement claim was not well-
founded.[65] Fee awards nevertheless still remain *relatively* uncommon, in light of
the statutory requirement that the case be exceptional.

Evidence from other countries suggests that *mandatory* fee-shifting from
loser to winner probably would deter a substantial portion of PAE suits (and is a
major reason why PAEs, while hardly absent, thus far have been less noticeable
in Europe).[66] Nevertheless, it's extremely unlikely that the United States would
seriously consider adopting such a rule anytime soon. Tradition means a lot to
lawyers (especially when it happens to coincide with their self-interest), and as a
matter of policy mandatory fee-shifting does carry a serious countervailing risk
of deterring some plaintiffs from bringing meritorious claims. A compromise position that Congress considered during 2014 and again in 2015, however, would

require courts to award fees to the prevailing party in a patent case unless the court "finds that the position and conduct of the nonprevailing party or parties were *reasonably justified* in law and fact or that special circumstances (such as severe economic hardship to a named inventor) make an award unjust" (emphasis added).[67] Just how often a court would conclude that the losing party's position wasn't "reasonably justified" is difficult to predict; I'd guess not too often, but that fee awards under this standard would become somewhat more common than under the current "exceptional" standard. On the other hand, one potential negative consequence of requiring the court to inquire into the losing party's justification for its position is that the inquiry itself results in an additional layer of litigation—lawyers refer to this as "satellite" litigation—though unless Congress required fee shifting in all cases (or in none), this problem is unavoidable. (Moreover, even when there is mandatory shifting, as in the UK, there often is satellite litigation on the question of whether the services provided and amounts paid were in fact reasonable.) Be that as it may, in my view the proposal would be worth trying out as a tool for deterring the sort of nuisance suits that the FTC Study has now brought to light, as well as other instances of bad conduct on the part of patent owners *and* infringers.

Possible Reforms: Procedure and Case Management

There are other measures that Congress or the courts could adopt to decrease the risk of abusive litigation without deterring legitimate suits from going forward. Some of these have been proposed in various patent reform bills that Congress has considered, but so far not enacted, since the AIA.

First, Congress could require that patent owners provide more details, when they commence litigation by filing a complaint alleging patent infringement, regarding which of the defendant's products infringe and how. One proposed bill, for example, would require the plaintiff to identify each allegedly infringing product, including its name or model number if any; to include "a clear and concise statement of . . . where each element of each claim identified . . . is found"; and to describe, "with detailed specificity, how each limitation of each claim . . . is met by the" allegedly infringing product.[68] Although this might seem burdensome to patent owners—particularly in comparison with the *very* simple complaints that owners were allowed to file until late 2015, when the Supreme Court's recommendation to delete an outdated "model" patent infringement complaint from the Federal Rules of Civil Procedure took effect—the type of information that would be required seems like just the sort of thing you'd expect a diligent owner to have at its disposal before invoking the power of the state to compel someone to appear in court. (Note that plaintiffs can, and often do, amend their complaints, as additional relevant information comes to light through discovery, so they wouldn't necessarily be locked in to a theory of the case that later proves untenable.) Requiring such specific allegations would enable courts to dispose of more cases on a pretrial motion to dismiss for failure to state a claim upon which relief may be granted, if the allegations don't meet even the minimal requirements for proceeding further.

Second, and relatedly, proposed legislation would require courts to "stay" (that is, hold off on requiring the parties to go forward with) the expensive discovery process I mentioned above until the court has resolved a motion to dismiss or a motion to transfer the action to another court.[69] (Earlier legislation would have gone further and stayed discovery pending the court's ruling on claim construction, a topic I discussed in Chapter 1.)[70] To be sure, some judges may chafe at what they view as interference with their independence to manage their own docket. Delaying discovery for a time nevertheless would reduce the incentive of Litigation PAEs or others to leverage the likely expense of compliance into a nuisance settlement. In addition, however, when discovery does begin, courts should require the parties early on to disclose information relevant to monetary damages.[71] Under current practice, the disclosure of such information often is deferred, but an early disclosure would help the parties to gauge how much money really is at stake, and encourage settlement when it appears that amount would barely cover the cost of litigating.[72]

Third, Congress could make it more difficult for patent owners to sue end users—a practice that PAEs have engaged in with some frequency, as we've seen. To illustrate, suppose that Patent Owner A sues End User B for infringement. If B is, say, a coffee shop or other small business, it probably has little familiarity with the patent system, or any idea about how the product it's using might infringe A's patent. Now, B could have a contractual arrangement with the manufacturer of the product (call it C) to indemnify B for any damages or other losses it suffers due to its use of infringing equipment; then again, it might not, or it might not be sure, or it might simply prefer to pay a small settlement to avoid the risks of litigation. Now suppose that C files an action for a declaratory judgment of noninfringment or invalidity, maybe in a different venue. (I talked a little about declaratory judgments in Chapters 1 and 3; they're the procedural tool the ACLU used to challenge Myriad's human gene patents.) Traditionally, the court in which this second action was filed would stay that second action until the first one terminated, which wouldn't do B much good if its goal was to avoid litigating altogether. Recently, however, the Federal Circuit held that "when a patent owner files an infringement suit against a manufacturer's customer and the manufacturer then files an action of noninfringement or patent invalidity," the court generally should stay the first suit, that is, the one filed against the customer.[73] The specific contours of this "customer stay" exception never-theless still remain a bit unclear. Enacting legislation to codify the exception and to render it mandatory in cases like the one described above, assuming the cus-tomer agrees to be bound by the outcome of the manufacturer's suit, would be a useful step.[74]

Other Reforms

Two other measures worth discussing are the enactment of laws regulating the content of demand letters, and proposed measures to require PAEs to dis-close the identity of the persons or entities that own them. As for the first, since 2013 over thirty state legislatures have enacted laws forbidding the "bad faith assertion of patent infringement," for example by transmitting a demand letter that fails to include the patent number, the name and address of the patent owner, and specific allegations concerning the allegedly infringing ac-tivity; or that offers to license the patent on "unreasonable" terms, or when the patent owner knows or should know that the claim of infringement lacks merit.[75] Whether these new laws are necessary or sufficient to combat abusive PAEs nevertheless remains to be seen, for at least three reasons. The first is that, even in the absence of such laws state attorneys-general in New York and Minnesota, as well as the FTC, were able to obtain settlements from MPHJ (the firm that sent out the scanner patent demand letters) using existing consumer protection and unfair competition laws.[76] Second, however, and potentially cutting in the opposite direction, is some residual uncertainty over whether state courts have jurisdiction to hear cases of this nature, which touch upon patent law; patent infringement cases can only be litigated in federal court, and the boundaries between state and federal jurisdiction over other cases in which patent issues may arise is not entirely clear.[77] Third, Federal Circuit case law in recent years has required persons asserting more traditional unfair competition claims premised on the wrongful assertion of IP rights to over-come *Noerr-Pennington* immunity, which, as we saw in Chapter 6, immunizes sham litigation from antitrust liability unless the litigation is both objectively and subjectively baseless.[78] Whether the Federal Circuit is right that *Noerr-Pennington* constrains claims based on laws other than antitrust is a matter the Supreme Court has yet to take up, but if it is, the impact of these state laws would appear to be rather limited. Not surprisingly, perhaps, aside from the actions noted above, neither the state attorneys-general nor private litigants appear thus far to have made much use of either the older or the new state laws to combat PAEs, though one early case filed against MPHJ in Vermont remained pending as of this writing.[79]

The second proposal arises from the fact, noted above, that many PAEs make use of the LLC form of corporate organization to obscure the identity of their shareholders and affiliates. Some commentators have argued that this use of the LLC form could enable the LLC's ultimate "parent" entity to extract more revenue from licensees because, for both legal and practical reasons, a defendant whose product is accused by (say) ten separate firms of infringing ten separate patents is exposed to greater aggregate holdup risk than is a defendant who is accused by one single firm owning all ten.[80] In addition, as noted earlier, the strategy could enable shareholders to better shield their own assets if, for example, a particular shell were ordered to pay attorneys' fees or other sanctions for misconduct.[81] Others speculate that public relations also could be a factor driving the use of the LLC form, because anonymity enables persons or firms that own shares in PAEs to deny their participation in activity that others condemn as trolling.[82]

Concerns over these matters led the USPTO in 2014 to propose a rule that would have required every patent applicant to identify any entity to whom it has assigned its patent, any "entity necessary to be joined in a lawsuit in order to have standing to enforce the patent," the "ultimate parent entity" of either of the preceding entities, and any entity that used any arrangement to temporarily divest itself or prevent the vesting of attributable ownership. The applicant would have needed to update this disclosure as necessary during patent prosecution, upon payment of postgrant maintenance fees, and in connection with any postgrant USPTO proceedings.[83] The agency later shelved the proposal, however, following the submission of mostly unfavorable comments on the part of patent owners who argued (among other things) that the requirements were too burdensome—which perhaps they were, applying as they would have to all patent applications, not just issued or asserted patents—and that the prescribed penalty for postgrant noncompliance (cancellation) exceeded the USPTO's authority. Congress nevertheless has considered enacting a somewhat similar proposal, albeit one that would be applicable only to patents that are asserted in litigation (and minus the cancellation penalty).[84]

The FTC Study sheds some further light on these transparency issues, at least as they relate to demand letters. Significantly, the agency found that few demand letter recipients received more than one letter from any PAE, let alone affiliated PAEs. Instead, as noted earlier in this chapter, the principal benefit of the LLC form appears to be that it helps PAEs segregate the revenue derived from the licensing of individual patents obtained from different former owners.[85] The FTC nevertheless recommends amending the Federal Rules of Civil Procedure along the lines proposed in some of the pending patent reform bills, to make it easier to identify the ultimate parent company in cases that proceed to litigation.[86] Although I find it hard to come up with any reason to oppose this proposal, the fact that PAEs mostly use the form for their own convenience in terms of segregating revenue also suggests that, if we have to choose, such transparency reforms probably shouldn't be a big priority item either.

Like other business entities, PAEs take advantage of the opportunities presented to them; but whether their pursuit of self-interest is consistent with the public interest is another story. Although it's possible that in some instances PAEs promote innovation by helping to ensure that inventors are compensated for their investment in R&D, at least three features of PAE behavior—the absence of technology transfer, their targeting of start-ups and end users, and their assertion of generally weak patents often in return for a nuisance settlement—suggest to me that PAEs often impose an unnecessary tax on business, both large and small, the cost of which ultimately is passed on to consumers in the form of higher prices (and potentially less innovation). Nevertheless, I've argued that the fix is not to outlaw patent licensing, which is often beneficial, or to require firms to work their patents. Instead, the better response is to reduce the opportunities for patent owners (whatever their specific organizational form or business model happens to be) to engage in socially costly forms of rent-seeking. To this end, the proposed reforms discussed in this chapter would reduce the ability of patent owners to leverage the high cost of litigation to wrest nuisance settlements from weak cases, while avoiding the risk of unduly chilling the assertion of rights in valuable inventions. Improvements to patent quality, particularly in the fields of software and business methods, would also help.

The good news is that, as of this writing, PAE activity appears to be on the wane due to a variety of factors, including both the Supreme Court's recent decisions on software and business method patent eligibility and the rise of administrative review as a method for challenging issued patents (see chapter 5). Assuming this trends persists—and is strengthened both by the recent reinterpretation of the federal venue statute as discussed earlier in this chapter, and perhaps by some of the reform proposals outlined above as well—the odds are good that within a few years' time the nation's second patent litigation explosion, like the first that petered out in the late nineteenth century, will soon pass into the mists of history. But I wouldn't count the PAE business model out for good. Like the trolls of myth and legend, PAEs may prove to be, if not immortal, at least hearty and long-lived. Some day in the distant future, after the patent system has undergone further changes we can scarcely now imagine, PAEs may be ready to return again, eager to spring from underneath the bridge precisely when we least expect them.

9

Smartphones and Other Complex Devices

I mentioned in the Prologue that, according to one estimate, there are 250,000 patents incorporated into the average smartphone. Whether that figure is right or not is debatable, but even if the estimate is off by, say, a factor of ten (and maybe only half the patents are valid), it seems inevitable that from time to time some of them are going to be infringed.[1] This is particularly so since, as the economist Paul Belleflamme points out, the smartphone market is "the archetypal example of . . . cumulative innovation," in that developments are both highly sequential (combining and improving upon that which went before) and complementary (their value depends upon their ability to interact with other features).[2] Now, since many of the relevant patent holders are themselves smartphone makers, that means they're also potential infringers of other smartphone makers' patents; moreover, as we've seen, in many countries including the United States anytime you file suit the other side gets to argue that your patent isn't valid after all. Given these risks, you might think that many firms would be inclined either to cross-license one another's patents, or even to tolerate some potentially infringing uses, on the theory that whatever they're giving up by not enforcing their patents to the max they're making up by not having to fend off similar demands themselves. And for a while, that's pretty much what happened, with the firms that competed in the nascent smartphone market of the early to mid-2000s all abiding by what might be characterized as an informal peace. Human nature being what it is, however, it shouldn't come as a big surprise that eventually someone would light the spark that would set the smartphone patent world ablaze. (The patent "arms race" metaphor that I've used before seems particular apt here.) Playing the role of Gavrilo Princip in the ensuing smartphone patent wars was the Finnish handset manufacturer Nokia, which in 2009 fired the first salvo by suing Apple for the infringement of ten Nokia patents. Apple in turn filed a counterclaim alleging that Nokia was infringing several Apple patents, and within a few months the two companies were tangling in four separate patent infringement proceedings in the United States, including one before the United States International Trade Commission (ITC), as well as actions in Germany and the United Kingdom.[3] (More about the ITC later in this chapter. Gavrilo Princip, in case you're scratching your head, was the fellow who in 1914 shot Archduke Franz Ferdinand, thus setting in motion World War I.)

Before long, litigation spanning ten countries had enmeshed just about all of the world's major smartphone makers, as well as some of the companies that provided them with key technologies—among them Samsung, Microsoft, Motorola Mobility, Ericsson, China's Huawei and ZTE, and Taiwan's HTC. (Features of Google's Android operating system were the target of some of the suits, which prompted Google to acquire Motorola Mobility in 2011 for $12.5 billion, mostly for its patent portfolio. Google sold off Motorola Mobility to smartphone maker Lenovo for just $2.9 billion in 2014.) Altogether, participants in the smartphone wars have asserted and challenged hundreds of patents, including some of Apple's most famous ones: its so-called "rubber-banding" patent (claiming a method which informs you that you've scrolled to the end of a list by causing the display to overscroll and bounce back);[4] the "slide-to-unlock" patent (claiming a method for unlocking a touchscreen phone by making a predefined hand gesture);[5] the "pinch-to-zoom" patent (which claims a method for enabling one type of pinch-to-zoom feature);[6] the "Steve Jobs" patent (which claims many of the features of the iPhone, and for which Steve Jobs himself was the first inventor listed on the application);[7] and design patents relating to the appearance of the iPhone and the iPad. I'll discuss the design patent litigation, which was the subject of a US Supreme Court opinion in December 2016, in some detail later in this chapter. Most of the lawsuits that made up the smartphone patent wars nevertheless have now terminated, either as a result of judgments or settlements—though according to blogger Florian Mueller, when the dust had settled only a small percentage of these actions resulted in clear victories for the parties that filed them.[8] Aside from the body count and the use of poison gas, maybe the World War I analogy isn't such a stretch.[9]

I titled this chapter "Smartphones and Other Complex Devices" not only because some of the litigation that made up the smartphone patent wars involved mobile devices such as tablets and e-book readers, but also because the issues I'm going to focus on here are relevant to the litigation and licensing of technologies used in all sorts of complex electronic products. Some of the most prominent patent disputes in recent years, for example, have involved patents on technologies that enable devices to communicate with one another or to perform in certain standardized ways. The so-called "standard-essential" patents (abbreviated "SEPs," and usually pronounced "seps," not "ess-ee-pees") at issue in these cases read on aspects of technical standards, like the wireless communications standards that are adopted by standard setting organizations (SSOs) such as the Institute of Electrical and Electronics Engineers (IEEE), the International Telecommunications Union (ITU), and the European Telecommunications Standards Institute (ETSI). Often these organizations require their members to disclose any patents they own that read on any aspect of a standard that the organization is considering or has adopted, and to commit to licensing those patents to third parties on fair, reasonable, and nondiscriminatory (FRAND) terms. (Sometimes the term of choice is simply "reasonable and nondiscriminatory," or "RAND," but the terms are used interchangeably and "FRAND" is currently the more popular. Similarly, SSOs are sometimes referred to in the alternative as standards *development* organizations, or SDOs, but SSO appears to be the more common usage. As you may have discerned by now, if you don't like acronyms, this chapter isn't for you.)

Often the resolution of cases involving technologies incorporated into complex devices hinges on issues we've discussed already, including patentable subject matter, nonobviousness, and claim construction. What this chapter will focus on, however, is what has become arguably the most contentious topic in patent litigation involving complex devices, both in the United States and abroad: remedies, particularly injunctions and damages. (This topic also happens to be my principal area of specialization in my academic writing.) Chapters 7 and 8 introduced some issues relating to the law of remedies, among them the question of whether courts generally should award the prevailing patent owner an injunction; whether NPEs and PAEs in particular should ever get injunctions; and whether courts should award enhanced (punitive) damages and attorneys' fees to the prevailing party. In this chapter, we'll see how these and other related issues are playing out in the world of complex devices. To set the stage, suppose that a typical smartphone really does embody 250,000—or even just 25,000—patents, and that my smartphone company has infringed *one* of them. Should the patent owner be able to enjoin me from selling the infringing phone, or should it settle for an ongoing royalty? Should it matter whether the patent owner is an NPE or PAE, or that the patent is standard-essential and subject to a FRAND commitment? What if it's standard-essential and *not* subject to a FRAND commitment? Are these even issues of patent law at all, or should they be addressed under antitrust law, or contract law, or something else? Furthermore, if the court is going to award damages in the form of a reasonable or FRAND royalty, how should it calculate that royalty—in other words, how can a court or anyone else possibly know what *one single patent out of 25,000* is worth? Are there any other forms of monetary compensation that might be better suited for this type of litigation?

I'll begin this chapter by discussing in a little more detail a couple of concepts from the world of economics that courts and commentators often invoke when discussing remedies for the infringement of complex device patents, namely *patent holdup* and *royalty stacking*. I'll then talk about the availability of injunctions in the United States and other countries, and how various bodies of law may play a role in deciding whether an injunction is appropriate. I'll conclude with a brief discussion of some of the difficult issues surrounding the calculation of damages for the infringement of complex devices, and the directions in which this body of law may be heading.

Patent Holdup and Royalty Stacking

When a new pharmaceutical product like the ones we talked about in Chapter 6 hits the market, it's typically covered by just one or a small number of patents.[10] Moreover, the drug companies that own these patents typically are practicing entities that use their patents to exclude, rather than license, competitors. By contrast, the PAEs we encountered in Chapter 8 typically assert software and telecommunications patents that are both complementary and sequential; and since PAEs don't make products, but rather seek to derive revenue from licensing, injunctions stand to benefit them only to the extent they provide additional bargaining power in licensing negotiations. The cases of interest for this chapter often have features common to both of these business models. On the one hand, the patent owners in most of the smartphone cases were practicing entities, which would suggest that, like drug companies, they'd benefit from injunctions to exclude competitors. And sometimes that's precisely what they wanted: Apple and Samsung, for example, sometimes sought injunctions against one another not as a means for extracting more licensing revenue, but rather for the purpose of keeping certain features exclusive to themselves. On the other hand, as noted above the number of patents that go into the typical smartphone is huge, and often smartphone makers want access to at least some of their competitor's features in order to make their own products marketable—especially, though not exclusively, if the patented technology is standard-essential. And in the world of complex device litigation more generally, not all of the plaintiffs are manufacturers of end products; some, like Qualcomm, manufacture components (and may engage in patent licensing as well), while others are mostly, or even exclusively, nonpracticing entities. On balance, then, it's probably fair to say that most of the time leverage, rather than exclusion, is the principal reason for seeking an injunction in these complex device cases, though there are some exceptions.

As discussed in Chapters 7 and 8, there are two principal economic reasons for protecting IP rights by means of injunctions. The first is that injunctions support the interest of patent owners (such as drug companies) in excluding competitors. If such exclusion is necessary to preserve the patent incentive, the public arguably benefits in the long run when courts preserve the owner's market exclusivity by granting injunctions. Second, and more broadly, injunctions conserve on information and adjudication costs. Here the theory is that, in comparison with the potential parties to a patent license, courts and other government agencies may not be very good at estimating how much a technology is worth, and therefore may be unable to ensure that a damages judgment will restore the prevailing patent owner to the position it would have occupied—and not a better nor a worse position—but for the infringement. Nevertheless, when the need for access is paramount (compulsory licenses for essential medicines might be an example), or when the availability of injunctions risks enabling the patent owner to negotiate a royalty that greatly exceeds the value of the invention in comparison with alternatives, the better practice *might* be to withhold injunctions and grant ongoing royalties instead, notwithstanding the valuation problem.

In the complex device cases in particular, this latter risk of enabling patent owners to extract excessive royalties could be substantial—particularly if the defendant has inadvertently infringed and cannot easily design around the infringing technology. (Think back to the BlackBerry case I mentioned in Chapter 8, for example.) Under these circumstances, a royalty negotiated under the threat of an injunction may reflect not only the technology's value over alternatives—its inherent worth—but also the "sunk" costs the defendant has already incurred, which will go to waste if it has to abandon that technology, and the incrementally higher costs of switching to a noninfringing alternative midstream.

The term commonly used for this phenomenon—using the threat of an injunction to extract royalties that exceed the value of the technology—is patent "holdup." I'll admit, the word "holdup" sounds pretty bad, conjuring up as it does the image of a bank robber or carjacker, but in economics, holdup (or opportunism) is simply a term used to describe taking advantage of another person who is, at least temporarily, locked in to a particular course of conduct.[11] Imagine, for example, two parties negotiating a contract whereby one agrees to provide the other with an ongoing supply of material the latter needs to complete a building project. The builder then begins incurring costs (transaction-specific investments) in reliance on the supplier keeping its end of the deal. Contract law protects the builder's interest by ensuring that if the supplier breaches, it will have to pay damages. But now suppose there's some ambiguity in the contract that the supplier can invoke as a reason for stalling, unless it receives some extra compensation. (Maybe the contract specified that the supplier would use its "best efforts" to stay on schedule, but didn't define the term; and because it's hard for the builder to monitor whether the supplier is actually using its best efforts, the supplier may have some additional leverage once the builder has begun incurring costs in reliance on having an adequate and timely supply of materials.) To be sure, the supplier may refrain from acting opportunistically if it cares about preserving a good reputation to attract future business; but if such reputational concerns aren't sufficient to overcome the temptation, the builder is subject to being held up *ex post.* This possibility makes the builder's project that much riskier. Thus, if there's no way to reduce the risk of holdup *ex ante* builders may be marginally less eager to take on new projects, or they'll factor the risk into the (lower) price they're willing to pay for supplies. Such precautions also threaten to harm suppliers, though, so you might think that the parties themselves would try, *ex ante,* to come up with ways to prevent either one from acting opportunistically *ex post.* And in fact there's a whole body of economics literature that explains various business practices as tools for fending off holdup: the parties could negotiate tighter contracts, for example, or develop ways to monitor one another's performance. Or maybe the builder will "vertically integrate" the supply and building functions into one single firm rather than relying on outsiders—though in that case it may need to develop tools for ensuring that its managers and employees avoid acting opportunistically when their individual self-interest conflicts with the firm's. As these examples suggest, however, developing and implementing tools for preventing holdup can be costly, and even then they aren't necessarily foolproof: surely you can't foresee and negotiate every possible contingency when negotiating a contract, at least not at acceptable cost. So in some instances the law may need to provide backups or default rules to address situations where private solutions just aren't feasible. For example, if a public utility is building a new transmission line and has acquired the right-of-way from every property owner but one, that last owner—the holdout—would be in a position to extract an extortionate price if the law didn't provide a means, through a process known in the United States as eminent domain, for forcing the owner to grant access at fair market value.

Seen in this light, a ban on injunctions might seem like a reasonable rule to adopt in cases in which patent owners would be tempted to practice holdup by using the threat of an injunction to extract an excessive royalty: that is, in cases in which it's hard for the user to negotiate a license up front (perhaps due to the combination of independent invention and the difficulty of conducting a thorough search of existing patents prior to a product launch), and the cost of redesigning the product to avoid infringement *ex post* would be enormous. As with the nonpatent examples of holdup, the concern is that, absent some way to prevent opportunism, companies that market new products incur an added risk (and, like our hypothetical builder, may be marginally less inclined to take on some new projects as a result). Further, to the extent patent owners succeed in extracting excessive royalties—royalties that are greater than the value of the invention over alternatives—society as a whole is worse off, because it's paying more for the invention than the invention is really worth. These are essentially the reasons I put forward in Chapter 8 for why PAEs (which, again, unlike the drug companies are not interested in market exclusivity) generally shouldn't be able to get injunctions; and much the same reasoning would seem to apply in complex device cases where the owner's interest lies in licensing and not exclusion. On this rationale, denying injunctive relief in the case of SEPs (which, by definition, are "essential" and therefore not easy to design around *ex post*) might seem particularly advisable.[12]

Some commentators nevertheless have critiqued this line of argument for a variety of reasons. In a couple of recent papers, for example, Alexander Galetovic, Stephen Haber, and Ross Levine (GHL) dispute the idea that holdup is a serious problem in the smartphone industry on the ground that the rapid growth, reductions in price, and increases in quality and innovation that characterize the industry are precisely what you *wouldn't* expect to find in a market plagued by holdup.[13] But to assume that holdup is a problem only in the (perhaps rare) cases in which royalties are so high that they measurably retard follow-up innovation may be taking too narrow a view of what holdup is. After all, even if the extent of holdup isn't such that it's likely to cause the whole system to stagnate, the public still stands to benefit from preventing patent owners from using injunctions to extract royalties that exceed the value of their inventions. GHL's thesis actually reminds me a bit of a similar argument that antitrust skeptics sometimes trot out, that because the price and cost of kerosene was falling throughout the late nineteenth century there was no need for Congress to enact antitrust laws to remedy monopolistic conduct.[14] It seems to me that by the same logic you could just as well argue that because we're now living in what may be the most peaceful period in human history,[15] we can eliminate our armed forces and police. Indeed, in the present context maybe the correct inference to draw from the absence of system-crashing holdup is not that injunctions don't contribute to holdup, but rather that it's the American courts' perceived reluctance, as discussed below, to grant injunctions that's helping *prevent* holdup from getting out of hand.

Some other critiques of the holdup thesis, however, arguably do counsel against turning what might be best thought of as a disposition against injunctions in complex device cases into an absolute rule. First, like our hypothetical supplier to the building trade, some patent owners may well be concerned about preserving a reputation for fair dealing, particularly if they want repeat business or are likely to find themselves on the receiving end of some deals.[16] Perhaps in such instances we shouldn't just *assume* that holdup is a serious problem. A second possible concern is that if it's too easy for inadvertent infringers to avoid injunctions, firms will have less of an incentive to develop more effective ways of searching for and clearing patent rights in advance of a product launch. Relatedly, there's also a potential problem in defining exactly what inadvertence *means* in this context. (Is a corporation an inadvertent infringer if one of its employees who had nothing to do with the allegedly infringing product was aware of the patent at issue?) This doesn't necessarily mean that inadvertence shouldn't matter in deciding whether an injunction is appropriate, but it does suggest that a standard that hinges on that concept may not be as straightforward in its application as one might initially assume. Third, if it's easy to avoid injunctions, infringers sometimes may have an incentive to delay obtaining a license and pay royalties for as long as possible. (Proponents of strong patent rights sometimes refer to this behavior on the part of infringers as "reverse holdup" or "holdout.")[17] Of course, if patent owners *eventually* are compensated in full, including for the time value of the money that the infringer delayed in paying, ultimately they're no worse off than they would have been absent the infringement; and US courts generally do award compounded prejudgment interest on patent damages awards. Not every country does, though, and SEP cases involving complex devices are not confined just to the United States. Moreover, delay may harm patent owners and benefit defendants if, for example, the rate used to calculate the interest due on a damages award is less than the patent owner's or the infringer's internal rate or return, or if other expenses such as attorneys' fees aren't awarded. (As we saw in Chapter 8, US courts generally don't award attorneys' fees, though of course in the event of delay both plaintiff's and defendants' fees continue to mount. With regard to fees, then, defendants benefit, relatively speaking, only if their own fees increase more slowly than do plaintiffs'.) In such cases, injunctions might be appropriate; alternatively, courts arguably should be able to award damages enhancements to make up for some of these otherwise uncompensable losses stemming from delay.[18]

Finally, it's important to keep in mind the principle economic reason for awarding injunctions: the concern that, because IP rights are hard to value, courts may not be up to the task of accurately compensating the patent owner for its loss by awarding an appropriate ongoing royalty. That fear could be misplaced, of course; even if not, if the courts' valuation errors are more or less random, over time they'd tend to cancel each other out, thus leaving society as a whole no better or worse off (though in individual case one party or the other may suffer). If on the other hand the courts' errors would be nonrandom and predictably under- or overcompensatory, it's conceivable that society would be better off if courts didn't even try to get it "right," but rather routinely awarded injunctions notwithstanding some risk of holdup—though as discussed in Chapter 7, undercompensatory awards would have the virtue of making consumers better off in the short run, and would have no ill effect in the long run if the patent incentive isn't all it's cracked up to be. Unfortunately, nobody really knows precisely how important the patent incentive is in many industries (and thus how important it is to value technology correctly), or how often courts over- or undervalue technology when they award ongoing royalties in lieu of injunctions (though I do think that the US practice of routinely enhancing the ongoing royalty rate is misguided, as discussed in Chapter 8). Suffice to say that US law, as reflected in the *eBay* case I discussed in the preceding chapter, appears to worry more about holdup than about valuation errors.

Another phenomenon that frequently comes up in discussions of smartphones and SEPs is "royalty stacking." In a casual sense, people sometimes use this term to refer to a situation in which, as Norman Siebrasse and I have put it, "a seller incurs an excessive royalty burden as a result of marketing a product incorporating multiple, separately-owned patents."[19] A slightly more technical description of the concept would go something like this. Suppose that, to produce some end product such as a phone, you need to license two patents owned by a single firm. (As we've seen, you'll surely need to license a lot more than two patents to sell a phone, but there's no reason to make this example more complicated than necessary.) You want to maximize your own profit from selling the phone to consumers, but the price you charge has to be at least high enough to cover your own costs, including the cost of licensing those two patents. Similarly, the patent owner wants to maximize its licensing revenue, which (let's assume) will be a percentage of the revenue you earn from selling phones; this means that the patent owner has a stake in ensuring that the price it charges for its patents isn't so high that it will cause *you* to charge a price that drives too many prospective customers away to your competitors. Neither of you knows precisely how consumers will respond to your new product, but you make your best guess and agree that you'll pay a royalty R. For simplicity, suppose that the royalty is $20, and that at this price you'll sell the phone for $100 and earn a profit of $10. Now suppose instead that the patents are owned by two separate companies (A and B), each of which demands the royalty it expects will maximize its own licensing revenue, without taking into account what the other is likely to charge. In turn, you have to factor this aggregate royalty burden into the price at which you sell the phone to consumers. Now, you might think that the aggregate royalty burden would be the same regardless of whether there are one or two patent owners—that is, that your aggregate royalty burden would be $20 either way, and your price and profits unaffected. In fact, though, as demonstrated nearly two centuries ago by the French economist Augustin Cournot, in cases like this the aggregate royalty burden is likely to be higher (for illustrative purposes, let's say $30), the resulting price of the end product will be higher (say, $105), and the overall profit lower (say, $5).[20] (Cournot obviously didn't know anything about smartphones, but the identity of the end product is irrelevant to the math. And in case you're wondering why you can't just raise the price of the end product to $110 and earn the same $10 profit—well, maybe you can, but typically if you raise the price you sell fewer units, and depending on the shape of the demand curve the profit-maximizing price may well be less than $110.)

In other words, your aggregate royalty burden is higher, and both you and (collectively) the patent owners are worse off, in comparison with the first scenario in which a single patent owner set a single profit-maximizing price for its two patents. The reason is that, in the second scenario, each owner's independent pricing decision imposes a cost—in economic terminology, an externality—on the other. In the first scenario, by contrast, the owner "internalizes" the externality by restraining its own pricing demand. Of course, in the actual market for smartphones there are not just two but maybe hundreds of patent owners with whom you may have to deal, which compounds the risk that the aggregate royalty burden will exceed the social optimum (that is, the royalty burden that would maximize social welfare consisting of the sum of patent owner profits, manufacturer profits, and consumer surplus). In theory, in the worst-case scenario the aggregate burden or "royalty stack," could exceed the price consumers are willing to pay for the end product (in which case, there's no point in your selling the product at all).

As with patent holdup, there's a healthy debate over whether or to what extent royalty stacking is a problem in the real world. A paper by Ann Armstrong, Joseph Mueller, and Tim Syrett estimates the aggregate royalty burden for the typical smartphone at about 30 percent of the selling price ($120 out of an estimated retail price of $400).[21] As the authors note, however, their estimate does not "account for a smartphone supplier's potential to reduce its cash payments for royalties through cross-licenses and pass-through or exhaustion of patent rights,"[22] an omission that some observers have criticized.[23] Others argue (as with some of the studies critical of holdup) that the empirical evidence simply doesn't support the royalty stacking thesis.[24] But even if these critiques are misguided, the fact (if it is a fact) that 30 percent of the price of the typical smartphone goes to pay patent royalties doesn't necessarily tell us very much. Maybe patent owners *are* restraining their demands, and 30 percent just happens to be the socially optimal aggregate royalty rate. (If anything, you might have expected the IP incorporated into a complex electronic device to cost *more* than the physical components.) Still, the possibility that firms may be charging royalties higher than the social optimum might counsel against routinely granting injunctions for the infringement of smartphone patents, since doing so would risk worsening the problem (though again, not granting an injunction might give rise to valuation problems instead). Moreover, while it's hard for me to see how courts could directly take the risk of royalty stacking into account in calculating damages—the court would somehow have to know what royalties everyone else is charging, and what the social optimum is—the concept may have some value at least as a sort of sanity check. For example, if a court is trying to determine the appropriate royalty an infringer should pay for one single patent, it might reject a proposal that (say) 2 percent of sales revenue is the right royalty, if the evidence shows that the patent in suit is only of average value compared to the other 25,000 for which the infringer may also owe royalties. Assessing a royalty rate that, if it were applied to the other patented inventions incorporated into the device, would result in the infringer shouldering an aggregate royalty burden of 50,000 percent surely fails the sanity check, suggesting that whatever the royalty should be for the infringed patent it must be substantially less than 2 percent. (In a sense, the "top-down" approach discussed later in this chapter *does* try to accomplish something along these lines, as we shall see.)

Injunctions Revisited

As I mentioned in Chapter 8, as a result of the US Supreme Court's 2006 decision in *eBay v. MercExchange* federal district courts are no longer obligated to award an injunction to the prevailing patent owner, and in about 25 percent of cases they don't. In my own scholarly writing, I've argued that, ideally, courts would consider whether to grant injunctions based on whether the factors that would make holdup a realistic possibility are present, rather than exclusively on the basis of the traditional "equitable" factors (irreparable harm, inadequacy of monetary damages, and so on); but whether this is right or not, my own sense is that the US courts' actual practice—granting injunctions to practicing entities like drug companies when they win at trial, but denying them to PAEs—is generally consistent with my recommendation.

But which outcome makes more sense when the owner of a complex device patent is a practicing entity, and the infringer is a competitor? In such a case, you might think that the outcome would hinge on whether the owner uses its patent to exclude or instead, as is sometimes the case in these markets, licenses the patent to its competitors (perhaps because it needs access to their patents as well). But even when the owner does prefer exclusivity to licensing, there's no guarantee that the court will enter an injunction, post-*eBay*. In lawsuits Apple filed against Samsung in the US District Court for the Northern District of California in 2011 and 2012, Apple requested both preliminary and, after prevailing on some of its claims at trial, permanent injunctions against certain models of Samsung phones and tablets. In a series of decisions arising out of these lawsuits, the Federal Circuit established the principle that, as part of the inquiry into whether the owner is likely to suffer "irreparable harm" in the absence of an injunction, the court should consider whether there is a "causal nexus" between the infringement and any loss of sales, consumer goodwill, or market share.[25] (The reason there was a "series" of decisions is that, when a court grants or denies a preliminary injunction pending trial, the losing side gets to file an immediate "interlocutory" appeal. In the two *Apple v. Samsung* cases, there were two interlocutory appeals, one for each case, and then after trial additional appeals from the final judgments.) In other words, the court seemed to be saying, given the many features, patented and non, that are embodied in the typical device, we shouldn't just *assume* that a company's lost sales, if any, were attributable to the infringement; in these specific cases, it was at least plausible that many consumers chose Samsung over Apple devices for a host of reasons not related to the patented features in suit. The Federal Circuit's more recent opinions in these cases nevertheless also have cautioned against denying an injunction just because the patent isn't the exclusive reason customers buy the product; it's enough if there's " 'some connection' between the patented features and the demand for the infringing products," which "may be shown in 'a variety of ways,' including, for example, 'evidence that a patented feature is one of several features that cause consumers to make their purchasing decisions,' 'evidence that the inclusion of a patented feature makes a product significantly more desirable,' and 'evidence that the absence of a patented feature would make a product significantly less desirable.' "[26] Exactly what all of this means may depend a lot on the individual judgment of the judges hearing the case. In one of the two *Apple v. Samsung* cases noted above, involving the "rubber-banding" and "pinch to zoom" patents among others, on remand from the Federal Circuit US District Judge Lucy Koh again denied Apple an injunction even though Apple wouldn't have licensed the patents to Samsung.[27] In the other case, involving among others the "slide to unlock" patent, the Court of Appeals strongly hinted that it thought an injunction was appropriate. As of mid-2017, the matter remained ongoing.[28]

None of the patents in the above two lawsuits were SEPs, but in cases involving SEPs US courts thus far have not been inclined to grant injunctions to the prevailing plaintiff. Doctrinally, the fact that the patent owner committed to license its SEPs on FRAND terms may amount to a concession on the part of the patent owner that there's an adequate remedy at law (damages in the form of the FRAND royalty).[29] And, again, the risk of holdup seems substantial, unless there's reason to think the defendant is somehow benefiting from undue delay in coming to terms.

Oddly, though, not *all* claims for the infringement of US patents are litigated in federal district court. Every year, somewhere between thirty and seventy infringement complaints are filed with the ITC, an agency established back in 1916 as the US Tariff Commission and charged with administering the US tariff system.[30] Section 337 of the Tariff Act—which in its original version was part of the infamous Smoot-Hawley Tariff Act of 1930, see Chapter 7—confers upon the agency the authority to exclude infringing imports from entry into the United States.[31] In particular, § 337 declares unlawful "[t]he importation into the United States, the sale for importation, or the sale within the United States after importation . . . of articles that . . . infringe a valid and enforceable United States patent."[32] True to its protectionist origins, however, the statute applies only "if an industry in the United States, relating to the articles protected by the patent . . . exists or is in the process of being established"; further, "an industry in the United States" is "considered to exist if there is in the United States, with respect to the articles protected by the patent . . . (A) significant investment in plant and equipment; (B) significant employment of labor or capital; or (C) substantial investment in its exploitation, including engineering, research and development, or licensing."[33] A firm that believes it qualifies as a domestic industry, and that products entering the United States from abroad are infringing its US patent, therefore can file a complaint with the ITC requesting that the agency commence an investigation. Eventually the investigation may result in a trial before an administrative law judge (ALJ) in which both the complaining party and the importer participate. The losing party can then appeal the ALJ's decision, called an "Initial Determination," to the full commission, and from there to the Federal Circuit.

For the most part, the ITC applies standard US patent law to determine if the patent in suit is valid and infringed; and, since the Patent Act itself prohibits the unauthorized importation and sale of patented goods, just about any patent matter the ITC investigates could be brought in federal district court instead. Technically, ITC investigations are "in rem" proceedings, meaning that they are directed against the imported goods themselves, rather than, as a civil action for patent infringement would be, against the individual or corporate entity that allegedly is causing the infringement. ("In rem" is the Latin term for "against the goods," and thus an in rem proceeding contrasts with a civil action "in personam," that is, "against the person.") This means that the complaining party in an ITC investigation doesn't have to prove that the court has jurisdiction over the person of, say, the manufacturer of the infringing goods, which may well be a foreign company that doesn't directly do any business in the United States.[34] Still, *some* entity has to be importing the goods into, and distributing them within, the United States, or else there's nothing to complain about, as far as US law is concerned; goods don't just magically show up on the store shelves in Poughkeepsie. So it would practically always be possible for the patent owner to file a civil action for infringement against the importer or distributor in federal court, even if an ITC investigation is also possible; and in fact, more often than not, patent owners who file ITC complaints also *do* file parallel civil actions for infringement.[35] One of the principal benefits of an ITC investigation, however, is that it proceeds faster than infringement litigation typically does, with most ITC matters terminating within eighteen months (not including any appeal to the Federal Circuit). Oh, and also, the *eBay* decision doesn't apply to the ITC.[36] The only sort of remedies the agency can order against infringing imports are cease-and-desist and "exclusion" orders, that is, injunction-like remedies forbidding the importation and distribution of infringing merchandise.[37] ITC proceedings therefore provide a convenient way for patent owners who figure they may not succeed in getting an injunction in federal court to obtain much the same thing from this alternative forum.

That said, even if you think (as I do) that the *eBay* rule is generally sound, you might also imagine that the availability of an ITC workaround isn't all that significant. After all, we're talking about fewer than a hundred ITC investigations per year, compared to about four thousand infringement actions. Moreover, as noted above the complainant has to be a "domestic industry," which on its face might seem to disqualify PAEs (which don't make or sell any patented products, foreign or domestic) and foreign firms (which receive over half of all US patents these days[38]). But these latter two assumptions aren't necessarily correct. Although the case law is heavily fact-specific, PAEs that have an ongoing patent licensing operation in the United States sometimes can qualify as industries; and US-based subsidiaries of foreign firms can qualify as "domestic."[39] Thus, since complex electronic devices such as smartphones often are manufactured abroad, even if they bear US brand names, you can have the paradoxical situation in which the domestic subsidiary of a foreign firm (such as Samsung) can invoke the ITC's jurisdiction to exclude allegedly infringing goods from being imported into the United States by a domestic firm (such as Apple). In fact, in 2013 the ITC sided with Samsung in a proceeding against Apple and was prepared to enter an order excluding certain Apple devices from entering the United States.[40] In this particular case, however, the patents in suit were standard-essential and subject to a FRAND commitment, and this fact in turn led to another twist arising from the president's power under the Tariff Act to veto any ITC exclusion order for "policy reasons."[41] Prior to 2013, the last time this had happened was in 1987,[42] but in 2013 the US Trade Representative—the individual to whom US presidents have in recent years delegated the veto power—decided against the exclusion order, citing the need for Apple to use the SEPs embodied in the devices and Samsung's FRAND commitment.[43]

To avoid holdup in future ITC cases, some commentators have argued that Congress should require the agency to follow *eBay*—or that the agency itself could find ways to approximate the decision's impact (for example, by delaying implementation of an exclusion order for a period of time necessary for the infringer to design around, and ordering the infringer to post a bond compensating the patent owner in the interim).[44] My own view is that having two parallel forums, US district courts and the ITC, both charged with hearing patent infringement disputes, simply invites a form of forum shopping (akin to PAEs' *en masse* filings in the Eastern District of Texas, as discussed in

Chapter 8). As a consequence, if it were up to me I would abolish the agency's jurisdiction over patent matters altogether—though I recognize that in the more populist, tariff-friendly environment into which the United States may now be headed, this probably isn't a feasible recommendation. More limited reforms like requiring the agency to follow *eBay* nevertheless would still be advisable.

In other countries where these types of cases are playing out, the law is, for now, more favorable to patent owners when it comes to granting injunctions. In Germany and Japan, for example—two of the most important jurisdictions for patent litigation outside of the United States—courts still view injunctions as pretty much a right to which the prevailing patent owner is entitled. And even in the UK, where (as in the United States) injunctions are viewed as a matter entrusted to the courts' equitable discretion, the way in which the legal standard is articulated makes it much more likely that a court will grant an injunction, even if the plaintiff is a PAE or a SEP owner.[45] Nonetheless, this doesn't mean that SEP owners always succeed in getting injunctions, even in places like Germany and Japan. (I'd say there's more than one way to skin a cat, if I wasn't such a cat lover.) In fact, there are at least three other bodies of law that a court conceivably might invoke to deny the prevailing patent owner an injunction, even in countries where injunctive relief remains the norm.

First, as noted earlier in this chapter, SSOs often require their members to commit to licensing any patents that are essential to the practice of SSO-adopted standards on FRAND terms. If so, then conceivably the act of seeking an injunction for the infringement of such a patent could amount to a breach of contract, at least where the alleged infringer itself has demonstrated its willingness to license on FRAND terms.[46] This theory has had some success in the United States, where a few courts have construed FRAND commitments as binding contracts for the benefit of third parties. (The most famous case to date is *Microsoft v. Motorola*, in which Microsoft accused Motorola of breaching its FRAND commitment by demanding royalties for the use of certain SEPs that far exceeded the patents' value.[47] I'll have a little more to say about this case at the end of this chapter.) Thus far, however, the contract argument hasn't met with as much success elsewhere. Moreover, until recently, SSO policies haven't *explicitly* stated that committing to grant a license on FRAND terms is inconsistent with later seeking an injunction, though in 2015 the IEEE did adopt a rule obligating its members to commit not to seek injunctions against willing licensees.[48] Nonetheless, even if the breach of contract argument is viable when there is an express FRAND commitment, it wouldn't have any bearing where no such commitment exists, e.g., for non-standard essential patents or for patents that read on so-called de facto standards that were arose without any central co-ordination by an SSO.

Second, antitrust (competition law) might preclude SEP owners from obtaining injunctive relief in some countries, though perhaps not the United States. As we saw in Chapter 6, although US antitrust law forbids monopolization, it's not an antitrust offense for a firm that has lawfully acquired monopoly power merely to exploit that power by charging an "unfair" or monopoly price; rather, the offense consists of acquiring, expanding, or preserving monopoly power through the predatory exclusion of competitors. Absent unusual circumstances, a patent owner's extraction of a high royalty under threat of an injunction (assuming that this were permissible under patent law) would seem more like lawful monopoly exploitation than unlawful monopoly expansion—though at the end of the day the weakness of an antitrust claim probably doesn't matter much, since *eBay* by itself likely would render the threat meaningless if the patent were a SEP or the owner a PAE.[49] Other countries, by contrast, may not follow *eBay* but might be inclined to apply antitrust in a more expansive fashion; in fact, decisions in Europe and in China have held that SEP owners may abuse their monopoly position by seeking injunctions against defendants who are willing to take licenses on FRAND terms.[50] Perhaps the most important recent decision came in a German patent infringement case between Huawei and ZTE, which eventually resulted in a judgment of the Court of Justice for the European Union setting out the conditions that market-dominant SEP owners must follow before they can lawfully seek injunctive relief.[51] As of this writing, the lower courts in Europe are still working through the precise application of these conditions, though even under a broad interpretation, the *Huawei* decision doesn't go as far as *eBay* in limiting injunctive relief. Due to lack of market power, for example, it probably wouldn't be a violation of European antitrust law in a run-of-the-mill, non-SEP case for a patent owner to seek an injunction, even if the owner happened to be an entity such as a PAE that wouldn't be likely to obtain one in the United States.

A third possibility that courts in a few countries have invoked to deny injunctive relief is a doctrine found in the civil law of some European and Asian countries known as "abuse of right." In the patent context, the doctrine might be roughly analogized to the US doctrine of patent misuse[52] in that it enables courts to restrain perceived abuses of patent rights when no other legal doctrine appears at hand. In two fairly recent decisions, courts in the Netherlands and Japan have invoked the doctrine to deny injunctions against an alleged infringer whom the courts understood to be willing to take a license to certain SEPs on FRAND terms.[53] (Both cases involved—guess who—Apple and Samsung, with Samsung as the plaintiff these times around.) Whether other courts will take up the somewhat amorphous doctrine as a tool for denying injunctions in SEP or other cases remains to be seen.

Damages

When the patent owner wins at trial, the court is likely to award damages to compensate for the infringing acts that have occurred through the date of judgment—and, if the court denies an injunction, an ongoing royalty to compensate for future acts of infringement, as discussed in Chapter 8. Sometimes these damages awards can be very high, totaling in the nine- and even ten-figure range. In the two *Apple v. Samsung* lawsuits that were litigated before Judge Koh, for example, the initial damages award in the case involving the rubber-banding and design patents exceeded $1 billion—later trimmed back to a mere $548 million[54]—while in the one involving among others slide-to-unlock the award came to $119 million, an amount that actually was viewed at the time as a loss for Apple.[55] (As of 2017, both cases were still pending. The award in the case involving the design patents probably will decrease further for reasons we'll get to shortly, but the Federal Circuit recently remanded the damages award in the other one so that the district court may consider whether a damages enhancement is appropriate.[56]) But the vast majority of patent damages awards are for far less. According to PricewaterhouseCoopers, in 2016 dollars the median award from 1997–2016 was $6.1 million[57]—hardly trivial, but not the stuff of headlines either—and for a variety of reasons including but not limited to market size, patent damages awards in other countries tend to be lower still.[58] Nonetheless, there's a lot of dissatisfaction these days with the state of patent damages law, particularly as it relates to complex products. (As I mentioned earlier, this is the area of patent law to which I devote most of my scholarly writing; and to my great pleasure, I've witnessed a tremendous increase in interest in this topic among practicing lawyers, judges, economists, patent owners, and even the Supreme Court just within the past five years or so.) So how *do* you determine the value of one or two patents out of the thousands that may be embodied in a typical smartphone?

Before trying to answer this question, it's important to note that courts in the United States and other countries typically take as their starting assumption the principle that the primary goal in awarding patent damages should be to restore the owner to the position it would have occupied, but for the infringement. This is pretty much the standard that applies in other types of tort cases as well, where the goal is to restore the injured party, to the extent money is capable of doing so, to the status he or she would have enjoyed had the injury never occurred. In patent law, this restorative goal also aligns with the theory that patents provide an incentive to invent: if damages *don't* restore the patent owner to the position it would have occupied absent the infringement, the patent incentive scheme is necessarily weakened. Of course, as I mentioned in Chapter 7, it's possible that the patent incentive wasn't really necessary to induce the creation of the invention in the first place, in which case it might seem that the public would be better served by undercompensating the patent owner (and, by necessity, encouraging some degree of infringement). Most patent scholars (including me) nevertheless adhere to the view that courts aren't in a very good position to determine how much of a reward would be necessary to maintain the appropriate incentive. To do so, a court not only would have to have credible information on the patent owner's R&D costs, but also some idea of the overall social value of the invention (the latter to ensure that we don't wind up rewarding people for investing huge sums of money into creating products that are no better than what's already on the market). But while something along these lines might be desirable in certain specific circumstances—for example, when a nation decides to order the compulsory licensing of a patented drug to stave off a public health emergency—the mainstream view is that this isn't the sort of inquiry we should saddle a judge (or jury) with in a normal, everyday patent infringement action. It also might seem to run contrary to separation-of-power and rule-of-law values, to have judges in effect encouraging people to infringe valid patents by deliberately keeping damages undercompensatory. Instead, as I've argued before, if the substantive law makes it too easy to obtain patents which confer little in the way of social value and for which the patent incentive is unnecessary, it's up to Congress and the USPTO to fix matters, not for the courts to take it upon themselves to undermine the existing rules.

There seems to be a rough consensus, then, that as a general rule patent damages should compensate the patent owner for the losses it suffered as a result of the infringement. But that doesn't necessarily exhaust the field. Another possible goal is deterrence—roughly, the idea that we should send a message that infringement doesn't pay—and one way to do this is to ensure that damages awards are large enough that the infringer winds up no better off for having infringed. Fortunately, compensatory damages (assuming they're accurately calculated) often should be sufficient to serve this deterrent purpose as well. Imagine, for example, that the defendant made ten infringing sales that we can confidently say otherwise would have gone to the patent owner, but that the patent owner would have made a higher profit on those sales than the infringer did. (The patent, after all, entitled the owner to a statutory monopoly; perhaps its cost of producing the patented good is lower than the infringer's too.) In such a case, the patent owner is entitled to recover its lost profit, and since this amount is higher than the profit the defendant earned on its infringing sales, an award of lost profits serves both a compensatory and a deterrent purpose.[59]

On the other hand, there may be cases in which the infringer's profit exceeds the profit the patent owner itself could have earned from sales of the patented good. If the patent owner is an NPE, for example, it wouldn't have made *any* sales absent the infringement, but rather would have earned money from licensing the patent (to the defendant or others). In these circumstances, US law would award the owner a "reasonable royalty," which you could think of as the royalty the owner would have earned had the defendant negotiated a license. As with lost profits, assuming that the court performs the calculation correctly, the award preserves the patent incentive by restoring the patent owner to the position it would have occupied but for the infringement. Or does it? Actually, an award of reasonable royalties may strike you as a little more "fictional" than a lost profits award, and for good reason. When the patent owner seeks a lost profits award, it has to prove that it would have made *x* number of sales absent the infringement; but how can we sure what sort of bargain the patent owner and the infringer would have struck if the infringer hadn't infringed? (As we'll see in a moment, courts have come up with various ways to try to estimate the terms of this hypothetical bargain, but none of them are perfect.) Moreover, unlike a lost profits award, an award of reasonable royalties doesn't appear to make the defendant any worse off for having infringed, and therefore might not seem an adequate deterrent. One response to this argument, however, is that the defendant *is* worse off for having infringed, to the extent it has to pay its attorneys' fees to defend itself in litigation; presumably those fees are higher than the fees that would have been incurred to negotiate a patent license. (As we saw in Chapter 8, the cost of litigating a patent infringement action ranges from hundreds of thousands to millions of dollars.) In addition, as we also saw in Chapter 8, in cases where the defendant intentionally infringed, it may be liable for enhanced damages and for its opponent's attorneys' fees, which remedies provide an additional layer of deterrence—as would an injunction, if as discussed earlier in this chapter the defendant engaged in the delaying practice known as holdout.

A final possibility, if you thought more deterrence was necessary, would be to take the profit the infringer earned from the sale of infringing products, and award the patent owner the portion of that profit attributable to the unauthorized use of the patented technology. (You would expect this amount to be greater than the amount of a reasonable royalty, since it's unlikely the infringer would have agreed to fork over its entire profit to the owner, but rather to split the profit from the use of the invention in some manner.) In fact, many countries do permit awards of the infringer's profits, as an alternative to an award of lost profits or a reasonable royalty, and US law used to as well. In 1946, however, Congress eliminated this remedy for the infringement of utility patents due to its perceived cost and complexity. And perhaps it's just as well: although deterring infringement sounds like a good idea, as discussed in Chapter 8, there may be reason to worry about *over*deterring firms from engaging in lawful conduct which, they fear, might be mistaken for infringement. Rewarding patent owners beyond the amount that their technology contributes to the state of the art also seems socially inefficient, for reasons discussed above in connection with patent holdup. Perhaps it's just as well, then, that the United States got rid of the disgorgement remedy—except that we didn't get rid of it altogether, but rather retained it as a remedy for *design* patent infringement only. As of late 2017, the question of how to calculate the design patent infringer's profits was again before the district court on remand from the Supreme Court in *Samsung v. Apple*, a case I'll come back to at the end of this chapter.

In patent cases generally, and complex device cases in particular, awards of reasonable royalties are more common than awards of lost profits for a variety of reasons,[60] one of them being the fact noted above that even practicing entities often license their patents and therefore can't really claim that the infringement cost them any lost sales. As also noted above, a common way of thinking about reasonable royalties is to imagine the bargain the patent owner and the infringer would have negotiated, but for the infringement. In theory, this construct makes sense if we're trying to restore the owner to the position it would have occupied but for the infringement, but in practice it's often quite difficult to achieve consensus on what such a bargain would have looked like. As I noted earlier in discussing the pros and cons of injunctions, estimating the value of patented inventions can be very difficult, in large part because that value resides in what the invention enables someone to do—the extra profits you could earn, or the costs you could avoid, in comparison with what you could earn or save by resorting to the next-best available noninfringing alternative. Moreover, since no *actual* negotiation really took place we can only make an educated guess as to how much the user would have been willing to pay, and how much the owner would have been willing to accept, had the parties actually negotiated a license. (Although it's possible that the owner has an established licensing program under which it makes its patent available to any and all takers at some standard rate, that's usually not the case. As Erik Hovenkamp and Jonathan Masur observe in a recent paper, the market for patents is different from, say, the market for toasters, which normally "involve[s] very little variability among the terms or scope of different transactions.")[61]

To assist in making that educated guess, the plaintiff and defendant in a patent infringement action will rely upon expert witnesses—usually economists, accountants, or people with expertise in patent licensing—who are allowed to offer an opinion as to the amount and structure of an appropriate reasonable royalty, provided that their testimony is admissible under the Federal Rules of Evidence. In particular, Rule 702 requires, among other things, that the opinion be based on "reliable principles and methods" which the expert "reliably" applies to the facts of the case. Courts actually have become somewhat more skeptical in recent years about what counts as a reliable methodology for purposes of assessing damages, but even so it's not unusual for testifying experts to disagree as to the amount of a reasonable royalty by factors of 20 to 1 or more (in at least one case, by a factor of 300 to 1!).[62] Such an embarrassingly broad range of admissible opinion is not a good thing. Economic analysis predicts that the greater the variance in possible outcomes, the less likely it is that the parties will settle (though to be sure, most patent cases, like most cases generally, ultimately do settle short of trial), and also that in cases that do settle the more risk-averse party will be more willing to accept a bad deal in order to reduce uncertainty. Uncertainty is further compounded by the fact that most patent infringement trials in the United States are jury trials.[63] (No other country in the world entrusts decisions in patent infringement actions to lay jurors, but in the United States the Seventh Amendment guarantees a right to trial by jury in "suits at common law" in federal court.) On the other hand, most patent cases are concentrated in just a few districts, which means that the judges often have some experience with patent matters even though there are no specialized patent trial courts as such, as there are in some other nations.

Anyway, the experts typically base their royalty estimates on a range of evidence, including the so-called *Georgia-Pacific* factors—a list of fourteen factors, first compiled in a 1970 patent case brought by the Georgia-Pacific Corporation, that are supposed to assist in constructing the terms of the hypothetical bargain that a willing licensor and licensee would have struck, prior to the date on which the infringement began.[64] The problem is that a list this long, which doesn't specify how much weight to give any single factor, provides experts with enormous room to maneuver—which in turn helps explain why their estimates often differ by such large margins. In recent years, however, some lawyers and scholars (again including me) have recommended that courts focus (and instruct juries) on just a handful of particularly relevant factors—in particular, *Georgia-Pacific* factor 2 ("the rates paid by the licensee for the use of other patents comparable to the patent in suit"); factors 8 through 10 (all of which relate to the value of the patented technology in comparison with alternatives); and factor 13 (apportionment, that is, "the portion of the realizable profit that should be credited to the invention as distinguished from non-patented elements, the manufacturing process, business risks, or significant features or improvements added by the infringer").[65] In fact, factor 2 (comparables) often appears to be the most persuasive in practice, though whether this is such a good idea is debatable. Critics argue that the use of comparables is circular, if the terms to which parties to another transaction agreed is in part a function of what they believed the court would award if the matter proceeded to trial, and those terms are then being used to influence what the court in the present action *should* do. Comparables also, presumably, reflect the parties' estimates of whether the patent at issue really is valid and infringed, but for purposes of trial the jury is instructed to assume that the parties would have bargained on the assumption that they *knew* the patent in suit was valid and infringed.[66] (This assumption is counterintuitive but economically correct, because it avoids a double discounting problem that otherwise would arise.)[67] Thus, unless the court instructs the jury to adjust the comparable rate accordingly (which courts generally don't do), an award based on a purported comparable risks undercompensating the patent owner. On the other hand, Hovenkamp and Masur wonder whether firms sometimes strategically hold out for higher rates—even to the point of rejecting some offers that in isolation would appear to be in both parties' interest—in order to use those rates as comparables in other litigation.[68] If so, this practice might tend to bias comparables in favor of *over*compensation, all other things being equal.

Perhaps the biggest problem with comparables, though, particularly in complex device cases, is that often there *is* no precisely comparable license to use as evidence of the terms to which the parties would have agreed to license the patent in suit. Particularly in the world of complex devices, patent owners often license portfolios of patents consisting of tens or even hundreds of individual patents. In litigation, by contrast, there are usually only one or at most a handful of patents in suit, which makes it difficult to use a much larger portfolio to determine the royalty. Although it might be tempting to assume that each patent in the portfolio is of equal value, so that you could just divide the aggregate portfolio rate by the number of patents in the portfolio to get a per-patent rate, that often isn't the case. I'll return to this issue in the context of the *Microsoft* and *Innovatio* litigation discussed below.

There are many other damages calculation problems of a more technical nature which I needn't go into in a book like this, but for which the interested reader can consult the works I've cited in the endnotes. Instead, I'll close this chapter with a brief discussion of three recent device cases that further illustrate some of the difficulties faced in accurately calculating damages. The first two are FRAND cases, and the third is the Apple design patent case.

The first case, *Microsoft Corp. v. Motorola, Inc.*,[69] arose following Microsoft's rejection of Motorola's offer to license two portfolios of patents Motorola represented as being essential to the IEEE's 802.11 wireless local area network standard and to the ITU's H.264 video coding standard. Motorola's asking price was 2.25 percent of the price of end products—Xbox units, laptops, phones—capable of practicing these patents.[70] In response, Microsoft filed suit for breach of contract, arguing that Motorola's commitment to license the patents at issue on FRAND terms constituted a binding promise for the benefit of third parties, and that the asking price was excessive (i.e., non-FRAND). In the course of a lengthy opinion, US District Judge James Robart reached several conclusions touching on the issues I've discussed in this chapter, among them (1) that Motorola was contractually bound to negotiate a license on FRAND terms; (2) that a royalty should reflect the value of the patented invention only, and not its holdup value; (3) that courts should avoid royalty stacking that would result in aggregate royalties exceeding the value of the device; (4) that the value of the patented invention over the next-best alternative is theoretically the correct measure of patent value, though one that may be difficult to estimate in practice; (5) the importance of carefully considering which purportedly comparable licenses are, in fact, comparable to the hypothetical license between the patent owner and the user; and (6) the importance of considering how important (or unimportant) the patent is to the user. On this last point in particular, the court noted that none of the Motorola patents at issue were of very high value; indeed, the patents relevant to the H.264 standard were used for a technology known as "video interlacing" which was largely obsolete by the date of trial. (Microsoft products such as the Xbox have to support this technology in order for Microsoft to promote these products as standard-compliant, but almost nobody actually uses it anymore.)

Ultimately the court relied heavily on the rates charged by certain patent "pools" as comparators. As Rob Merges has succinctly put it, "[p]atent pools are industry-wide agreements, often accompanied by administrative structures, to centralize all firms' patents for automatic out-licensing or to cross-license each others' patents."[71] Each contributor to the pool (and sometimes third parties as well) therefore gets to use any or all of the pooled patents, in exchange for an agreed-upon royalty that is divided among the contributors in some manner proportionate to their contributions. Relevant to the *Microsoft* case, for example, there are patent pools for both the H.264 and 802.11 standards, each of which charges a uniform royalty and distributes the proceeds to contributing patent owners on a per-patent basis. (As I noted above, on one view according each patent equal value is not optimal, since some patents are likely more valuable than others. Indeed, even when all of the patents are standard-essential, such that a user needs to have access to all of them to market a standard-compliant product, some of the patents are still likely to be more or less valuable than others; the number of consumers who actually make use of certain standardized features such as video interlacing, for example, may be minuscule. Nevertheless, patent pools often do accord each patent equal value because doing so greatly reduces the cost of administering the pool.) Membership in a pool is entirely voluntary, however, and Motorola itself was not a member of either pool, presumably because it expected to fare better as an outsider to the arrangement; as an outsider, it could try to extract higher royalties for its own patents, though it wouldn't enjoy the offsetting benefit of accessing pool members' patents at the pooled rate. Ultimately, though, the court concluded that Motorola's patents contributed so little to either the H.264 or 802.11 standard that a FRAND royalty for Motorola's H.264 patents would have been just three times the estimated per-patent rate charged by the H.264 pool, and that the FRAND rate for the 802.11 patents (taking into account two other proposed comparables as well) was less than twice the 802.11 pool rate. The FRAND royalty for the patents at issue therefore amounted to just 0.555 cents per unit for the products using the H.264 SEPs, and 3.471 cents per unit for the 802.11 SEPs[72]—a far cry from the $3 or more that Motorola had sought for the sale of each Xbox.[73]

The second case, *In re Innovatio IP Ventures LLC Patent Litigation*,[74] involved a portfolio of 802.11 patents owned by Innovatio IP Ventures, a PAE. (This is the company that, as I mentioned in Chapter 8, initially filed suit against coffee shops, hotels, and other small businesses for making wireless Internet access available to their customers.) Eventually Cisco Systems and other firms that made the allegedly infringing equipment used by these businesses intervened as defendants, and the case proceeded to a nonjury trial on damages *prior to* a trial on liability. (This procedure, known as "reverse bifurcation," is unusual but arguably makes sense in a case like this where the principal obstacle to settlement may be the parties' very different views as to an appropriate royalty.)

In the course of yet another lengthy opinion, Judge James Holderman mostly agreed with the methodology used in *Microsoft* to estimate the FRAND royalty, which he summarized as involving three steps:

> First, a court should consider the importance of the patent portfolio to the standard, considering both the proportion of all patents essential to the standard that are in the portfolio, and also the technical contribution of the patent portfolio as a whole to the standard . . . . Second, a court should consider the importance of the patent portfolio as a whole to the alleged infringer's accused products . . . . Third, the court should examine other licenses for comparable patents to determine a RAND rate to license the patent portfolio, using its conclusions about the importance of the portfolio to the standard and to the alleged infringer's products to determine whether a given license or set of licenses is comparable.[75]

One difference, however, was that in this case the judge didn't think the 802.11 pool was a good comparator, given the small number of SEP owners that participated in it and the relatively high value of Innovatio's patents compared to Motorola's. (Specifically, the judge cited a 1998 study finding that "the top 10 percent of all electronics patents account for 84 percent of the value in all electronics patents,"[76] and concluded that the patents in suit fell into the top 10 percent of all 802.11 SEPs. They therefore were entitled to a proportionate share of the assumed 84 percent of the value of these patents.) Rejecting the parties' other proposed comparables as well, the judge instead adopted a so-called top-down approach to royalty calculation that involved (1) taking the average price of a WiFi chip—the smallest saleable component that embodied the patented technologies in suit—for the duration of the patents' terms ($14.85); (2) multiplying this number by the average profit margin of chip makers (12.1 percent), for a per-chip profit of $1.80 (the royalty base); (3) multiplying this number by 84 percent, for reasons stated above; and (4) multiplying that number by 19/300, reflecting his estimate that there were 3,000 SEPs per chip, of which 300 are in the top 10 percent and 19 of which were in suit. This brought the total royalty to 9.56 cents per chip.[77] As with *Microsoft v. Motorola*, commentators viewed the amount of the adjudicated royalty here as a victory for the manufacturers, given Innovatio's initial demand for a royalty amounting to as much as $40 per chip.[78] The case settled not long after.

Both cases arguably achieved reasonable solutions to the problem of determining how to value a small number of patents out of thousands. First, as illustrated by *Microsoft*, the rate charged by a patent pool can be a useful tool for determining patent royalties in complex device cases. Firms contributing patents to a pool are likely to be both licensors and licensees of the pooled patents, and their goals in setting a pool rate therefore should align with at least some of the goals of the court in setting damages: ensuring that compensation is adequate to preserve the incentive to invent and in some sense proportionate to the contribution, and avoiding holdup and royalty stacking. To be sure, pools have their disadvantages as well. As noted above, the pool rate is likely to be the same for all patents within the pool, but this rough-and-ready measure may not accurately reflect the value of any single patent over alternatives; moreover, the pool rate may appear lower than it really is because pool contributors are receiving as compensation not only the royalties due for their own patents, but also the value of access to other contributors' patents. As in *Microsoft*, however, a court can make adjustments to account for these characteristics of pool rates— by doubling or tripling the pool rate, for example, in recognition of the fact that a pool outsider such as Motorola doesn't gain the in-kind benefits of access to other pooled patents, or perhaps by adjusting the rate up or down to reflect the value of the patent in suit in comparison with the average patent within the pool. Similarly, a top-down approach like the one used in *Innovatio*—whereby the court determines the total "pot" from which royalties would be paid, and then divides it up in rough proportion to the relative value of the patents in suit—also reduces the risk of holdup and stacking. And as long as the pot is determined correctly, this approach also more or less ensures that damages are awarded in a manner that is roughly proportionate to the (relative) value of the patents in suit.

To be sure, neither of the two courts' approaches is perfect, either in theory or in execution. In my academic writing, for example, I've noted some possible technical flaws in both Judge Robart's use of pool rates and in Judge Holderman's top-down approach—though at the end of the day these may not have mattered a great deal in either case.[79] (Arguably, the errors favored the patent owners, who nonetheless wound up getting a lot less than they had hoped for.) I've also suggested that the top-down approach in particular would benefit from efforts to develop better or more current estimates of the number of valid and essential patents embodied in various technical standards, the distribution in value among those patents, and the percentage of revenue from sales of devices that typically goes toward paying royalties. (On this last point, more studies addressing the subject of the Armstrong et al. paper I noted earlier in this chapter would be welcome.) At the same time, however, it's important to recognize that any standards for awarding patent damages must simultaneously balance two considerations, namely accuracy and administrability. All things being equal, for reasons I've alluded to elsewhere in this chapter it would be nice if those standards always led to *accurate* determinations of the royalty the parties actually would have negotiated absent the infringement. But all things aren't equal: at some point, the investment of more time and money to achieve just a little more accuracy may not be worth it; indeed, it may not even be feasible to try, since at some point we run up against intractable gaps in the available information from which the hypothetical bargain is constructed. Thus in some of my recent academic work I've proposed that courts consider developing simpler, more predictable rules that may be "good enough" under the circumstances—and which might have the added benefit of narrowing the often wide gap I noted above between competing expert opinions. Procedural reforms such as requiring the parties to disclose their damages theories at an earlier stage in the litigation than is now common, as well as the use of neutral, court-appointed experts to supplement the experts retained by the parties, also may assist in resolving some disputes earlier and at lower cost.[80]

I'll close this chapter with a short discussion of *Samsung Elecs. Co. v. Apple Inc.*, which as of the end of 2017 is the Supreme Court's most recent foray into the law of patent damages (and complex devices). As noted earlier, one of the two civil actions Apple filed against Samsung in the Northern District of California involved some Apple design patents (along with a handful of utility patents including the rubber-banding patent). Design patents, as noted in Chapter 1, cover novel, nonobviousness, and ornamental (nonfunctional) industrial design, and historically they've been of much less importance than utility (invention) patents, at least in the United States. Fewer than one out of every ten US patents issued is a design patent. In the late 2000s, however, Apple succeeded in obtaining design patent protection for different aspects of the design of the iPhone. The illustrations here come from three of the patents in suit.

The first is taken from US Design Patent No. D618,677 and covers the design elements of the front face of the iPhone. The second, D593,087, covers the phone's "bezel" or rim, while D604,305 claims the "the ornamental design for

Figure 9.1 Apple Design Patents at Issue in *Samsung v. Apple*

a graphic user interface for a display screen or portion thereof." A jury found the three patents valid and infringed by certain makes of Samsung phones, and the Federal Circuit affirmed. These issues were hotly contested—and, as of this writing, the USPTO is reconsidering the validity of D'677—but the thorniest issue of all was how to calculate the monetary award to which Apple was entitled.

The reason for that thorniness was an obscure provision of the Patent Act dating back to the nineteenth century. In two related cases involving a patent for a carpet design, the Supreme Court in 1885 and 1886 held that (as in a utility patent case) the successful patent owner was entitled to recover its lost profit "due to" the infringing design. In these particular cases, however, the owner was unable to prove that it would have made *any* additional profit absent the infringement—the defendants had lots of noninfringing alternatives available to them—and thus was entitled to recover only "nominal" damages in the amount of six cents per defendant.[81] Several members of Congress apparently thought this was unfair, so in 1887 Congress enacted a law making it easier for design patent owners to recover an award of the infringer's profits. (Recall that this disgorgement remedy used to be available for utility patent infringement too, but in utility patent cases the patentee was entitled only to recover the profit the infringer earned over and above what it would have earned from use of the next-best alternative, which was hard to estimate.) Anyway, the law Congress passed in 1887 is now codified, with some modifications not relevant here, in § 289 of the Patent Act.[82] It reads as follows:

> Whoever during the term of a patent for a design, without license of the owner, (1) applies the patented design, or any colorable imitation thereof, to any article of manufacture for the purpose of sale, or (2) sells or exposes for sale any article of manufacture to which such design or colorable imitation has been applied shall be liable to the owner to the extent of his *total profit*, but not less than $250, recoverable in any United States district court having jurisdiction of the parties.

Nothing in this section shall prevent, lessen, or impeach any other remedy which an owner of an infringed patent has under the provisions of this title, but he shall not twice recover the profit made from the infringement.

I've highlighted two words in the above, "total profit." Although the statute isn't exactly a model of clarity, on what probably is the most obvious reading it appears to say that the owner of a design patent is entitled to recover the total profit the defendant earned on sales of the infringing "article of manufacture," or $250 (an amount that's never been updated, by the way, in all these years). In other words, there's no apportionment: the defendant has to give up its "total profit" on sales of the "article," and not (as in a utility patent case) only the profit that was attributable to the use of the infringing feature.

As a general proposition, this "total profit" rule makes little economic sense: maybe in some instances all or most of the profit earned from sales of the "article" is attributable to the infringing design, but that hardly seems like a sound presumption across the board. Indeed, if the relevant article comprises several patented components, it seems unlikely that all the profit could be due to one single design patent; and what if there were two or more design patents embodied in the article? Should the defendant have to disgorge its total profit twice? (Case law since 1887 has made it clear that design patents can read on parts of larger products, and that products may embody multiple design patents, as was the case in *Samsung*.)[83]

Thankfully, Congress didn't change the apportionment rule for utility patents, but when in 1946 it eliminated disgorgement in the latter class of cases it nevertheless chose to keep the total profit rule in place for design patents—where, at the end of the day, it probably didn't do a *great* deal of harm, given the relative infrequency of and low stakes involved in typical design patent cases. Then along came *Apple v. Samsung*, where as you can imagine the "total profit" from sales of the infringing "article" could be enormous. Still, there's a potential out: the statute doesn't explicitly provide any guidance for determining what the "article of manufacture" *is* to which the infringing design is affixed. In the case of comparatively simple fare like a carpet design, perhaps it's obvious that the "article" is the carpet. But in the case of a smartphone, what's the article? Is it the entire smartphone? Or just some component, such as the exterior or the screen? Should it matter whether these components can be sold separately?

To make a long story short, the district court in *Apple* concluded, and the Federal Circuit affirmed, that the term "article of manufacture" here meant the entire end product, i.e., the smartphone. Samsung therefore was required to pay Apple its entire profit from the sale of infringing phones, which amounted to $399 million. In December 2016, however, the Supreme Court reversed, holding that the relevant article of manufacture *doesn't* have to be the end product, but rather can be just a component.[84] The Court nonetheless left it up to the Federal Circuit to take the first crack at devising a test for determining what the relevant "article of manufacture" is for purposes of § 289. Moreover, whatever the article turns out to be, the patent owner will be entitled to all of the profits attributable to it, even if the patented design is only one of the article's many features—which from an economic perspective still seems like overkill, though not as bad as what the Federal Circuit's equation of the article with the end product would have permitted.

As of this writing, how all of this will play out with regard to Apple and Samsung remains to be seen; maybe the relevant article of manufacture will turn out to be just the exterior of the phone, and the relevant profit will be only a small percentage of $399 million. The bigger question, though, is how these rules will apply in other design patent cases, in the world of both complex devices and other products (for example, athletic shoes and equipment). Prior to the Supreme Court's decision in *Samsung*, some people were worried that "design patent trolls" would be the next big thing in patent law; and while the decision should ease these fears to some extent, whether the law ultimately will settle on a broad or narrow definition of "article of manufacture" remains for now an open (e-)book.

More generally, for both design and utility patents, the law of remedies surely will continue to evolve, both in the United States and abroad, in the years to come. If I had to guess, I'd say that eventually other countries will adopt, by one means or another, some sort of discretionary, *eBay*-like standard for injunctive relief, while US courts increasingly will be receptive to substantive and procedural measures to render damages calculation more predictable and less complex. Perhaps we'll see less of an emphasis on the formal, adversarial approach and more use of court-appointed experts, damages arbitration, and consensus-based SSO policies to guide us along. Then again, I could be wrong; the world of patent law surely has more surprises in store than any of us are capable of foreseeing. For we may not know when the next spark will flare, but there are sure to be new skirmishes to be fought, truces to be negotiated, and tactics to be refined in anticipation of the next patent war to end all wars.

CONCLUSION

The large amount of research that has already occurred when no researcher had sure knowledge that patent protection would be available
suggests that legislative or judicial fiat as to patentability will not deter
the scientific mind from probing into the unknown any more than
Canute could command the tides. Whether respondent's claims are
patentable may determine whether research efforts are accelerated by
the hope of reward or slowed by want of incentives, but that is all.
— *Diamond v. Chakrabarty*, 447 U.S. 303 (1980) (Burger, C. J.)

If you've made it to the end of this book, you now know a lot more about patents than does the average person—or even the average lawyer, judge, or member of Congress, for that matter. You may have agreed with most of what I had to say, when, as I often have, I've strayed from pure description to analysis or opinion; or from time to time you may have thought I was completely off my nut. But whatever your own conclusions may be, I hope that next time the topic of the day has something to do with patents—whether you're reading a news item on the latest salvo in the smartphone wars, or hearing how a friend of a friend received an ominous letter from a patent troll, or discussing the price of prescription drugs with your doctor, pharmacist, or elected representative—you'll be better equipped both to evaluate and critique what you're being told and to contribute to the discussion. Maybe on occasion you'll even convince your conversation partners to rethink their views. And who knows? Should our paths ever cross in the months or years to come, maybe you'll succeed in convincing *me* that I *was* off my nut when, say, I suggested that the case against gene patents wasn't all that convincing, or that the United States could reconcile reasonably strong patent protection for drugs with a single-payer health care system. Stranger things have happened.

But if this book has any one, central message other than "think for your-self," it's that there's so much we *don't* know for sure, even after all these years of granting, revoking, licensing, and fighting over patents. Do patents really spur invention, disclosure, and innovation? Do they, on balance, benefit the public by speeding up discoveries, or do they mostly serve to limit public access to things that would have been invented anyway? A lot depends on context, of course, on the contingencies of history. Ever since the invention of writing, if not earlier, some sort of patent system might have been possible in theory; Aristotle for one floated (and rejected) the concept of granting "honors for those who discover something advantageous to the state." But even if patents or other honors had been offered to inventors in ancient Greece or some other advanced civilization of the day, it's hard to imagine that they would have had a substantial impact on everyday life until much more recent times; even now, scholars are divided on the issue of whether patents played much of a role in spurring the Industrial Revolution just a couple of centuries ago.[1] And for all we know, patents may turn out to be unnecessary in some artificial intelligence–dominated world only a few decades away—if not sooner or, as the minority of economists who count themselves among the patent abolitionists would have it, already.

So maybe there are no universal lessons to be learned. For reasons I've recounted in this book, however, I think that in the environment we currently inhabit there are contexts in which patents probably play a positive role in fostering the innovations that improve our lives, and others in which they make less of a contribution; and that by making use of the (imperfect) tools that economics and other disciplines have to offer we can improve the system at the margins. But let's not overstate our case. The reality may be that, while patents are ubiquitous in the modern world, the policies and practices that governments over the years have adopted to strengthen or weaken patent rights may not be anywhere near as central to the innovation landscape as those of us in the thick of it sometimes would like to imagine.[2]

I'll close by noting that when I started teaching patent law many years ago I used to ridicule Chief Justice Burger's statement from *Chakrabarty* quoted at the beginning of this concluding chapter. The "that is all" part in particular always got my goat, for it seemed to suggest that patents had at best only a marginal impact on the progress of the useful arts; and if that's all there is, as Peggy Lee would put it, then why bother having a patent system at all? As the years have passed, however, I've come to see that maybe the chief was right—that, as Kevin Kelly writes, in large part the *technium* tends to evolve according to its unique path and timetable.[3] Perhaps the best the law can do is move it along a little faster or smoother than it otherwise might go. A rather humble mandate, perhaps; but at a time in which humility often seems to be in short supply, a bit refreshing for all that.

NOTES

Prologue

1. *See* Crate & Barrel, Simmons Full Beautyrest Luxury Firm Mattress, http://www. crateandbarrel.com/simmons-full-beautyrest-luxury-firm-mattress/s408032 (accessed Dec. 12, 2016); Select Comfort Co., Annual Report (Form 10-K) (Jan. 3, 2015); U.S. Patent No. 7,461,424 ("Method and apparatus for a pillow including foam pieces of various sizes").

2. *See* Alec Bank, *How Nike Used the Olympics to Beat Adidas to Market with Flyknit Technology,* Highsnobiety (Aug. 4, 2016), http://www.highsnobiety.com/2016/08/04/nike-flyknit-vs-adidas-primeknit/.

3. U.S. Patent No. 8,074,172 (filed Jan. 5, 2007).

4. In what appears to be a calculated gamble to encourage the development of a wider network for the support of electric cars, Tesla in 2014 announced it was dedicating all of its patents to the public domain. For discussion, *see* Jorge L. Contreras, *Patent Pledges,* 47 Ariz. St. L.J. 543 (2015) (noting, among other things, that Toyota followed suit with respect to "nearly 5,700 patents covering fuel cells for hydrogen-powered vehicles"). *See also* Christina Rogers, *A Shape-Shifting Car? Patent Filings Point to Auto Industry's Future,* Wall St. J., Sept. 18, 2017, https://www.wsj.com/articles/new-way-to-track-auto-innovation-patent-filings-1505732436.

5. *See, e.g., Split Pivot, Inc. v. Trek Bicycle Corporation,* 154 F.Supp.3d. 769 (W.D. Wis. 2015); Complaint, *dw-link Incorporated v. Giant Bicycle, Inc.,* No. 2:13-cv-00801 (C.D. Cal. Feb. 5, 2013); *HTC Corp. v. Gemalto* [2013] EWHC 1876 (Pat.) (Eng.) (smart cards).

6. *See Ass'n for Molecular Pathology v. Myriad Genetics, Inc.,* 133 S. Ct. 2107 (2013).

7. Actually, the number of US patents granted annually to domestic inventors per capita is not all that much higher than it was from roughly the post-Civil War period to the early part of the Great Depression. Today, however, well over half of all US patents are awarded to foreign inventors, and the total number of patents per capita is more than twice that experienced in the past. *See* B. Zorina Khan, *Facts and Fables: A Long-Run Perspective on the Patent System,* Cato Unbound (Sept. 10, 2014), http://www.cato-unbound.org/2014/09/10/b-zorina-khan/facts-fables-long-run-perspective-patent-system; *U.S. Patent Activity: Calendar Years 1790 to the Present,* U.S. Pat. & Trademark Off., http://www.uspto.gov/web/offices/ac/ido/oeip/taf/h_counts.htm (last visited Sept. 27, 2016).

8. *U.S. Patent Activity: Calendar Years 1790 to the Present,* U.S. Pat. & Trademark Off., http://www.uspto.gov/web/offices/ac/ido/oeip/taf/h_counts.htm (last visited Sept. 27, 2016).

9. *See* Chris Barry et al., PwC 2017 Patent Litigation Study: Change on the Horizon? 4 (reporting "[a]pproximately 5,100" filings from October 1, 2015 to September 30, 2016); Brian C. Howard & Jason Maples, Lex Machina 2016 Patent Litigation Year in Review i, 2 (2017) (reporting 4,537 patent cases filed in calendar year 2016). Again, though, as a matter of history, there have been times in the past when the number of patent lawsuits per capita exceeded what we are experiencing today. *See* Christopher Beauchamp,

The First Patent Litigation Explosion, 125 YALE L. J. 848, 851–53 (2016) (". . . it seems likely that the volume of patent litigation in the late nineteenth-century United States routinely exceeded the number of suits filed during most of the twentieth century. And it is even possible that there were years in the nineteenth century when the *absolute* quantity of patent litigation approached or matched the levels of that during the early twenty-first") (emphasis in original).

10. *See Golan v. Holder*, 132 S. Ct. 873, 888 (2012); *cf.* Ned Snow, *The Meaning of Science in the Copyright Clause*, 2013 BYU L. REV. 259 (2013) (arguing that the dominant eighteenth-century meaning of "Science" was somewhat narrower).

11. *Id.* at 79–80 (1958).

12. For a good popular account, *see* DAVID WARSH, KNOWLEDGE AND THE WEALTH OF NATIONS: A STORY OF ECONOMIC DISCOVERY (W.W. Norton & Co. 2006).

13. JONATHAN HAIDT, THE RIGHTEOUS MIND: WHY GOOD PEOPLE ARE DIVIDED BY POLITICS AND RELIGION (Pantheon Books 2012).

14. *See* Naomi Hawkins, *An Exception to Infringement for Genetic Testing-Addressing Patient Access and Divergence Between Law and Practice*, 43 INT'L REV. INTELL. PROP. & COMPETITION L. 641, 646 (2012) (stating that, in Europe, gene patents "are largely ignored, and are essentially irrelevant within the system of diagnostic testing development and delivery within the" UK National Health Service). Hawkins argues, however, that problems could arise if gene patent owners began seeking licenses, and she recommends that European states formally adopt an infringement exception for diagnostic testing, rather than excluding genes from patentability altogether. *See id.* at 649–51.

Chapter 1

1. *See* WORLD INTELL. PROP. ORG., 2016 WORLD INTELLECTUAL PROPERTY INDICATORS 70–72 (2016), www.wipo.int/edocs/pubdocs/en/wipo_pub_941_2016.pdf (reporting, among other things, that more than 2.6 million US patents were in force in 2015). Note that when I state that the big five granted more than 1 million patents in 2015, some of those grants may have been for the same inventions since (as discussed in the text) a patent granted in one country is enforceable only in that country.

2. For a critique of some of patent law's allegedly gendered assumptions, *see, e.g.,* Dan L. Burk, *Feminism and Dualism in Intellectual Property Law*, 15 AM. U.J. GENDER SOC. POL'Y & L. 183, 193–94 (2007).

3. *See id.*

4. *See, e.g.,* EDWARD JUNG, SOMETHING FOR EVERYONE: BUILDING INCENTIVES FOR INNOVATION ECOSYSTEMS (2013), https://www.ineteconomics.org/uploads/papers/Jung-Paper.pdf; Ronald J. Riley, *Pressure on the American Patent System: Part 4: Privatizing the PTO*, ABOUT, http://theinventors.org/library/weekly/aa080497.htm (last visited Oct. 7, 2016).

5. *See, e.g.,* Dennis Crouch, *Cross-Border Patents*, PATENTLY-O (Nov. 21, 2010), http://www.patentlyo.com/patent/2010/11/cross-border-inventors.html (stating, with respect to US patents, that "[t]he number of inventors per patent has been steadily increasing over the past forty years. Patents issued during the past six months, have an average of 2.7 inventors per patent. In all, 68 percent of these patents list multiple inventors with 13 percent listing five or more inventors. Prior to 1990, most patents listed only one inventor"). US patent law requires that anyone who contributed to the conception of the invention be listed as a joint inventor. *See, e.g., Bard Peripheral Vascular, Inc. v. W.L. Gore & Assocs.*, 670 F.3d 1171, 1179–80 (Fed. Cir. 2012) *reaff'd in relevant part*, 682 F.3d 1003, 1005 n.1 (Fed. Cir. 2012) (en banc), *cert. denied*, 133 S.Ct. 932 (Jan. 14, 2013).

6. *See* Steve Jobs, CEO, Apple Inc. & Pixar Animation Studios, Commencement Address at Stanford University (June 12, 2005), http://news.stanford.edu/news/2005/june15/jobs-061505.html.

7. *See* Mark Lemley, *The Myth of the Sole Inventor*, 110 MICH. L. REV. 709, 711 (2012). For other recent discussions of simultaneous or cumulative invention, *see, e.g.,* JOSEPH HENRICH, THE SECRET OF OUR SUCCESS: HOW CULTURE IS DRIVING HUMAN EVOLUTION, DOMESTICATING OUR SPECIES, AND MAKING US SMARTER 322–23 (Princeton University

Press 2016); Kevin Kelly, What Technology Wants ch. 7 (Penguin Books 2011); Brian Merchant, The One Device: The Secret History of the iPhone 90 (Little, Brown & Co. 2017); Steven Sloman & Philip Fernbach, The Knowledge Illusion: Why We Never Think Alone 199–200 (Riverhead Books 2017).

8. *See id.* at 712–33. For extended analysis of whether Bell actually stole the key idea behind the telephone from his rival Elisha Gray, however, *see* Seth Shulman, The Telephone Gambit: Chasing Alexander Graham Bell's Secret (2008).

9. Graham v. John Deere Co., 383 U.S. 1, 15 & n.7 (1966). As a reviewer of an earlier draft noted, "if 'genius' means that you have an IQ above 140 (1 in 200) it might mean that there are plenty of geniuses on the team doing the . . . research"). Fair point, though my own view is that we should reserve the term "genius" for a more select group of unusually creative and insightful people.

10. *Dawson v. Dawson*, 710 F.3d 1347, 1360 (Fed. Cir. 2013) (Reyna, J. dissenting) (quoting *Mergenthaler v. Scudder*, 11 App. D.C. 264, 276 (D.C. Cir.1897)).

11. From 1836 to 1870, the US Patent Act required inventors to submit models of their inventions "in all cases in which admit[ted] of a representation by model." Patent Act of 1836 § 6, 5 Stat. 117, 119 (1836) (quoted in Kendall J. Dood, *Patent Models and the Patent Law:1790–1880 (Part I)*, 65 J. Pat. Off. Soc'y 187, 187 (1983)). The current law permits the Director of the USPTO to require submission of a model, *see* 35 U.S.C. § 114 (2012), but in practice this is rare. It is common, however, for inventors in the field of biotechnology to submit specimens of biological materials in order to comply with patent law's enablement requirement. *See* 37 C.F.R. § 1.802 (2012).

12. The assumption that a given drug is covered by one single patent isn't necessarily accurate, however. *See, e.g.*, Lisa Larrimore Ouellette, *How Many Patents Does It Take to Make a Drug? Follow-on Pharmaceutical Patents and University Licensing*, 17 Mich. Telecom. & Tech. L. Rev. 299, 300 (2010) (stating that "most small-molecule drugs are protected by multiple patents. The average was nearly 3.5 patents per drug in 2005, with over five patents per drug for the best-selling pharmaceuticals; these numbers have increased over time"). And over time, there may be multiple patents owned by different entities on new formulations, methods of delivery, or other variations or combinations of existing drugs. *See* Andrew Christie et al., *Patents Associated with High-Cost Drugs in Australia*, 8 PLoS One 1, Apr. 2013, http://journals.plos.org/plosone/article?id=10.1371/journal.pone.0060812 (in a study of the fifteen costliest drugs in Australia over a twenty-year period, reporting a mean of forty-nine patents per drug).

13. *See* U.S Pat. & Trademark Off., Manual of Patent Examining Procedure § 2106 (9th ed. 2015) [hereinafter MPEP], for more detailed definitions. The MPEP is a document published by the USPTO and used by patent lawyers, agents, and examiners for guidance on how to draft and examine patent applications.

14. *See* Stuart Graham & Saurabh Vishnubhakat, *Of Smart Phone Wars and Software Patents*, 27 J. Econ. Persp., Winter 2013, at 67, 73.

15. *See* AIPLA, 2017 Report of the Economic Survey I-87 to I-88; *see also id.* at 30 (reporting medians).

16. I shouldn't overstate how difficult it is merely to get the application through the Patent Office, however. The patent grant rate in the United States has been estimated to be between 70 and 85 percent, *see* Gideon Parchomovsky & Michael Mattioli, *Partial Patents*, 111 Colum. L. Rev. 207, 215 n.25 (2011) (citing two separate studies providing these figures); *cf.* Michael Carley et al., *What Is the Probability of Receiving a U.S. Patent?*, 17 Yale J. L. & Tech. 203, 203 (2015) (reporting, based on analysis of 2.15 million US applications from 1996 through mid-2013, a 55.8 percent grant rate not including applications that are split off into new (continuation) applications after earlier rejections, but that 71.2 percent of all initial applications eventually result in at least one patent when continuations are taken into account), though it's possible the percentage has gone down in the last few years as a result of some changes to patent law discussed later in this and other chapters. Nevertheless, many granted patents may be easy to design around or otherwise lack substantial commercial value.

17. There are widely differing estimates of the percentage of patents that are commercialized. *Compare* Peter Lee, *Transcending the Tacit Dimension: Patents, Relationships, and Organizational*

Integration in Technology Transfer, 100 Cal. L. Rev. 1503, 1507 n.13 (2012) (citing studies for
the proposition that about half of all granted patents are commercialized), *with* Paul J. Heald
& Susannah Chapman, *Veggie Tales: Pernicious Myths About Patents, Innovation, and Crop
Diversity in the Twentieth Century*, 2012 U. Ill. L. Rev. 1051, 1060, 1078–79 (2012) (noting
that "[a] key assumption in the patenting debate is that only a small percentage of patents are
ever commercialized," perhaps as low as 2–5 percent, but that "hard evidence of commercialization rates has been elusive to gather" because the lower estimate is "a guess based on
licensing and litigation rates, while the higher estimates" of up to 50 percent "are based on
interviews and surveys of inventors and firms, and not analyses of entire consumer markets").
Heald and Chapman report an average 16 percent commercialization rate for patented vegetable varieties, excluding corn, and a 48 percent rate for apples. *See id.* at 1079–80. Of course,
even if the percentage of patents that are commercialized is in the higher range of about
50 percent, the percentage that is *successfully* commercialized in the sense of turning a profit
would, presumably, be much lower.

18. *See Ill. Tool Works, Inc. v. Indep. Ink, Inc.*, 547 U.S. 28, 28–29 (2006).

19. Another common situation in which a patent owner cannot practice its own patent, without
other conditions being in place, is where the patent improves upon another patented technology. In such a case, the owner of the improvement patent must obtain permission from
the first (dominant) patent in order to practice the improvement. This is referred to as the
"blocking patents" scenario (see Chapter 7).

20. *See AIPLA, supra* note 15, at I-112 to -122 (reporting mean costs through appeal of $627,000
for cases with less than $1 million at stake, $1.456 million with $1-$10 million at stake,
$2.374 million with $10-$25 million at stake, and $3.831 million with more than $25 million
at stake); *id.* at 41 (reporting medians); *id.* at I-161 (comparing cost of asserting versus cost of
defending).

21. *See* John R. Allison et al., *Our Divided Patent System*, 82 U. Chi. L. Rev. 1073, 1099–100,
1124–26 (2015) (reporting, based on analysis of all patent infringement actions filed in
federal district court in 2008–09, an overall invalidation rate of 42.6 percent for all patents
litigated to judgment, but also noting the uncertainty whether patents litigated to judgment
are representative of all patents or even of all litigated patents); *see also* John R. Allison & Mark
A. Lemley, *Empirical Evidence on the Validity of Litigated Patents*, 26 AIPLA Q. J. 185, 205–207
(1998).

22. *See* Mark A. Lemley, *Rational Ignorance at the Patent Office*, 95 Nw. U. L. Rev. 1495, 1510
(2001).

23. *See generally* U.S. Gov't Accountability Off., GAO-16-490, Intellectual Property:
Patent Office Should Define Quality, Reassess Incentives, and Improve Clarity
(2016); U.S. Gov't Accountability Off., GAO-16-479, Intellectual Property:
Patent Office Should Strengthen Search Capabilities and Better Monitor
Examiners' Work (2016).

24. *See* Joan Farre-Mensa et al., *The Bright Side of Patents* (USPTO Econ. Working Paper Series
No. 2015-5, 2016), http://www.uspto.gov/sites/default/files/documents/Patents%20
030216%20USPTO%20Cover.pdf (based on a study of 45,817 first-time patent applications
filed by US start-ups since 2001, posited a causal relationship between approval of the application and a start-up's subsequent ability to "create jobs, enjoy faster sales growth, innovate
more," and to go public or be acquired; and stating that "[t]he effect was more pronounced
in the IT sector than in biotech," given that start-ups in the latter field "tend to be founded
by experienced scientists, the quality of whose research can be evaluated using a variety of
sources such as academic publications and … grants"); *see also* Stuart J. H. Graham et al., *High
Technology Entrepreneurs and the Patent System: Results of the 2008 Berkeley Patent Survey*, 24
Berkeley Tech. L. J. 1255, 1270 n.44, 1280 (2009); Bronwyn H. Hall & Dietmar Harhoff,
Recent Research on the Economics of Patents 21–22 (Nat'l Bureau of Econ. Research, Working
Paper no. 17773, 2012), http://www.nber.org/papers/w17773; Sebastian Hoenen et al., *The
Diminishing Signaling Value of Patents Between Early Rounds of Venture Capital Financing*, 43
Res. Pol'y 956, 982 (2014); Clarisa Long, *Patent Signals*, 69 U. Chi. L. Rev. 625, 678 (2002).

25. *See* F. M. Scherer, *The Innovation Lottery, in* Expanding the Boundaries of Intellectual
Property: Innovation Policy for the Knowledge Society 3 (Dreyfuss et al. eds.,

Oxford University Press 2001). *See also* Mark A. Lemley, *The Surprising Resilience of the Patent System*, 95 Tex. L. Rev. 1, 40–42 (2016) (noting other theories of "why people obtain patents and then do nothing with them," including vanity, rewarding employee creativity, and social norms).

26. *See Madey v. Duke University*, 307 F.3d 1351, 1362 (Fed. Cir. 2002) (quotation omitted).

27. *See* 35 U.S.C. § 271(e)(1); *Merck KGaA v. Integra Lifesciences I, Ltd.*, 545 U.S. 193 (2005) (holding that the use of a patented invention in preclinical tests that might ultimately lead to an FDA submission did not infringe because the tests were "reasonably related to the development and submission of information" to the FDA).

28. *See* Christopher A. Cotropia & Mark A. Lemley, *Copying in Patent Law*, 87 N. C. L. Rev. 1421, 1451–57 (2009). There are a variety of arguably plausible reasons for not exempting inadvertent infringement, among them that doing so might discourage firms from reading patents or increase the costs of administering and adjudicating patent disputes. Intent nevertheless can be relevant when the defendant is accused of inducing or contributing to someone else's unauthorized manufacture, use, or sale of the patented invention, or in some instances (as discussed in Chapter 8) for purposes of assessing monetary damages.

29. *See* MPEP, *supra* note 13, § 901.04. A complete list of INID numbers can be found at MPEP § 901.05(b).

30. The title should be as "short and specific as possible" and may not exceed 500 characters. *Id.* § 606. Words such as "new" or "improvement" are no longer used in titles.

31. *See* 35 U.S.C. § 115 (2012). There are some exceptions in the case of a joint inventor or inventor under an obligation of assignment who refuses to execute the oath. *See id.*

32. *See id.* § 118.

33. *Id.* § 113.

34. *Id.* § 112.

35. Under U.S. law, there is a third disclosure requirement which obligates the inventor to disclose her "best mode"—her preferred method or embodiment of carrying out the invention. *See id.* § 112(a) (stating that " [t]he specification. . . shall set forth the best mode contemplated by the inventor or joint inventor of carrying out the invention"). As a result of recent changes to U.S. patent law, however, this requirement, though still technically in place, is largely unenforceable. Most other countries do not have a best mode requirement.

36. Technically, "peripheral claiming" is the established U.S. method of claiming. Some other countries apply a variation of so-called "central claiming," under which the inventor claims only the "core" of his or her invention, and the courts ultimately determine how far beyond the core the inventor's rights extend. In theory, the U.S. practice might seem easier to administer, but in practice even determining whether an allegedly infringing invention falls within the claimed periphery frequently cannot be conclusively determined absent litigation.

37. An electrolyte is "a substance which dissolves in water or another suitable medium to give a solution capable of conducting an electric current." I Supplement to the Oxford English Dictionary 925 (1972). Gatorade and other sports beverages contain electrolytes. In the "Detailed Description of the Invention," the Fregley et al. patent states that "electrolytes of the composition can be selected, for example, from the group consisting of sodium, potassium, phosphate, bicarbonate, sulfate, chloride, calcium, and magnesium." U.S. Patent No. 5,089,477 (filed Oct. 9, 1990). Glycerol is a trihydroxy sugar alcohol that is sometimes used, *inter alia*, as a sweetening agent. *See* Dorland's Illustrated Medical Dictionary 803 (31st ed. 2007); Stedman's Medical Dictionary 820 (28th ed. 2006). According to the patent, glycerol is the ingredient that renders the claimed beverage an improvement over Gatorade.

38. There is an exception to this principle, known as the doctrine of equivalents, but we can gloss over that for present purposes.

39. *See* J. Jonas Anderson & Peter S. Menell, *Informal Deference: An Historical, Empirical, and Normative Analysis of Patent Claim Construction*, 108 Nw. U. L. Rev. 1, 40–41 tbl.3 (2013) (showing that claim construction reversal rates peaked at 44.2 percent in 2004, but were down to 20.4 percent in 2011).

40. *See Markman v. Westview Instruments, Inc.*, 517 U.S. 370 (1996).

41. *Nautilus, Inc. v. Biosig Instruments, Inc.*, 134 S. Ct. 2120, 2130 (2014). This case overturned the Federal Circuit's standard under which a claim was indefinite only if it was "insolubly ambiguous."

42. *See, e.g., MedImmune, Inc. v. Genentech, Inc.*, 549 U.S. 118, 137 (2007) (holding that a patent licensee is "not required . . . to break or terminate its . . . license . . . before seeking a declaratory judgment . . . that the patent was invalid, unenforceable, or not infringed"); *Hewlett-Packard Co. v. Acceleron LLC*, 587 F.3d 1358, 1364 (Fed. Cir. 2009) (interpreting *MedImmune* to stand for a shift toward a more generalized analysis of "case-and-controversy"). Practice in other countries can vary quite a bit. Some permit virtually anyone to file a lawsuit challenging patent validity, at any time, while others are more restrictive. *See generally* Thomas F. Cotter, Comparative Patent Remedies: A Legal and Economic Analysis (Oxford University Press 2013).

43. *See* John R. Allison et al., *Understanding the Realities of Modern Patent Litigation*, 92 Tex. L. Rev. 1769, 1779–80 (2014) (stating that "more than 90 percent of lawsuits settle before the court resolves summary judgment or tries the case," and that others settle pending appeal); Mark A. Lemley, *Where to File Your Patent Case*, 38 AIPLA Q. J. 401, 404–05 & tbl.1 (2010) (reporting that, of all 21,667 patent infringement cases filed from January 1, 2000 to March 17, 2010, 75.5 percent settled; 15 percent were litigated to judgment; and the rest were either consent judgments or are classed as "indeterminate"); J. Shawn McGrath & Kathleen M. Kedrowski, *Trends in Patent Damages*, A. B. A: Sec. Litig. 3, http://www.docs.piausa.org/ABA/07-06-01-ABA-Report-On-Patent-Damages.pdf (last visited Oct. 9, 2016) (reporting that 3–4 percent of patent infringement actions filed from 2000 to 2006 went to trial). Courts sometimes dispose of cases on the basis of dispositive pretrial motions, such as motions to dismiss or motions for summary judgment—the latter when pretrial discovery discloses that there is no "genuine issue of material fact" to be tried, such that one party or the other is entitled to judgment as a matter of law.

44. *See* Chris Barry et al., PwC, 2012 Patent Litigation Study: Litigation Continues to Rise amid Growing Awareness of Patent Value 9 (2012), http://patentlyo.com/media/docs/2013/03/2012-patent-litigation-study.pdf; *see also* Allison et al., *supra* note 43, at 1779.

45. Allison et al.'s research suggests that the bias against foreign patent plaintiffs reported in Kimberly A. Moore, *Xenophobia in American Courts*, 97 Nw. U. L. Rev. 1497 (2003), no longer appears to be an issue, though they note that this effect "may be driven in full or in part by selection effects." *See* Allison et al., *supra* note 43, at 1796–97.

46. *See* Thomas F. Cotter & John M. Golden, *Empirical Studies Relating to Patents—Remedies*, *in* Research Handbook on the Economics of Intellectual Property Law (Peter S. Menell et al., eds., Edward Elgar Publishing forthcoming 2018) (manuscript at 14, 16–17), http://papers.ssrn.com/sol3/papers.cfm?abstract_id=2665680 (discussing empirical studies reporting median patent damages awards in the United States ranging from $688,000 to $2 million, and studies from France, Japan, and China reporting average awards many magnitudes lower); *see also* Cotter, *supra* note 42, at 259, 309–10 n.95, 354–55.

47. For more discussion on some of the critiques, *see* Ashby Jones, *Critics Fault Court's Grip on Appeals for Patents*, Wall. St. J. (July 6, 2014, 7:10 pm).

48. *See* Paris Convention for the Protection of Industrial Property art. 4, Mar. 20, 1883, 21 U.S.T. 1583.

49. Patent Cooperation Treaty, June 19, 1970, 28 U.S.T. 7645.

50. A majority of members of the European Union have agreed to implement a new Unitary Patent system, however, which may take effect in the ratifying members sometime in 2018 (though Brexit may complicate matters).

51. Leahy-Smith America Invents Act, Pub. L. No. 112–29, 125 Stat. 284 (2011) (codified in scattered sections of 35 U.S.C.).

52. *See generally* Dennis Crouch, *Patent Reform: Patent Act of 2005*, Patently-O (June 9, 2005), http://patentlyo.com/patent/2005/06/patent_reform_p.html.

53. As we'll see in the next chapter, it wasn't always the case, everywhere, that someone had to be an inventor to obtain a patent. Some of the earliest patents awarded in Italy and in England were to people who "imported" a new invention from another country. *See generally*

CHRISTINE MACLEOD, INVENTING THE INDUSTRIAL REVOLUTION: THE ENGLISH PATENT SYSTEM, 1660–1800, at 13 (1988). Today, defenders of strong IP rights might call such importation "theft." Whether this is the right way to think about the issue—I'm inclined to think it's not—for present purposes the point is moot, since no country awards this type of patent anymore. Everybody's laws stipulate than only inventors—or the firms to which inventors have assigned their rights—may obtain utility patents.

54. Of course, if small inventors develop a disproportionate share of great inventions, but are likely to be disadvantaged by a first-to-file rule, perhaps the first-to-invent rule provides the greater public benefit as well. Most patent scholars, including me, think this is not the case, though others are less certain whether the overall impact on social welfare will be positive or negative. *See* David S. Abrams & R. Polk Wagner, *Poisoning the Next Act? The America Invents Act and Small Inventors,* 65 STAN. L. REV. 517, 562–63 (2013).

55. The statement in the text is a slight overstatement. Most countries afford a one-year grace period if the inventor discloses her invention at an international exhibition such as a world's fair, which used to be an important way of attracting attention to new technology, or if someone (a rogue employee, for example) discloses the invention without the inventor's permission. Japan recently introduced a general six-month grace period. *See* COTTER, *supra* note 42, at 292 & n.12.

56. *See* Florian Mueller, *Video of Steve Jobs's iPhone Presentation Kills Apple's Photo Gallery Touch Patent in Germany,* FOSS PATENTS (Sept. 27, 2013, 7:31 PM), http://www.fosspatents.com/2013/09/video-of-steve-jobss-iphone.html.

57. *See Broad Inst., Inc. v. Regents of Univ. of Cal.,* Patent Interference No. 106,048 (DK) (PTAB Feb. 15, 2017) (concluding that Broad's claims, "which are all limited to CRISPR-Cas9 systems in a eukaryotic environment, are not drawn to the same invention as UC's claims, which are all directed to CRISPR-Cas9 systems not restricted to any environment"). Both teams hold patents and patent applications on different aspects of CRISPR-Cas 9, which had resulted in some confusion over whether other researchers must obtain licenses from one or the other or both. *See* Amy Dockser Marcus et al., *Crispr Patent-Holders Move Toward Easing Access to Gene-Editing Technology,* WALL ST. J., July 8, 2017, https://www.wsj.com/articles/crispr-patent-holders-move-toward-easing-access-to-gene-editing-technology-1499527983?mg=prod/accounts-wsj.

58. In addition, as noted in the text there is a federal statute that prevents the U.S. government from issuing patents on nuclear weapons. *See* 42 U.S.C. § 2181(a) (2012). The AIA also introduced two new categories of nonpatentable subject matter, tax planning methods and human organisms. I will discuss these in more detail in subsequent chapters.

59. *See Therasense, Inc. v. Becton Dickinson & Co.,* 649 F.3d 1276 (Fed. Cir. 2011) (en banc).

60. For a further discussion on this point, *see* COTTER, *supra* note 42, at 87–88, 174 & n.47.

61. *See id.;* Jason Rantanen, *Trends in Inequitable Conduct,* PATENTLY-O (Sept. 20, 2013), http://www.patentlyo.com/patent/2013/09/trends-in-inequitable-conduct.html.

62. The terms are not exactly synonymous. "Capable of industrial application" rules out the patentability of games, for example, but utility doesn't. For more information on this difference, *see* World Intell. Prop. Org. [WIPO], *"Industrial Applicability" and "Utility" Requirements: Commonalities and Differences,* Standing Committee on the Law of Patents, Ninth Session, SCP/9/5 (Mar. 17, 2005), http://www.wipo.int/edocs/mdocs/scp/en/scp_9/scp_9_5.pdf.

63. The utility requirement is so loosely enforced, however, that sometimes patents on fantastic inventions are approved. For one particularly egregious example, *see* U.S. Patent No. 5,676,977 (filed May, 31, 1996) (titled "Method of curing AIDS with tetrasilver tetroxide molecular crystal devices"). You'll have no problem finding it in that happy hunting ground for conspiracy theorists known as the Internet. For a sober assessment of the (lack of) benefits of using tetrasilver tetroxide—a swimming pool disinfectant—to cure AIDS by electrocuting the HIV virus, consult the website of AVERT, a leading international HIV and AIDS charity based in the United Kingdom, titled *Cure for AIDS. Is There a Cure for HIV/AIDS?,* AVERT, http://www.avert.org/cure-aids.htm (last updated Jan. 26, 2016).

64. 15 F.Cas. 1018 (C.C.D. Mass. 1817). The case is not a Supreme Court case, but rather hearkens back to a time when U.S. Supreme Court justices "rode circuit" to conduct trials and hear appeals when the Supreme Court was not in session.

65. *Id.* at 1019.
66. *See Scott & Williams, Inc. v. Aristo Hosiery Co.,* 7 F.2d 1003 (2d Cir. 1925) (seamless stockings); *Brewer v. Lichtenstein,* 278 F. 512 (7th Cir. 1922) (gambling games); *Rickard v. Du Bon,* 103 F. 868 (2d Cir. 1900) (tobacco leaves).
67. *See Juicy Whip, Inc. v. Orange Bang, Inc.,* 185 F.3d 1364 (Fed. Cir. 1999). The supposedly fraudulent invention was a beverage dispenser that made it appear as if the syrup and water had been premixed, which supposedly induces impulse purchases, when in fact the syrup and water were mixed at the point of sale (a feature that was more desirable from the standpoint of hygiene). Notice the odd position of the defendant in such a case, who must argue that the invention it allegedly is using is unpatentable because it is immoral!
68. 42 U.S.C. § 2181 (2012).
69. *See* Rick Weiss, *US Denies Patent for Part-Human Hybrid,* WASH. POST, Feb. 13, 2005, at A3; Press Release 98-6, U.S. Pat. & Trademark Off., Facts on Patenting Life Forms Having a Relationship to Humans (Apr. 1, 1998), http://www.uspto.gov/news/pr/1998/98-06.jsp.
70. *See, e.g.,* Convention on the Grant of European Patents, art. 53, Oct. 5, 1973, 1065 U.N.T.S. 199, as amended Nov. 29, 2000, http://www.epo.org/law-practice/legal-texts/epc.html.
71. *See Brenner v. Manson,* 383 U.S. 519 (1966).
72. *See, e.g., In re Brana,* 51 F.3d 1560 (Fed. Cir. 1995).
73. 421 F.3d 1365 (Fed. Cir. 2005).
74. More specifically, for an invention to be "useful" there must be a basis for concluding that it has both a *specific* utility—it provides "a well-defined and particular benefit to the public," rather than merely being a member of a class of things that in general are useful—and a *substantial* utility, meaning that the invention has some "'real-world' value" that "'provides an immediate benefit to the public.'" *Id.* at 1371 (citations omitted).
75. *See* 35 U.S.C. § 102(a)(1) (2012).
76. Tony Mauro, *High Court Case Could Imperil Pending Patents,* LAW.COM, Nov. 28, 2006, http://www.law.com/jsp/article.jsp?id=900005552268&High_Court_Case_Could_Imperil_Pending_Patents&slreturn=20130827164100 [https://advance.lexis.com/search?crid=b828944f-c971-4ec6-9fd4-fe4049dc0a7c&pdsearchterms=LNSDUID-ALM-NTLAWJ-900005468095&pdmfid=1000516&pdisurlapi=true]
77. For discussion, *see* Michael Abramowicz & John F. Duffy, *The Inducement Standard of Patentability,* 120 YALE L. J. 1590 (2011).
78. Letter from Thomas Jefferson to Isaac McPherson (Aug. 13, 1813), *reprinted in* THE COMPLETE JEFFERSON 1011, 1016 (Saul Padover ed. 1943).
79. *See Hotchkiss v. Greenwood,* 52 U.S. (11 How.) 248 (1851). As John Duffy has pointed out, however, it wasn't as if no one had ever thought to make doorknobs from porcelain before. What was unusual about the knob was that it had a dovetailed cavity in which a screw was formed by pouring molten metal. The technique, which had recently been invented by someone else in a nearby town, had previously been used only with wooden and metal knobs. *Hotchkiss* therefore stands for the proposition that an invention may be obvious when its sudden appearance is likely attributable to an exogenous technological development—here, the invention of the new technique for fastening knobs to screws. *See* John F. Duffy, *A Timing Approach to Patentability,* 12 LEWIS & CLARK L. REV. 343, 351–52 (2008).
80. *See Graham v. John Deere,* 383 U.S. 1, 15 & n.7 (1966).
81. *Id.* at 11, 15 & n.7.
82. *See, e.g., In re Klein,* 647 F.3d 1343, 1348 (Fed. Cir. 2010). *Graham* itself did not hold that all of the prior art categories that are relevant for purposes of novelty are also relevant for purposes of nonobviousness, but subsequent lower court decisions have effectively established this principle. Many foreign patent systems impose some further limitations on the classes of prior art that are relevant to nonobviousness (inventive step), but we need not go into these technicalities here.
83. *Graham,* 694 U.S. at 17.
84. *See id.* The PHOSITA is presumed, unrealistically, to be familiar with all of the relevant prior art.
85. *See id.* at 17–18.
86. *Jacobellis v. Ohio,* 378 U.S. 184, 197 (1964) (Stewart, J., concurring).

87. See *ACS Hosp. Sys., Inc. v. Montefiore Hospital.*, 732 F.2d 1572, 1577 (Fed. Cir. 1984).
88. See Gregory N. Mandel, *Patently Non-Obvious: Empirical Demonstration that the Hindsight Bias Renders Patent Decisions Irrational*, 67 Ohio St. L. J. 1391 (2006). Professor Mandel's follow-up study, however, suggested that while hindsight bias is certainly a risk, the TSM test actually did little to relieve it. *See* Gregory N. Mandel, *Patently Non-Obvious II: Experimental Study on the Hindsight Bias Issue Before the Supreme Court in* KSR v. Teleflex, 9 Yale J. L. & Tech. 1, 5 (2007).
89. See U.S. Patent No. 6,143,347 (filed May 14, 1999), "Early season not from concentrate orange juice and process of making." *Id.* Claim 1 read: "A method of preparing early season not from concentrate orange juice, comprising the steps of: harvesting a very early season orange cultivar selected from the group consisting of a cultivar within the Seleta family of cultivars, a Westin cultivar, a Ruby Nucellar cultivar, or a combination of these very early season cultivars, said harvesting being very early in the harvesting season for orange fruit, namely no later than the harvesting season of Hamlin orange fruit in the growing territory; extracting juice from a volume of said very early season oranges of said harvesting step; collecting the resulting extracted orange juice as an early season orange juice having a Color Number of at least 33 CN units, said Color Number being greater than Hamlin orange juice harvested at the time of said harvesting step; and blending said extracted early season orange juice with another orange juice source in order to provide a not from concentrate orange juice product having a Color Number in excess of 33 CN units, while also exhibiting sensory qualities substantially equivalent to the sensory qualities of Hamlin orange juice." *Id.* Claim 27 recited the juice prepared in accordance with this method. *Id.* The other forty-five claims were for other variations on the method and product. For discussion of the controversy surrounding the patent, *see, e.g.,* Betsy McKay, *Orange Growers Get Squeezed by Disputed Tropicana Patent*, Wall St. J., http://www.wsj.com/articles/SB1030994533639457595 (updated Sept. 3, 2002, 12:01 am).
90. 175 F.3d 994 (Fed. Cir. 1999).
91. See *id.* at 999.
92. See Fed. Trade Comm'n, To Promote Innovation: The Proper Balance of Competition and Patent Law and Policy, ch. 4, at 11 (Oct. 2003) (quoting USPTO Deputy Commissioner for Patent Examination Policy Stephen Kunin), https://www.ftc.gov/sites/default/files/documents/reports/promote-innovation-proper-balance-competition-and-patent-law-and-policy/innovationrpt.pdf.
93. See *supra* note 16; European Patent Office (EPO), Annual Report 2011—Statistics and Trends: Granted Patents in 2011, http://www.epo.org/about-us/annual-reports-statistics/annual-report/2011/statistics-trends/granted-patents.html (reporting a 47 percent grant rate in 2011 in the EPO).
94. See Mark A. Lemley & Bhaven Sampat, *Is the Patent Office a Rubber Stamp?*, 58 Emory L. J. 181, 185 n.23 (2008).
95. 550 U.S. 398 (2007).
96. *Id.* at 414.
97. See *id.* at 418–21.
98. *Id.* at 421.
99. See *id.* at 416–18; *see also* John F. Duffy, *Inventing Invention: A Case Study of Legal Innovation*, 86 Tex. L. Rev. 1, 12 (2007).
100. See Jason Rantanen, *The Federal Circuit's New Obviousness Jurisprudence: An Empirical Study*, 16 Stan. Tech. L. Rev. 709, 737 (2013). Pre-*KSR* cases are those decided ten years or less prior to the Supreme Court's decision to hear the case; post-*KSR* are those decided five years or less after the Court issued its opinion. *See id.* at 726–27 & n.86. In appeals from USPTO determinations of obviousness (i.e., cases like *Dembiczak*) the percentages finding nonobviousness are 17 percent before and 4 percent after. *Id.* at 737. For explanation of why the percentages in this latter group of appeals are, predictably, higher, *see id.* at 733–35.
101. See *Samsung Elecs. Co. v. Apple Inc.*, 137 S. Ct. 429 (2016), *rev'g* 786 F.3d 983 (Fed. Cir. 2015).
102. See Pat. Tech. Monitoring Team (PTMT), U.S. Pat. & Trademark Off., U.S. Patent Statistics Chart: Calendar Years 1963–2015, http://www.uspto.gov/web/offices/ac/ido/oeip/taf/us_stat.htm (last modified Oct. 15, 2016, 8:09 pm).

103. Prior to May 13, 2015, the term was fourteen years from the date of grant.
104. *See* WIPO, *supra* note 1, at 140.
105. *See* 35 U.S.C. §§ 161–64 (2012).
106. *See* 7 U.S.C. §§ 2321–2582.
107. *See* International Convention for the Protection of New Varieties of Plants, Dec. 2, 1961, 815 U.N.T.S. 89. I'll discuss the UPOV treaties in a little more detail in Chapter 7.
108. *See e.g., Farmer's Privilege Under Attack,* GRAIN 1–2 (June 15, 2003), https://www.grain.org/article/entries/103-farmers-privilege-under-attack.
109. *See* PAT. TECH. MONITORING TEAM (PTMT), *supra* note 102; *see also Issued Certificates,* U.S. DEP'T OF AGRIC., https://www.ams.usda.gov/services/plant-variety-protection/issued-certificates (last visited Oct. 15, 2016).
110. *See J. E. M. Ag Supply, Inc. v. Pioneer Hi-Bred Int'l, Inc.,* 534 U.S. 124 (2001).
111. There are others of less importance to this book, such as the "utility models" that some countries (but not the United States) afford for minor innovations, and the "right of publicity" that some states confer against unauthorized uses of a person's name, likeness, or other indicia of identity for purposes of trade.

Chapter 2

1. There are many varieties of utilitarianism, the details of which need not concern us here. Concerns over the inability to quantify "utility," or subjective pleasure, lead economists to prefer "wealth" maximization to utility maximization as a social welfare criterion, with wealth defined as the amount an individual would be willing to pay for an asset. The wealth maximization criterion has its own drawbacks, however, as one might readily imagine.
2. There's a lot more to the story, of course. Initially, copyright was more a tool for censorship than for the promotion of new works of authorship. *See generally* Thomas F. Cotter, *Gutenberg's Legacy: Copyright, Censorship, and Religious Pluralism,* 91 CAL. L. REV. 323 (2003).
3. *See, e.g.,* Ted Sichelman & Sean O'Connor, *Patents as Promoters of Competition: The Guild Origins of Patent Law in the Venetian Republic,* 49 SAN DIEGO L. REV. 1267, 1275–75 (2012).
4. It was not a smooth transition. Charles Dickens lampooned the difficulty facing English inventors in obtaining patents in his 1850 spoof *A Poor Man's Tale of a Patent.* For an argument, moreover, that the Statute of Monopolies hardly killed off royal trading privileges, many of which continued to be granted post-1623, see Thomas B. Nachbar, *Monopoly, Mercantilism, and the Politics of Regulation,* 91 VA. L. REV. 1313 (2005).
5. On the question of whether patents play a useful role in encouraging disclosure, specifically, the empirical evidence to date suggests that the technical information disclosed in patents is more important in industries such as pharmaceuticals and less so in fields such as software. *See* Bronwyn H. Hall & Dietmar Harhoff, *Recent Research on the Economics of Patents,* Nat'l Bureau Econ. Res. WORKING PAPER 1773, at 16–18 (Jan. 2012), http://www.nber.org/papers/w17773 (based on existing empirical studies, reporting that patent disclosure is most useful with respect to pharmaceuticals and chemicals); Mark A. Lemley, *Ignoring Patents,* 2008 MICH. ST. L. REV. 19 (asserting that patent disclosure is less important in telecommunications and information technology because researchers in those fields generally don't read patents); Lisa Larrimore Ouellette, *Do Patents Disclose Useful Information?,* 25 HARV. J. L. & TECH. 531, 534 (2012) (reporting that 64 percent of surveyed nanotechnology researchers claimed to read patents, that 70 percent of those who read patents did so in search of technical information, and that of those "60 percent found useful technical information").
6. As of this writing, the issue of inequality seems to be looming larger with every passing day—a development that was perhaps heralded by the surprising best-seller status of Thomas Piketty's 2013 book *Capital. See* THOMAS PIKETTY, CAPITAL IN THE TWENTY-FIRST CENTURY (Arthur Goldhammer tr., Harvard University Press 2013); *see also* ROBERT J. GORDON, THE RISE AND FALL OF AMERICAN ECONOMIC GROWTH: THE U.S. STANDARD OF LIVING SINCE THE CIVIL WAR ch. 18 (Princeton University Press 2016). Indeed, some research suggests that, for many people, fairness and equality often are more important than efficiency and wealth creation. For discussion, *see* Neil Irwin, *A More Efficient World That People May Not Want,* N.Y. TIMES, July 3, 2016; *see also Does Inequality*

Matter?, ECONOMIST: ECONS. BY INVITATION (Jan. 21, 2011), http://www.economist.com/economics/by-invitation/questions/how_does_inequality_matter [https://web.archive.org/web/20150429115054/http://www.economist.com/economics/by-invitation/questions/how_does_inequality_matter]; Anna Bernaske, *Income Inequality, and Its Cost*, N. Y. TIMES (June 25, 2006), http://www.nytimes.com/2006/06/25/business/yourmoney/25view.html.

Of course, as I try to stress throughout this book, things are often more complicated than they may first appear. If a monopolist patent owner happens to be a publicly traded corporation, lots of middle- and working-class people may own shares in that corporation, if not directly then through their pension funds. So it's possible that the transfer of income from consumers to producers really is, at some point, a wash, if the producers ultimately are owned by the consumers. Nevertheless, monopoly still results in a short-term deadweight loss which (absent some countervailing long-run virtue) is an unambiguous social bad.

7. *See, e.g.,* W. KIP VISCUSI ET AL., ECONOMICS OF REGULATION AND ANTITRUST 76–78 (2d ed. 1995).

8. An exception arises when there are economies of scale in production, such that one firm can supply a product at lower cost than would be possible if there were many sellers of that product. In such a case, known as a "natural monopoly," it may make more sense to tolerate the monopoly and regulate its price. This is the conventional rationale for public utility regulation. Another possibility is that there are economies of scale on the demand side, meaning that consumers actually prefer a standardized product that enables them to interact with other consumers using the very same product. These "network effects" or "network externalities" exist in some markets, such as the market for Internet operating systems.

9. *See* JOSEPH A. SCHUMPETER, CAPITALISM, SOCIALISM, AND DEMOCRACY (Harper & Bros. 3d ed. 1950). The lesson that some people draw from Schumpeter's analysis is that there is no point in regulating monopoly because doing so reduces the incentive to become a (temporary) monopolist through the introduction of new products and services. Other economists, by contrast, have emphasized the benefits of competition as a spur to innovation, a view usually associated with Kenneth Arrow. *See* Kenneth J. Arrow, *Economic Welfare and the Allocation of Resources for Invention, in* THE RATE AND DIRECTION OF INVENTIVE ACTIVITY: ECONOMIC AND SOCIAL FACTORS 609, 620–21 (Richard R. Nelson ed., 3d. prtg. 1976, Princeton University Press 1962). Some contemporary economic research posits that competition's effect on innovation takes the form of an inverted "U," meaning that, up to a point, innovation increases with competition before decreasing. *See* Philippe Aghion et al., *Competition and Innovation: An Inverted "U" Relationship*, 120 Q. J. ECON. 701, 706–07 (2005); *see also* Erik Hovenkamp, *Patent Prospect Theory and Competitive Innovation* (Apr. 15, 2016) (unpublished paper), http://papers.ssrn.com/sol3/papers.cfm?abstract_id=2765478 (summarizing recent research as showing that "aggregate innovation is maximized somewhere in between monopoly and perfect competition; that is, the market should be relatively competitive, but not too competitive").

10. For an accessible discussion by an economic journalist, *see* DAVID WARSH, KNOWLEDGE AND THE WEALTH OF NATIONS: A STORY OF ECONOMIC DISCOVERY (W.W. Norton & Co. 2006).

11. Ronald Coase's articles *The Theory of the Firm*, 4 ECONOMICA 386 (1937), and *The Problem of Social Cost*, 3 J. L. & ECON. 1 (1960), are often cited as the foundational works in transaction-cost economics. Oliver Williamson extended transaction-cost economics to contract structure in works such as THE ECONOMIC INSTITUTIONS OF CAPITALISM: FIRMS, MARKETS, RELATIONAL CONTRACTING (1985). Both Coase and Williamson were awarded Nobel Prizes in economics.

12. *See* Thomas F. Cotter, *Patent Holdup, Patent Remedies, and Antitrust Responses*, 34 J. CORP. L. 1151, 1169–70 (2009) (discussing the literature on the Cournot Complements Problem).

13. *See generally* Michael A. Heller & Rebecca S. Eisenberg, *Can Patents Deter Innovation? The Anticommons in Biomedical Research*, 280 SCI. 698 (1998).

14. Though sometimes contractual promises, if enforceable, may reach beyond what patent law would permit (for example, by restraining the owner of a patented article from using it in certain ways or from reselling it, even though patent law's exhaustion doctrine would permit these activities). Chapter 7 touches on a few of the contemporary issues surrounding the exhaustion doctrine.

15. *See generally* MICHELE BOLDRIN & DAVID K. LEVINE, AGAINST INTELLECTUAL MONOPOLY (2008).

16. *See id.* at 137–44.

17. Michele Boldrin & David K. Levine, *The Case Against Patents* 17 (Fed. Reserve Bank St. Louis Res. Division, Working Paper No. 2012-035A, 2012), https://research.stlouisfed.org/wp/2012/2012-035.pdf (citing Michele Boldrin et al., *Competition and Innovation*, 1 CATO PAPERS ON PUBLIC POLICY 109 (2011)).

18. *See* BODRIN, *supra* note 15, at 192–98; *see also* Boldrin & Levine, *supra* note 17, at 16–19.

19. *See* Wesley M. Cohen et al., *Protecting Their Intellectual Assets: Appropriability Conditions and Why U.S. Manufacturing Firms Patent (or Not)* (Nat'l Bureau Econ. Res., Working Paper No. 7552, 2000), http://www.nber.org/papers/w7552; *see also* Bronwyn H. Hall & Dietmar Harhoff, *Recent Research on the Economics of Patents* 12–15 (Nat'l Bureau Econ. Res., Working Paper No. 1773, 2012), http://www.nber.org/papers/w17773 (concluding, based on a survey of the existing empirical literature, that "the patent system provides clear incentives for innovation in only a few sectors," including "pharmaceutical, biotechnology, and medical instrument areas, and possibly specialty chemicals . . . but that firms and industries do respond to its presence, both by making use of the system and by sometimes tailoring their innovative strategies to its presence").

20. Josh Lerner, *Patents in a Time of Turmoil*, 2 W.I.P.O. J. 28, 32 (2010).

21. Stuart Graham & Saurabh Vishnubhakat, *Of Smart Phone Wars and Software Patents*, 27 J. ECON. PERSP. 67, 70 (2013).

22. For a popular account, *see* DAVA SOBEL, LONGITUDE: THE TRUE STORY OF THE LONE GENIUS WHO SOLVED THE GREATEST SCIENTIFIC PROBLEM OF HIS TIME (1995).

23. *See* Steve Lohr, *Netflix Awards $1 Million Prize and Starts a New Contest*, N. Y. TIMES: BITS (Sept. 21, 2009, 10:15 AM), http://bits.blogs.nytimes.com/2009/09/21/netflix-awards-1-million-prize-and-starts-a-new-contest/; *see also* Matt Richtel, *Awarder of Space Prize to Add Others*, N. Y. TIMES (Feb. 1, 2007), http://www.nytimes.com/2007/02/01/business/01prize.html.

24. Another is the risk that the funder will renege and refuse to pay the prize. For discussion of historical examples, including the British government's foot-dragging in actually paying out the promised longitude prize to John Harrison, *see* B. Zorina Khan, *Inventing Prizes: A Historical Perspective on Innovation Awards and Technology Policy*, 89 BUS. HIST. REV. 631 (2015); *see also* Benjamin N. Roin, *Intellectual Property Versus Prizes: Reframing the Debate*, 81 U. CHI. L. REV. 999 (2014). For discussion of the comparative advantages and disadvantages of prizes, patents, grants, and tax credits as tools for encouraging innovation, *see* Daniel J. Hemel & Lisa Larrimore Ouellette, *Beyond the Patents-Prizes Debate*, 92 TEX. L. REV. 303 (2013).

25. An insight that can be traced back at least as far as Adam Smith, who observed that prizes "would hardly ever be so precisely proportioned to the merit of the invention as" patents, for "if the invention be good and such as is profitable to mankind, he will probably make a fortune by it; but if it be of no value he also will reap no benefit." ADAM SMITH, LECTURES ON JURISPRUDENCE 83 (R.L. Meek et al., eds., Oxford University Press 1978) (quoted in Khan, *supra* note 24, at 659 n.87). In theory, one possible way to retain the virtues of patents while reducing their social costs would be for the government to institute a buyout program, under which it would offer to buy up patents at a premium over their private value and then dedicate them to the public domain. To determine that value, the government could hold an auction, announcing in advance that it would award the patent to the highest bidder in a randomly selected sample of x percent of cases; that bidder would then buy the patent and charge whatever it liked. In all other cases, the government would pay a specific premium over, say, the third highest bid. *See* Michael Kremer, *Patent Buyouts: A Mechanism for Encouraging Innovation*, 113 Q. J. ECON. 1137 (1998). So far, however, no government has taken up this proposal. For discussion and citation to this and other relevant literature on prizes and buyouts, *see, e.g.,* Michael Abramowicz, *Perfecting Patent Prizes*, 56 VAND. L. REV. 115 (2003); Hemel & Ouellette, *supra* note 24.

26. *See* Orphan Drug Act, 21 U.S.C. § 360aa (2012). For discussions, *see, e.g.,* Gary A. Pulsinelli, *The Orphan Drug Act: What's Right with It*, 15 SANTA CLARA COMP. & HIGH TECH. L. J.

299 (1999); *see also* David Duffield Rohde, *The Orphan Drug Act: An Engine of Innovation? At What Cost?* 55 FOOD & DRUG L. J. 125 (2000). On a related note, in December 2016 President Obama signed into law the 21st Century Cures Act, H.R. 34, 114th Cong., 2d Sess. (enacted Dec. 13, 2016), which promises to increase federal funding for cancer research and other purposes. For discussion, *see, e.g.,* Jennifer Steinhauer & Robert Pear, *Sweeping Health Measure, Backed by Obama, Passes Senate,* N. Y. TIMES, Dec. 7, 2016, http://www.nytimes.com/2016/12/07/us/politics/21st-century-cures-act-senate.html.

27. *See* Owen Barder et al., *Advance Market Commitments: A Policy to Stimulate Investment in Vaccines for Neglected Diseases,* ECONOMISTS' VOICE (Feb. 2006), https://economics.mit.edu/files/6809.

28. *See* GAVI ALLIANCE SECRETARIAT, ADVANCE MARKET COMMITMENT FOR PNEUMOCOCCAL VACCINES ANNUAL REPORT – 1 APRIL 2012 TO 31 MARCH 2013 (2013), http://www.gavi.org/library/gavi-documents/amc/.

29. *See* Edmund W. Kitch, *The Nature and Function of the Patent System,* 20 J. L. & ECON. 265 (1977).

30. *See* Mark F. Grady & Jay I. Alexander, *Patent Law and Rent Dissipation,* 78 VA. L. REV. 305 (1992).

31. *See* F. Scott Kieff, *Coordination, Property, and Intellectual Property: An Unconventional Approach to Anticompetitive Effects and Downstream Access,* 56 EMORY L. J. 327, 415–19 (2006). Other scholars argue that patent law could do more to promote commercialization, for example, by conditioning patents on efforts to commercialize or by awarding protection to persons who commercialize a forgotten technology. *E.g.,* Ted Sichelman, *Commercializing Patents,* 62 STAN. L. REV. 341 (2010); *see, e.g.,* Benjamin N. Roin, *Unpatentable Drugs and the Standards of Patentability,* 87 TEX. L. REV. 503, 509–10 (2009) (arguing that "motivating the creation of an invention . . . can still be critical for encouraging the subsequent investment in its development").

32. *See generally* Roger L. Beck, *The Prospect Theory of the Patent System and Unproductive Competition,* 5 RES. L. & ECON 193 (1983); Robert P. Merges & Richard R. Nelson, *On the Complex Economics of Patent Scope,* 90 COLUM. L. REV. 839 (1990). John Duffy takes issue with Beck's treatment of the invention of cellophane, however. *See* John F. Duffy, *Rethinking the Prospect Theory of Patents,* 71 U. CHI. L. REV. 439, 488 n.141 (2004).

33. SCHUMPETER, *supra* note 9.

34. *See supra* note 9.

35. In many countries, however, including now the United States, an exception is sometimes available for someone who invented first and chose to keep an invention as a trade secret rather than to seek patent protection. For discussion, *see* U.S. PATENT & TRADEMARK OFFICE, REPORT TO CONGRESS: REPORT ON THE PRIOR USER RIGHTS DEFENSE (2012), http://www.uspto.gov/aia_implementation/20120113-pur_report.pdf.

36. *But see* Mark A. Lemley, *The Myth of the Sole Inventor,* 110 MICH. L. REV. 709, 757 (2012) (noting research by Professor Benjamin Roin to the effect that racing may deter some innovation in the pharmaceutical industry) (citing Roin, *supra* note 31, at 545).

37. *See* Lemley, *supra* note 36.

38. *See* John Golden, *Principles for Patent Remedies,* 88 TEX. L. REV. 505, 528 (2010); *see also* Cristiano Nisoli et al., *Colloquium: Artificial Spin Ice: Designing and Imaging Magnetic Frustration,* 85 REV. MOD. PHYS. 1473, 1473 (2013) ("Frustration in the presence of competing interactions is ubiquitous in the physical sciences and is a source of degeneracy and disorder, giving rise to new and interesting physical phenomena"). Golden uses the term "frustration" to describe the inability of a system of patent remedies—damages and injunctions for infringement—to achieve all of the possible goals of the patent system, but the point seems applicable to other aspects of patent law as well. *See* Golden, *supra,* at 527–29.

39. Locke's treatise can be found in many editions and is also freely available on the Internet from sources such as Project Gutenberg. *See* JOHN LOCKE, SECOND TREATISE OF GOVERNMENT (1690), https://www.gutenberg.org/files/7370/7370-h/7370-h.htm. In addition, there are many interpretations of Locke's theory of property and of its relevance to intellectual property law. Professor Wendy Gordon's article *A Property Right in Self-Expression: Equality and Individualism in the Natural Law of Intellectual Property,* 102 YALE L. J. 1533 (1993), sets

forth an understanding of Locke that I find persuasive, while also noting some other possible interpretations. Robert P. Merges's book JUSTIFYING INTELLECTUAL PROPERTY (Harvard University Press 2011) presents an extended defense of intellectual property rights that draws on both Locke and Kant. William W. Fisher III's essay *Theories of Intellectual Property, in* NEW ESSAYS IN THE LEGAL AND POLITICAL THEORY OF PROPERTY 168 (Stephen Munzer ed., 2001), presents a more skeptical view that is more consistent with my own.

40. LOCKE, *supra* note 39, ¶ 27. The premise of self-ownership follows from the more fundamental assumption that we owe a duty to God not to destroy ourselves and hence not to consent to our own enslavement. *See id.*, ¶ 23.

41. *See id.* ¶¶ 28, 32.

42. The first modern copyright statute dates from 1710, after Locke's death, though prior to that time the Crown granted exclusive rights to the Stationer's Guild under a series of Licensing Acts. Locke advocated amending these acts to confer a time-limited exclusive right on authors and publishers—basically, a copyright law—but it's not clear whether he believed his theory of property acquisition applied to works of authorship. For discussion, *see* Justin Hughes, *Locke's 1694 Memorandum (and More Incomplete Copyright Historiographies)*, 27 CARDOZO ARTS & ENTER. L. J. 555 (2010).

43. Among the other reasons to doubt the Lockean theory as a basis for IP rights are the difficulty of defining exactly what the "commons" consists of in this context; the inability of the Lockean theory to determine how rights over improvements of others' ideas should be apportioned; and whether a greater investment of labor requires stronger, longer, or more durable rights (and if so, how we measure such investments).

44. I suppose you could argue that your teachers agreed to teach you in exchange for whatever compensation they were paid, on the understanding that they would have no further claim upon you thereafter; so in that sense your ride isn't free. (You may not have paid them yourself, but someone—taxpayers, your family, whoever—did so on your behalf.) Locke, in other words, doesn't require that your debt be paid on a per-use basis. My point, though, is that we all benefit from whatever fund of human knowledge to which we have been granted access, and that nobody seriously entertains the notion that throughout our lives we should have to keep tabs on whether we have free-ridden on some long-distant contribution to that fund. For millennia, human culture has evolved through the sharing of knowledge, much of it presumably without any formal system or expectation of compensation.

45. MERGES, *supra* note 39, at 41–67; Gordon, *supra* note 39, at 1566–78.

46. In German, *Von der Unrechtmäßigkeit des Büchernachdrucks, in* 4 IMMANUEL KANTS WERKE 213 (Artur Buchenau & Ernst Cassirer eds., 1922).

47. For discussion, *see* Thomas F. Cotter, *Pragmatism, Economics, and the Droit Moral*, 76 N. C. L. REV. 1 (1997), from which a portion of the discussion in the text is drawn.

48. MERGES, *supra* note 39, at 72.

49. *Id.* at 70, 83.

50. *Id.* at 70.

51. *Id.* at 82.

Chapter 3

1. The paper that presented these results is Jeff M. Hall et al., *Linkage of Early-Onset Familial Breast Cancer to Chromosome 17q21*, 250 SCI. 1684 (1990). A team headed by Gilbert Lenoir confirmed these results and also uncovered a link between the posited gene and ovarian cancer. *See* Steven A. Narod et al., *Familial Breast-Ovarian Cancer Locus on Chromosome 17q21–q23*, 338 LANCET 82 (1991); King, Mark Skolnick, and other actors in this saga are profiled in Kevin Davies & Michael White's 1996 book BREAKTHROUGH: THE RACE TO FIND THE BREAST CANCER GENE. A more recent source of important background information on the discovery and patenting of BRCA1 and BRCA2 is E. Richard Gold & Julia Carbone, *Myriad Genetics: In the Eye of the Policy Storm*, 12 (4 Suppl.) GENETICS MED. 39 (2010).

2. "BRCA" stands for breast cancer, and use of the number "1" reflected the belief, which proved to be correct, that research would uncover at least one other gene that plays a role in

causing breast cancer. King has stated that "BRCA" also stands for Berkeley, California and for Paul Broca, a nineteenth-century anatomist who was among the first to postulate a hereditary role in the transmission of breast cancer. *See* William Check, *BRCA: What We Now Know*, CAP TODAY (Sept., 2006), http://www.captodayonline.com/Archives/feature_stories/0906BRCA.html.

3. The papers presenting these results are Yoshio Miki et al., *A Strong Candidate for the Breast and Ovarian Cancer Susceptibility Gene BRCA1*, 266 SCI. 66 (1994), and P. Andrew Futreal et al., *BRCA1 Mutations in Primary Breast and Ovarian Carcinomas*, 266 SCI. 5182 (1994).

4. *See* Richard Wooster et al., *Localization of a Breast Cancer Susceptibility Gene, BRCA2, to Chromosome 13q12–13*, 265 SCI. 2088 (1994).

5. *See* Richard Wooster et al., *Identification of the Breast Cancer Susceptibility Gene BRCA2*, 378 NAT. 789 (1995).

6. *See* S. V. Tavtigian et al., *The Complete BRCA2 Gene and Mutations in Chromosome 13q-Linked Kindreds*, 12 NAT. GENETICS 333 (1996).

7. *BRCA1 and BRCA2: Cancer Risk and Genetic Testing*, NAT'L CANCER INST. (Apr. 1, 2015), http://www.cancer.gov/cancertopics/factsheet/Risk/BRCA.

8. A good source for assisting the educated nonspecialist in understanding the underlying science is Reinhard Renneberg's book BIOTECHNOLOGY FOR BEGINNERS (Arnold L. Demain eds., Renate FitzRoy & Jackine Jones trans., Academic Press, 1st ed. 2007). I have relied upon this source, among others, in writing the text above.

9. For discussion of why there remains substantial uncertainty as to the precise number, even after the sequencing of the human genome, *see* Mihaela Pertea & Steven L. Salzberg, *Between a Chicken and a Grape: Estimating the Number of Human Genes*, 11 GENOME BIOLOGY 206 (2010).

10. *See, e.g.*, Shi-Lung Lin et al., *Intronic MicroRNA (miRNA)*, 2006 J. BIOMED. BIOTECH. 26818; Justin J.-L.Wong et al., *Orchestrated Intron Retention Regulates Normal Granulocyte Differentiation*, 154 CELL 583 (2013); Shao-Yao Ying et al., *Intron-mediated RNA Interference, Intronic MicroRNAs, and Applications*, 629 METHODS MOLECULAR BIOLOGY 203, 205 (2010).

11. *See* Meena Kishore Sakarkhar et al., *Distribution of Exons and Introns in the Human Genome*, 4 SILICO BIOLOGY 387 (2004).

12. U.S. Patent No. 5,747,282 (issued May 5, 1998).

13. *Id.* One commentator has described the argument that "isolated DNA is not the same as the natural DNA" as scientific nonsense: for one thing, the process of isolating DNA does not create an artificial molecule—the body's own cells isolate DNA all the time, in the process of turning it into proteins. Steven Salzberg, *Private companies own your DNA—again*, FORBES (July 31, 2011, 5:06 PM), https://www.forbes.com/sites/stevensalzberg/2011/07/31/private-companies-own-your-dna-again/#69ad545b7ea7. True, the body's own cells isolate DNA to make proteins, as described in the text above, but the cells do not isolate the DNA from other cellular components which naturally accompany a native human sequence or protein. As defined in the patent, the term "isolated" effectively means "isolated from the human body," though as noted in the text some ambiguities remain.

14. *See* Christopher M. Holman, *Will Gene Patents Impede Whole Genome Sequencing?: Deconstructing the Myth that 20 percent of the Human Genome Is Patented*, 2 IP THEORY Iss. 1, Article 1. (2012).

15. 90 U.S. 566 (1874). *See also Cochrane v. Badische Anilin & Soda Fabrik*, 111 U.S. 293 (1884) (stating, as one ground for finding the patent in suit not infringed, that it covered an artificial but chemically identical version of a naturally produced dye).

16. 1889 Dec. Comm'r Pat. 123, 125 (1889). In much the same vein, *see id.* at 126–27 ("the fiber, when it is made free, is in nowise changed or different from its natural construction. There is no chemical combination effected by the treatment which frees it by which the fiber becomes something new or different from the fiber in its natural state . . . . [T]he fiber not only is old . . . but it is a natural product and can no more be the subject of a patent in its natural state when freed from its surroundings than wheat which has been cut by a reaper or by some new method of reaping can be patented as wheat cut by such a process").

17. *Id.*

18. *See* Christopher Beauchamp, *Patenting Nature: A Problem of History*, 16 STAN. TECH. L. REV. 257, 274–75 (2013).

19. *See, e.g., In re Merz,* 97 F.2d 599 (C.C.P.A. 1938) ("artificial ultramarine . . . substantially free from color dulling floatable impurities"); *In re Ridgway,* 76 F.2d 602 (C.C.P.A. 1935) (purified alpha alumina); *In re Marden,* 47 F.2d 957 (C.C.P.A. 1931) (ductile uranium); *In re Marden,* 47 F.2d 958 (C.C.P.A. 1931) (ductile vanadium); *General Electric Co. v. DeForest Radio Co.,* 28 F.2d 641 (3d Cir. 1928) ("substantially pure tungsten").

20. 283 U.S. 1 (1931). *See also Hartranft v. Wiegmann,* 121 U.S. 609 (1887); *Anheuser-Busch Brewing Ass'n v. United States,* 207 U.S. 556 (1908).

21. The leading biography of Hand is Gerald Gunther's LEARNED HAND: THE MAN AND THE JUDGE (Alfred A. Knopf, 1994). And yes, "Learned" was his real name—actually, his middle name. Early in his career he abandoned use of his first name, "Billings." "Learned" was his mother's maiden name.

22. 189 F. 95 (C.C.S.D.N.Y. 1911).

23. Actually, it wasn't as pure as Takamine and his assistant, Keizo Uenaka, thought; what they had extracted and isolated was a mixture of epinephrine and a biosynthetic precursor, nor-epinephrine. For discussion, *see* Joan W. Bennett, *Adrenalin and Cherry Trees,* 4 MOD. DRUG DISCOVERY, No. 12, 47 (2001), http://pubs.acs.org/subscribe/archive/mdd/v04/i12/html/12timeline.html; and Walter Sneader, *The Discovery and Synthesis of Epinephrine,* 14 DRUG NEWS PROSPECT 491, 493–94 (2001).

24. Jon M. Harkness, *Dicta on Adrenalin(e): Myriad Problems with Learned Hand's Product-of-Nature Pronouncements in* Parke-Davis, 93 J. PAT. & TRADEMARK OFF. SOC'Y 363 (2011).

25. *See Parke-Davis Co. v. H.K. Mulford & Co.,* 196 F. 496 (2d Cir. 1912). More precisely, the court affirmed the judgment that certain claims were valid and infringed, and reversed as to some of the other claims (including Claim 1 of the '177 Patent), not because it disagreed with Hand's reasoning but rather because "we are not now willing to enter into an examination of claims which it is not necessary to pass upon in order fully to dispose of the controversy at bar." *Id.* at 500.

26. The Patent Office granted other purified-hormone patents that included claims similar in format to Takamine's, but the judicial decisions of the 1920s and 1930s (cited *supra* note 19) tended to follow the more restrictive view reflected in the *American Wood Products* dicta and *Latimer. See* Beauchamp, *supra* note 18, at 296–302.

27. *See Merck & Co., Inc. v. Olin Mathieson Chemical Corp.,* 253 F.2d 156 (4th Cir. 1958).

28. U.S. Patent No. 4,259,444 (issued Mar. 31, 1981) ("Microorganisms Having Multiple Compatible Degradative Energy-generating Plasmids and Preparation Thereof").

29. To date, concerns over potential environmental consequences have prevented the use of *Pseudomonas putida* and other recombinant microorganisms in bioremediation outside the laboratory environment. *See* Fu-Min Menn, et al., *Genetically Engineered Microorganisms and Bioremediation,* in BIOTECHNOLOGY SET 441 (2d ed., 2001).

30. The path to the Supreme Court was a little more complicated than suggested in the text. While Chakrabarty's application was pending, another set of inventors (Bergy et al.) filed an application claiming, among other things, "[a] biologically pure culture of the microorganism *Streptomyces vellosus* . . . said culture being capable of producing the antibiotic lincomycin . . . ." The Board of Patent Appeals and Interferences rejected the Bergy application for the same reason it had rejected Chakrabarty's (no living things!), and Bergy appealed to the CCPA. The CCPA decided Bergy's appeal first, concluding that the pure culture of *Streptomyces* was not a product of nature and that nothing in the Patent Act barred the patentability of living things. Based on this precedent, the CCPA shortly thereafter issued a similar ruling in favor of Chakrabarty. Now it was the USPTO's turn to appeal its two losses, but the Supreme Court, which had just decided a case involving the patentability of mathematical algorithms (*Parker v. Flook,* discussed in Chapter 5) sent both cases back to the CCPA for reconsideration in light of *Flook.* The lower court stuck to its guns, and the USPTO once again asked the Supreme Court to hear the two cases. The Court agreed, though while they were pending the owner of the Bergy application (perhaps sensing a loss) decided to abandon its bacteria claim. Chakrabarty would continue on alone.

31. *See Diamond v. Chakrabarty,* 447 U.S. 303 (1980).

32. *Id.* at 308.

33. *Id.* at 309 (quoting *Hearing on H.R. 3760 Before Subcommittee No. 3 of the House Committee on the Judiciary,* 82th Cong., 1st Sess., 37 (1951)).

34. 333 U.S. 127 (1948).
35. Chakrabarty, 447 U.S. at 310.
36. *Id.* at 316–17.
37. *See, e.g.,* Calestous Juma, Innovation and Its Enemies: Why People Resist New Technologies 282 (Oxford University Press 2016) (stating that *Chakrabarty* "played a decisive role in the emergence of the biotechnology industry by making it possible to patent inventions arising from living forms"); Margo A. Bagley, *Academic Discourse and Proprietary Rights: Putting Patents in Their Proper Place,* 47 B. C. L. Rev. 217, 235 (2006) ("By expanding the scope of patent-eligible subject matter to comprise living organisms, including the genetically engineered bacteria at issue in the case, *Chakrabarty* jump-started the fledgling biotechnology industry and further fueled National Institutes of Health funding of university research in the life sciences").
38. Commentators identify the first two as U.S. Patent No. 4,322,499 (issued Mar. 30, 1982) (titled "Adenocorticotropin-lipotropin Precursor Gene" and claiming a recombinant cDNA sequence), and U.S. Patent No. 4,363,877 (issued Dec. 14, 1982) (titled "Recombinant DNA Transfer Vectors" and claiming a recombinant DNA sequence). *See, e.g.,* Eric J. Rogers, *Can You Patent Genes? Yes and No,* 93 J. Pat. & Trademark Off. Soc'y 19, 19 n.3 (2011); *see also* Andrew W. Torrance, *Gene Concepts, Gene Talk, and Gene Patents,* 11 Minn. J.L. Sci. & Tech. 157, 176–77 (2010).
39. *See* Brief for the United States as Amicus Curiae in Support of Neither Party at 4–5, *Ass'n for Molecular Pathology v. USPTO,* No. 2010-1406 (Fed. Cir. Oct. 29, 2010) ("Applicants eventually began to seek, and PTO began to grant, patents directed not only to synthetic DNA molecules such as cDNAs but also to isolated but otherwise unaltered genomic DNA itself— that is, genomic material excised from an organism's genome and isolated from the cellular environment in which it normally occurs, but without material change to its naturally occurring chemical structure and function. The first such patents claimed genes directly, without the rubric of isolation or purification. *See, e.g.,* U.S. Patent No. 4,472,502 (1984) (claiming the *Lactobacillus* bacteria malolactic gene). The first patent using the term 'isolated DNA' appears to have issued in 1987, although it was directed to a recombinant vector rather than genomic DNA. *See* U.S. Patent No. 4,680,264, claim 27 (1987). It is believed that PTO issued the first patent claiming isolated but otherwise unmodified human genomic DNA in the same period").
40. *See Amgen, Inc. v. Chugai Pharm. Co.,* 927 F.2d 1200 (Fed. Cir. 1991).
41. *See, e.g.,* Rebecca S. Eisenberg, *Patenting the Human Genome,* 39 Emory L.J. 721, 727 (1990).
42. *See* Utility Examination Guidelines, 66 Fed. Reg. 1092, 1093 (USPTO Jan. 5, 2001) (stating that "an inventor's discovery of a gene can be the basis for a patent on the genetic composition isolated from its natural state and processed through purifying steps that separate the gene from other molecules naturally associated with it," and that "where the application discloses a specific, substantial, and credible utility for the claimed isolated and purified gene, the isolated and purified gene composition may be patentable").
43. *See* Kyle Jensen & Fiona Murray, *Intellectual Property Landscape of the Human Genome,* 310 Sci. 239 (2005).
44. *See* Holman, *supra* note 14 (noting that the Jensen & Murray study found that 20 percent of U.S. patents contained claims that explicitly mentioned human gene sequences or proteins coded for by those sequences, and arguing among other things that the authors failed to appreciate the distinction between "mentioning" and "claiming" those sequences).
45. Myriad did threaten to file suit against four Canadian provinces but ultimately did not do so. *See* Gold & Carbone, *supra* note 1, at 25–28. Meanwhile, the EU and other national bodies largely followed the same route as the United States in permitting patents to issue on isolated sequences, so the United States was hardly an outlier.
46. *See* Gold & Carbone, *supra* note 1.
47. 549 U.S. 118 (2007).
48. The plaintiffs raised some other arguments based on constitutional law, but none of the courts involved in the *Myriad* litigation found it necessary to address these issues.
49. *See* Rebecca S. Eisenberg, *Diagnostics Need Not Apply,* 21 B. U. J. Sci. & Tech. L. 256, 279 (2015).

50. *See Ass'n for Molecular Pathology v. USPTO*, 702 F.Supp.2d 181 (S.D.N.Y. 2010). In a footnote, Judge Sweet recalled a time when Hand "turned his back on the author of this opinion arguing before him on behalf of the Government . . . ." Revenge is Sweet.

51. *Ass'n for Molecular Pathology v. USPTO*, 689 F.3d 1303, 1328 (Fed. Cir. 2012).

52. *Ass'n for Molecular Pathology v. Myriad Genetics, Inc.*, 133 S. Ct. 2107, 2120 (2013).

53. The Court made a few errors, none of them crucial to the outcome. *See* Steven Salzberg, *Supreme Court Gets Decision Right, Science Wrong, on Gene Patents*, FORBES (June 13, 2013, 3:21 PM), http://www.forbes.com/sites/stevensalzberg/2013/06/13/supreme-court-gets-decision-right-science-wrong/#3ffd333612cc.

54. *Myriad*, 133 S. Ct. at 2118.

55. The English jurist Sir Robin Jacob expressed precisely this point in *Aerotel Ltd. v. Telco Holdings Ltd.*, [2006] EWCA Civ. 1371: "Patents are essentially about information as to what to make or do."

56. *Id.* at 2119.

57. *See id.* The Court also noted that "[i]n rare instances, a side effect of a viral infection of a cell can be the random incorporation of fragments of the resulting cDNA, known as a pseudogene, into the genome" but stated that "[t]he possibility that an unusual and rare phenomenon *might* randomly create a molecule similar to one created synthetically through human ingenuity does not render a composition of matter nonpatentable." *Id.* at 2119 n.8 (emphasis added).

58. I for one have a hard time imagining the decision coming out differently even if Myriad had used a "closed" claim that would have excluded the BRCA gene plus Justice Thomas's hypothetical additional nucleotide from its scope. Interesting, in a recent opinion the High Court of Australia cited the informational equivalence between DNA and cDNA as a reason for concluding that *neither* falls within the scope of patentable subject matter in that country. *See* D'Arcy v. Myriad Genetics Inc., [2015] HCA 35 (Australia).

59. 133 S. Ct. at 2116.

60. *See, e.g.*, John P. Walsh et al., *View from the Bench: Patents and Material Transfers*, 309 SCI. 2002 (2005).

61. *See* Holman, *supra* note 14, at 7–10.

62. This appears to be the USPTO's view. *See* USPTO, *Nature-Based Product Examples* (Dec. 16, 2014), https://www.uspto.gov/sites/default/files/documents/mdc_examples_nature-based_products.pdf.

63. *See* Jensen & Murray, *supra* note 43.

64. *See* Bhaven Sampat & Heidi L. Williams, *How Do Patents Affect Follow-On Innovation? Evidence from the Human Genome* (Nat'l Bureau Econ. Res. Working Paper No. 21666, 2015), http://www.nber.org/papers/w21666.pdf; *cf.* Alberto Galasso & Mark Schankerman, *Patents and Cumulative Innovation: Evidence from the Courts* (Nat'l Bureau Econ. Res. Working Paper No. 20269, 2014), http://www.nber.org/papers/w20269.pdf.

65. For discussion, *see* John Conley, *ACLU v. Myriad Genetics, Round 2: The Problem of Governance by Guidance*, GENOMICS L. REP. (June 9, 2016), http://www.genomicslawreport.com/index.php/2016/06/09/aclu-v-myriad-genetics-round-2-the-problem-of-governance-by-guidance/#more-13606.

66. *See* Gold & Carbone, *supra* note 1, Appendix B: Detailed Legal Analysis of Gene Patents, Competition Law and Privacy Law. French national law does not permit gene patents, but may be contrary to EU law on this point, while German national law permits gene patents but "restricted to the particular function associated with the protein that the gene produces." Notably, the European Patent Office issues gene patents that can be validated in any member of the European Patent Convention, including France and Germany. For discussion of the interface of patents and universal care health, see Chapters 6 and 7 of this book.

67. *See* Eisenberg, *supra* note 49, at 279 ("If the marker for disease susceptibility is not in a coding region of the gene, the cDNA version will not do the job").

Chapter 4

1. *See* Mark F. Grady & Miles I. Alexander, *Patent Law and Rent Dissipation*, 78 VA. L. REV. 305, 309 (1992). To be more precise, Grady and Alexander's theory is that patent doctrine works

to avoid "rent dissipation," that is, patent races among both would-be pioneers and would-be improvers. The theory predicts that laws of nature will be unpatentable because (1) there will be no race to improve a "perfect" solution, and (2) if laws of nature were patentable, there would be a rent-dissipating race to discover laws of nature. To be honest, the first part of the argument strikes me as silly. Einstein certainly "improved" Newton's law of universal gravitation, and if someone ever succeeds in unifying relativity with quantum physics we'll have an improvement over Einstein. And certainly there are numerous, practically infinite, *practical applications* of the law of gravity.

2. *See* Michael Steven Green, *Copyrighting Facts*, 78 IND. L. J. 919, 954, 956 (2003). Actually, Green argues that scientists shouldn't be able to *copyright* laws of nature (such as the theory of relativity), because they benefit more from the enhancement to their reputation from allowing their theories to be tested than from selling copyrighted works describing those theories. The logic of Green's argument, such as it is, would appear to apply to patent protection as well.

3. *See, e.g., In re Cruciferous Sprout Litig.*, 301 F.3d 1343 (Fed. Cir. 2002) (holding that a claimed method for preparing a food product rich in glucosinolates—a naturally occurring substance that induces the production of enzymes that reduce the risk of developing cancer—was inherent in the prior art, because people had been preparing such foods, which include broccoli and cauliflower, for millennia, albeit without knowing about their role in fighting cancer when harvested prior to the two-leaf stage).

4. For an accessible discussion of the cosmological constant, *see* BRIAN GREENE, THE HIDDEN REALITY: PARALLEL UNIVERSES AND THE DEEP LAWS OF THE COSMOS ch.6 (2011).

5. *See* OFFICE OF PATENT LEGAL ADMINISTRATION, U.S. PAT. & TRADEMARK OFF., EVALUATING SUBJECT MATTER ELIGIBILITY UNDER 35 USC § 101: AUG. 2012 UPDATE, at 29, http://www.uspto.gov/sites/default/files/patents/law/exam/101_training_aug2012.pdf.

6. *Id.* at 33.

7. *See* Rebecca S. Eisenberg, *Diagnostics Need Not Apply*, 21 B.U. J. SCI. & TECH. L. 256, 262–63, 265–66 (2015).

8. *See, e.g.*, Daniel Closa & Gaëtan Beaucé, *Medical Methods Under the European Patent Convention* (26–30 Nov. 2012), http://www.zbm-patents.eu/pdf/EPO_Medical_methods_EPO.pdf.

9. *See Morton v. N.Y. Eye Infirmary*, 17 F. CAS. 879 (C.C.S.D.N.Y. 1862); *see also Ex parte Brinkerhoff*, 24 Dec. Comm'r 349 (1883) (Patent Office decision holding that methods for treating disease are unpatentable). For further discussion, *see* Katherine J. Strandburg, *Legal but Unacceptable: Pallin v. Singer and Physician Patenting Norms, in* INTELLECTUAL PROPERTY AT THE EDGE: THE CONTESTED CONTOURS OF IP 321, 324 (Rochelle Cooper Dreyfuss & Jane C. Ginsburg, eds., 2014) (discussing cases).

10. *See Legislation: PTO Assails Bills to Limit Patents on Medical Procedures*, 50 BNA PAT. TRADEMARK & COPYRIGHT JOURNAL 737, 737 (1995) (stating that, "[a]lthough the Patent and Trademark Office has issued patents on medical and diagnostic procedures since the 1950s," until recently these patents had been "uncommon and rarely enforced"); William D. Noonan, *Patenting Medical and Surgical Procedures*, 77 J. PAT. & TRADEMARK OFF. SOC'Y 651 (1995) (documenting a small number of medical procedure patents as early as 1925); Strandburg, *supra* note 9, at 324.

11. *See* Strandburg, *supra* note 9, at 325–36.

12. *See* Am. Med. Ass'n, *Reports of Council on Ethical and Judicial Affairs*, 1995 PROC. AM. MED. ASS'N ANN. MTG. 200–06 [hereinafter Am. Med. Ass'n, *Reports*]; Am. Med. Ass'n, *Resolutions*, 1994 PROC. AM. MED. ASS'N ANN. MTG. 388, 390.

13. *See* Am. Med. Ass'n, *Reports, supra* note 12, at 204–05. Medical practitioners who develop effective new techniques also can hope for more customers, fame, and perhaps having their name associated with the techniques (as with the Heimlich maneuver or the Mohs skin cancer surgery technique).

14. *See* Strandburg, *supra* note 9, at 339–41.

15. After a district court found his patent invalid and noninfringed, Pallin wound up agreeing to a consent order dismissing his case. *See id.* at 335.

16. *See* 35 U.S.C. § 287(c):

(1) With respect to a medical practitioner's performance of a medical activity that constitutes an infringement under section 271(a) or (b), the provisions of sections 281, 283, 284, and 285 shall not apply against the medical practitioner or against a related health care entity with respect to such medical activity.

(2) For the purposes of this subsection:

(A) the term "medical activity" means the performance of a medical or surgical procedure on a body, but shall not include (i) the use of a patented machine, manufacture, or composition of matter in violation of such patent (ii) the practice of a patented use of a composition of matter in violation of such patent, or (iii) the practice of a process in violation of a biotechnology patent.

(B) the term "medical practitioner" means any natural person who is licensed by a State to provide the medical activity described in subsection (c)(1) or who is acting under the direction of such person in the performance of the medical activity.

(C) the term "related health care entity" shall mean an entity with which a medical practitioner has a professional affiliation under which the medical practitioner performs the medical activity, including but not limited to a nursing home, hospital, university, medical school, health maintenance organization, group medical practice, or a medical clinic.

(D) the term "professional affiliation" shall mean staff privileges, medical staff membership, employment or contractual relationship, partnership or ownership interest, academic appointment, or other affiliation under which a medical practitioner provides the medical activity on behalf of, or in association with, the health care entity.

(E) the term "body" shall mean a human body, organ or cadaver, or a nonhuman animal used in medical research or instruction directly relating to the treatment of humans.

(F) the term "patented use of a composition of matter" does not include a claim for a method of performing a medical or surgical procedure on a body that recites the use of a composition of matter where the use of that composition of matter does not directly contribute to achievement of the objective of the claimed method ....

The provision applies only to patents based on applications filed after September 30, 1999, so it wouldn't have applied to Dr. Pallin even if his case hadn't settled.

17. *O'Reilly v. Morse*, 56 U.S. 62, 112 (1853).

18. Indeed, it would have covered practices that were in the prior art, such as the use of light for signaling—though no one would have known this at the time, James Clerk Maxwell not yet having published his famous equations as of 1853. *See* Norman Siebrasse, *The Rule Against Abstract Claims: History and Principles*, 26 R. C. P. I. 205, 221 (2011).

19. *See id.* at 113.

20. The Telephone Cases, 126 U.S. 1, 531 (1888).

21. *See id.* at 537–39.

22. *See State Street Bank & Trust Co. v. Signature Financial Group, Inc.*, 149 F.3d 1368, 1373 (Fed. Cir. 1998); *In re Alappat*, 33 F.3d 1526, 1544 (Fed. Cir. 1994) (en banc); *see also* U.S. PAT. & TRADEMARK OFF., MANUAL OF PATENT EXAMINING AND PROCEDURE § 2106, at 2100–11 (8th rev. ed. 2006) (defining "useful" as limited to a practical application, "tangible" as mean "not abstract," and "concrete" as meaning "substantially repeatable").

23. 548 U.S. 124 (2006) (per curiam).

24. *Id.* at 128–29 (Breyer, J., dissenting). As described in the Federal Circuit's opinion, because folate and cobalamin assist in metabolizing homocysteine, scientists previously had "assayed homocysteine to screen for cobalamin and folate deficiency," but "[t]hese direct homocysteine assays were unreliable. Then researchers at University Patents Inc. (UPI) discovered a relationship between elevated levels of total homocysteine and a deficiency in either cobalamin or folate .... Total homocysteine includes free and protein-complexed homocysteine and also includes homocysteine derivatives homocystine and homocysteine-cysteine." *Metabolite Labs., Inc. v. Lab. Corp. of Am. Holdings*, 370 F.3d 1354, 1358 (Fed. Cir. 2004), *cert. dismissed*, 548 U.S. 124 (2006) (per curiam).

25. *See Lab. Corp. of Am. Holdings v. Metabolite Labs., Inc.*, 546 U.S. 975 (2005). The Court rephrased the question from LabCorp's own somewhat more pugnacious wording: "Whether

a method patent setting forth an indefinite, undescribed, and non-enabling step directing a party simply to 'correlat[e]' test results can validly claim a monopoly over a basic scientific relationship used in medical treatment such that any doctor necessarily infringes the patent merely by thinking about the relationship after looking at a test result." Petition for a Writ of Certiorari, *Lab. Corp. of Am. Holdings v. Metabolite Labs., Inc.*, 2004 WL 2505526 (2004) (No. 04-607).

26. *Lab. Corp. of Am. Holdings v. Metabolite Labs., Inc.*, 548 U.S. 124 (2006) (per curiam).
27. *Id.* at 124, 136–37 (Breyer, J., dissenting).
28. *See id.*
29. 132 S. Ct. 1289 (2012).
30. *See id.* at 1293–94, 1301, 1303.
31. *Id.* at 1294.
32. *Id.* at 1297–98.
33. *Id.* at 1294.
34. *Id.* at 1298.
35. For example, subsequent to the Supreme Court's opinion in *Mayo* but prior to its opinion in *Myriad*, the Federal Circuit's *Myriad* decision had affirmed the invalidation of certain method claims asserted by Myriad on the ground that the steps of comparing a patient's BRCA sequences to wild-type sequences and analyzing the differences involved nothing more than "abstract ideas" or "mental steps." *See Ass'n for Molecular Pathology v. USPTO*, 689 F.3d 1303, 1309, 1333–35 (Fed. Cir. 2012), *aff'd in part, rev'd in part on other grounds*, 133 S. Ct. 2107 (2013). The court subsequently invalidated two other similar method claims in a case Myriad filed against competitors that had entered the market following the Supreme Court decision, *see In re BRCA1- and BRCA2-Based Hereditary Cancer Test Patent Litig.*, 774 F.3d 755, 763–65 (Fed. Cir. 2014). *See also Genetic Techs. Ltd. v. Merial L.L.C.*, 818 F.3d 1369, 1378 (Fed. Cir. 2016) (stating that *Mayo* "rejected diagnostic and therapeutic method claims that combined routine and conventional physical implementation of a law of nature with a simple mental process step"); *Ariosa Diagnostics, Inc. v. Sequenom, Inc.*, 809 F.3d 1282, 1285 (Fed. Cir. 2015) (stating that "abstract ideas are essentially mental steps"), *cert. denied*, 136 S. Ct. 2511 (2016).
36. The leading paper is Kevin Emerson Collins, *Propertizing Thought*, 60 SMU L. REV. 317 (2007); *see also* Thomas F. Cotter, *A Burkean Perspective on Patent Eligibility*, 22 BERKELEY TECH. L. J. 855, 881 (2007).
37. For discussion of the "constitutional avoidance" doctrine, *see, e.g.*, Andrew Nolan, *The Doctrine of Constitutional Avoidance: A Legal Overview* (Sept. 2, 2014), https://www.fas.org/sgp/crs/misc/R43706.pdf.
38. The leading paper is John R. Thomas, *Liberty and Property in Patent Law*, 39 HOUS. L. REV. 569, 570 (2002); *see also* Cotter, *supra* note 36, at 881–82; Thomas F. Cotter, *A Burkean Approach to Patentable Subject Matter, Part II: Reflections on the (Counter) Revolution in Patent Law*, 11 MINN. J. L. SCI. & TECH. 365, 377 (2010).
39. As discussed in the Federal Circuit's opinion in *LabCorp*, "[a]fter cobalamin became available in tablet form . . . doctors could simply order a total homocysteine test and, without identifying the deficient vitamin, treat elevated levels of total homocysteine with a tablet containing both cobalamin and folate." *Metabolite Labs., Inc. v. Lab. Corp. of Am. Holdings*, 370 F.3d 1354, 1358 (Fed. Cir. 2004), *cert. dismissed*, 548 U.S. 124 (2006) (per curiam).
40. Such a rule, by the way, arguably would be consistent with the position the US government took in *Mayo*, which proposed "that virtually any step beyond a statement of a law of nature itself should transform an unpatentable law of nature into a potentially patentable application sufficient to satisfy § 101's demands." *Mayo*, 132 S. Ct. at 1303. The Court rejected this proposal on the ground that it would have rendered the "'law of nature' exception to § 101 patentability a dead letter," *id.* —a conclusion that appears a *bit* overstated, since as we've just seen even a narrow exception would protect *some* liberty and autonomy interests. To be sure, it might seem ridiculously easy for claim drafters to draft around such an exclusion by simply adding an extra nonmental or non–autonomy-evading step or two (though such ease in drafting around is arguably a good thing, if you think that the incentive to discover and commercialize correlations like the ones at issue in *LabCorp* and *Mayo* otherwise will suffer).

On the other hand, if separate persons perform the diagnosis and treatment steps, it's possible that, for some claims that include both steps, *no one* would be liable for infringing, *see* Christopher M. Holman, *Caught Between a Rock and a Hard Place: How* Limelight *Compounds the Challenges Facing Biotechnology Innovators After* Mayo *and* Myriad, 33 BIOTECHNOLOGY L. REP. 135, 137–38 (2014); Rachel E. Sachs, *Innovation Law and Policy: Preserving the Future of Personalized Medicine*, 49 U. C. DAVIS L. REV. 1881, 1917, 1921–23 (2016), though under the most recent case law involving so-called "divided infringement," as long as one single entity (say, a hospital) directs or controls the performance of all the steps, that entity could be liable.

41. As the district court noted. *See Mayo*, 132 S. Ct. at 1296 ("The District Court also accepted Prometheus' view that a doctor using Mayo's test could violate the patent even if he did not actually alter his treatment decision in the light of the test. In doing so, the court construed the claim's language, 'indicates a need to decrease' (or 'to increase'), as not limited to instances in which the doctor actually decreases (or increases) the dosage level where the test results suggest that such an adjustment is advisable").

42. *See id.* at 1295 ("At the time the discoveries embodied in the patents were made, scientists already understood that the levels in a patient's blood of certain metabolites, including, in particular, 6–thioguanine and its nucleotides (6–TG) and 6–methyl–mercaptopurine (6–MMP), were correlated with the likelihood that a particular dosage of a thiopurine drug could cause harm or prove ineffective . . . . But those in the field did not know the precise correlations between metabolite levels and likely harm or ineffectiveness. The patent claims at issue here set forth processes embodying researchers' findings that identified these correlations with some precision").

43. *See* Eisenberg, *supra* note 7, at 269–70.

44. I'm actually not sure when the tablets came on the market; the example is hypothetical only.

45. *See In re BRCA1- and BRCA2-Based Hereditary Cancer Test Patent Litig.*, 774 F.3d. at 763–65.

46. *See* 788 F.3d 1371 (Fed. Cir. 2015), *cert. denied*, 136 S. Ct. 2511 (2016); U.S. Patent No. 6,258,540 B1 (issued July 10, 2001).

47. *See id.* at col. 1; Y. M. Dennis Lo et al., *Presence of Fetal DNA in Maternal Plasma and Serum*, 350 LANCET 485 (1997).

48. *Ariosa*, 788 F.3d at 1373.

49. *See id.* at 1373–74.

50. *See id.* at 1376.

51. *See id.* at 1376–78.

52. *Id.* at 1378–79.

53. *See id.* at 1379. By way of contrast, however, consider *Rapid Litig. Mgt. Ltd. v. CellzDirect, Inc.*, 827 F.3d 1042 (Fed. Cir. 2015). For a long time, scientists have been able to freeze human liver cells (hepatocytes), thaw them, and by using something called density gradient fractionation separate those that are "viable" for research purposes from those that have been damaged by the freezing technique. It was long believed, however, that even the viable cells could be frozen and thawed only once before they too became unfit for use. After scientists discovered that some of the viable cells nonetheless would remain viable after refreezing, they claimed a process involving the steps of (1) using density gradient fractionation to separate viable from nonviable cells; (2) preserving the viable ones; and (3) refreezing the viable cells for future use, for which about 70 percent would prove fit after being thawed a second time. Characterizing the process as "a new and useful laboratory technique for preserving hepatocytes," the Federal Circuit held that the claim recited patentable subject matter, distinguishing it from the unpatentable method claims at issue in cases like *Ariosa* or *Myriad* on the ground that the latter "amounted to nothing more than observing or identifying the ineligible concept itself." Moreover, according to the court, while "[t]he individual steps of freezing and thawing were well known, . . . a process of preserving hepatocytes by repeating those steps was itself far from routine and conventional."

54. *Ariosa*, 809 F.3d at 1290 (Dyk, J., concurring in the denial of a petition for rehearing en banc); *see also* ROBERT P. MERGES & JOHN F. DUFFY, PATENT LAW AND POLICY: CASES AND MATERIALS 151–52 (6th ed. 2013) (discussing the "'Nature's Library' Fiction"); Siebrasse, *supra* note 18, at 212, 226 (citing English and Canadian case law to the effect that

"the law is indifferent as to whether the inventive ingenuity lies in the conception or the implementation").

55. *See* U.S. Pat. & Trademark Off., Subject Matter Eligibility Examples: Life Sciences, ex. 29 (May 6, 2016), http://www.uspto.gov/sites/default/files/documents/ieg-may-2016-ex.pdf.

56. *See* Christopher M. Holman, *Mayo, Myriad, and the Future of Innovation in Molecular Diagnostics and Personalized Medicine*, 15 N. C. J. L. & Tech. 639, 646–47 (2014); Amalia Issa, *Personalized Medicine and the Practice of Medicine in the 21st Century*, 10 McGill J. Med. 53 (2007).

57. Nicholas J. Schork, *Personalized Medicine: Time for One-Person Trials*, 520 Nature 609 (2015), http://www.nature.com/news/personalized-medicine-time-for-one-person-trials-1.17411#/imprecision. I thank Colleen Chien for bringing this article and the materials cited *infra* notes 65 and 66 to my attention.

58. *See also* Kevin Emerson Collins, *Patent-Ineligibility as Counteraction*, 94 Wash. U. L. Rev. 955 (2017) (arguing that, in theory, the narrower interpretation of *Mayo* also could serve a utilitarian purpose of counteracting what would otherwise be patent law's more favorable treatment of diagnostic inference patents, which he believes inherency and overbreadth doctrines alone do not adequately police).

59. *See* Sec'y's Advisory Comm. on Genetics, Health & Soc'y, Dep't of Health & Human Servs., Gene Patents and Licensing Practices and Their Impact on Patient Access to Genetic Tests 34 (2010), http://osp.od.nih.gov/sites/default/files/SACGHS_patents_report_2010.pdf.

60. *See id.*; Sachs, *supra* note 40, at 1889–90, 1894–95.

61. *See* Food & Drug Admin., U.S. U.S. Dep't of Health & Human Servs., Framework for Regulatory Oversight of Laboratory Developed Tests (LDTs), Draft Guidance (2014), http://www.fda.gov/downloads/medicaldevices/deviceregulationandguidance/guidancedocuments/ucm416685.pdf; Sachs, *supra* note 40, at 1889–99.

62. *See* Eisenberg, *supra* note 7, at 285–86; Sachs, *supra* note 40, at 1923–30.

63. *See* U.S. Food & Drug Admin., *Discussion Paper on Laboratory Developed Tests (LDTs)*, Jan. 13, 2017, https://www.personalizedmedicinebulletin.com/wp-content/uploads/sites/6/2017/02/LDT_discussionpaper.pdf; Antoinette F. Konski, *FDA Hits "Pause" on Regulation of LDTs*, Personalized Med. Bull., Feb. 12, 2017, https://www.personalizedmedicinebulletin.com/2017/02/12/fda-hits-pause-on-regulation-of-ldts/.

64. *See* Eisenberg, *supra* note 7, at 285; Sachs, *supra* note 40, at 1929–30.

65. *See, e.g,* Office of the Press Sec'y, The White House, Fact Sheet: President Obama's Precision Medicine Initiative (Jan. 30, 2015), https://www.whitehouse.gov/the-press-office/2015/01/30/fact-sheet-president-obama-s-precision-medicine-initiative (outlining an initiative to increase federal support for, among other things, identification of the "genomic drivers in cancer").

66. *See* Anne B. Laakmann, *The New Genomic Semicommons*, 5 UC Irvine L. Rev. 1001, 1035–39 (2015); W. Nicholson Price II, *Big Data, Patents, and the Future of Medicine*, 37 Cardozo L. Rev. 1401, 1439–52 (2016); Sachs, *supra* note 40, at 1932–36.

Chapter 5

1. As far as I know, Shakespeare was the first person to coin the term "star-crossed lovers," as an astrology-driven metaphor for lovers whose plans are foiled by external circumstances. *See* William Shakespeare, Romeo and Juliet, act I, prologue ("From forth the fatal loins of these two foes, A pair of star-cross'd lovers take their life"). He pretty clearly didn't invent the concept.

2. I should stress that the "abstract ideas" concept in patent law is only analogous, not identical, to the abstraction concept in copyright law. For an insightful discussion of four different ways in which patent case law has used the term "abstract idea," *see* Kevin Emerson Collins, *Bilski and the Ambiguity of "An Unpatentable Abstract Idea,"* 15 Lewis & Clark L. Rev. 37, 62 (2011) (enumerating "basic tool" claims, "[c]laims written in excessively general language," "[c]laims describing insufficiently tangible embodiments," and "[c]laims reciting newly invented mental processes").

3. For accessible discussions of the concepts introduced in this portion of the text, *see, e.g.,* WALTER ISAACSON, THE INNOVATORS: HOW A GROUP OF HACKERS, GENIUSES, AND GEEKS CREATED THE DIGITAL REVOLUTION (2014); MARK A. LEMLEY ET AL., SOFTWARE AND INTERNET LAW (4th ed. 2011); John W.L. Ogilvie, Note, *Defining Computer Program Parts Under Learned Hand's Abstractions Test in Software Copyright Infringement Cases,* 91 MICH. L. REV. 526 (1992).

4. *See Gottschalk v. Benson,* 409 U.S. 63, 67 (1972) (explaining that "decimal 53 is represented as 0101 0011 in BCD [binary coded decimal notation], because decimal 5 is equal to binary 0101 and decimal 3 is equivalent to binary 0011"). BCD notation is often easier for humans to comprehend than are pure binary numbers.

5. The full text of the opinion in *Honeywell Inc. v. Sperry Rand Corp.,* 180 U.S.P.Q. 673 (D. Minn. Oct. 19, 1973), can be accessed at http://www.ushistory.org/more/eniac/index.htm.

6. *See* 17 U.S.C. § 117, as amended.

7. *See, e.g., Finisar Corp. v. DirecTV Grp., Inc.,* 523 F.3d 1323, 1340 (Fed. Cir. 2008) (stating that such claims are not subject to invalidation for lack of definiteness as long as the body of the patent discloses the underlying algorithm "in any understandable terms including as a mathematical formula, in prose . . . or as a flow chart, or in any other manner that provides sufficient structure").

8. *See Williamson v. Citrix Online, LLC,* 792 F.3d 1339, 1357 (Fed. Cir. 2015) (en banc) (holding that even if a claim doesn't use the word "means," it is a means-plus-function claim if the claim itself doesn't recite the structure by which the function is to be carried out); *Advanced Ground Information Sys. v. Life360, Inc.,* 830 F.3d 1341 (Fed. Cir. 2016) (applying *Williamson*). For discussion of the role that functional claiming has played in software patents, at least prior to *Williamson, see* Kevin Emerson Collins, *Patent Law's Functionality Malfunction and the Problem of Overbroad, Functional Software Patents,* 90 WASH. U. L. REV. 1399 (2013); Mark A. Lemley, *Software Patents and the Return of Functional Claiming,* 2013 WIS. L. REV. 905 (2013). For more recent updates, *see* Kevin Emerson Collins, *The* Williamson *Revolution in Software's Structure,* 31 BERKELEY TECH. L. REV. 1597 (2016); Paul R. Gugliuzza, *Early Filing and Functional Claiming,* 96 B.U. L. REV. 1223 (2016).

9. For discussion, *see* Kevin Emerson Collins, Williamson v. Citrix Online: *And Now Comes the Difficult Part,* PATENTLY-O, June 21, 2015, http://patentlyo.com/patent/2015/06/collins-williamson-difficult.html.

10. *See Nautilus, Inc. v. Biosig Instruments, Inc.,* 134 S. Ct. 2120 (2014).

11. 409 U.S. 63 (1972), *rev'g* 441 F.2d 682 (C.C.P.A. 1971). The facts presented in the text above are drawn from the Supreme Court and lower court opinions.

12. *Id.* at 73.

13. *See id.* at 64, 71.

14. 437 U.S. 584 (1978).

15. *Id.* at 585.

16. *Id.* at 590.

17. 450 U.S. 175 (1981).

18. U.S. Patent No. 4,344,142 (publicized Aug. 10, 1982), cl. 1, col. 7.

19. *See Diehr,* 450 U.S. at 178.

20. *See id.* at 183 (quoting *Cochrane v. Deener,* 94 U.S. 780, 787–88 (1877)).

21. *See id.* at 191–92.

22. *In re Alappat,* 33 F.3d 1526, 1544 (Fed. Cir. 1994) (en banc).

23. *In re Beauregard,* 53 F.3d 1583 (Fed. Cir. 1995).

24. *AT&T Corp. v. Excel Commc'ns, Inc.,* 172 F.3d 1352 (Fed. Cir. 1999).

25. *See* U.S. PAT. & TRADEMARK OFF., MANUAL OF PATENT EXAMINING AND PROCEDURE § 2106, at 2100–11 (8th rev. ed. Aug. 2006).

26. U.S. CONST. amend. VIII, § 8. In his opinion in *Bilski v. Kappos,* Justice Stevens discusses some of the evidence often put forward in support of the proposition that, in the eighteenth and nineteenth centuries, the term "useful arts" referred to "manufacturing and similar applied trades," as opposed to "method[s] for organizing human activity." *Bilski v. Kappos,* 561 U.S. 593, 628, 632–35 (2010) (Stevens, J., concurring).

27. *See* Michael Risch, *America's First Patents*, 64 FLA. L. REV. 1279, 1296 (2012); *cf. Bilski*, 561 U.S. at 628–29, 638 (Stevens, J., concurring) (describing early patents on methods of doing business as, among other things, "rare").

28. Justice Stevens makes a similar observation in *Bilski*, 561 U.S. at 630. For discussion of the mail-order catalogue, *see, e.g.*, ROBERT J. GORDON, THE RISE AND FALL OF AMERICAN ECONOMIC GROWTH: THE U.S. STANDARD OF LIVING SINCE THE CIVIL WAR 90–92 (Princeton University Press 2016) (stating that Ward "deserves the credit for revolutionizing rural commerce").

29. *See* John R. Allison & Starling D. Hunter, *On the Feasibility of Improving Patent Quality One Technology at a Time: The Case of Business Methods*, 21 BERKELEY TECH. L. J. 729, 731 n.1 (2006).

30. *See* U.S. PAT. & TRADEMARK OFF., PATENT TECHNOLOGY MONITORING TEAM (PTMT), PATENT COUNTS BY CLASS BY YEAR 1995–2015, https://www.uspto.gov/web/offices/ac/ido/oeip/taf/cbcby.htm. The United States still uses the USPC for design and plant patents. US patents also bear International Patent Classification (IPC) numbers, which much of the rest of the world uses. For a scholarly overview of the patent classification process within the USPTO, *see* Saurabh Vishnubhakat, *The Field of Invention*, 45 HOFSTRA L. REV. 899 (2017), https://papers.ssrn.com/sol3/papers.cfm?abstract_id=2857155.

31. *See* USPTO WHITE PAPER, AUTOMATED FINANCIAL OR MANAGEMENT DATA PROCESSING METHODS (BUSINESS METHODS) 6–7 (2000), https://www.uspto.gov/sites/default/files/web/menu/busmethp/whitepaper.pdf.

32. *See* Allison & Hunter, *supra* note 29.

33. PTMT, *supra* note 30.

34. USPTO White Paper, *supra* note 31, at 5.

35. *See id.*

36. *Id.* at 7.

37. *State St. Bank & Tr. Co. v. Signature Fin. Grp., Inc.*, 149 F.3d 1368, 1375 (Fed. Cir. 1998).

38. *Id.* at 1373–75.

39. 76 U.S.P.Q.2d 1385 (B.P.A.I. 2005) (per curiam).

40. *See* PTMT, *supra* note 30.

41. The USPTO granted 147,517 utility patents in 1998 and 219,614 in 2010. *See* U.S. PAT. & TRADEMARK OFF., PTMT, U.S. PATENT STATISTICS CHART CALENDAR YEARS 1963–2015, http://www.uspto.gov/web/offices/ac/ido/oeip/taf/us_stat.htm.

42. Stuart J. H. Graham & David C. Mowery, *The Use of Intellectual Property in Software: Implications for Open Innovation, in* OPEN INNOVATION: RESEARCHING A NEW PARADIGM 184, 189 (Henry Chesbrough et al., eds., 2006).

43. James Bessen, *A Generation of Software Patents*, 18 B. U. J. SCI. & TECH. L. 241, 251 (2012) (stating further that "[a]dditionally, at least some novel aspect of the invention should reside in the software").

44. Lemley, *supra* note 8, at 937 n.134; *see also* Stuart Graham & Saurabh Vishnubhakat, *Of Smart Phone Wars and Software Patents*, 27 J. ECON. PERSP. 67, 75 (2013) ("[A]n accurate 'software patent' definition is elusive because many patents have software elements mixed with non-software elements").

45. *See* Graham & Mowery, *supra* note 42, at 190. The full list, using their designations as of January 1, 2015, includes 345 (Computer Graphics Processing and Selective Visual Display Systems); 358 (Facsimile and Static Presentation Processing); 382 (Image Analysis); 704 (Data Processing: Speech Signal Processing, Linguistics, Language Translation, and Audio Compression/Decompression); 707 (Data Processing: Database, Data Mining, and File Management or Data Structures); 709 (Electrical Computers and Digital Processing Systems: Multicomputer Data Transferring); 710 (Electrical Computers and Digital Data Processing Systems: Input/Output); 711 (Electrical Computers and Digital Processing Systems: Memory); 713 (Electrical Computers and Digital Processing Systems: Support); 714 (Error Detection/Correction and Fault Detection/Recovery); 715 (Data Processing: Presentation Processing of Document, Operator Interface Processing, and Screen Saver Display Processing); and 717 (Data Processing: Software Development, Installation, and Management). In a later paper, Graham and Vishnubhakat used a more

finely grained technique, focusing on specific class-subclass pairs identified by USPTO experts as "likely to contain patents applications or issued patents containing some element of either general purpose software or software that is specific to some form of hardware." Graham & Vishnubhakat, *supra* note 44, at 75. They use these data to compare allowance and rejection rates for software versus nonsoftware patents, however, and do not report specific numbers of software patent grants.

46. Graham & Mowery, *supra* note 42, at 190.

47. Gabison focuses on fourteen classes, including five that are not in Graham and Mowery's set (Class 324 (Electricity: Measuring and Testing), 369 (Dynamic Information Storage or Retrieval), 700 (Data Processing: Generic Control Systems or Specific Applications), 701 (Data Processing: Vehicles, Navigation, and Relative Location), 703 (Data Processing: Structural Design, Modeling, Simulation, and Emulation)), and excluding Class 382. *See* Garry A. Gabison, *Spotting Software Patent Innovation in a Patent Assertion Entity World*, 8 HASTINGS SCI. & TECH. L. J. 99, 121 n.32 (2015).

48. *See id.* at 122.

49. *See* Bessen, *supra* note 433, at 252–53 (estimating the number of software patents granted in 2011 as about 40,000, "based on USPTO technology classes that are titled data processing (classes 700–707 and 715–717) and several other classes that are reliant on software and in which software companies obtain patents (341, coded data generation or conversion; 345, computer graphics processing; 370, multiplex communication; 375, digital communications; 380, cryptography; 381, audio signal processing; 382, image analysis; 726, information security; and 902, electronic funds transfer)"). Note that Bessen, unlike Graham & Mowery and Gabison, includes Class 705 patents within the mix. As Allison and Tiller note, most of the business method patents of significance can be viewed as a category of software patents. *See* John R. Allison & Emerson H. Tiller, *The Business Patent Myth*, 18 BERKELEY TECH. L. J. 987, 991 n.8 (2003).

50. *See* James Bessen & Robert M. Hunt, *An Empirical Look at Software Patents*, 16 J. ECON. & MGT. STRATEGY 157 (2007) (identifying 167,438 software patents granted from 1976 through 2002, including just under 25,000 in 2002). Bessen and Hunt used the following search query:

(("software" in specification) OR ("computer" AND "program" in specification))
AND (utility patent excluding reissues)
ANDNOT ("chip" OR "semiconductor" OR "bus" OR "circuit" OR "circuitry" in title)
ANDNOT ("antigen" OR "antigenic" OR "chromatography" in specification)
Id. at 185.

51. For review and critique of the existing studies as of 2006, *see* Anne Layne-Farrar, *Defining Software Patents: A Research Field Guide* (Feb. 15, 2006), *available at* http://papers.ssrn.com/abstract=1818025.

52. *See* John F. Duffy, *Why Business Method Patents?*, 63 STAN. L. REV. 1247 (2011).

53. *See* U.S. Patent No. 5,443,036 (filed Nov. 2, 1993).

54. *See* U.S. Patent No. 6,058,941 (filed June 18, 1999).

55. *See* U.S. Patent No. 6,368,227 (filed Nov. 17, 2000). For other examples in this genre, *see, e.g.*, U.S. Patent No. 5,851,117 (filed Apr. 23, 1997) (patenting a method for training a janitor); U.S. Patent No. 6,014,975 (filed June 6, 1995) (patenting a shaving method); U.S. Patent No. 6,607,389 (filed Dec. 3, 2001) (patenting a method for selecting a jury). James Gleick's article *Patently Absurd*, which appeared in the *New York Times* on March 12, 2000, and cited among other questionable patents Amazon's one-click shopping patent discussed in the text above, probably played a role in igniting interest in the subject among the general public. *See* James Gleick, *Patently Absurd*, N. Y. TIMES, Mar. 12, 2000, http://www.nytimes.com/2000/03/12/magazine/patently-absurd.html.

56. AIA, § 14.

57. *See* U.S. Patent No. 5,960,411 (filed Sept. 12, 1997). Many people derided Amazon's suit against Barnes & Noble for infringing this patent, which was filed in October 1999 (just in time for the holiday shopping season) and resulted in the entry of a preliminary injunction against B&N. The Federal Circuit later vacated the injunction, citing substantial questions about the patent's validity, and the parties settled. In 2010, however, the USPTO ultimately

upheld the patent, which Amazon had slightly narrowed during reexamination. *See* Dennis Crouch, *Amazon One-Click Patent Slides Through Reexamination*, PATENTLY-O (Mar. 10, 2010), http://patentlyo.com/patent/2010/03/amazon-one-click-patent-slides-through-reexamination.html.

58. *See* U.S. Patent No. 5,797,127 (filed Dec. 31, 1996).

59. *See* John R. Allison et al., *Patent Litigation and the Internet*, 2012 STANFORD TECH. L. REV. 3, ¶ 5 n.15 (2012). *See also* JAMES BESSEN & MICHAEL J. MEURER, PATENT FAILURE: HOW JUDGES, BUREAUCRATS AND LAWYERS PUT INNOVATORS AT RISK, 194–98 (2008) (providing other examples of potentially very broad software claims).

60. Allison & Tiller, *supra* note 49, at 998. Similarly, a study by Allison & Hunter following the USPTO's establishment of a "Second Pair of Eyes Review" (SPER) program in March 2000, under which all applications falling into primary Class 705 were assigned to *two* examiners, concluded that the program only marginally improved patent quality in that class—and that inventors responded to the initiative by drafting their applications to avoid that primary classification, thus leading the authors to question whether "attempting patent reform one technology at a time is the best approach." Allison & Hunter, *supra* note 29, at 738. *See also* Starling D. Hunter III, *Have Business Method Patents Gotten a Bum Rap? Some Empirical Evidence*, 6 J. INFO. TECH. THEORY & APPLICATION 1 (2004) (concluding that Class 705 patents were of no lower quality than patents in other data processing classes); Layne-Farrar, *supra* note 51, at 25–28 (comparing the results of other studies on patent quality).

61. *See* John R. Allison et al., *Our Divided Patent System*, 82 U. CHI. L. REV. 1073, 1086–87, 1092, 1097 (2015) (based on a review of all patent litigation filed in federal district court during the years 2008–09, reporting that software patents—inventions "in which the claims cover data processing . . . the actual manipulation of data . . . and not merely transmission, receipt, or storage of data," including "software business methods"—comprised "the single largest category of decided cases, accounting for more than one-third of all outcomes in our data set," but that "software patents prevailed in only 30 out of 223 cases, or 13.5 percent," with an invalidation rate of 45.3 percent, or 56.4 percent for software business method patents); Allison et al., *supra* note 59, at ¶ 6 (based on a study of 1,093 Internet-related patents issued through 1999, reporting that such patents were "between 7.5 and 9.5 times more likely to end up in infringement litigation, depending on the model we used," and that "[w]ithin the category of Internet patents, those on business models were litigated at a significantly higher rate than those on business techniques;" on the other hand, there was "no significant difference" in win rates in comparison with non-Internet patents). *See also* BESSEN & MEURER, *supra* note 59, at 22, 193 (reporting that "[s]oftware patents are more than twice as likely to be litigated as other patents" and business method patents nearly seven times more); *cf.* Bessen, *supra* note 43, at 259–60.

62. *See* John R. Allison et al., *Patent Quality and Settlement Among Repeat Patent Litigants*, 99 GEO. L. J. 677, 695–97 (2011) (reporting that software patents constituted 74.1 percent of the most-litigated patents, defined as those asserted eight or more times between January 2000 and February 2009, but that their win rate was only 12.9 percent).

63. *See, e.g.*, BESSEN & MEURER, *supra* note 59, at 199.

64. *See id.* at 199–200.

65. *See, e.g.*, Bessen & Hunt, *supra* note 50; Bronwyn H. Hall & Megan MacGarvie, *The Private Value of Software Patents*, 39 RES. POL'Y 994 (2010).

66. *See eBay Inc. v. MercExchange, L.L.C.*, 126 S. Ct. 1837 (2006). The Court didn't explicitly say that the defendant is entitled to a judgment for damages for future, as opposed to merely for past, acts of infringement, but the decision has been so interpreted.

67. *Id.* at 397 (Kennedy, J., concurring). Another case, *Microsoft Corp. v. AT&T Corp.*, 550 U.S. 437 (2007), involved a technical issue of statutory interpretation—concerning the applicability of U.S. patent law to conducts occurring outside the United States—which hinged on whether software exported from the US to the UK constituted a "component" of a patented invention. The underlying patent was on "an apparatus for digitally encoding and compressing recorded speech," which Microsoft allegedly caused third parties to infringe because the installation of Microsoft Windows software code on a computer would "enable[] a computer to process speech in the manner claimed by that patent." *Id.* at 441–42. The

question of whether software-related inventions like the one at issue recited patentable subject matter didn't come up, but the Court did state in passing that while software on a disk
could be a "component" of a patentable invention, software in the abstract ("the instructions
themselves, detached from any medium") was merely an "an idea without physical embodiment." *Id.* at 447–49.

68. *In re Bilski*, 545 F.3d 943, 949 (Fed. Cir. 2008) (en banc), *aff'd on other grounds*, 561 U.S. 593
    (2010).
69. *See id.*
70. *See id.* at 953–57.
71. *See id.* at 963–66.
72. *See id.* at 959–61. Also left undecided was what exactly a "particular machine" is. The *Alappat*
    decision had stated that any general-purpose computer became a "particular machine"
    once it ran a program, but, in the wake of *Bilski*. the USPTO came around to the view that
    this was no longer the law—though a combination of two programmed general-purpose
    computers *would* be a particular machine. *See* Thomas F. Cotter, *A Burkean Perspective on
    Patent Eligibility, Part II: Reflections on the (Counter) Revolution in Patent Law*, 11 MINN. J. L.
    SCI. & TECH. 365, 368 n.8 (2010) (citing sources). Formalities, anyone?
73. 561 U.S. 593 (2010).
74. *See id.* at 601–08.
75. *See id.* at 608–09. Justice Kennedy also noted that, in 1999, Congress had enacted 35 U.S.C.
    §273 exempting Person A from infringement liability in a case in which Person B invents
    and patents a business method that Person A had independently invented and used as a
    trade secret for more than one year prior to the date on which Person B filed her patent
    application. In Justice Kennedy's view, this provision evidenced Congress's understanding
    that business methods were patent-eligible. The exception has since been expanded to cover
    prior trade secret uses of inventions in addition to business methods. *See id.* at 594–95, 607–
    08; 35 U.S.C. § 273.
76. *See id.* at 609–13. The reference to "fundamental economic practice" was a quote from Judge
    Rader's separate opinion rejecting Bilski's application when the case was before the Federal
    Circuit.
77. *See Bilski*, 561 U.S. at 613–57 (Stevens, J., concurring).
78. For what it's worth, in yet another (brief) opinion Justice Breyer also observed that no
    member of the Court supported the Federal Circuit's now-dead standard of limiting the
    inquiry into whether a claimed invention is "useful, concrete, and tangible." *See id.* at 657,
    659–60 (Breyer, J., concurring).
79. *See* U.S. PAT. & TRADEMARK OFF., INTERIM GUIDANCE FOR DETERMINING SUBJECT
    MATTER ELIGIBILITY FOR PROCESS CLAIMS IN VIEW OF *BILSKI V. KAPPOS* (July 27,
    2010), https://www.uspto.gov/sites/default/files/patents/law/exam/bilski_guidance_
    27jul2010.pdf. Of possible interest, these guidelines include for reference all nine of the
    claims at issue in *Bilski*.
80. 717 F.3d 1269 (Fed. Cir. 2013) (en banc).
81. *See* 717 F.3d at 1292 (Rader, C.J., concurring in part and dissenting in part). The method
    claim didn't explicitly mention the use of a computer, and the judges were divided on the
    issue of whether that claim nevertheless did require use of a computer. *Compare id.* at 1312
    (Rader, C. J., concurring in part and dissenting in part) *with id.* at 1327, 1329–32 (Linn, J.,
    dissenting).
82. *Id.* at 1285 (Lourie, J., concurring).
83. 134 S. Ct. 2347 (2014).
84. *Id.* at 2355 (citation omitted).
85. *Id.* at 2356.
86. *Id.* at 2357.
87. *Id.* at 2358–59 (citation omitted).
88. *Id.* at 2360.
89. *See* James Cosgrove, *Are Business Method Patents Dead? It Depends on Who's Applying for Them*,
    IP WATCHDOG (Aug. 4, 2015), http://www.ipwatchdog.com/2015/08/04/are-business-
    method-patents-dead-it-depends-on-whos-applying-for-them/id=60077; Robert R Sachs, *A*

Survey of Patent Invalidations Since Alice, LAW360 (Jan. 13, 2015), http://www.law360.com/
articles/604235/a-survey-of-patent-invalidations-since-alice; Robert R. Sachs, *Two Years
After Alice: A Survey of the Impact of a "Minor Case" (Part 2)*, BILSKI BLOG (June 20, 2016),
http://www.bilskiblog.com/blog/2016/06/two-years-after-alice-a-survey-of-the-impact-of-
a-minor-case-part-2.html. As you can see, the preceding three sources are all blog posts or
newspaper articles. As of this writing, I'm not aware of any published studies by economists or
academics.

90. *See* CHRIS BARRY ET AL., PwC 2017 PATENT LITIGATION STUDY: CHANGE ON THE
HORIZON? 7; Saurabh Vishnubhakat et al., *Strategic Decision Making in Dual PTAB and
District Court Proceedings*, 31 BERKELEY TECH. L. J. 45, 83–84 (2017). In addition, the
cost of litigating an IPR to judgment is lower than the cost of challenging validity in court,
see AIPLA, 2017 REPORT OF THE ECONOMIC SURVEY I-163 (reporting mean costs of
$451,000 through appeal for post-grant proceedings, compared with $627,000 just for cases
with less than $1 million at stake); *id.* at 43 (reporting a median cost of litigating a post-
grant proceeding through trial and appeal of $350,000), and the challenger benefits from a
more favorable burden of proof and standard of claim construction. *See* 35 U.S.C. § 316(e);
Cuozzo Speed Techs., Inc. v. Lee, 136 S. Ct. 2131 (2016).

91. *See* 35 U.S.C. § 321.

92. *See id.* § 311(b), 314(a).

93. *See* AIA, § 18(d)(1).

94. *See id.* § 18(a)(1)(B).

95. *See* U.S. PAT. & TRADEMARK OFF., PATENT TRIAL AND APPEAL BOARD STATISTICS 2,
10–11 (Mar. 31, 2017), https://www.uspto.gov/sites/default/files/documents/AIA%20
Statistics_March2017.pdf (reporting 2,406 institutions, and 1,277 findings of total or partial
invalidity, out of 4,563 completed IPR petitions; and 243 institutions, and 156 findings of
total or partial invalidity, out of 446 completed CBM petitions); *see also* BRIAN C. HOWARD,
LEX MACHINA PATENT TRIAL AND APPEAL BOARD (PTAB) 2017 REPORT 1 (reporting, as
of June 11, 2017, 2,847 institutions of IPRs and CBMs, and 1,295 findings of total or partial
invalidity, out of 5,374 petitions filed and terminated as of May 31, 2017). As one perceptive
blogger has noted, however, there is a time lag in statistics like these, since the USPTO has
six months to decide whether to institute—and if it decides not to, the matter immediately
comes to an end—but up to one and a half years to conclude any resulting trials; the end
result of reporting only on completed cases may be an underreporting of the percentage of
petitions instituted. *See* Michael E. Sander, *By the Numbers: Is the USPTO Underreporting
the Rate They Institute IPRs and CBMs?*, PATENTLY-O, May 16, 2016, http://patentlyo.com/
patent/2016/05/numbers-underreporting-institute.html.

96. *See* HOWARD, *supra* note 95, at 9; USPTO, *supra* note 95, at 10–11, 14.

97. *See* Robert R. Sachs, *#AliceStorm: April Update and the Impact of* TC Heartland *on Patent
Eligibility*, BILSKI BLOG, June 1, 2017, http://www.bilskiblog.com/blog/2017/06/
alicestorm-april-update-and-the-impact-of-tc-heartland.html [hereinafter Sachs, *April
Update*]; Robert R. Sachs, *AliceStorm Update for Fall 2016*, BILSKI BLOG, Oct. 19, 2016,
http://www.bilskiblog.com/blog/2016/10/alicestorm-update-turbulence-and-troubles-
.html; Robert R. Sachs, *Two Years After* Alice: *A Survey of the Impact of a "Minor Case"
(Part 1)*, BILSKI BLOG, June 16, 2016, http://www.bilskiblog.com/blog/2016/06/two-
years-after-alice-a-survey-of-the-impact-of-a-minor-case.html.

98. *See* Sachs, *April Update, supra* note 97.

99. The diagnostic methods case is *Rapid Litig. Mgt. Ltd. v. CellzDirect, Inc.*, 827 F.3d 1042 (Fed.
Cir. 2015), discussed in Chapter 4 n.53.

100. DDR Holdings, LLC v. Hotels.Com, L.P., 773 F.3d 1245, 1248–49 (Fed. Cir. 2014).

101. *Id.* at 1257–59.

102. *Enfish, LLC v. Microsoft Corp.*, 822 F.3d 1327, 1330 (Fed. Cir. 2016).

103. *Id.* at 1333, 1336.

104. *See Planet Bingo, LLC v. VKGS LLC*, 576 Fed. App'x. 1005 (Fed. Cir. 2014).

105. The EPO applies this standard, however, in determining whether the claimed invention
demonstrates an inventive step—the analogue to the nonobviousness standard in the
United States—while applying a comparatively minimalist approach to patentable subject

matter. *See* Case T 0258/03, Hitachi, ¶ 4.6 (EPO Bd. App., Apr. 21, 2004); *see also* Dan Burk, *The Inventive Concept in* Alice Corp. v. CLS Bank Int'l, 45 IIC 865 (2014) (noting the arguable convergence between the US and EPO approaches); Thomas F. Cotter, *A Burkean Perspective on Patentable Eligibility*, 22 BERKELEY TECH. L. J. 855, 887–90 (2007) (discussing *Hitachi*). The USPTO has defined "technological inventions," which are not subject to CBM review, along similar lines, namely as inventions in which "the claimed subject matter as a whole recites a technological feature that is novel and unobvious over the prior art; and solves a technical problem using a technical solution" 37 C.F.R. § 42.301(b). The definition nevertheless fails to elaborate on what the word "technical" means. The Federal Circuit has held, however, that based on *Alice*, "the presence of a general purpose computer to facilitate operations through uninventive steps does not," by itself, render an invention "technical" or "technological." *See Versata Dev. Grp., Inc. v. SAP Am., Inc.*, 793 F.3d 1306, 1326 (Fed. Cir. 2015).

106. *See* Cotter, *supra* note 722, at 373–74.

Chapter 6

1. *See* Press Release, *Special Comm. on Aging, U.S. Senate, Valeant Pharmaceuticals' Business Model: The Repercussions for Patients and the Health Care Systems* (Apr. 27, 2016), http://www.aging.senate.gov/press-releases/valeant-pharmaceuticals-business-model-the-repercussions-for-patients-and-the-health-care-systems.

2. *See* News Release, Office of US Senator from Minn. Amy Klobuchar, *Klobuchar Calls for Judiciary Hearing and Investigation into at Least 400 Percent Increase of EpiPen Packs* (Aug. 20, 2016), http://www.klobuchar.senate.gov/public/2016/8/klobuchar-calls-for-judiciary-hearing-and-investigation-into-at-least-400-percent-increase-of-epipen-packs. For discussion, *see, e.g.*, Cynthia Koons & Robert Langreth, *How Marketing Turned the EpiPen into a Billion-Dollar Business*, BLOOMBERG BUS. WEEK (Sept. 23, 2015), http://www.bloomberg.com/news/articles/2015-09-23/how-marketing-turned-the-epipen-into-a-billion-dollar-business; Andrew Pollack, *Mylan Raised EpiPen's Price Before the Expected Arrival of a Generic*, N. Y. TIMES (Aug. 24, 2016), http://www.nytimes.com/2016/08/25/business/mylan-raised-epipens-price-before-the-expected-arrival-of-a-generic.html.

   To be clear, list prices aren't necessarily the prices that all consumers pay. "Middlemen" such as insurers and pharmacy benefits managers (PBMs) often negotiate rebates or discounts. Consumers without insurance or those with high deductibles nevertheless can winding up paying up to the list price; and even with insurance sometimes the price consumers pay for the generic can be higher than they pay for the brand-name device. For discussion, see Jonathan D. Rockoff, *Behind the Push to Keep Higher-Priced EpiPen in Consumers' Hands*, WALL ST. J., Aug. 7, 2017, https://www.wsj.com/articles/behind-the-push-to-keep-higher-priced-epipen-in-consumers-hands-1502036741; Denise Roland & Peter Loftus, *Insulin Prices Soar While Drugmakers' Share Stays Flat*, WALL ST. J., Oct. 7, 2016, http://www.wsj.com/articles/insulin-prices-soar-while-drugmakers-share-stays-flat-1475876764; Joseph Walker, *Middlemen Faulted in Drug Prices*, WALL ST. J., Oct. 3, 2016, topics.wsj.com/documents/print/WSJ_-B001-20161003.pdf. Moreover, efforts to cast the blame for high drug prices on middlemen, as Mylan's CEO attempted to do, *see* Walker, *supra*, strike me as largely a distraction; the drug company ultimately decides what to charge and has no reason to set a list price above or below what it expects to be its profit-maximizing price. Similarly, while FDA Commissioner Scott Gottlieb has argued that a misguided antitrust settlement encourages drug companies to use rebates rather than discounts when negotiating with PBMs, and thus contributes to higher list prices than might otherwise be the case to non-PBMs, *see* Scott Gottlieb, *How Congress Can Make Drug Pricing More Rational*, FORBES, Sept. 12, 2016, http://www.forbes.com/sites/scottgottlieb/2016/09/12/how-congress-can-make-drug-pricing-more-rational/#132f19b32f6b, I'm skeptical that resolving the problem of high drug prices ultimately hinges on this issue.

3. *See* Peter Loftus & Gary Fields, *Costly Hepatitis C Drugs Force Prisons to Ration Care*, WALL ST. J. (Sept.13, 2016, 1:34 PM), http://www.wsj.com/articles/high-cost-of-new-hepatitis-c-drugs-strains-prison-budgets-locks-many-out-of-cure-1473701644.

4. *See* Peter B. Bach, *Why Drugs Cost So Much*, N. Y. Times (Jan. 14, 2015), http://www.nytimes.com/2015/01/15/opinion/why-drugs-cost-so-much.html ("Eli Lilly charges more than $13,000 a month for Cyramza, the newest drug to treat stomach cancer. The latest medicine for lung cancer, Novartis's Zykadia, costs almost $14,000 a month. Amgen's Blincyto, for leukemia, will cost $64,000 a month.") (formatting omitted).

5. *See* Katie Thomas, *A Push to Lower Drug Prices That Hit Insurers and Employers the Hardest*, N. Y. Times (Sept. 8, 2016), http://www.nytimes.com/2016/09/09/business/express-scripts-urges-narrower-coverage-of-anti-inflammatory-drugs.html ("Humira, made by AbbVie, and Enbrel, made by Amgen, each carry a monthly list price of just over $4,000, and each have increased those prices by about 130 percent from 2011 to 2016, according to the Gold Standard Drug Database compiled by Elsevier Clinical Solutions").

6. *See id.; see also Developments in the Prescription Drug Market: Oversight Before the Full H.Comm. on Oversight & Gov't Reform*, 114th Congress (Feb. 4, 2016), https://oversight.house.gov/hearing/developments-in-the-prescription-drug-market-oversight/.

7. *See* Gretchen Morgenson, *How Valeant Cashed in Twice on Higher Drug Prices*, N. Y. Times (July 29, 2016), http://www.nytimes.com/2016/07/31/business/how-valeant-cashed-in-twice-on-higher-drug-prices.html ("On June 18, 2015, for example, Valeant raised the price of Glumetza, its diabetes drug, to $3,432 from $572, according to Truven Health Analytics. And about a month later, on July 31, 2015, Valeant hiked Glumetza's price again to $5,148. Zegerid, a treatment for acid reflux and other stomach problems, is another example. During the third quarter of 2015, Valeant increased its price twice, raising it to $3,034 from $421 .... And in late July of last year, Valeant increased the price of Cuprimine, a treatment for Wilson's disease, a toxic accumulation of copper in the liver and other organs, to $26,189 from $6,547").

8. *See* Andrew Pollack, *Drug Goes from $13.50 a Tablet to $750, Overnight*, N. Y. Times (Sept. 20, 2015), http://www.nytimes.com/2015/09/21/business/a-huge-overnight-increase-in-a-drugs-price-raises-protests.html; Andrew Pollack & Matthey Goldstein, *Martin Shkreli All but Gloated Over Huge Drug Price Increases, Memos Show*, N. Y. Times (Feb. 2, 2016), http://www.nytimes.com/2016/02/03/business/drug-makers-calculated-price-increases-with-profit-in-mind-memos-show.html.

9. *See* Julie Creswell et al., *Drug C.E.O. Martin Shkreli Arrested on Fraud Charges*, N. Y. Times (Dec. 17, 2015), http://www.nytimes.com/2015/12/18/business/shkreli-fraud-charges.html. As of this writing, the matter remains pending.

10. *See* Express Scripts Lab, Express Scripts 2016 Drug Trend Report 31 (Feb. 2017), http://lab.express-scripts.com/lab/~/media/29f13dee4e7842d6881b7e034fc0916a.ashx.

11. *See* Robert Langreth & Rebecca Spalding, *Shkreli Was Right: Everyone's Hiking Drug Prices*, Bloomberg (Feb. 2, 2016, 4:00 am), http://www.bloomberg.com/news/articles/2016-02-02/shkreli-not-alone-in-drug-price-spikes-as-skin-gel-soars-1-860.

12. US Centers for Medicare and Medicaid, *National Health Expenditure Projections 2016–2025*, https://www.cms.gov/Research-Statistics-Data-and-Systems/Statistics-Trends-and-Reports/NationalHealthExpendData/Downloads/proj2016.pdf.

13. *See* European Medicines Agency, *Adrenaline Auto-injectors Article-31 referral - Annex I* (Aug. 26, 2015), http://www.ema.europa.eu/docs/en_GB/document_library/Referrals_document/Adrenaline_31/WC500165691.pdf; Pauline Fréour, *Aux États-Unis, le prix d'un stylo-injecteur fait scandale*, Figaro (Sept. 2, 2016), http://sante.lefigaro.fr/actualite/2016/09/02/25352-etats-unis-prix-dun-stylo-injecteur-fait-scandale (stating that a pair of EpiPen injectors in France cost 75 euros); Sheryl Ubelacker, *EpiPen Price in Canada Not Spiked as in U.S.*, Waterloo Record (Aug. 26, 2016), http://www.therecord.com/news-story/6825766-epipen-price-in-canada-not-spiked-as-in-u-s-/.

14. Marcia Angell, *Why Do Drug Companies Charge So Much? Because They Can*, Wash. Post (Sept. 25, 2015), https://www.washingtonpost.com/opinions/why-do-drug-companies-charge-so-much-because-they-can/2015/09/25/967d3df4-6266-11e5-b38e-06883aacba64_story.html.

15. *See* Centers for Medicare and Medicare Servs., *National Health Expenditure Data—Historical* (Dec. 6, 2016), https://www.cms.gov/research-statistics-data-and-systems/statistics-trends-and-reports/nationalhealthexpenddata/nationalhealthaccountshistorical.html; OECD Data, *Health Spending* (2017), https://data.oecd.org/healthres/health-spending.

htm. Focusing just on pharmaceuticals, Americans spend approximately $1,100 per person per year, about $100 more than the Swiss and $300 or more than anyone else. *See* OECD Data, *Pharmaceutical Spending* (2017), https://data.oecd.org/healthres/pharmaceutical-spending.htm.

16. *Compare* Kenneth D. Kochanek et al., *Mortality in the United States 2016*, NCHS Data Brief, No. 293, Dec. 2017, https://www.cdc.gov/nchs/data/databriefs/db293.pdf (life expectnay in 2016 was 78.6 years), *with* Elizabeth Arias et al.,65 Nat'l Vital Statistics Reports, No. 8, Nov. 2016, tbl.21 (historical data), https://www.cdc.gov/nchs/data/nvsr/nvsr65/nvsr65_08.pdf. According to one estimate, the average increase in life expectancy attributable to drugs that were granted FDA priority-review status and approved between 1979 and 1998 was 4.7 months. *See* Frank R. Lichtenberg, *Pharmaceutical Knowledge-Capital Accumulation and Longevity, in* Measuring Capital in the New Economy 237, 241 n.7, 264 (Carol Corrado et al. eds., University Chicago Press 2005) (explaining that "priority-review approvals" are "considered by the FDA to represent "significant improvement compared to marketed products, in the treatment, diagnosis, or prevention of a disease," and accounted for 42 percent of approvals of new molecular entities from 1990 to 2001). The most important contribution to US life expectancy over the past century, however, is probably not medicine but rather sanitation, which resulted in the near-elimination of cholera, typhus, and other water-borne illnesses. *See* Robert J. Gordon, The Rise and Fall of American Economic Growth: The U.S. Standard of Living Since the Civil War 244–45 (Princeton University Press 2016).

17. *See, e.g.,* Angell, *supra* note 14. Although Angell is more critical of the drug companies than are many other researchers—stating in the *Washington Post* article, for example, that "there is very little innovation at the big drug firms"—she notes that the research arms of European drug companies "are often located in the United States, not only because this is their profit center but because they want to be near universities that receive generous [National Institute of Health] funding"). *See also 2016 Global R&D Funding Forecast*, 58 R&D Mag., Jan. 1, 2016, at 15 (reporting expected R&D funding in the life sciences, of which "the biopharmaceutical sector . . . accounts for about 85 percent," as $71.1 billion in the United States and $169.3 billion globally for 2016).

18. Express Scripts Lab, *supra* note 10, at 31.

19. *See* Gordon, *supra* note 16, at 487–88; Aaron Carroll, *Chart: Life Expectancy at Birth and Health Care Spending Per Capita*, The Incidental Economist Blog (Nov. 21, 2013, 12:15 pm), http://theincidentaleconomist.com/wordpress/chart-life-expectancy-at-birth-and-health-care-spending-per-capita/; Esteban Ortiz-Ospina & Max Roser, *Financing Healthcare*, https://ourworldindata.org/financing-healthcare/; *see also* James Banks & James P. Smith, *International Comparisons in Health Economics: Evidence from Aging Studies*, 4 Ann. Revs. Econ. 57, 79 (2012) (concluding that "until very old age, the United States ranks poorly on all health indicators with the exception of self-reported subjective health status"); James Banks et al., *Disease and Disadvantage in the United States in England*, 295 JAMA 2037 (2006) (concluding that "US residents are much less healthy than their English counterparts and these differences exist at all points of the [socioeconomic status] distribution," despite much higher per capita spending in the United States). Some studies have reported that cancer patients in the United States have higher survival rates than in Europe, *see, e.g.,* Tomas Philipson et al., *An Analysis of Whether Higher Health Care Spending in the United States Versus Europe Is 'Worth It' in the Case of Cancer*, 31 Health Aff. 667 (2012), though other researchers argue that data on survival rates are not comparable, *see* Sharon Begley, *Is High Spending on Cancer Care Worth It?*, Reuters (Apr. 9, 2012, 4:24 pm), http://www.reuters.com/article/2012/04/09/us-cancercare-idUSBRE8380SA20120409. Other studies have tried to quantify the lack of health insurance on mortality rates, *see, e.g.,* Andrew P. Wilper et al., *Health Insurance and Mortality in U.S. Adults*, 99 Am. J. Pub. Health 2289 (2009) (estimating up to 45,000 deaths in 2005 associated with lack of health insurance), but these conclusions too have been questioned.

20. Elisabeth Rosenthal, *The Soaring Cost of a Simple Breath*, N. Y. Times (Oct. 13, 2013), http://www.nytimes.com/2013/10/13/us/the-soaring-cost-of-a-simple-breath.html [hereinafter Rosenthal, *Breath*]. In 2013–14 Rosenthal published a series of articles in the *New York Times* on the high cost of US health care, and more recently has published a book, Elisabeth

ROSENTHAL. AN AMERICAN SICKNESS: HOW HEALTHCARE BECAME BIG BUSINESS AND HOW YOU CAN TAKE IT BACK (Penguin Press 2017).

For discussion of reporting requirements for anticipated shortages of drugs and the FDA's plans for responding to such shortages, *see* VALERIE JEPSEN, PREVENTING AND MITIGATING DRUG SHORTAGES: FDA's AND MANUFACTURERS' ROLES (Mar. 31, 2016), www.fda.gov/downloads/Drugs/NewsEvents/UCM493617.pdf; *see also* Peter Loftus, *Shortages of Simple Drugs Thwart Treatment*, WALL ST. J., July 1, 2017, https://www.wsj.com/articles/shortages-of-simple-drugs-thwart-treatments-1498906805?mg=prod/accounts-wsj.

21. *See* ROSENTHAL, *supra* note 20, at 302; Anne B. Martin et al., *National Health Spending in 2014: Faster Growth Driven by Coverage Expansion and Prescription Drug Spending*, 35 HEALTH AFF. 150 (2016).

22. *See* Michael A. Carrier & Carl J. Minniti III, *The Untold EpiPen Story:How Mylan Hiked Prices by Blocking Rivals*, 102 CORNELL L. REV. ONLINE 53 (2017).

23. For useful discussions, from a variety of perspectives, of the R&D process leading up to the approval of a new drug, *see, e.g.,* MARCIA ANGELL, THE TRUTH ABOUT THE DRUG COMPANIES: HOW THEY DECEIVE US AND WHAT TO DO ABOUT IT 22–30 (2004); Iain Cockburn & Rebecca Henderson, *Public-Private Interaction and the Productivity of Pharmaceutical Research* (Nat'l Bureau Econ. Research, Working Paper no. 6018, 1997); E. Ray Dorsey, *Funding of US Biomedical Research, 2003–2008*, 303 JAMA 137 (Jan. 13, 2010); J. P. Hughes et al., *Principles of Early Drug Discovery*, 162 BRIT. J. PHARMACOLOGY 1239 (2011); Ashley Stevens et al., *The Role of Public-Sector Research in the Discovery of Drugs and Vaccines*, 364 NEW ENG. J. MED. 535 (2011); *The Drug Development Process*, U.S. FOOD & DRUG ADMIN, http://www.fda.gov/ForPatients/Approvals/Drugs/default.htm (last updated June 24, 2015); Benjamin Zycher et al., *Private Sector Contributions to Pharmaceutical Science: Thirty-Five Summary Case Histories*, 17 AM. J. THERAPEUTICS 101 (2010).

24. Federal law requires that the recipient of federal funding share the proceeds of commercialization with the individual inventors, and though it doesn't specify percentages, a common practice is for the inventors to receive a one-third share. Of course, if patents are unnecessary to promote invention or disclosure, and the reason to allow universities to obtain these exclusive rights is to promote commercialization, evidence that exclusive rights are unnecessary to promote commercialization would suggest that the public actually doesn't gain anything from patenting. For an interesting proposal that in effect would prevent recipients of federal funds from enforcing patents in cases in which industry was willing to accept nonexclusive licenses to commercialize the technology, *see* Ian Ayres & Lisa Larrimore Ouellette, *A Market Test for Bayh-Dole Patents*, 102 CORNELL L. REV. 271 (2017).

25. *See* Brian J. Love, *Do University Patents Pay Off? Evidence from a Survey of University Inventors in Computer Science and Electrical Engineering*, 16 YALE J. L. & TECH. 285 (2013).

26. *See, e.g., Brenner v. Manson*, 383 U.S. 519 (1966); *Janssen Pharmaceutica v. Teva Pharms. USA Inc.*, 583 F.3d 1317 (Fed. Cir. 2009).

27. *See Trends, Charts, Maps*, CLINICALTRIALS.GOV, https://clinicaltrials.gov/ct2/resources/trends; *see also* ANGELL, *supra* note 23, at 29 (reporting that over 80,000 trials, involving 2.3 million participants, were ongoing in the US in 2001); Stephan Ehrhardt et al., *Research Letter: Trends in National Institutes of Health Funding for Clinical Trials Registered in ClinicalTrials.gov*, 314 JAMA 3566 (Dec. 15, 2015) (reporting 18,400 new clinical trials in 2014).

28. The FDA's website reports a 70 percent rate, *see* U.S. FOOD & DRUG ADMIN., *supra* note 23, while a recent empirical study by Di Masi et al. reports a 60 percent rate, *see* Joseph DiMasi et al., *Innovation in the Pharmaceutical Industry: New Estimates of R&D*, 47 J. HEALTH ECON. 20 (2016). Hay et al. report that success rates vary considerably depending on factors such as the type of drug, the disease, and the size of the sponsoring firm. They also argue that a more insightful statistic is not the approval rate per *drug*, but rather the approval rate per *indication*, since some drugs are tested for multiple indications and may prove safe and effective for only some of them. *See* Michael Hay et al., *Clinical Development Success Rates for Investigational Drugs*, 32 NATURE BIOTECHNOLOGY 40 (2014).

29. *See* sources cited *supra* note 28.

30. *See* sources cited *supra* note 28.

31. *See* Hay et al., *supra* note 28, at 42.

32. *See* U.S. Food & Drug Admin., Approved Drug Products with Therapeutic Equivalence Evaluations (Orange Book), http://www.fda.gov/Drugs/InformationOnDrugs/ucm129662.htm.

33. *See* DiMasi et al., *supra* note 28, at 24 (reporting an average of 96.8 months from start of clinical testing to marketing approval); Zycher et al., *supra* note 23, at 105 (asserting that the time from drug discovery to NDA takes on average 10–15 years).

34. *See* 35 U.S.C. § 156(g)(6)(A). If an extension would result in the drug being subject to patent protection for more than fourteen years following FDA approval, the extension must be reduced accordingly. *See id.* § 156(c)(3).

35. *See* 21 U.S.C. §§ 355(c)(3)(E)(ii), 355(j)(5)(F)(ii).

36. *See* Ehrhardt et al., *supra* note 27.

37. *See, e.g.*, Ben Goldacre, Bad Pharma: How Drug Companies Mislead Doctors and Harm Patients 213–16 (Faber and Faber Inc. 2012); John LaMattina, *Pharma Controls Clinical Trials of Their Drugs. Is This Hazardous to Your Health?*, Forbes (Oct. 2, 2013), http://www.forbes.com/sites/johnlamattina/2013/10/02/pharma-controls-clinical-trials-of-their-drugs-is-this-hazardous-to-your-health/#1664220b189d; Peter Whorisky, *As Drug Industry's Influence over Research Grows, So Does the Potential for Bias*, Wash. Post. (Nov. 24, 2012), https://www.washingtonpost.com/business/economy/as-drug-industrys-influence-over-research-grows-so-does-the-potential-for-bias/2012/11/24/bb64d596-1264-11e2-be82-c3411b7680a9_story.html.

38. *See* Pharm. Researchers & Mfrs. Am. (PhRMA), 2016 Profile: Biopharmaceutical Research Industry 33, 36, 53; *see also supra* note 17.

39. As of 2016, several states were considering legislation that would require drug companies to disclose such information. For discussion, *see, e.g.*, Rachel Sachs, *Pharmaceutical Transparency Bills: Targeting Disclosure Purposefully*, Harv. L.: Bill of Health Blog (Apr. 13, 2016), http://blogs.harvard.edu/billofhealth/2016/04/13/pharmaceutical-transparency-bills-targeting-disclosures-purposefully/.

40. DiMasi et al., *supra* note 28, at 22.

41. *See id.*

42. *See id.* at 25–26. All of these numbers, which are reported in 2013 dollars, are considerably higher than the authors' previous estimates of $802 million (in 2001 dollars) as reported in a 2003 study of (mostly) NMEs, *see* Joseph A. DiMasi et al., *The Price of Innovation: New Estimates of Drug Development Costs*, 22 J. Health Econ. 151, 166 (2003), and of approximately $1.3 billion (in 2005 dollars) as reported in a 2007 study of both NMEs and NBEs; *see* Joseph A. DiMasi & Henry G. Grabowski, *The Cost of Biopharmaceutical R&D: Is Biotech Different?*, 28 Managerial & Decision Econ. 469, 476–77 (2007). It's possible that the differences reflect in part the higher cost incurred in recent years to complete clinical testing. *See* DiMasi et al., *supra* note 28, at 21.

43. *See* Jerry Avorn, *The $2.6 Billion Pill—Methodologic and Policy Considerations*, 372 New Eng. J. Med. 1877, 1878 (2015); Aaron E. Carroll, *$26 Billion to Develop a Drug? New Estimate Makes Questionable Assumptions*, N. Y. Times (Nov. 18, 2014), http://www.nytimes.com/2014/11/19/upshot/calculating-the-real-costs-of-developing-a-new-drug.html?rref=upshot&abt=0002&abg=1&_r=0; Donald Light & Rebecca Warburton, *Demythologizing the High Costs of Pharmaceutical Research*, 6 BioSocieties 34, 40–41 (2011). Light and Warburton pegged the cost of developing a new drug at as little as $43 million in 2000 dollars.

44. *See* DiMasi et al., *supra* note 28, at 30. For other responses to Light & Warburton from, or on behalf of, DiMasi et al., *see* Letter from Kenneth I. Kaitin, Dir. & Research Professor, Tufts Ctr. for the Study of Drug Dev., to Supporters and Friends (Mar. 2011), http://csdd.tufts.edu/news/complete_story/internal_news (containing Dr. DiMasi's response to Light and Warburton's article); Joseph A. DiMasi et al., *Reply: Extraordinary Claims Require Extraordinary Evidence*, 24 J. Health Econ. 1034 (2005) [hereinafter DiMasi et al., *Extraordinary*]; Joseph A. DiMasi et al., *Reply: Setting the Record Straight on Setting the Record Straight: Response to the Light and Warburton Rejoinder*, 24 J. Health Econ. 1049 (2005).

45. *See* Christopher Paul Adams & Van Vu Brantner, *Spending on New Drug Development*, 19 Health Econ. 130, 131–32 (2010); Christopher P. Adams & Van V. Brantner, *MARKET*

WATCH: Estimating the Cost of New Drug Development: Is It Really $802 Million?, 25 HEALTH
AFFAIRS 420, 420 (2006). For further comparison, see also JORGE MESTRE-FERRANDIZ
ET AL., THE R&D COST OF A NEW MEDICINE (Dec. 2012), https://www.ohe.org/
publications/rd-cost-new-medicine (reviewing studies through 2012, and estimating the
mean cost of developing a new drug at $1.5 billion in 2011 dollars); Vinay Prasad & Sham
Mailankody, *Research and Development Spending to Bring a Single Cancer Drug to Market and
Revenues After Approval*, 177 JAMA INTERNAL MED. 1569 (2017) (estimating the cost to develop a cancer drug at $648 million).

46. *See* DiMasi et al., *supra* note 28, at 30–31.

47. TOPHER SPIRO ET AL., CTR. FOR AM. PROGRESS, ENOUGH IS ENOUGH: THE TIME HAS
COME TO ADDRESS SKY-HIGH DRUG PRICES 6 (Sept. 2015) (quoting Carroll, *supra* note
43); *see also* Avorn, *supra* note 43, at 1877–78; Light & Warburton, *supra* note 43, at 46.

48. *See* Stevens et al., *supra* note 23; *see also* Cockburn & Henderson, *supra* note 23; Andrew
A. Toole, *The Impact of Public Basic Research on Industrial Innovation; Evidence from the
Pharmaceutical Industry*, 41 RES. POL'Y 1 (2012). DiMasi and certain coauthors have published
work arguing that, based on case histories, the drug companies also have contributed to basic
research on an important scale. *See* Zycher et al., *supra* note 23.

49. See sources cited *supra* note 43.

50. *See* PHARM. RESEARCHERS & MFRS. AM. (PhRMA), *supra* note 38, at 47.

51. For discussion and citation to the relevant literature, *see* Michael Abramowicz, *Perfecting
Patent Prizes*, 56 VAND. L. REV. 115 (2003); Benjamin N. Roin, *Intellectual Property versus
Prizes: Reframing the Debate*, 81 U. CHI. L. REV. 999 (2014).

52. *See, e.g.*, THOMAS F. COTTER & JEFFREY D. HARRISON, LAW AND ECONOMICS: POSITIVE,
NORMATIVE AND BEHAVIORAL PERSPECTIVES 591–95 (3d ed. 2014).

53. In the UK, for example, the National Health Service decides which drugs the public health
system will make available and at what price based on its assessment of such factors as the
benefits of treatment and the drug company's need to recover its investment in R&D. *See*
U.K. DEP'T OF HEALTH, THE PHARMACEUTICAL PRICE REGULATION SCHEME 2014 (Dec.
2013), https://www.gov.uk/government/uploads/system/uploads/attachment_data/
file/282523/Pharmaceutical_Price_Regulation.pdf. Many other countries also take into
account the price charged for the drug in other comparable countries. For discussion of
various practices around the world, *see, e.g.*, ROSENTHAL, *supra* note 20, at 307–17; Penny
S. Bonner & Jill M. Daley, *Pharmaceutical Pricing and Reimbursement in Canada: An Overview
for Innovative Drug Manufacturers*, WHO'S WHO LEGAL (Feb. 2010), http://whoswholegal.
com/news/features/article/27744/pharmaceutical-pricing-reimbursement-canada-
overview-innovative-drug-manufacturers; Olga Khazan, *Why Medicine Is Cheaper in
Germany*, ATLANTIC (May 22, 2014), http://www.theatlantic.com/health/archive/
2014/05/why-medicine-is-cheaper-in-germany/371418/; Akane Takayama & Mamoru
Narakawa, *Pharmaceutical Pricing and Reimbursement in Japan: For Faster, More Complete
Access to New Drugs*, 50 THERAPEUTIC INNOV. & REG. SCI. 361 (2016). To the extent, if
any, that other countries *don't* fully compensate drug companies for undertaking risky R&D
and the United States does, the familiar assertion that US consumers "subsidize" foreign
consumers is accurate. The companion argument, however, that if only foreign countries
raised their prices, drug companies could lower the prices they charge US consumers, makes
no economic sense. Because FDA law generally prevents the large-scale importation of
drugs from a low-price country (such as Canada) to a high-price country (such as the United
States), the profit-maximizing price at which a drug is sold in the United States for the most
part doesn't depend on the price charged anywhere else. I return to the subject of importation in Chapter 7.

54. *See* Hannah Brennan et al., *A Prescription for Excessive Drug Pricing: Leveraging Government
Patent Use for Health*, 18 YALE J. L. & TECH. 275 (2016).

55. *See* Liyan Chen, *The Most Profitable Industries in 2016*, FORBES (Dec. 21, 2015, 4:19 PM),
http://www.forbes.com/sites/liyanchen/2015/12/21/the-most-profitable-industries-
in-2016/#202f45107a8b (asserting that, based on data provided by FactSet, "pharma generic" came in first with a 30 percent net margin projected for 2016, and "pharma major"
fourth at 24.6 percent); Liyan Chen, *Best of the Biggest: How Profitable Are the World's Largest*

Companies?, Forbes (May 13, 2014, 9:50 am), http://www.forbes.com/sites/liyanchen/ 2014/05/13/best-of-the-biggest-how-profitable-are-the-worlds-largest-companies/ #2b1e2f364c33 ("With an astounding 42 percent profit margin, Pfizer (No. 45) leads the top ten drug companies which have an average of 19 percent profit margin—the highest of all five industries"). *Cf.* F.M. Scherer, *The Pharmaceutical Industry—Prices and Progress*, 351 New Eng. J. Med. 927, 929 (2004) (stating that "there is an element of fallacy" in describing pharma as among the most profitable industries because outlays for R&D are in substance investments which should "be included in the company's assets and then depreciated over an appropriate time period. When they are not, the capital base to which profits are related in standard measures tends to be undervalued, and percentage returns on that capital base are overstated"). Scherer cites a 1993 study estimating that "the true returns on investment by the pharmaceutical industry during the 1980s were only 2 to 3 percent higher, on average, than 'normal' competitive rates of return, which were estimated to average roughly 10 percent" and states that "[w]hether the differential has remained within that range in recent years has not been tested by broadly accepted analyses." *Id.* at 929 & nn.19–21.

56. *See Pharmaceutical Marketing*, DrugWatch, https://www.drugwatch.com/manufacturer/ marketing/ (last modified Aug. 25, 2015); Michelle Llamas, *Selling Side Effects: Big Pharma's Marketing Machine*, DrugWatch, [https://web.archive.org/web/20160518074706/ https://www.drugwatch.com/manufacturer/marketing/]; Ana Swanson, *Big Pharmaceutical Companies Are Spending Far More on Marketing Than Research*, Wash. Post: Wonkblog (Feb. 11, 2015), https://www.washingtonpost.com/news/wonk/wp/2015/02/11/big- pharmaceutical-companies-are-spending-far-more-on-marketing-than-research/; *see also* Gretchen Morgenstern, *Big Pharma Spends on Share Buybacks, but R&D? Not So Much*, N. Y. Times, July 14, 2017, https://www.nytimes.com/2017/07/14/business/big-pharma- spends-on-share-buybacks-but-rd-not-so-much.html?mcubz=2&_r=0.

57. *See* Brennan et al., *supra* note 54, at 326–30.

58. *See, e.g.*, Merrill Goozner, The $800 Million Pill: The Truth Behind the Cost of New Drugs 241–43 (2004); Light & Warburton, *supra* note 43, at 37 (pointing out that, perversely, the cost of conducting clinical trials for drugs that offer few advantages over alternatives may be higher than the cost for breakthrough drugs because the former trials may need to study very large populations in order to tease out statistically significant correlations of comparative effectiveness). *Contra* Joseph A. DiMasi & Laura B. Faden, *Competitiveness in Follow-On Drug R&D: A Race or Imitation?*, 10 Nature Revs.: Drug Discovery 23 (2011) (arguing that most me-too drugs are the result of patent races, not imitation); Henry I. Miller, *Critics of 'Me-Too Drugs' Need to Take a Chill Pill*, Wall St. J. (Jan. 1, 2014, 5:13 pm), http://online.wsj.com/news/articles/SB10001424052702303293 604579256263038269796.

59. *See* Brennan, *supra* note 54, at 319 n.211.

60. Nonobviousness, in other words, is only loosely tied to any concept of social value, and while this might seem like a defect of the patent system generally, it's hardly obvious (no pun in- tended) how patent examiners could predict, far in advance of any clinical studies, what the social value of an invention eventually will turn out to be. Requiring that examination be deferred until after the completion of clinical studies seems unworkable as well, not only be- cause it would require significant changes to the patent statute's definition of "prior art," but also because, as Ben Roin notes, drug companies are reluctant to go forward with clinical testing until they have a patent in hand. *See* Benjamin N. Roin, *Unpatentable Drugs and the Standards of Patentability*, 87 Tex. L. Rev. 503, 536–39 (2009).

61. *See, e.g., Ariad Pharm., Inc. v. Eli Lilly & Co.*, 598 F.3d 1336, 1345–48 (Fed. Cir. 2010) (en banc).

62. *See* 35 U.S.C. § 287(c) (2012).

63. *See, e.g., Sun Pharm. Indus. v. Eli Lilly & Co.*, 611 F.3d 1381, 1384–85 (Fed. Cir. 2010).

64. *See Schering Corp. v. Geneva Pharm., Inc.*, 339 F.3d 1373, 1379 (Fed. Cir. 2003) ("In general, a limitation or the entire invention is inherent and in the public domain if it is the 'natural result flowing from' the explicit disclosure of the prior art").

65. For discussion, *see* Mark A. Lemley & Kimberly A. Moore, *Ending Abuse of Patent Continuations*, 84 B. U. L. Rev. 63, 81–83 (2004).

66. For discussion of the concept of "bioequivalence" with regard to small-molecule compounds, *see FDA Ensures Equivalence of Generic Drugs*, U.S. Food & Drug Admin. (Aug. 2002), http://www.fda.gov/Drugs/EmergencyPreparedness/BioterrorismandDrugPreparedness/ucm134444.htm:

     One way scientists demonstrate bioequivalence is to measure the time it takes the generic drug to reach the bloodstream and its concentration in the bloodstream in 24 to 36 healthy, normal volunteers. This gives them the rate and extent of absorption—or bioavailability—of the generic drug, which they then compare to that of the pioneer drug. The generic version must deliver the same amount of active ingredients into a patient's bloodstream in the same amount of time as the pioneer drug.

67. *See* 21 U.S.C. § 355(j)(5)(F)(ii) (2012).
68. *See, e.g.*, 21 U.S.C. 355(j)(2)(A)(vii) (required certifications with regard to patent holders); 21 U.S.C. 355(j)(5)(B)(iv) (180-day exclusivity period).
69. Although you might expect that requiring the patent owner to provide an enabling disclosure of its invention would overcome the challenges of producing biosimilars, in practice, the enabling disclosure isn't sufficient to enable easy reproduction of the specific biologic product for which the owner obtains FDA marketing approval. For discussion, *see* W. Nicholson Price II & Arti Rai, *Manufacturing Barriers to Biologics Competition and Innovation*, 101 Iowa L. Rev. 1023 (2016).
70. *See* U.S. Food & Drug Admin., Off. of Generic Drugs, 2016 OGD Annual Report https://www.fda.gov/downloads/Drugs/DevelopmentApprovalProcess/HowDrugsareDevelopedandApproved/ApprovalApplications/AbbreviatedNewDrugApplicationANDAGenerics/UCM542929.pdf.
71. 15 U.S.C. §§ 1, 2.
72. For recent discussion and citation to sources, *see* Caleb Nelson, *The Legitimacy of (Some) Federal Common Law*, 101 Va. L. Rev. 1, 45–48 (2015).
73. *See Bus. Elecs. Corp. v. Sharp Elecs. Corp.*, 485 U.S. 717, 732 (1988) ("The Sherman Act adopted the term 'restraint of trade' along with its dynamic potential. It invokes the common law itself, and not merely the static content that the common law had assigned to the term in 1890.") (Scalia, J.).
74. *United States v. Grinnell Corp.*, 384 U.S. 563, 570–71 (1966).
75. Though, as of 2017, calls for a more "populist" approach to antitrust seem to be increasing. For critical discussion, *see* D. Daniel Sokol, *A Better Deal for Antitrust?*, Antitrust & Comp. Pol'y Blog, July 25, 2017, http://lawprofessors.typepad.com/antitrustprof_blog/2017/07/a-better-deal-for-antitrust.html.
76. *Grinnell Corp.*, 384 U.S. at 571.
77. *See* Willard K. Tom & Joshua A. Newberg, *Antitrust and Intellectual Property: From Separate Spheres to Unified Field*, 66 Antitrust L. J. 167, 178–84 (1997).
78. U.S. Dep't of Justice & Fed. Trade Comm'n, Antitrust Guidelines for the Licensing of Intellectual Property § 2.1 (2017).
79. *See* 35 U.S.C. § 271(e)(1) (2012).
80. *See id.* § 271(e)(2).
81. *See* Chris Barry et al., PwC, 2017 Patent Litigation Study: Change on the Horizon? 7.
82. *See* AIPLA, 2017 Report of the Economic Survey I-128; *see also id.* at 42 (reporting medians of $500,000 and $1.1 million, respectively, considerably less than in 2013 and 2015). The small sample size may have something to do with the variation over time.
83. If the generic firm started selling infringing products before the conclusion of trial, of course, the brand-name would be entitled to damages for these infringing sales. Nevertheless, one reason sometimes cited in defense of reverse-payment settlements is that the brand-name firm might not be able to collect from the generic firm, maybe because the latter declares bankruptcy or is otherwise able to shield its assets. In fact, though, the generic drug industry came in first in Forbes's most recent listing of most profitable industries, see sources cited *supra* note 55, though presumably some generic firms are in better shape than others.

84. For further discussion on this point, *see* Thomas F. Cotter, *Antitrust Implications of Patent Settlements Involving Reverse Payments: Defending a Rebuttable Presumption of Illegality in Light of Some Recent Scholarship*, 71 Antitrust L. J. 1069 (2004). There's also the argument that reverse-payment settlements aren't really that unusual, because, even in the more commonplace situation where the defendant pays the plaintiff to settle litigation, the plaintiff is giving something up—say, the chance of recovering $10 million instead of the $7 million the defendant is willing to pay in settlement. What arguably makes reverse-payment settlements of ANDA litigation different, though, is that the plaintiff is bestowing upon the defendant a benefit it wouldn't have enjoyed if the defendant had won at trial. *See* Michael A. Carrier, *Payment After* Actavis, 100 Iowa L. Rev. 7, 26 (2014).

85. *See* Aaron Edlin et al., *Activating* Actavis, 28 Antitrust, Fall 2013, at 16, 20; Aaron Edlin et al., Actavis *and Error Costs—A Reply to Critics*, 14 Antitrust Source, Oct. 2014, at 4, http://www.crai.co.uk/sites/default/files/publications/Actavis-and-error-costs-a-reply-to-critics.pdf.

86. *See* Fed. Trade Comm'n, Bureau of Competition, Agreements Filed with the Federal Trade Commission under the Medicare Prescription Drug, Improvement, and Modernization Act of 2003: Overview of Agreements Filed in FY 2014: A Report by the Bureau of Competition, exhibit 1 (2016), https://www.ftc.gov/system/files/documents/reports/agreements-filled-federal-trade-commission-under-medicare-prescription-drug-improvement/160113mmafy14rpt.pdf.

87. *See* C. Scott Hemphill & Bhaven N. Sampat, *Drug Patents at the Supreme Court*, 339 Sci. 1386, 1387 (2013); C. Scott Hemphill & Bhaven N. Sampat, *When Do Generics Challenge Drug Patents?*, 8 J. Empirical Legal Stud. 613, 643 (2011); *see also* Fed. Trade Comm'n, Generic Drug Entry Prior to Patent Expiration: An FTC Study 13, 16 & n.8 (2002), http://www.ftc.gov/sites/default/files/documents/reports/generic-drug-entry-prior-patent-expiration-ftc-study/genericdrugstudy_0.pdf (reporting that, when ANDA litigation was pursued to judgment, "generic applicants prevailed in 73 percent of the cases (22 out of 30), and brand-name companies prevailed 27 percent of the time (8 out of 30)").

88. *FTC v. Actavis, Inc.*, 133 S. Ct. 2223, 2226 (2013).

89. *Id.* at 2236–37.

90. *Id.* at 2236.

91. *See In re Loestrin 24 Fe Antitrust Litigation*, 814 F.3d 538 (1st Cir. 2016); *King Drug Co. v. SmithKline Beecham*, 791 F.3d 388 (3d Cir. 2015).

92. *See* Fed. Trade Comm'n, Pay-for-Delay: How Drug Company Pay-Offs Cost Consumers Billions 2 (2010), http://www.ftc.gov/sites/default/files/documents/reports/pay-delay-how-drug-company-pay-offs-cost-consumers-billions-federal-trade-commission-staff-study/100112payfordelayrpt.pdf.

93. *See Abbott Labs. v. Teva Pharmaceuticals USA, Inc.*, 432 F. Supp.2d 408 (D. Del. 2006).

94. *See New York ex rel. Schneiderman v. Actavis PLC*, 787 F.3d 638 (2d Cir. 2015), *cert. dismissed*, 136 S. Ct. 581 (Mem) (2015). Not all the cases have been favorable to the antitrust plaintiffs, however. In *Mylan Pharms. Inc. v. Warner Chilcot Public Ltd. Co.*, 838 F.3d 421 (3d Cir. 2016), for example, the court affirmed a judgment in favor of the defendants, who had engaged in a pattern of substituting different forms of an acne medication, based on evidence that the defendants (1) lacked market power, given the availability of substitute medications; and (2) had not engaged in anticompetitive conduct, given among other matters problems with earlier versions of their product. For a critique, *see* Michael A. Carrier & Steve D. Shadowen, *Product Hopping: A New Framework*, 92 Notre Dame L. Rev. 167, 196–98 (2016).

95. For a recent paper expressing this view, and arguing that a better response to product hopping is to reform the Hatch-Waxman Act, *see* Dennis Carlton et al., *A Critical Evaluation of the FTC's Theory of Product Hopping as a Way to Promote Competition* (July 8, 2016) (unpublished paper) (available at http://ssrn.com/abstract=2808822).

96. *See* Carrier & Minniti, *supra* note 22. In another paper, Carrier, Levidow, and Kesselheim argue that Turing's change to a restricted distribution system, which made it more difficult for potential competitors to obtain samples of the drug for bioequivalence studies, may have

violated antitrust law. *See* Michael Carrier et al., *Using Antitrust Law to Challenge Turing's Daraprim Price Increase*, 31 BERKELEY TECH. L. J. 1379 (2017).

97. *See* U.S. GOV'T ACCOUNTABILITY OFFICE, GAO-10-201, BRAND-NAME PRESCRIPTION DRUG PRICING: LACK OF THERAPEUTICALLY EQUIVALENT DRUGS AND LIMITED COMPETITION MAY CONTRIBUTE TO EXTRAORDINARY PRICE INCREASES 18 (2009). More recently, the GAO has noted the possibility that consolidation in the generic drug industry may be contributing to increases in the price of some generic drugs. *See* U.S. GOV'T ACCOUNTABILITY OFFICE, GAO-16-706, GENERIC DRUGS UNDER MEDICARE: PART D GENERIC DRUG PRICES DECLINED OVERALL, BUT SOME HAD EXTRAORDINARY PRICE INCREASES 24 (2016). More recently still, the Department of Justice has been investigating alleged price fixing with regard to certain generic drugs. *See* Tom Schoenberg et al., *U.S. Generic Drug Probe Seen Expanding After Guilty Pleas*, BLOOMBERG.COM, Dec. 14, 2016, https://www.bloomberg.com/news/articles/2016-12-14/u-s-files-first-charges-in-generic-drug-price-fixing-probe.

98. *See, e.g.*, Carrier & Minniti, *supra* note 22; Robin Feldman et al., *Empirical Evidence of Drug Pricing Games—A Citizen's Pathway Gone Astray*, 20 STANFORD TECH. L. REV. 39 (2017).

99. *See* Prof'l Real Estate Inv'rs, Inc. v. Columbia Pictures Indus., 508 U.S. 49 (1993).

100. *See* 15 U.S.C. §§ 18, 18a (2012).

101. *See* WILLIAM B. VOGT & ROBERT TOWN, ROBERT WOOD JOHNSON FOUND., HOW HAS HOSPITAL CONSOLIDATION AFFECTED THE PRICE AND QUALITY OF HOSPITAL CARE? 1 (2006), http://www.rwjf.org/en/library/research/2006/02/how-has-hospital-consolidation-affected-the-price-and-quality-of.html ("By the mid-1990s, hospital merger and acquisition activity was nine times its level at the start of the decade."); Kate Pickert, *Fewer Hospitals May Lead to Higher Prices*, TIME (July 23, 2013), http://swampland.time.com/2013/07/23/fewer-hospitals-may-lead-to-higher-prices/ (citing data provided by Professor Martin Gaynor and from the American Hospital Association).

102. *See* Cory Capps & David Dranove, *Market Concentration of Hospitals*, AHIP COVERAGE 2 (June 2011).

103. *See* CORY CAPPS, FEDERAL HEALTH PLAN MERGER ENFORCEMENT IS CONSISTENT AND ROBUST 36 (2009) http://www.bateswhite.com/media/pnc/7/media.227.pdf (America's Health Insurance Plans' public comment submitted to the Department of Justice and the Federal Trade Commission on the Horizontal Merger Guidelines Review Project); Mark E. Rust, *From HCQIA to ACA: The 180° Arc of Provider Antitrust Concerns in Healthcare Over 25 Years*, 33 J. LEG. MED. 21, 29–30 (2012).

104. *See* Thomas L. Greaney, *Chicago's Procrustean Bed: Applying Antitrust Law in Health Care*, 73 ANTITRUST L. J. 857, 858–59 (2004) ("Chicago [School]'s tendency to brush over market imperfections in health care often causes tribunals to miss important features of health care markets and misjudge the impact of antitrust claims").

105. VOGT & TOWN, *supra* note 101, at 4.

106. *See* MARTIN GAYNOR & ROBERT TOWN, ROBERT WOOD JOHNSON FOUND., THE IMPACT OF HOSPITAL CONSOLIDATION—UPDATE (June 2012), www.rwjf.org/content/dam/farm/reports/issue_briefs/2012/rwjf73261. For example, one of the studies Gaynor and Town reviewed, Deborah Haas-Wilson and Christopher Garmon's *Hospital Mergers and Competitive Effects: Two Retrospective Analyses*, 18 INT'L J. ECON. BUS. 17 (2011), concluded that a 2000 merger of two suburban Chicago entities, Evanston Northwestern Healthcare Corporation and Highland Park Hospital, allowed the merged entity to charge significantly higher prices than would have been possible absent the merger; Haas-Wilson and Garmon further concluded that the merger did not result in the merged entity accepting significantly more complicated cases or improving quality, either of which could provide an alternative explanation for the increase in price. (They also reported that another merger occurring at about the same time in Waukegan, Illinois, did not exhibit these price effects.) More recently, Dafny et al. report that, based on their study of hospital mergers across geographic markets, "hospitals gaining system members in-state (but not in the same geographic market) experience price increases of 7–10 percent relative to control hospitals...." Leemore Dafny et al., *The Price Effects of Cross-Market Hospital Mergers* 3 (Nat'l Bureu of Econ. Research Working Paper No. 22106, 2016). In a similar vein, Matthew Lewis and

Kevin Pflum report, based on "data on out-of-market acquisitions occurring across the US from 2000–2010," that "prices at hospitals acquired by out-of-market systems increase by about 17 percent more than unacquired, stand-alone hospitals," while "the prices of nearby competitors to acquired hospitals increase by around 8 percent." Matthew S. Lewis & Kevin E. Pflum, *Hospital Systems and Bargaining Power: Evidence from Out-of-Market Acquisitions,* 22 RAND J. ECON. 691 (2016).

107. *See* Gregory Curfman, *Everywhere, Hospitals Are Merging—But Why Should You Care?,* HARV. HEALTH BLOG (Apr. 1, 2015, 5:00 PM), http://www.health.harvard.edu/blog/everywhere-hospitals-are-merging-but-why-should-you-care-201504017844 (reporting ninety-eight hospital mergers in 2013 and ninety-five in 2014); Kaufman Hall, *Hospital Merger and Acquisition Activity Continues Upward Momentum, According to Kaufman Hall Analysis,* https://www.kaufmanhall.com/news/hospital-merger-and-acquisition-activity-continues-upward-momentum-according-kaufman-hall (112 in 2015, 102 in 2016).

108. *See* Roger Feldman, *Antitrust Policy in Health Care, in* INSTITUTE OF MEDICINE OF THE NATIONAL ACADEMIES, THE HEALTH CARE IMPERATIVE: LOWERING COSTS AND IMPROVING OUTCOMES: WORKSHOP SERIES SUMMARY 314–19 (Pierre L. Yong et al. eds. 2010).

Another practice that arguably works to shield hospitals from competition are the certificate-of-need (CON) laws in force in thirty-six states and the District of Columbia. Although the evidence is mixed, economists have argued that these laws work to the advantage of incumbent hospitals by imposing barriers to entry in the construction of new facilities. *See* U.S. DEP'T OF JUSTICE & FED. TRADE COMM'N, IMPROVING HEALTH CARE: A DOSE OF COMPETITION 22 (2004). For more recent work, *see, e.g.,* Traci L. Eichmann & Rexford E. Santerre, *Do Hospital Chief Executive Officers Extract Rents from Certificate of Need Laws?,* 37 J. HEALTH CARE FIN. 1, 2, 12 (2011); Maureen K. Ohlhausen, *Certificate of Need Laws: A Prescription for Higher Costs,* 30 ANTITRUST 50 (2015); *see also* TRACY YEE ET AL., HEALTH CARE CERTIFICATE-OF-NEED LAWS: POLICY OR POLITICS? NAT. INST. FOR HEALTH CARE REFORM RES. BRIEF NO. 4 at 2 (2011) (although the evidence of the effect of CONs on health care costs has been inconclusive, the process of obtaining a CON "often takes several years," and CONs "tend to be heavily influenced by political relationships").

109. *See* Ctrs. for Medicare & Medicaid Servs. *Medicare Provider Charge Data,* CMS.GOV, http://www.cms.gov/Research-Statistics-Data-and-Systems/Statistics-Trends-and-Reports/Medicare-Provider-Charge-Data/ (last modified Nov. 11, 2016, 11:12 AM); Dan Munro, *Healthcare's Story of the Year for 2013: Pricing Transparency,* FORBES (Dec. 15, 2013),http://www.forbes.com/sites/danmunro/2013/12/15/healthcares-story-of-the-year-for-2013-pricing-transparency/ (noting a similar effort in New York). Until recently, only California made such information public. *See* Jaime A. Rosenthal et al., *Availability of Consumer Prices from U.S. Hospitals for a Common Surgical Procedure,* 173 JAMA INTERNAL MED. 427 (2013) (reporting that "[n]ine top-ranked hospitals (45 percent) and 10 non–top-ranked hospitals (10 percent) were able to provide a complete bundled price" for a common procedure, total hip arthroplasty (THA) and that "[t]he range of complete prices was wide for both top-ranked ($12,500–$105,000) and non–top-ranked hospitals ($11,100-$125,798)").

110. *See* Medicare, Medicaid, *Children's Health Insurance Programs; Transparency Reports and Reporting of Physician Ownership or Investment Interests,* 78 FED. REG. 9458 (Feb. 8, 2013) (codified at 42 C.F.R. pts. 402 and 403) (requiring affected groups to report their data by March 31, 2014). For discussion, *see, e.g.,* Nicole Fisher, *The Sunshine Act Is Finally Final,* FORBES (Feb. 11, 2013, 9:49 AM), http://www.forbes.com/sites/aroy/2013/02/11/the-sunshine-act-is-finally-final/#2c1b4f9565b0. In December 2013, GlaxoSmithKline announced that it would voluntarily cease paying doctors to promote its drugs. *See* Jonathan D. Rockoff & Hester Plumridge, *Drug Firms Curb Ties to Doctors,* WALL ST. J. (Dec. 18, 2013, 7:09 PM), http://www.wsj.com/articles/SB10001424052702304858104579263640414302348.

111. Steven Brill, *Bitter Pill: Why Medical Bills Are Killing Us,* TIME, Mar. 4, 2013, at 16, 34.

112. U.S. GOV'T ACCOUNTABILITY OFFICE, GAO-12-126, MEDICARE: LACK OF PRICE TRANSPARENCY MAY HAMPER HOSPITALS' ABILITY TO BE PRUDENT PURCHASERS OF IMPLANTABLE MEDICAL DEVICES 29 (2012).

113. *See* Rosenthal, *supra* note 20, at 175–77; *see also id.* at 190–92 (discussing pricing transparency).
114. *See* Josh Cothran, *US Health Care: Who Pays?*, Cal. Health Care Found. (Dec. 2015), http://www.chcf.org/publications/2015/12/data-viz-hcc-national (showing the percentages of various health care costs that are paid out-of-pocket and that are funded by private or public insurers or other payors); Scherer, *supra* note 55, at 928–29.
115. Abhijit Banerjee & Esther Duflo, Poor Economics: A Radical Rethinking of the Way to Fight Global Poverty 148 (Public Affairs 2011).
116. *See* William Fleischman et al., *Association Between Payments from Manufacturers of Pharmaceuticals to Physicians and Regional Prescribing: Cross Sectional Ecological Study*, 354 BMJ 1 (2016).
117. *See* Brennan et al., *supra* note 54, at 285 ("Healthcare payors are often statutorily required to cover new drugs. For example, state Medicaid programs must cover drugs offered by any manufacturer that enters into a rebate agreement with the federal government . . . . Medicare Part D Plans, as well as private health insurance plans serving the individual and small group markets, have more leeway, but they still must cover a minimum number of drugs in each category and class . . . . Public programs and private payors receiving federal funds are also subject to nondiscrimination requirements that may limit their latitude to create restrictive formularies"); Bach, *supra* note 4. *See also* Rosenthal, *supra* note 20, at 20, 221–22 (arguing that private insurers often do not have an adequate incentive to negotiate for lower prices). Insurers sometimes have argued that they'd have more leverage negotiating prices if they were allowed to bargain collectively or to merge, but the courts so far haven't been persuaded. In 2017, the DOJ successfully blocked two proposed mergers between major health insurers, one between Anthem and Cigna and another between Humana and Aetna.
118. *See* 42 U.S.C. §§ 1395l(t)(14)(A)(iii), 1395w-111(i). For criticism, *see, e.g.*, Brill, *supra* note 111, at 46; *Medicare: A Plan B for Part D*, L. A. Times (Dec. 21, 2012), http://articles.latimes.com/2012/dec/21/opinion/la-ed-medicare-prescription-drug-negotiated-prices-20121221 (noting, *inter alia*, that the Veteran's Administration, unlike Medicare, is allowed to bargain).
119. *See* Nat'l Comm'n on Physician Payment Reform, Report of the National Commission on Physician Payment Reform 7–8, 11–12, 15–16, 18–19 (Mar. 2013) [hereinafter Payment Reform], http://physicianpaymentcommission.org/report/ ; *see also* Rosenthal, *supra* note 20, at 34–39 (discussing strategic billing).
120. *See* 26 U.S.C. § 5000a (2012).
121. *See, e.g.*, Henry J. Aaron, *How to Rescue Obamacare As Insurers Drop Out*, Wash. Post (Aug. 19, 2016), https://www.washingtonpost.com/opinions/how-to-rescue-obamacare-as-insurers-drop-out/2016/08/19/edb038b2-6641-11e6-be4e-23fc4d4d12b4_story.html?utm_term=.893b682fd4cf.
122. For discussion, *see, e.g.*, Nancy Folbre, *The Single-Payer Alternative*, N. Y. Times (Nov. 25, 2013, 12:01 am), http://economix.blogs.nytimes.com/2013/11/25/the-single-payer-alternative/; Robert H. Frank, *Why Single Payer Health Care Saves Money*, N. Y. Times, July 7, 2017, https://www.nytimes.com/2017/07/07/upshot/why-single-payer-health-care-saves-money.html?mcubz=2; Sanjoy Mahajan, *Transaction Costs: The American Way*, Freakonomics: Blog (Nov. 12, 2013, 12:02 pm), http://freakonomics.com/2013/11/12/transaction-costs-the-american-way/; Uwe E. Reinhardt, *Waste vs. Value in American Health Care*, N. Y. Times (Sept. 13, 2013, 12:01 am), http://economix.blogs.nytimes.com/2013/09/13/waste-vs-value-in-american-health-care/; *see also* Payment Reform, *supra* note 115, at 8 (stating that "[a]lthough Medicare's administrative costs are only 2 percent, those of private insurance companies and health plans routinely reach 13 percent or more").
123. For discussion and citations to the relevant statutory provisions, *see* Robin Feldman, *Regulatory Property: The New IP*, 40 Colum. J. L. & Arts 53 (2016); John R. Thomas, *The End of "Patent Medicines"? Thoughts on the Rise of Regulatory Exclusivities*, 70 Food & Drug L. J. 39 (2015).
124. *See* Goldacre, *supra* note 37, at 57; Feldman, *supra* note 123, at 78–79.
125. For discussion, *see, e.g.*, Feldman, *supra* note 123, at 92–93; Michael Hiltzik, *The Little-Known FDA Program That's Driving Drug Prices Higher*, L. A. Times, Sept. 23, 2015, http://www.

latimes.com/business/hiltzik/la-fi-mh-the-little-known-fda-program-20150923-column. html; Aaron S. Kesselheim & Daniel H. Solomon, *Incentives for Drug Development—The Curious Case of Colchicine*, 362 New Eng. J. Med. 1484 (2010); Thomas, *supra* note 123, at 44; Ryan M. Mott, *Colchicine, Guaifenesin, and the Constitutionality of FDA Market Exclusivity for Approval Pioneers* (Mar. 19, 2012) (unpublished paper), https://works.bepress.com/ ryan_mott/1/.

126. For discussion, *see, e.g.*, Rosenthal, *supra* note 20, at 93, 99, 101–04, 312, 315–17; Goldacre, *supra* note 37, at 130; Steven Grossman, *FDA Should Consider Cost in Some Decisions*, The Health Care Blog (Oct. 5, 2011), http://thehealthcareblog.com/blog/ 2011/10/05/fda-should-consider-cost-in-some-decisions/ (arguing that "FDA . . . plays a role (however unintentionally) in exacerbating the crisis in affordable cancer care" and that it "may need to find ways to favor less effective or riskier products only because they can be made available at a market-driven price").

127. *See, e.g.*, Scott Alexander, *Reverse Voxsplaining: Drugs vs. Chairs*, Slate Star Codex (Aug. 29, 2016), http://slatestarcodex.com/2016/08/29/reverse-voxsplaining-drugs-vs-chairs/; Greg Ip, *A Cure for Swelling Drug Prices: Competition*, Wall St. J. (Aug. 31, 2016, 2:06 pm), http://www.wsj.com/articles/a-cure-for-swelling-drug-prices-competition-1472662484.

128. *See, e.g.*, Rosenthal, *supra* note 20, at 89, 132–33; Conor Friedsdorf, *Ted Cruz's Best Idea for Overhauling the FDA*, Atlantic (Dec. 18, 2015), http://www.theatlantic.com/politics/ archive/2015/12/ted-cruzs-best-idea-for-overhauling-the-fda/421158/ and sources cited *supra* note 127. The recently enacted 21st Century Cures Act, which among other things increases federal funding for the NIH, doesn't go this far but it does permit the FDA to consider "real world evidence," defined as "data regarding the usage, or the potential benefits or risks, of a drug derived from sources other than clinical trials," in deciding whether to approve a new drug. H.R. 34, 114th Cong., 2d Sess.§ 3022 (enacted Dec. 13, 2016).

129. *See* Center for Responsive Politics, *Influence & Lobbying: Health*, OpenSecrets.org, http://www.opensecrets.org/lobby/indus.php?id=H&year=2016.

130. *See Sorrell v. IMS Health Inc.*, 564 U.S. 552 (2011).

131. *See Thompson v. Western States Med. Center*, 535 U.S. 357 (2002).

132. *See* 21 C.F.R. § 202.1 (2014) (regulations relating to prescription drug advertising); U.S. Food & Drug Admin., Guidance for Industry: Consumer-Directed Broadcast Advertisements (2002), http://www.fda.gov/RegulatoryInformation/Guidances/ ucm125039.htm.

133. For views on the legality of restrictions on drug advertising, *see* Symposium, *Commercial Speech and Public Health*, 21 HealthMatrix: J. L. & Med. 1, 7–189 (2011). According to the World Health Organization, the only other country in the world that permits direct-to-consumer drug advertising is New Zealand. *See* Gary Humphreys, *Direct-to-Consumer Advertising Under Fire*, 87 Bull. World. Health Org. 576, 576 (2009). For one recent controversy, *see* Alan Schwarz, *The Selling of Attention Deficit Disorder*, N. Y. Times, Dec. 15, 2013, at A1 (noting that "The rise of A.D.H.D. diagnoses and prescriptions for stimulants over the years coincided with a remarkably successful two-decade campaign by pharmaceutical companies to publicize the syndrome and promote the pills to doctors, educators and parents," resulting in a level of diagnosis that one researcher describes as "unprecedented and unjustifiable").

    On the other hand, one reform often championed by the political right—tort reform, such as the adoption of damages caps—doesn't appear to have a major impact on reducing health care costs, according to some studies. For a review of the empirical evidence and an argument that reform of liability standards, as opposed to policies such as damages caps, could have an impact on controlling costs, *see* Michael Frakes, *The Surprising Relevant of Medical Malpractice Law*, 82 U. Chi. L. Rev. 317 (2015). I'm also skeptical about another proposal championed by the right, namely permitting the sale of health insurance policies across state lines on the grounds (among others) that it wouldn't affect the majority of policies; that insurers aren't showing much interest in exploiting the existing opportunities to sell across state lines permitted under the ACA; and that, if such sales became common, they would threaten a "race to the bottom" among insurers. For discussion, *see, e.g.*, Michael Hiltzik, *Selling Health Insurance Across State Lines Is a Favorite GOP 'Reform.' Here's Why It Makes*

No Sense, L. A. TIMES, Nov. 14, 2016, www.latimes.com/business/hiltzik/la-fi-hiltzik-insurance-state-lines-20161114-story.html; Bruce Japsen, *Sorry, Trump: Selling Health Insurance Across State Lines Wouldn't Lower Costs*, FORBES, Oct. 10, 2016, http://www.forbes.com/sites/brucejapsen/2016/10/10/sorry-trump-selling-health-insurance-across-state-lines-wouldnt-lower-costs/; Margot Sanger-Katz, *The Problem with G.O.P. Plans to Sell Health Insurance Across State Lines*, N. Y. TIMES, Aug. 31, 2015, http://www.nytimes.com/2015/09/01/upshot/the-problem-with-gop-plans-to-sell-health-insurance-across-state-lines.html.

134. *See* Alexander Lane, *Obama Invokes Republican Icons on Health Care*, POLITIFACT (Mar. 5, 2009, 6:39 PM), http://www.politifact.com/truth-o-meter/statements/2009/mar/05/barack-obama/Obama-goes-back-to-his-Republican-roots-on-health-/ (substantiating the claim that Roosevelt championed a national health care program).

135. *See* F.A. HAYEK, THE ROAD TO SERFDOM 125 (University of Chicago Press, 50th anniv. ed. 1994) [1944]:

> Where, as in the case of sickness and accident, neither the desire to avoid such calamities nor the efforts to overcome their consequences are as a rule weakened by the provision of assistance—where, in short, we deal with genuinely insurable risks—the case for the state's helping to organize a comprehensive system of social insurance is very strong. There are many points of detail where those wishing to preserve the competitive system and those wishing to supercede it by something different will disagree on the details of such schemes; and it is possible under the name of social insurance to introduce measures which tend to make competition more or less ineffective. But there is no incompatibility in principle between the state's providing greater security in this way and the preservation of individual freedom.

136. For details on such an alternative approach, *see* JAY BHATTACHARYA ET AL., BEST OF BOTH WORLDS: UNITING UNIVERSAL COVERAGE AND PERSONAL CHOICE IN HEALTH CARE 33 (2013), http://www.aei.org/papers/health/healthcare-reform/best-of-both-worlds-report/ (proposing a move away from reliance on group plans in favor of portable, long-term individual policies, coupled with a subsidy for the poor to buy such policies); John H. Cochrane, *What to Do When ObamaCare Unravels*, WALL ST. J. (Dec. 25, 2013, 3:51 PM), http://online.wsj.com/news/articles/SB10001424052702304866904579265932490593594 (similar).

Chapter 7

1. *See* Louis J. Hoffman, *Countries in Which the Patent Cooperation Treaty (PCT) Does Not Apply*, HOFFMAN PATENT FIRM (Feb. 24, 2015), http://www.valuablepatents.com/non-pct-countries/. Hoffman asserts that eleven countries had no patent laws in force as of 2015, but of these four (Afghanistan, Maldives, Myanmar, and Vanuatu) are WTO members (Afghanistan only since July 2016). For reasons discussed later in this chapter, as a result of their WTO membership, these four should have functioning patent systems in place soon, if they don't already.

2. Of course, even when there is a domestic patent system, inventors in small countries may have a robust incentive to obtain patents in larger markets. For discussion, *see* Jonathan Barnett, *Patent Tigers: The New Geography of Global Innovation* (Sept. 22, 2016) (unpublished paper), http://papers.ssrn.com/abstract=2842350 (arguing that the US patent system has supported innovation in emerging market economies such as Taiwan and Israel).

3. Petra Moser, *Patents and Innovation: Evidence from Economic History*, 27 J. ECON. PERSP. 23, 25 (2013) (citing ERIC SCHIFF, INDUSTRIALIZATION WITHOUT NATIONAL PATENTS: THE NETHERLANDS 1868–1912; SWITZERLAND 1850–1907 (Princeton University Press 1971)).

4. *See id.* at 30–31; Petra Moser, *How Do Patent Laws Influence Innovation? Evidence from Nineteenth-Century World's Fairs*, 95 AM. ECON. REV. 1214, 1221 (2005).

5. On this last point, *see, e.g.*, Alan O. Sykes, *TRIPs, Pharmaceuticals, Developing Countries, and the Doha "Solution"*, 3 CHI. J. INT'L L. 47 (2002).

6. Lee Branstetter et al., *Do Stronger Intellectual Property Rights Increase International Technology Transfer? Empirical Evidence from US Firm-Level Data*, 12 Q. J. ECON. 321 (2006). For other

studies or reports in this vein, *see, e.g.,* Mercedes Delgado et al., *Intellectual Property Protection and the Geography of Trade,* 3 J. INDUS. ECON. 733 (2006) (finding increased trade flows in IP-intensive sectors following the domestic implementation of international IP treaty provisions); Richard C. Levin et al., *Appropriating the Returns from Industrial Research and Development,* 18 BROOKINGS PAPERS ON ECONOMIC ACTIVITY 783, 798 (1987) (stating that "[s]ome developing countries require, as a condition of entry, that US firms license technology to a host-country firm, and some patents are filed primarily to permit such licensing").

7. *See* Albert G. Z. Hu & I. P. L. Png, *Patent Rights and Economic Growth: Evidence from Cross-Country Panels of Manufacturing Industries,* 65 OXFORD ECON. PAPERS 675 (2013).

8. *See* Margaret Kyle & Yi Qian, *Intellectual Property Rights and Access to Innovation: Evidence from TRIPs* (Nat'l Bureau of Econ. Res., Working Paper No. 20799, 2014), http://www.nber.org/papers/w20799.

9. Yi Qian, *Do National Patent Laws Stimulate Domestic Innovation in a Global Patenting Environment? A Cross-Country Analysis of Pharmaceutical Patent Protection, 1978–2002,* 89 REV. ECON. & STATS. 436 (2007). *See also* Iain Cockburn et al., *Patents and the Global Diffusion of New Drugs,* CEP DISCUSSION PAPER NO. 1298 (Sept., 2014) (based on a study of 642 new drugs in seventy-six countries from 1983 to 2002, concluding that patents, along with other institutional factors, accelerated the introduction of new drugs into developing countries).

10. *See* Daniel Gervais, *TRIPS and Development, in* INTELLECTUAL PROPERTY, TRADE, AND DEVELOPMENT: STRATEGIES TO OPTIMIZE DEVELOPMENT IN A TRIPs-PLUS ERA 3, 33 (Daniel J. Gervais, ed., Oxford University Press 2007) (concluding that "sufficient IP protection is an essential component of increased inward FDI and trade flows in IP-sensitive goods for countries above a certain economic development threshold"); KEITH E. MASKUS, INTELLECTUAL PROPERTY RIGHTS IN THE GLOBAL ECONOMY 169, 199–205 (Inst. for Int'l Econ., 2000) (concluding that IPRs, in combination with an open economy, foreign direct investment, and human capital development, can enhance economic growth in developing countries).

11. *See* Thomas F. Cotter, *Market Fundamentalism and the TRIPs Agreement,* 22 CARDOZO ARTS & ENT. L. J. 307, 35 (2004) (stating that "most observers who have considered the issue have concluded that it will take much more than strong patent rights to induce this type of research," and that "[e]ven in the United States, it took the Orphan Drug Act to make research into some drugs with relatively small demand profitable"); F. M. Scherer, *Patents, Monopoly Power, and the Pricing of Pharmaceuticals in Low-Income Nations* (HKS Faculty Research Working Paper Series RWP13-029, 2013), https://research.hks.harvard.edu/publications/getFile.aspx?Id=975 (manuscript at 14–16). As noted in Chapter 2, the Orphan Drug Act, 21 U.S.C. § 360aa, provides drug companies with additional government funding for research into diseases that affect relatively small numbers of people and seven years of exclusive marketing rights for any resulting drugs.

12. *See* Jonathan M. Barrett, *Do Patents Matter? Empirical Evidence on the Incentive Thesis, in* HANDBOOK ON LAW, INNOVATION AND GROWTH 178, 191–92 (Robert E. Litan ed., Edward Elgar 2011); Gervais, *supra* note 10, at 33.

13. *See* BUREAU INTERNATIONAL DES EXPOSITIONS, THE EXPOS, http://www.bie-paris.org/site/en/expos/about-expos/expo-categories.

14. This portion of the text principally relies on STEPHEN P. LADAS, PATENTS, TRADEMARKS, AND RELATED RIGHTS: NATIONAL AND INTERNATIONAL PROTECTION 59–60 (Harvard University Press 1975); Michael Blakeney, *The International Protection of Industrial Property: From the Paris Convention to the Agreement on Trade-Related Aspects of Intellectual Property Rights (the TRIPS Agreement),* WIPO NATIONAL SEMINAR ON INTELLECTUAL PROPERTY FOR FACULTY MEMBERS AND STUDENTS OF AJMAN UNIVERSITY (Apr. 2004), http://www.wipo.int/edocs/mdocs/arab/en/wipo_ip_uni_dub_04/wipo_ip_uni_dub_04_1.doc; and PAPERS RELATING TO THE FOREIGN RELATIONS OF THE UNITED STATES, 1872, 42d Cong., 3d Sess., H.R. Ex. Docs. VI, part 1, at 44–63 (1873).

15. *See* Paris Convention for the Protection of Industrial Property, July 14, 1967, 21 U.S.T. 1583, art. 2.

16. *See id.* art. 4.

17. Actually, Paris Convention article 4bis in effect requires that, if a given country measures the patent term from the date of filing, it must be the date of actual filing in that country, not the priority date (date of filing in the first country). But the Convention doesn't say anything about what the term must be in years.

18. *See id,* art. 28(1) ("Any dispute between two or more countries of the Union concerning the interpretation or application of this Convention, not settled by negotiation, may, by any one of the countries concerned, be brought before the International Court of Justice by application in conformity with the Statute of the Court,4 unless the countries concerned agree on some other method of settlement").

19. *See* WORLD TRADE ORG., https://www.wto.org/.

20. Paul R. Krugman, *Is Free Trade Passé?*, 1 J. ECON. PERSP. 131, 132 (1987).

21. In this regard, studies in psychology and behavioral economics show that people often feel worse about a downward departure from the status quo than they feel good about an upward departure of equivalent monetary value, a phenomenon known as the "endowment effect." Philosophers also posit that we value certain things in different ways, such that trading one of them (say, a valued pet) for another (or for money) is inconsistent with the way in which we value them. For discussion, *see* Thomas F. Cotter, *Legal Pragmatism and the Law and Economics Movement*, 84 GEO. L. J. 2071, 2113, 2128–29 (1996).

22. For discussion, *see, e.g.,* Ronald D'Amico & Peter Z. Schochet, *The Evaluation of the Trade Adjustment Assistance Program: A Synthesis of Major Findings* (2012), https://www.mathematica-mpr.com/~/media/publications/PDFs/labor/TAA_Synthesis.pdf.

23. For discussion, *see* Tyler Cowen, *Income Inequality Is Not Rising Globally. It's Falling.*, N. Y. TIMES, July 19, 2014, https://www.nytimes.com/2014/07/20/upshot/income-inequality-is-not-rising-globally-its-falling-.html?mcubz=2. As for my speculation that, at some point, free trade might risk undermining the political stability that makes free trade possible in the first place, it recently came to my attention that a book I read long ago (and had largely forgotten) can be understood as arguing a similar point. *See* KARL POLANYI, THE GREAT TRANSFORMATION: THE POLITICAL AND ECONOMIC ORIGINS OF OUR TIME (Beacon Press 1944) (advancing, among other things, the "double movement" thesis).

24. *See* Robert Pollin et al., *Global Apparel Production and Sweatshop Labour: Can Raising Retail Prices Finance Living Wages?*, 28 CAMBRIDGE J. ECON. 153 (2004).

25. For discussion, *see, e.g.,* Drusilla K. Brown et al., *Pros and Cons of Linking Trade and Labor Standards* (2002), www.tulane.edu/~dnelson/PEReformConf/BDS-Pros.pdf; Samira Salem & Faina Rozental, *Labor Standards and Trade: A Review of Recent Empirical Evidence*, 4 J. INT'L COMM. & ECON. 63 (2012), https://www.usitc.gov/journals/LaborStandardsandTrade_final%209_12.pdf.

26. The discussion in this portion of the text largely follows Thomas J. Dillon, Jr., *The World Trade Organization: A New Legal Order for World Trade?*, 16 MICH. J. IN'TL L. 349 (1995); *see also* WORLD TRADE ORG., THE GATT YEARS: FROM HAVANA TO MARRAKESH, https://www.wto.org/english/thewto_e/whatis_e/tif_e/fact4_e.htm; WORLD TRADE ORG., THE URUGUAY ROUND, https://www.wto.org/english/thewto_e/whatis_e/tif_e/fact5_e.htm; and WORLD TRADE ORG., UNDERSTAND THE WTO: THE AGREEMENTS, https://www.wto.org/english/thewto_e/whatis_e/tif_e/agrm1_e.htm.

27. Dillon, *supra* note 26, at 354.

28. For an overview of the EU and the EEA, *see* DELEGATION OF THE EUROPEAN UNION TO THE U.S., THE EUROPEAN UNION THROUGH THE YEARS, http://www.euintheus.org/who-we-are/timeline/. For an overview of EFTA, *see* THE EUROPEAN FREE TRADE ASSOCIATION, http://www.efta.int/. For an overview of NAFTA, *see* OFF. OF THE U.S. TRADE REPRESENTATIVE, NORTH AMERICAN FREE TRADE AGREEMENT (NAFTA), https://ustr.gov/trade-agreements/free-trade-agreements/north-american-free-trade-agreement-nafta.

29. A. David Demiray, *Intellectual Property and the External Power of the European Community: The New Extension*, 16 MICH. J. INT'L L. 187, 201–02 (1994).

30. *See* Peter Yu, *TRIPs and Its Discontents*, 10 MARQ. INTELL. PROP. L. J. 369, 371–73 (2006) [hereinafter Yu, *Discontents*]. Yu notes that efforts to revise the Paris Convention in the early

1980s had fizzled, in large part due to disagreements between the developing countries, which sought concessions regarding the scope of patent protection, and the developed countries, which resisted. Four years later, however, the developed countries successfully fought to include IP in GATT's agenda, and to increase the overall level of protection, in part because in the trade forum they could offer trade concessions as an inducement for increased IP protection. *See* Peter K. Yu, *Currents and Crosscurrents in the International Intellectual Property Regime*, 38 LOY. L. A. L. REV. 323, 357–58 (2004).

31. *See* Yu, *Discontents, supra* note 30, at 371–76.

32. *See* Agreement on Trade-Related Aspect of Intellectual Property Rights, art. 3, Apr. 15, 1994, Marrakesh Agreement Establishing the World Trade Organization, Annex 1C, 33 I.L.M. 1197 (1994) [hereinafter TRIPS]. There are a few small exceptions not relevant here.

33. *See id.* art. 4.

34. *See id.* arts. 2(1), 9(1).

35. *See id.* arts. 41–61.

36. *Id.* art. 27(1).

37. *See id.* art. 27(1) n.5 ("For the purposes of this Article, the terms 'inventive step' and 'capable of industrial application' may be deemed by a Member to be synonymous with the terms 'non-obvious' and 'useful' respectively").

38. *Id.* art. 27(2) (3).

39. *See* MICHELE BOLDRIN & DAVID K. LEVINE, AGAINST INTELLECTUAL MONOPOLY 216–17 (Cambridge University Press 2008).

40. US courts arguably do apply fact-specific patent doctrines relating to matters such as claim construction, nonobviousness, and enablement somewhat differently depending on the field of technology. For discussion, *see* DAN L. BURK & MARK A. LEMLEY, THE PATENT CRISIS AND HOW THE COURTS CAN SOLVE IT (University of Chicago Press 2009).

41. *See* TRIPS art. 6 (stating that, subject to certain qualifications, nothing in the agreement "shall be used to address the issue of the exhaustion of intellectual property rights").

42. For further reading, *see, e.g.,* Herbert Hovenkamp, *Post-Sale Restraints and Competitive Harm: The First Sale Doctrine in Perspective*, 66 NYU ANN. SURVEY AM. LAW 487, 539–46 (2011).

43. 137 S. Ct. 1523 (2017).

44. For an accessible discussion of the FDA rules, *see* Erika Lietzan, *Demystifying Drug Importation after* Impression v. Lexmark, PATENTLY-O, June 6, 2017, https://patentlyo.com/patent/2017/06/demystifying-importation-impression.html. The FDA's principal concern is safety, but if we abstract from this concern and assume that consumers would find the products sold abroad and domestically to be identical, or at least adequate substitutes, the economic question raised by the exhaustion is whether the law should permit or forbid price discrimination. National exhaustion permits patent owners to price discriminate, by charging higher prices in countries where it is profitable and legal to do so, and lower prices elsewhere. Under a system of international exhaustion, by contrast, price discrimination tends not to work very well, because intermediaries can engage in what economists refer to as "arbitrage," meaning that they can buy at a relatively low price in one market and then resell in another. Subject to the availability of supply and transportation costs, widespread arbitrage tends to even out the price charged in multiple markets, thus frustrating efforts to price discriminate and reducing prices in what would otherwise be the high-price countries. One concern about a regime of international exhaustion is that drugs are often sold at much lower prices in developing countries, see Scherer, supra note 11, so if international exhaustion and the ensuing arbitrage forced the drug companies to charge (more or less) the same price everywhere in the world, the companies' likely response would be either to raise prices in developing countries, if they could, or to withdraw certain products from those countries altogether. From the standpoint of global welfare, then, it may be better if the developed world follows a regime of national or regional exhaustion than a regime of international exhaustion. *See* Daniel J. Hemet & Lisa Larrimore Ouellette, *Trade and Tradeoffs: The Case of International Patent Exhaustion*, 116 COLUM. L. REV. SIDEBAR 17 (2016). Nevertheless, as long as FDA law also forbids the unauthorized importation of drugs into the United States, perhaps *Impression Products* will have only a negligible impact on global welfare.

45. *See* Cotter, *supra* note 11, at 314–15.
46. *See id.*
47. *See* 35 U.S.C. § 273.
48. *See* 42 U.S.C. § 7608; 35 U.S.C. § 203; 7 U.S.C. § 2404.
49. *See Paice LLC v. Toyota Motor Corp.*, 504 F.3d 1293, 1313 n.13 (Fed. Cir. 2007).
50. *See* Colleen Chien, *Cheap Drugs at What Price to Innovation: Does the Compulsory Licensing of Pharmaceuticals Hurt Innovation?*, 18 BERKELEY TECH. L. J. 853, 876 (2003).
51. Thomas F. Cotter & John M. Golden, *Empirical Studies Relating to Patents—Remedies, in* RESEARCH HANDBOOK ON THE ECONOMICS OF INTELLECTUAL PROPERTY LAW (Peter Menell et al., eds., Edward Elgar Publishing forthcoming 2018) (citing F. M. SCHERER, THE ECONOMIC EFFECTS OF COMPULSORY PATENT LICENSING 66–75 (NYU Monograph Series in Fin. & Econ., 1977)). *See also* IRINA HARACOGLOU, COMPETITION LAW AND PATENTS: A FOLLOW-ON INNOVATION PERSPECTIVE IN THE BIOPHARMACEUTICAL INDUSTRY 56 (Edward Elgar, 2008); Chien, *supra* note 50, at 874–80.
52. Paris Convention, art. 5A.
53. The text here follows my discussion in Cotter, *supra* note 11, at 312–13 nn.25, 26.
54. The TRIPS Agreement doesn't define the terms "developing country" and "least-developed country." The WTO states that "[a]bout two thirds" of its members are developing countries. *See* WORLD TRADE ORG., UNDERSTANDING THE WTO: DEVELOPING COUNTRIES, https://www.wto.org/english/thewto_e/whatis_e/tif_e/dev1_e.htm. In addition, "[t]he WTO recognizes as least-developed countries (LDCs) those countries which have been designated as such by the United Nations. There are currently 48 least-developed countries on the UN list, 36 of which to date have become WTO members." WORLD TRADE ORG., UNDERSTANDING THE WTO: LEAST DEVELOPED COUNTRIES, https://www.wto.org/english/thewto_e/whatis_e/tif_e/org7_e.htm.
55. *See* Sue Ann Mota, *The World Trade Organization: An Analysis of Disputes*, 25 N. C. J. INT'L L. & COM. REG. 75, 93–94 (1999).
56. *See* William J. Fisher III & Cyrill P. Rigamonti, *The South Africa AIDS Controversy: A Case Study in Patent Law and Policy* (2005), https://cyber.harvard.edu/people/tfisher/South%20Africa.pdf.
57. *See* Thomas F. Cotter, *Introduction to IP Symposium*, 14 FLA. J. INT'L L. 147, 148 n.1 (2001), and sources cited therein.
58. This portion of the text is adapted in part from Cotter, *supra* note 57, at 151.
59. *See* Donald G. McNeil, Jr., *A Nation Challenged: The Drug; A Rush for Cipro, and the Global Ripples*, N. Y. TIMES (Oct. 17, 2001), http://www.nytimes.com/2001/10/17/world/a-nation-challenged-the-drug-a-rush-for-cipro-and-the-global-ripples.html?_r=0.
60. WORLD TRADE ORG., DECLARATION ON THE TRIPs AGREEMENT AND PUBLIC HEALTH (Nov. 14, 2001), https://www.wto.org/english/thewto_e/minist_e/min01_e/mindecl_trips_e.htm. The WTO Ministerial Conference in 2001 addressed several other issues as well, most of them not directly relevant to IP. For an overview, *see generally* WORLD TRADE ORG., THE DOHA DECLARATION EXPLAINED, https://www.wto.org/english/tratop_e/dda_e/dohaexplained_e.htm#trips; WORLD TRADE ORG., THE DOHA IMPLEMENTATION DECISION EXPLAINED, https://www.wto.org/english/tratop_e/dda_e/implem_explained_e.htm#trips.
61. The General Council is "the WTO's highest-level decision-making body in Geneva." WORLD TRADE ORG., THE WTO GENERAL COUNCIL, https://www.wto.org/english/thewto_e/gcounc_e/gcounc_e.htm.
62. *See* WORLD TRADE ORG., DECISION OF THE GENERAL COUNCIL OF 30 AUGUST 2003, IMPLEMENTATION OF PARAGRAPH 6 OF THE DOHA DECLARATION ON THE TRIPS AGREEMENT AND PUBLIC HEALTH (Sept. 1, 2003), https://www.wto.org/english/tratop_e/trips_e/implem_para6_e.htm.
63. *See* WORLD TRADE ORG., DECISION REMOVES FINAL OBSTACLE TO CHEAP DRUG IMPORTS (Aug. 30, 2003), https://www.wto.org/English/news_e/pres03_e/pr350_e.htm.
64. The TRIPS Council did agree in November 2005 to extend the transition period for LDCs from January 1, 2006, to July 1, 2013. *See* WORLD TRADE ORG., POOREST COUNTRIES GIVEN MORE TIME TO APPLY INTELLECTUAL PROPERTY RULES, http://www.wto.org/english/

news_e/pres05_e/pr424_e.htm. Since the LDCs already had until January 1, 2016, to conform their patent and trade secret laws as they related to pharmaceutical products, all this meant was that they could delay implementing the rest of the agreement (the parts relating to copyright, trademarks, and so on) until 2013. The WTO thereafter further extended both of these extensions, to July 1, 2021 and January 1, 2033, respectively.

65. *See* World Trade Org., Decision of the General Council of 6 December 2005, Amendment of the TRIPS Agreement (Dec. 8, 2005), https://www.wto.org/english/tratop_e/trips_e/wtl641_e.htm; World Trade Org., Members OK Amendment to Make Health Flexibility Permanent (Dec. 6, 2005), https://www.wto.org/english/news_e/pres05_e/pr426_e.htm. "Bis," in case you're wondering, is the Latin word for "twice," and when international treaties are revised it's commonly used to designate an article that will come in between two other articles that the drafters don't want to renumber.

66. *See* Peter Kenny, *Amended TRIPS Agreement Close To Ratification, Says WTO's Azevêdo*, Intell. Prop. Watch, Nov. 25, 2016, http://www.ip-watch.org/2016/11/25/amended-trips-agreement-close-ratification-says-wtos-azevedo/; World Trade Org., *Dominica Accepts TRIPS Amendment to Ease Poor Countries' Access to Affordable Medicines*, Nov. 28, 2016, https://www.wto.org/english/news_e/news16_e/trip_28nov16_e.htm.

67. *See* World Trade Org., Notification Under Paragraph 2(a) of the Decision of 30 August 2003 on the Implementation of Paragraph 6 of the Doha Declaration on the TRIPs Agreement and Public Health—Rwanda, IP/N/9/RWA/1, Doc. Num. 07-3075 (July 19, 2007), https://docs.wto.org/dol2fe/Pages/FE_Search/FE_S_S006.aspx?Query=(%20@Symbol=%20ip/n/9/*%20)&Language=ENGLISH&Context=FomerS criptedSearch&languageUIChanged=true#; Notification Under Paragraph 2(c) of the Decision of 30 August 2003 on the Implementation of Paragraph 6 of the Doha Declaration on the TRIPs Agreement and Public Health—Canada, IP/N/10/CAN/1, Doc. Num. 07-4285 (October 8, 2007), https://docs.wto.org/dol2fe/Pages/FE_Search/FE_S_S006.aspx?Query=(%20@ Symbol=%20ip/n/10/*%20)&Language=ENGLISH&Context=FomerScriptedSearch&lang uageUIChanged=true#. The WTO maintains a dedicated webpage for notifications at https://www.wto.org/english/tratop_e/trips_e/public_health_e.htm, from which the interested reader can verify that the only two notifications to date have been the two cited above.

68. Reed Beall & Randall Kuhn, *Trends in Compulsory Licensing of Pharmaceuticals Since the Doha Declaration: A Database Analysis*, 9 PLoS Med. 1, 4 (2012), http://journals.plos.org/plosmedicine/article/asset?id=10.1371/journal.pmed.1001154.PDF. The authors also note that the extension of the TRIPS compliance deadline for LDCs wasn't as meaningful as one might have expected either, since "in practice a great many LDCs accelerated their compliance timelines well ahead of 2016, particularly since most were preparing for a 2006 deadline." *Id.* at 2.

69. For discussion, *see, e.g.*, Sam Halabi, *International Intellectual Property Shelters*, 90 Tul. L. Rev. 903, 925–27 (2016).

70. *See* Beall & Kuhn, *supra* note 688. In 2012, however, India required the compulsory licensing of a cancer drug made by Bayer. *See* William J. Bennett, Note, *Indian Pharmaceutical Patent Law and the Effects of* Novartis AG v. Union of India, 13 Wash. U. Global Stud. L. Rev. 535, 546 n.57 (2014); Jodie Liu, Note, *Compulsory Licensing and Anti-Evergreening: Interpreting the TRIPs Flexibilities in Sections 84 and 3(d) of the Indian Patent Act*, 56 Harv. Int'l L. J. 207 (2015). So far, India hasn't issued any more compulsory licenses. *See* Shamnad Basheer, *Patent Pledge: Caving in on Compulsory Licensing?*, Spicy IP Blog (Mar. 15, 2016), http://spicyip.com/2016/03/patent-pimping-caving-in-on-compulsory-licensing.html. And, in 2012, the High Court of Kenya held that "the fundamental right to life, human dignity, and health" under the Kenyan Constitution trumped the operation of a Kenyan law that prohibited the copying of AIDS drugs. *See P. A. O. v. Att'y Gen.*, Pet'n No. 409 of 2009, Apr. 20, 2012, reprinted in 43 IIC 717 (2012).

71. On the reduction in prices of drugs in developing countries, *see, e.g.*, Scherer, *supra* note 11, at 9–11. On India's decision to invalidate Novartis's patent on Gleevec on the ground that it failed to satisfy a requirement under Indian law that a new form of an existing compound must demonstrate enhanced efficacy over that compound, *see* Bennett, *supra* note 70; Liu, *supra* note 70.

72. *See* Cotter, *supra* note 11, at 334–35 (citations omitted).

73. *See* Reed F. Beall, *Patents and the WHO Model List of Essential Medicines (18th Edition): Clarifying the Debate on IP and Access*, WIPO GLOBAL CHALLENGES BRIEF (2016), http://www.wipo.int/edocs/mdocs/mdocs/en/wipo_gc_ip_ge_16/wipo_gc_ip_ge_16_brief.pdf. Beall notes, however, that "[i]n the long-term, the proportion of patented products on the [WHO list] will likely increase."

74. *See* Cotter, *supra* note 11, at 334; Beall & Kuhn, *supra* note 70, at 7 (stating that middle-income countries "face considerable pressure from internal industrial lobbies and foreign governments to honor intellectual property rights").

75. *See* Kyle & Qian, *supra* note 8; Cockburn et al., *supra* note 9. The Cockburn et al. study also notes, however, that while "stronger patent rights and the absence of price regulation" promote the faster launching of drugs, "[t]his highlights the basic tradeoff countries face between making new drug therapies available and making them affordable." Cockburn et al., *supra* note 9, at 26.

76. REPORT OF THE UNITED NATIONS SECRETARY-GENERAL'S HIGH-LEVEL PANEL ON ACCESS TO MEDICINES: PROMOTING INNOVATION AND ACCESS TO HEALTH TECHNOLOGIES 7, 31–32 (Sept., 2016), http://www.unsgaccessmeds.org/s/UNSG-HLP-Report-FINAL-12-Sept-2016.pdf [hereinafter UN REPORT].

77. *See* TPP arts. 18.48(2) (in the case of drug patents, requiring members to make available an undefined "adjustment of the patent term to compensate the patent owner for unreasonable curtailment of the effective patent term as a result of the marketing approval process"); *id.* arts. 18.50, 18.52 (disclosure of clinical data); *id.* arts. 18.51, 18.52 (linkage), https://medium.com/the-trans-pacific-partnership/intellectual-property-3479efdc7adf. *See also* UN REPORT, *supra* note 76, at 25–26 (listing TRIPS-Plus provisions found in various bilateral and plurilateral agreements).

78. *See* TPP arts. 9.18 et seq., https://medium.com/the-trans-pacific-partnership/investment-c76dbd892f3a.

79. *See, e.g., Investor-State Attacks on Public Interest Policies: Access to Medicines*, PUBLIC CITIZEN (Mar. 30, 2015), https://www.citizen.org/documents/tpp-investment-chapter-and-access-to-medicines.pdf.

80. UN REPORT, *supra* note 76, at 10.

81. *Id.* at 36.

82. Beall, *supra* note 73, at 4.

83. *See* UN REPORT, *supra* note 76, at 37.

84. *See* DRUGS FOR NEGLECTED DISEASES INITIATIVE, AN INNOVATIVE APPROACH TO R&D FOR NEGLECTED PATIENTS: TEN YEARS OF EXPERIENCE AND LESSONS LEARNED BY DNDi 18, 20 (Jan., 2014). DNDi describes itself as "an independent, international not-for-profit R&D organization, [which] was established in 2003. Within 10 years and with a budget of approximately EUR 182.5 million, the initiative has delivered six new treatments for neglected diseases and established a solid drug development pipeline, including 12 new chemical entities (NCEs) in preclinical and clinical development." *Id.* at 2.

85. *See* UN REPORT, *supra* note 76, at 35.

86. *See id.* at 22, 37.

87. For intelligent discussion of many of the obstacles to improving health care in developing countries, *see* ABHIJIT BANERJEE & ESTHER DUFLO, POOR ECONOMICS: A RADICAL RETHINKING OF THE WAY TO FIGHT GLOBAL POVERTY ch. 3 (Public Affairs 2011).

88. More precisely, Article 5(1) of UPOV 1978 provides that the breeder (rightholder) has the right to authorize "the production for purposes of commercial marketing," "the offering for sale," and "the marketing of reproductive or vegetative propagating material, as such, of the variety." "Article 5(1) of the '78 Act provides, by implication, the ability of a farmer to save seeds for personal uses, but not subsequent resale," otherwise known as the farmer's privilege. A. Bryan Endres & Carly E. Giffin, *Necessity Is the Mother, But Protection May Not Be the Father of Invention: The Limited Effect of Intellectual Property Regimes on Agricultural Innovation*, 14 COLUM. SCI. & TECH. L. REV. 203, 213 (2012). The texts of the treaties themselves can be accessed at http://www.upov.int/upovlex/en/acts.html.

89. UPOV 1991 renders the farmer's privilege optional because article 15(2) of the 1991 Act, titled "Exceptions to the Breeder's Right," provides that members *may* adopt an "optional

exception" that would "within reasonable limits and subject to the safeguarding of the legitimate interests of the breeder, restrict the breeder's right in relation to any variety in order
to permit farmers to use for propagating purposes, on their own holdings, the product of
the harvest which they have obtained by planting, on their own holdings, the protected
variety."

90. *See* 7 U.S.C. § 2543 ("Except to the extent that such action may constitute an infringement
under subsections (3) and (4) of section 2541 of this title, it shall not infringe any right here-
under for a person to save seed produced by the person from seed obtained, or descended
from seed obtained, by authority of the owner of the variety for seeding purposes and use
such saved seed in the production of a crop for use on the farm of the person, or for sale as
provided in this section").

91. *See Bowman v. Monsanto Co.*, 133 S. Ct. 1761 (2013).

92. For a critical analysis, *see Ten Reasons Not to Join UPOV*, GAIA/GRAIN (May 15, 1998),
https://www.grain.org/article/entries/1-ten-reasons-not-to-join-upov.

93. *See, e.g.,* Endres & Giffin, *supra* note 88, at 213–15.

94. WIPO, *Traditional Knowledge*, http://www.wipo.int/tk/en/. A small portion of the text above
is adapted from Cotter, *supra* note 57. Another topic related to TK that is beyond the scope of
the present work is whether certain special protections for geographical indications, which
under TRIPs are limited to wines and spirits (e.g., *Cognac* as indicative of a distilled spirit
emanating from the Cognac region of France), should be extended to products like Basmati
rice and Darjeeling tea. Discussions on this issue at the WTO have stalled, as have discussions
over whether the WTO should take a position on the protectability of TK. *See* World Trade
Org., Doha WTO Ministerial 2001: Ministerial Declaration (Nov. 20, 2001), art. 19, https://
www.wto.org/english/thewto_e/minist_e/min01_e/mindecl_e.htm; World Trade
Org., TRIPs: Reviews, Article 27.3(b), and Related Issues: Background and the
Current Situation, https://www.wto.org/english/tratop_e/trips_e/art27_3b_back-
ground_e.htm; World Trade Org., TRIPs: Geographic Indications: Background
and the Current Situation: Extending the Higher Level of Protection
Beyond Wines and Spirits, https://www.wto.org/english/tratop_e/trips_e/gi_back-
ground_e.htm#protection/.

95. For discussion of some of the disputes, and of the relevant legal and policy arguments, *see,
e.g.,* James Boyle, Shamans, Software, and Spleens: Law and the Construction
of the Information Society 128–30 (Harvard University Press 1996); Paul Kuruk,
*Regulating Access to Traditional Knowledge and Genetic Resources: The Disclosure Requirement
as a Strategy to Combat Biopiracy,* 17 San Diego Int'l L. J. 1, 12–14 (2015); Stephen
R. Munzer & Kair Raustiala, *The Uneasy Case for Intellectual Property Rights in Traditional
Knowledge,* 27 Cardozo Arts & Ent. L. J. 37 (2009); Madhavi Sunder, *The Invention of
Traditional Knowledge,* 70 L. & Contemp. Probs. 97 (2007).

96. Reasonable minds also may differ on how frequently situations like the hypothetical one
described in the text, which advocates of protection for TK refer to as "biopiracy," actually occur or have occurred. At the same time, one may sometimes be skeptical of the
claims of Western companies that the improvement they've made over TK is really novel or
nonobvious. India was successful in having the neem-related patent invalidated, for example,
and it has since increased efforts to document its TK precisely to prevent the patentability
of products or methods that are actually in the prior art. *See* Kuruk, *supra* note 95, at 13;
Munzer & Raustiala, *supra* note 95, at 50, 52.

97. Convention on Biological Diversity (CBD), https://www.cbd.int/convention/
text/.

98. Convention on Biological Diversity, Text of Nagoya Protocal, https://www.
cbd.int/abs/text/default.shtml.

99. CBD art. 8(j). Article 2 of the Convention defines "Biological diversity" to mean "the variability among living organisms from all sources including, inter alia, terrestrial, marine and
other aquatic ecosystems and the ecological complexes of which they are part; this includes
diversity within species, between species and of ecosystems." It also defines "Sustainable
use" to mean "the use of components of biological diversity in a way and at a rate that does
not lead to the long-term decline of biological diversity, thereby maintaining its potential to
meet the needs and aspirations of present and future generations."

100. *Id.* art. 15. Article 2 defines "[g]enetic resources" to mean "genetic material of actual or potential value," and "[g]enetic material" as "any material of plant, animal, microbial or other origin containing functional units of heredity"; Article 2 also defines "[c]ountry of origin of genetic resources" as "the country which possesses those genetic resources in in-situ conditions," and "[i]n-situ conditions" as "conditions where genetic resources exist within ecosystems and natural habitats, and, in the case of domesticated or cultivated species, in the surroundings where they have developed their distinctive properties."

101. Nagoya Protocol, arts. 5–7.

102. *See* Convention on Biological Diversity, List of Parties, https://www.cbd.int/information/parties.shtml

103. *See* Regulation (EU) No. 511/2014 of the European Parliament and of the Council of 16 April 2014 on Compliance Measures for Users from the Nagoya Protocol on Access to Genetic Resources and the Fair and Equitable Sharing of Benefits Arising from their Utilization in the Union, 2014 O.J. (L 150) 59, http://eur-lex.europa.eu/legal-content/EN/TXT/PDF/?uri=CELEX:32014R0511&from=EN.

Chapter 8

1. *See* Brenda Sandburg, *Trolling for Dollars*, The Recorder (July 30, 2001), http://www.therecorder.com/id=900005370205/Trolling-for-Dollars?slreturn=20160702204836; Joff Wild, *The Real Inventors of the Term "Patent Troll" Revealed*, IAM Blog (Aug. 22, 2008), http://www.iam-media.com/blog/detail.aspx?g=cff2afd3-c24e-42e5-aa68-a4b4e7524177.

2. For a sampling of sources, *see, e.g.,* Dennis Crouch, *Watch the #StopBadPatents Commercial*, Patently-O Blog (Apr. 28, 2014), http://patentlyo.com/patent/2014/04/watch-stopbadpatents-commercial.html (linking to the television ad sponsored by "StopBadPatents.com"); LastWeekTonight, *Last Week Tonight with John Oliver* (Apr. 19, 2015), https://www.youtube.com/watch?v=3bxcc3SM_KA; Mike Masnick, *This American Life Followup on Patents Reveals Intellectual Ventures Is Even Slimier than Previously Believed*, TechDirt (June 3, 2013, 12:56 pm), https://www.techdirt.com/articles/20130603/11295023297/this-american-life-followup-patents-reveals-intellectual-ventures-is-even-slimier-than-previously-believed.shtml; Stop Bad Patents, http://stopbadpatents.com/ (last visited Dec. 16, 2016); PBS NewsHour, *U.S. Innovators Dogged by Money-Grubbing 'Patent Trolls'*, May 26, 2016, https://www.youtube.com/watch?v=33qEghEs6X4; Mark Summerfeild, *Parody: Hitler Receives a Threat from a Patent Troll*, Patentology (June 16, 2013), http://blog.patentology.com.au/2013/06/parody-hitler-receives-threat-from.html; Laura Sydell, *Taking the Battle Against Patent Trolls to the Public*, NPR: All Tech Considered (Aug. 30, 2013, 5:21 pm), http://www.npr.org/sections/alltechconsidered/2013/08/30/217272814/taking-the-battle-against-patent-trolls-to-the-public# (linking to a radio ad sponsored by "StopBadPatents.com"); *411: When Patents Attack Transcript*, This American Life (July 22, 2011), http://www.thisamericanlife.org/radio-archives/episode/441/transcript; *496: When Patents Attack . . . Part 2! Transcript*, This American Life (May, 31, 2013), http://www.thisamericanlife.org/radio-archives/episode/496/transcript.

3. *See* Ali Sternberg, *Obama Acknowledges Patent Troll Problem [w/ Transcript]*, Pat. Progress (Feb. 14, 2013), http://www.patentprogress.org/2013/02/14/obama-acknowledges-patent-troll-problem-w-transcript/ (linking to video).

4. Fed. Trade Comm'n, Patent Assertion Entity Activity: An FTC Study 1 (Oct. 2016) [hereinafter "FTC Study"].

5. A more detailed discussion of the issues discussed in this chapter will be presented in Chapter 5 of a book I am currently coauthoring with Professor Colleen Chien and Judge Richard Posner, titled *Redesigning Patent Law*. We hope this book will be published some time in 2018. I am the principal drafter of Chapter 5 of that work, and Chapter 8 of this book draws on largely the same body of research.

6. FTC Study, *supra* note 4, at 2, 38–40 (describing the study's methodology). The agency also conducted a separate Wireless Case Study involving analysis of information from six wireless manufacturers and five NPEs. *See id.* at 40, 102–123.

7. *Id.* at A-1.

8. *Id.* at 3. While many observers previously had speculated that there were a wide variety of PAE business models, according to the agency, the data revealed "far more organizational homogeneity . . . than expected." *Id.* at 42 (noting in addition that a 2011 FTC report had "described 'many types of actors' and 'evolving' business models"). For other efforts to classify PAEs or NPEs, *see, e.g.,* Mark A. Lemley & A. Douglas Melamed, *Missing the Forest for the Trolls,* 113 Colum. L. Rev. 2117, 2125–27 (2013) (dividing "patent trolls" into three categories: "lottery-ticket" trolls that own a single patent and "hope[ ] to strike it big in court"; "bottom feeders" who are "interested in quick, low-value settlements for a variety of patents"; and "patent aggregators" like Intellectual Ventures, which appear to be identical to the firms the FTC refers to as Portfolio PAEs); Kristen Osenga, *Formerly Manufacturing Entities— Piercing the "Patent Troll" Rhetoric,* 47 Conn. L. Rev. 435 (2014) (arguing that "formerly manufacturing entities" that continue to license their patents after they cease manufacturing are a benign type of patent troll); *see also* Christopher A. Cotropia et al., *Unpacking Patent Assertion Entities (PAEs),* 99 Minn. L. Rev. 649, 654 (2014) (classifying patent owners as "Operating Company, University, Individual Inventor, Patent Aggregator, Technology Development Company, Failed Start-Up, IP Holding Subsidiary of an Operating Company, or Patent Holding Company"); Erik N. Hovenkamp & Thomas F. Cotter, *Anticompetitive Patent Injunctions,* 100 Minn. L. Rev. 871 (2016) (discussing "diagonally integrated" NPEs that manufacture products, which may or may not be patented, while using other patents to exclude competitors); Raymond Millien, *Landscape 2013: Who Are the Players in the IP Marketplace?,* IPWatchdog (Jan. 23, 2013), http://www.ipwatchdog.com/2013/01/23/ip-landscape/id=33356/; Malte Köllner & Paul Weber, *Trolls and Their Consequences: An Evolving IP Ecosystem,* Mitteilungen der deutchsen Patentanwälte 106 (March 2014). Note also that some patent aggregators (RPX Corporation is perhaps the largest) are defensive in nature, in that they buy patents and license them to subscribers for defensive purposes only—that is, to assert only in retaliation for an infringement suit brought by another patent owner. As noted in the text above, however, retaliation doesn't work well for NPEs, which (since they don't market any products) are unlikely to be liable themselves for patent infringement.

   For a critique of the FTC study, *see* Joshua D. Wright & Douglas H. Ginsburg, *The FTC PAE Study: A Cautionary Tale About Making Unsupported Policy Recommendations,* Public Domain, ABA Antitrust Section Newsletter of the Intell. Prop. Committee (Nov. 2016) (criticizing the agency for making policy recommendations on the ground that "because the full population of PAEs is not identified in any publicly available data set, its results are based upon a potentially unrepresentative sample, making it inappropriate to extrapolate its findings to PAEs as a whole"). For my response, stating among other things that "the findings may not be representative of all PAEs—but they do appear to give us an unprecedented window into the characteristics of the ones that, at least individually, have the most economic impact," *see* Thomas F. Cotter, *Wright and Ginsburg on the FTC's PAE Study,* Comparative Patent Remedies Blog, Dec. 12, 2016, http://comparativepatentremedies.blogspot.com/2016/12/wright-and-ginsburg-on-ftcs-pae-study.html.

9. *Id.* at 3.

10. *Id.* at 45.

11. *See id.* at 3–4, 45.

12. *Id.* at 2–4.

13. *See id.* at 5, 74–75, 135.

14. *See id.* at 85–87.

15. *See* 3 Roger M. Milgrim & Eric E. Bensen, Milgrim on Licensing § 18.06 (Matthew Bender rev. ed. 2015) ("Without doubt, the most common form of consideration for licenses of patents, know-how, trade secrets and trademarks is what is known as running royalty"). The use of lump-sum royalties was more pronounced among Litigation PAEs (99 percent) than Portfolio PAEs (84 percent). *See* FTC Study, *supra* note 4, at 86–87.

16. *See* FTC Study, *supra* note 4, at 47–53.

17. *See id.* at 46–47, 49, 56, 58–61.

18. *See id.* at 60–63.
19. *See id.* at 66; Complaint, In the Matter of MPHJ Tech. Investments, LLC, Docket No. C-4513 (Fed. Trade Comm'n Mar. 13, 2015), https://www.ftc.gov/system/files/documents/cases/150317mphjtechcmpt.pdf; Decision and Order, In the Matter of MPHJ Tech. Investments, LLC, Docket No. C-4513 (Fed. Trade Comm'n Mar. 13, 2015), https://www.ftc.gov/system/files/documents/cases/150317mphjtechdo.pdf. In 2015, the PTAB invalidated the primary patent at issue, and the Federal Circuit recently affirmed. *See MPHJ Tech. Investments, LLC v. Ricoh Ams. Corp.,* 847 F.3d 1363 (Fed. Cir. 2017).
20. *See* CHRIS BARRY ET AL., PwC 2017 PATENT LITIGATION STUDY: CHANGE ON THE HORIZON? 4 (reporting "[a]pproximately 5,100" filings from October 1, 2015 to September 30, 2016, amounting to a compound annual growth rate from 1991 of 6.0 percent, compared to a compound annual growth rate in the number of patents issued of 4.9 percent); BRIAN C. HOWARD & JASON MAPLES, LEX MACHINA 2016 PATENT LITIGATION YEAR IN REVIEW i, 2 (2017) (reporting 4,537 patent cases filed in calendar year 2016). If I were to hazard to guess, it would be that the Supreme Court's software and business method case law discussed in Chapter 5 is a major reason for the decline.
21. Christopher Beauchamp, *The First Patent Litigation Explosion,* 125 YALE L. J. 848, 848 (2016).
22. For discussion, *see, e.g.,* Colleen V. Chien, *Reforming Software Patents,* 50 HOUS. L. REV. 325, 344–50 (2012); Gerard N. Magliocca, *Blackberries and Barnyards: Patent Trolls and the Perils of Innovation,* 82 NOTRE DAME L. REV. 1809 (2007); Robert P. Merges, *The Trouble with Trolls: Innovation, Rent-seeking, and Patent Law Reform,* 24 BERKELEY TECH. L. J. 1583, 1592–96 (2009).
23. *See* Cotropia et al., *supra* note 8, at 693 (reporting that "Large Aggregators + Patent Holding Companies" accounted for 17.80 percent of filings in 2010 and 43.93 percent in 2012, although the percentage of alleged infringers involved in PAE suits rose only from 34.06 percent to 39.45 percent during that time); Sara Jeruss et al., *The America Invents Act 500: Effects of Patent Monetization Entities on US Litigation,* 11 DUKE L. & TECH. REV. 358, 361 (2012) (based on a random sample of 100 actions filed each year from 2007 to 2011, reporting that "patent monetization entities" (PMEs) initiated 40 percent of all patent infringement actions in 2011, up from 22 percent five years earlier); *see also* Robin Feldman et al., *The AIA 500 Expanded: The Effects of Patent Monetization Entities* 7 (U.C. Hastings Research Paper No. 45, 2013), http://ssrn.com/abstract=2247195 (in a follow-up study to Jeruss et al., reporting that PMEs initiated 58.7 percent of all patent infringement actions in 2012). RPX Corporation reports that NPEs (not distinguished from PAEs) filed more than 60 percent of all patent infringement actions, involving over half of all unique defendants, in 2012, 2013, 2014, and 2015. *See, e.g.,* RPX CORP., 2015 NPE ACTIVITY: HIGHLIGHTS 6 (2016), https://www.rpxcorp.com/wp-content/uploads/sites/2/2016/01/RPX-2015-NPE-Activity-Highlights-FinalZ.pdf; RPX CORP., 2014 NPE LITIGATION REPORT 6, 12 (2015), http://www.rpxcorp.com/wp-content/uploads/2014/12/RPX_Litigation_Report_2014_FNL_03.30.15.pdf [hereinafter RPX CORP., 2014 NPE REPORT]; RPX CORP., 2013 NPE LITIGATION REPORT 39 (2014), https://www.rpxcorp.com/wp-content/uploads/2014/01/RPX-2013-NPE-Litigation-Report.pdf; RPX CORP., 2012 NPE ACTIVITY REPORT (2013), http://patentlyo.com/media/docs/2013/07/0BF995E82CFF591EE80EFE8AC69259E7.pdf. One outlier is a 2013 Government Accounting Office (GAO) report concluding that "PMEs and likely PMEs brought 17 percent of all lawsuits in 2007 and 24 percent in 2011," a difference that is statistically insignificant, but that operating company filings fell from 76 percent to 59 percent, a difference that is statistically significant. *See* U.S. Gov't Accountability Office, GAO-13-465, Intellectual Property: Assessing Factors that Affect Patent Infringement Litigation Could Help Improve Patent Quality 17 (2013).
24. *See* FTC Study, *supra* note 4, at 102.
25. *See* Collen V. Chien, *Turn the Tables on Patent Trolls,* FORBES (Aug. 9, 2011, 11:37 PM), http://www.forbes.com/sites/ciocentral/2011/08/09/turn-the-tables-on-patent-trolls/.
26. James Bessen et al., *The Private and Social Costs of Patent Trolls,* 34 REGULATION, Winter 2011–12, at 26.
27. James E. Bessen & Michael J. Meurer, *The Direct Costs from NPE Disputes,* 99 CORNELL L. REV. 388, 410–11 (2014).

28. *See, e.g.,* David L. Schwartz & Jay P. Kesan, *Essay: Analyzing the Role of Non-Practicing Entities in the Patent System,* 99 Cornell L. Rev. 426, 441–45 (2014) (questioning the inclusion of transfers of income from operating companies to NPEs as a social cost and whether the data underlying the second of the two studies is representative); Joshua D. Wright & Douglas H. Ginsburg, *Patent Assertion Entities and Antitrust: A Competition Cure for a Litigation Disease?,* 79 Antitrust L. J. 501, 513 n.52 (2014) (raising technical objections to the stock market reaction study).

29. *See* Lemley & Melamed, *supra* note 8, at 2167.

30. *See* Christopher A. Cotropia & Mark A. Lemley, *Copying in Patent Law,* 87 N. C. L. Rev. 1421, 1451–57 (2009).

31. *See, e.g.,* William F. Lee & A. Douglas Melamed, *Breaking the Vicious Cycle of Patent Damages,* 101 Cornell L. Rev. 385, 388 (2016) (stating that, in many fields, "including key high-tech fields like information technology . . . [a] profusion of overlapping and unclear patent rights . . . make full patent preclearance—i.e., avoiding infringement by obtaining in advance licenses to all relevant patents—literally impossible in many situations and, in others, so costly that it is not feasible as a practical matter"); Christina Mulligan & Timothy B. Lee, *Scaling the Patent System,* 68 NYU Ann. Survey Am. Law 289 (2015) (arguing that with regard to software "patent clearance by all firms would require many times more hours of legal research than all patent lawyers in the United States can bill in a year"). *But see* Ted Sichelman, *Are There Too Many Patents to Search? A Response,* New Priv. L. Blog (July 2, 2015), https://blogs.law.harvard.edu/nplblog/2015/07/02/are-there-too-many-patents-to-search-a-response-ted-sichelman/ (arguing that Mulligan and Lee exaggerate the difficulty of preclearance).

32. *See* FTC Study, *supra* note 4, at 7, 49, 90.

33. *See* AIPLA, 2017 Report of the Economic Survey I-136 to I-141; *see also id.* at 42 (reporting median costs of $200,000 and $500,000 for suits with less than $1 million at stake, and more for higher-stakes disputes).

34. *See* FTC Study, *supra* note 4, at 90–92, 119 (noting, in addition, that Wireless Manufacturers, *see supra* note 6, often granted royalty-free licenses in exchange for the licensee's agreement to cross-license its own technology to the manufacturer).

35. *See* Barry et al., *supra* note 20, at 15, 17 (reporting that, from 1997 to 2016, practicing entities "enjoy[ed] an 11 percent premium in their overall success rate" in comparison with NPEs); John R. Allison et al., *How Often Do Patent Assertion Entities Win Patent Suits?,* 32 Berkeley Tech. L. J. (forthcoming 2017) (based on analysis of all patent lawsuits filed in 2008–09, reporting that NPEs made up approximately 25 percent of patent litigants but won only 14.4 percent of their cases litigated to judgment; the win rate for operating companies was 30.6 percent); *see also* John R. Allison et al., *Patent Quality and Settlement Among Repeat Patent Litigants,* 99 Geo. L. J. 677 (2011) (reporting that patent plaintiffs "who sue eight or more times on the same patents . . . overwhelmingly" lose when they go to trial); Michael Risch, *Patent Troll Myths,* 42 Seton Hall L. Rev. 457, 460–61 (2012) (based on a study of the "ten most litigious NPEs," reporting that "trolls almost never won infringement judgments").

36. *See* FTC Study, *supra* note 4, at 6, 74, 78.

37. *See In re Innovatio IP Ventures LLC v. MEI-GSR Holdings LLC,* No. 3:11–CV–00343–LRH–WGC, 2011 WL 6812541, at *1 (D. Nev. Dec. 27, 2011).

38. *See* Colleen V. Chien, *Startups and Patent Trolls,* 17 Stan. Tech. L. Rev. 461, 474–77 (2014); Lauren Cohen et al., *Patent Trolls: Evidence from Targeted Firms* (Harv. Bus. School Working Paper No. 15-002, 2016), http://ssrn.com/abstract=2464303.

39. *See* Cohen et al., *supra* note 38; Stephen Kiebczak et al., *The Effect of Patent Litigation and Patent Assertion Entities on Entrepreneurial Activity,* 45 Res. Pol'y 218 (2015); Roger Smeets, *Does Patent Litigation Reduce Corporate R&D? An Analysis of US Public Firms* (Apr. 28, 2014), https://papers.ssrn.com/sol3/papers.cfm?abstract_id=2443048.

40. *See* FTC Study, *supra* note 4, at 26–27 & nn.95–97; *id.* at 100; *see also* Bessen & Meurer, *supra* note 27, at 410–11 (estimating that, at most, 20 percent of defendants' payments to NPEs go to patentees); Risch, *supra* note 35, at 461 ("the evidence does not support a theory that NPEs incentivize investment by providing a market for patents," though they do "provide a better way for individual inventors to enforce their patents than bringing lawsuits themselves").

41. *See VE Holding Corp. v. Johnson Gas Appliance Co.,* 917 F.2d 1574 (Fed. Cir. 1990), interpreting 28 U.S.C. § 1400(b); *Beverly Hills Fan. Co. v. Royal Sovereign Corp.,* 21 F.3d 1558, 1565 (Fed Cir. 1994).

42. *See* J. Jonas Anderson, *Court Competition for Patent Cases,* 163 U. Pa. L. Rev. 631, 671–74 (2015); Daniel Klerman & Greg Reilly, *Forum Selling,* 89 S. Cal. L. Rev. 241, 255–57. For other sources documenting this portion of the text, *see generally* Brian Howard, Lex Machina, 2015 End-of-Year Trends (2016), https://lexmachina.com/lex-machina-2015-end-of-year-trends/ (reporting 2,540 of the 5,830 patent cases filed in calendar year 2015 were filed in the Eastern District of Texas); Paul R. Gugliuzza, *The New Federal Circuit Mandamus,* 45 Ind. L. Rev. 343 (2012) (on the court's reluctance to transfer); Matthew Sag, *IP Litigation in U.S. District Courts: 1994–2014,* 101 Iowa L. Rev. 1065, 1081–85, 1100–02 (2016) (on joinder of defendants); David O. Taylor, *Patent Misjoinder,* 88 N. Y. U. L. Rev. 652 (2013) (on joinder of defendants).

43. *See* Barry et al., *supra* note 20, at 22. *But see* Brian C. Howard, Lex Machina 2014 Patent Litigation Year in Review 25 (reporting median damages of $8.7 million in the Eastern District from 2005 to 2014), http://pages.lexmachina.com/rs/lexmachina/images/2014%20Patent%20Litigation%20Report.pdf.

44. *See* Barry et al., *supra* note 20, at 24 (reporting that NPEs accounted for 38 percent of the 195 identified decisions rendered in patent actions in the Eastern District from 1997 to 2017); FTC Study, *supra* note 4, at 81 (reporting that the Litigation PAEs studied filed 54 percent of their cases in the Eastern District); RPX Corp., 2014 NPE Report, *supra* note 23, at 4 (reporting that 48 percent of all NPEs cases filed in 2014 were filed in the Eastern District); U.S. Gov't Accountability Office, GAO-13-465, *supra* note 23, at 24.

45. *See* Bruce Berman, *For Samsung Charity Begins at "Home," Marshall, Texas,* IP CloseUp (Feb. 25, 2015), https://ipcloseup.com/2015/02/25/for-samsung-charity-begins-at-home-marshall-texas/; Jonas Anderson, *Court Competition for Patent Cases,* 163 U. Pa. L. Rev. 631, 653–54 (2015); Klerman & Reilly, *supra* note 42, at 273–74 (suggesting in addition that some of the judges simply find patent litigation more intellectually interesting than other cases, and may enjoy the prestige that comes from national notoriety).

46. *See* TC Heartland LLC v. Kraft Foods Group Brands LLC, 137 S. Ct. 1514 (2017).

47. *See* Colleen V. Chien & Michael Risch, *Recalibrating Patent Venue,* 77 Md. L. Rev. (forthcoming 2018) (manuscript at 28–29); *see also In re Cray,* 871 F.3d 1355 (Fed. Cir. 2017) (holding that venue requires "a physical place in the district" of "sufficient permanence," and "not solely a place of the defendant's employee"),

48. *See* Barry et al., *supra* note 20, at 24; Lauren Cohen et al., *Patent Trolling Isn't Dead—It's Just Moving to Delaware,* Harv. Bus. Rev., June 28, 2017, https://hbr.org/2017/06/patent-trolling-isnt-dead-its-just-moving-to-delaware.

49. *See* Thomas F. Cotter, Erik Hovenkamp & Norman Siebrasse, *Switching Costs, Path Dependence, and Patent Holdup* (Mar. 2, 2018), https://papers.ssrn.com/sol3/papers.cfm?abstract_id=3127933.

50. *See* Ian Austen, *BlackBerry Maker Reaches Deal in Patent Dispute,* N. Y. Times (Mar. 3, 2006), http://www.nytimes.com/2006/03/03/technology/03cnd-blackberry.html?_r=1&bl.

51. 547 U.S. 388 (2006).

52. For empirical studies on the percentage of cases in which courts award injunctions post-*eBay* and the specific factors that appear to be most important, *see* Christopher B. Seaman, *Permanent Injunctions in Patent Litigation After eBay,* 101 Iowa L. Rev. 1949 (2016).

53. *See, e.g., ActiveVideo Networks, Inc. v. Verizon Comm'ns, Inc.,* 694 F.3d 1312, 1341 (Fed. Cir. 2012) (quoting *Amado v. Microsoft Corp.,* 517 F.3d 1353, 1361–62 (Fed. Cir. 2008)); *see also Paice LLC v. Toyota Motor Corp.,* 504 F.3d 1293 (Fed. Cir. 2007).

54. *See* Christopher B. Seaman, *Ongoing Royalties in Patent Cases After eBay: An Empirical Assessment and Proposed Framework,* 23 Tex. Intell. Prop. L. J. 203, 238–39 & tbl. 5 (2015) (reporting mean and median postjudgment royalty rates of 1.84 and 1.34 times the mean and median prejudgment royalty rates, respectively).

55. *See ActiveVideo Networks, Inc.,* 694 F.3d at 1342 (requiring the defendant to pay a royalty of $2.74 per subscriber for the use of certain interactive television patents, even though the patent owner received only $0.17 per subscriber from another company and the court recognized that the defendant never would have agreed to such an amount *ex ante*).

56. *See* Thomas F. Cotter, *Patent Holdup, Patent Remedies, and Antitrust Remedies*, 34 J. Corp. L. 1151, 1181–82, 1188 n.172 (2009); *see also* Mark A. Lemley, *Ongoing Confusion over Ongoing Royalties*, 76 Mo. L. Rev. 695, 704–05 (2011).

57. *See* 35 U.S.C. § 284 (2012); *Halo Electronics, Inc. v. Pulse Electronics, Inc.*, 136 S. Ct. 1923 (2016).

58. *See generally* Christopher B. Seaman, *Willful Patent Infringement and Enhanced Damages After* In re Seagate: *An Empirical Study*, 97 Iowa L. Rev. 417, 465–471 (2012).

59. 136 S. Ct. 1923.

60. *See* Michael Feldman & Mark A. Lemley, *"Characteristic of a Pirate": Willfulness and Treble Damages* (Stan. Pub. Law Working Paper No. 2811773, 2016), https://papers.ssrn.com/abstract_id=2811773.

61. *See generally* Thomas F. Cotter, *An Economic Analysis of Enhanced Damages and Attorney's Fees for Willful Patent Infringement*, 14 Fed. Cir. B.J. 291 (2004).

62. *Halo Elecs.*, 136 S. Ct. 1936, 1938 (Breyer, J., concurring).

63. *See* 35 U.S.C. § 285 (2012).

64. 134 S. Ct. 1749 (2014).

65. *See* Scott Flanz, Octane Fitness: *The Shifting of Patent Attorneys' Fees Moves into High Gear*, 19 Stan. Tech. L. Rev. 329, 343–44 (2016); *see also* Hannah Jiam, *Fee-Shifting and* Octane Fitness: *An Empirical Approach Toward Understanding "Exceptional"*, 30 Berkeley Tech. L.J. 611 (2015); Darin Jones, *A Shifting Landscape for Shifting Fees: Attorney-Fee Awards in Patent Suits After* Octane *and* Highmark, 90 Wash. L. Rev. 505 (2015).

66. *See* Christian Helmers et al., *Is There a Patent Troll Problem in the U.K.?*, 24 Fordham Intell. Prop. Media & Ent. L. J. 509, 510 (2014); Brian J. Love et al., *Patent Assertion Entities in Europe*, in Patent Assertion Entities and Competition Policy (D. Daniel Sokol ed., 2017); *see also* Joint Research Center, Patent Assertion Entities in Europe. Their impact on innovation and knowledge transfer in ICT markets 44 (Nikolaus Thumm & Garry Gabison eds. 2016), publications.jrc.ec.europa.eu/repository/bitstream/JRC103321/lfna28145enn.pdf.

67. *See* Innovation Act, H.R. 9, Rep. No. 114–235, 114th Cong. § 3(b) (2015), https://www.congress.gov/bill/114th-congress/house-bill/9/text#toc-H7E6F9EAE8263402492511BD54A562B0B.

68. *See* Innovation Act, H.R. 9, 114th Cong. § 3(a) (reported July 29, 2015), https://www.congress.gov/bill/114th-congress/house-bill/9/text#toc-H7E6F9EAE8263402492511BD54A562B0B; *see also* Patent Act, S. 1137, 114th Cong. § 3(b) (reported Sept. 8, 2015), https://www.congress.gov/bill/114th-congress/senate-bill/1137?q={%22search%22%3A[%22\%22s1137\%22%22]}&resultIndex=1 (similar). *See generally* FTC Study, *supra* note 4, at 12–13.

69. *See* Innovation Act, H.R. 9, § 3(b); PATENT Act, S. 1137, § 5; *see also* FTC Study, *supra* note 4, at 10–11.

70. *See* Innovation Act, H.R. 3309, 113th Cong. § 3(d) (introduced Oct. 23, 2013).

71. *See* U.S. Dist. Ct., N.D. Cal., Patent Local Rules (Jan. 17, 2017), at 7, http://patentlyo.com/media/2017/02/Patent_Local_Rules_1-2017.pdf; Stuart Graham et al., *Final Report of the Berkeley Center for Law & Technology Patent Damages Workshop*, Tex. Intell. Prop. L. J. (forthcoming 2017) (manuscript at 14–16) (surveying current experiments with early disclosure); Gaston Kroub, *An Important Approach to Early Patentee Damages Disclosure*, Law360 (Mar. 27, 2013), http://www.law360.com/ip/articles/424432; Randall R. Rader, *The State of Patent Litigation*, Eastern District of Texas Judicial Conference, at 26 (Sept. 27, 2011), http://patentlyo.com/media/docs/2011/09/raderstateofpatentlit.pdf; *see also* FTC Study, *supra* note 4, at 11.

72. *See* Colleen V. Chien, *Holding Up and Holding Out*, 21 Mich. Telecomm. & Tech. L. Rev. 1, 26 (2014) (graphic showing that for small-stakes disputes, the median costs of litigating as reported by AIPLA often exceed the value of the case).

73. *In re Nintendo of Am., Inc.*, 756 F.3d 1363, 1365 (Fed. Cir. 2014).

74. *See* Innovation Act, H.R. 9, § 5; PATENT Act, S. 1137, § 4. For further discussion of the customer stay exception, *see* Colleen V. Chien & Edward Reines, *Why Technology Customers Are Being Sued En Masse for Patent Infringement and What Can Be Done*, 49 Wake Forest L. Rev. 235 (2014); Brian J. Love & James C. Yoon, *Expanding Patent Law's Customer Suit Exception*, 93 B. U. L. Rev. 1605 (2013); FTC Study, *supra* note 4, at 12.

75. For overviews of the state laws, *see* Qian Huang et al., *Navigating the Landscape of Anti-trolling Legislation*, INTELL. PROP. MAG. 54 (June 2016), https://www.pillsburylaw.com/siteFiles/ Publications/054_056IPM_June_2016Feat.pdf; *2016 Patent Troll Legislation*, NAT CONF. OF STATE LEGISLATURES (July 12, 2016), http://www.ncsl.org/research/financial-services-and-commerce/2016-patent-troll-legislation.aspx.

76. For discussion, *see* Paul R. Gugliuzza, *Patent Trolls and Preemption*, 101 VA. L. REV. 1579, 1580–81, 1599–600 (2015).

77. *See* Gunn v. Minton, 133 S. Ct. 1059, 1065 (2013) (holding that a claim is within the exclusive subject matter of the federal courts, if federal law creates the cause of action or if the federal issue "is: (1) necessarily raised, (2) actually disputed, (3) substantial, and (4) capable of resolution in federal court without disrupting the federal-state balance approved by Congress"). In *Gunn* itself, the Court held that state, not federal, courts had jurisdiction to hear a legal malpractice claim arising from a lawyer's alleged mishandling of a patent case. *Id.* at 1068–69.

78. *See* 800 Adept, Inc. v. Murex Sec., Ltd., 539 F.3d 1354, 1370 (Fed. Cir. 2008); *Dominant Semiconductors SDN BHD v. Osram GmbH*, 524 F.3d 1254, 1260 n.5 (Fed. Cir. 2007). For a critical view of the Federal Circuit's application of *Noerr-Pennington* to claims alleging bad faith assertion of IP rights, *see* Gugliuzza, *supra* note 76.

79. *E.g.*, Ruling on Motion to Stay, Motion to Amend, and Motion to Dismiss, State of Vermont v. MPHJ Tech. Invs., LLC, No. 282-5-13 Wncv (Vt. Sup. Ct., Aug. 28, 2014), https://www. vermontjudiciary.org/20112015%20Tcdecisioncvl/2014-11-4-8.pdf; *see* Joshua K. Dalton & Sarah K. Paige, *Finding the Right Way to Deal with Patent Demand Letters*, LAW360 (Sept. 8, 2016), https://www.law360.com/corporate/articles/836518/finding-the-right-way-to-deal-with-patent-demand-letters (discussing some background on the respondent in the Vermont case and details about another pending case in the District of Maryland).

80. *See* Lemley & Melamed, *supra* note 8, at 2159–60 (arguing that PAEs facilitate "double dipping" because (1) an accused who might negotiate a portfolio license with a single owner cannot readily do so when ownership is divided among many, perhaps unknown, owners; and (2) due to flaws in patent damages law, the damages awarded for the infringement of even a single patent may sometimes include some of the value of other components, such that multiple infringement actions relating to the same product expose the defendant to more risk than would a single action involving multiple patents); *see also* Taurus IP v. DaimlerChrysler, 726 F.3d 1306, 1328–29 (Fed. Cir. 2013) (affirming award of attorneys' fees against a losing PAE, where the evidence showed, among other things, that in a previous action an affiliated company had misled the defendant into believing that it was settling all claims relating to certain products); EXEC. OFFICE OF THE PRESIDENT, PATENT ASSERTION AND U.S. INNOVATION 4 (June 2013), https://www.whitehouse.gov/sites/default/files/docs/ patent_report.pdf (stating that PAEs "may hide their identity by creating numerous shell companies and requiring those who settle to sign non-disclosure agreements, making it difficult for defendants to form common defensive strategies (for example, by sharing legal fees rather than settling individually)).

81. *See, e.g.*, David Rogers, *The State of Patent Trolls in 2015*, INSIDE COUNS. (July 10, 2015), http://www.insidecounsel.com/2015/07/10/the-state-of-patent-trolls-in-2015; Amy Schatz, *Tech Firms and Universities Spar Over Patent Troll Bill*, RECODE (Mar. 23, 2014, 4:02 PM), http://recode.net/2014/03/23/tech-firms-and-universities-spar-over-patent-troll-bill/.

82. *See* Mike Masnick, *Nathan Myhrvold's Intellectual Ventures Using Over 1,000 Shell Companies to Hide Patent Shakedown*, TECHDIRT (Feb. 18, 2010, 7:44 AM), https://www.techdirt. com/articles/20100217/1853298215.shtml (accusing Intellectual Ventures of doing this). Relatedly, the original patent owner may be an operating company that, for strategic reasons, would prefer not to openly sue a competitor, and thus assigns certain patents to a so-called "privateer," who agrees to enforce the patent and share the proceeds with the assignee.

83. *See* Changes to Require Identification of Attributable Owner, 79 Fed. Reg. 4,105 (Jan. 24, 2014).

84. *See* Innovation Act, H.R.9, 114th Cong. §4 (reported July 29, 2015), https://www.congress.gov/ bill/114th-congress/house-bill/9/text#toc-H7E6F9EAE8263402492511BD54A562B0B;

Patent Act, S. 1137, 114th Cong. § 10 (reported Sept. 8, 2015), https://www.congress.gov/bill/114th-congress/senate-bill/1137?q={%22search%22%3A[%22\%22s1137\%22%22]}&resultIndex=1.

85. *See* FTC Study, *supra* note 4, at 52, 60–63, 66–67.
86. *See id.* at 11. Federal Rule of Civil Procedure 7.1 already requires any nongovernmental corporate party in any federal civil action to identify "any parent corporation and any publicly held corporation owning 10 percent or more of its stock" and to update this information as necessary. Similarly, parties to USPTO administrative proceedings such as IPRs must disclose the "real party in interest," 37 C.F.R. § 42.8 (2016), a term that the rule leaves undefined but which so far has been interpreted to require consideration of various factors identified in other contexts to determine if a judgment precludes another party from litigating a matter again. *See* Office Patent Trial Practice Guide, 77 Fed. Reg. 48,756, 48,759 (Aug. 14, 2012) (citing *Taylor v. Sturgell*, 553 U.S. 880 (2008)). None of these existing rules expressly requires the identification of "grandparent" corporations or beyond, however, or of subsidiaries or sister companies; and Rule 7.1 does not apply at all to noncorporate entities. For discussion, *see* 5 CHARLES ALAN WRIGHT & ARTHUR R. MILLER, FEDERAL PRACTICE & PROCEDURE § 1197 (3d ed. 2004). The requirements under consideration, therefore, would be considerably more burdensome on litigants than is any existing rule. On the other hand, a firm that was served only with a demand letter would remain unable in many cases to identify the demander's ultimate parent entity, up until the point (if ever) that a complaint is filed—though another proposed bill would have required any entity submitting more than twenty demand letters involving the same patent within a single year to disclose its ultimate parent entity to the USPTO. *See* H.R. 1896, 114th Cong. § 2 (introduced Apr. 20, 2015), https://www.congress.gov/bill/114th-congress/house-bill/1896/text.

Chapter 9

1. The number is *at least* in the tens of thousands. One recent study, for example, reports that there were 314,490 patent-filing entities—entities, mind you—in a database of US patents granted from 2006 to 2012 in "14 classifications related most closely to smartphones." JOEL R. REIDENBERG ET AL., PATENTS AND SMALL PARTICIPANTS IN THE SMARTPHONE INDUSTRY 3 (Jan. 15, 2015), http://www.wipo.int/export/sites/www/ip-competition/en/studies/clip_smartphone_patent.pdf. Another study identified "251 technical interoperability standards implemented in a modern laptop computer, and estimates that the total number of standards relevant to such a device is much higher." Brad Biddle et al., *How Many Standards in a Laptop? (And Other Empirical Questions)*, 2010 INT'L TELECOMM. UNION SEC. TELECOMM. STANDARDIZATION KALEIDOSCOPE ACAD. CONF. PROC. 123, http://papers.ssrn.com/abstract=1619440. As discussed in the text above, each such standard may incorporate numerous patented technologies—as illustrated by Judge James Holderman's conclusion, in a case I discuss later in this chapter, that 3,000 was a "credible account of the number of patents potentially" essential to the IEEE's 802.11 standard. *In re Innovatio IP Ventures, LLC Patent Litig.*, Case No. 11 C 9308, 2013 WL 5593609, at *43 (N.D. Ill. Oct. 3, 2013).
2. *See* Paul Belleflamme, *The Smartphone Patent Wars: Nothing Really Surprising . . .* , IPDIGIT (Nov. 28, 2013), http://www.ipdigit.eu/2013/11/the-smartphone-patent-wars-nothing-really-surprising/.
3. Academics are usually hesitant to cite Wikipedia because it's not subject to any sort of formal oversight or peer review, but the WIKIPEDIA page titled *Smartphone Patent Wars*, available at https://en.wikipedia.org/wiki/Smartphone_patent_wars, appears to be a well-sourced reference for the first three or four years of the smartphone wars. Its coverage appears less than complete for 2013 and thereafter, however. Another useful source for detailed information on many of the cases that made up the smartphone wars is Florian Mueller's blog *FOSS Patents*, available at http://www.fosspatents.com/.
4. U.S. Patent No. 7,469,381 ("List scrolling and document translation, scaling, and rotation on a touch-screen display").
5. U.S. Patent No. 8,046,721 ("Unlocking a device by performing gestures on an unlock image").

6. U.S. Patent No. 7,844,915 ("Application programming interfaces for scrolling operations").

7. U.S. Patent No. 7,479,949 ("Touch screen device, method, and graphical user interface for determining commands by applying heuristics").

8. *See* Florian Mueller, *Analysis of 222 Smartphone Patent Assertions: More than 90 Percent Go Nowhere, Rest Lacks Impact*, FOSS PATENTS (Oct. 1, 2014), http://www.fosspatents.com/2014/10/analysis-of-222-smartphone-patent.html.

9. Well, okay—the World War I analogy may be a *bit* of a stretch. Few, if any, of the participating companies have been decimated in the smartphone wars; and for successful companies like Apple and Samsung, even the occasional multimillion dollar patent infringement judgment is, relatively speaking, just a drop in the bucket.

10. The assumption, however, that a given drug is covered by one single patent isn't necessarily accurate. *See supra* Chapter 1 n.12.

11. The foundational work on holdup is usually attributed to Oliver Williamson, co-recipient of the 2009 Sveriges Riksbank Prize in Economic Sciences in Memory of Alfred Nobel. *See, e.g.,* OLIVER E. WILLIAMSON, THE ECONOMIC INSTITUTIONS OF CAPITALISM: FIRMS, MARKETS, RELATIONAL CONTRACTING 61 (1985); *see also* Oliver Hart, *Incomplete Contracts, in* 2 THE NEW PALGRAVE DICTIONARY OF ECONOMICS 752 (John Eatwell et al. eds., 1987); Paul Joskow, *Transaction Cost Economics, Antitrust Rules, and Remedies*, 18 J.L. ECON. & ORG. 95, 102–03 (2002); Paul L. Joskow, *Asset Specificity, in* 1 THE NEW PALGRAVE DICTIONARY OF ECONOMICS AND THE LAW 107 (Peter Newman ed. 1998); Benjamin Klein et al., *Vertical Integration, Appropriable Rents, and the Competitive Contracting Process*, 21 J.L. & ECON. 297 (1978); Benjamin Klein, *Transaction Cost Determinants of "Unfair" Contractual Arrangements*, 70 AM. ECON. REV. 356, 356–57 (1980). *See generally* Oliver E. Williamson, *The Vertical Integration of Production: Market Failure Considerations*, 61 AM. ECON. REV. 112 (1971).

12. Though not all of them are really (technically) essential, or essential to most consumers; and there may be competing standards. Nonetheless, even if switching to a different standard is technically feasible, it may be unduly costly once a product has been launched.

13. *See* Alexander Galetovic et al., *An Empirical Examination of Patent Holdup*, 11 J. COMP. L. & ECON. 549 (2015); Alexander Galetovic et al., *Patent Holdup: Do Patent Holders Hold Up Innovation?* (Hoover IP²,Working Paper No. 14011, 2014), http://hooverip2.org/wp-content/uploads/ip2-wp14011-paper.pdf. *But see* Rudi Bekkers, *Concerns and Evidence for Ex-Post Hold-Up with Essential Patents* (Sept. 22, 2015) (unpublished paper), https://papers.ssrn.com/sol3/papers.cfm?abstract_id=2663939 (stating that, "[w]hile it has been argued that hold-up is a theoretical risk only, and does not manifest itself in 'real world' scenarios," there have been "a number of recent, seminal court cases in which the judge determined that for essential patents, fees were demanded that wildly exceeded what the court ultimately deemed to be a FRAND royalty rate").

14. *See, e.g.,* DOMINICK ARMENTANO, ANTITRUST AND MONOPOLY: ANATOMY OF A POLICY FAILURE 58–60 (2d ed. 1982).

15. *See* STEVEN PINKER, THE BETTER ANGELS OF OUR NATURE: WHY VIOLENCE HAS DECLINED (2011).

16. *See, e.g.,* Damien Geradin, *Reverse Hold-Ups: The (Often Ignored) Risks Faced by Innovators in Standardized Areas, in* THE PROS AND CONS OF STANDARD SETTING 101, 111–12 (Swedish Comp. Auth. Ed. 2010), http://www.konkurrensverket.se/.

17. *E.g., id.* at 101, 105.

18. To be sure, in its recent *Halo* decision (discussed in Chapter 8) the Supreme Court held that enhanced damages aren't intended to serve a compensatory purpose; but, in practice, a modest damages enhancement in a case in which a "willful" infringer unduly delayed paying would make up for some of the otherwise uncompensable harm caused by the delay, as well as having some deterrent value. For discussion, *see* Thomas F. Cotter, *Enhanced Damages for the Infringement of Standard Essential Patents*, COMPARATIVE PATENT REMEDIES BLOG (Dec. 1, 2016), http://comparativepatentremedies.blogspot.com/2016/12/enhanced-damages-for-infringement-of.html.

19. Norman V. Siebrasse & Thomas F. Cotter, *The Value of the Standard*, 101 MINN. L. REV. 1159, 1161 (2017); *see also* Thomas F. Cotter, *Patent Holdup, Patent Remedies, and Antitrust*

Responses, 34 J. Corp. L. 1151, 1169–70 (2009); Mark A. Lemley & Carl Shapiro, *Patent Holdup and Royalty Stacking*, 85 Tex. L. Rev. 1991, 2013 (2007).

20. Augustin Cournot, Researches into the Mathematical Principles of the Theory of Wealth 99–104 (Augustus M. Kelly ed., Nathaniel T. Bacon trans., 1897) (1838).

21. Ann Armstrong et al., *Surveying Royalty Demands for the Components within the Modern Smartphone 2* (May 29, 2014) (unpublished paper), http://ssrn.com/abstract=2443848.

22. *Id.* at 4.

23. *See, e.g.*, Keith Mallinson, *Stacking the Deck in Analysis of Smartphone Patent Licensing Costs*, WiseHarbor (Sept. 19, 2014), http://www.wiseharbor.com/pdfs/Mallinson%20on%20 Intel's%20Smartphone%20Royalty%20Stack%2019Sept2014.pdf.

24. *See, e.g.*, Alexander Galetovic & Kirti Gupta, *Royalty Stacking and Standard Essential Patents: Theory and Evidence from the World Mobile Wireless Industry* (Hoover IP² Working Paper No. 15012, 2016), http://hooverip2.org/wp-content/uploads/ip2-wp15012-paper.pdf; *see also* Jorge Contreras, *Patents, Technical Standards, and Standards-Setting Organizations: A Survey of the Empirical, Legal, and Economics Literature, in* 2 Research Handbook on the Economics of Intellectual Property Law (Peter Menell & David L. Schwartz, eds., forthcoming 2018) (manuscript at 14–15 & n.10), http://papers.ssrn. com/abstract_id=2641569 (surveying the empirical literature on stacking).

25. The first two Federal Circuit opinions on causal nexus were rendered in appeals from orders relating to motions for preliminary injunctions. *E.g., Apple Inc. v. Samsung Elecs. Co.*, 695 F.3d 1370 (Fed. Cir. 2012); *Apple Inc. v. Samsung Elecs. Co.*, 678 F.3d 1314 (Fed. Cir. 2012).

26. *Apple Inc. v. Samsung Elecs. Co.*, 809 F.3d 633, 641 & n.1 (Fed. Cir. 2015) (quoting *Apple Inc. v. Samsung Elecs. Co.*, 735 F.3d 1352, 1364, 1368 (Fed. Cir. 2013)).

27. *See Apple Inc. v. Samsung Elecs. Co.*, No. 11–CV–01846–LHK, 2014 WL 976898, at *21 (N.D. Cal. Mar. 6, 2014).

28. *See Apple Inc. v. Samsung Elecs. Co.*, 809 F.3d 633 (Fed. Cir. 2015). After this decision was handed down, another panel of the Federal Circuit held that the patents in suit were invalid, *see Apple Inc. v. Samsung Elecs. Co.*, 816 F.3d 788, 793 (Fed. Cir. 2016), but then in October 2016 the court overruled this decision en banc, *see* Apple Inc. v. Samsung Elecs. Co., 839 F.3d 1034, 1063 (Fed. Cir. 2016) (en banc).

29. *See Microsoft Corp. v. Motorola, Inc.*, No. C10–1823JLR, 2012 WL 5993202 (W. D. Wash. Nov. 30, 2012) (holding that Motorola is not entitled to injunctive relief for Microsoft's alleged infringement of patents subject to a FRAND commitment and reiterating that Microsoft is a third-party beneficiary of Motorola's contractual promise to license the patents on FRAND terms); *Apple, Inc. v. Motorola, Inc.*, 869 F. Supp. 2d 901, 913–15 (N.D. Ill. 2012) (Posner, J., sitting by designation) (holding that Motorola was not entitled to injunctive relief), *aff'd in part, rev'd in part, vacated in part, and remanded*, 757 F.3d 1286 (Fed. Cir. 2014).

30. *See* 19 U.S.C. § 1337(a) (2012). For detailed scholarly discussions of the ITC, *see, e.g.*, Colleen V. Chien, *Patently Protectionist? An Empirical Analysis of Patent Cases at the International Trade Commission*, 50 Wm. & Mary L. Rev. 63 (2008); Colleen V. Chien & Mark A. Lemley, *Patent Holdup, the ITC, and the Public Interest*, 98 Cornell L. Rev. 1 (2012); Robert W. Hahn & Hal J. Singer, *Assessing Bias in Patent Infringement Cases: A Review of International Trade Commission Decisions*, 21 Harv. J. L. & Tech. 457 (2008); Sapna Kumar, *The Other Patent Agency: Congressional Regulation of the ITC*, 61 Fla. L. Rev. 529 (2009). For numbers of case filings, *see* U.S. Int'l Trade Comm'n, Section 337 Statistics: Number of New, Completed, and Active Investigations by Fiscal Year (Updated Quarterly) (July 14, 2017), https://www. usitc.gov/intellectual_property/337_statistics_number_new_completed_and_active.htm; U.S. Int'l Trade Comm'n, Section 337 Statistics: Number of 337 Investigations Brought by NPEs (Updated Quarterly) (July 14, 2017), https://www.usitc.gov/intellectual_property/ 337_statistics_number_section_337_investigations.htm [hereinafter ITC NPE Update]; U.S. Int'l Trade Comm'n, Section 337 Statistics: Types of Unfair Acts Alleged in Active Investigations by Fiscal Year (Updated Annually), https://www.usitc.gov/intellectual_pro-perty/337_statistics_types_unfair_acts_alleged_active.htm.

31. *See* Chien, *supra* note 30, at 72–80 (discussing the statutory history, as well as some of the advantages of proceeding before the agency); *see also* A Lawyer's Guide to Section

337 INVESTIGATIONS BEFORE THE U.S. INTERNATIONAL TRADE COMMISSION 5–6 (Tom M. Schaumberg ed., 2d ed. 2012).

32. 19 U.S.C. § 1337(a)(1)(B).

33. *See id.* §§ 1337(a)(2) (3).

34. *See* Chien, *supra* note 30, at 73–74.

35. *See* Chien & Lemley, *supra* note 30, at 28 & n.152; *see also* Chien, *supra* note 30, at 70 (reporting that "65 percent of ITC cases studied had a district court counterpart").

36. *See Spansion, Inc. v. Int'l Trade Comm'n,* 629 F.3d 1331, 1359 (Fed. Cir. 2010).

37. More specifically, upon finding a violation, the ITC "shall direct that the articles concerned . . . be excluded from entry into the United States, unless, after considering the effect of such exclusion upon the public health and welfare, competitive conditions in the United States economy, the production of like or directly competitive articles in the United States, and United States consumers, it finds that such articles should not be excluded from entry." 19 U.S.C. § 1337(d)(1).

38. *See* U.S. PATENT & TRADEMARK OFFICE, U.S. PATENT STATISTICS, CALENDAR YEARS 1963–2015 (2016), https://www.uspto.gov/web/offices/ac/ido/oeip/taf/us_stat.pdf (foreigners accounted for approximately 52 percent of all US patent grants in 2015).

39. *See* Chien & Lemley, *supra* note 30, at 14–15, 26 (stating that, although "section 337 was created to keep foreign pirates out of American markets, recent PAE cases have targeted domestic companies almost twice as often as foreign ones (209 times versus 123 times, respectively)," and that "nearly every patentee can bring an ITC complaint, and nearly every accused infringer is a potential ITC defendant, converting the ITC into a mainstream venue in which to file patent grievances") (citations omitted). The ITC itself reports that twelve out of seventy-one investigations filed from fiscal year 2016 through the second quarter of fiscal year 2017 were brought by NPEs. *See* ITC NPE Update, *supra* note 30.

40. *See* Commission Opinion, Certain Electronic Devices, Inv. No. 337-TA-794 (U.S. Int'l Trade Comm'n July 5, 2013) (public version) 41–64, 107–14; *see also* Notice of Final Determination, Certain Electronic Devices, Inv. No. 337-TA-794, 78 Fed. Reg. 34,699 (U.S. Int'l Trade Comm'n June 4, 2013).

41. *See* 19 U.S.C. § 1337(j)(2).

42. *See* J. Gregory Sidak, *International Trade Commission Exclusion Orders for the Infringement of Standard-Essential Patents,* CRITERION ECONS.141 & n.116 (2016), https://www.criterioneconomics.com/docs/itc-exclusion-orders-for-standard-essential-patents.pdf (citing to Presidential Disapproval of Determination of the U.S. Int'l Trade Comm'n, Certain Dynamic Random Access Memories, Inv. No. 337-TA-242, 52 Fed. Reg. 46,011 (Dec. 3, 1987)).

43. *See* Letter from Michael B. G. Froman, Exec. Office of the President of the U.S. Trade Rep., to Irving A. Williamson, Chairman, U.S. Int'l Trade Comm'n (Aug. 3, 2013) (quoting U.S. DEP'T OF JUSTICE & U.S. PAT. & TRADEMARK OFF., POLICY STATEMENT ON REMEDIES FOR STANDARDS-ESSENTIAL PATENTS SUBJECT TO VOLUNTARY F/RAND COMMITMENTS 7–8 (Jan. 8, 2013), www.justice.gov/atr/public/guidelines/290994.pdf), https://ustr.gov/sites/default/files/08032013%20Letter_1.PDF (stating that "whether public interest considerations counsel against a particular exclusion order depends on the specific circumstances at issue," but that "to mitigate against patent hold-up, exclusionary relief from the Commission based on FRAND-encumbered SEPs should be available only" when, for example, " 'a putative licensee refuses to pay what has been determined to be a FRAND royalty, or refuses to engage in a negotiation to determine F/RAND terms,' " or " 'is not subject to the jurisdiction of a court that could award damages' ").

44. *See* Colleen V. Chien & Mark A. Lemley, *Patents and the Public Interest,* N. Y. TIMES (Dec. 13, 2011), http://www.nytimes.com/2011/12/13/opinion/patents-smartphones-and-the-public-interest.html.

45. For discussion of the availability of injunctions for patent infringement outside the United States, *see* THOMAS F. COTTER, COMPARATIVE PATENT REMEDIES: A LEGAL AND ECONOMIC ANALYSIS (Oxford University Press 2013); Thomas F. Cotter, *The Comparative Law and Economics of Standard-Essential Patents and FRAND Royalties,* 22 TEX. INTELL. PROP. L. J. 311 (2014).

46. For discussion of contract law as a possible limitation on the right to seek injunctive relief and the reception (or not) of this theory in different jurisdictions, *see* Cotter, *supra* note 45, at 315–19; Benjamin C. Li, Note, *The Global Convergence of FRAND Licensing Practices: Towards "Interoperable" Legal Standards*, 31 BERKELEY TECH. L. J. 429, 440–42 (2016); *see also* Reto M. Hilty & Peter R. Slowinski, *Standardessentielle Patente—Perspectiken außerhalb des Kartellrechts*, 2015 GRUR INT. 781 (proposing that the EU should adopt a regulation that would interpret FRAND commitments made to SSOs as contracts for the benefit of third parties).

47. No. C10-1823JLR, 2013 WL 6000017 (W.D. Wash. Nov. 12, 2013), *aff'd*, 795 F.3d 1024 (9th Cir. 2015).

48. *See, e.g.,* Institute of Electric and Electronics Engineers Standards Association (IEEE-SA) Standards Board Bylaws 6.2, *available at* http://standards.ieee.org/develop/policies/bylaws/sect6-7.html. Traditionally, though, SSOs haven't wanted to be too explicit about the meaning of FRAND, given the difficulty of achieving consensus among their members and of determining in advance precisely what a FRAND royalty would be, as well as the possibility that even attempting to do so might subject SSO members to antitrust liability for price fixing. *See* Cotter, *supra* note 455, at 312 n.2.

49. *See id.* at 333–37 (noting, in addition, that it's something of an open question whether *Noerr-Pennington* immunity would shield SEP owners from liability for merely seeking an injunction, unless the infringement litigation was a sham). That said, and despite the reservations about US antitrust law that I express in the text, in two cases the FTC has invoked its authority under § 5 of the FTC Act to require firms that had acquired or were about to acquire other firms that owned SEPS to commit to forgoing injunctive relief for the infringement of those SEPs. *See In the Matter of Motorola Mobility LLC and Google Inc.*, FTC File No. 12-0120 (July 23, 2013), https://www.ftc.gov/enforcement/cases-proceedings/1210120/motorola-mobility-llc-google-inc-matter; *In the Matter of Robert Bosch GmbH*, FTC File No. 121-0081, 11, 13–14 (Apr. 24, 2013), https://www.ftc.gov/enforcement/cases-proceedings/1210081/bosch-robert-bosch-gmbh.

50. For discussion, *see* Cotter, *supra* note 455; Li, *supra* note 45, at 442–51.

51. *See* Case C-170/13, *Huawei Technologies Co. v. ZTE Corp.* (CJEU 2015), http://curia.europa.eu/juris/liste.jsf?num=C-170/13.

52. The misuse doctrine renders a patent unenforceable if the owner has, well, "misused" it in some way, for example by conditioning a license on the licensee's agreement not to purchase some other product from a competitor, in a way that harms competition. The doctrine often dovetails with antitrust law, but its precise contours remain murky. For discussion, *see, e.g.,* Thomas F. Cotter, *Four Questionable Rationales for the Patent Misuse Doctrine*, 12 MINN. J.L. SCI. & TECH. 457 (2011).

53. *Samsung Electronics Co., Ltd. v. Apple Japan Godo Kaisha* [Intellectual Prop. High Ct.] May 16, 2014, no. 10043; Rechtbank's-Gravenhage, Mar. 14, 2012, Nos. 11-2212, 11-2213, 11-2215 (*Samsung Elecs. Co. v. Apple Inc.*) (Neth.), http://uitspraken.rechtspraak.nl/inziendocument?id=ECLI:NL:RBSGR:2012:BV8871. For discussion, *see, e.g.,* Cotter, *supra* note 45, at 322–27; Yuzuki Nagakoshi & Katsuya Tamai, *Japan Without FRANDs? Recent Developments on Injunctions and FRAND-Encumbered Patents in Japan*, 44 AIPLA Q. J. 243 (2016).

54. *See* Joe Mullin, *Supreme Court Takes up* Apple v. Samsung, *First Design Patent Case in a Century*, ARS TECHNICA (Mar. 21, 2016), http://arstechnica.com/tech-policy/2016/03/supreme-court-could-slash-apples-548m-win-against-samsung/.

55. *See, e.g.,* Florian Mueller, *Apple wins $119 million in patent damages from Samsung, wanted $2.2 billion: mixed verdict*, FOSS PATENTS (May 2, 2014), http://www.fosspatents.com/2014/05/apple-wins-119-million-in-patent.html.

56. *See Apple Inc. v. Samsung Elecs. Co.*, 839 F.3d 1034, 1063 (Fed. Cir. 2016) (en banc), *cert. denied*, 138 S. Ct. 420 (2017).

57. *See* CHRIS BARRY ET AL., PwC 2017 PATENT LITIGATION STUDY: CHANGE ON THE HORIZON? 9, 29, https://www.pwc.com/us/en/forensic-services/publications/assets/2016-pwc-patent-litigation-study.pdf.

58. *See generally* Cotter, *supra* note 45; Thomas F. Cotter & John M. Golden, *Empirical Studies Relating to Patents—Remedies, in* Research Handbook on the Economics of Intellectual Property Law (Peter Menell et al., eds., Edward Elgar Publishing, forthcoming 2018).

59. The astute reader may ask how we know that a lost profits award will make the infringer worse off. The answer is that if the evidence shows that the patent owner would have made *x* more sales absent the infringement, this necessarily means that the infringer wouldn't have made those sales; but if the infringer could have made and distributed the product at lower cost than the patent owner, then, absent the infringement, the owner would have licensed the infringer rather than making and selling the product itself. Put another way, in cases in which the owner can prove lost profits, it's fair to infer that those lost profits are greater than the profit the defendant earned because otherwise the owner would be seeking a reasonable royalty instead. Conceivably, the parties could have believed, incorrectly, that the infringer was less efficient than the patent owner, and in that case they wouldn't have agreed to any royalty *ex ante*. But then the patent owner's lost profits will be less than the infringer's profits, and the patent owner will probably seek a reasonable royalty anyway instead of lost profits, so even then the point made in the text still holds.

60. *See* Barry et al., *supra* note 57, at 11.

61. Erik Hovenkamp & Jonathan S. Masur, *Reliable Problems from Unreliable Patent Damages*, 25 Tex. Intell. Prop. L. J. (forthcoming 2017) (manuscript at 9), https://papers.ssrn.com/sol3/papers.cfm?abstract_id=2825236.

62. John C. Jarosz & Michael J. Chapman, *The Hypothetical Negotiation and Reasonable Royalty Damages: The Tail Wagging the Dog*, 16 Stan. Tech. L. Rev. 769, 809 (2013).

63. *See* Barry, *supra* note 57, at 6.

64. *See Georgia-Pacific Corp. v. U.S. Plywood Corp.*, 318 F. Supp. 1116, 1120 (S.D.N.Y. 1970), *modified*, 446 F.2d 295 (2d Cir. 1971).

65. *See* Thomas F. Cotter, *Patent Damages Heuristics*, 25 Tex. Intell. Prop. L. J. (forthcoming 2017) (manuscript at 31), https://papers.ssrn.com/sol3/papers.cfm?abstract_id=2809917 (manuscript at 31); *see also* Fed. Circuit Bar Ass'n, Model Patent Jury Instructions (Jan. 2016) (proposing that courts instruct juries to "consider all the facts known and available to the parties at the time the infringement began," but that "[s]ome of the kinds of factors that you may consider in making your determination are: (1) The value that the claimed invention contributes to the accused product. (2) The value that factors other than the claimed invention contribute to [the accused product]. (3) Comparable license agreements, such as those covering the use of the claimed invention or similar technology"), https://fedcirbar.org/IntegralSource/Model-Patent-Jury-Instructions; Daralyn J. Durie & Mark A. Lemley, *A Structured Approach to Calculating Reasonable Royalties*, 14 Lewis & Clark L. Rev. 627 (2010).

66. *See* Hovenkamp & Masur, *supra* note 61 (manuscript at 16–18); *see also* Cotter, *supra* note 65 (manuscript at 31–34).

67. I've explained the double discounting problem elsewhere as follows, citing an example found in Stephen Kalos & Jonathan D. Putnam, *On the Incomparability of "Comparable": An Economic Interpretation of "Infringer's Royalties,"* 9 J. Proprietary Rts. 2, 4–5 (1997). Suppose that:

> as of the date of infringement both parties expect that (1) the defendant would earn $1 million in additional profit from a course of conduct that the plaintiff believes would infringe her patent; and (2) there is an 80 percent probability of validity and an (independent) 70 percent probability that the proposed use would infringe. On these facts, the parties would agree to a license in the amount of $560,000 (that is, $1 million x 0.7 x 0.8). If the parties go to trial instead, the plaintiff's expected payoff also must be discounted to reflect the probability that the court will find the patent invalid or not infringed. If those probabilities are the same as they would have been as of the date of infringement, the plaintiff's expected payoff is 56 percent of whatever damages she expects to recover at trial if she wins. If she expects to recover $1 million, her expected payoff is, again, $560,000, the same as if the parties had agreed to a license (ignoring, for present purposes, any differences attributable to the time value of

money). If the court were to award her only $560,000, her expected payoff from going to trial would be $313,600 (that is, $560,000 x 0.7 x 0.8), which means she is worse off than she would have been, but for the infringement. (COTTER, *supra* note 45, at 135–36 n.240)

68. *See* Hovenkamp & Masur, *supra* note 61 (manuscript at 21–29) (discussing this and other related problems with the use of comparables).

69. *See Microsoft Corp. v. Motorola, Inc.*, Case No. C10-1823JLR, 2013 WL 2111217 (W.D. Wash. Apr. 25, 2013), *aff'd*, 795 F.3d 1024 (9th Cir. 2015). Portions of the text here are adapted from Cotter, *supra* note 46.

70. *See id.* at *2.

71. Robert P. Merges, *Of Property Rules, Coase, and Intellectual Property*, 94 COLUM. L. REV. 2655, 2662 n.27 (1994).

72. *Microsoft*, 2013 WL2111217, at *83–101.

73. *See id.* at *65. Following the nonjury trial to determine the amount and range of a FRAND royalty for the two portfolios, the court conducted a jury trial on Microsoft's claim for damages resulting from Motorola's alleged breach of its contractual duty of good faith and fair dealing, which resulted in a $14.5 million jury award to Microsoft. The Ninth Circuit thereafter affirmed the final judgment in Microsoft's favor. *See* 795 F.3d 1024 (9th Cir. 2015).

74. No. 2303, 2013 WL 5593609 (N.D. Ill. Oct. 3, 2013).

75. *Id.* at *6.

76. *See id.* at *43 (stating that "Dr. Leonard adjusted the value attributable to Innovatio's patents in each of those cases by relying on a 1998 article finding that the top 10 percent of all electronics patents account for 84 percent of the value in all electronics patents. (*See* DTX-192, Mark Schankerman, *How Valuable is Patent Protection? Estimates By Technology Field*, 29 RAND J. ECON. 77, 94 tbl.5 & n.12 (1998).)").

77. *See id.* at *12–18, 37–43.

78. *See* Fiona Scott Morton & Carl Shapiro, *Patent Assertions: Are We Any Closer to Aligning Reward to Contribution?, in* 16 INNOVATION POLICY AND THE ECONOMY 89, 123 (William R. Kerr et al. eds., University of Chicago Press 2016).

79. For a more recent use of a top-down approach as a check on rates derived from the use of comparables, *see* Mr. Justice Birss's opinion in *Unwired Planet International Ltd. v. Huawei Technologies Co.*, [2017] EWHC 711 (Eng.).

80. For further discussion of some of the ideas presented in this paragraph, *see, e.g.*, Cotter, *supra* note 65.

81. *Dobson v. Hartford Carpet Co.*, 114 U. S. 439, 444 (1885); *see also Dobson v. Dornan*, 118 U. S. 10, 17 (1886)

82. For a brief discussion of the history leading up to the enactment of the predecessor statute to § 289, *see Samsung Elecs. Co. v. Apple Inc.*, 137 S. Ct. 429, 432–33 (2016).

83. *See id.* at 431, 435–36 (citing *Ex parte Adams*, 84 Off. Gaz. Pat. Office 311 (1898), and *Application of Zahn*, 617 F.2d 261, 268 (C.C.P.A.1980)).

84. *See id.* at 434–35.

Conclusion

1. For discussion of conflicting views on the effect of patents on the Industrial Revolution, *see* James E. Bessen & Michael J. Meurer, *Of Patents and Property*, 31 REGULATION, Winter 2008–09, at 18.

2. *See* Mark A. Lemley, *The Surprising Resilience of the Patent System*, 95 TEX. L. REV. 1 (2016).

3. *See* KEVIN KELLY, WHAT TECHNOLOGY WANTS (Penguin Books 2011).

INDEX

damages (*cont.*)
  lost profits v. reasonable royalty, 246–47.
    (*See also* lost profits, reasonable royalty)
  total profit, 247–48
  underlying principles in the patent
    context, 245–46
declaratory judgments
  MedImmune, Inc. v. Genentech, Inc., 83
design patents
  disgorgement/total profit, 255–56
  generally, 34, 254
  global grant practices, 34
  See also Apple v. Samsung litigation
DiMasi, Grabowski & Hanson drug development
    studies
  critiques, 147–48
  generally, 145–47, 203
disclosure, 23–24
drug pricing
  Mylan N.V., 139
  reports on price increases, 139–40
  role of patents, 148–51
  Turing Pharmaceuticals, 139
drug research
  cost, 145–47
  federally-funded, 141–42
  privately-funded, 142

eBay Inc. v. MercExchange, L.L.C.
  holding, 130
  impact on injunctive relief, 239
Eastern District of Texas venue
  generally, 217–18
  effect on patent litigation outcomes, 218
Edison, Thomas, 2
Eisenberg, Rebecca, 82, 103
enhanced damages
  *Halo Electronics, Inc. v. Pulse Electronics,
    Inc.*, 221–22
evergreening patents, 163–64

fair, reasonable, and nondiscriminatory
    ("FRAND") licensing, 231
  RAND licensing, 231
  impact on injunctive relief, 240, 242, 244
  *In re Innovatio IP Ventures LLC Patent
    Litigation*, 252–53
  Microsoft v. Motorola, 243, 250–52
  See also patent pools
Feldman, Roger, 167
Food & Drug Administration,
  ANDA, 151, 158
  approval process, 170
  generally, 142–43
  investigational new drugs, 143–44
free trade,
  generally, 180–83

General Agreement on Tariffs and Trade
    ("GATT"), 184–85
  European Union ("EU"), 185
  North American Free Trade Agreement
    ("NAFTA"), 183
  Smoot-Hawley Tariff Act of 1930, 184

Gabison, Garry, 126
Gates Foundation, 51
generic drugs
  Abbott Labs. v. Teva Pharm. USA, Inc., 164–65
  anticompetitive behavior, 157–161
  generally, 151–52
  *New York ex rel. Schneiderman v. Actavis
    PLC*, 164
  relative costs, xvii
  reverse payment settlements, 161–63
  FTC v. Actavis, Inc., 162–63
genes, 64–66
  discovery of DNA, 64
  protein coding, 67
  RNA, 66

Gold, Richard & Julia Carbone, 83
Golden, John, 54
Grady, Mark & Miles Alexander, 94
Graham, Stuart & David Mowery, 126
Graham, Stuart & Saurabh Vishnubhakat, 4, 49
Greaney, Thomas, 167
Green, Michael, 94

Haidt, Jonathan, xx, xxv
von Hayek, Friedrich, 171
health insurance, 168–69
Heller, Michael & Rebecca Eisenberg, 46
Honeywell Inc. v. Sperry Rand Corp., 115
Hovenkamp, Erik & Jonathan Masur, 248, 250
Hu, Albert & I.P.L. Png, 176

infant industry, 181–82
injunctive relief
  consequences in the smartphone context, 235
  economic rationale for use in intellectual
    property, 236–37
  generally, 219–20
  internationally, 243–44
  See also eBay, Inc. v. MercExchange LLC
  for standard-essential patents, 244
Inter Partes Reviews ("IPRs")
  constitutionality, 136
  generally, 136
international patent law
  Agreement on Trade-Related Aspects of
    Intellectual Property Rights ("TRIPs"),
    180–81, 185–91, 194–96
  Paris Convention, 179–180
  Patent Cooperation Treaty ("PCT"), 179